BUSINESS MATHEMATICS
Concepts and Applications

Note to the Student

Dear Student,

If you winced when you learned the price of this textbook, you are experiencing what is known as "sticker shock" in today's economy. Yes, textbooks are expensive, and we don't like it anymore than you do. Many of us here at Kent have sons and daughters of our own attending college, or we are attending school part time ourselves. However, the prices of our books are dictated by the cost factors involved in producing them. The costs of paper, designing the book, setting it in type, printing it, and binding it have risen significantly each year along with everything else in our economy. You might find the following table to be of some interest.

Item	1967 Price	1986 Price	The Price Increase
Monthly Housing Expense	$114.31	$686.46	6.0 times
Monthly Automobile Expense	82.69	339.42	4.1 times
Loaf of Bread	.22	1.00	4.6 times
Pound of Hamburger	.39	1.48	3.8 times
Pound of Coffee	.59	2.45	4.2 times
Candy Bar	.10	.40	4.0 times
Men's Dress Shirt	5.00	25.00	5.0 times
Postage	.05	.22	4.4 times
Resident College Tuition	294.00	1,581.00	5.4 times

Today's prices of college textbooks have increased only about 2.8 times 1967 prices. Compare your texts sometime to a general trade book, i.e., a novel or nonfiction book, and you will easily see significant differences in the internal design, quality of paper, and binding. These features of college textbooks cost money.

Textbooks should not be looked on only as an expense. Other than your professors, your textbooks are your most important source for what you hope to learn in college. What's more, the textbooks you keep can be valuable resources in your future career and life. They are the foundation of your professional library. Like your education, your textbooks are one of your most important investments.

We are concerned, and we care. Please write to us at the address below with your comments. We want to be responsive to your suggestions, to give you quality textbooks, and to do everything in our power to keep their prices under control.

Wayne A. Barcomb
President

Kent Publishing Company
20 Park Plaza
Boston, MA 02116

BUSINESS MATHEMATICS

Concepts and Applications

Robert E. Swindle, D.B.A.
Glendale College

Elizabeth M. Swindle
Rio Salado College

Kent Publishing Company
A Division of Wadsworth, Inc.
BOSTON, MASSACHUSETTS

Executive Editor : Richard C. Crews

Editor : Read Wickham

Production Editor: Carolyn Ingalls

Interior Designer: Outside Designs

Cover Designer: Steve Snider

Manufacturing Manager: Linda Siegrist

Kent Publishing Company
A Division of Wadsworth, Inc.

Printed in the United States of America

1 2 3 4 5 6 7 8 9 — 91 90 89 88 87

Library of Congress Cataloging-in-Publication Data

Swindle, Robert. E.
  Business mathematics.

  Includes index.
  1. Business mathematics.   2. Business mathematics—
Problems, exercises, etc.   I. Swindle, Elizabeth M.
II. Title.
HF5691.S85   1987   512'.1   86-27441
ISBN 0-534-07572-X

Preface

Before asking their students to buy a particular textbook, instructors make many comparisons in an endeavor to select the one that offers the most promise as an effective learning tool and invaluable reference source. They seek comprehensive coverage of new materials and respond positively to new approaches to traditional problems — provided that the fundamentals are thoroughly presented.

In this sense, many of the features of this book are similar to those of competing publications.

- All of the **traditional segments** are included — ranging from a fast-paced coverage of basic calculations to an extensive presentation of retail mathematics, from payroll computations to securities analysis, from electronic funds transfers to tables and graphs.
- The **time-tested pattern** of following clearly stated concepts with related applications and reinforcing exercises is adhered to religiously.
- **Answers** to selected problems are placed in an appendix.
- **Terms** are highlighted within the chapters and brought together in an alphabetically arranged **glossary** near the back of the book.
- Selected **tables and equations** are also in an appendix, to prevent clutter within the chapters and to enable easy access during tests.

But the first edition of any textbook is much like a new kid on the block; to gain prominence in a well-established market, a new book must prove itself with well-defined features that are clearly superior to competing publications. The authors' response to such a formidable challenge is reflected in the following features:

- An **algebraic approach** is applied wherever practical, but a reliance on symbols is avoided wherever their use would result more in confusion than clarity.
- Most students enjoy learning new applications for their hand-held **calculators**, and these materials cater to that receptiveness. Every segment of every chapter is oriented toward calculator applications with accompanying diagrams of entries and displays — most heavily in the early chapters, but also as practical in later chapters with newly introduced concepts and relatively complex manipulations. All problems are designed accordingly — no easily identifiable answers, no over-simplification of problems, no contrived situations to derive even answers, no outdated methods for "proving" answers.
- Rather than overwhelm readers with a conglomeration of prices, discounts, transportation costs, markups, and markdowns, the **elements of retail mathematics** are segmented sequentially as they relate to (1) manufacturers' prices and discounts, (2) exchanges of products between manufacturers and retailers, and (3) retail operations. The objective of this strategic approach to retailing is not only to enable readers to work with different types of invoices, but is also to establish a firm understanding of just which companies assess what charges against which firms and which companies

extend certain types of discounts to others, as well as the underlying reasons for doing so.

- The three chapters on **compound interest** provide instruction in related equations and table applications, but those chapters are designed primarily to provide insight into the interrelationships of compound amount, present value of compound amount, amount of and present value of annuities, sinking funds, and amortization. The thrust is toward comprehension rather than rote manipulation.

- The business transactions that form the basis of the many problems throughout this textbook reflect an unusually **high level of authenticity**, having been based on either the authors' collective experience in business and in teaching or taken from the actual records of U.S. corporations.

The overriding feature that distinguishes this book from the others, however, might be called the "judgment factor" — thorough explanations without excessive verbiage; numerous examples, applications, and exercises without the inclusion of space fillers or busywork; comprehensive coverage in a functional format of manageable length. Through the combined efforts of the authors, their colleagues, the editors, the reviewers, and the production staff at Kent Publishing Company, *Business Mathematics: Concepts and Applications* is presented as a carefully selected and prepared learning package that is both rigorous and rewarding.

Acknowledgments

Many key people at Kent Publishing Company were involved in the planning, designing, and production of this book, as reflected on the copyright page. We thank them very much for their efforts and also extend special appreciation to the following reviewers for their invaluable comments and suggestions:

Alec Beaudoin, *Triton College*
Mark Hinds, *New York City Technical College*
Arthur Hirshfield, *Bronx Community College*
William Small, *Spokane Community College*
Richard Whiston, *Hudson Valley Community College*

R.E.S. and E.M.S.

CONTENTS

x   Contents

BUSINESS MATHEMATICS
Concepts and Applications

1 Whole Numbers and Fractions

Upon completion of this foundational chapter, you will be able to

- understand the relationships between whole numbers and fractions
- read and write numbers in the millions, billions, and trillions
- label the essential elements of problems in addition, subtraction, multiplication, and division
- perform fundamental math operations on electronic calculators
- identify mixed numbers, as well as proper, improper, and mixed fractions
- reduce fractions to the lowest terms
- apply ratios in number comparisons

Stop! Don't do what so many students do when beginning such courses as Business Mathematics. Don't assume that because you know a whole number from a fraction and a mixed number from its decimal equivalent, you may safely skip to more challenging areas of the book. You may understand the relatively simple concept of whole numbers, but do you have insight into the composition of whole numbers? The manipulation of fractions is easy also, but are you familiar with the many subtleties involved? Do you know, for instance, that using fractions often enables us to derive more accurate answers than does using decimal numbers? Do you also know that fractions are easily manipulated on electronic calculators?

WHOLE NUMBERS

We use whole numbers in business when speaking or writing about total entities:

    2 (whole) aircraft
    500 (whole) dollars
    2,500 (whole) cases of canned goods
    38 (whole) hours per week
    65,000 (whole) pounds
    528 (whole) employees

But the number 528 (the last number listed) is actually the sum of several other numbers:

500 (100 + 100 + 100 + 100 + 100)

20 (10 + 10)

8 (1 + 1 + 1 + 1 + 1 + 1 + 1 + 1)

In contemplating the number 528, we know that the 8 stands for 8 people because it is in the ones (units) position, that 20 stands for 2 times 10 because the 2 is in the tens position, and that the 5 represents 5 times 100 because the 5 is in the hundreds position. Correspondingly, we may refer to the number 528 rather than an itemized list of 100 + 100 + 100 + 100 + 100 + 10 + 10 + 1 + 1 + 1 + 1 + 1 + 1 + 1 + 1.

Now, as you study the numerical positions presented in Figure 1.1, notice that a million is 1,000 thousand, that a billion is 1,000 million, and that a trillion is 1,000 billion. Because many businesses and governments often deal in millions, billions, and even trillions of dollars, it is important that you be able to identify, read, and write numbers at each of these levels.

A. Five hundred twenty-eight
B. Six hundred fifty-one thousand,
   five hundred twenty-eight
C. Twenty million,
   six hundred fifty-one thousand,
   five hundred twenty-eight

Figure 1.1
Numerical Positions —
Whole Numbers

	Trillions	Billions	Millions	Thousands	Hundreds Tens Units
A					528
B				651	528
C			20	651	528
D		453	120	651	528
E	2	453	120	651	528

D. Four hundred fifty-three billion,
   one hundred twenty million,
   six hundred fifty-one thousand,
   five hundred twenty-eight
E. Two trillion,
   four hundred fifty-three billion,
   one hundred twenty million,
   six hundred fifty-one thousand,
   five hundred twenty-eight

Although the placement of decimals is discussed in the following chapter, we will not present basic instruction in the addition, subtraction, multiplication, and division of whole numbers. So that you will be able to comprehend the related terminology when it is used throughout the text, however, the following labeling and computer applications may prove helpful.

Addition

523	addend
+118	addend
641	sum

Calculator	
Entries	**Display**
5 2 3	523
+	523
1 1 8	118
=	641

Subtraction

1,190	minuend
−1,021	subtrahend
169	difference

Calculator	
Entries	**Display**
1 1 9 0	1,190
−	1,190
1 0 2 1	1,021
=	169

Multiplication

625	multiplicand
×36	multiplier
22,500	product

Calculator	
Entries	**Display**
6 2 5	625
×	625
3 6	36
=	22,500

Division

$$\begin{array}{r} 625 \\ \text{Divisor } 36\overline{)22,500} \end{array}$$ quotient / dividend

Calculator	
Entries	**Display**
2 2 5 0 0	22,500
÷	22,500
3 6	36
=	625

CLASSIFICATION OF FRACTIONS

In business transactions we usually do not enjoy the convenience of dealing totally with whole numbers. The average weight of a case of 48/2 (48 six-ounce cans) tuna might weigh 27-1/2 pounds rather than an even 27 pounds. Similarly, an employee may have worked 47-1/2 hours last week, with the time in excess of 40 hours being paid at 1-1/2 the hourly (whole) rate.

Proper fractions include such numbers as 1/2, 3/4, 5/8, and 15/16, those in which the numerator (the figure above the line) is smaller than the denominator (the figure below the line), and they always denote a portion of a whole.

Figure 1.2
Proper Fractions

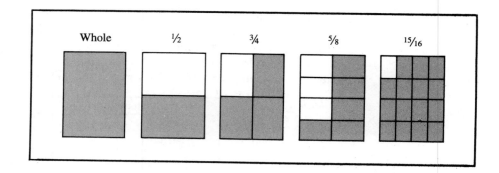

To determine 1/2, we divide the whole by 2 (the denominator) and shade 1 section (the numerator). To determine 3/4, we divide the whole by 4 (the denominator) and shade 3 areas (the numerator). To determine 5/8, we divide the whole by 8 (the denominator) and shade in 5 areas (the numerator), and so on.

To illustrate the equivalency of fractions such as 1/2, 2/4, 4/8, and 8/16, we may use the same divisions (denominators) as in the previous example.

Figure 1.3
Equivalency of Fractions

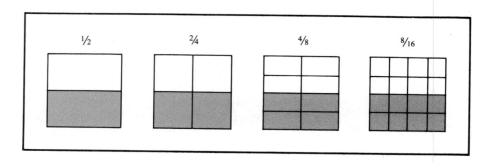

No matter how you divide the square (the whole), the size of the shaded areas remains identical. To maintain the equivalency of a fraction, therefore, we may multiply or divide both the numerator and denominator by the same number (except zero).

$$\frac{4 \times 3}{8 \times 3} = \frac{12}{24}$$

$$\frac{4 \div 2}{8 \div 2} = \frac{2}{4} = \frac{1}{2}$$

Improper fractions are those in which the numerator is larger than the denominator: 3/2, 5/2, 5/4. **Mixed numbers** are combinations of whole numbers and fractions: 1-1/2, 2-1/2, 1-1/4. Notice that the following improper fractions and mixed numbers are equivalent.

Figure 1.4
Conversion of Fractions

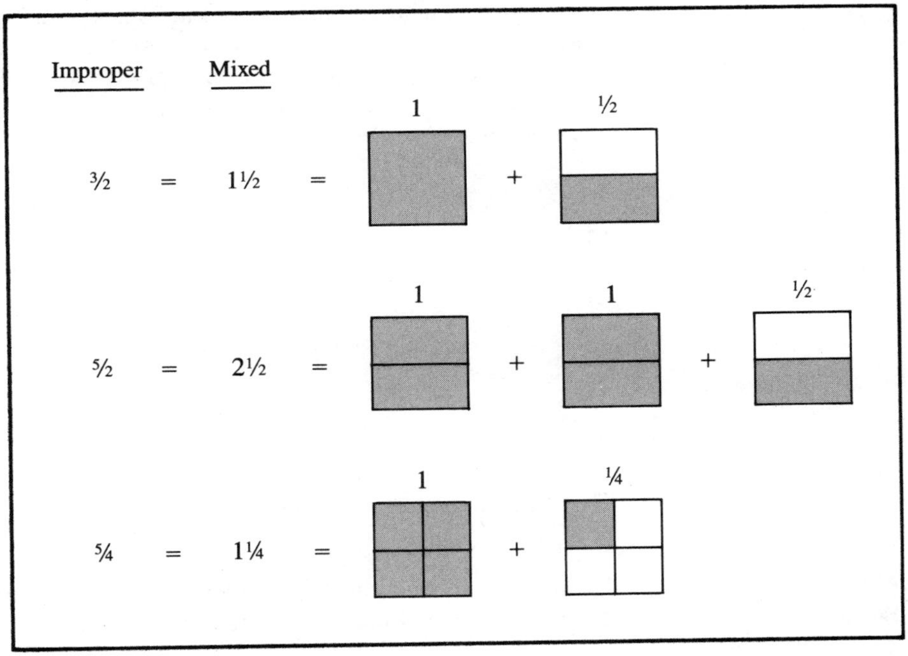

To **convert improper fractions to mixed numbers**, we divide the numerator by the denominator and place any remainder over the denominator:

$$\frac{13 \text{ (numerator)}}{2 \text{ (denominator)}} = 13 \div 2 = 6\frac{1}{2}$$

$$\frac{12}{3} = 12 \div 3 = 4$$

$$\frac{17}{3} = 17 \div 3 = 5\frac{2}{3}$$

To **convert mixed numbers to improper fractions**, we multiply the whole number by the denominator, add the numerator, and place the sum over the denominator.

$$6\frac{1}{2} = \frac{(6 \times 2) + 1}{2} = \frac{13}{2}$$

$$5\frac{2}{3} = \frac{(5 \times 3) + 2}{3} = \frac{17}{3}$$

Remember that when multiplication or division is combined in the same part of an equation with addition or subtraction, the multiplication and/or division must be completed before we add or subtract. In converting 6-1/2 to an improper fraction, for example, we multiply 6 times 2 before adding the 1.

A **complex fraction** is a number in which the numerator and/or denominator is a fraction:

$$\frac{3/5}{4}$$

$$\frac{10}{1/5}$$

$$\frac{3/16}{1/8}$$

The manipulation of fractions is discussed in the following four sections.

ADDITION OF FRACTIONS

The addition of fractions having identical denominators is easy; we simply add the numerators and keep the same denominator:

Figure 1.5
Addition of Fractions

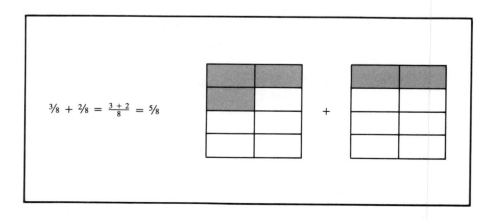

$$\frac{3}{8} + \frac{2}{8} = \frac{3+2}{8} = \frac{5}{8}$$

When the denominators of our fractions differ, on the other hand, we must find the **lowest common denominator**, a number that is divisible by the denominators of the fractions being added.

$$\frac{3}{8} + \frac{1}{4} = \frac{3 + 2}{8} = \frac{5}{8}$$

Since both 8 and 4 will divide evenly into 8, the number 8 becomes our common denominator. The numerator 3 remains unchanged because it was stated in 8ths to begin with, and 1/4 is converted to its equivalent value in 8ths by multiplying both the numerator and the denominator by 2:

$$\frac{1 \times 2}{4 \times 2} = \frac{2}{8}$$

Having stated both fractions in terms of 8ths, we simply add the numerators (3 + 2) and maintain the denominator (8). To assure complete understanding, also consider the following examples:

APPLICATION 1

$$\frac{2}{3} + \frac{1}{9} = \frac{6 + 1}{9} = \frac{7}{9}$$

APPLICATION 2

$$1\frac{5}{7} + \frac{5}{21} = \frac{12}{7} + \frac{5}{21} = \frac{36 + 5}{21} = \frac{41}{21} = 1\frac{20}{21}$$

APPLICATION 3

$$1\frac{1}{3} + 5\frac{2}{5} = \frac{4}{3} + \frac{27}{5} = \frac{20 + 81}{15} = \frac{101}{15} = 6\frac{11}{15}$$

When we have an improper fraction as an answer, as in the second and third applications, we can increase clarity by converting it to a mixed number:

$$\frac{41}{21} = 41 \div 21 = 1\frac{20}{21}$$

$$\frac{101}{15} = 101 \div 15 = 6\frac{11}{15}$$

Also, for added clarity, we reduce answers to the **lowest terms** as explained under equivalency of fractions so that 4/64 equals 1/16.

$$\frac{4}{64} = \frac{4 \div 4}{64 \div 4} = \frac{1}{16}$$

If we fail to notice that both 4 and 64 are divisible by 4 (the greatest common divisor) and divide by 2 instead, a second calculation is required to derive the lowest terms.

$$\frac{4}{64} = \frac{4 \div 2}{64 \div 2} = \frac{2}{32}; \quad \frac{2}{32} = \frac{2 \div 2}{32 \div 2} = \frac{1}{16}$$

Seeing that our first answer can be further reduced, we divide the elements of the fraction by 2. Also consider the following examples:

APPLICATION 1

$$\frac{63}{81} = \frac{63 \div 9}{81 \div 9} = \frac{7}{9}$$

(or)

$$\frac{63}{81} = \frac{63 \div 3}{81 \div 3} = \frac{21}{27}; \quad \frac{21}{27} = \frac{21 \div 3}{27 \div 3} = \frac{7}{9}$$

APPLICATION 2

$$\frac{30}{48} = \frac{30 \div 6}{48 \div 6} = \frac{5}{8}$$

(or)

$$\frac{30}{48} = \frac{30 \div 2}{48 \div 2} = \frac{15}{24}; \quad \frac{15}{24} = \frac{15 \div 3}{24 \div 3} = \frac{5}{8}$$

APPLICATION 3

$$\frac{17}{6} = 2\frac{5}{6}$$

As illustrated in Application 3, the reduction of answers to lowest terms includes the conversion of improper fractions to mixed numbers.

Finding the **lowest common denominator (LCD)** sometimes requires extra effort, as in the following problem:

$$\frac{1}{30} + \frac{2}{45} + \frac{3}{25} = ?$$

Begin by arranging the denominators in a row. Divide the denominators by the highest possible divisors, excluding the number 1, provided that two or more denominators may be divided evenly. Write the quotients and any indivisible numbers below the dividends. Continue to divide each row by the highest divisor until no two numbers may be divided evenly by the same number.

5	30	45	25
3	6	9	5
	2	**3**	**5**

The number 5 divides into the original denominators 6, 9, and 5 times. The divisor 3 then divides into the first two numbers 2 and 3 times, with number 5 remaining unchanged. We cannot continue our calculation further because 2, 3, and 5 are prime numbers.[1] We then multiply the numbers at the left and at the bottom to derive the LCD:

$5 \times 3 \times 2 \times 3 \times 5 = 450$

Dividing the original denominators by 2 instead of 5 would have resulted in one extra calculation but would also have derived the correct answer:

2	30	45	25
5	15	45	25
3	3	9	5
	1	**3**	**5**

$LCD = 2 \times 5 \times 3 \times 3 \times 5 = 450$

Notice in our final calculation that we ignored the number one; to multiply any number by one is to leave the number unchanged. The number 450 is our lowest common denominator; that is, the lowest number that is divisible by 30, 45, and 25, which enables us to complete the original problem. For example, to change 1/30 to its equivalent of 15/450, we multiply both the numerator and denominator by 15. When we have converted each fraction to its

---

[1] A prime number, you will recall, is one that is divisible by only itself and 1 — such as 1, 2, 3, 5, 7, and 11.

equivalent fraction in terms of the common denominator (450), we simply add the numerators.

Also consider the following sets of numbers.

APPLICATION 1. 5, 6, 3

$$
\begin{array}{c|ccc}
3 & 5 & 6 & 3 \\
\hline
 & 5 & 2 & 1
\end{array}
$$

$LCD = 3 \times 5 \times 2 = 30$

APPLICATION 2. 15, 28, 36

$$
\begin{array}{c|ccc}
3 & 15 & 28 & 36 \\
4 & 5 & 28 & 12 \\
\hline
 & 5 & 7 & 3
\end{array}
$$

$LCD = 3 \times 4 \times 5 \times 7 \times 3 = 1{,}260$

We can simplify the addition of mixed numbers by positioning the addends in columns:

EXAMPLE 1

$$
\begin{array}{ll}
1\dfrac{5}{8} & 1\dfrac{10}{16} \\[2ex]
2\dfrac{3}{16} & 2\dfrac{3}{16} \\[2ex]
 & 3\dfrac{13}{16}
\end{array}
$$

EXAMPLE 2

$$
\begin{array}{ll}
2\dfrac{3}{5} & 2\dfrac{12}{20} \\[2ex]
6\dfrac{1}{20} & 6\dfrac{1}{20} \\[2ex]
5\dfrac{7}{10} & 5\dfrac{14}{20} \\[2ex]
 & 13\dfrac{27}{20} = 14\dfrac{7}{20}
\end{array}
$$

Reducing to lowest terms the fractional part of the answer (27/20) in the second illustration gives us 1-7/20. We then add the whole numbers (13 and 1) to derive our answer (14-7/20).

SUBTRACTION OF FRACTIONS

Much of the procedure for the addition of fractions applies equally to subtraction:

$$5\frac{3}{8} - 2\frac{2}{3} = 5\frac{9}{24} - 2\frac{16}{24} = 4\frac{33}{24} - 2\frac{16}{24} = 2\frac{17}{24}$$

As with addition, we begin by stating both fractions in terms of a common denominator. The only difference is that we then subtract rather than add. Notice that in this problem it is necessary to borrow a whole number, reducing the whole number in the minuend by one and increasing the fractional part of that number by one (24/24 + 9/24 = 33/24). Also consider the following examples:

APPLICATION 1

$$16\frac{2}{3} - \frac{3}{5} = 16\frac{10}{15} - \frac{9}{15} = 16\frac{1}{15}$$

APPLICATION 2

$$42\frac{1}{2} - 13\frac{5}{8} = 42\frac{4}{8} - 13\frac{5}{8} = 41\frac{12}{8} - 13\frac{5}{8} = 28\frac{7}{8}$$

APPLICATION 3

$$8\frac{1}{4} - 7\frac{1}{8} = 8\frac{2}{8} - 7\frac{1}{8} = 1\frac{1}{8}$$

The addition and subtraction of fractions with their decimal equivalents is presented in Chapter 2.

MULTIPLICATION OF FRACTIONS

Multiplication of fractions is considerably easier than are addition and subtraction, and, except for mixed numbers, multiplication is easily executed with electronic calculators. We (1) reduce our fractions through cancellation wherever possible, (2) multiply across, and (3) reduce answers to their lowest terms.

$$\frac{2}{3} \times 4 = \frac{2}{3} \times \frac{4}{1} = \frac{8}{3} = 2\frac{2}{3}$$

No cancellations are possible in this problem, so we simply multiply the two numerators (2 × 4) and our two denominators (3 × 1), giving us 8/3, which we reduce to 2 2/3. Also consider the following example:

$$\frac{5}{9} \times \frac{7}{21} \times \frac{3}{10} = \frac{\overset{1}{\cancel{5}}}{\underset{3}{\cancel{9}}} \times \frac{\overset{1}{\cancel{7}}}{\underset{3}{\cancel{21}}} \times \frac{\overset{1}{\cancel{3}}}{\underset{2}{\cancel{10}}} = \frac{1}{18}$$

In this second illustration we divide 5 and 10 by 5, reducing them to 1 and 2 respectively. We then divide 9 and 3 by 3, reducing them to 1 and 3 — although we could just as well have divided 3 and 21 by 3, reducing them to 1 and 7. Finally, we divide 7 and 21 by 7, reducing them to 1 and 3. With no further reductions possible, we cross multiply our new numerators (1 × 1 × 1) and our new denominators (3 × 3 × 2), resulting in a product of 1/18 which is not reducible. As illustrated in this multiplication problem, we may cancel either diagonally or vertically, but not horizontally.

What would happen, you might wonder, if we worked the problem without reducing the fractions through cancellations? We would simply end up working with larger numbers.

$$\frac{5}{9} \times \frac{7}{12} \times \frac{3}{10} = \frac{5 \times 7 \times 3}{9 \times 21 \times 10} = \frac{105}{1890} = \frac{105 \div 105}{1890 \div 105} = \frac{1}{18}$$

When **multiplying mixed numbers**, we should first convert the mixed number to an improper fraction before proceeding with the multiplication.

$$8\frac{2}{3} \times \frac{1}{5} = \frac{26}{3} \times \frac{1}{5} = \frac{26}{15} = 1\frac{11}{15}$$

Also consider the following multiplication problems.

APPLICATION 1

$$\frac{3}{16} \times \frac{8}{15} \times \frac{7}{8} = \frac{\overset{1}{\cancel{3}}}{16} \times \frac{\overset{1}{\cancel{8}}}{\underset{5}{\cancel{15}}} \times \frac{7}{\underset{1}{\cancel{8}}} = \frac{7}{80}$$

APPLICATION 2

$$\frac{5}{15} \times \frac{4}{9} \times \frac{9}{12} \times \frac{3}{8} = \frac{\overset{1}{\cancel{5}}}{\underset{3}{\cancel{15}}} \times \frac{\overset{1}{\cancel{4}}}{\underset{1}{\cancel{9}}} \times \frac{\overset{1}{\cancel{9}}}{\underset{\underset{1}{\cancel{3}}}{\cancel{12}}} \times \frac{\overset{1}{\cancel{3}}}{8} = \frac{1}{24}$$

APPLICATION 3

$$1\frac{4}{5} \times 3\frac{9}{12} \times 16 = \frac{\overset{3}{\cancel{9}}}{\underset{1}{\cancel{5}}} \times \frac{\overset{9}{\cancel{45}}}{\underset{\underset{1}{\cancel{4}}}{\cancel{12}}} \times \frac{\overset{4}{\cancel{16}}}{1} = \frac{108}{1} = 108$$

Other symbols for multiplication include dots and parentheses.

$4 \times 6 = 24$

$4 \cdot 6 = 24$

$4(6) = 24$

$4(3 + 3) = 4 \times 6 = 24$

As illustrated in the final equation, any calculations within parentheses must take place before continuing with the remainder of the problem.

We may use calculators in the multiplication of fractions — by first multiplying the numerators and then dividing by the denominators (Approach A) or by mixing our multiplication and division (Approach B). (The numbers displayed on your calculator may differ from those shown below, depending on the make and model being used.)

The Problem
$$\frac{3}{5} \times \frac{7}{8} \times \frac{5}{6} =$$

Approach A		Approach B	
Entries	**Display**	**Entries**	**Display**
3	3.	3	3.
×	3.	÷	3.
7	7.	5	5.
×	21.	×	0.6
5	5.	7	7.
÷	105.	÷	4.2
5	5.	8	8.
÷	21.	×	0.525
8	8.	5	5.
÷	2.625	÷	2.625
6	6.	6	6.
=	0.4375	=	0.4375

Although the manipulation of fractions on calculators often results in answers with decimals, further discussion of decimal numbers is reserved for Chapter 2.

DIVISION WITH FRACTIONS

The division of fractions, after inversion of the divisor, is actually multiplication. Division is easier, however, because it involves only two fractions.

$$\frac{3}{8} \div \frac{5}{16} = \frac{3}{\overset{}{\underset{1}{8}}} \times \frac{\overset{2}{\cancel{16}}}{5} = \frac{6}{5} = 1\frac{1}{5}$$

We invert the divisor by changing 5/16 to 16/5 (the reciprocal) and then multiplying the two fractions. When we divide, either with whole numbers or with fractions, we are determining the number of times the divisor will go into the dividend.

$$3 \div \frac{3}{4} = \overset{1}{\cancel{3}} \times \frac{4}{\underset{1}{\cancel{3}}} = 4$$

This calculation tells us that 3/4 will go into the whole number 3 four times. Similarly, the answer to the following problem tells us that 1/4 will go into the fraction 3/4 three times.

$$\frac{3}{4} \div \frac{1}{4} = \frac{3}{\underset{1}{\cancel{4}}} \times \frac{\overset{1}{\cancel{4}}}{1} = \frac{3}{1} = 3$$

In considering the following examples, note that, as with multiplication, mixed numbers must be converted to improper fractions before beginning the calculations.

APPLICATION 1

$$\frac{9}{16} \div \frac{4}{5} = \frac{9}{16} \times \frac{5}{4} = \frac{45}{64}$$

APPLICATION 2

$$\frac{9}{15} \div 3\frac{3}{5} = \frac{\overset{1}{\cancel{9}}}{\underset{3}{\cancel{15}}} \times \frac{\overset{1}{\cancel{5}}}{\underset{2}{\cancel{18}}} = \frac{1}{6}$$

APPLICATION 3

$$9\frac{1}{5} \div 3\frac{1}{7} = \frac{\overset{23}{\cancel{46}}}{5} \times \frac{7}{\underset{11}{\cancel{22}}} = \frac{161}{55} = 2\frac{51}{55}$$

Once the divisor has been inverted, multiplication may be performed with calculators, as explained on page 13.

Other symbols that denote division are the underscore and diagonal.

$$\frac{1}{2} = 1 \div 2$$

$$\frac{3}{8} = 3 \div 8$$

$$\frac{1/2}{3/8} = \frac{1}{2} \div \frac{3}{8}$$

Every fraction represents a division problem, therefore, with the numerator (dividend) being divided by the denominator (divisor).

RATIOS

A **ratio** is a comparison in lowest terms of two related numbers. Rather than explain that the stockholders have invested $340,000 in a corporation that has $85,000 in outstanding debts, it is clearer to state that for every dollar of outstanding debt the stockholders have invested four dollars.

$340,000 : $85,000

$$\frac{340,000}{85,000} : \frac{85,000}{85,000}$$

$$4 : 1$$

In comparing two numbers such as these, we divide each side of the resulting equation by the lower of the two numbers (in this case by 85,000). The answers derived will always be a one juxtaposed to a higher number. In this example we have a four-to-one ratio.

As illustrated in the following applications, the placement of the numbers (left versus right) is unimportant.

APPLICATION 1. Economy cars (12,704,160) versus large cars (794,010)

$$\frac{12,704,160}{794,010} = \frac{794,010}{794,010} = 16:1$$

Calculator	
Entries	**Display**
1 2 7 0 4 1 6 0	12,704,160.
÷	12,704,160.
7 9 4 0 1 0	794,010.
=	16.

APPLICATION 2. Housing starts this year (32,000); last year (64,000)

$$\frac{32,000}{32,000} = \frac{64,000}{32,000} = 1:2$$

Calculator	
Entries	**Display**
6 4 0 0 0	64,000.
÷	64,000.
3 2 0 0 0	32,000.
=	2.

Sixteen times as many small cars were sold as large ones, and twice as many new houses were built last year than are scheduled for construction this year.

For expediency in calculating ratios, simply divide the larger number by the smaller number and compare the quotient with one. Rather than write the entire equation in Application 1, for instance, you may divide the number of economy cars (the larger number) by the number of large cars (the smaller number) and compare the resulting answer with one.

From the preceding examples, we can see that a ratio is actually a fraction — that housing starts were one-half (32,000/64,000) the number this year as last and that only 1/16 (794,010/12,704,160) as many large cars were sold as economy cars. Because ratios are fractions (a/b), we may sometimes obtain lower numbers by reducing the fractions.

APPLICATION 1

$$50:75 = \frac{50}{75} = \frac{2}{3} = 2:3$$

APPLICATION 2

$$90 : 225 = \frac{90}{225} = \frac{18}{45} = \frac{2}{5} = 2 : 5$$

Ratios are discussed further in Chapter 2, Decimal Notation, and in Chapter 18, Financial Ratios.

EXERCISES (as assigned by your instructor)

1-1 What position in the number 831 does the number 1 occupy? the number 3? the number 8?

1-2 In the number 6,250, what does the figure 2 actually represent?

1-3 Be prepared to read or write the following numbers:

a. 12,500	d. $2,500,000,000	g. $5,323,461.20
b. 6,245.50	e. $42,111,500	h. $145,621.00
c. 610,218.20	f. $810,444.25	

1-4 In addition, what do we call the numbers being added? the total?

1-5 In subtraction, what do we call the number being subtracted? the number from which another number is being subtracted? the answer?

1-6 What do we call numbers that are being multiplied? the answers?

1-7 In division, what do we call the number being divided by another number? the number being divided into another number? the answer?

1-8 How does a proper fraction differ from an improper fraction?

1-9 Cite three fractions that are the equivalent of 1/4.

1-10 Convert the following improper fractions to mixed numbers:

a. 10/3 =	d. 16/3 =	g. 21/6 =
b. 8/5 =	e. 12/8 =	h. 19/8 =
c. 13/2 =	f. 15/4 =	i. 43/24 =

1-11 Convert the following mixed numbers to improper fractions:

a. 1 1/2 =	d. 10 5/6 =	g. 2-1/8 =
b. 23 1/3 =	e. 2 6/17 =	h. 5-7/9 =
c. 3 2/3 =	f. 33 1/3 =	i. 16-3/4 =

1-12 Reduce the following fractions to the lowest terms.

a. 6/18 =	f. 21/30 =	k. 5-15/135 =
b. 8/45 =	g. 27/45 =	l. 1-13/14 =
c. 3/42 =	h. 73/9 =	m. 6-8/72 =
d. 16/24 =	i. 4/3 =	n. 11/8 =
e. 16/64 =	j. 1-4/8 =	o. 12/144 =

1-13 Determine the lowest common denominator (LCD) for the following sets of numbers

a. 48 and 15	f. 12, 30, and 56
b. 33, 11, and 6	g. 15 and 4
c. 4, 8, 15, and 3	h. 2, 5, and 9
d. 16, 30, 25, and 10	i. 8, 6, 7, 5, and 4
e. 12, 30, 9, and 15	j. 16, 9, 6, and 3

1-14 Complete the following problems in addition and reduce all answers to the lowest terms.

a. 1/8 + 5/8 =	h. 1/8 + 3/4 + 5/16 =
b. 3/4 + 5/8 =	i. 2-1/9 + 1/5 =
c. 4/5 + 1/5 =	j. 18 + 3-1/5 =
d. 7/5 + 3/8 =	k. 15-1/3 + 25/8 =
e. 9/16 + 1/8 + 3/4 =	l. 12-1/3 + 15-3/4 =
f. 1/32 + 3/16 + 5/8 =	m. 5-3/5 + 3-3/4 =
g. 1-1/3 + 5/9 =	n. 3-3/5 + 5-2/15 + 1-3/10 =

1-15 Complete the following problems in subtraction and reduce all answers to the lowest terms.

a. 7/8 − 1/4 =	h. 21-1/3 − 5-1/2 =
b. 5/6 − 3/8 =	i. 5-3/11 − 7/9 =
c. 3/5 − 2/7 =	j. 5 − 1-2/3 =
d. 9/11 − 3/7 =	k. 4-2/5 − 2/7 =
e. 3/5 − 1/3 =	l. 3-13/15 − 4/5 =
f. 5 − 1-3/4 =	m. 6-1/5 − 2-5/7 =
g. 4-3/9 − 2-1/9 =	n. 16 − 2-1/8 =

1-16 Complete the following problems in multiplication and reduce all answers to lowest terms.

a. $4/9 \times 7/8 =$

b. $21/23 \times 2/7 =$

c. $4/5 \times 3/5 =$

d. $20/51 \times 3/5 =$

e. $9/11 \times 5/6 =$

f. $3/28 \times 4/9 \times 3/8 =$

g. $10/33 \times 11/20 \times 3/5 =$

h. $320 \times 3/4 =$

i. $8/9 \times 3/7 \times 3/4 =$

j. $16/19 \times 5/8 \times 1/2 =$

k. $2\text{-}3/8 \times 3/4 =$

l. $1\text{-}1/3 \times 2\text{-}1/6 =$

m. $16\text{-}1/5 \times 3\text{-}4/9 =$

n. $3\text{-}7/8 \times 1\text{-}7/9 =$

1-17 Complete the following problems in division and reduce all answers to lowest terms.

a. $1/4 \div 1/4 =$

b. $3/5 \div 1/3 =$

c. $13/14 \div 3/8 =$

d. $6/20 \div 3/25 =$

e. $9/4 \div 12/8 =$

f. $5\text{-}7/8 \div 3\text{-}3/4 =$

g. $16 \div 3\text{-}1/4 =$

h. $27\text{-}6/7 \div 7\text{-}2/9 =$

i. $2\text{-}4/7 \div 2/3 =$

j. $2\text{-}3/11 \div 1\text{-}1/3 =$

k. $1\text{-}6/19 \div 5/8 =$

l. $3\text{-}3/10 \div 1/15 =$

m. $15\text{-}1/2 \div 1\text{-}1/4 =$

n. $3\text{-}1/9 \div 1\text{-}1/9 =$

1-18 Restate the following numerical comparisons in the simplest possible terms:

a. 14,641 to 73,205
b. 1,021,830 to 340,610
c. Of a total of 384 employees, 64 are minorities.
d. Total income of the Underwood Corporation was $1,440,000, with $1,200,000 being from normal operations and the balance from other, unrelated sources.
e. Of a total of 12,768 rail shipments last year, 1,824 were routed via the Burlington Northern.

1-19 Solve the following word problems, reducing your answers to lowest terms.

a. If Company A has wheat amounting to 3-7/8 barge loads and Company B has wheat totaling 5-4/5 barge loads, how many barges will be required to transport both shipments?
b. If administrative expenses are 1/8 of all company expenses and executive salaries consume 1/2 of all administrative expenses, what fraction of total expenses are the executive salaries?

c. If a jeweler has 7/8 of an ounce of white gold and an order for a ring that requires 1/4 of an ounce, how much gold will remain upon completion of the ring?

d. If one business partner receives 1/3 of all profits and a second partner receives 1/6, what fraction of profits remains for the third partner?

e. If a shipment from Company A constitutes 1/3 of a total railcar load and a shipment from Company B is only 1/4 the amount shipped by Company A, the shipment by Company B is what fractional amount of the total railcar load?

f. If 1,200 cases of food weigh 20-1/4 pounds each and 500 weigh 22-1/2 pounds each, what is the total weight of the entire shipment?

g. Kapt Kitt cat food did weigh 25-1/2 pounds per case. How much does it now weigh, having been reduced 4-1/8 pounds per case by switching from tin cans to aluminum cans?

h. A service station has two underground tanks with a capacity of 20,000 gallons each. If one tank is 3/4 empty and the other is 5/8 empty, how much gasoline does the station have available?

i. If a refinery has available for shipment 230,521 gallons of leaded gasoline and 691,563 gallons of unleaded gasoline, what is the ratio (stated in lowest terms) of the two types of fuel?

j. Make a simple comparison of the sale of 132,489 sleeping bags this year compared to 44,163 last year.

2 Decimal Notation

The materials in this second chapter represent a logical extension of those in Chapter 1 and will enable you to

- recognize the function of stated and assumed decimals
- label the values of digits that are positioned to the right of decimals
- recognize and disregard insignificant zeros
- add, subtract, multiply, and divide decimal numbers — both manually and with calculators
- use short-cut methods for performing chain multiplication and division problems on calculators
- multiply and divide by tens and multiples of tens by simply repositioning decimals
- convert decimals to fractions and fractions to decimals
- identify aliquot parts and the decimal equivalents of other commonly used fractions
- increase the accuracy of sensitive calculations by applying fractions rather than their decimal equivalents
- recognize when, how, and where to round numbers

Although no discussion of decimals was included in Chapter 1, decimal notation is implicit in a discussion of whole numbers. Rather than placing decimals after whole numbers, however, we simply assume their presence.

Rather than	We write
300. employees	300 employees
$5,000.	$5,000
15. days	15 days
15.1/2 days	15-1/2 days

We do not ignore the omitted decimals, but, for convenience, we do not show them.

The presence of decimals is essential, on the other hand, when dealing with decimal fractions.

Rather than	We state
15-1/2	15.5
160-1/1000	160.001
1/8	0.125
$255-1/2	$255.50

SIGNIFICANT AND INSIGNIFICANT ZEROS

When zeros at the left of decimals (such as 0.125) are not preceded by significant non-zero digits, those zeros have no value. To multiply another number by 0.125 is to ignore the cosmetic zero and to multiply by .125. Similarly, when zeros at the right of decimals are not followed by a significant non-zero digit, they have no value. To multiply another number by $255.50, for example, results in the same answer as when multiplying by 255.5 (without the zero). The insignificant zeros are eliminated in the following numbers.

With insignificant zeros	With insignificant zeros removed
003.16	3.16
0.1250	.125
506.210	506.21
453.0001	453.0001
453.1000	453.1

When zeros are standing alone, therefore, either to the far left of decimals or the far right of decimals, we may ignore them. Otherwise, they are essential to our mathematical calculations and interpretations. Note that no commas are used to separate digits to the right of decimals.

The position of digits to the right of decimals is illustrated in Figure 2.1.

Figure 2.1
Numerical positions for fractional values

			Tenths	Hundredths	Thousandths	Ten thousandths
A	0	.	1			
B	0	.	0	1		
C	0	.	0	0	1	
D	0	.	0	0	0	1

In Row A we have one tenth (1/10 of one); B is one one-hundredth (1/100 of one); Row C is one one-thousandth (1/1,000 of one); and Row D is one ten-thousandth (1/10,000 of one). All zeros to the right of the decimals in Figure 2.1 are significant because they are followed by a significant digit — the number 1. Also consider the following examples:

The number	Interpreted as
0.5	five tenths (or) one half
2.5	two and one half
2.50	two and one half (zero is insignificant)
2.51	two and 51/100ths
2.515	two and 515/1,000ths
2.5151	two and 5,151/10,000ths

As with whole numbers, the farther a digit is to the left of a fractional number, the greater its value. As illustrated in Figure 2.1, the first position following a decimal is one tenth of a whole, the second digit is 1/100 of a whole, and so on. Also consider the following numerical comparisons:

$0.5 > 0.25$

$0.75 > 0.5$

$0.75 > 0.7256$

The number 0.5 (50%) is greater than the double-digit number 0.25 (25%). Similarly, 0.75 is greater than 0.5. The number 0.75 in the final example is greater than 0.7256; the 7s in the 10ths position of this third set of numbers are identical, so we look to the 100ths position and see that 5 (in the first number) is greater than 2 (in the second number).

ADDITION AND SUBTRACTION OF DECIMAL NUMBERS

To add numbers manually, we first align the decimals. When adding electronically, the calculator aligns them for us.

	Addition	*Manual Calculation*
	$1.121 + 23.5 =$	1.121
		23.5
		24.621

Calculator	
Entries	**Display**
[1] [.] [1] [2] [1]	1.121
[+]	1.121
[2] [3] [.] [5]	23.5
[=]	24.621

Also consider the following problem.

APPLICATION 1

	Manual		
Addition	*Calculations*		

		Calculator	
		Entries	**Display**

$230 + 16.02 +$
$3.2 + 451$

Manual Calculations:
```
  230.
   16.02
    3.2
  451.
  _____
  700.22
```

Calculator	
Entries	**Display**
[2][3][0]	230.
[+]	230.
[1][6][.][0][2]	16.02
[+]	246.02
[3][.][2]	3.2
[+]	249.22
[4][5][1]	451
[=]	700.22

To subtract one number from another also requires an alignment of decimals, both the assumed decimals and those that are shown.

Subtraction	Manual Calculations
$16.21 - 3.80$	16.21 −3.80 ‾‾‾‾‾ 12.41

Calculator	
Entries	**Display**
[1][6][.][2][1]	16.21
[−]	16.21
[3][.][8]	3.8
[=]	12.41

Whether we enter the zero in 3.80 is inconsequential; being an insignificant digit, it has absolutely no effect on our answer. Also consider the following problem:

APPLICATION 2

Subtraction	Manual Calculation
$4,816 - 356.21$	4,816.00 −356.21 ‾‾‾‾‾‾‾ 4,459.79

Calculator	
Entries	**Display**
[4][8][1][6]	4,816.
[−]	4,816.
[3][5][6][.][2][1]	356.21
[=]	4,459.79

Notice that the assumed decimal in the minuend (4,816) need not be included in the calculator entry.

MULTIPLICATION WITH DECIMALS

We need not align decimals when multiplying, but we must adjust the decimals in answers to reflect the position of decimals in the multiplicands and in the multipliers — except, of course, when using calculators.

	Manual		
Multiplication	*Calculations*		
32.50 × 2.10	32.5		

	×2.1	
	325	
	650	
	68.25	

Calculator		
Entries		**Display**
$\boxed{3}\boxed{2}\boxed{.}\boxed{5}$		32.5
$\boxed{\times}$		32.5
$\boxed{2}\boxed{.}\boxed{1}$		2.1
$\boxed{=}$		68.25

The decimal in the answer is moved two places from the extreme right because there is one significant digit to the right of the decimal in both the multiplicand and the multiplier (1 + 1 = 2 decimal places to the left). Whether we multiply 32.5 by 2.1 or 2.1 by 32.5 is of no importance, since either arrangement will result in the correct answer. As a matter of expediency during manual calculations, however, the larger number is normally placed at the top and the smaller number at the bottom. Notice that the insignificant zeros in both of the numbers being multiplied are disregarded in actual calculation. Also consider the following problem.

APPLICATION 3

	Manual	
Multiplication	*Calculation*	
3,215.26	3,215.26	
×2.061	×2.061	
	321526	
	1929156	← one space
	643052	← two spaces
	6626.65086	

Calculator		
Entries		**Display**
$\boxed{3}\boxed{2}\boxed{1}\boxed{5}\boxed{.}\boxed{2}\boxed{6}$		3,215.26
$\boxed{\times}$		3,215.26
$\boxed{2}\boxed{.}\boxed{0}\boxed{6}\boxed{1}$		2.061
$\boxed{=}$		6,626.65086

Because we have a total of five digits to the right of decimals in the numbers being multiplied (26 and 061), we move the decimal in the answer five places from the extreme right. Also, rather than entering a row of zeros when multiplying by the zero in the multiplier, we simply begin the next row of figures an extra place (two places) to the left.

Chain multiplication can be rapidly performed on some calculators. Rather than repeatedly entering the same multiplier, after the initial calculation we simply enter the multiplicand and strike the equal (=) key. To multiply 326, 451, and 1,820 by 0.35, for example, we begin by multiplying 0.35 by 326. Thereafter, we need enter only the 451 and 1,820.

First calculation

0.35×326

Calculator	
Entries	**Display**
. 3 5	0.35
×	0.35
3 2 6	326.
=	114.1

Second calculation

0.35×451

Entries	**Display**
4 5 1	451.
=	157.85

Third calculation

$0.35 \times 1,820$

Entries	**Display**
1 8 2 0	1,820.
=	637.

In chain multiplication, it is important to remember which number acts as a constant — the first number entered or the second one. In the above calculations, the first number entered (the multiplier 0.35) is the constant. If that arrangement does not work with your calculator, try entering the constant after the multiplicand (326×0.35). In either event, the second and third calculations will be the same as illustrated here.

DIVISION WITH DECIMALS

In the division of decimal numbers, we move the decimal in the divisor (if there is a decimal within the number) to the extreme right of the divisor to create a whole number; that is, we multiply the divisor by 10 or by multiples of 10. We then move the decimal in the dividend, stated or assumed, the same number of places to the right; whatever action we take with the divisor, we must take identical action with the dividend. Then, after having calculated an answer, we move the decimal in the dividend directly upward into the answer.

	Manual	Calculator	
Division	*Calculations*	**Entries**	**Display**

	8.1
9.72 ÷ 1.2	12. ⟌ 97.2
	96
	12
	12

Calculator	
Entries	**Display**
[9] [.] [7] [2]	9.72
[÷]	9.72
[1] [.] [2]	1.2
[=]	8.1

Notice in the manual calculation that the decimal is moved to the right of the divisor (1.2 to 12). Correspondingly, we moved the decimal in the dividend one space (9.72 to 97.2). Then, after dividing, we move the newly positioned decimal in the dividend directly upward into the answer, resulting in a quotient of 8.1. Also consider the following problem.

APPLICATION 4

	Manual
Division	*Calculation*

	4.88
2.5864 ÷ 0.53	53 ⟌ 258.64
	212
	466
	424
	424
	424

Calculator	
Entries	**Display**
[2] [.] [5] [8] [6] [4]	2.5864
[÷]	2.5864
[.] [5] [3]	0.53
[=]	4.88

To move the decimal in the divisor completely to the right involves moving it two places (0.53 to 53.), which necessitates movement of the decimal in the dividend two places (2.5864 to 258.64). Following our division calculations, we move the decimal directly upward from the dividend into the quotient, giving us 4.88 as the answer.

Chain division, the division of more than one number by the same divisor, can be accomplished on some calculators without repeatedly entering the divisor. To divide 12 into 276, 972, and 1,344, we first divide 276 by 12. Thereafter, we simply enter 972 and 1,344 and follow each number with an equal sign (=) entry.

First Calculation

276 ÷ 12

Calculator	
Entries	**Display**
[2] [7] [6]	276.
[÷]	276.
[1] [2]	12.
[=]	23.

Second Calculation

$972 \div 12$

Entries	Display
9 7 2	972.
=	81.

Third Calculation

$1,344 \div 12$

Entries	Display
1 3 4 4	1,344.
=	112.

In chain division, entries are made in the normal manner; that is, (1) entering the dividend, (2) entering the division sign, (3) entering the divisor, and (4) entering the equal sign. For subsequent problems involving the same divisor, only the dividend and the equal sign need be entered.

TENS AND MULTIPLES OF TENS

When **multiplying with 10** or **multiples of 10**, we may derive the answers by simply moving the decimals to the right.

$753 \times 10 = 7,530$ one space

$753 \times 100 = 75,300$ two spaces

$753 \times 1,000 = 753,000$ three spaces

In multiplying 753 by 10, we move the assumed decimal one place to the right by adding one zero. In multiplying by 100, we move the assumed decimal two places to the right by adding two zeros, and so on. Also consider the following calculations.

$753.61 \times 10 = 7,536.1$ one space

$753.61 \times 100 = 75,361$ two spaces

$753.61 \times 1,000 = 753,610$ three spaces

The decimal was moved one place in the first equation and two places in the second equation without the necessity of adding zeros. To move the decimal three places to the right in the third equation, on the other hand, required the addition of one zero. Because decimals are stated only when needed to separate whole numbers from fractional numbers, the decimals in the second and third answers are assumed.

To **multiply by fractional decimals of 10** or **multiples of 10**, on the other hand, requires that the decimal be moved to the left.

$915.82 \times 0.1 = 91.582$ one space

$915.82 \times 0.01 = 9.1582$ two spaces

$915.82 \times 0.001 = 0.91582$ three spaces

Because we are multiplying 915.82 by 1/10th in the first example, our answer is only 1/10th of the multiplicand, and, as the multipliers become progressively smaller, it follows that our answers become smaller also.

When **dividing with 10** or **multiples of 10**, we move the decimal to the left.

$753 \div 10 = 75.3$ one space

$753 \div 100 = 7.53$ two spaces

$753 \div 1,000 = 0.753$ three spaces

To **divide by fractional decimals of 10** or **multiples of 10** requires that the decimal be moved in the opposite direction, to the right.

$915.82 \div 0.1 = 9,158.2$ one space

$915.82 \div 0.01 = 91,582$ two spaces

$915.82 \div 0.001 = 915,820$ three spaces

One zero was added to the third equation so that the decimal could be moved three places to the right. Because decimals are stated only when needed to separate whole numbers from fractional numbers, the decimals in the second and third answers are assumed.

CONVERTING DECIMALS TO FRACTIONS

To change decimal numbers to fractions, we simply state the numbers to the right of decimals (except for preceding zeros) as our numerators and include as our denominators the number 1 plus as many zeros as there are significant digits to the right of the decimal:

Decimal fraction	Conversion	Fractional equivalent
0.3	$\dfrac{3}{1+0}$	$\dfrac{3}{10}$
0.03	$\dfrac{3}{1+00}$	$\dfrac{3}{100}$
0.003	$\dfrac{3}{1+000}$	$\dfrac{3}{1,000}$
0.0003	$\dfrac{3}{1+0000}$	$\dfrac{3}{10,000}$

To assure comprehension, also consider the following examples:

Decimal fraction	Fractional equivalent
3.1	3-1/10
4.25	4-25/100 = 4-1/4
10.125	10-125/1,000 = 10-1/8
216.4500	216-45/100 = 216-9/20

CONVERTING FRACTIONS TO DECIMALS

Every fraction is, in essence, a division problem:

$$\frac{1}{2} = 1 \div 2 = 0.5$$

$$\frac{3}{4} = 3 \div 4 = 0.75$$

$$\frac{7}{8} = 7 \div 8 = 0.875$$

Because of the widespread use of electronic calculators and computers, which are programmed for decimal notation, such conversions are commonplace.

An **aliquot part** is a part of a number by which the number can be divided evenly, that is, without leaving a remainder. The numbers 2 and 5 are aliquot parts of 10, for instance, in that they may be divided evenly into 10. Aliquot parts of 100 (such as 5, 10, 25, and 50) are of special importance in business computations. These and other frequently used fraction-decimal equivalents should be memorized.

Table 2.1
Commonly used Fraction-Decimal Equivalents

1/2 = 0.5	1/3 = 0.333[1]	1/4 = 0.25	1/5 = 0.2	1/8 = 0.125
	2/3 = 0.667[1]	3/4 = 0.75	2/5 = 0.4	3/8 = 0.375
			3/5 = 0.6	5/8 = 0.625
			4/5 = 0.8	7/8 = 0.875

[1]Rounding to the thousandths position, as is done here, may be too severe for some business calculations. See "Rounding Numbers" on page 32.

The halves, thirds, quarters, and fifths are easily recalled; and, if you can remember that 1/8 is 0.125, you can mentally calculate that three times 0.125 is 0.375, that five times 0.125 is 0.625, and so on. Then, rather than keying fractions into your calculations, you may enter the decimal equivalents.

USING FRACTIONS FOR INCREASED ACCURACY

Although we rely heavily on decimal notation in business transactions, decimals occasionally result in less accurate answers. In taking one third of $23,750, for example, using a fraction as the multiplier results in a significantly more accurate answer than when using the decimal equivalent — even when we carry the decimal number to five places.

$$\$23,750 \times \frac{1}{3} = \$7,916.67$$

$$\$23,750 \times 0.33333 = \$7,916.59$$

The first answer is within 1/3 cent of being accurate, as we can see with the following check, whereas the second answer is off by almost eight cents.

$$\$7,916.67 \times 3 = \$23,750.01$$

$$\$7,916.59 \times 3 = \$23,749.77$$

The first check shows a difference of one cent, which when divided by 3, reflects an inaccuracy of 1/3 cent. In contrast, the second answer differs from $23,750 by 23 cents, which, when divided by 3, reflects a variance of 7-2/3 cents.

When dealing with large numbers especially, we should work with fractions rather than decimals. In multiplying $45,145 by 2/3, for example, key your calculator or program your computer first to multiply the number by 2 and then to divide by 3, or first to divide the number by 3 and then to multiply by 2.

Multiplication first

$45,145 \times 2 \div 3$

Calculator	
Entries	**Display**
4 5 1 4 5	45,145.
×	45,145.
2	2.
÷	90290.
3	3.
=	30,096.66667

Division first

$45,145 \div 3 \times 2$

Entries	**Display**
4 5 1 4 5	45,145.
÷	45,145.
3	3.
×	15,048.33333
2	2.
=	30,096.66667

Notice that the displayed (calculator) answer ends with the figure 7 with rounding having occurred automatically.

ROUNDING NUMBERS

The preceding calculation would result in an endless string of 6s if performed manually. In programming calculators, however, manufacturers include either 3 or 4 extra decimal places (called "guard digits") to the right of the displayed numbers. They are unseen but are reflected in the displayed answers. Because the first guard digit to the right of the displayed area was a 6 in this instance, the last displayed digit was changed from a 6 to a 7, which corresponds to the following guidelines:

Guidelines for Rounding Fractional Amounts
1. The last digit to be stated (arrows below) is called the "round-off" digit.
2. The digit following the round-off digit (underscored below) is the "test" digit.
3. If the test digit is 5 or greater, we increase the round-off digit by 1.
4. If the test digit is 4 or lower, we leave the round-off digit unchanged.
5. Thereafter, we disregard the test digit and all digits to the right of it.

Number	Rounded
↓	
18.435	18.4
29.582	29.6
↑	

We may round fractional amounts to 10ths, 100ths, or 1,000ths, as illustrated below, or even further from the decimal if desired.

Original amount	10ths	100ths	1,000ths
16.142	16.1	16.14	16.142
23.6851	23.7	23.69	23.685
330.16	330.2	330.16	330.160
45.1638	45.2	45.16	45.164

In rounding to the 10ths position, we increase the number in the 10ths position if the following digit (the one in the 100ths position) is 5 or greater and leave it unchanged if the following number is less than 5. The key number in rounding to the 100ths position is the following digit, the one in the 1,000ths position, and so on.

When multiplying or dividing by numbers such as 15-2/3, the decimal equivalent of 15.66666666667 will result in more accurate answers than the number 15.67 — significantly so when dealing in large denominations over extended periods of time. In most business transactions, however, and certainly when dealing with total amounts of money, we round to the 100ths position.

For ease of interpretation, we sometimes round very large numbers. Rather than burden readers with seven- to ten-digit numbers, for example, we can specify that all figures are stated in thousands of dollars.

Actual amounts	Stated in thousands
$79,500	$79.5
$152,320	$152.3
$5,115,556	$5,115.6

The second number is stated as $152.3 rather than $152.4 because the following digit (a 2) is lower than 5. Conversely, the third number is rounded upward to $5,115.6 because the following digit (a 5) is 5 or higher.

EXERCISES (as assigned by your instructor)

2-1 Rewrite the following numbers and enter the assumed decimals:

    a. 250   b. $1,500   c. $47   d. 1-1/2

2-2 Be prepared to read or write the following numbers:

    a. 0.5   b. 1.006   c. 3.020   d. 14.5001

2-3 Use either a $>$ or $<$ in each of the following sets of numbers to indicate which is the greater. (Example: $6 > 3$ and $6 < 12$)

a. 0.0555   0.110

b. 0.731   0.9

c. 0.11120   0.1213

d. 1.2305   1.3204

e. 3.875   3.785

f. 0.333   0.2999

2-4 Add the following numbers:

a. $16.1 + 23 + 1.21 =$

b. $18 + 22.25 + 0.111 =$

c. $15.001 + 112\text{-}1/2 + 5.25 =$

d. $21.210 + 0.335 + 19.1 =$

e. $255.5 + 133.20 + 168 + 10 =$

f. $22.2 + 583.93 + 18.6 + 55.01 =$

g. $1.110 + 15.293 + 12.2 + 880 =$

h. $16.123 + 18.1 + 1.555 + 1.1 =$

2-5 Perform the following subtractions:

a. $181.1 - 16.33 =$

b. $0.9 - 0.875 =$

c. $4{,}876.14 - 3{,}868.10 =$

d. $16.228 - 16.189 =$

e. $5{,}220 - 432.1 =$

f. $16.419 - 12.221 =$

g. $67{,}220 - 33{,}113.25 =$

h. $575.22 - 472.88 =$

i. $5{,}221.21 - 4{,}999.19 =$

j. $32{,}115 - 9{,}899.3 =$

k. $3{,}255.11 - 2{,}155.78 =$

l. $44{,}210 - 38{,}111.5 =$

2-6 Multiply the following decimal numbers:

a. $16.1 \times 121 =$

b. $321.6 \times 0.15 =$

c. $16.222 \times 2.1 =$

d. $221.21 \times 0.011 =$

e. $32.5 \times 1.6 =$

f. $2{,}200 \times 0.125 =$

g. $16{,}120 \times 5.5 =$

h. $13{,}010.10 \times 2.22 =$

i. $2{,}500 \times 1.25 =$

j. $1{,}682.2 \times 0.5 =$

k. $32{,}000 \times 0.17 =$

l. $161.1 \times 23.2 =$

2-7 Divide the following decimal numbers and round your answers to the cents (100ths) position.

a. $8.35 \div 0.5 =$

b. $140.3 \div 16.1 =$

c. $1{,}983.55 \div 14\text{-}1/2 =$

d. $3{,}810.212 \div 3 =$

e. $16.5 \div 2.31 =$

f. $293.56 \div 0.05 =$

g. $1{,}000 \div 12\text{-}1/4 =$

h. $19{,}180.50 \div 3.10 =$

2-8 Using chain multiplication with your calculator, perform the following calculations:

a. Multiply the following numbers by 25 and round your answers to the cents (100ths) position: 16,121; 25.223; 92,010.50; 221.25

b. Multiply the following numbers by 23-1/4 and round your answers to the tenths position: 16.21; 333.5; 980; 65,111.50; 22,141.00

c. Divide the following numbers by 35 and round the answers to the cents (100ths) position: 16,221; 230.45; 222.2; 110,255.50; 5.005

d. Divide the following numbers by 12-1/2 and round the answers to the tenths position: 211.25; 5,060.11; 24.818.25; 100,080; 242.755

2-9 Manually solve the following problems through movement of the decimals. Do not round the answers.

a. $1,212.60 \times 10 =$ f. $16,183.2 \times 100 =$

b. $31.25 \times 0.1 =$ g. $818.08 \times 0.01 =$

c. $1,945.606 \times 1,000 =$ h. $3,502.5 \div 10 =$

d. $75,414 \div 0.10 =$ i. $25,610 \div 100 =$

e. $25,415,600 \div 1,000 =$ j. $3,156 \div 0.01 =$

2-10 Convert the following decimals to fractions and reduce to lowest terms:

a. $0.5 =$ e. $0.05 =$ i. $0.250 =$

b. $3.5 =$ f. $5.15 =$ j. $16.67 =$

c. $1.003 =$ g. $3.00080 =$ k. $5.25 =$

d. $3.125 =$ h. $8.40 =$ l. $14.75 =$

2-11 Convert the following fractions to their decimal equivalents and round to the 1,000ths position:

a. $1/9 =$ e. $2/7 =$ i. $1/6 =$

b. $3/11 =$ f. $9/13 =$ j. $15/17 =$

c. $3/7 =$ g. $21/51 =$ k. $19/25 =$

d. $16/17 =$ h. $53/8 =$ l. $17/29 =$

2-12 Through observation only, convert the following fractions to their decimal equivalents and round the repeating numbers to the 1,000ths position.

a. $1/2 =$ e. $2/3 =$ i. $3/8 =$

b. $7/8 =$ f. $1/3 =$ j. $1/2 =$

c. $3/4 =$ g. $1/5 =$ k. $3/5 =$

d. $1/4 =$ h. $4/5 =$ l. $1/8 =$

2-13 Perform the following multiplication and division problems, using the decimal equivalents of the multipliers and the divisors and rounding to the cents (100ths) position.

a. $750 \times 1/2 =$

b. $1,609.50 \times 2/3 =$

c. $1,200 \div 1/4 =$

d. $950.50 \div 1/5 =$

e. $1,350 \times 1/8 =$

f. $56.12 \times 1/100 =$

g. $1,955.60 \div 1/10 =$

h. $15,200 \div 7/8 =$

2-14 Division C of the Marcor Corporation had sales of $17,223.15 for the first week of August; $23,555.20 for the second week; $19,650.90 for the third week; and $20,990.11 for the fourth week. What were the total sales in August for this one division?

2-15 If James Mason produced 23-1/2 units during an 8-hour shift and Ramsey Clarke produced 24-1/8 units, what was their combined output for the shift?

2-16 If the distance for delivering packages was 13.1 miles for one trip, 23 miles for a second trip, and 48.5 miles for a third trip, what was the total mileage?

2-17 How much of $42,151 in sales will a company have left after paying a broker's commission of $2,950.57?

2-18 What is the total amount of an invoice for 550 cases of canned goods priced at $13.50 per case?

2-19 If an item priced at $17 per case is discounted $1.50 per case, how much must the buyer pay for a shipment of 2,000 cases?

2-20 If the state government is assessing a property tax of $1.25 for each unit of merchandise in a company warehouse, how much tax must be paid for each of the following batches of merchandise: 23,000 cases in Warehouse A; 45,150 cases in Warehouse B; and 115,200 cases in Warehouse C?

2-21 The financial manager at Robbins Manufacturing has alloted $20,000 for the purchase of gifts for guests at an open house to celebrate the dedication of a line of new products. If each gift costs $6.25, how many may be purchased?

2-22 Part-time employee A earned $118.13, employee B earned $161.44, and employee C earned $210.00. If each of these three employees holds a job that pays $5.25 per hour, how many hours did each employee work?

2-23 Department A has total square footage of 3,500; Department B has 2,135 square feet; and Department C has 2,112-1/2 square feet. What is the total square footage for all three departments?

2-24 Of the $230,661.12 in sales for September, Nortex corporation has customer returns totaling $2,150.16. What was the company's net (actual) sales for the month?

2-25 If a department store paid the manufacturer $650 for a dinette set, priced it at $925, but eventually reduced the price by $125, how much profit (ignoring related expenses) did the store realize?

2-26 If a real estate broker receives $4,550 commission for the sale of a residence and pays the salesperson one fourth of that amount, how much of the commission does the broker have left?

2-27 If a buyer agrees to pay $85,500 for a home plus $2,100 in closing costs, and makes a down payment of $21,375, how much is still owed on the property?

2-28 Convert the following numbers to millions of dollars, rounding to the tenths position.

a. $663,894   c. $15,778,213   e. $783,537

b. $8,438,938   d. $111,783   f. $463,204,928

3 Basic Algebra

LEARNING OBJECTIVES

The word *algebra* has very broad meanings, being used to define introductory courses in the subject as well as extremely complicated applications in graduate courses at the university level. A working knowledge of the basic concepts presented here will suffice for most business applications, and comprehension of these materials will enable you to

- comprehend the rationale of mathematics involving signed numbers
- add, subtract, multiply, and divide with signed numbers
- interpret and apply the various forms and symbols that are used in the multiplication and division of signed numbers
- solve algebraic equations
- apply algebraic concepts to a wide variety of business problems
- recognize and solve problems having elements that are directly or indirectly proportional
- interpret and apply exponential notation.

All business math books contain algebraic solutions to problems, but relatively few include the word "algebra" in the chapter headings, the indexes, or even within the related chapters. The authors rely instead on such terms as "review of equations" or "application of formulas."

Why is this so? Haven't students been required to take courses in algebra? Shouldn't they be expected to apply the acquired knowledge to business transactions? Unfortunately, many people have become so fearful of higher mathematics that they automatically recoil from the mere mention of the word "algebra."

Such a reaction is self-defeating, because many business problems can be solved most easily through the use of simple algebra. Simple? Yes, simple. Only a limited knowledge of algebra is required to solve most business problems, and, rather than attempting to deceive readers with substitute names and formula manipulations that must be memorized, we are labeling the chapter "Basic Algebra" and demonstrating the practical applications of algebra to a wide range of business computations.

ADDITION OF SIGNED NUMBERS

The signs that apply in regular mathematics are also used in algebraic equations. The plus sign (+) specifies that a number is positive or that it is to be added to another number or numbers, and, as in arithmetic, a number is assumed to be positive when it is not preceded by a sign.

$5 = +5$

Also as in arithmetic and as illustrated with the accompanying scale, positive numbers that are added result in sums that are positive — even when not preceded by a plus sign. Figure 3.1 illustrates the equation $5 + 3 = 8$:

Figure 3.1
Addition of positive numbers

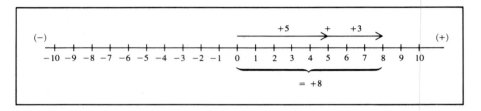

When adding negative numbers, on the other hand, the sum is negative. Figure 3.2 illustrates the equation $(-5) + (-3) = -8$:

Figure 3.2
Addition of negative numbers

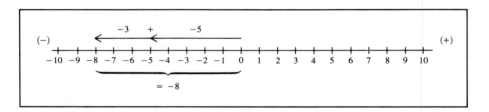

When adding two numbers of mixed signs (plus and minus), the answer is the difference between the two numbers preceded by the sign of the largest number. Figure 3.3 illustrates the equation $(+5) + (-3) = 5 - 3 = 2$:

Figure 3.3
Addition of numbers with mixed signs

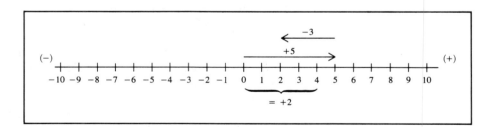

The positive 5 takes us up the scale 5 points, and the negative 3 brings us back 3 points, resulting in a positive 2.

The addition of more than two numbers of mixed signs requires that we find the difference between the total positive numbers and the total negative numbers and then precede the difference with the dominant sign. Or we may derive separate totals for the positive and the negative numbers and then find the difference.

EXAMPLES. Addition of Signed Numbers

$$19 + (-3) + (-5) + 10 = 21$$
$$61 + 9 + (-3) + 5 = 72$$
$$12 + 3 + (-8) = 7$$
$$(-21) + (-18) + 3 = -36$$
$$(-7) + (-3) + 5 = -5$$
$$15 + (-15) + 21 = 21$$

SUBTRACTION OF SIGNED NUMBERS

Although the subtraction of signed numbers is actually performed by addition, the rationale is slightly more difficult to grasp than that of algebraic addition. The difference between a positive 5 and a positive 3 is 2, as shown in Figure 3.4:

Figure 3.4
Subtraction of numbers with like signs

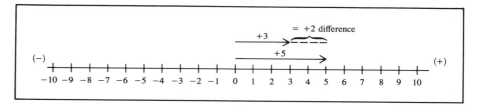

We find the difference between two positive numbers or two negative numbers by changing the sign of the subtrahend and then adding.

$$(+5) - (+3) = (+5) + (-3) = 2$$

$$(-3) - (-2) = (-3) + (+2) = (-1)$$

Correspondingly, the difference between a positive 5 and a negative 2 is 7 as shown in Figure 3.5:

Figure 3.5
Subtraction of numbers with mixed signs

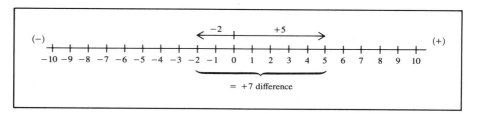

As before, we change the sign of the subtrahend and add.

$$(+5) - (-2) = (+5) + (+2) = 7$$

To illustrate this concept further, let's assume that a business lost $2,000 in

January, an amount that must be offset before working toward the goal of a $5,000 profit for February. As already diagramed (although in dollars rather than thousands of dollars), the business would have to earn $7,000 — the $5,000 profit objective *plus* the $2,000 (−2,000) loss. To account for the $2,000 loss, therefore, we change the negative sign to a positive sign and add. Also consider the following examples:

EXAMPLES. Subtraction of Signed Numbers

$$(+16) - (+8) = (16) + (-8) = 8$$
$$(-30) - (-10) = (-30) + (+10) = -20$$
$$(-12) - (+8) = (-12) + (-8) = -20$$
$$(12) - (6) = (12) + (-6) = 6$$

MULTIPLICATION OF SIGNED NUMBERS

Algebraic multiplication is accomplished in the same manner as regular multiplication. When multiplying numbers with identical signs, the answer is always positive.

$$(+5) \times (+4) = +20$$

$$(-5) \times (-4) = +20$$

When multiplying numbers with different (mixed) signs, the answer is always negative.

$$(+5) \times (-4) = -20$$

$$(-5) \times (+4) = -20$$

The answers to multiplication problems involving more than two numbers may be either positive or negative. If the equation includes an even count of negative numbers (or no negative numbers at all), the answer is positive.

$$(6) \times (-3) \times (-2) = +36$$

$$(7) \times (3) \times (2) = +42$$

When the equation includes an odd count of negative numbers, on the other hand, the answer is negative.

$$(3) \times (-8) \times (2) = -48$$

$$(-4) \times (10) \times (2) = -80$$

In algebraic equations, the times ($\times$) sign is often replaced by centered dots, parentheses, or simply omitted.

Stated as	Calculated as
$6 \cdot 3 =$	$6 \times 3 =$
$6(3) =$	$6 \times 3 =$
$(6)(3) =$	$6 \times 3 =$
$5x =$	$5 \times x =$
$5(3 - 1) =$	$5 \times (3 - 1) =$

Signed numbers within parentheses must be calculated first. In the final equation, it is only after performing the subtraction within the parentheses $(3 - 1 = 2)$ that we multiply the difference by 5.

If the numbers within parentheses are related to different symbols, or if one is related to a symbol and the other is not, we must deal with them separately. As illustrated in the following equation, we cannot add $2A$ and $2T$ and derive a meaningful answer any more than we can add 2 apples and 2 tangerines and declare the sum to be 5 tangapples. Instead, we multiply each of the numbers by 5:

$$5(2A + 3T) = 10A + 15T$$

Symbols such as A and T are frequently called *variables,* in that they represent quantities that may assume any value. This multiplication process is known as "factoring," and it takes place only when a number immediately precedes the first parenthesis.

Multiplication

$$3(x - 0.4) = 3x - 1.2$$

Subtraction

$$3 - (x - 0.4) = 3 - x + 0.4$$

Because a sign (a minus sign) separates the 3 from the parenthetical numbers in the second equation, no multiplication is involved; however, we must follow specific rules regarding the removal of grouping symbols.

Table 3.1
Rules for removing parentheses or other grouping symbols such as braces and brackets

1. If a positive sign precedes the grouping symbol, no sign changes are necessary; simply remove it and proceed with the stipulated operations.

$$a + 2(3a - 2) = a + 6a - 4 = 7a - 4$$

2. If a negative sign precedes the grouping symbol, change the signs within the group; that is, change positive signs to negative and negative signs to positive.

$$a - 2(3a - 2) = a - 6a + 4 = -5a + 4$$

3. If there are two or more grouping symbols, delete the inner ones first.

$$[6 + 2(2a - 4)] = [6 + 4a - 8] = 4a - 2$$

Also consider the following examples:

EXAMPLES. Multiplication of Signed Numbers

$$(8) \times (4) = 32 \qquad\qquad 13 \cdot 2 = 26$$
$$(9)(3) = 27 \qquad\qquad (-7)(-4) = 28$$
$$(-8)(5) = -40 \qquad\qquad (-5)(6) = -30$$
$$(2)(-5)(3) = -30 \qquad\qquad (5)(2)(-2)(-1) = 20$$
$$5(3 + 1) = 5 \times 4 = 20 \qquad -3(6 - 1) = (-3) \times (5) = -15$$
$$5(3A + 2B) = 15A + 10B \qquad -6(2Y + 3Z) = -12Y - 18Z$$

DIVISION OF SIGNED NUMBERS

As with multiplication, the answers in algebraic division are positive when the dividend and divisor have the same signs and negative when the signs are mixed.

Same signs	Mixed signs
$16 \div 4 = 4$	$(16) \div (-4) = -4$
$(-16) \div (-4) = 4$	$(-16) \div (4) = -4$

The division sign may be replaced with a diagonal or underscore.

Stated as	Calculated as
2/3	$2 \div 3 =$
$\dfrac{3}{4}$	$3 \div 4 =$

The following examples will help clarify these relationships:

EXAMPLES. Division with Signed Numbers

$$(3)/(4) = 0.75 \qquad (15) \div (-3) = -5$$
$$(-12) \div (-4) = 3 \qquad (-24) \div (12) = -2$$
$$(-1) \div (+1) = -1$$

Now, before dealing further with algebraic equations, the following summary of the rules for addition, subtraction, multiplication, and division might prove helpful:

Table 3.2
Summary of Rules for Calculating Signed Numbers

Addition	Find the difference between the total positive numbers and the total negative numbers, and prefix this answer with the sign (positive or negative) of the group having the greatest value.	$(+5) + (-3) + (-6) =$ $(+5) + (-9) = -4$
Subtraction	Change the sign (from positive to negative or from negative to positive) of the subtrahend and then add.	$(+5) - (-4) =$ $(+5) + (+4) = +9$
Multiplication	After finding the product through regular multiplication, assign a positive prefix if the factors being multiplied are all positive or if an even number of negative factors are included. Precede the answer with a negative prefix only when an uneven number of negative factors are included.	$(+5)(+3) = +15$ $(+3)(-2) = -6$ $(+3)(-4)(-2) = +24$ $(+5)(-2)(+6) = -60$
Division	Following regular division of two numbers, assign (or assume) a positive prefix if both the dividend and the divisor are of the same sign (both positive or both negative). Assign a negative prefix when the signs are mixed.	$(+6) \div (+3) = +2$ $(-15) \div (-3) = +5$ $(+10) \div (-5) = -2$

ALGEBRAIC EQUATIONS

When we do not know the value of a given number, we may substitute a symbol for the unknown; the substitute may be any letter of the alphabet or even a question mark.

$$5 + 4 = x$$

$$5 + 4 = ?$$

$$5 + 4 = 9$$

Until we have solved the equation and determined that the answer is 9, we may use either the x, the ?, or any other symbol to designate the unknown value.

Now let's restate the equation so that the answer is not quite so obvious.

$5 + x = 9$

Although we can see that the value of x is 4, because we know that the difference between 9 and 5 is 4, we may use this equation to illustrate the means of solving an algebraic problem. Such equations are like an old-fashioned scale, necessitating that we keep both sides equal to maintain a balance, as shown in Figure 3.6:

Figure 3.6
Equality of equations

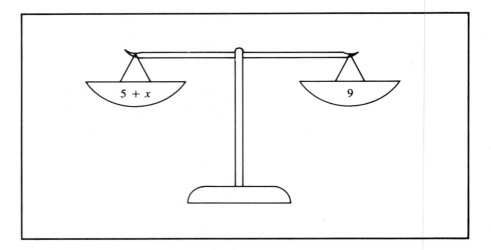

Our objective is to alter both sides of the equation to where the symbol (the unknown x) stands alone. To eliminate the positive 5 from the left, we must add a minus 5; and, to maintain a balance on both sides of the equal sign, we must also add a minus 5 to the right side.

$$\begin{array}{rcr} 5 + x = & 9 \\ -5 \qquad = & -5 \\ \hline x = & 4 \end{array}$$

The minus 5 on the left side cancels the plus five $[(+5) + (-5) = 0]$, leaving only the x; and the minus 5 on the right side reduces the 9 to 4 $(9 - 5 = 4)$, giving us our answer $(x = 4)$. We can then check the answer by plugging the newly found value of x into our original equation.

$5 + x = 9$

$5 + 4 = 9$

In the preceding equation we eliminated a positive 5 to the left of the equal sign by introducing a negative 5. When the number to be eliminated is negative instead, we introduce a positive number of the same numeric value.

$$
\begin{aligned}
x - 6 &= 5 \\
+\ 6 &= +6 \\
\hline
x &= 11
\end{aligned}
$$

Adding a positive 6 on the second line cancels the minus 6 $[(-6) + (+6) = 0]$, and, in adding a positive 6 to the right side of the equation we maintain the necessary balance and change the value from 5 to 11 $(5 + 6 = 11)$. These moves leave the x alone on one side of the equal sign, indicating that our answer (the value of x) is 11.

We should note at this point that any number preceding an algebraic symbol actually means that the symbol is being multiplied by that number.

$x = 1 \cdot x$ (one times x)

$2x = 2 \cdot x$ (two times x)

$3x = 3 \cdot x$ (three times x)

When the symbol in an original equation is being multiplied, we again eliminate that value (isolate the symbol) by doing just the opposite of multiplication — that is, by dividing.

$3x = 15$

$$\frac{3x}{3} = \frac{15}{3}$$

$x = 5$

We reduce $3x$ to $1x$ through division by dividing both sides by 3, resulting in x $(3x \div 3 = 1x = x)$ on the left side of the equal sign and 5 $(15 \div 3 = 5)$ on the opposite side. The value of our unknown x is 5.

Finally, when our unknown (the x in these examples) is being divided, we isolate the symbol (our unknown variable) by doing just the opposite, that is, by multiplying the factor by the same numeric value.

$$\frac{x}{3} = 15$$

$$\frac{3x}{3} = 3 \cdot 15$$

$x = 45$

To eliminate the 3 in $x/3$, we multiply both sides of the equation by 3. The threes on the left side are canceled ($3 \div 3 = 1$), leaving just the x; and the 3 times 15 on the right side gives us a product of 45, so that $x = 45$.

In the preceding examples, we have eliminated numbers with symbols on the left side of the equations. Now let's consider a problem where we must also cancel numbers with symbols to the right of the equal sign.

(1) $2x + 5 = 11 - x$

(2) $\quad\quad -5 = -5 \quad\quad$ (place -5 on both sides)

(3) $\underline{x \quad\quad\quad\quad + x}$ (place $+x$ on both sides)

(4) $3x \quad\quad = \quad 6$

$\quad\quad 3x = 6$

(5) $\dfrac{3x}{3} = \dfrac{6}{3}$

(6) $x = 2$

In Step 2 we eliminate the positive 5 on the left side of the equation by introducing a minus 5 to both sides. In Step 3 we eliminate the negative x on the right side by introducing a positive x to both sides. The resulting equation in Step 4 is achieved by adding $2x$ and $1x$ (giving us $3x$) and by subtracting 5 from 11 (giving us 6). Then, because the $3x$ actually represents 3 times x (multiplication), we use division to eliminate the 3 by dividing both sides by 3. We have determined that the value of x, the unknown variable, is 2.

Solutions to the following examples require the use of each of these several approaches, with the adjustments being placed within the equations.

Addition and division required

$$3x + 5 = 16 + 4$$

$$3x + 5 - 5 = 16 + 4 - 5$$

$$3x = 15$$

$$\frac{3x}{3} = \frac{15}{3}$$

$$x = 5$$

Division required

$$5x = 25$$

$$\frac{5x}{5} = \frac{25}{5}$$

$$x = 5$$

Addition required

$$x - 2 = 10 - 3x$$

$$x - 2 + 2 + 3x = 10 - 3x + 2 + 3x$$

$$4x = 12$$

$$\frac{4x}{4} = \frac{12}{4}$$

$$x = 3$$

Multiplication
required

$$\frac{x}{5} = 45$$

$$\frac{5x}{5} = 45 \times 5$$

$$x = 225$$

Rather than adding and subtracting terms on both sides of an equation in order to maintain equality, we may take a shortcut by transposing these terms; that is, by shifting a term from one side of an equation to the other and changing its sign.

$$x - 4 = 12$$

$$x = 12 + 4 \quad \text{(moving the 4 to the right and changing the sign)}$$

$$x = 16$$

$$3x + 6 = 10 - x$$

$$3x + x = 10 - 6 \quad \text{(switching the 6 and the } x \text{ and changing their signs)}$$

$$4x = 4$$

$$x = 1$$

Note that this form of transposition applies only to addition and subtraction.

Since division is the inverse operation of multiplication, we may also simplify our operations when performing these operations. We simply drop the coefficient (5 is the coefficient of x in the number $5x$) and divide the other side of the equation by the value of that coefficient.

$$2x + 3x = 35$$

$$5x = 35$$

$$x = 7$$

$$x + \frac{x}{3} = 44 \quad \left(\frac{x}{3} \text{ is the same as } \frac{1}{3}x \right)$$

$$\frac{4}{3}x = 44$$

$$x = \overset{11}{\cancel{44}} \cdot \frac{3}{\underset{1}{\cancel{4}}} \quad \text{(to divide by a fraction, invert and multiply)}$$

$$x = 33$$

Rather than solving for just one unknown, as in the preceding examples, let's consider problems that involve **two unknowns** which require two equations. We begin the following problem by reducing the two lines into just one equation, and, in so doing, we restate the problem in terms of just one unknown.

The problem

$$x + 2y = 6$$

$$2x - y = 7$$

Restated

$$x + 2y = 6$$
$$4x - 2y = 14$$
$$\overline{5x \quad\quad = 20}$$
$$x \quad\quad = 4$$

Electing to remove the y's, we multiply the second line by 2, restating the equation as $(4x - 2y = 14)$. When we add the two equations, the $-2y$ cancels the $+2y$, leaving only the x's, with the remaining values easily manipulated to determine that $x = 4$. Then, to determine the value of y, we restate the original equation (the first one because it is the simplest to work with) and replace the previously unknown x with the figure 4.

Original

$$x + 2y = 6$$

(or)

Original

$$x + 2y = 6$$

Restated

$$4 + 2y = 6$$
$$-4 \quad\quad\quad -4$$
$$\overline{\quad\quad 2y = 2}$$
$$y = 1$$

Restated

$$4 + 2y = 6$$

$$2y = 6 - 4$$

$$y = 1$$

Also consider the following examples.

EXAMPLE 1

Original

$$x + 4y = -8$$
$$4x + 2y = 10$$

Restated

$$-4x - 16y = 32 \quad \text{(first line times } -4\text{)}$$
$$\underline{4x + 2y = 10}$$
$$-14y = 42$$
$$-y = 3$$

To convert the $-y$ to a $+y$, we multiply both sides of the equation by -1.

$$-y = 3$$
$$(-y)(-1) = 3(-1)$$
$$y = -3$$

We then solve for x by plugging our newly found value for y into the first (the easier) of the two original equations.

Original

$$x + 4y = -8$$

Restated

$$x + 4(-3) = -8$$
$$x - 12 \qquad = -8$$
$$\underline{+ 12 \qquad\qquad +12}$$
$$x \qquad\qquad = \quad 4$$

(or)

Original

$$x + 4y = -8$$

Restated

$$x + 4(-3) = -8$$
$$x - 12 \qquad = -8$$
$$x \qquad\qquad = -8 + 12$$
$$x \qquad\qquad = 4$$

Proof

$$x + 4y = -8$$
$$4 + 4(-3) = -8$$
$$4 - 12 = -8$$

EXAMPLE 2. If a company sells two grades of chemicals, Grade A priced at 84¢ and Grade B at 72¢, how many gallons of each grade must be combined to produce a 90-gallon mixture to form a new product valued at 80¢ per gallon?

Here we have two unknowns; that is, we must determine the number of gallons of each grade that is to be included in the mixture. Labeling Grade A as "A" and Grade B as "B" (which is much clearer than using x and y), we have the following two-line equation:

(1) $A + B = 90$
(2) $0.84 A + 0.72 B = 0.80(90)$

To reduce the equation to one unknown, we may either multiply the top line by -0.84 or -0.72. Choosing -0.84 to eliminate the $+0.84A$, we multiply all three elements in the first line by -0.84, restate the second line without alteration, and then add the two equations.

(1) $-0.84A + -0.84B = -75.6$ (first line times -0.84)
(2) $\underline{0.84A + \quad 0.72B = \quad 72.0}$
$\qquad\qquad -0.12B = \quad -3.6$
$\qquad\qquad\qquad B = 30$ gallons
$\qquad\quad A = 90 - 30 = 60$ gallons

We may also state this problem in a fashion that will enable us to solve for just one unknown. Rather than define Grade B separately from Grade A, we define it in terms of Grade A. Knowing that we need a total mixture of 90 gallons, we define Grade B as 90 gallons minus whatever amount is required for Grade A, giving us the following one-line equation:

(1) $0.84A + 0.72(90 - A) = 0.8(90)$
(2) $0.84A + 64.8 - 0.72A = 72$
(3) $\underline{\qquad -64.8 \qquad\qquad -64.8 \qquad}$
(4) $0.84A \qquad\quad -0.72A = 7.2$
(5) $\qquad\qquad\quad 0.12A = 7.2$
(6) $\qquad\qquad\qquad A = 60$ gallons

If 60 gallons of Grade A are added, 30 gallons of Grade B will be required to produce 90 gallons of final product ($60 + 30 = 90$), which we may test by plugging the answer (60 gallons) into the original equation.

(1) $0.84(60) + 0.72(90 - 60) = 0.8(90)$
(2) $0.84(60) + 0.72(30) = 0.8(90)$
(3) $50.4 + 21.6 = 72.0$

First, to illustrate just how simple it is to form easy-to-solve algebraic equations from word problems, let's consider the following exercises:

APPLICATION 1. Three times what number is 81?

$$\text{(1)} \quad 3 \cdot x = 81$$

$$\text{(2)} \quad \frac{3x}{3} = \frac{81}{3}$$

$$\text{(3)} \quad x = 27$$

APPLICATION 2. The number 35 added to what other number equals 42?

(1) $35 + x =$ 42
(2) -35 -35 *(or)* $35 + x = 42$
(3) $\overline{\hphantom{-35} \quad x = \quad 7}$ $x = 42 - 35$
                                                            $x = \;\; 7$

APPLICATION 3. What number plus 16 equals 50?

(1) $x + 16 =$ 50
(2) $- 16$ -16 *(or)* $x + 16 = 50$
$\overline{\quad x \quad\quad = \quad 34}$ $x \quad\quad = 50 - 16$
                                                        $x \quad\quad = 34$

APPLICATION 4. What number when added to three times the same number totals 24?

(1) $x + 3x = 24$
(2) $4x = 24$
(3) $x = \;\; 6$

APPLICATION 5. If 6 is subtracted from two times a number and the remainder is 24, what is the number from which 6 is subtracted?

(1) $2x - 6 =$ 24
(2) $+ 6$ $+6$
(3) $\overline{2x \quad\quad = \quad 30}$

$$\text{(4)} \quad \frac{2x}{2} = \frac{30}{2}$$

$$\text{(5)} \quad x = 15$$

(or)

$$(1)\ 2x - 6 = 24$$
$$(2)\ 2x = 24 + 6$$
$$(3)\ 2x = 30$$
$$(4)\ \ x = 15$$

Treating the unknown number as x, the word *times* as a multiplication sign, and the words *equal* and *is* as equal signs, these word problems are converted to algebraic equations almost automatically. Now, applying the same logic, let's consider some additional situations.

APPLICATION 6. We do not know the weekly salary of Employee A, but we are aware that Employee B earns \$225, which is three times the amount earned by Employee A. How much money does Employee A earn?

Using A for Employee A's salary, we have

$3A = \$225$ (3 times A's salary is \$225)

$A = \$75$ (both sides divided by 3)

We may test our accuracy by replacing A in the original equation with the answer \$75, that is, by multiplying 3 times 75:

$$3A = 225$$

$$3 \cdot 75 = 225$$

$$225 = 225$$

APPLICATION 7. Partner A and Partner B realized \$10,400 net profit from their business during August. If Partner B's share is three fifths that of Partner A, how much money will Partner A receive?

With fractions	With decimals

With fractions

$$A + \frac{3}{5}A = 10,400$$

$$\frac{8}{5}A = 10,400$$

$$\frac{\cancel{5}}{\cancel{8}} \cdot \frac{\cancel{8}}{\cancel{5}}A = 10,400 \times \frac{5}{8}$$

$$A = \$6,500$$

With decimals

$$A + .6A = 10,400$$

$$1.6A = 10,400$$

$$A = \$6,500$$

(To divide by fractions, as you will recall from Chapter 1, we must invert the multiplier before actually multiplying.)

We may test our accuracy by replacing A in the original equation:

$$6,500 + 0.6(6,500) = 6,500 + 3,900 = \$10,400$$

APPLICATION 8. A retailer bought a refrigerator from the manufacturer, added a profit of one fifth of the amount paid, and sold the unit for \$1,020. How much did the retailer pay for the refrigerator?

With fractions

$$x + \frac{1}{5}x = 1,020$$

$$\frac{6}{5}x = 1,020$$

$$\frac{\cancel{5}}{\cancel{6}} \cdot \frac{\cancel{6}}{\cancel{5}}x = 1,020 \times \frac{5}{6}$$

$$x = \$850$$

With decimals

$$x + .2x = 1,020$$

$$1.2x = 1,020$$

$$x = \$850$$

Then, by plugging the \$850 into the original equation, we find the answer to be accurate:

$$850 + \frac{1}{5}(850) = 850 + 170 = \$1,020$$

APPLICATION 9. The western Division of Marcourt, Inc. sold a total of 425 units last month for \$5,181.25, with sales consisting of Product A (priced at \$12.50 per unit) and Product B (priced at \$11.75 per unit). How many units of each product were sold during the month?

Original equation

$$A + B = 425$$
$$12.5A + 11.75B = 5,181.25$$

Restated

$$\begin{array}{r} -12.5A - 12.5B = -5,312.50 \\ \underline{12.5A + 11.75B = 5,181.25} \\ -0.75B = -131.25 \\ B = 175 \end{array}$$

We may now solve for A by plugging our value for B into the original equation.

Original

Restated

$A + B = 425$

$A + 175 = 425$
$A = 425 - 175 = 250$ units

Finally, we may test our answers by plugging both values into the original equation.

Original

$12.5(250) + 11.75(175) = 5,181.25$

Restated

$3,125.00 + 2,056.25 = 5,181.25$

APPLICATION 10. Ramco Industries employs 340 people in two divisions. Division B has 60 fewer employees than Division A. How many people are employed in each division?

$A + (A - 60) = 340$ Solve for B:

$A + A - 60 = 340$ $340 - 200 = 140$

$2A = 340 + 60$

$A = 200$ employees

Proof

$200 + (200 - 60) = 340$

$200 + 140 = 340$

PROPORTION
PROBLEMS

Some numerical relationships are directly proportional to other numerical combinations. If we know that $680 will earn interest of $85 during a one-year
period, for example, we can determine the amount of interest that $1,200
would earn without even knowing the rate of interest being paid.

Amount invested	Amount earned
680	85
1,200	x

Our equation is

$$\frac{680}{1200} = \frac{85}{x}$$

$$\frac{(1200)680x}{1200} = \frac{85(1,200)x}{x}$$ Multiply both sides by 1,200 and by x
to eliminate the denominators.

$$680x = 85(1,200)$$

$$680x = 102,000$$

$$x = \$150$$

If we had placed our initial figures in a different arrangement, the answer
would still be the same.

Amount invested	680	1,200
Amount earned	85	x

$$\frac{680}{85} = \frac{1,200}{x}$$

$$\frac{680x(85)}{85} = \frac{1,200x(85)}{x}$$

$$680x = 1,200(85)$$

$$680x = 102,000$$

$$x = \$150$$

A more expedient approach to proportional problems is termed **cross multi-plication.** Simply pair the elements diagonally and place them on opposite sides of an equal sign.

$$680 \quad 1{,}200$$
$$85 \quad x$$

$$680x = 1{,}200(85)$$

$$680x = 102{,}000$$

$$x = \$150$$

When investing a greater amount of money under identical conditions, as in the preceding example, we would expect the amount earned to be greater also; that is, we would expect the relationships to be directly proportional. However, not all such relationships are directly proportional; some are indirectly proportional instead. If we can produce 1,200 units in ten days with five machines, for example, we would expect an increase in the number of machines used to reduce the number of days required rather than to consume a greater number of days. Because the numeric combinations are indirectly proportional, we multiply across rather than diagonally.

Days	Machines
10	5
x	8

$$8x = 10 \times 5$$

$$8x = 50$$

$$x = 6.25$$

$$x = 6\text{-}1/4 \text{ days}$$

When solving proportional problems, therefore, it is important to check the logic of the expected answer, to determine whether an increase in one variable will result in a corresponding increase in another variable (directly proportional) or a decrease in the other variable (indirectly proportional).

EXPONENTIAL NOTATION

Some business transactions, including several interest computations later in this book, require the application of exponents. The concept is simple; the power of a number, which is considered to be "one" if unstated, is noted by a superscript (a small, raised number) immediately following the number to which it is related.

3 = 3 [the superscript (3^1) being unstated]

$3^2 = 3 \times 3 = 9$

$4^2 = 4 \times 4 = 16$

$5^3 = 5 \times 5 \times 5 = 125$

$10^4 = 10 \times 10 \times 10 \times 10 = 10,000$

If your calculator has a (y^x) key, you may use it in place of chain multiplication. Consider the value of 8^5.

Manual computation

$8 \times 8 \times 8 \times 8 \times 8 = 32,768$

Calculator	
Entries	**Display**
8	8.
y^x	8.
5	5.
=	32,768.

As this example shows, exponential notation represents a convenient type of shorthand when dealing with large numbers, and the calculator provides an expedient method of interpretation.

EXERCISES (as assigned by your instructor)

3-1 In solving the following problems in addition, you are to assume the plus sign in positive answers.

a. $(-21) + (-3) =$

b. $(3) + (12) =$

c. $30 + (-20) =$

d. $(12) + (-15) =$

e. $10 + 15 + (-5) =$

f. $(-12) + (-4) - (3) =$

g. $8 + (-3) + (-4) =$

h. $(-10) + (-5) + 20 =$

i. $(14) + (-7) + (-5) + 8 =$

j. $(-8) + (-5) + (-6) + 16 =$

3-2 In solving the following problems in subtraction, you are to assume the plus sign in positive answers.

a. $(15) - (7) =$ d. $(-50) - (-15) =$ g. $0.5 - (-0.25) =$

b. $(-12) - 6 =$ e. $(-21) - (-7) =$ h. $5y - (-3y) =$

c. $17 - (-18) =$ f. $3x - 2x =$ i. $(-27) - (+3) =$

3-3 In solving the following problems in multiplication, you are to assume the plus sign in positive answers.

a. $8 \cdot 5 =$ d. $(9)(-2)(2) =$ g. $5(3 + 2) =$

b. $(-3)(-2)(8) =$ e. $(7)(-3) =$ h. $6(x - 10) =$

c. $-5(30) =$ f. $(-2)(-9)(-3) =$ i. $-3(x - 5) =$

3-4 In solving the following problems in division, you are to assume the plus sign in positive answers.

a. $(20) \div (4) =$ i. $30/(-5) + (-1) =$

b. $0.22/1.1 =$ j. $-42/7 =$

c. $-20/(10)(-5) =$ k. $30/-6 =$

d. $(-16) \div (-4) =$ l. $12/-2(0.5) =$

e. $16/(8)(2) =$ m. $63/9 =$

f. $24/(-6)(2) =$ n. $-84/6 =$

g. $(-54) \div (6) =$ o. $(-48)/(-12) =$

h. $80 \div (-5) =$

3-5 Solve the following algebraic equations:

a. $16 + x = 11$ i. $3(4 - 2x) = 0$

b. $55 = 5x$ j. $-8x + 12 - x = 16$

c. $2(3 + 2) = x$ k. $143 + 37 = 9x$

d. $x - 12 = 25$ l. $44 = x \div 11$

e. $x/45 = 5$ m. $N - 20 = 35$

f. $2 + (18 \div 3) = x$ n. $3x + 2 + x = 18 + 2x$

g. $3x - 5 = 15 + x$ o. $2x - (3x - 2) = 0$

h. $-80 + 3x = 106$

3-6 Determine the values of both unknowns.

a. $2x + 10y = 30$
$6x + 15y = 60$

b. $x + y = 20$
$3x + 6y = 12(3)$

c. $x + y = 60$
$3x + 5y = 84$

d. $5x + 12y = 9$
$10x + 9y = 33$

3-7 If we add a number to three times the same number and derive a sum of 316, what is the number that we began with?

3-8 If we subtract 41 from four times another number and the remainder is 283, what is the number?

3-9 If we divide 1,318 into two parts and the difference between the parts is 702, what is the value of each of the parts?

3-10 If the total investment in a partnership by Partner A and Partner B is $360,500 and Partner A invested $110,200 more than Partner B, how much money did Partner A invest?

3-11 If Jim Snodgrass has four times as many years' service with XYZ Company as Martha Bayer has, and the difference in their seniority is 12 years, how many years' seniority does Snodgrass have?

3-12 If three numbers total 455, and if the second number is two times as great as the first, and if the third number is four times as great as the first, what are the three numbers?

3-13 At Smythe Electric the plant manager scheduled production for July 15 of 15,000 cases of fruit cocktail. If the employees on Line 14 produced only seven-eighths as many cases as produced on Line 15, how many cases were produced on each of the two lines?

3-14 The commission for a sale of property is $2,025. If the selling agent receives only three-fifths of the amount retained by the broker, how much does the broker make on the transaction? (Ignore related costs that the broker would experience.)

3-15 A total of 1,204 new homes was built in the city last year, with two and one-half times as many being built on the west side as on the east side. How many homes were built on the east side?

3-16 Of the 2,695 units sold last month, how many were sold by Marti Coleman if Jerry Adams sold twice as many as she did and Robbin Radzatz sold half as many as Marti? (Only three salespeople are in the employ of the company.)

3-17 Of a total of 77 new automobiles that were sold during December, Virginia Brown sold two and one-half times as many as Virgil Appleton, and Rex Allen sold four cars fewer than Appleton. How many automobiles did Appleton sell?

3-18 A computer that is now being sold for $2,284 has been discounted by four fifths of the original price. What was the original price?

3-19 If the mixture in a truck carrying 53-1/4 tons of ready-to-pour cement consists of 3-3/4 as much sand as gravel, plus one ton of cement mix, how much sand and gravel were used?

3-20 Of a total U.S. work force of 90 million people, there are approximately 3-1/2 times as many nonunion employees as those that belong to unions. How many unionized employees are there?

3-21 During the entire year, Discount Tire Company sold 5,046 truck tires. During the second quarter (second three-month period) they sold 1-1/4 times as many as during the first quarter. During the third quarter they sold 125 fewer tires than during the first quarter, and during the fourth quarter they sold 20 more tires than in the first quarter. How many tires were sold during the first quarter?

3-22 How many shares of Stock A at $27.50 and Stock Z at $30.125 per share did an investor buy if a total of 350 shares was purchased at a total value (excluding brokerage fees and taxes) of $10,150?

3-23 A total of 118 dress shirts amounting to $2,074.65 was sold in the men's department last month. If short sleeve shirts were priced at $16.50 each and long sleeve shirts at $19.95, how many of each kind were sold?

3-24 If a theater sells a total of 350 tickets totaling $5,715, how many $18 dollar tickets were sold for Section A and how many $15 tickets were sold for Section B?

3-25 A store manager wishes to produce a mixture of unsalted peanuts and raisins totaling 120 pounds and costing approximately $2.15 per pound. If the store pays $2.30 per pound for the peanuts and $1.80 per pound for the raisins, how many pounds of each must be combined?

3-26 If 24 construction workers can complete a project in 8 days, how many days will it take 30 workers to complete an identical project?

3-27 If a savings and loan institution paid Tolson Electronics $75 interest during a three-month period on a deposit of $2,500, how much interest will be paid during the current three-month period on a beginning balance of $3,250 — assuming that the interest rate is unchanged?

3-28 Bradshaw Corporation paid $2,510 in property taxes last year on a commercial property that has since been increased in value from $80,000 to $82,500. How much can they expect to pay in property taxes this year, assuming that the tax rate is unchanged?

3-29 If 75,200 gallons of fuel oil filled a storage tank to the 23-1/4-foot level, how many gallons will be required to reach the 40-foot level?

3-30 If a moving van is driven 330 miles in six hours, how far can we expect it to be driven in twelve hours, assuming the same number and duration of stops and identical driving conditions?

3-31 If 18 machines can produce 2,220 units in 8 hours, how many hours will it take 22 machines to produce the same number of units? (Round your answer to the 10th position.)

3-32 Compute manually the values of the following numbers:

a. $5^2 =$ d. $2^5 =$ g. $4^4 =$

b. $2^2 =$ e. $3^3 =$ h. $10^5 =$

c. $5^5 =$ f. $6^2 =$ i. $12^2 =$

3-33 Using a calculator, restate the following values in regular terms:

a. $16^2 =$ d. $11^5 =$ g. $12^7 =$

b. $20^5 =$ e. $15^6 =$ h. $25^5 =$

c. $14^3 =$ f. $180^3 =$ i. $5^8 =$

4 Percentage Applications

LEARNING OBJECTIVES

Mastering the concepts in Chapter 4 will enable you to

- apply your understanding of our money system to your use of percents
- convert percents to decimals before beginning mathematical operations
- convert decimals to percents for convenient interpretation of solutions
- utilize the percent key on calculators
- change percents to fractions and fractions to percents
- solve percentage problems algebraically or with formulas
- determine the percent of increase (decrease) in the comparison of numerical values
- identify the types of business expenses that are commonly categorized as "overhead"
- distribute overhead expenses among the various segments of a business enterprise on the basis of several established criteria

Commissions earned by sales personnel are generally calculated by employers as a percent of total sales. The interest that banks pay is figured as a percentage of the amounts deposited, and the interest that banks collect is a percentage of the amounts loaned. The discounts that manufacturers offer are almost always figured as a percentage of their regular prices. Retailers establish their prices by adding either a percentage of the costs they pay or the prices they charge, and they sometimes discount their prices in an inverse manner.

Similarly, employees pay income taxes and Social Security contributions as percents of their gross income. Consumers are taxed a fixed percent on many of the goods and services that they purchase, and they pay real estate taxes as a percent of the assessed value of their properties. They make mortgage payments based on fixed or adjustable rates (percents) of the unpaid balances, and they pay interest on automobile loans as percents of the amounts borrowed. The list goes on and on; percentage applications are not only important in commerce but also in our everyday lives as consumers and taxpayers.

RELATED CONCEPTS

Our dollar is based on the decimal system, as explained in Chapter 2. Decimals are used to separate whole dollars from fractional amounts of dollars, and we conveniently refer to the parts as *cents*. Historically, in fact, the word *percent* was spelled *per cent*, as two words rather than one, which means "per hundred." Correspondingly, the cents position is the 100ths position following the decimal:

$$1\cent = 0.01 = \frac{1}{100}$$

$$25\cent = 0.25 = \frac{25}{100} = \frac{1}{4}$$

$$50\cent = 0.5 = \frac{5}{10} = \frac{1}{2}$$

Notice that in converting cents to dollars, we move the decimal two places to the left and discard the cent sign.

In **converting percents to decimals**, we must take identical action.

Percents to decimals

$1\% = 0.01$

$25\% = 0.25$

$50\% = 0.5$

You will recall from Chapter 2 that decimals are assumed to follow whole numbers. When fractional amounts are involved (except when stated as fractions), decimals are used to separate whole numbers and related fractional amounts.

With fractions	With decimals
1-1/2%	1.5%
4-3/4%	4.75%

Percents include decimals whether stated or assumed, and we convert percents to their decimal equivalents by moving decimals two places to the left and discarding the percent sign.

Percents	Decimal equivalents
1.5%	0.015
4.75%	0.0475

In moving decimals two places to the left, we are actually dividing by 100.

$$1.5\% = 1.5 \div 100 = 0.015$$

$$4.75\% = 4.75 \div 100 = 0.0475$$

We **convert decimals to percents** in an inverse manner, that is, by moving the decimal two places to the right and adding a percent sign.

$$0.32 = 32\%$$

$$1.575 = 157\frac{1}{2}\% = 157.5\%$$

$$0.05 = 5\%$$

$$0.055 = 5\frac{1}{2}\% = 5.5\%$$

In moving the decimal two places to the right, we are actually multiplying by 100.

$$0.32 \times 100 = 32.0$$

If your calculator has a **percent (%) key**, you may use it rather than multiplying by 100. Compare the following equation with the calculator application.

The problem:

$$38.4 \div 120 = 0.32 = 32\%$$

Calculator	
Entries	**Display**
③ ⑧ . ④	38.4
÷	38.4
① ② ⓪	120.
%	32.

By entering the percent (%) sign rather than the equal (=) sign, we derive "32" (as in 32%) rather than "0.32."

Changing percents to fractions is similar to changing decimals to fractions, as discussed in Chapter 2. After converting a percent to its decimal equivalent by dividing by 100 (moving the decimal two places to the left) and removing the percent sign, we state the fractional values (numbers to the right of the decimals) as fractions

Percent	Decimal equivalent	Fraction	Lowest terms
50%	0.5	5/10	1/2
5%	0.05	5/100	1/20
0.5%	0.005	5/1000	1/200

Fifty percent (0.5) becomes 5/10 because the 5 is in the 10ths position; 0.05 becomes 5/100ths because the five is in the 100ths position, and so on.

To **change a fraction to a percent**, we divide the numerator by the denominator and multiply by 100 (move the decimal two places to the right).

Fraction	Decimal	Percent
1/2	1 ÷ 2 = 0.5	50%
1/20	1 ÷ 20 = 0.05	5%
1/200	1 ÷ 200 = 0.005	0.5%

APPLICATION 1. Convert the following percents to decimals.

150% = 1.5	12-1/2% = 0.125
25% = 0.25	3-1/8% = 0.03125
3% = 0.03	16.5% = 0.165

APPLICATION 2. Convert the following decimals to percents.

0.03 = 3%	3.0 = 300%
0.1 = 10%	1.0 = 100%
0.005 = 0.5%	1.25 = 125%

APPLICATION 3. Convert the following percents to proper fractions.

5% = 0.05 = 5/100	1-1/2%=0.015 = 15/1,000
0.5% = 0.005 = 5/1,000	1-2/3%=0.01667=1,667/10,000
60.5% = 0.605 = 605/1,000	4-3/8%=0.04375=4,375/100,000

APPLICATION 4. Convert the following fractions to percents.

1/2 = 0.5 = 50%	1/8 = 0.125 = 12.5%
1/3 = 0.333 = 33 1/3%	1/7 = 0.14285 = 14.3%
3/4 = 0.75 = 75%	3/5 = 0.6 = 60%

THE BASIC EQUATION   Most percentage problems fit nicely within the following equation:

$$BR = P$$

B Base, the whole of whatever is being considered — the total population, the total amount of a sale, the total number of products manufactured

R   Rate, a number that is always related to the percent (%) sign or the word *percent*

P   Percentage, which is defined as "part of a whole"

In discussing one fifth of a pie, for example, the pie would be the base, the percent would be the rate, and the piece would be the percentage.

Similarly, if 160 miles of transit line are to be built, only 20 percent of which has been completed, we can determine that 32 miles are now operational.

$$BR = P$$

$$160 \times 0.20 = P$$

$$160 \times 0.2 = 32 \text{ miles}$$

Calculator	
Entries	**Display**
1 6 0	160.
×	160.
. 2	0.2
=	32.

To compute percentage, therefore, we simply multiply the base times the rate.

Let's build on the preceding example by assuming that we know the number of miles of track presently in operation and the total miles to be built but do not know what percent of the total project is already completed.

$$BR = P$$

$$160R = 32$$

$$R = 32 \div 160$$

$$R = 0.2 = 20\%$$

Calculator	
Entries	**Display**
3 2	32.
÷	32.
1 6 0	160.
%	20.

We enter those numbers that are known (B and P) and solve algebraically to determine the unknown (R). As explained earlier, the percent sign is our final calculator entry when solving for rate.

If we know instead that 20 percent of the project is completed and that 32 miles are now operational, we can determine the total miles planned.

$$BR = P$$

$$B\,0.20 = 32$$

$$B = 32 \div 0.2$$

$$B = 160 \text{ miles}$$

Calculator	
Entries	**Display**
3 2	32.
÷	32.
. 2	0.2
=	160.

Again we enter the known values (R and P) and solve algebraically for the unknown (B).

Some people find the **formula approach** convenient when working percentage problems.

Figure 4.1

The percentage pyramid

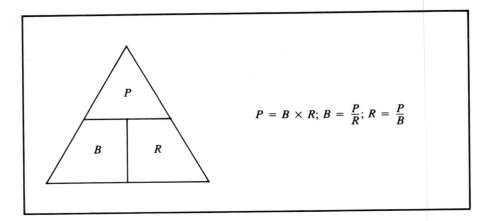

If we think of the three letters as parts of a pyramid, it seems natural to place "P" at the pinnacle, "B" at the base, and "R" at the right. It is then easy to remember that "P" is derived by multiplying "B" times "R," that "B" is computed by dividing "P" by "R," and that "R" is calculated as "P" divided by "B."

APPLICATION 1. If the work force of a city consists of 1,393,651 people, 6.3 percent of whom are unemployed, approximately how many people are unemployed?

$$BR = P$$
$$1,393,651 \times 0.063 = P$$
$$1,393,651 \times 0.063 = 87,800$$

APPLICATION 2. If the statewide labor force is 1,406,501 people, 95,079 of whom are unemployed, what is the rate of employment?

$$1,406,501 - 95,079 = 1,311,422$$
$$BR = P$$

$$1,406,501R = 1,311,422$$
$$R = 0.9324 = 93.2\%$$

APPLICATION 3. If a real estate salesperson receives a commission of $8,640 based on 6 percent of the selling price of a property, what was the selling price?

$$BR = P$$
$$B \times 0.06 = 8,640$$
$$B = \$144,000$$

APPLICATION 4. If 30 percent of a work force of 2,160 people voted for a union, how many of the employees are opposed to the union?

$$BR = P$$
$$2,160 \times 0.30 = P$$
$$2,160 \times 0.30 = 648$$
$$2,160 - 648 = 1,512$$
(*or*)
$$100\% - 30\% = 70\%$$
$$2,160 \times 0.70 = P$$
$$1,512 = P$$

APPLICATION 5. If the 23,152 women who work at Ramco Corporation constitute 32 percent of the work force, how many people are employed at the company?

$$BR = P$$
$$B \times 0.32 = 23,152$$
$$B = 72,350$$

APPLICATION 6. If at the end of one year a friend repays a personal loan of $3,500 with a check for $3,780, what rate of interest was charged?

$$3,780 - 3,500 = 280$$
$$BR = P$$
$$3,500R = 280$$
$$R = 0.08 = 8\%$$

PERCENT OF INCREASE OR DECREASE

Business people make many comparisons — comparing this year's sales with sales for the preceding year, this month's expenses with those for earlier periods, and so forth. They do so by finding the difference between the two related numbers and dividing the difference by the earlier figure. If sales for this year total $250,921 and sales for last year were $213,456, we subtract last year's sales from this year's sales and divide the difference by the sales figure for the earlier year.

Increased sales

Current year	$250,921
Preceding year	$213,456
Difference	$ 37,465

37,465 ÷ 213,456 =

0.1755162656 = 17.6%

Calculator	
Entries	**Display**
2 5 0 9 2 1	250,921.
−	250,921.
2 1 3 4 5 6	213,456.
=	37,465.
÷	37,465.
2 1 3 4 5 6	213,456.
=	.1755162656

A decrease in value from one time period to the next is calculated in an identical manner. In the following example, company sales for the current year declined $13,904 from the preceding year.

Decreased sales

Current year	$610,011
Preceding year	623,915
Difference	($ 13,904)

−13,904 ÷ 623,915 =

−0.022285087 = (2.2%)

Calculator	
Entries	**Display**
6 1 0 0 1 1	610,011.
−	610,011.
6 2 3 9 1 5	623,915.
=	−13.904.
÷	−13,904.
6 2 3 9 1 5	623,915.
=	−.022285087

Enclosure of the answer with parentheses denotes a decrease. These calculations are illustrated further in the following applications.

APPLICATION 1. If a grocer increases the price on 10-ounce cans of enchilada sauce from 57¢ to 61¢, what is the rate of increase?

New price	0.61
Original price	0.57
Difference	0.04 ÷ 0.57 = 0.070175 = 7%

APPLICATION 2. If the population of a community declined from 32,150 persons ten years ago to 24,010 today, what has been the percent of decrease?

Currently	24,010
Ten years ago	32,150
Difference	−8,140 ÷ 32,150 = −0.2532 = 25.3%

APPLICATION 3. Rossmore, Inc., a retailing firm, had sales of $1,250,335 last year compared to $1,315,620 the previous year. What was the rate of change?

$$\begin{array}{ll}
\text{Last year} & 1,250,335 \\
\text{Preceding year} & \underline{1,315,620} \\
\text{Difference} & -65,285 \div 1,315,620 = -0.04962 = (5\%)
\end{array}$$

APPLICATION 4. If you earned $33,000 last year, compared to $30,000 the preceding year, and the rate of inflation was 7 percent, were you better or worse off last year?

$$\begin{array}{ll}
\text{Last year} & 33,000 \\
\text{Preceding year} & \underline{30,000} \\
& 3,000 \div 30,000 = 0.1 = 10\%
\end{array}$$

$$10\% - 7\% = 3\% \text{ better off}$$

DISTRIBUTION OF OVERHEAD

Accountants may identify certain expenses with specific areas of a business, such as charging Department A for wages and salaries paid, for supplies consumed, and for computer time utilized by employees within that department. On the other hand, certain expenses termed **overhead** are not readily assignable to specific departments such as rental payments on buildings, utility expenses, and insurance premiums. Therefore, some pattern must be established to assign a fair share of such expenses to each department in proportion to the benefits derived.

A distribution of overhead **as a percentage of total floor space** is an allocation method that is commonly used. The distribution of a utility bill of $5,000 among four departments would be computed as follows:

Department	Square feet of floor space	Percentage equation		Total expense	Departmental expense
A	3,000	$\dfrac{3,000}{12,000}$	×	5,000	1,250.00
B	2,500	$\dfrac{2,500}{12,000}$	×	5,000	1,041.67
C	3,200	$\dfrac{3,200}{12,000}$	×	5,000	1,333.33
D	3,300	$\dfrac{3,300}{12,000}$	×	5,000	1,375.00
Total	12,000				$5,000.00

We compute the percent of total footage in Department A by dividing the square footage in that department (3,000) by total square footage in the building (12,000), giving us 0.25 or one fourth, which we multiply by the total expense of $5,000 to derive the $1,250 that is chargeable to that specific department. Upon completion of similar calculations for the remaining departments, we add the individual allocations to make certain that the total equals the amount of expense that is being distributed ($5,000 in this example).

Also consider the following calculator functions for the same problem:

Calculator Applications			
Dept. A		**Dept. B**	
Entries	**Display**	**Entries**	**Display**
3 0 0 0	3,000.	2 5 0 0	2,500.
÷	3,000.	÷	2,500.
1 2 0 0 0	12,000.	1 2 0 0 0	12,000.
×	0.25	×	.2083333333
5 0 0 0	5,000.	5 0 0 0	5,000.
=	1,250.	=	1,041.666667

Dept. C		**Dept. D**	
Entries	**Display**	**Entries**	**Display**
3 2 0 0	3,200.	3 3 0 0	3,300.
÷	3,200.	÷	3,300.
1 2 0 0 0	12,000.	1 2 0 0 0	12,000.
×	.26755555556	×	0.275
5 0 0 0	5,000.	5 0 0 0	5,000.
=	1,333.333334	=	1,375.

Notice that in each operation we are dividing by 12,000 and multiplying by 5,000. To avoid such unnecessary repetition, we may first divide 5,000 by 12,000 and then chain multiply by the square footage of each department.[1]

[1] To understand the rationale for dividing 5,000 by 12,000, consider the original equation:

$$\frac{3,000}{12,000} \times 5,000 = 1,250$$

As you will recall from our discussion of fractions in Chapter 1, we may multiply or divide in any order; that is, we may (1) divide 3,000 by 12,000 and then multiply by 5,000; (2) multiply 3,000 by 5,000 and then divide by 12,000; or (3) divide 5,000 by 12,000 and then multiply by 3,000. The third approach is most beneficial in this calculation because it enables us to simplify the related calculations for Departments B, C, and D.

Calculator Applications					
Dept. A			**Dept. B**		
Entries	**Display**		**Entries**	**Display**	
5 0 0 0	5,000.		2 5 0 0	2,500.	
÷	5,000.		=	1,041.666667	
1 2 0 0 0	12,000.				
×	.4166666667				
3 0 0 0	3,000.				
=	1,250.				

Dept. C		**Dept. D**	
Entries	**Display**	**Entries**	**Display**
3 2 0 0	3,200.	3 3 0 0	3,300.
=	1,333.333333	=	1,375.

If your calculator does not perform chain multiplication, you may divide 5,000 by 12,000 and store the resulting quotient (0.4166666667) in memory (M+). Then multiply 3,000 by memory recall (RM); 2,500 by RM; 3,200 by RM; and 3,300 by RM.

Distribution of expenses by the **number of employees** that work in the various departments of a business is sometimes appropriate, depending on the intensity and pattern of employment at a particular company. Except for using employees as our criterion for distribution, rather than square footage, the calculations are identical to those in the preceding section.

Department	Number of employees	Percentage equation		Total expense	Departmental expense
A	33	33/120	×	5,000	1,375.00
B	25	25/120	×	5,000	1,041.67
C	22	22/120	×	5,000	916.67
D	40	40/120	×	5,000	1,666.67
Total	120				$5,000.01

The resulting distribution differs drastically from the preceding one based on floor space. The one cent by which the total of all four departments is over-stated may be subtracted from either of the expense figures so that every cent of the $5,000 expense will be distributed. As before, you may avoid needless repetition by first dividing 5,000 by 120 and then chain multiplying 33, 25, 22, and 40.

An allocation **based on sales** often provides an equitable method of distributing such overhead expenses as advertisements. **Net sales** are the total revenues received from the sale of goods or services after adjustments have been made for any items that were returned for credit. Continuing with the $5,000 figure, assume that this amount was spent for advertising during a one-month period — an expense that cannot be identified directly with any of three sales divisions. Further assume that net sales were as listed here for each product group:

Group	Net sales	Percentage equation		Total expense		Departmental expense
A	$120,300	$\dfrac{120,300}{625,635}$	×	5,000	=	961.42
B	310,220	$\dfrac{310,220}{625,635}$	×	5,000	=	2,479.24
C	195,115	$\dfrac{195,115}{625,635}$	×	5,000	=	1,559.34
Total	$625,635					$5,000.00

You will find it productive to review this chapter to whatever extent necessary to assure complete understanding. The concepts presented here apply to our later discussion of interest rates as well as to several other areas of the book.

EXERCISES (as assigned by your instructor)

4-1 Convert the following percents to their decimal equivalents:

a. 3% =	f. 3-1/4% =	k. 250% =	p. 16-1/3% =
b. 32% =	g. 25-1/8% =	l. 1,000% =	q. 9% =
c. 400% =	h. 16% =	m. 21.5% =	r. 6.5% =
d. 20% =	i. 100% =	n. 6.75% =	s. 1/2% =
e. 1-1/2% =	j. 200% =	o. 1.1% =	t. 50% =

4-2 Convert the following decimal numbers to percents:

a. 0.5 =	f. 2.0 =	k. 1.375 =	p. 17-1/2 =
b. 0.50 =	g. 3.25 =	l. 1.1 =	q. 0.04 =
c. 0.05 =	h. 16-1/4 =	m. 0.1 =	r. 0.045 =
d. 0.005 =	i. 2.25 =	n. 0.01 =	s. 1.25 =
e. 0.2 =	j. 20 =	o. 31.75 =	t. 0.0625 =

4-3 Change the following percents to fractions and reduce to lowest terms.

a. 45% =	f. 2.5% =	k. 7% =	p. 9/4% =
b. 10% =	g. 8-1/4% =	l. 35% =	q. 1/2% =
c. 5% =	h. 110% =	m. 12.5% =	r. 7-1/2% =
d. 100% =	i. 0.5% =	n. 0.25% =	s. 2% =
e. 3-1/2% =	j. 1/4% =	o. 5% =	t. 25% =

4-4 Change the following fractions to percents (with percent signs) and round your answers to 10ths of a percent:

a. 1/3 =	f. 3/8 =	k. 2/3 =	p. 3-1/3 =
b. 3/4 =	g. 2/4 =	l. 1/15 =	q. 5/8 =
c. 1/5 =	h. 1/6 =	m. 7/8 =	r. 1-1/4 =
d. 2/5 =	i. 1/10 =	n. 1/16 =	s. 7/12 =
e. 1/8 =	j. 1/2 =	o. 1/7 =	t. 5/6 =

4-5 Solve the following percentage problems:

a. $92.75 is what percent of $700?
b. 150% of what number is $1,462.50?
c. What is 3-1/4 percent of $1,500?
d. What percent is $15,990 of $24,600?
e. What number is 12 percent less than 829? (Round to 100ths position.)
f. Three fifths of what number is 990?
g. What number is 16 percent more than 850?
h. $8,772.75 is what percent of $350,910.00?
i. Exactly 12 percent of all sales by Nortex Corporation were written off as bad debts, totaling $33,038.88. What were the total sales for the year?
j. What amount did a sales person receive on the sale of merchandise priced at $199.95 if the commission rate is 15 percent of the selling price?

k. How much money must a purchaser have to make a down payment of 15 percent on an automobile priced at $10,275?

l. Of the total market value of all outstanding stock, 13-1/2 percent valued at $168,750 is in preferred stock. What is the value of the common stock outstanding?

m. If a business charged a customer $33.50 in late charges in the payment of an invoice totaling $1,675.00, what percent of the amount was the penalty charge?

n. The state sales tax is 5 percent of the sales price of merchandise. What is the total amount (merchandise and tax) that must be paid on the purchase of merchandise valued at $521.95?

o. If dividends of $4.60 are paid per share this year, representing 8 percent of the market value of Marcor common stock, what is the current market value (price) of the stock?

p. Total sales last month were $452,620, of which 13-1/2 percent were cash sales. What dollar amount of sales were made on credit?

q. If a credit customer made a down payment of 20 percent on the purchase of a $255 item, what is the outstanding credit balance?

r. Worthington Industries, Inc. spent $74,745 in print advertising this year, which was 13-1/4 percent more than for last year. How much money did the company spend on this type of advertising last year?

s. If the average employee at Hurley Electronics earns a gross income of $1,260 per month, from which the company deducts $504, what percent of total income is the average employee's take-home pay?

t. At a commission rate of 4-1/4 percent, the top sales person earned $3,168.75. What was the total amount of sales realized by this one employee?

u. Officials of the Amalgamated Clothiers Union suffered a one-year decline of 16-1/2 percent in last year's membership of 85,200. What is the total membership at this time?

v. The ABC grocery chain realized a profit during November of $75,096.70, which equaled 3-1/2 cents of every dollar taken in. What was the total value of company sales during this one-month period?

w. A contractor charged the federal government $92.56 for a product that cost the company $35.60 to produce. What percent profit did the company receive?

x. A. J. Clark and Company, a food broker in San Francisco, received a commission check from California Canners for $8,520. At a commission rate of 3 percent, what is the total value of sales made by the brokerage company for this one-month period?

y. If the holder of a patent receives a 3-1/2 percent royalty on all sales of a new product, what amount of royalties should be received for sales during March totaling $850,210?

z. A large corporation paid federal income taxes of $186,750 last year on net income totaling $450,000. What was the effective tax rate for the year?

4-6 In finding the following percents of increase or decrease, round your answers to tenths of a percent where practical to do so:

a. If the manager of a computer "supermarket" lowers the price of a computer package from $1,490 to $1,284.38, what is the percent decrease?

b. The number of revenue (paid) passenger miles flown by all U.S. airlines this year totaled 259,643,870, compared to 281,305,274 for the preceding year. What was the rate of change?

c. Operating profits of Western Transports, Inc., a trucking firm, are forecast at $155,820.00 for the current year. If the projection is accurate, what will be the rate of change from last year's profits of $144,523.05?

d. In 1973 many of the oil producing countries increased the average price of a barrel of crude oil from $2.60 to $11.00. What was the percent of increase?

e. If major oil companies are now charging retailers 85 cents per gallon for regular gasoline but announce an immediate increase to 91 cents per gallon, what is the percent of increase?

f. Production workers agreed to wage cuts of 50 cents per hour on an average wage of $18.20 per hour. What was the rate of change?

g. If the average wage of production workers was increased during the year from $23.75 to $25.65 per hour, compared to an annual inflation rate of 7.5 percent, how much better or worse off from a percentage standpoint were the employees at the end of the year?

h. General expenses last year were $43,721.16, compared to $52,625.23 for the current year. What is the rate of change?

i. The utility bill for Plant A changed from $2,820.20 to $3,666.26 upon the start of operations at a nuclear power plant. What was the rate of change?

j. The store manager has directed that the shelf price of 17-ounce house-brand sweet peas be changed from 35 cents per can to 3/1.00 (three for one dollar). What is the rate of change?

4-7 What amount of a $3,560 electric bill should be charged to Department A on the basis of the number of employees, if 16-1/4 percent of the total company work force is located in Department A?

4-8 What amount of a $1,600.15 insurance bill should be charged to Department B if distribution is based on square footage? Total footage of production facilities is 35,610, of which 5,768.82 is located in Department B.

4-9 If monthly rental fees for a department store total $12,620, what amounts are to be charged to the shoe department (1,200 square feet) and to appliances (2,010 square feet), provided that overhead is distributed on the basis of square footage for the entire store (54,210 square feet)?

4-10 Distribute $17,210 in computer expenses among the following divisions according to dollars of sales volume: Western Division, $45,182.68; Midwest Division, $104,025.24; Southern Division, $73,553.20; Eastern Division, $39,928.88. (Show all computations, even though using a calculator.)

5 Producers' Prices and Discounts

LEARNING OBJECTIVES

Mastery of the materials in Chapter 5 will prepare you for the next two chapters by enabling you to

- identify the individual elements commonly used in marketing channels
- describe the functions and interactions of marketing intermediaries
- distinguish between list prices and discounted prices
- explain the difference between trade discounts and cash discounts
- understand and define such credit terms and abbreviations as ordinary dating, receipt of goods (ROG), after arrival (AA), and end of month (EOM)
- explain the rationale for variations in the terms of sale
- apply trade discounts, cash discounts, and extended charges
- describe the rationale and mechanism for price protection
- itemize discounts and apply short-cut methods for deriving net values
- perform basic calculations for the preparation and interpretation of invoices

A study of commerce quite naturally begins with a discussion of the prices that producers charge, simply because most commercial transactions originate with the producers of goods and services. The study is continued in Chapter 6 (Transportation Costs and Invoices) and Chapter 7 (Retail Transactions) as we follow the flows of products and the related transactions.

FLOWS OF COMMERCE

Figure 5.1 outlines the four patterns of distribution that are commonly used to channel products from manufacturers to consumers, with all other participants being routinely referred to as "marketing intermediaries" or "middlemen."

The word *producer* may be applied to businesses where either goods or services are produced. Also, a producer of one class of products may be the customer of a producer of another class of products, such as a pencil manufacturer buying wood from a lumber company and a computer manufacturer buying integrated circuits from an outside supplier. For purposes of clarity, however, we are

FIGURE 5.1

Channels of Distribution

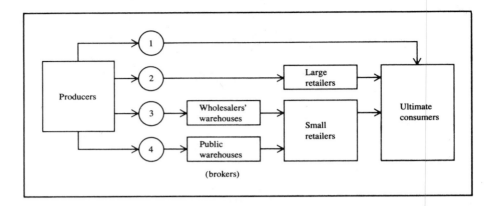

confining this presentation to the flow of goods from a single producer to an ultimate (final) consumer.

1. The first line in Figure 5.1 illustrates those uncommon situations in which producers sell directly to consumers with such appeals as "direct from factory to you" and "why don't you visit our factory showroom." The word "showroom" suggests a retailing area in which potential customers may inspect the merchandise. In essence, these producers are performing their own retailing function.

2. The second line of Figure 5.1 includes one marketing intermediary, the retailer. Many producers sell directly to retailers, especially to large retailers, without the involvement of wholesalers or brokers. **Retailers**, by definition, make the final sales to consumers. When retailers do not use the services of wholesalers, it is usually because they perform a similar function as an integral part of their own operations; that is, they order large quantities shipped to central locations from where they distribute relatively small quantities to their individual retail outlets.

3. The third line of figure 5.1 adds another class of intermediary, the wholesaler. **Wholesalers** are in business for themselves, independent of producers and retailers. They normally buy from producers in large quantities and sell to retailers in relatively small quantities. They take physical possession of the products and assume complete responsibility for their resale.

4. Line 4 of Figure 5.1 illustrates still another common arrangement. Many producers contract with **brokers** to perform the selling function in various parts of the country. A retailer routinely mails purchase orders for a wide variety of products to a single broker. The broker, in turn, either orders the items from producers for delayed delivery or has the items delivered promptly from local warehouse stocks. In either event, the producer ships products to public warehouses for eventual delivery to retailers. Producers normally compensate brokers for their sales and clerical activities on a commission

basis, payable monthly, as a percentage of the value of the merchandise sold — payments that producers normally absorb as a routine and necessary cost of doing business.

In many instances, therefore, several different companies may become involved in the channeling of products from manufacturer to consumer. Multiple factors also influence the prices that manufacturers charge. After accounting for all costs and expenses, which sometimes include brokers' commissions, manufacturers must add a profit factor to the prices they charge. Transportation charges must also be considered, and discounts are sometimes offered.

TRADE DISCOUNTS

List prices are the base prices that producers publish, usually in the form of price lists. These lists may range from one page to entire catalogs of prices, and, at many companies, list prices are subject to frequent or continuous discounts. Rather than undergo the costly process of revising and reissuing existing price quotations, a producer may simply announce discounts in the price of one, several, or all products. A producer may issue a bulletin to its business customers, for example, to announce a temporary discount of $2.00 per case off the list price of 24/1 Blue Ridge elberta peaches. The "24" represents the number of cans per case, and the "1" specifies that the contents of each can weigh approximately one pound. A wholesaler or retailer ordering 1,000 cases of the item would be charged $33,500, assuming a list price of $35.50 per case.

1,000 cs @ $35.50 = $35,500
Discount   −2,000
                             $33,500

The producer may decide to offer the $2 discount on this particular item for all orders received (or postmarked) from March 1 through 20. The manufacturer's bulletin might also include information about **price protection**, which would grant the discount on purchases made a week or two before the starting discount date, advising either (1) that refunds would be made automatically or (2) that the buyers must submit refund requests. The rationale for offering price protection is as encouragement to business customers (such as grocery chains) to place their orders regularly rather than await the announcements of trade discounts.

Some producers offer **chain discounts** as enticements for their business customers to order merchandise in large quantities. An order for 500 units of a product might carry a discount of 5 percent, for instance, with a second discount of 3 percent offered for orders of 1,000 or more units. Assuming a list price of $20, the discounted (per-unit) prices in the following three orders differ significantly.

Number of units ordered		List Price per unit	Dollar amount	Per unit price
250		$20	$5,000	$20.00
500		$20	$10,000	
	Less 5%		−500	$19.00
			$9,500	
1,000		$20	$20,000	
	Less 5% and 3%		−1,570	$18.43
			$18,430	

Observe the competitive advantage that the high-volume purchaser (1,000 units) has over the buyer of small quantities (250 units), a difference of $1.57 per unit. Manufacturers may legally offer quantity discounts only when they can demonstrate cost savings related to the processing of relatively large orders.

In applying **chain discounts**, we do not simply add the discounts and multiply. For the 1,000-unit transactions illustrated here, we must apply the first discount, deriving a net value, and then apply the second discount.

First discount   1,000 units × $20 = $20,000
                            $20,000 × 0.05 = −1,000
                                                      $19,000

Second discount $19,000 × 0.03   −570
                                                   $18,430

An easier approach to the computation of discounts is to multiply the list price or amount by the complement of the discount, which is the difference between the discount and one. If a 5 percent discount is to be offered, as in the 500-unit purchase, the buyer is actually paying 95 percent of the list price (100% − 5% = 95%).

$10,000 × 0.95 = $9,500

Calculator	
Entries	**Display**
1 0 0 0 0	10,000.
×	10,000.
. 9 5	0.95
=	9,500.

If chain discounts of 5 percent and 3 percent are offered, as in the 1,000-unit purchase, we may simplify our calculations by multiplying the $20,000 by 95 percent (100% − 5% = 95%) and by 97 percent (100% − 3% = 97%).

$20,000(0.95)(0.97) = $18,430

Calculator	
Entries	**Display**
2 0 0 0 0	20,000.
×	20,000.
. 9 5	0.95
×	19,000.
. 9 7	0.97
=	18,430.

In transactions involving chain discounts, it is often instructive to the producer, the wholesaler, and the retailer to know the **equivalent discount**, that is, the actual rate of discount being offered. What is being asked, in essence, is this: What percent is the discount of the amount being discounted?

Amount to be discounted − net amount = Amount of discount

$20,000 − 18,430 = 1,570

Base × Rate = Percentage

$20,000R = $1,570

R = 0.0785 = 7.85%

Calculator	
Entries	**Display**
2 0 0 0 0	20,000.
−	20,000.
1 8 4 3 0	18,430.
=	1,570.
÷	1,570.
2 0 0 0 0	20,000.
=	0.0785

A more expedient method of calculating the equivalent (actual) rate of discount is to multiply the complements of the discounts and subtract the product from one.

(0.95)(0.97) = 0.9215

1.0 − 0.9215 = 0.0785 = 7.85%

Calculator	
Entries	**Display**
. 9 5	0.95
×	0.95
. 9 7	0.97
=	0.9215
M+ or STO	0.9215
1	1.
−	1.
MR or RCL	0.9215
=	0.0785

In buying 1,000 units with discounts of 5 percent and 3 percent, the purchaser is receiving an actual discount of 7.85 percent. The following applications serve to illustrate these concepts through a broader range of transactions.

APPLICATION 1. What amount should the manufacturer bill a hardware company for 850 bulk-pack drills @ $2.65 each?

$850 \times 2.65 = \$2,252.50$

APPLICATION 2. If Stay Fresh cling peaches are listed at $22.50 per case, what amount should the packer charge a chain store for the purchase of 2,500 cases, assuming that the order is placed during a period when a trade discount of $1.25 per case is in effect?

$$
\begin{array}{lr}
2,500 \times 22.50 = & 56,250 \\
\text{Discount} & \underline{-3,125}\ (2,500 \times 1.25) \\
\text{Net Amount} & \$53,125
\end{array}
$$

APPLICATION 3. If a wholesaler orders 1,000 cartons of 6/4 oz yarn at $1.25 per carton, subject to discounts of 8 percent and 5 percent, what is the net amount?

$1,000 \times 1.25 = 1,250$
$1,250(0.92)(0.95) = \$1,092.50$

APPLICATION 4. If items are purchased totaling $2,850 (list), what is the net amount after allowing successive discounts of 10 percent, 7 percent, and 3 percent?

$2,850(0.9)(0.93)(0.97) = \$2,313.89$

APPLICATION 5. What is the equivalent discount received by the buyer in Application 4?

$2,850.00 - 2,313.89 = 536.11$
$BR = P$
$2,850R = 536.11$
$R = 0.1881087719 = 18.8\%$
(or)
$(0.9)(0.93)(0.97) = 0.81189$
$1.0 - 0.81189 = 0.1881 = 18.8\%$

CASH DISCOUNTS AND EXTENDED CHARGES

A **cash discount** is a deduction from the net amount that a business may take (deduct) for paying promptly. The common terms of sale within the giant food industry, for example, are "2/10, n/30," which means that the seller is extending credit to the business buyer and that the buyer may deduct 2 percent from the net amount of the invoice (bill) if payment is made within ten days from the date of the invoice. No cash discount should be taken when payment is made after the ten-day period. The "n/30" specifies that if not paid within the discount period the net amount of the invoice becomes due within thirty days from the date of the invoice. The seller considers the buyer delinquent if thirty days elapse with no payment forthcoming.

To illustrate, assume that a wholesaler has purchased 500 cases of canned goods at $24.50 per case and that payment is made within the discount period.

$$500 \times 24.50 = \quad 12{,}250 \text{ net amount}$$
$$12{,}250 \times 0.02 \quad \underline{-245} \text{ cash discount}$$
$$\$12{,}005 \text{ payment}$$

The buyer is entitled to deduct $245 and issue a check to the seller for the balance of $12,005.

The end date of a discount period is figured by adding to the current date the number of days allowed. Under the standard terms of "2/10," the final payment dates for earning discounts on invoices dated January 12, 15, and 25 are as follows:

Invoice date	Final discount date	Computation
January 12	January 22	12 + 10 = 22
January 15	January 25	15 + 10 = 25
January 25	February 4	6 days in January 4 days in February

In computing discount periods, remember that April, June, September, and November have only 30 days and that February has 28 days except for Leap Year (every presidential election year in the United States) when it has 29 days.

Terms may vary with respect to the percent of discount offered and the length of the discount period. Under terms of "2/10, 1/20, n/30," for instance, the buyer may deduct 2 percent if paid within ten days of the date of the invoice but only 1 percent if paid within the second ten-day period. Other terms may apply as well.

Receipt of goods (ROG) and **after arrival (AA)** are synonymous; the discount period does not begin until the products have reached the buyer's warehouse. When products are shipped under regular terms from the West Coast to the Midwest or East Coast, for instance, the buyers would often have to pay for their orders before receiving them. To offset the competitive disadvantage that Midwest or East Coast buyers would experience in relation to buyers located closer to the point of shipment, the manufacturer offers special terms to distant buyers.

For a purchase of 2,250 units at $4.25 each under terms of "1-1/2/10, n/30, ROG," the buyer should remit $9,419.06 if paid by August 15, assuming that the shipment was received at its destination on August 5.

$$2{,}250 \times 4.25 \qquad = \$9{,}562.50 \text{ net amount}$$
$$9{,}562.50 \times 0.015 = \underline{-143.44} \text{ cash discount}$$
$$\$9{,}419.06 \text{ payment}$$

Terms of **end of month (EOM)**, which is sometimes referred to as **prox** (an abbreviation for the Latin word *proximo*), indicates that a discount period of ten days begins the first day of the following month. For an invoice dated January 5, under terms of "2/10, EOM," for example, the buyer may deduct 2 percent from the net amount of the invoice if payment is made by February 10. When an invoice is dated the 26th of the month or later, however, the buyer has an extra month to pay; that is, discount periods begin the first day of the second month. If an invoice is dated April 28 under terms of "2/10, EOM," for instance, the buyer may deduct 2 percent from the net amount of the invoice if payment is made by June 10. Because of the legal implications involved, EOM terms should reflect the number of days that may elapse before payment becomes delinquent, as in "2/10, n/30, EOM." When no such limitation is specified, a 20-day grace period is commonly assumed to follow the discount period.

When buyers do not send payment within the discount periods, one of two situations probably exists: First, the business customer may have fallen behind in his or her bookkeeping chores. Second, and more likely, the company may be short of funds. Buyers may postpone payment for 20 days under the usual terms of sale before payment becomes past due, but, as you will read in Chapter 8, the annualized interest rate that buyers effectively pay for this privilege is in excess of 30 percent. The failure of a buyer to pay promptly, therefore, usually denotes severe financial circumstances. When a customer does not qualify as credit worthy, a C.O.D. transaction becomes a possibility, as discussed in the following chapter.

You might wonder why some producers offer credit terms that differ so drastically from those offered by other companies. Industry patterns usually dictate the terms of sale. If competing companies are offering terms of "2/10, n/30," any company offering lesser terms will suffer decreased sales. Even worse consequences might occur if a company offers relatively liberal terms as a way of gaining sales, in that competitors will usually be forced to offer identical terms with decreased revenues resulting for all concerned. A widely accepted practice, on the other hand, is to offer more lenient terms of sale on a one-time basis for new businesses and in connection with the sale of slow-moving stock and odd-lot merchandise that is of substandard quality.

Rather than rewarding buyers for paying promptly, producers within some industries penalize buyers for paying late. **Extended charges** of "net 10 days + 1-1/2% in 30 days" means that a buyer of 100 $15-items remits only the full (net) amount of the invoice if payment is made within the ten-day period but includes a penalty payment of $22.50 if the check is mailed after that date.

$$100 \times 15 \quad = \quad 1{,}500.00 \text{ net amount}$$
$$1{,}500 \times 0.015 = \quad \underline{+22.50} \text{ extended charge}$$
$$\$1{,}522.50 \text{ payment}$$

In either event, whether business buyers are rewarded for paying promptly or are penalized for paying late, bills that are past due should be subject to interest charges. Sellers do not want buyers to use money that is due them without being charged for the privilege, so they routinely ask delinquent buyers to sign short-term notes so that the eventual payments received will include accrued interest.

Buyers with cash-flow problems sometimes make **partial payments** as a way of earning at least part of the cash discounts and also as a way of appeasing their creditors. Whatever the buyer's reasons may be, partial payments within discount periods are entitled to the prevailing cash discounts. If Aramco, Inc. owes $3,200 in payment of an invoice dated August 5 under terms of "2/10, n/30," a payment of $1,500 on or before August 15 would be credited as $1,530.61, leaving a balance due of $1,669.39.

$$100\% - 2\% = 98\%$$

$$BR = P$$

$$B \times 0.98 = 1{,}500$$

$$0.98B = 1{,}500$$

$$B = 1{,}530.61 \text{ credited}$$
$$\text{to account}$$

$$3{,}200.00 - 1{,}530.61 = \$1{,}669.39$$
$$\text{balance due}$$

Calculator	
Entries	**Display**
1 5 0 0	1,500.
÷	1,500.
. 9 8	0.98
=	1,530.61
M+ or STO	1,530.61
3 2 0 0	3,200.
−	3,200.
RM or RCL	1,530.61
=	1,669.39

(or)

$$0.98x = 1{,}500$$

$$x = 1{,}530.61$$

If a cash discount of 2 percent applies, the $1,500 payment must be considered 98 percent of some amount; therefore, we ask the following question: Ninety-eight percent of what amount (our unknown B) equals $1,500? Having made the calculation, we credit the buyer's account just as though payment of $1,530.61 had been made. The unpaid balance must be paid by September 4 (26 days in August and 4 in September = 30 days) before it will be classified as "past due." The following examples illustrate these concepts more thoroughly.

APPLICATION 1. If a retailer contracts for 50 boxes of cast iron skillets (six skillets to the box) at $30.50 per box, under terms of "3/10, n/30," what amount should the buyer pay on July 12? Assume that the invoice was dated July 3.

$$50 \times 30.50 = 1,525.00 \text{ net amount}$$
$$1,525.00 \times 0.03 = \underline{\quad 45.75} \text{ cash discount}$$
$$\$1,479.25 \text{ payment}$$

APPLICATION 2. If an invoice for merchandise totaling $1,600 is dated August 10 under terms of "2/10, n/30," what amount should the buyer remit if payment is made August 22?

The net amount of $1,600 because the payment was made after the discount period had elapsed.

APPLICATION 3. An invoice dated March 20 carries terms of "2/10, 1/20, n/30." If total value of the listed items is $3,650, what amount should the buyer remit if payment is mailed April 2?

3,650.00 net amount
$$\underline{-36.50} \text{ cash discount } (3,650 \times 0.01)$$
$3,613.50 payment

APPLICATION 4. As a clerk in the accounts payable department, by what date must you pay an invoice dated September 29, under terms of "2/10, EOM," if you are to earn the 2 percent cash discount?

By November 10 (an extra month because dated later than the 25th).

APPLICATION 5. By what date should the buyer make payment on an invoice dated January 15 under terms of "2/10, n/30, ROG" to earn the full cash discount, provided the merchandise was received on January 27?

By February 6 (4 days + 6 days = 10 days).

APPLICATION 6. What amount would you pay for goods valued at $850 on an invoice dated April 5 under terms of "net 10 days + 1%" if payment is made on April 26?

850.00 net amount
$$850.00 \times 0.01 = \underline{+8.50} \text{ extended charge}$$
$858.50 payment

APPLICATION 7. If you receive a check for $1,000 on July 10 in partial payment of an invoice dated July 2, by what amount will you reduce the balance due in the customer's account? The terms are "1-1/2/10, net 30."

$$100\% - 1\text{-}1/2\% = 98\text{-}1/2\%$$
$$BR = P$$
$$B \times 0.985 = 1,000$$

$$0.985B = 1,000$$
$$B = \$1,015.23$$
(or)
$$0.985x = 1,000$$
$$x = \$1,015.23$$

ALL FACTORS
CONSIDERED

In considering all of the elements that comprise a producer's invoice, we should cite two important points. First, the net amount of an invoice does *not* include freight charges; any freight charges that might have been added to the computation must be subtracted before a net figure is derived as the basis for cash discounts and broker's commissions. Second, broker's commissions, when applicable, are computed on the net amount of the invoice but are not included in the final amounts that business customers must pay.

As an illustration, assume that you are a packer of canned chicken and turkey and that on August 2 you have shipped ten 12/50 case packs at $64.05 each. A trade discount of 5 percent is in effect for orders of ten or more packs, and terms of sale are "2/10, n/30." Freight charges total $125.50, which the buyer is to pay, and the broker's commission on this private label product is only 2-1/2 percent. What amount must the retailer pay, provided that payment is made on August 10?

10 case packs × $64.05	$640.50 total amount
640.50 × 0.05	−32.03 trade discount
	$608.47 net amount
	125.50 freight charges
608.47 × 0.02	−12.17 cash discount
	$721.80 payment

Notice that the rate of discount is itemized, a recommended practice that reduces the necessity for phone calls and letters seeking clarification of your computations.

A broker's commission of $15.21 would be computed at the end of the month and paid along with earnings for other sales during that period.

Net amount × Rate = Commission

$608.47   × 0.025 = $15.21

Also consider the varying circumstances in the following applications.

APPLICATION 1. A retailer has purchased through a broker (3% commission rate) 150 cartons of Product A at $12.25 per unit and 500 cartons of Product B at $16.75 each. Freight charges, which the seller is to pay and then charge to the retailer, total $520.16, and terms of sale are "2/10, 1/20, n/30" on an invoice dated May 6. Product A carries a trade discount of 5 percent, and Product B is subject to successive discounts of 5 percent and 3 percent. If payment is made on May 20, what amount should the retailer pay?

Product A	150 ctns @ $12.25	1,837.50	
	1,837.50 × 0.05	−91.88	$1,745.62
Product B	500 ctns @ $16.75	8,375.00	
	8,375.00 × 0.05	−418.75	
		7,956.25	
	7,956.25 × 0.03	−238.69	7,717.56

Net amount	9,463.18
Freight	520.16
Cash discount 9,463.18 × 0.01	−94.63
Payment	$9,888.71

(Brokerage: 9,463.18 × 0.03 = $283.90)

APPLICATION 2. A retailer receives a carload shipment (3,000 cases of canned goods at $28.75 per case) on October 23, relating to Invoice 26158 dated October 7 of the current year. A promotional allowance (trade discount) of $2.50 per case is presently in effect. Freight charges are being paid separately by the retailer, and the transaction was consummated without the assistance of a broker. If terms are "2/10, n/30 AA," (a) what is the last day that payment can be made to earn a cash discount, and (b) what would be the amount of payment on that date?

a. The last discount day is November 2 (8 days in October plus two in November equal 10 days after arrival of the shipment).

b. 3,000 CS × $28.75 $86,250
   3,000 CS × $2.50   −7,500 trade discount
                       $78,750 net amount
   78,750 × 0.02   −1,575 cash discount
                       $77,175 payment

APPLICATION 3. A manufacturer shipped an order on December 20 that included 220 boxes of merchandise that were invoiced on December 22 at a total amount of $10,320 — including freight charges of $420. If terms of sale are "2/10, EOM" and if a broker's commission of 1-1/2 percent must eventually be paid, (a) when is the last day the cash discount may be taken, (b) when would payment become due if not paid within the discount period, and (c) exactly how much money will the manufacturer realize from the sale (including freight but excluding brokerage) if payment is made within the discount period?

a. The last day of discount period is January 10.
b. January 30 (January 10 + 20 days).
c. $10,320 − $420 = $9,900.00 net amount
   9,900 × 0.02   −198.00 cash discount
   9,900 × 0.015   −148.50 commission
                        420.00 freight
                       $9,973.50

APPLICATION 4. If an invoice is dated July 28 under terms of "2/10, n/30, EOM" in the amount of $16,450, what is the balance due after the buyer makes a $10,000 payment on August 15?

$$100\% - 2\% = 98\%$$

$$0.98x = 10,000$$

$$x = 10,204.08$$

$$16,450.00 - 10,204.08 = \$6,245.92$$

The discount date is extended 30 days to September 10 because the invoice is dated after the 25th of the month.

Chapter 6 builds on the materials covered here by explaining the special mathematics that are involved in computing transportation charges and by bringing all of these concepts together in the preparation and interpretation of invoices.

EXERCISES (as assigned by your instructor)

5-1 Essay questions:

a. List the names of three prominent retailing firms within the United States.
b. What are the functions of a wholesaler?
c. What are the differences between wholesaling operations and those of brokers?
d. How do some large retailers manage to operate without the assistance of either wholesalers or brokers?
e. What are list prices?
f. What is the difference between a list price and a net price?
g. Why do many companies routinely issue trade discounts rather than publish new list prices?
h. What is the difference between a trade discount and a cash discount?
i. What is meant by the acronym ROG? EOM? AA?
j. Explain why multiple discounts of 4 percent and 3 percent do or do not represent an equivalent discount of 7 percent.
k. What did the authors mean when they stated that chain discounts are sometimes related to the quantities purchased?
l. Are quantity discounts a form of discrimination against small companies? Explain your answer.
m. What is price protection? Who receives it? What is the rationale for such provisions?
n. What action should a seller take when a buyer does not pay within the discount period?

o. Why do the provisions of cash discounts differ so drastically from one industry to another?

p. Wouldn't it be expedient for sellers to switch from costly terms of sale? Rather than rewarding business customers for paying promptly, for example, wouldn't it be good business to penalize them for paying late?

q. What does it mean, specifically, when the authors advise that cash discounts and brokers' commissions are stated as a percentage of the net amount of an invoice? How do freight charges enter into the computation?

r. Who pays a broker's commission (if any), the seller or the buyer?

5-2 Trade discounts (round percent answers to the 10ths position):

a. What is the net amount of an invoice for 500 units at $16.50 per unit?

b. What is the net price of an item that lists at $26.25 after multiple discounts of 15 percent and 12-1/2 percent have been applied?

c. Find the net price of an item that lists for $48.20 and is subject to chain discounts of 16 percent, 12 percent, and 8 percent.

d. In Problem 5-2c, what is the equivalent discount of the multiple discounts?

e. What is the actual percent discount received by a retailer who buys products from a price list that is subject to chain discounts of 17 percent, 13 percent, and 5-1/2 percent?

f. What is the amount of discount (in dollars and cents) of 500 cartons of foodstuff that list for $31.75 per unit, with a per-unit discount of 60 cents?

g. In Problem 5-2f, what percent is the discount?

h. If a retailer pays $37.83 for an item that has been discounted 22 percent from the list price, what was the list price?

i. An item that a manufacturer lists at $35.50 is sold to a retailer for $27.10 each. By what percent was the item discounted?

j. What is the net amount of an invoice for 500 units @ $38.80 each with multiple discounts of 12 percent, 9 percent, and 5 percent?

k. What is the list price of an item that sells for $72.07 after applying trade discounts of 10 percent, 5 percent, and 3 percent?

l. If an item that lists at $140.50 is subject to chain discounts of 30 percent and 20 percent, what per-unit price must a retailer pay?

m. If an order is valued at $16,702 on the basis of list prices which are still subject to discounts of 15 percent and 10 percent, what is the total amount of the discounts?

n. What is the net amount of a $65 item following discounts of 13 percent, 7-1/2 percent, and 5 percent?

o. If a manufacturer raises the list price of a $47.90 item by 5 percent but continues to allow multiple discounts of 10 percent and 7 percent, what is the new net price of the item?

p. As the owner of a hardware store, you can buy push brooms at $55 per dozen from one wholesaler but at $4.88 each with a 7 percent discount from another wholesaler. Which purchase is the least expensive and by how much?

q. A manufacturer has applied what rate of discount off the list price if an item that lists at $118.20 is offered at $98.70?

r. Appliance City, a large retailing chain, has contracted with a Japanese firm for 1,000 video recorders at $950 each, less discounts of 15 and 10 percent. What is the net amount of the invoice that the distributor will mail to Appliance City?

s. A wholesaler offers High Marks pencils at $46.08 per gross (twelve dozen), less a 5 percent discount for purchases of at least ten gross and an additional 3 percent discount on purchases of at least twenty gross. (a) What is the net amount of the invoice for twenty gross? (b) What is the net price per pencil on the purchase?

t. If teacups are listed by a manufacturer at $150 per dozen and are subject to discounts of 8 percent and 4 percent, what is the per-unit price that retailers must pay?

5-3 Cash discounts and extended charges:

a. What amount should a retailer remit for an invoice with a net amount of $2,500 that is dated June 21 and carries terms of "2/10, n/30," provided payment is made on July 1?

b. If a manufacturer's invoice is for 500 integrated circuits priced at $16.50 per unit, what amount should the credit people there expect to receive on an invoice dated June 20 that is paid on July 1 under terms of "1/10, n/60"?

c. If the terms of sale on an invoice dated March 10 for merchandise that is valued at $65,000 (after two trade discounts have been applied) are "3/10, 1-1/2/20, n/30 EOM," what amount should the buyer remit on March 25?

d. If a large retailing company receives on September 25 a railcar that is loaded with merchandise and that is related to the manufacturer's invoice of September 14 for $105,000 which carries terms of "2/10, n/30 AA," (a) what is the last day of the discount period and (b) what amount should be remitted if payment is made by that date?

e. If the net amount of an invoice is $85,750 under terms of "3/10, 2/20, n/30," what is the balance due the seller if the buyer makes payment of $50,000 on March 7? The invoice is dated February 25 of the current year (a Leap Year).

f. What amount should a wholesaler pay a manufacturer for goods with a net value of $42,950 if terms are "net 10 days + 1%"? The invoice is dated January 15, and payment is to be made on January 30.

g. If you were employed in the accounts payable section of the accounting department at Rutgers International, what payment would you authorize for the receipt of a shipment valued at $92,000 under terms of "2/10 EOM"? The invoice is dated April 28, and payment will be made on June 6.

h. A packing company shipped goods with a net value of $5,650 on May 10. If the company issued an invoice on May 12 with terms of "2/10, 1/20, n/30," (a) what is the last date that payment can be made to earn a 2 percent discount, (b) what is the last day to earn a 1 percent discount, and (c) what amount should be paid if payment is withheld until June 15?

i. If payment is made August 16 on an invoice for $16,500 dated July 25, under terms of "15 days + 1-1/2% in 30 days," what amount should be remitted?

j. What is the last day on which payment can be made without foregoing the cash discount if terms are "2% EOM, n/30" and the invoice date is March 15?

5-4 Comprehensive discount problems:

a. What amount should a retailer pay for the following items under terms of "2/10, n/30" if the invoice is dated December 10 and payment is on December 18?

100 6/48	OZ CRUNCHY WHOLE SWEET PICKLES	$13.46 PER CASE
150 6/48	OZ CRUNCHY FRESH CUCUMBER CHIPS	10.10
75 12/22	OZ CRUNCHY FR PACK KOSHER DILLS	10.28

The retailer used his own truck to pick up the items.

b. A small retailer dropped by a public warehouse to pick up the following items that your company had in storage there. Standard terms of sale are "3/10, 2/20, n/30," and freight and handling charges of 85 cents per case are added to the invoice. If both items are subject to a 5 percent discount, what is the correct amount of payment on your invoice dated June 25 if the retailer mails a check to your company on July 15?

25 CTNS 12/1.25   OZ PAN RICH BROWN GRAVY CONCENTRATE
$7.56 CTN

125 CTNS 12/1-5/8   OZ PAN RICH CHICKEN GRAVY CONCENTRATE
8.12 CTN

c. If 300 cases of Product A list at $22.50 each and 500 cases of Product B list at $26.85 each, as reflected on the seller's invoice dated March 14, what amount must the retailer remit on April 8 under terms of "2% EOM, 30 days"? A trade discount of 5 percent applies to all orders of 250 or more cases, and a second discount of 2-1/2 percent applies to orders of 500 or more cases — even when the same order includes mixed items. Transportation costs of $245 are to be added to the invoice, and a broker is entitled to a 3 percent commission on the sale.

d. A retailer has the choice of buying 500 cases of 24/8 OZ Campbell's

Old Fashion bean soup at $8.50 per carton, including delivery, or placing an order with a broker for delivery from a local warehouse at $7.75. Terms of sale for either purchase would be "3/10, n/30," but the order placed with the broker would also involve a handling and delivery charge of 75 cents per carton. Which is the better choice, and what is the difference in total costs, provided that the retailer pays during the discount period?

e. Six dinette sets are listed by the manufacturer (including delivery), subject to commercial discounts of 7 percent, 5 percent, and 2 percent. The invoice is dated August 3, under terms of "5/10, EOM, 60 days," is subject to a broker's commission of 1-1/2 percent, and is paid on September 8.

(a) What is the net amount of the invoice?
(b) What is the equivalent discount?
(c) What is the brokerage payment?
(d) What amount must the buyer pay?

6 Transportation Costs and Invoices

The materials in this chapter, which help bridge the gap between the operations of manufacturers and retailers, will enable you to

- recognize and describe the documents normally involved in the sale and shipment of products from a manufacturer to a retailer or wholesaler
- apply the abbreviations F.O.B. and F.A.S. in a legally correct manner
- apply freight rates on a per cwt., per M, and per ton basis
- compute freight costs in connection with minimum weight requirements
- calculate weight-break points between sets of weight-rate combinations
- minimize shipping costs by pooling certain shipments
- process shipments on a C.O.D. and a shipper's order basis
- apply for refunds of overcharges by transportation companies
- prepare and interpret various types of invoices
- figure the amount of money that brokers remit to their principals (when selling products for them) or collect from their principals (when buying products for them)

Having considered in the preceding chapter the prices that producers charge and the discounts that they offer, let's focus on two areas of common interest to both sellers and buyers — transportation costs and invoices. Before a purchase agreement can be reached, a determination must be made as to who is to pay the shipping charges, either the shipper (consignor) or the receiver (consignee). Whether or not any transportation charges appear on the seller's invoice depends on prior agreement between the two parties. In either case, it is important that the employees on both ends of such transactions have a working knowledge of freight rates and a thorough understanding of invoices.

So that you may keep the seller-buyer relationship in proper perspective, consider the following steps and documents that are involved in a typical manufacturer-retailer transaction:

1. The retailer submits a **purchase order** to a manufacturer, specifying the items being ordered and the related prices.
2. The manufacturer releases the merchandise and transfers responsibility to the transportation company upon signing a **bill of lading** (shipping agreement) by representatives of both the manufacturer and the transportation company.
3. The carrier (rail, truck, air, or steamship company) mails to the manufacturer a **P-bill** (meaning "prepaid bill") if the shipping charges are to be prepaid, depending on prior agreement between the manufacturer and the retailer.

4. The carrier delivers the shipment and mails a **freight bill** (invoice) to the buyer (consignee), a document that is either marked prepaid (paid by the manufacturer) or collect (buyer is to send a check to the carrier for shipping charges), again depending on prior agreement.[1]
5. The manufacturer mails an **invoice** (bill) to the buyer (retailer or wholesaler) for the total value of the goods purchased, which may or may not include any prepaid shipping charges.

Keep in mind that shipping charges and the dollar amount of the goods being shipped are separate considerations, and that buyers and sellers may handle transportation costs in a variety of ways.

FREE ON BOARD

You may already know that F.O.B. stands for "free on board," but do you understand the implications involved? To be used properly, this abbreviation should be related to a specific location. Terms of "F.O.B. Chicago" for a shipment from Chicago to Atlanta would mean that the buyer in Atlanta must pay the shipping costs. Moreover, the buyer would assume responsibility for the shipment the moment a bill of lading were signed in Chicago and would be required to file a claim with the transportation company for any short or damaged items.

If, instead, terms for the same shipment were "F.O.B. Atlanta," the seller (shipper) would pay the freight charges and file the claim for any short or damaged items reported by the buyer (consignee). If the term "F.O.B." is listed on a bill of lading without the location being specified, it is treated legally as though it read "F.O.B. point of origin." Although shippers occasionally show on bills of lading such notations as "F.O.B. plant" (referring to the manufacturer's factory) and "F.O.B. buyer's warehouse," it is advisable from a legal standpoint to be more specific; the seller may have more than one factory, and the buyer may have warehouses in several cities, with the transportation charges varying drastically from one location to another.

The term "F.A.S." (free along side) is used in connection with marine shipments. If a shipment from Honolulu, Hawaii, were destined for Fullerton, California, for example, the shipping papers might read "F.A.S. Port of Los Angeles." Accordingly, the shipper in Honolulu would pay the freight (steamship) charges and retain liability for the shipment until it was unloaded on the dock in Los Angeles, and the consignee would assume complete responsibility for movement of the shipment from "along side" the ship to the inland city of Fullerton.

Before proceeding to the next section, determine who must pay the freight charges in the following situations:

---

[1] The word *freight* may be defined as "goods or merchandise being shipped" and as "the amount that a transportation company charges for moving materials from one location to another."

APPLICATION 1

Situation: The terms for a shipment from Chicago to Mobile are "F.O.B. Mobile."
Answer: The seller pays the freight charges.

APPLICATION 2

Situation: The bill of lading for a shipment from Denver, Colorado, to Tucson, Arizona, carries terms of "F.O.B. Denver."
Answer: The buyer (consignee) in Tucson pays.

APPLICATION 3

Situation: A shipment from Indianapolis, Indiana, to Detroit, Michigan, simply reflects the abbreviation "F.O.B."
Answer: The abbreviation would be interpreted as "F.O.B. Indianapolis," with the buyer (consignee) in Detroit paying all freight charges.

APPLICATION 4

Situation: A 20,000-pound shipment of canned goods from Ponce, Puerto Rico, to Cleveland, Ohio, reads "F.A.S. Port Newark."
Answer: The seller (shipper) pays for transportation from Ponce to Port Newark, and the buyer (consignee) in Cleveland pays the inland freight charges.

FREIGHT RATES

Freight rates are simply the prices that transportation companies charge for the movement of materials, the size of the rate depending on the distance involved, the value and fragility of the items being shipped, and the weight or size of the whole shipment. **Tariffs** are the price lists that transportation companies publish, usually in pamphlet form for different categories of freight — such as canned goods, lumber, steel, livestock, and fresh citrus products.

Most rates are quoted "cwt." (per hundred weight), the "c" designating "100" and "wt" being an abbreviation for "weight." For a 200-pound shipment rated at $2.50 per cwt., for example, we divide the weight by 100 (move the assumed decimal two places to the left) and multiply the quotient by the rate.

$$\frac{200 \times 2.50}{100} = 2.00 \times 2.50 = \$5$$

Calculator	
Entries	**Display**
2 0 0	200.
×	200.
2 . 5	2.5
÷	500.
1 0 0	100.
=	5.

We may multiply first and then divide (as shown in the calculator entries), or we may divide first and then multiply — without altering the answer.

If a rate is quoted "per M" instead, we divide the weight by 1,000 and multiply (or multiply first and then divide), so that the freight charge for a 22,500-pound shipment at $15.75 per M would be $354.38.

$$\frac{22,500 \times 15.75}{1,000}$$

$$= 22.500 \times 15.75 = \$354.38$$

Calculator	
Entries	**Display**
$\boxed{2}\boxed{2}\boxed{.}\boxed{5}$	22.5
$\boxed{\times}$	22.5
$\boxed{1}\boxed{5}\boxed{.}\boxed{7}\boxed{5}$	15.75
$\boxed{=}$	354.375

We may simplify our calculations, as shown in the calculator entries, by first dividing mentally (moving the decimal three places to the left) and then entering 22.5 times 15.75.

When freight rates are quoted on a "per ton" basis, we divide the weight by 2,000 (the number of pounds in a ton) and multiply the quotient by the freight rate. Accordingly, a 100,000-pound shipment rated at $250 per ton would total $12,500:

$$\frac{100,000 \times 250}{2,000}$$

$$= 50 \times 250 = \$12,500$$

Calculator	
Entries	**Display**
$\boxed{1}\boxed{0}\boxed{0}\boxed{0}\boxed{0}\boxed{0}$	100,000.
$\boxed{\times}$	100,000.
$\boxed{2}\boxed{5}\boxed{0}$	250.
$\boxed{\div}$	25,000,000.
$\boxed{2}\boxed{0}\boxed{0}\boxed{0}$	2,000.
$\boxed{=}$	12,500.

Also consider the following situations.

APPLICATION 1. What is the cost of a shipment weighing 1,500 pounds if the freight rate is $6.15 per cwt.?

$$\frac{1,500 \times 6.15}{100} = 15.00 \times 6.15 = \$92.25$$

APPLICATION 2. Compute the freight charges on a 65-pound shipment that is subject to a freight rate of $10.50 per cwt.

$$\frac{65 \times 10.50}{100} = 0.65 \times 10.50 = \$6.83$$

APPLICATION 3. What will be the total amount of a freight bill for 60,152 pounds @ $12.15 per M?

$$\frac{60{,}152 \times 12.15}{1{,}000} = 60.152 \times 12.15 = \$730.85$$

APPLICATION 4. Determine the freight charge for a rail carload of steel coils weighing 120,000 pounds that is rated at $75.25 per ton.

$$\frac{120{,}000 \times 75.25}{2{,}000} = 60 \times 75.25 = \$4{,}515$$

MINIMUM WEIGHTS

Although transportation companies commonly publish "any quantity" (AQ) rates, which apply to shipments regardless of the total weight involved, most rates are subject to minimum-weight requirements. For example, a rate of $1.75 per cwt. might impose a minimum weight requirement of 20,000 pounds, in which case a shipper would be billed for 20,000 pounds or the actual weight shipped, whichever is greater. To illustrate, assume that Producer A is shipping 18,000 pounds of materials and that Producer B is shipping 23,500 pounds.

	Weight	Rate cwt.	Freight charges
Producer A	18,000		
	as		
	20,000	1.75	350.00
Producer B	23,500	1.75	411.25

Calculator	
Entries	**Display**
2 0 0	200.
×	200.
1 . 7 5	1.75
=	350.
Entries	**Display**
2 3 5	235.
×	235.
1 . 7 5	1.75
=	411.25

Because Producer A's products weigh less than the minimum-weight requirement, the shipment is billed as though 20,000 pounds were being shipped. Producer B is billed at the actual weight, because 23,500 pounds exceeds the minimum-weight requirement. Producer A must either pay for 2,000 pounds of so-called "phantom freight" or delay shipment until an additional 2,000 pounds or more can be added to the load.

Transportation companies routinely offer rates on a sliding-scale basis, relating progressively lower rates with progressively higher minimun weights, so that, with certain limitations, the heavier the shipment, the lower the rate. Consider the following combinations of minimum weights and related rates that apply to the movement of a particular product from City A to City Z:

Freight rates — City A to City Z

Minimum weight	Rate per cwt.
10,000	1.95
20,000	1.80
30,000	1.69

A **weight-break point** exists between any two weight-rate combinations, which is the particular weight at which it becomes less costly for the shipment to be billed (priced) at the next higher minimum rate in order to benefit from a lower rate. In the preceding schedule of rates, a shipment weighing 19,000 pounds, if billed at the actual weight, would cost more than a shipment weighing 20,000 pounds (the next higher minimum weight).

19,000 @ 1.95 cwt. = $370.50

20,000 @ 1.80 cwt. = $360.00

Logic dictates, therefore, that the smaller shipment be billed as 20,000 pounds.

19,000

as

20,000 @ 1.80 cwt. = $360.00

Rather than making separate calculations for shipments of varying weight, we may identify with the following calculations the weight-break point between the 10,000-pound and the 20,000-pound rates:

Minimum weight	Rate cwt.
10,000	1.95
20,000	1.80

$$195x = 20,000 \times 180$$

$$x = 18,461.53846 = 18,462 \text{ pounds}$$

We are asking, in essence, what weight at the $1.95 rate is equal to 20,000 pounds at $1.80. We may simplify our calculation to a significant degree by disregarding all decimals except the one in the answer, and the answer, you will notice, is rounded upward to even pounds.

Having determined the weight-break point, we know that shipments weighing more than 10,000 pounds but less than 18,462 should be billed at their actual weights. Shipments weighing more than 18,462 pounds, on the other hand, should be billed at the higher minimum (20,000 pounds) and at the lower rate ($1.80 per cwt.).

Using the following weight-rate combinations, consider the five related applications.

Minimum weight	Rate cwt.
7,000	$7.50
11,000	6.85
15,000	6.49

APPLICATION 1. What is the freight charge for a 6,500-pound shipment?

6,500
as
7,000 @ 7.50 = $525

APPLICATION 2. What is the weight-break point between the 11,000-pound rate and the 15,000-pound rate?

$685x = 15,000 \times 649$
$x = 14,212$ pounds

Application 3. What is the lowest weight-rate combination for a $14,500-pound shipment?

14,500
as
15,000 @ 6.49 = $973.50

(above the weight-break point of 14,212 pounds)

APPLICATION 4. What is the lowest rate combination for a 13,225-pound shipment?

13,225 @ 6.85 = $905.91

(billed at the actual weight because less than the weight-break point of 14,212 pounds)

APPLICATION 5. What are the freight charges for a 16,000-pound shipment?

16,000 @ 6.49 = $1,038.40

POOL SHIPMENTS

When destination points are reasonably aligned with each other, so that trucks or railcars need not be routed far out of their way to stop at one or more points en route to a more distant destination, we say that the stop-off points (for partial unloading or loading) are intermediate to the final destination. Under such circumstances, two or more shipments may be pooled (combined) and billed at the rate that applies to the most distant point. Consider the following weight-rate combinations as related to a 7,000-pound shipment from point of origin to Point X and a 14,000-pound shipment to Point Y, with Point X being intermediate to Point Y and Points X and Y being intermediate to Point Z.

Point X		Point Y		Point Z	
Minimum weight	Rate cwt.	Minimum weight	Rate cwt.	Minimum weight	Rate cwt.
8,000	2.50	10,000	3.15	10,000	3.40
12,000	2.35	20,000	2.75	15,000	3.22
18,000	2.05	25,000	2.62	22,000	3.01
Stop charge: $40.00					

If shipped separately, we have a total charge of $641.
Point X: 7,000
     as
     8,000 @ 2.50 = $200
Point Y: 14,000 @ 3.15 =   441
                    $641

If the two shipments are combined, instead, we have a total charge of $617.50.
Points X and Y: 7,000 + 14,000 = 21,000 pounds
           21,000 @ 2.75 = $577.50
           Stop charge   40.00 (Point X)
                   $617.50

Although products for the closer Point X are subject to a rate for the more distant Point Y, the combined weight of the two shipments qualifies the entire shipment for the higher minimum weight (20,000 pounds) and a relatively low rate ($2.75 compared to $3.15). Even when adding a stop charge of $40.00

for partial unloading at Point X, the combined shipments costs $23.50 less than for two separate shipments ($641.00 − $617.50 = $23.50).

Using the same rate schedule, consider the following situations.

APPLICATION 1. Compare the costs of pooling the following two orders as opposed to shipping them separately.

Point X: 12,000 pounds
Point Z: 8,000 pounds

Separately:

Point X: 12,000 @ 2.35 = $282.00
Point Z: 8,000
    as
   10,000 @ 3.40 = 340.00
        $622.00

X and Z combined:

20,000 @ 3.22 = $644.00
Stop charge   40.00
     $684.00

A difference of $62.00 ($684.00 − 622.00 = $62.00).

APPLICATION 2. With the objective of minimizing shipping costs, should the following two orders be pooled or shipped separately: 5,000 pounds for Point Y and 16,000 pounds for Point Z?

Separately:

Point Y: 5,000
    as
   10,000 @ 3.15 = $315.00
Point Z: 16,000 @ 3.22 = 515.20 $830.20

Y and Z combined:

21,000
  as
22,000 @ 3.01 = $662.20
Stop charge   40.00   702.20
       $128.00

The combined shipments result in the lower charge.

APPLICATION 3. Should all or either of the following three shipments be combined: Point X, 9,000 pounds; Point Y, 18,000 pounds; Point Z, 10,500 pounds?

All three points shipped separately:

Point X: 9,000 @ 2.50 = $ 225
Point Y: 18,000
        as
     20,000 @ 2.75 =   550
Point Z: 10,500 @ 3.40 =   ___357
                 $1,132

Point X separately, Points Y and Z combined:

Point X: 9,000 @ 2.50 = $225.00
Y and Z: 28,500 @ 3.01 =   857.85
Stop charge   ___40.00 (at Point Y)
              $1,122.85

Y separately, X and Z combined:

Point Y: 18,000
        as
     20,000 @ 2.75 = $550.00
X and Z: 19,500 @ 3.22 =   627.90
Stop charge   ___40.00
              $1,217.90

X and Y combined, Z separately:

X and Y: 27,000 @ 2.62 = $707.40
Point Z: 10,500 @ 3.40 =   357.00
Stop charge   ___40.00 (at Point X)
              $1,104.40

X, Y, and Z combined:

37,500 @ 3.01 = $1,128.75
Two stop charges ___80.00 (at points X and Y)
            $1,208.75

The lowest cost of $1,104.40 is achieved by pooling Points X and Y and shipping Point Z separately.

C.O.D. AND SHIPPER'S ORDER

When shippers do not wish to extend credit terms to certain buyers, they may instruct truckers to collect on delivery (C.O.D.) for the value of the merchandise. Truckers charge fees for performing this type of service, the size of the fee depending on the amount of money that the driver is to collect from the consignee. The total amount of a C.O.D. normally includes the collection fee and all related freight charges, depending on instructions from the consignor to the trucker at the time of shipment.

To illustrate, Marvin Manufacturing Company may sell $5,000 worth of merchandise to Salem Groceries. Knowing that the prepaid freight charges will total $250 and that the C.O.D. fee will be $16, Marvin Manufacturing may direct the trucking company to collect $5,266 (5,000 + 250 + 16 = 5,266). Before sending the shipment on a C.O.D. basis, however, the shipper would secure agreement from Salem Groceries to pay this amount at the actual time of delivery.

For a railcar shipment, on the other hand, Marvin Manufacturing would use a special shipping document, a **shipper's order bill of lading**, the original of which would be sent to a bank at the destination city as specified by Salem Groceries, and rail representatives would release the railcar for unloading only after Salem Groceries had made payment to the bank, secured the original bill of lading from the bank, endorsed the document on the back, and surrendered it to the proper rail representative. Under terms of C.O.D., we are paying truckers to perform a collection function, whereas shipper's order bills of lading are normally used in connection with rail shipments, with bankers performing the collection function in close cooperation with carrier representatives.

REFUNDS AND BALANCE-DUE ADJUSTMENTS

When transportation companies compute freight charges incorrectly, companies that have paid the charges must request refunds. They do so by itemizing in letters the amounts charged, amounts that should have been charged, and the refunds due. For a 10,000-pound shipment billed at $6.25 per cwt. when the correct rate is $4.85, the following explanation would be appropriate.

On your Freight Bill 16128 an incorrect rate was applied:

Reads: 10,000 @ 6.25 = $625
Should read: 10,000 @ 4.85 = 485
Refund due: $140

We are enclosing the original freight bill and requesting a prompt refund.

Identifying such mistakes before payment and issuing checks in the correct amounts is a more desirable situation, of course. A similar format is used by carrier representatives when they issue balance-due freight bills to collect for any undercharges that have been identified.

SELLERS' INVOICES

Invoices, which are bills that sellers present to buyers, reflect all of the financial detail and many of the physical elements involved in seller-buyer transactions. Many people deal with invoices: Personnel at the seller's place of business must prepare and mail invoices, collect the amounts due, and occasionally adjust invoice records. Employees at transportation companies must be able to interpret invoices in connection with any claims filed for lost or damaged merchandise, and people at the buyer's place of business must be familiar with all types of entries if they are to pay the correct amounts and avoid paying either too early or too late.

It is imperative, therefore, that business people have at least a working knowledge of invoices. The format for invoices varies drastically, but most of the forms have common elements — seller's name and address (printed on the forms); office and warehouse addresses; billing and shipping dates; and various columns and boxes for itemizing the products that are being sold, the prices being charged, and any discount and taxes that are applicable.

The "ship to" address in Figure 6.1 is the same as the "sold to" address. The terms of sale authorize Baldour Industries to deduct one percent of the net amount of the invoice (1% of $542.34) if payment is made by October 10 and show that freight charges of $19.84 have been prepaid by the seller and added to the invoice for a delivery made by Central Couriers.

The sample invoice in Figure 6.2 indicates that the Conodec Corporation has shipped 1,100 drill bits to an address in Chicago that differs from the address to which the invoice is being mailed. Terms are C.O.D., with the express company assuming responsibility for collecting $8,267.85 at the time of delivery (before releasing the merchandise to Crystaline Corp.).

BROKER'S COMMISSION

If brokers were involved with either of the sales represented in Figure 6.1 or 6.2, they would be entitled to a percentage of the net amounts of the respective invoices. Assuming a commission rate of 3 percent for both sales, the computations would be as follows:

Figure 6.1: $542.34 × 0.03   = $16.27

Figure 6.2: $8,235.00 × 0.03 = $247.05

In some transactions, especially those involving the buying and selling of commodities, a broker may effect the sale, make collection from the buyer, deduct the established commission, and remit the balance to the principal. To illustrate, let's assume that the Nardoff Brokerage Company sells 3,000 cases of product that is manufactured by Happy Valley Canners. The price is $25 per case, with no trade or cash discounts involved; freight charges total $1,650, F.O.B. the Happy Valley warehouse; and the broker's commission is 2 percent of net sales.

MONTIEL SUPPLY COMPANY

1649 Circle Drive, N.W.
Buchanan, Michigan 49107

(616) 697-8131

INVOICE NO.	95113
INVOICE DATE	9/15/86

SOLD TO: Baldour Industries, Inc.   SHIP TO:
          501 Wickham Road   Same
          Melbourne, FL 32901

ACCOUNT NO. 58012

CUSTOMER ORDER	SHIPPED VIA	FREIGHT	TERMS OF PAYMENT
16309	Central Couriers	FOB Buchanan	1% Tenth Prox

UNITS ORDERED	UNITS SHIPPED	BACK ORDERED	ITEM NUMBER AND DESCRIPTION	LIST PRICE	NET PRICE	NET AMOUNT
12	12		310 ROM DRILL PRESS	19.95	13.31	159.72
6	6		322 ROM MOTO TOOL	39.95	26.65	159.90
6	6		410 ROM MOTO TOOL	49.95	33.32	199.92
24	24		586 ROM 1/32 COLET	1.25	0.95	22.80

AMOUNT OF SALE	SALES TAX	SHIPPING COST	PAY THIS AMOUNT
$ 542.34	$ 0.00	$ 19.84	$ 562.18

FOR PROPER CREDIT—RETURN REMITTANCE COPY WITH PAYMENT.
Subject to terms and conditions on this and reverse side of invoice.

Figure 6.1
Sample Invoice

THE CONODEC CORPORATION

3299 SAN FERNANDO ROAD
LOS ANGELES CA 90065
(213) 258-7777 258-7778

PLEASE RECORD ACCOUNT
NUMBER ON YOUR CHECK
ACCOUNT NUMBER

INVOICE NUMBER
006915

INVOICE DATE
8/22/86

034775

SOLD TO: CRYSTALINE CORP
          300 WEST MADISON STREET
          CHICAGO IL 60606

SHIPPED TO: CRYSTALINE CORP
             6512 WEST JACKSON BLVD
             CHICAGO IL 60606

ORDER DATE	SHIPPING DATE	SHIPPED BY	YOUR ORDER NO.	F.O.B.	TERMS
8-18-86	8-21-86	AIR EXPRESS	A-12319	LA	COD

QUANTITY	DESCRIPTION	PRICE	AMOUNT
300	1 MM BULK PACK DRILL BITS	5.25	1,575.00
400	1¼ MM BULK PACK DRILL BITS	6.15	2,460.00
400	1½ MM BULK DRILL BITS	10.50	4,200.00
			$8,235.00

ANY RETURNED MERCHANDISE
SUBJECT TO A 10% RESTOCKING CHARGE

COLLECT ON DELIVERY
MERCHANDISE $ 8,235.00
SHIPPING 28.50
C.O.D. FEE 4.35
TOTAL $ 8,267.85

Figure 6.2
Sample Invoice

3,000 @ $25 $75,000 collected
Related expense   −1,650 freight
Total amount $73,350
$75,000 × 0.02   −1,500 commission
Balance $71,850 to principal

Rather than Happy Valley Canners issuing an invoice to the business customer, Nardoff Brokerage pays the trucker and bills the customer for $75,000. Upon collection of that amount, Nardoff deducts the $1,650 freight payment and $1,500 commission (2% of the value of the merchandise) and remits the balance of $71,850 to Happy Valley Canners.

Many brokers specialize in purchasing products for their principals rather than selling products. If, for example, Gerber Brothers (a brokerage company) purchased for Silver Supply Company 750 units of sterling silver wire for 65.5 cents per unit under terms of "EXTENDED PAYMENT TIME EXTRA, F.O.B. DELIVERED" on a commission basis of 3-1/4 percent, Gerber would make payment to the seller and send a bill to Silver Supply Company for $507.22.

750 units @ $0.655 $491.25 paid
491.25 × 0.0325   +15.97 commission
Total due $507.22 from principal

Gerber Brothers, acting as broker for Silver Supply company, makes the purchase, pays the seller, and bills Silver Supply Company for the value of the merchandise plus the commission earned.

APPLICATION 1. Tillie Lawson, a commission merchant, sold 1,000 bushels of apples for Nakano Farms, her principal, for $8.50 a bushel (F.O.B. delivered) and paid shipping charges of $365.00. If Lawson charges a commission of 3 percent, what amount of money should she remit to Nakano Farms?

1,000 @ 8.50 $8,500 net value
Related expense   −365 freight
Total amount $8,135 collected
8,500 × 0.03   −255 commission
Balance due $7,880 to principal

After collecting from the buyer for the value of the merchandise, the commission merchant deducted the amount paid the transportation company and the commission earned and sent a check for the balance to the principal.

APPLICATION 2. Samuel Snyder, a purchasing agent, bought a truckload of lettuce for Ralston Produce, paying $1,800 for the lettuce and an additional

$250 for freight. At a commission rate of 2 percent, how much money should Snyder collect from Ralston Produce?

Truckload	$1,800	net value
Related expense	250	freight
1,800 × 0.02	36	commission
Total due	$2,086	from principal

The purchasing agent should send a bill to the principal for the value of the produce, freight charges, and commission.

EXERCISES (as assigned by your instructor)

6-1 What is a bill of lading?

6-2 What is a freight bill?

6-3 What is meant by the following terms:

a. "F.O.B. Pittsburgh," for a shipment from Pittsburgh to Indianapolis?
b. "F.O.B." for a shipment from Los Angeles to San Francisco?
c. "F.A.S. Mobile" for a shipment from Puerto Rico to Atlanta?
d. "F.O.B. BUYER'S WAREHOUSE" which is located in Chicago?
e. "F.O.B. PLANT" for a shipment from Detroit to Louisville?
f. "F.O.B. PORT NEWARK" for a shipment from Port Newark to Cleveland?

6-4 Compute freight charges under the following conditions:

a. 35,200 pounds @ $21.50 per cwt.
b. Sixty-five pounds @ $4.50 per cwt.
c. 16,500 pounds @ $15.75 per M.
d. 145,000 pounds of steel bars at $450 per ton.
e. 17,500 pounds at $2.35 per cwt., subject to a minimum weight requirement of 18,000 pounds.

6-5 Use these weight-rate combinations to respond to the questions that follow.

Point X	
Minimum weight	Rate cwt.
7,000	4.25
10,000	3.80
12,000	3.65

a. What is the weight-break point between 7,000 pounds and 10,000 pounds?

b. What are the freight charges for a shipment weighing 8,500 pounds?

c. What are the freight charges for a 9,000-pound shipment?

d. What are the freight charges for a 10,505-pound shipment to Point X?

6-6 Use the following weight-rate combinations in responding to the questions that follow:

Point X		Point Y		Point Z	
Minimum weight	Rate cwt.	Minimum weight	Rate cwt.	Minimum weight	Rate cwt.
7,000	4.25	8,000	4.60	7,000	5.12
10,000	3.80	10,000	4.25	10,000	4.86
12,000	3.65	12,000	4.10	15,000	4.70
Stop charge $50.00					

a. What is the lowest-cost way to ship 5,500 pounds to Point X and 4,200 pounds to Point Y — separately or combined? (Show your computations.)

b. What is the lowest cost to ship 8,500 pounds to Point X, 5,000 pounds to Point Y, and 7,100 pounds to Point Z?

6-7 Respond to the following questions:

a. What is the purpose of sending a shipment C.O.D.?

b. What elements may be included in a C.O.D.?

c. What document should a seller use when shipping a railcar load of merchandise to a customer when the customer's credit rating is unacceptable?

6-8 What statement would be appropriate for a company to explain to a transportation firm that a 5,000-pound shipment was billed at $8.50 per cwt. when it should have been billed as 6,000 pounds at $6.85 per cwt.?

6-9 Heffernan and Levene sold a carload of potatoes (commonly referred to in business as "spuds") to Central Markets for $3,875, F.O.B. the Central Market warehouse in Chicago. If Heffernan and Levene, a commission merchant that charges a rate of 3-1/2 percent, paid the related freight charges of $350, how much money must the company remit to Farmer's Co-op, the principal?

6-10 Rudolph Sikes & Sons, Inc., a purchasing agent, contracted with a farmer to purchase 6,000 boxes of navel oranges from a grower for $5.25 per box. Sikes & Sons paid the grower an additional $625 for transporting the oranges to Wilson Produce. At a commission rate of 3 percent, what amount must Sikes & Sons collect from Wilson Produce for whom the oranges were purchased?

6-11 After storing 1,500 boxes of bananas in his warehouse for two days at a daily storage rate of 15 cents per box, Frank Todd, a commission merchant, sold the entire lot for $10.75 per case. Considering a commission rate of 7 percent based on the selling price, what amount must he remit to the principal?

6-12 If Margaret Reed purchased for Save-Way Markets 250 boxes of apples at $5.50 per case and 500 boxes of oranges at $4.75 per box, a transaction that involved an additional outlay of $180 in shipping charges, what was her rate of commission if a check for $4,230 was received from Save-Way Markets?

6-13 The Commodities Exchange sold for Charles Hansen, a small meat packer in Minnesota, 150 cases of canned meat at $37.25 per case, a price that included shipping charges of $1.75 per case. At a commission rate of 5 percent, how much money did Hansen, the principal, receive?

7 Retail Transactions

LEARNING OBJECTIVES

The materials in this chapter, combined with those in the preceding two chapters, will help you comprehend the intricacies of producer-retailer interactions so that you will be able to

- work with manufacturer's prices from the retailer's perspective
- understand and describe the components and rationale for markups at the retail level
- add markup to costs to derive retail prices
- apply the basic retail equation to derive retailers' costs, markups, and prices
- determine the rate of markup as either a percent of cost or as a percent of price
- compute equivalent rates of markup by converting the rate of markup on cost to the markup on price — and vice versa
- mark down retail prices
- identify those points below which retailers should never lower their prices
- calculate break-even points in terms of the number of units that must be sold at a specified price in order to cover variable costs and related overhead
- apply unit pricing to a wide variety of products
- compute the sales taxes that retailers must collect

The materials in this chapter are a logical extension of those in the preceding two chapters. Having dealt with the prices and discounts offered by producers, the transportation costs involved in moving products to retailers and wholesalers, and the related invoices, we now turn our attention to the final link in the chain — the retail transactions.

Even before making purchase decisions, retailers must relate the prices that they are to pay (their costs) with the prices that they are to charge. The spread between these two figures must be sufficient not only to cover the cost of the products, but also to cover the retailer's operational expenses and to provide a reasonable profit. Moreover, these same elements must be given special consideration when offering products at sale prices.

RETAILER'S COSTS, MARKUPS, AND PRICES

Three basic elements are involved in retail pricing:

1. *Cost* — the amounts that retailers pay for products
2. *Markup* — the amounts that retailers add to costs to establish the prices they charge consumers
3. *Price* — the prices that retailers charge consumers

117

If, for example, Sunlight Grocers orders 200 cases of 48/6 (48 six-ounce cans) Starkist Light Chunk Tuna at $37.75 per case, plus freight charges of $130.00, the cost to the company is 80 cents per can.

(1) $130.00 ÷ 200 cases = 0.65 freight per case

(2) $\dfrac{37.75 + 0.65}{48 \text{ cans}} = \dfrac{38.40}{48} = 0.8 = 80 \text{ cents per can}$

To this cost Sunlight Grocers must add a markup that is sufficient to contribute a fair share to such expenses as wages and salaries, rent, insurance, taxes, and electricity — all of the expenses involved in shelving the tuna, protecting the product from theft and damage, making the sale, and processing the paperwork. Included also, as mentioned earlier, must be a profit factor; the overriding objective of conducting a business is, after all, the realization of profits.

Assuming that Sunlight Grocers adds a markup of 8 cents per can, we have a retail price of 88 cents per can.

Cost + Markup = Price

0.80 + 0.08 = 0.88 = 88¢ per can

The figure 88¢ is called the **retail price** because it is the price that retailers charge you and me, the ultimate consumers. **To compute price** when cost and markup are known, therefore, we simply add cost and markup.

To determine cost when markup and price are known, we subtract markup from price.

Cost = Price − Markup

(or)

C = P − M

To derive markup when cost and price are known, we subtract cost from price.

Markup = Price − Cost

(or)

M = P − C

These concepts are illustrated in the following applications.

APPLICATION 1. If a retailer pays $5,000 for 200 household coffee grinders and adds a per unit markup of $5, what is the retail price?

$$\$5{,}000 \div 200 = \$25 \text{ each}$$
$$C + M = P$$
$$\$25 + \$5 = \$30$$

APPLICATION 2. If a manufacturer ships 100 cases (48 cans per case) of apple-sauce to a retailer for $36.00 per case, including freight, which the retailer sells for 81 cents per can, what amount of markup is being added to the retailer's cost?

$$\$36.00 \div 48 \text{ cans each} = 75\text{¢ per can}$$
$$P - C = M$$
$$0.81 - 0.75 = 0.06 = 6\text{¢}$$

APPLICATION 3. What is the retailer's cost for a product that carries a retail price of $95.95 and includes a markup of $14.95?

$$P - M = C$$
$$\$95.95 - \$14.95 = \$81.00$$

MARKUP ON COST OR PRICE

If retailers make a practice of adding markups that do not cover costs and expenses, not to mention contributions to profits, they will eventually go bankrupt. If retailers add markups that are too high, on the other hand, they will eventually be forced out of business by competitors who charge lower prices. Correspondingly, retailers who operate in competitive environments must contain their costs and align their prices to a significant degree with those of competing companies.

In some business sectors, such as within the canned-goods industry, companies base their **markups on cost**, that is, on the prices that they pay packing companies for the products they must resell. As guidelines for basing prices on costs, the marketing personnel in many firms use average industry costs, prices, and markups that are published periodically in trade magazines. To illustrate the concept of markup based on cost, let's assume that the marketing manager of a retail grocery chain wishes to realize a markup on cost of 13 percent for 6-ounce cans of Sockeye salmon that cost $1.75 per can when purchased from a Seattle packer.

$$C + M = P$$

$$1.75 + 0.13(1.75) = P$$

$$1.75 + 0.2275 = 1.9775 = \$1.98$$

If markup is 13 percent of cost and cost is \$1.75, it follows that markup is 13 percent of \$1.75. Or, more simply, we may compute price when markup is based on cost by multiplying cost by one plus the percent markup.

$$1.00 + 0.13 = 1.13$$

$$1.75 \times 1.13 = 1.9775 = \$1.98$$

Rather than multiplying \$1.75 by 13 percent and then adding the product to the cost, the one in "1.13" has the effect of including the cost in the answer — requiring only one calculation rather than two.

In contrast, let's assume that the owner of an apparel shop can sell a particular garment at \$150 after having added a 35 percent **markup based on price**. How much can the retailer afford to pay the manufacturer for such a garment?

$$C + M = P$$

$$C + 0.35(150) = 150.00$$

$$C + 52.50 = 150.00$$

$$C = 150.00 - 52.50$$

$$C = \$97.50$$

Knowing that price is \$150 and that markup is 35 percent of price, we simply multiply 150 by 0.35 to determine that markup is \$52.50; and, because cost is the difference between price and markup, we subtract to determine cost. The following examples will reinforce your understanding of these relationships.

APPLICATION 1. If cost is \$17.50 and markup is 14 percent of cost, what is the selling price?

$$C + M = P \qquad\qquad 1.00 + 0.14 = 1.14$$
$$17.50 + 0.14(17.50) = P \quad or \quad 17.50 \times 1.14 = \$19.95$$
$$17.50 + 2.45 = \$19.95$$

APPLICATION 2. If price is \$175 and markup is 12 percent of price, what is cost?

$$C + M = P$$
$$C + 0.12(175) = 175$$
$$C + 21 = 175$$
$$C = 175 - 21$$
$$C = \$154$$

APPLICATION 3. If a retailer pays a manufacturer $5,300 for 200 cartons of merchandise, what price must the retailer charge for each item to realize a markup on cost of 16 percent?

$$5,300 \div 200 = 26.50 \text{ per unit}$$
$$C + M = P$$
$$26.50 + 0.16(26.50) = P$$
$$26.50 + 4.24 = \$30.74$$

APPLICATION 4. If a retailer must charge $1,910 for an item, in order to be competitive with other retailers selling the same product, how much can the retailer afford to pay a manufacturer for the item if the markup on price is 8 percent?

$$C + M = P$$
$$C + 0.08(1,910) = 1,910$$
$$C + 152.80 = 1,910$$
$$C = 1,910 - 152.80$$
$$C = \$1,757.20$$

DETERMINING THE RATE OF MARKUP

Retailers that purchase goods from the same producers are subject to the same costs, except for quantity discounts and variations in shipping charges, because federal law requires producers to offer identical prices to all business customers. Retailers may also determine the prices that other retailers are charging by simply reading their ads or walking through their stores. Knowing their competitors' costs and prices, retailers may calculate the amount of markup being applied. If, for example, another retailer's cost for an item is $140 and the selling price is $210, we can determine the percent of **markup on cost** by dividing markup by cost. First, we compute the amount of markup.

$$P - C = M$$

$$210 - 140 = \$70$$

Second, assuming that the pattern within the particular retailing segment is to base markups on cost, we may calculate the rate of markup by dividing the amount of markup by cost.

$$M_c = \frac{M}{C} = \frac{70}{140} = 0.5 = 50\%$$

When, in any problem situation, we want to know what percent one number is of another number, we divide by the other number. To determine the percent that 70 is of 140, we divide 70 by 140.

If, instead, the pattern within this particular retail market is to base **markup on price**, we determine the rate of markup by dividing markup by price.

$$M_p = \frac{M}{P} = \frac{70}{210} = 0.33333 = 33\text{-}1/3\%$$

In either calculation, markup on cost or markup on price, we are dealing with an item that the retailer bought for $140 and sold for $210. When computing markup on cost, however, we derive a significantly higher rate (50%) than for markup on price (33-1/3%).

APPLICATION 1. If a retailer pays a manufacturer $55 for an item that is to be sold for $75.90, what is the rate of markup based on cost?

$$P - C = M$$
$$75.90 - 55.00 = 20.90$$

$$M_c = \frac{M}{C} = \frac{20.90}{55.00} = 0.38 = 38\%$$

APPLICATION 2. If an item that cost the retailer $2,119.00 is priced at $4,555.85, what is the percent of markup on price?

$$P - C = M$$
$$4,555.85 - 2,119.00 = 2,436.85$$

$$M_p = \frac{M}{P} = \frac{2,436.85}{4,555.85} = 0.535 = 53\text{-}1/2\%$$

APPLICATION 3. If a retailer buys 3,000 coffee makers at a unit price of $14.50, what is the markup on cost as related to a retail price of $18.85?

$$P - C = M$$
$$18.85 - 14.50 = 4.35$$

$$M_c = \frac{M}{C} = \frac{4.35}{14.50} = 0.3 = 30\%$$

APPLICATION 4. If the markup is $3,500 and the retail price is $6,500, what is the rate of markup on cost?

$$P - M = C$$
$$6,500 - 3,500 = 3,000$$

$$M_c = \frac{M}{C} = \frac{3,500}{3,000} = 1.1666 = 116.7\%$$

APPLICATION 5. If the cost is $122.00 and the markup $30.50, what is the rate of markup on price?

$$C + M = P$$
$$122.00 + 30.50 = 152.50$$

$$M_p = \frac{M}{P} = \frac{30.50}{152.50} = 0.2 = 20\%$$

The rates of markup differ drastically from one retail segment to another. Women's apparel generally carries a higher markup than that for men's apparel, for example, because women's shops typically carry a wider variety of clothing that is subject to more frequent changes in design. Retailers who deal in furniture add higher markups than appliance dealers because wooden furniture consumes more display space, requires more maintenance, and damages more easily than an appliance. Furniture dealers also add higher markups than grocers do because of a relatively low rate of turnover; consumers buy groceries several times a week but purchase furniture only every few years or so.

Rates of markup differ even from one grocery item to another. People buy more cling peaches than they do bing cherries, for instance, forcing grocers to add relatively high markups to the cost of cherries. Most grocery items are priced (marked up) at a rate that will, in effect, charge each item a rental fee based on the amount of shelf space consumed — in terms of both space and time.

DETERMINING COST AND PRICE

In the preceding section we calculated price when both the markup and the cost were known. When only the percent of markup is known, however, a **determination of cost** requires some simple algebra. If a retailer knows that a competitor is selling an item for **$36.95** and realizes that the standard markup on such items is approximately 10 percent of cost, he may estimate the competitors's cost.

$$C + M = P$$

$$C + 0.10C = 36.95$$

$$1.10C = 36.95$$

$$C = 33.5909 = \$33.59$$

Our unknown C for cost is similar to an unknown X, which, when added to 10 percent of C, gives us $1.10C$.

If cost is $33.59, it follows that a 10 percent markup on cost amounts to $3.36:

$$C \times \%M_c = M$$

$$33.59 \times 0.10 = \$3.36$$

We may then establish proof of our calculations by plugging the newly derived figures into the basic retail equation.

$$C + M = P$$

$$33.59 + 3.36 = 36.95$$

$$36.95 = 36.95$$

A **determination of price** also begins with the basic retail equation and the application of simple algebra. To illustrate, assume that a retailer has paid 85 cents for an item and wishes to add the usual markup of 12 percent of price. Because price (P) is our unknown, we state markup as 12 percent of P.

$$C + M = P$$

$$0.85 + 0.12P = P$$

$$0.85 = P - 0.12P$$

$$0.85 = 0.88P$$

$$0.9659 = P$$

$$97¢ = P$$

Rounding our answer to the cents position, we have a price of 97 cents per unit. We may then prove our answer by plugging the newly derived price into the original equation.

$$C + M = P$$

$$0.85 + 0.12(0.97) = 0.97$$

$$0.85 + 0.12 = 0.97$$

$$0.97 = 0.97$$

Also consider the following retail situations.

APPLICATION 1. If a retailer prices an item at $250, which includes a markup on cost of 20 percent, how much did the retailer pay for the item?

$$C + M = P$$
$$C + 0.20C = 250.00$$
$$1.20C = 250.00$$
$$C = \$208.33$$

Proof:
$$C + M = P$$
$$208.33 + 0.2(208.33) = 250.00$$
$$208.33 + 41.67 = 250.00$$
$$250 = 250$$

APPLICATION 2. How much can a retailer afford to pay the manufacturer for an item that is to be priced at $36.95 if a 12 percent markup on cost is to be realized?

$$C + M = P$$
$$C + 0.12C = 36.95$$
$$1.12C = 36.95$$
$$C = \$32.99$$

Proof:
$$C + M = P$$
$$32.99 + 0.12(32.99) = 36.95$$
$$32.99 + 3.96 = 36.95$$
$$36.95 = 36.95$$

APPLICATION 3. If a retailer pays the manufacturer $82.60 per unit and adds a markup of 15 percent of price, what is the retail price?

$$C + M = P$$
$$82.60 + 0.15P = P$$
$$82.60 = P - 0.15P$$
$$82.60 = 0.85P$$
$$\$97.18 = P$$

Proof:
$$82.60 + 0.15(97.18) = 97.18$$
$$82.60 + 14.58 = 97.18$$
$$97.18 = 97.18$$

APPLICATION 4. What price must a retailer charge for an item that cost 64 cents if a markup of 26 percent of price is to be realized?

$$C + M = P$$
$$0.64 + 0.26\,P = P$$
$$0.64 = P - 0.26P$$
$$0.64 = 0.74P$$
$$86¢ = P$$

Proof:
$$0.64 + 0.26(0.86) = 0.86$$
$$0.64 + 0.22 = 0.86$$
$$0.86 = 0.86$$

EQUIVALENT RATES OF MARKUP

We may convert a markup on cost to the **equivalent markup on price** by using the standard retail equation and plugging in any price. If we know that a retailer is using a markup on cost of 30 percent, for example, we can make cost one dollar (or any other amount) and determine the equivalent markup on price.

$$C + M = P$$

$$1.00 + 0.30(1.00) = P$$

$$1.00 + 0.30 = 1.30$$

$$M_p = \frac{M}{P} = \frac{0.30}{1.30} = 23.1\%$$

A 30 percent markup on cost is the same as a 23.1 percent markup on price. In essence, we determined the unknown markup on price by dividing the known markup on cost by the sum of one dollar and the percent of markup.

$$\frac{\text{Known } M_c}{1.00 + M_c} = \frac{0.30}{1.00 + 0.30} = \frac{0.30}{1.30} = 23.1\%$$

If we know the markup on price, instead, we may determine the **equivalent markup on cost** by plugging in one dollar (or any other amount) for price and performing a similar calculation. Building on the same example, let's assume that we know that the markup on price is 23.1 percent but that we do not know the equivalent markup on cost.

$$C + M = P$$

$$C + 0.231(1.00) = 1.00$$

$$C + 0.231 = 1.00$$

$$C = 1.00 - 0.231$$

$$C = 0.769$$

$$M_c = \frac{M}{C} = \frac{0.231}{0.769} = 0.3 = 30\%$$

In essence, we are finding the equivalent markup on cost by dividing the known markup on price (M_p) by the difference of one dollar and the markup on price.

$$M_c = \frac{M_p}{1.00 - M_p} = \frac{0.231}{1.00 - 0.231} = \frac{0.231}{0.769} = 0.3 = 30\%$$

APPLICATION 1. If a retailer typically adds to cost a markup of 6 percent of price, what percent of cost is the markup?

$$C + M = P$$
$$C + 0.06(1.00) = 1.00$$
$$C + 0.06 = 1.00$$
$$C = 1.00 - 0.06$$
$$C = 0.94$$

$$M_c = \frac{M}{C} = \frac{0.06}{0.94} = 0.064 = 6.4\%$$

APPLICATION 2. What markup on price is the equivalent of a 14 percent markup on cost?

$$C + M = P$$
$$1.00 + 0.14(1.00) = P$$
$$1.14 = P$$

$$M_p = \frac{M}{P} = \frac{0.14}{1.14} = 12.3\%$$

(or)

$$M_p = \frac{M}{1 + M_c} = \frac{0.14}{1.00 + 0.14} = \frac{0.14}{1.14} = 12.3\%$$

APPLICATION 3. If the markup on an item is 8 percent of price, what percent is the markup on cost?

$$C + M = P$$
$$C + 0.08(1.00) = 1.00$$
$$C + 0.08 = 1.00$$
$$C = 1.00 - 0.08$$
$$C = 0.92$$

$$M_c = \frac{M}{C} = \frac{0.08}{0.92} = 8.7\%$$

(*or*)

$$M_c = \frac{M_p}{1.00 - M_p} = \frac{0.08}{1.00 - 0.08} = \frac{0.08}{0.92} = 8.7\%$$

APPLICATION 4. Retailer No. 1, who has been adding a markup of 12 percent to the cost of a particular product, has found that Retailer No. 2 has been adding an 11 percent markup on price. Assuming that the product costs the retailers the same amount, which retailer's price is higher?

Retailer No. 1

$$C + M = P$$
$$1.00 + 0.12(1.00) = P$$
$$1.12 = P$$

$$M_p = \frac{M}{P} = \frac{0.12}{1.12} = 10.7\%$$

(*or*)

$$M_p = \frac{M}{1 + M_c} = \frac{0.12}{1.00 + 0.12} = \frac{0.12}{1.12} = 10.7\%$$

Retailer No. 2 has a higher markup (11% of price) than Retailer No. 1 (10.7% of price).

MERCHANDISE MARKDOWNS

A **markdown** is a reduction in a retail price. Retailers cannot always maintain their original prices, of course; they sometimes must reduce them in order to increase sales and to sell slow-moving stocks. If Jarvis Footware marks down the prices of a select batch of men's shoes by 15 percent, for example, a pair that was priced at $69.00 will be marked at the reduced price of $58.65.

$$100\% - 15\% = 85\%$$

$$\$69.00 \times 0.85 = \$58.65$$

When a 15 percent discount is applied, it follows that the customer will pay only 85 percent of the original price. Also consider the following two transactions.

APPLICATION 1. What is the reduced price of a self-defrost refrigerator that was priced at $750 after a price reduction of 7 percent has been applied?

$$1.00 - 0.07 = 0.93$$
$$750 \times 0.93 = \$697.50$$

APPLICATION 2. If the cost of the refrigerator in Example 1 is $450, what is the new percent markup on cost?

$$C + M = P$$
$$450 + M = 697.50$$
$$M = 697.50 - 450.00$$
$$M = 247.50$$

$$M_c = \frac{M}{C} = \frac{247.50}{450.00} = 55\%$$

APPLICATION 3. Compute the reduced price on the following items after an across-the-board markdown on price of 25 percent.

Unit Price		1.00 − 0.25		Discounted price
$7.25	×	0.75	=	$5.44
12.50	×	0.75	=	9.38
16.21	×	0.75	=	12.16
9.30	×	0.75	=	6.98

Do not forget to use chain multiplication, as explained on page 26, when using a calculator to solve such problems.

BREAK-EVEN POINT

Prices can be reduced only so far, of course, before retailers begin to lose money. At the very least, the price charged for a product should be high enough to recover variable costs, that is, those costs that are directly related to the production or the purchase and handling of a particular product. The variable cost of a product represents a floor below which prices should not fall. Otherwise, the greater the sales volume, the greater the resulting losses.

To actually break even, however, prices should be high enough to also cover a fair share of related overhead. Overhead costs, which remain relatively constant at varying production and sales volumes, are frequently referred to as "fixed costs"; and, as explained in Chapter 4, overhead includes costs that are not readily assignable to specific departments — costs such as rental payments, utility bills, and insurance premiums. Also as explained in Chapter 4, overhead may be prorated among various products and departments on the basis of floor space, number of employees, amount of total sales, or a number of other criteria.

To illustrate the concept of a break-even point, let's assume that a retailer pays $25 per unit for a product to be priced at $30 per unit, a product to which total overhead of $50,000 has been distributed. The following formula may be used to derive the break-even point:

$$\text{Break-even point} = \frac{\text{Overhead}}{\text{Retail price} - \text{variable cost}}$$

$$BEP = \frac{50,000}{30 - 25} = \frac{50,000}{5} = 10,000 \text{ units}$$

Each unit sold at $30 contributes $5 ($30 − $25 = $5) toward overhead, with total sales of 10,000 units required to completely cover the $50,000 overhead. Profits begin to accumulate only on products sold in excess of 10,000 units. Also consider the following situations.

APPLICATION 1. If a retailer pays $110.00 for an item that has related expenses of $4.75 per item, what is the lowest price that should be charged?

$$\text{Cost} + \text{direct expenses} = \text{variable cost}$$
$$110.00 + 4.75 = \$114.75$$

APPLICATION 2. In Application 1, what is the break-even point at a retail price of $129.00, assuming total overhead of $85,000 assigned to the product?

$$\frac{\text{Overhead}}{\text{Price} - \text{variable cost}} = \frac{85,000}{129.00 - 114.75}$$

$$= \frac{85,000}{14.25} = 5,964.9 = 5,965 \text{ units}$$

APPLICATION 3. If the overhead assigned to a particular product is $1,500, the retailer's variable cost is $3.25 per unit, and the selling price is $3.75 per unit, what is the break-even point?

$$\frac{\text{Overhead}}{\text{Price} - \text{Variable cost}} = \frac{1,500}{3.75 - 3.25}$$

$$= \frac{1,500}{0.50} = 3,000 \text{ units}$$

APPLICATION 4. In relation to the situation in Example 3, compute the new break-even point following a 10 percent markdown of the retail price.

$$3.75 - 0.10(3.75) =$$
$$3.75 - 0.38 = \$3.37$$

$$\frac{1,500}{3.37 - 3.25} = \frac{1,500}{0.12} = 12,500 \text{ units}$$

In the final example, a markdown of just 10 percent has more than quadrupled the number of units that the retailer must sell just to break even on the cost of carrying this one item. Will the lower price result in such high sales? If not, such a reduction would be ill-conceived — unless, of course, the item were being used as a "loss leader" to attract customers who might also purchase other items.

UNIT PRICING

So that their customers will not need calculators to compare prices, many grocers now provide unit pricing by placing small cards on the edges of shelves to show the per-ounce prices. Without unit pricing, imagine the difficulty of comparing the prices of two boxes of detergent.

4 lb 8 oz Tide $3.79:

(1) 4 lb 8 oz = 72 oz (4 × 16 + 8 = 72)

(2) $3.79 ÷ 72 oz = 0.0526 = 5.26¢ per oz

9 lb 3 oz Tide $7.49:

(1) 9 lb 3 oz = 147 oz (9 × 16 + 3 = 147)

(2) $7.49 ÷ 147 oz = 0.051 = 5.10¢ per oz

First we state the weight in terms of ounces. We then divide the price per box by the number of ounces of product within the box. As we would expect, buyers of the larger box of detergent will pay less per ounce than persons who choose the smaller box, but only a small fraction of a cent less. This example is based on actual prices posted at a grocery store at the time this book is being written, as are the following price comparisons.

APPLICATION 1. How much money per ounce can a consumer save by purchasing the larger of the following two cans of pineapple chunks?

8 oz can @ 55¢ each
20 oz can @ 91¢ per can

0.55 ÷ 8 = 6.88¢ per oz
0.91 ÷ 20 = <u>4.55¢</u> per oz
$\overline{2.33}$ = 2-1/3¢ per oz

20 oz × 2-1/3¢ = 47¢

APPLICATION 2. What is the savings per ounce between the same two cans of
pineapple chunks if based on the net weight of the contents, that is, on
the actual (net) weight of the pineapple chunks without the weight of the
juice included? The net weight is 5-1/4 ounces and 14 ounces.

5-1/4 oz @ 55¢ each
    14 oz @ 91¢ each

0.55 ÷ 5.25 = 10.48¢ per oz
0.91 ÷ 14.00 = <u>6.50¢</u> per oz
$\overline{}$ 3.98¢ per oz (almost 4¢ per oz)

APPLICATION 3. When price is the main consideration, which is the better buy,
the 14-ounce or the 24-ounce bottle of Heinz catsup?

14 oz @ 81¢
24 oz @ $1.27

0.81 ÷ 14 = 5.79¢ per oz
1.27 ÷ 24 = <u>5.29¢</u> per oz
$\overline{}$ 0.50¢ per oz

The larger bottle is priced lower by one-half cent per ounce.

APPLICATION 4. Compare prices of the following boxes of detergent:

(1) 9 lb 3 oz box of *Ajax* @ $4.69
(2) 20 lb box of *All* $12.99
(3) 147 oz box of generic @ $4.17

(1) 9 lb 3 oz = 147 oz (9 × 16 + 3 = 147)
     $4.69 ÷ 147 = 3.19¢ per oz

(2) 20 lb = 320 oz (20 × 16 = 320)
     $12.99 ÷ 320 = 4.06¢ per oz

(3) $4.17 ÷ 147 = 2.84¢ per oz

The generic (no brand) product is the lowest cost per ounce, with the heavy
(20 pound) box of *All* being the highest cost — both by a wide margin.

SALES TAX A final transaction at the retail level, after the prices of items being sold have been entered into a cash register, is to add a sales tax. The percent of this tax varies among the fifty states, ranging from no tax at all to as high as 6 or 7 percent of the value of the items being sold. Assuming a tax of 5 percent on an item priced at $150.00, the total to be paid by the customer is $157.50.

Price × Tax rate = Tax
  150.00 × 0.05 = $7.50

  Price + Tax = Total
150.00 + 7.50 = $157.50

The retailer collects $157.50 from the customer and eventually remits the $7.50 tax to the state government. A short-cut method of computation is to add mentally 100 percent (the number "one") to the tax rate before multiplying. Using the same item and tax rate, we have

100% + 5% = 105% (mental calculation)

$150 × 1.05 = $157.50 (manual or electronic calculation)

We have derived the same answer with only one calculation rather than two. Such computations are unnecessary, of course, when using electronic cash registers that automatically compute and add sales tax to the value of items being sold. At stores with less sophisticated registers, employees use tax tables to find the applicable amounts of tax to be added — proceeding down the columns in a table to $150, for example, to determine that the correct tax is $7.50. On big-ticket items such as automobiles, refrigerators, stereos, and television sets, on the other hand, sales personnel must calculate the applicable tax. The following transactions include a variety of related situations.

APPLICATION 1. At a tax rate of 4 percent, what is the total charge for two items priced at $15.25 and $19.95?

  15.25 + 19.95 = 35.20
  35.20 × 0.04 = 1.41
  35.20 + 1.41 = $36.61

APPLICATION 2. If you were a salesperson at an auto dealership, what would you tell a customer who asked for the total amount of money required for a used car priced at $2,450 that is subject to a state tax of 6 percent on both new and second-owner vehicles?

  2,450 × 1.06 = $2,597

APPLICATION 3. A customer has purchased $23.25 worth of products at a small grocery store, of which only $15.00 are nonfood items that are subject to a 5 percent sales tax. What is the total amount to be collected from the customer?

$$15.00 \times 0.05 = 0.75$$
$$23.25 + 0.75 = \$24.00$$

APPLICATION 4. If a customer pays $1,728.05 for an item, including a sales tax of 7 percent, what was the price of the item before the tax was added?

(a) $100\% + 7\% = 107\%$
(b) $BR = P$
$$1.07B = 1,728.05$$
$$B = \$1,615.00$$

(*or*)

$$X + 0.07X = 1,728.05$$
$$1.07X = 1,728.05$$
$$X = \$1,615.00$$

APPLICATION 5. A local garage charged a customer $78.40 for a tune-up, which included $55.00 for labor and $23.40 for parts. What was the total bill, assuming a 5 percent state sales tax?

$55.00 labor
 23.40 parts
$78.40
  1.17 tax $(23.40 \times 0.05 = 1.17)$
$79.57 total

Notice in the final example that the sales tax was applicable only for the parts used. In most states, sales taxes are assessed only on the sale of material items — not on services (such as hair styling, home deliveries, and legal counsel) or on labor (such as installation charges, office maintenance, and auto repair).

EXERCISES

7-1 If a retailer orders 1,000 cases of 24/8 (24 eight-ounce jars) of Folgers instant coffee at $94.13 per case, with related freight costs of $125, what is the retailer's unit cost?

7-2 For an item that the retailer pays $84.20 and sells for $88.41,

a. What is the amount of markup?
b. What is the percent of markup based on cost?
c. What is the rate of markup on price?

7-3 If a manufacturer bills a retailer $28.32 per unit for a 1,500-unit order, assuming that the price includes all shipping costs, at what price must the retailer sell each item to realize a 15 percent markup on cost?

7-4 What is the retail price of an item that cost the retailer $423.00 and includes a markup of $50.76?

7-5 What is the retailer's cost for a pair of men's shoes priced at $65.00 that carries a markup of $9.75?

7-6 If cost is $146.80 and a markup of 12-1/2 percent of cost is added, what is the selling price?

7-7 If the retail price is $895.00 and a markup of 12 percent of price had been added, how much did the retailer pay for the item?

7-8 If City Center Appliances pays the manufacturer $8,000 for ten refrigerators and pays freight charges of $50 per unit, what must the retail price be for the retailer to realize an 8 percent markup on cost?

7-9 What is the highest price that City Center Appliances can accept from the manufacturer for washing machines that, to be competitively priced, cannot be tagged at a price of more than $629 if a return on price of at least 5 percent is to be realized?

7-10 A retailer paid the manufacturer $5,100 (including shipping charges) for six television sets that were sold to consumers for $1,045.50 each. What was the rate of markup on cost?

7-11 If a retailer pays $1,025.00 for a product that is to be sold at the retail level for $1,209.50, what is the rate of markup on price?

7-12 If a retailer pays $245.00 for an item and adds a markup of 15 percent of cost, what is the rate of markup on the retailer's selling price?

7-13 If a retailer's rate of markup on price is 23 percent, what is the equivalent markup on cost?

7-14 What is the equivalent markup on price of an item that carries a 25 percent markup on cost?

7-15 What is the cost of an item that carries a retail price of $180.00, assuming that the markup is 16 percent of the retail price?

7-16 What is the retail price of an item that cost the retailer $3,060, to which a markup on cost of 45 percent was added?

7-17 If the manufacturer charges $620.00 per unit, to which the retailer adds a markup on price of 17 percent, what is the retail price?

7-18 A product that carries a 33 percent markup on cost carries a price of $645.05 at the retail level. What price did the retailer pay for the item?

7-19 What price must a retailer charge for an item that cost 45 cents, assuming a markup of 13 percent of the retail price?

7-20 If a retailer adds to cost a markup of 8-1/2 percent of the selling price, what is the equivalent markup on cost?

7-21 If a competitor is adding to cost a markup on price of 38 percent, what is the equivalent markup on cost?

7-22 What percent markup on price is equivalent to a 40 percent markup on cost?

7-23 If all items in a retail store are to be lowered 23 percent during a pre-Christmas sale, what will be the newly adjusted price for an item that was priced at $149.90?

7-24 What prices will the following items carry following an across-the-board markdown of 15 percent? (Round your answers upward to the nearest nickel.)

a. $15.95
b. $42.50
c. $120.95

7-25 If fixed costs are $50,000, variable costs are $16.20, and the retail price is $25.00, how many items must be sold to cover both variable and fixed costs relating to the item?

7-26 If an item that was priced at $245.00 is marked down 20 percent, what is the new break-even point — assuming fixed costs of $100,000 and per-unit variable costs of $175.25?

7-27 What is the unit price of the following sizes of Date Bran breakfast cereal? (Round your answer to the 100ths position.)

a. 15 oz $1.69
b. 20 oz $2.09
c. 25-1/2 oz $2.49

7-28 Which of the following three items is the wiser purchase, assuming that low price is the primary objective? (Round your answer to the 10ths position.)

a. 12 oz $1.45
b. 18 oz $1.99
c. 24 oz $2.69

7-29 What is the per-ounce saving between the following two sizes of Taster's Choice regular instant coffee? (Round your answer to the 10ths position.)

a. 4 oz @ $3.15
b. 8 oz @ $5.79

7-30 At a rate of 6 percent, what is the sales tax on an item that retails at $42.95?

7-31 What is the total charge for taxable items priced at $16.25, $19.95, and $42.25 — assuming a state sales tax of 4 percent?

7-32 What is the total cost to a buyer for a motorboat priced at $7,500, if the state sales tax is 6-1/2 percent?

7-33 With a sales tax of 6 percent, except for food items, what is the total amount to be collected from a customer who is purchasing $62.50 of groceries and $22.25 of nonfood items?

7-34 If a used car is priced at $4,326, including a state sales tax of 3 percent, what is the before-tax price of the car?

7-35 Men's shirts at a fashionable department store were marked down 20 percent from a regular price of $28.50. If a customer buys two shirts and has the sleeves shortened, what is the total cost — assuming a state sales tax of 6 percent and an alteration charge of $4.50 per shirt?

8 Simple Interest

The successful completion of materials in this chapter will enable you to

- understand and describe the terms *principal, rate, time,* and *interest*
- apply the simple-interest equation to loan transactions
- compute in a single equation the amount of a loan
- distinguish between and compute both ordinary and exact interest
- compute both the exact and the approximate number of days between a loan date and a related maturity date
- determine algebraically either the interest, principal, rate, or time of a loan, when three elements are known but one element is unknown
- process partial payments on loans to determine the amount of payments to be applied toward a reduction in principal and to determine the amounts required to pay off loans
- compute the monthly payments and total finance charges on installment purchases
- determine the number of days in credit accounting cycles in charge accounts and compute average daily balances and related interest charges

Interest is a charge for borrowing money. Rather than paying cash for new automobiles, for instance, many purchasers pay for them partially with cash down payments or trade-ins and then finance the balance owed with borrowed money. In turn, they make monthly payments to reduce the principal (amount borrowed) and to pay the lender (interest) for the privilege of using the borrowed money.

The word *simple* does not mean that simple interest computations are easy to comprehend, but specifies instead that the interest is being computed strictly on the original amount of money that is borrowed. Compound interest differs from simple interest in this respect, as explained in Chapter 10.

THE SIMPLE-INTEREST EQUATION

The simple-interest equation involves four elements: principal, rate, time, and interest:

Principal × rate × time = interest

(or, more simply)

$$Prt = I$$

Principal is the beginning amount, the quantity of money that is borrowed (loaned) on which an interest charge is computed. **Rate** is the designated percent of the principal that the lender collects as rent for the borrower's use of the money. **Time** is the number of days, months, or years that the borrower uses the money; time is stated either in whole years (1, 2, ... 20), number of months in a year (3/12, 6/12, 8/12), or number of days of a year (45/360, 156/360, ... 270/365). The total days in a year may be either 360, 365, or 366, as explained later in this chapter.

To illustrate the application of the simple interest equation, assume that a consumer purchases an $8,000 automobile, makes a down payment of $2,000, and finances the $6,000 balance over a four-year period at 12 percent simple interest.

$$Prt = I$$

$$6,000 \times 0.12 \times 4 = I$$

$$6,000 \times 0.12 \times 4 = \$2,880$$

The **amount of a loan** is the total money that must be repaid, including principal and interest.

Principal + Interest on the principal = Amount

(or, more simply)

$$P + Prt = A$$

$$6,000 + 2,880 = \$8,880$$

Rather than dealing with separate equations, we may use this single equation to solve the entire problem:

$$P + Prt = A$$

$$6,000 + (6,000 \times 0.12 \times 4) = A$$

$$6,000 + 2,880 = \$8,880$$

This equation simply adds to principal (*P*) the computed interest (*Prt*), giving us the total amount of principal and interest (*A*) that must be repaid.

With the borrower having to repay a principal of $6,000 and interest of $2,880, each **monthly payment** must be $185.

4 years × 12 months each = 48-month loan

Amount ÷ Months = Monthly payment

8,880 ÷ 48 = $185 per month

APPLICATION 1. What is the interest charge on a loan of $5,000 that is to be repaid at the end of two years on the basis of 11-1/2 percent simple interest?

$Prt = I$

$5,000 \times 0.115 \times 2 = \$1,150$

APPLICATION 2. What is the amount of a four-year loan of $18,750 at 13 percent simple interest?

$P + Prt = A$

$18,750 + (18,750 \times 0.13 \times 4) = A$

$\qquad 18,750 + 9,750 = \$28,500$

APPLICATION 3. If a consumer makes a down payment of $300 on a refrigerator priced at $1,150 and pays the balance over a one-year period at 8 percent simple interest, what will be the amount of each monthly payment?

$1,150 - 300 = 850$ balance due

$P + Prt = A$

$850 + (850 \times 0.08 \times 1) = A$

$\qquad 850 + 68 = \$918$

$918 \div 12$ mo $= \$76.50$

ORDINARY AND EXACT INTEREST

Time is always stated in terms of years or fractional parts of years, as mentioned earlier. When the terms of loans involve fractional parts of years (days or months), however, the time designation depends on whether we are using ordinary or exact interest.

Ordinary interest, also called "approximate interest" and "banker's interest," simplifies interest computations by treating all months as though they contain 30 days. Even though a year actually has 365 days, except for leap year, which has 366, we assume a 360-day year (12 months × 30 days = 360) when computing ordinary interest.

To compute a loan from June 15, 1987, to July 20, 1988, we may use the following procedure to find the difference (in days) between the two dates:

	Year	Month	Day
Maturity date	88	7	20
Loan date	87	6	15
Difference	1	1	5

$360 + 30 + 5 = 395$ days

July is the seventh month of the year, and June is the sixth. The term of the loan is the sum of one year, one 30-day month, and five days, which is stated as 395/360. Also consider a loan from August 15, 1987, to December 5, 1988:

	Year	Month	Day
		11	35
Maturity date	88	~~12~~	~~5~~
Loan date	87	8	15
Difference	1	3	20

$$360 + 90 + 20 = 470 \text{ days}$$

Being unable to subtract 15 days from 5 days, we borrow one month, decreasing the months from 12 to 11 and increasing the days from 5 to 35. Our answer reveals the term of the loan to be one year, three 30-day months, and 20 days, which is stated in the simple-interest equation as 470/360.

In contrast, **exact interest** is based on the actual number of days in the months and years, necessitating that we remember that April, June, September, and November have 30 days and that all of the other months have 31 days, except February. February has 28 days except for leap years (presidential election years in the United States), at which time it has 29 days. Correspondingly, each leap year includes 366 days as opposed to the usual 365.

To illustrate, let's compute the term of a loan for exact interest from April 15 to August 20 of the same year.

$$
\begin{array}{rl}
\text{April} & 15 \ (30 - 15 = 15) \\
\text{May} & 31 \\
\text{June} & 30 \\
\text{July} & 31 \\
\text{August} & \underline{20} \\
& 127 \text{ days}
\end{array}
$$

The beginning day is not included in the computation, but the ending day is counted.

Table 8.1 in Appendix A provides a convenient alternative to month-by-month computations of terms for exact interest. Referring to the same 127-day loan, we move to the column for April and then move downward to the 15th row to see that April 15 is the 105th day of the year. Upon finding, in a similar manner, that August 20 is the 232nd day, we subtract and find the difference between the two numbers to be 127 days (232 − 105 = 127).

If the principal of the loan is $10,000 and the rate of simple interest is 12 percent per annum (per year), we may calculate the exact interest to be charged:

$Prt = I$

$10,000 \times 0.12 \times 127/365$

$= \$417.53$

Calculator	
Entries	**Display**
1 0 0 0 0	**10,000.**
×	**10,000.**
. 1 2	**0.12**
×	**1,200.**
1 2 7	**127.**
÷	**152,400.**
3 6 5	**365.**
=	**417.5342466**

Notice in the time (t) designation that when computing exact interest, we use not only the exact number of days in the term of the loan (127 days in this instance), but also the exact number of days in a year (365, except for leap year).

If the term of a loan is in excess of one year, the time designation becomes an improper fraction. For a loan of $5,000 from August 10, 1986, that was repaid on February 10, 1988, at 12 percent exact interest, we show time as 549/365.

$1986 = 143 \ (365 - 222)$
$1987 = 365$
$1988 = \underline{\ \ 41} \ (31 + 10)$
$\qquad \quad 549$

$Prt = I$

$5,000 \times 0.12 \times 549/365$

$= \$902.47$

Calculator	
Entries	**Display**
5 0 0 0	**5,000.**
×	**5,000.**
. 1 2	**0.12**
×	**600.**
5 4 9	**549.**
÷	**329,400.**
3 6 5	**365.**
=	**902.465753**

APPLICATION 1. Determine time (t) in computing ordinary interest for a loan issued on July 12, 1988, to be repaid on August 31, 1989.

	Year	Month	Day
Maturity date	89	8	31
Loan date	88	7	12
	1	1	19

$$360 + 30 + 19 = 409/360$$

APPLICATION 2. Determine time (t) in computing ordinary interest for a loan issued on April 5, 1986, that is to be repaid January 10, 1988.

	Year	Month	Day
	87	13	
Maturity date	88	1	10
Loan date	86	4	5
	1	9	5

$$360 + 270 + 5 = 635/360$$

APPLICATION 3. Without the use of a table, compute the exact number of days between July 10 and December 15.

July 21 (31 − 10 = 21)   Oct 31
Aug 31   Nov 30
Sep 30   Dec 15
                                     158 days

APPLICATION 4. Using Table 8.1 in Appendix A and assuming that this is a leap year, determine the exact number of days between January 23 and August 5.

Aug 5 = 217th day
Jan 23 = 23rd day
           194 + 1 = 195 days

APPLICATION 5. Using Table 8-1 in the appendix, determine the exact number of days between August 15, 1985, and February 10, 1987.

1985 = 138 (365 − 227)
1986 = 365
1987 =   41 (41 − 0)
          544 days

APPLICATION 6. Compute the amount of interest that must be paid for a $500 loan from July 1, 1986, to be repaid on March 15, 1988, assuming that approximate interest of 10 percent is to be charged.

	Year	Month	Day
	87	15	
Maturity date	88	3	15
Loan date	86	7	1
Difference	1	8	14

$$360 + 240 + 14 = 614$$

$Prt = I$
$500 \times 0.10 \times 614/360 = \$85.28$

APPLICATION 7. Under terms of exact interest of 12 percent, what is the interest charge for a $1,600 loan from a finance company on May 20 that is to be repaid on August 20 of the same year?

May 11 (31 − 20 = 11) $Prt = I$
Jun 30 $1{,}600 \times 0.12 \times 92/365 = \$48.39$
Jul 31
Aug <u>20</u>
    92 days

APPLICATION 8. Rather than paying a $500 invoice within ten days to take advantage of a 2 percent cash discount, a merchant made payment at the end of the thirty-day grace period. What was the approximate rate of interest the merchant effectively paid for the privilege of using the $500 an extra twenty days?

Missed discount: $500 \times 0.02 = \$10$

$Prt = I$
$500R\ 20/360 = 10$
$27.7778R = 10$
$R = 0.36 = 36\%$

DETERMINING PRINCIPAL, RATE, AND TIME

In addition to figuring interest, as in the preceding examples, we may compute principal, rate, and time — provided that we know the three remaining variables — just as we did with base, rate, and percentage in Chapter 4. If we know that the rate of simple interest is 18 percent, for instance, and that the term is two years and the interest charge $223.20, we may **determine principal**.

$$Prt = I$$

$$P \times 0.18 \times 2 = 223.20$$

$$0.36P = 223.20$$

$$P = \$620$$

Having plugged the known variables into our interest equation, we use simple algebra to solve for the unknown principal (P).

If we know, instead, that the principal is $620; the term, two years; and the interest, $223.20; we may **determine the rate** of interest being charged.

$$Prt = I$$

$$620 \times r \times 2 = 223.20$$

$$1240r = 223.20$$

$$r = 0.18 = 18\%$$

Similarly, the **term of the loan** can be determined by plugging into our equation the principal, rate, and interest.

$$Prt = I$$

$$620 \times 0.18t = 223.20$$

$$111.6t = 223.20$$

$$t = 2 \text{ years}$$

Also consider the varying elements in the following transactions.

APPLICATION 1. If a merchant sells an item for $1,000, accepts a down payment of $250, and finances the balance for one year at 11-1/2 percent simple interest, how much interest will the buyer pay?

Price − down payment = balance due
1,000 − 250 = 750

$$Prt = I$$
$$750 \times 0.115 \times 1 = I$$
$$\$86.25 = I$$

APPLICATION 2. If the owner of a small business secures a loan for 15-1/2 percent simple interest, on which $5,115 was earned by the bank over a three-year period, what was the amount borrowed?

$$Prt = I$$
$$P \times 0.155 \times 3 = 5,115$$
$$0.465P = 5,115$$
$$P = \$11,000$$

APPLICATION 3. If a consumer secured a personal loan for $1,500 from a credit union at a rate of 14 percent, on which interest of $52.50 was paid, for what term was the money borrowed?

$$Prt = I$$
$$1,500 \times 0.14t = 52.50$$
$$210t = 52.50$$
$$t = 0.25$$

Because time is stated in years, 0.25 represents one fourth of a year or three months.

APPLICATION 4. If a customer pays interest of $243.75 for financing a $1,250 purchase for two years, what rate of interest is being charged?

$$Prt = I$$
$$1,250 \times r \times 2 = 243.75$$
$$2,500r = 243.75$$
$$r = 0.0975 = 9\text{-}3/4\%$$

APPLICATION 5. A dealer sold a used car to a customer for $2,000 accepting a down payment and a note for the balance. If the balance due was financed at 8 percent for a period of one and one-half years, at which time the buyer will have made payments totaling $1,960, how much was the down payment?

$$P + Prt = A$$
$$P + (P \times 0.08 \times 1.5) = 1,960$$
$$P + 0.12P = 1,960$$
$$1.12P = 1,960$$
$$P = 1,750$$

Price − Principal = Down payment
2,000 − 1,750 = $250

You may be wondering why interest rates fluctuate to such a significant degree. The market (current) rate of interest depends on supply and demand. Increases in the supply of available money, as manipulated by the Federal Reserve Board, result in lower rates, and decreases are accompanied by higher rates. Conversely, increases in the demand for money (increased borrowing by consumers, businesses, and governments) exert an upward pressure on interest rates, whereas a slack in borrowing eventually results in lower rates.

PARTIAL PAYMENTS

Many loan agreements permit borrowers to make partial payments whenever they wish, as a way of reducing interest charges, in which case the United States Rule comes into play. Because of numerous lawsuits resulting from various methods of crediting partial payments, the Supreme Court established this rule as the legal standard for such transactions.

The reason that borrowers sometimes make partial payments voluntarily is, of course, to reduce the amount of interest paid. A **three-step procedure** is used:

1. Compute the interest on the principal ($Prt = I$) from the first day of the loan to the date of partial payment.
2. Subtract the accrued interest charge from the partial payment.
3. Apply the balance (payment less accrued interest) to the principal.

The same steps apply to all partial payments, with interest being computed on only the unpaid balance from one payment to the next. Or, if you prefer, the interest may first be added to the previous balance due and the total reduced by the amount of the payment.

To determine the total **amount owed on the payoff date**, the interest is added to the unpaid balance.

1. Compute the interest on the principal ($Prt = I$) from the date of the last payment to the date of the payoff date.
2. Add the accrued interest to the balance due following the last partial payment.

Any partial payments that are less than the accrued interest may pacify the lender but will not serve to reduce the principal; such payments are simply held by lenders until future payments are received. The following problem illustrates these procedures in the processing of two partial payments and one final payment.

If the seller of a home accepts at the time of purchase a note (a type of I.O.U.) from the buyer for $5,000 in lieu of cash, to earn simple interest of 11 percent per annum and for repayment in full (principal plus interest) in five years, a partial payment of $1,000 one year later will be treated as follows:

First payment

Principal $5,000
Rate 11%
Time 1 year

a. Interest: $Prt = I$
   $5,000 \times 0.11 \times 1 = 550$

b. Payment $-$ Interest $=$ Credit
   $1,000 - 550 = 450$

c. Principal $-$ Credit $=$ Balance due
   $5,000 - 450 = \$4,550$

Now assume that the borrower sends a second check to the seller six months later in the amount of $2,000.

Second payment

Principal $4,550
Rate 11%
Time 1/2 year

a. Interest: $Prt = I$
   $4,550.00 \times 0.11 \times 6/12 = 250.25$

b. Payment $-$ Interest $=$ Credit
   $2,000.00 - 250.25 = 1,749.75$

c. Principal $-$ Credit $=$ Balance due
   $4,550.00 - 1,749.75 = \$2,800.25$

Interest is computed on $4,550, the balance after the first payment, that is, on the amount of money the borrower was actually using between the first and second payments.

Finally, assume that the buyer telephones the seller seven months later, requesting a payoff figure effective that same day.

Final payment

Principal $2,800.25
Rate 11%
Time 7/12

a. Interest: $Prt = I$
   $2,800.25 \times 0.11 \times 7/12 = 179.68$

b. Principal $+$ Accrued Interest $=$ Payoff amount
   $2,800.25 + 179.68 = \$2,979.93$

Adding the interest that has accrued during the most recent seven-month period to the balance remaining after the second payment results in a settlement figure of $2,979.93. Bankers in some states impose an indirect penalty on the prepayment of installment loans through imposition of the Rule of 78, a provision that is explained in Chapter 9.

APPLICATION 1. What is the balance due on a personal three-year loan of $2,500 following a payment of $1,000 at the end of the eighth month under terms of 8-1/2 percent?

   a. $2,500.00 \times 0.085 \times 8/12 = 141.67$
   b. $1,000.00 - 141.67 = 858.33$
   c. $2,500.00 - 858.33 = \$1,641.67$

APPLICATION 2. Continuing with the situation in Application 1, what is the payoff amount four months later, that is, at the end of the first year of the loan?

a. $1{,}641.67 \times 0.085 \times 4/12 = 46.51$
b. $1{,}641.67 + 46.51 = \$1{,}688.18$

APPLICATION 3. Continuing with the situation in Applications 1 and 2, how much interest did the borrower pay during the term of the loan?

$141.67 + 46.51 = \$188.18$

APPLICATION 4. What is the payoff amount on July 12 for a loan of $6,000 on January 15, assuming a rate of 12 percent approximate interest?

	Year	Month	Day
		6	42
Maturity date	0	~~7~~	~~12~~
Loan date	0	1	15
		5	27 = 177 days

a. $6{,}000 \times 0.12 \times 177/360 = 354$
b. $6{,}000 + 354 = \$6{,}354$

APPLICATION 5. In the preceding situation, what would the payoff be if exact interest were used?

Jan 16	Apr 30	Jun 30
Feb 28	May 31	Jul 12
Mar 31		178 days

(or)

Table 8.1: $193 - 15 = 178$ days

a. $6{,}000 \times 0.12 \times 178/365 = 351.12$
b. $6{,}000 + 351.12 = \$6{,}351.12$

A comparison of the answers in Examples 4 and 5 reveals a higher payoff amount under approximate interest, which may be the reason that bankers prefer to use ordinary (banker's) interest on the loans that they extend to borrowers and exact terms on the interest that they pay depositors.

INSTALLMENT PLANS

Retailers and financial institutions routinely finance **durable goods** such as refrigerators, television sets, and automobiles, products that have useful lives of more than three years. Consumers, after making down payments either in the form of cash or trade-ins, repay the balances owed in installments, usually on a monthly basis. Using **add-on interest**, lenders add simple interest charges to the amounts to be financed and divide by the number of payment periods to determine the size of the payments.

For example, Scott Motors allowed Jerry's Audio Company $3,770 as a trade-in on the replacement of a used panel truck for a new one priced at $14,550. With the trade-in serving as a down payment, Scott Motors arranged monthly payments of $443.18 on a three-year loan at 16 percent simple interest.

Amount to be financed

Price	$14,550
Trade-in	−3,770
Balance due	$10,780

Interest to be added

$$Prt = I$$

$10,780 \times 0.16 \times 3 = \$5,174.40$

Size of payments

Amount financed	$10,780.00
Add-on interest	5,174.40
Total due	$15,954.40
Monthly payment	$443.18 (15,954.40 ÷ 36 months)

From an inverse perspective, the buyer may compare monthly payments with the amount to be financed at the time of purchase to determine the amount of interest charged.

Total payments	$15,954.48 (443.18 × 36 months)
Amount financed	10,780.00
Interest charged	$5,174.48

The simple interest equation ($Prt = I$) may be used to determine the rate of interest being applied (16 percent). As explained in the following chapter, however, the effective (actual) rate of interest when borrowers make periodic payments is much higher than when they are permitted to use the entire amount borrowed for the full term of a loan.

APPLICATION 1. John Cordova bought a 1/3 carat diamond engagement ring priced at $1,250. The jeweler required a down payment of $500 and accepted the balance in 18 monthly installments with carrying charges of 12 percent simple interest. How much money must John pay every month?

Amount to be financed

Price	$1,250
Down payment	−500
Balance due	$750

Interest to be added

$Prt = I$
$750 \times 0.12 \times 1.5 = \$135$

Size of payments

Amount financed	$750
Add-on interest	135
	$885
Monthly payment	$49.17 ($885 ÷ 18 months)

APPLICATION 2. If Leta Snodgrass made a down payment of $400 on a $2,620 personal computer and agreed to pay the balance in monthly payments of $118.40 for two years, what is the total amount of interest she will be paying?

Amount to be financed

Price	$2,620
Down payment	400
Amount financed	$2,220

Interest charged

Total payments	$2,841.60 ($118.40 × 24 months)
Amount financed	2,220.00
Interest charged	$621.60

APPLICATION 3. In the preceding situation, what rate of simple interest was applied in computing the add-on interest?

$Prt = I$
$2,220 \times r \times 2 = 621.60$
$4,440r = 621.60$
$r = 0.14 = 14\%$

CHARGE ACCOUNTS   Charge accounts differ from installment plans in that they need never be completely paid off. Charge accounts are also referred to as "open-account credit" and "open-end credit" because unpaid balances may continue indefinitely as long as borrowers continue purchasing products on credit and continue making only partial payments each month.

Because charge accounts are so prevalent in modern business, a working knowledge of related computations is important to business students and to consumers generally. Usury laws, that place upper limits on the rate of interest that stores and other lenders may charge, vary among the 50 states, but most of these laws have been liberalized to such an extent during earlier periods of soaring interest rates that they represent little or no constraint on lenders today.

The monthly interest rates that many department stores charge may be annualized by multiplying them by 12 months:

Monthly rate		Annual rate
1.583%	× 12 =	19%
1.75%	× 12 =	21%

Merchants generally allow a 20- to 30-day grace period between the billing date and the due date, during which time no interest charges are imposed — provided that the account is paid in full for the preceding month. If only the required minimum payment is made, instead, interest charges are continued on the balance due and begin on new purchases at the time they are charged. No interest-free grace period is extended on newly purchased items, therefore, when unpaid charges are carried forward from one month to the next.

If the entire balances of charge accounts are not fully paid by specified due dates, the finance charge is computed each month on the **average daily balance**. After adding the purchases and subtracting any payments, each day's balance in the account during the billing cycle is added. Then, to derive the average daily balance, the sum of the daily balances is divided by the number of days in the cycle.

Assume, for example, that a customer paid in full the statement for the preceding month, the billing date being August 27.[1] Assume further that the customer charges purchases on August 31 totaling $65, purchases on September 10 totaling $120, and purchases on September 21 totaling $175. The next bill shows a "billing cycle closing date" of September 24 and a payment due date of October 19, and no interest charges will be assessed if the customer makes payment in full by October 19.

To illustrate the process for computing interest on charge accounts, let's assume instead that the customer began this most recent accounting cycle with a balance due of $150. At a monthly interest rate of 1.583 percent (19 percent annually), the store will add to the next bill interest charges of $4.71.

---

[1] Billing dates vary, depending on a person's name. Rather than mailing all statements at the end of each month, merchants avoid such panic situations by mailing statements to customers whose names begin with certain letters of the alphabet on one day, other letters on another day, and so on.

Days in the billing cycle

Aug 4 (31 − 27)
Sep 24 (1 through 24)
   28 days

Average daily balance

Time period	Number of days		Balance due		Total
Aug 28 − Aug 30	3	×	150	=	450
Aug 31 − Sep 9	10	×	215 (150 + 65)	=	2,150
Sep 10 − Sep 20	11	×	335 (215 + 120)	=	3,685
Sep 21 − Sep 24	4	×	510 (335 + 175)	=	2,040
	28				$8,325

$8,325 ÷ 28 = $297.32 ADB

Interest calculation

ADB	Monthly rate		Interest charge
$297.32	× 0.01583	=	$4.71

First, we determine the number of days between the preceding and current closing dates. Second, we calculate the average daily balance for the billing cycle. Third, we multiply the average daily balance by the monthly interest rate. Correspondingly, this customer's bill would be $514.71.

Balance due	$150.00
Purchases	360.00
Interest	4.71
Total	$514.71

Because of the unpaid balance that was carried forward from the previous bill, interest charges began for the balance due on the first billing day of the new cycle and began immediately on subsequent purchases as they occurred throughout the billing cycle.

APPLICATION 1. If the previous billing cycle closed on May 24 and the billing cycle closing date on the current bill is June 25, how many days are there in the current billing cycle?

May 7 days (31 − 24)
Jun 25 days
   32 days

APPLICATION 2. Continuing with the situation in Application 1, assume that the customer purchased on May 31 an item costing $250, purchased on June 10 items totaling $100, and purchased on June 20 products totaling $160. If the customer had an outstanding balance of $300 carried from the previous billing period, what is the average daily balance in the current period?

May 25 – May 30	6 days	300 (balance)	1,800
May 31 – Jun 9	10 days	550 (300 + 250)	5,500
Jun 10 – Jun 19	10 days	650 (550 + 100)	6,500
Jun 20 – Jun 25	6 days	810 (650 + 160)	4,860
	32		18,660

18,660 ÷ 32 = $583.13 ADB

APPLICATION 3. Continuing with the preceding example, what is the total of the customer's current bill if the annual interest rate is 21 percent?

Annual rate ÷ 12 = monthly rate
21% ÷ 12 = 1.75%
$583.13 × 0.0175 = $10.20

Previous balance	$300.00
Purchases	510.00
Interest	10.20
Total	$820.20

Notice that the monthly rate is used even though the billing cycle is not exactly one month.

APPLICATION 4. In the preceding Application, what will be the balance due at the beginning of the next billing cycle, provided that this customer submits the minimum payment of 15 percent of the total?

820.20 × 0.15 = $123.03 payment
820.20 – 123.03 = $697.17 balance

The subject of simple interest is continued in the following chapter, in which bank discounts, the discounting of notes, and early payments are discussed.

EXERCISES (as assigned by your instructor)

8-1 If a consumer makes a down payment of $250 on a $1,050 television set and finances the balance,

a. How much interest will be charged over a two-year period at a rate of 9 percent simple interest?

b. What will be the amount of the monthly payments?

8-2 If an individual secures a consumer loan of $750, to be repaid in 12 monthly payments at 15 percent simple interest, what is the total amount the consumer will have paid the lender at the end of the year?

8-3 Compute the amount of interest involved in each of the following situations:

Principal	Rate	Time
a. $1,600	8%	2 years
b. $23,000	9-1/4%	3 months
c. $735	16-1/2%	1-1/2 years
d. $1,100	10-1/2%	15 months

8-4 Compute the approximate number of days in the following sets of dates:

Loan date	Maturity date
a. February 2, 1986	August 2, 1986
b. February 2, 1988	August 2, 1988 (1988 is a leap year)
c. January 15, 1988	July 10, 1990
d. December 15, 1986	February 30, 1987
e. September 23, 1986	March 13, 1989

8-5 Determine the exact number of days in the following sets of dates, without the use of a table:

Loan date	Maturity date
a. March 12	August 12
b. January 30	June 30
c. January 15, 1988	June 10, 1989 (1988 is a leap year)
d. February 12	September 10
e. July 7, 1986	March 12, 1988 (1988 is a leap year)

8-6 Using Table 8.1 in Appendix A, compute the exact number of days in the following sets of dates:

Loan date	Maturity date
a. March 27	September 12
b. February 15, 1988	February 20, 1989 (1988 is a leap year)
c. October 10, 1987	June 15, 1988
d. June 1, 1986	December 15, 1989

8-7 For a loan of $17,500 from March 19 to December 23 at 11-1/2 percent simple interest,

a. What amount of ordinary interest is to be collected by the lender?
b. What amount of exact interest would be collected?

8-8 If a business borrows $12,000 at 9-1/4 percent ordinary interest, what is the total amount that must be repaid at the end of three and one-half years?

8-9 For a loan of $5,000 to a friend on June 15, what amount should be repaid on September 21 at 8 percent simple interest? Use exact time and assume that this is a leap year.

8-10 Under exact terms, what is the total interest due on a $750 loan dated January 1 that is repaid on December 31 of this year (a leap year) at simple interest of 10-1/2 percent?

8-11 Enter the missing data in each of the following loan situations, using banker's rates:

Principal	Rate	Time	Interest
a. $1,650	9%	3 months	_____
b. $21,200	10-1/4%	_____	$5,432.50
c. $10,500	8%	1 year	
d. $50,000	_____	23 months	$7,187.50
e. _____	6-3/4%	1.5 years	$11,137.50
f. $1,640	12%	60 days	_____
g. $23,000	14%	_____	$805.00

8-12 If a borrower repays $11,430 at the end of two years, which includes

$2,430 interest at a rate of 13-1/2 percent, what was the principal of the loan?

8-13 The owner of a small business borrowed $50,000 and repaid a total of $59,500 two years later. What was the rate of interest?

8-14 A banker loaned $25,000 to a small business owner, who repaid $29,375, including principal and interest at 14 percent approximate. What was the term of the loan?

8-15 An individual repaid $728 to a finance company for a six-month loan of $650. What rate of interest was charged?

8-16 If a dealership sold an ultralight aircraft for $7,500, on which the buyer made payments for three years totaling $4,865, including principal plus simple interest of 13 percent, what amount was financed?

8-17 If a friend borrows $5,000 on July 10 under terms of exact interest at 9 percent per annum, makes a $1,500 payment on August 18 and a second payment of $1,000 on December 12, what is the pay-off amount on March 3 of the following year?

8-18 The seller of a house agrees to let the buyer pay $5,000 of a $15,000 down payment over a two-year period — the first payment of $1,250 six months after the loan date of August 12, a second payment of $1,250 twelve months after the loan date, and the balance at the end of the second year — under terms of 12 percent ordinary interest.

a. What is the balance due following the first payment?
b. What is the balance due following the second payment?

8-19 A complete Sony audio system featuring eight speakers was offered for $1,125.00 with a minimum 20 percent down and 24 easy monthly payments. Using add-on interest of 12-1/2 percent, what is the amount of each monthly payment?

8-20 The Harringtons purchased an air-conditioning unit for $3,500, including installation. Their down payment consisted of a trade-in of $125 on the old unit plus a check for $575. If the balance is paid off in 20 monthly installments of $175 each, how much money are the Harringtons paying in finance charges?

8-21 In Exercise 8-20, what rate of simple interest did the seller use in computing the monthly payments?

8-22 If a credit card customer has a balance of $540 in a department store account after having made a payment the preceding month,

a. What is the average daily balance if the closing period for the earlier month was August 27 and the closing date for the most recent month was September 28 with the customer having made the following purchases:

$150.00 on August 31
$132.50 on September 5
$78.21 on September 20

b. At a rate of 1.75 percent per month, what amount of interest will be added to the current bill?

c. What amount must be paid to clear the account?

d. If the customer does not pay the entire amount by the due date of the current bill, when will interest charges begin on a $200 purchase on October 4?

9 Bank Discounts and APR

LEARNING OBJECTIVES

Continuing with the subject of simple interest, the materials in this chapter will enable you to

- calculate the principal and proceeds of loans that are being discounted
- determine the effective rate of interest on discounted loans
- describe the distinctions between promissory notes and the various forms of drafts
- find the maturity dates of promissory notes and drafts
- discount noninterest-bearing and interest-bearing notes
- figure the amount of interest and the proceeds of discounted notes
- describe the concept and purpose of *annual percentage rate*
- compute the annual percentage rate for credit purchases through charge accounts and installment plans
- calculate the charges, pay-off amounts, and effective rates of interest when terms of the Rule of 78 are applicable

The simple interest charges discussed in the preceding chapter pertained to the types of loans that consumers typically secure from such lending institutions as banks, finance companies, and credit unions, as well as their credit purchases from merchants in the form of installment plans and charge accounts. In contrast, the materials presented in this chapter are related to the discounted loans that bankers extend to their business customers. Provisions of Regulation Z (Truth in Lending) and the Rule of 78 are also included.

DISCOUNTED LOANS

When dealing with individuals, bankers typically lend them the entire principal (P), compute interest on the principal (Prt), and eventually collect from the borrower the amount (A) of the transaction, which is the sum of principal and interest.

$$P + Prt = A$$

When bankers extend commercial loans, on the other hand, they regularly discount the loans by collecting the interest in advance.

Principal − Interest on the principal = Proceeds

(or, more simply)

$$P - Prt = P'$$

As previously defined, *principal* is the amount of money on which interest is computed. Unlike the transactions in Chapter 8, in which interest was added to principal to determine the maturity value of a loan, the principal of a discounted loan is also the maturity value of the loan, the amount that the borrower must repay. The *Prt* part of the equation is the same as before, and **proceeds (P′)** is the actual amount of money that the borrower receives from the bank. The term *bank discount* pertains to the interest that the bank collects in advance, that is, at the beginning of the loan term.

If on July 1 Hyatte Electronics borrows $50,000 from a bank for six months and the bank discounts the loan at 14 percent, Hyatte Electronics will receive proceeds of only $46,000.

$$P - Prt = P'$$

$$50,000 - (50,000 \times 0.14 \times 6/12) = P'$$

$$50,000 - 3,500 = \$46,500$$

Calculator	
Entries	**Display**
5 0 0 0 0	50,000.
×	50,000.
. 1 4	0.14
×	7,000.
6	6.
÷	42,000.
1 2	12.
=	3,500.
STO or M+	3,500.
5 0 0 0 0	50,000.
−	50,000.
RCL or RM	3,500.
=	46,500.

After the bank deducts $3,500 interest charges for six months on $50,000, Hyatte Electronics has only $46,500 at its disposal on July 1. The principal becomes the maturity value, essentially, in that the company is actually borrowing only $46,500 and assuming an obligation to repay that amount plus interest (46,500 + 3,500 = 50,000).

Another way of approaching bank discounts is similar to the short-cut method of applying trade discounts, as explained in Chapter 5. Rather than multiply the price by the percent of discount and then subtracting, we simply multiply the price by the difference between 100 percent and the percent of discount. To refresh your memory, consider an item priced at $12 with a 5 percent discount.

$$100\% - 5\% = 95\%$$

$$\$12 \times 0.95 = \$11.40 \text{ net price}$$

We may **calculate the proceeds of discounted loans** in the same fashion; that is, by multiplying the principal by the difference between 100% (or one) and the product of rate and time.

$$P(1 - rt) = P'$$

$$50,000(1 - 0.14 \times 6/12) = P'$$

$$50,000(1 - 0.07) = P'$$

$$50,000 \times 0.93 = \$46,500$$

Calculator	
Entries	**Display**
$\boxed{.}\boxed{1}\boxed{4}$	0.14
$\boxed{\times}$	0.14
$\boxed{6}$	6.
$\boxed{\div}$	0.84
$\boxed{1}\boxed{2}$	12.
$\boxed{=}$	0.07
$\boxed{STO}$ or $\boxed{M+}$	0.07
$\boxed{1}$	1.
$\boxed{-}$	1.
$\boxed{RCL}$ or $\boxed{RM}$	0.07
$\boxed{=}$	0.93
$\boxed{\times}$	0.93
$\boxed{5}\boxed{0}\boxed{0}\boxed{0}\boxed{0}$	50,000.
$\boxed{=}$	46,500.

The calculator computations can be simplified by recognizing that the difference between 1.00 and 0.07 is 0.93 and, rather than using the storage capabilities of the calculator, multiplying that figure by the principal (0.93 × 50,000 = 46,500). Although both equations are equally appropriate, the authors favor the first formula ($P - Prt = P'$) because it is easier to understand and to recall.

We may **calculate the principal of discounted loans** through use of either of the two formulas. The managers at Hyatte Electronics may need precisely $50,000 on July 1, rather than the $46,500 balance after interest has been deducted. Having identified the proceeds (P'), the principal (P) becomes the unknown.

$$P - Prt = P'$$

$$P - (P \times 0.14 \times 6/12) = 50,000$$

$$P - 0.07P = 50,000$$

$$0.93P = 50,000$$

$$P = \$53,763.44$$

(or)

$$P(1 - rt) = P'$$

$$P(1 - 0.07) = 50,000$$

$$0.93P = 50,000$$

$$P = \$53,763.44$$

By borrowing \$53,763.44 (the principal), the managers at Hyatte Electronics will receive proceeds of \$50,000. The bank will deduct interest of \$3,763.44 for the six-month loan (in advance), and Hyatte Electronics will pay the bank \$53,763.44 at the end of the term.

The **effective rate of a discounted loan** differs from the stated rate because the borrower does not have the privilege of using the entire principal. The stated rate in the preceding situation is 14 percent, whereas the effective (actual) rate is 15-1/10 percent.

$$\text{Principal} - \text{Proceeds} = \text{Interest}$$

$$53,763.44 - 50,000 = 3,763.44$$

$$Prt = I$$

$$50,000r \,(6/12) = 3,763.44$$

$$25,000r = 3,763.44$$

$$r = 15.1\%$$

Principal is the \$50,000 that the borrower actually received, *rate* is the unknown value and the basis of computation, *time* is six months, and *interest* is the difference between the principal of the loan and the proceeds. Because the bank withheld \$3,763.44 interest from the amount of the loan, the effective rate is 1-1/10 percent higher than the stated rate.

In these and the following transactions, notice that approximate (banker's) interest is applied.

APPLICATION 1. If the bank discounts a three-month, \$150,000 loan at 14-1/2 percent simple interest,

a. What amount will the borrower actually receive from the bank?

$$P - Prt = P'$$
$$150,000 - (150,000 \times 0.145 \times 3/12) = P'$$
$$150,000 - 5,437.50 = \$144,562.50$$

(or)

$$P(1 - rt) = P'$$
$$P[1 - (0.145 \times 3/12)] = P'$$
$$150,000(1 - 0.03625) = P'$$
$$150,000 \times 0.96375 = \$144,562.50$$

b. What amount must the borrower repay at the end of the term?

The principal of $150,000.

c. What amount of interest will the banker deduct from the principal?

$$\text{Principal} - \text{Proceeds} = \text{Interest}$$
$$150,000.00 - 144,562.50 = 5,437.50$$

d. What will be the effective rate of interest?

$$Prt = I$$
$$144,562.50 \times r \times 3/12 = 5,437.50$$
$$36,140.625r = 5,437.50$$
$$r = 15\%$$

APPLICATION 2. If the managers of an amusement park need $25,000 two months before opening the park for the summer, in order to buy supplies and to perform certain maintenance functions, what amount of money should they request from the banker if the current discount rate is 12 percent?

$$P - Prt = P'$$
$$P - (P \times 0.12 \times 2/12) = 25,000$$
$$P - 0.02P = 25,000$$
$$0.98P = 25,000$$
$$P = \$25,510.20$$

(or)

$$P(1 - rt) = P'$$
$$P[1 - (0.12 \times 2/12)] = 25,000$$
$$P[1 - 0.02] = 25,000$$
$$0.98P = 25,000$$
$$P = \$25,510.20$$

APPLICATION 3. In Application 2, what amount must the borrower repay at the end of the term?

The principal of $25,510.20.

APPLICATION 4. If the net amount of an invoice is $8,750, subject to terms of 2/10, n/30, and with added freight charges of $350, how much money must the retailer borrow from a bank in order to take advantage of the cash discount? The current discount rate at the retailer's bank is 11 percent per annum. The invoice is dated January 2, and the term of the loan will run from the end of the discount period to the end of the 30-day grace period. (Round the answer to even thousands of dollars.)

$$100\% - 2\% = 98\%$$
$$8{,}750 \times 0.98 = 8{,}575$$
$$8{,}575 + 350 = 8{,}925 \text{ (amount due)}$$
$$30 \text{ days} - 10 \text{ days} = 20/360 \text{ days (time)}$$
$$P - Prt = P'$$
$$P - (P \times 0.11 \times 20/360) = 8{,}925$$
$$P - 0.0061111111P = 8{,}925$$
$$0.99388889P = 8{,}925$$
$$P = 8{,}979.88 = \$9{,}000 \text{ (rounded to even thousands)}$$

(or)

$$P(P - rt) = P'$$
$$P[P - (0.11 \times 20/360)] = 8{,}925$$
$$P[P - 0.0061111111P] = 8{,}925$$
$$0.9938888889P = 8{,}925$$
$$P = 8{,}979.88 = \$9{,}000 \text{ (rounded to even thousands)}$$

DISCOUNTING NOTES   The word **note** encompasses a variety of financial instruments such as promissory notes and sight drafts. These documents are, essentially, promises to pay specific amounts of money within prescribed time periods, with or without interest charges. Notes are classified as **negotiable instruments** in that they represent claims on present or future payments that may be transferred from an individual or institution to other individuals or institutions.

Promissory notes involve two parties: the maker or drawer of the note (the debtor) and the individual or corporation that is extending credit (the payee). In most business transactions involving promissory notes, the maker is usually the buyer and the payee is the seller. As mentioned in Chapter 5, when the sellers of products and services experience difficulty collecting outstanding debts from customers, they sometimes ask the customers to sign notes promising to pay outstanding amounts of money (including interest) within prescribed time frames. Such an arrangement is illustrated in Figure 9.1, in which Brown-Foreman, Inc. (the payee) sold merchandise on credit to Ruby L. McIntosh (the drawer), to be paid from Ruby's account at First National Bank by July 30 (the stated due date), provided that Ruby signed and forwarded the original of the note to her bank. Although McIntosh is legally the maker of the note, personnel within the credit department at Brown-Foreman, Inc. actually prepared the document and mailed it to her (the buyer) for authorization of payment.

FIGURE 9.1

Promissory Note

```
$ 500.00--                    PLACE Phoenix, Arizona  DATE   June 20, 1987

        One month                   AFTER DATE  I   PROMISE TO PAY TO

THE ORDER OF       Brown-Foreman, Inc. (Payee)

---------------------Five Hundred 00/100--------------------------------------- DOLLARS

PAYABLE AT        First National Bank (Payor)

VALUE RECEIVED WITH INTEREST AT      16%        PER ANNUM

NO.    82    DUE    July 30, 1987       Ruby L. McIntosh
                                        Ruby L. McIntosh (maker)
```

Unlike a note, which involves only a drawer and a payee, a **draft** (also called "bill of exchange") is a written order by the first party (the drawer, who is usually the seller) for the second party (the drawee, who is usually the buyer) to pay a specified sum of money to a third party (usually the seller's bank). As illustrated in Figure 9.2, authorized personnel at Jarvis Exporters (drawer, seller) has prepared (drawn, drafted) a note (draft, bill of exchange) and mailed it to LaMar Importers (drawee, buyer) requesting essentially that LaMar accept the note for immediate (at sight) payment to the bank designated by LaMar Importers (drawee).

FIGURE 9.2

Draft (Bill of Exchange)

```
$ 1,000.00                       DATE      April 5, 1987

          At sight                                          PAY TO

THE ORDER OF       First National Bank of Illinois (payee)

---------------------One Thousand---------------------------------------- DOLLARS

VALUE RECEIVED AND CHARGE TO ACCOUNT OF

TO   LaMar Importers (drawee)          JARVIS EXPORTERS, INC. (drawer)

No.    131      Bordeaux, France         R. B. Mason
                                         R. B. Mason, Treasurer
```

Because **sight drafts** are payable upon their receipt, without extensions of credit, no interest charges are involved. **Time drafts**, on the other hand, are those that are payable "after sight." For a draft that is payable 30 days after sight, as illustrated in Figure 9.3, the stated amount becomes due 30 days after the drawee (buyer, debtor) receives and accepts the draft.

As shown, a representative for J. C. Spencer (the drawee) has accepted the obligation by so indicating in handwriting on the face of the draft — entering the word *accepted*, the representative's signature, and the current date. Accordingly, the stated amount of \$3,000 becomes due on December 22, *exactly* 30 days following the date of acceptance. Because neither of the drafts in Figures 9.2 or 9.3 specifies an interest charge, both documents are referred to as noninterest-bearing notes.

The discounting of notes takes place when the drawers of time drafts (the sellers) choose to forego part of the money owed them rather than wait for future payments. The **discounting of non-interest-bearing notes** requires only one step, the deduction of interest by a bank, with the seller receiving the difference between the interest charged and the face value of the note. If Company Y draws a note on Company Z for \$1,000 dated August 8 with interest-free terms of "90 days after sight," Company Y may simply hold the note and collect the full face value at the end of 90 days. Assuming that Company Z (drawee, buyer) accepts the note on August 11, Company Y should collect \$1,000 on November 9.

Aug	20	(31 − 11)
Sept	30	
Oct	31	
Nov	9	(due date)
	90 days	

FIGURE 9.3
Time Draft

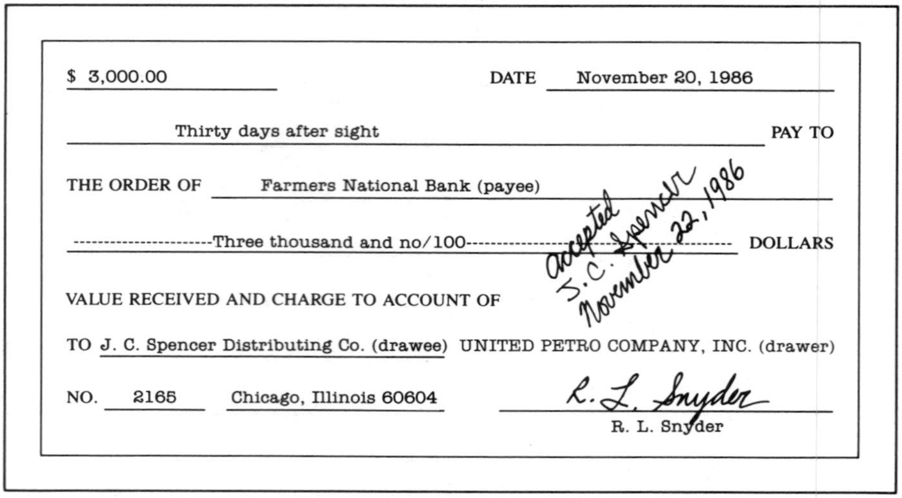
$ 3,000.00 DATE November 20, 1986

Thirty days after sight PAY TO

THE ORDER OF Farmers National Bank (payee)

---------------------Three thousand and no/100--------------------- DOLLARS

VALUE RECEIVED AND CHARGE TO ACCOUNT OF

accepted
J.C. Spencer
November 22, 1986

TO J. C. Spencer Distributing Co. (drawee) UNITED PETRO COMPANY, INC. (drawer)

NO. 2165 Chicago, Illinois 60604

R. L. Snyder
R. L. Snyder

We compute time on the basis of exact interest when stated in days but in even months when stated in months, so that a three-month note dated April 15 would mature on July 15.

If the managers at Company Y need the money immediately, on the other hand, they may discount the note at a bank. Assuming a current bank discount rate of 14 percent, Company Y would receive proceeds of $965.

$$P - Prt = P'$$

$$1,000 - (1,000 \times 0.14 \times 90/360) = P'$$

$$1,000 - 35 = \$965$$

You will recognize that this computation is identical to the discounted loans discussed earlier in this chapter. In effect, the bank has extended a $1,000 loan to Company Y and deducted $35 interest in advance. Rather than collecting the face value of the note from Company Y (the corporation that presented the note to the bank), however, the bank will collect $1,000 (the face value of the note) from Company Z (drawee, buyer) at the end of the term.

If, instead, Company Y holds the note for 30 days before discounting it at a bank, the proceeds will be $976.67.

$$P - Prt = P'$$

$$1,000 - (1,000 \times 0.14 \times 60/360) = P'$$

$$1,000.00 - 23.33 = \$976.67$$

The time (t) designation in discounting transactions is the amount of time between the discount date at the bank and the maturity date of the note; in this case, it is 60 days ($90 - 30 = 60$).

The **discounting of interest bearing notes** requires a two-step computation. First, we determine the amount (A) of the note, which is the maturity value, the sum of principal and interest. Second, we discount that amount. If, for example, Company Y sells $5,000 of merchandise to Company Z with an interest rate of 12 percent "60 days after sight" and an acceptance date of July 28, the maturity date is September 26 (July, 3; August, 31; September, 26) and the maturity value is $5,100.

Step 1: Maturity value

$$P + Prt = A$$

$$5,000 + (5,000 \times 0.12 \times 60/360) = A$$

$$5,000 + 100 = 5,100$$

Assume further that Company Y discounts the note the same day it is accepted, at a bank rate of 14 percent.

Step 2: Discount the maturity value

$$A - (Art) = P'$$

$$5,100 - (5,100 \times 0.14 \times 60/360) = P'$$

$$5,100 - 119 = \$4,981$$

Company Y sacrifices not only the $100 interest that would have been earned by holding the note to maturity, but also an extra $19 ($5,000 − 4,981 = $19), resulting from the bank's having discounted the maturity value at a rate that was 2 percent higher than the rate specified in the note (14% − 12% = 2%). How much money did the bank earn for the lending service provided? The interest collected by the bank was the difference between the maturity value of the note (the amount collected from Company Z at the end of 60 days) and the proceeds to the seller (5,100 − 4,981 = $119).

If, instead, Company Y held the 60-day note for 15 days before discounting it, the time designation in Step 2 (the discount equation) would be 45/360 (60 − 15 = 45):

$$A - Art = P'$$

$$5,100 - (5,100 \times 0.14 \times 45/360) = P'$$

$$5,100.00 - 89.25 = \$5,010.75$$

Company Y earned interest on the face value of the note for 15 days, resulting in proceeds that are $29.75 higher than when the note was discounted immediately upon its acceptance. Keep in mind that notes may be drawn under terms of either approximate or exact interest but that bankers typically use approximate (ordinary, banker's) interest when discounting them. The following examples provide a wide variety of discounting situations.

APPLICATION 1. Brooks Tool Company secured an 18-month loan of $12,000 from Farmers Trust National Bank, which the bank discounted at 15 percent.

a. What were the proceeds to the borrowing company?

$$P - Prt = P'$$
$$12,000 - (12,000 \times 0.15 \times 18/12) = P'$$
$$12,000 - 2,700 = \$9,300$$

b. What amount of interest was paid by Brooks Tool Company?

$2,700

c. If the loan date is January 15 of the current year, what is the maturity date next year?

July 15

d. What amount must Brooks Tool Company pay the bank at maturity?

$12,000

APPLICATION 2. The managers at Globe Products, Inc. need $60,000, which they have secured at a local bank at 12 percent simple interest, to maintain a positive cash flow during the next 90 days.

a. What amount must be borrowed if the company is to receive proceeds of exactly $60,000 following the bank discount?

$$P - Prt = P'$$
$$P - (P \times 0.12 \times 90/360) = 60,000$$
$$P - 0.03P = 60,000$$
$$0.97P = 60,000$$
$$P = \$61,855.67$$

b. What amount must Globe Products pay the bank at maturity?

$61,855.67

APPLICATION 3. If a small-business operator borrows $10,000 from a local bank for three months, to be discounted at 16 percent simple interest, what is the effective rate of interest?

$$P - Prt = P'$$
$$10,000 - (10,000 \times 0.16 \times 3/12) = P'$$
$$10,000 - 400 = 9,600$$

$$P'rt = I$$
$$9,600 \times r \times 3/12 = 400$$
$$2,400r = 400$$
$$r = 16\text{-}2/3\%$$

APPLICATION 4. Hartz Plastics, Inc. sold products valued at $100,000 to Interstate Automotive Corporation, accepting $50,000 in cash and a 90-day promissory note dated March 10 for the balance. Hartz discounted the note at the bank on March 20 at a rate of 16 percent.

a. What were the proceeds received by Hartz?

90 days − 10 days = 80 days remaining

$$P - Prt = P'$$
$$50,000 - (50,000 \times 0.16 \times 80/360) = P'$$
$$50,000.00 - 1,777.78 = \$48,222.22$$

b. How much interest did the bank collect in advance?

$1,777.78

APPLICATION 5. Connector Corporation mailed a bill of exchange dated April 8 to Norbert Simes Company for $20,000 plus 14 percent per annum payable to First National Bank 90 days after sight.

a. If the acceptance date is April 12, what is the maturity date?

Apr 18 (30 − 12)
May 31
Jun 30
Jul 11 (maturity date)
     90 days

b. What amount will be payable to First National Bank at maturity?

$$P + Prt = A$$
$$20,000 + (20,000 \times 0.14 \times 90/360) = A$$
$$20,000 + 700 = 20,700$$

c. If the financial manager at Connector Corporation discounts the note at 16 percent on April 25, what proceeds will be realized?

Step 1: Amount = 20,700 (preceding question)
Step 2: April 12 to April 25 = 13 days
         90 days − 13 days = 77 days

$$A - Art = P'$$
$$20,700 - (20,700 \times 0.16 \times 77/360) = P'$$
$$20,700.00 - 708.40 = \$19,991.60$$

d. How much money will the bank collect from Norbert Simes Company at maturity?

$20,700

e. How much interest will the bank realize from having discounted the note?

$$20,700.00 - 19,991.60 = \$708.40$$

ANNUAL PERCENTAGE RATE (APR)

As shown in this and the preceding chapter, creditors may compute interest charges in numerous ways — on outstanding balances, on the original amounts of loan, by interest deducted in advance, on exact or approximate terms. Loan transactions are further complicated by variations in the amounts of money involved and the time periods for which funds are borrowed. In response to widespread abuses by creditors in the manipulation and obfuscation of these variables, the U.S. Congress enacted the Truth-in-Lending Act in 1969 requiring creditors such as banks, finance companies, credit-card companies, and retailers to disclose sufficient information to enable consumers to make informed decisions regarding the assumption of credit obligations.[1]

Provisions of the Act, as issued by the Federal Reserve Board under the title Regulation Z, require that lenders clearly disclose the effective (actual) interest rate on all loan agreements. Furthermore, conversion of interest rates to annual percentage figures, which must be accurate to within one fourth of one percent (0.25 percent), enables borrowers to identify the cost of using each one dollar of credit for one year.[2]

The **annual percentage rate (APR)** is the common denominator with which consumers may assess and compare loan offers. Procedures for determining APR vary for charge accounts and installment purchases. For charge accounts (including credit-card accounts), the APR is computed and stated on an annualized basis by multiplying the periodic rates (monthly, weekly, daily) by the number of periods in one year. Because department stores and banks usually charge interest on a monthly basis, we simply multiply their periodic rates by 12 months. If the rate is expressed in terms of weeks or days, instead, we multiply by 52 and 365, respectively.

---

[1] The Act also prohibits lenders from seeking from applicants information concerning age, sex, marital status, child-bearing plans, color, religion, national origin, or other criteria that might discourage applicants or result in loan refusals or terms different from those offered to applicants with similar credit records. Females may open accounts in their own names, rather than that of their spouses, provided that through their own incomes or resources they qualify for credit. Lenders must also combine *all* of a woman's income with that of her spouse when checking her qualifications for jointly requested loans — even when the woman is pregnant or when her income is from a part-time job.

[2] In addition to the manner in which interest charges are assessed, Regulation Z requires that all finance charges be fully disclosed to borrowers — in writing. Finance charges often include extra accounting costs incurred in credit transactions, fees for credit investigations, insurance coverage, bank discounting, collection costs, and bad debt write-offs.

Rate		Periods		APR
1.75% per month	×	12	=	21%
0.4% per week	×	52	=	20.8%
0.06% per day	×	365	=	21.9%

Because the computations of APR on installment purchases are relatively complex, the Federal Reserve Board has simplified the process for lenders through the issuance of tables. The figures within the body of Table 9.1 in Appendix A represent the finance charge per $100 of credit, with different tables available for quarterly, monthly and weekly payment plans. Use of this monthly table reduces the **procedure for computing APR** to two steps:

1. Divide the finance charge by the total amount being financed, to derive the finance charge per dollar, and then multiply the quotient by $100 to determine the charge for each $100 of credit.
2. Proceed down the column at the far left of the table to the number of payments involved and then read across that row to the quotient that is closest in value to the answer determined in Step 1.

The rate identified in Step 2 is the annual percentage rate.

To illustrate, assume that the advertised price of a Maximax personal computer is $875, with a down payment of $75 and finance charges of $176. The balance is to be paid in 18 monthly payments.

$$Step\ 1: \frac{\text{Finance charges}}{\text{Amount financed}} \times 100 = \frac{176}{800} \times 100 = 22$$

Step 2: Moving down the left column in Table 9.1 in Appendix A to 18 payments and proceeding across that row for several pages to 22.05, the closest value to 22.00, the APR at the top of the column is 26.25 percent

Because the value derived in Step 1 (22.00) is at variance with the closest value in the table (22.05), the APR of 26.25 percent is only an approximation. Most lenders use tables to compute APR because the results are always in compliance with the law (within one fourth of one percent of the true percent), rather than rely on any of the several complex formulas that are available for computing approximations that are only slightly more accurate.

A comparison of the simple interest rate of 14-2/3 percent with the APR of 26-1/4 percent in this transaction reveals a difference of a little more than 11-1/2 percent.

$$Prt = I$$
$$800 \times r \times 18/12 = 176$$
$$1,200r = 176$$
$$r = 14\text{-}2/3\%$$

$$
\begin{array}{r}
26\text{-}1/4 \\
-14\text{-}2/3 \\
\hline
11\text{-}7/12\%
\end{array}
$$

Unlike a regular loan, in which the borrower maintains possession of the entire principal ($800) for the duration of the loan (18 months), the amount of borrowed money to which this borrower has access declines with each monthly installment payment. The true (effective) rate of interest being charged, as based on the actual amount of borrowed funds remaining in the borrower's possession each month, is 26-1/4 percent (the APR). In making credit decisions regarding the purchase of the Maximax computer, consumers may accurately compare the equivalent rate of 26-1/4 percent with APRs disclosed by other retailers in connection with the credit terms they offer.

APPLICATION 1. Find the APR for an interest rate on a charge account for 1-1/2 percent per month.

$$1.5 \times 12 = 18\%$$

APPLICATION 2. Mr. and Mrs. Cleaves purchased a deluxe 23.9 cubic foot refrigerator-freezer for $1,125.00. They financed the appliance with a down payment of $125.00 and an agreement to pay the balance in 12 monthly installments of $92.88. What APR should the seller disclose in the contract?

Finance charges:

Installment payment	$92.88
Number of payments	×12
Total amount to pay	$1,114.56
Less amount financed	1,000.00
Interest charged	$114.56

Step 1: $\dfrac{\text{Finance charges}}{\text{Amount financed}} \times 100 = \dfrac{114.56}{1,000.00} \times 100 = 11.456$

Step 2: The closest value to 11.456 in Row 12 of Table 9.1 is 11.45, which reveals at the top of the column an APR of 20.50 (20-1/2) percent.

APPLICATION 3 In Application 2, how does the APR compare with the simple interest rate?

$$Prt = I$$
$$1{,}000 \times r \times 1 = 114.56$$
$$1{,}000r = 114.56$$
$$r = 11\text{-}1/2\%$$
$$20\text{-}1/2\% - 11\text{-}1/2\% = 9\% \text{ difference}$$

RULE OF 78

The Rule of 78, in those states where its use is permitted, enables lenders to impose restrictive conditions on loans that are paid off before the maturity dates. This rule has the effect of assessing higher interest charges during the early months of loans than during later periods. The rationale for this rule is that borrowers have command over more dollars during the early periods, before they have repaid much of the money; and, because the cost of preparing short-term loans is just as great as for long-term transactions, lenders are entitled to higher returns for loans that are paid early.

The term *Rule of 78* came about because many installment purchases are for one year and because the sum of 12 months is 78:

$$1 + 2 + 3 + 4 \dots + \dots + 11 + 12 = 78$$

Then, reversing the numbers of the months as our numerators and using the sum as our denominator, 12/78 of the interest is charged the first month, 11/78 the second month, and so on. If the interest charge on an installment loan is $250, for example, $38.46 of that amount would be related to the first month and $35.26 to the second month, totaling $73.72 for the two-month period.

Interest for first month: $250 \times 12/78 = \$38.46$
Interest for second month: $250 \times 11/78 = \underline{35.26}$
Interest for first two months: $\$73.72$

(or)

$$250 \times \frac{12 + 11}{78} = 250 \times \frac{23}{78} = \$73.72$$

From the perspective of the borrower, the amount of interest to be rebated if paying off the loan at the end of the second month would be $176.28.

$$\text{Amount} \times \frac{\text{Months remaining}}{\text{Sum of months}}$$

$$= \frac{1 + 2 + 3 + 4 + 5 + 6 + 7 + 8 + 9 + 10}{1 + 2 + 3 + 4 + 5 + 6 + 7 + 8 + 9 + 10 + 11 + 12} = \frac{55}{78}$$

$$250 \times \frac{55}{78} = \$176.28$$

Multiplying total interest by the sum of the months remaining over 78, we find the rebate (the balance of the interest due the borrower):

$176.28 rebate
  73.72 earned by lender
$250.00 interest on original contract

Assume, instead, that the lender pays off the loan at the end of the tenth month.

Interest for the last two months =

$$250 \times \frac{1 + 2}{78} = 250 \times \frac{3}{78} = \$9.62$$

In paying the loan just two months early, the borrower reduces the interest payment by only $9.62.

The terms for installment loans may differ, of course, so that the denominator in the equation may vary from 78.

6 months = 1 + 2 + 3 + 4 + 5 + 6 = 21

18 months = 1 + 2 + 3 ... + 17 + 18 = 171

The task of adding periods in excess of 12 months may be eliminated by use of the following formula, with n being the number of monthly payments involved in a contract.

$$\frac{n(n + 1)}{2}$$

$$18 \text{ months} = \frac{18(18 + 1)}{2} = \frac{18 \times 19}{2} = \frac{342}{2} = 171$$

The Truth in Lending Act requires that lenders state in writing the methods for computing rebates for the early payment of consumer loans.

APPLICATION 1. How much of a total of $275 interest will the lender charge during the first three months of a six-month loan under the Rule of 78?

$$275 \times \frac{6 + 5 + 4}{1 + 2 + 3 + 4 + 5 + 6} =$$

$$275 \times \frac{15}{21} = \$196.43$$

APPLICATION 2. For a loan contract carrying interest charges of $98.50, how much interest will the lender rebate to the borrower for paying off the loan at the end of the seventh month rather than at the end of one year?

Months remaining $= 12 - 7 = 5$

$$\text{Interest rebated} = 98.50 \times \frac{1 + 2 + 3 + 4 + 5}{1 + 2 + 3 \ldots + 12} =$$

$$98.50 \times \frac{15}{78} = \$18.94$$

APPLICATION 3. If a consumer has an obligation to make six monthly payments of $64.20, with each payment including $4.20 interest, how much interest can be saved by paying off the loan at the end of the fifth month (one month early), assuming that the Rule of 78 is applicable?

Total interest $= 4.20 \times 6 = 25.20$

Interest saved $= 25.20 \times \dfrac{1}{21} = \$1.20$

APPLICATION 4. Realizing that the sum of the number of payments for 12 months is 78, what is the sum of 15 months?

$78 + 13 + 14 + 15 = 120$

(or)

$$\frac{n(n+1)}{2} = \frac{15(15 + 1)}{2} = \frac{15 \times 16}{2} = \frac{240}{2} = 120$$

APPLICATION 5. If a consumer makes a down payment of $250 on the purchase of a $1,150 refrigerator that is subject to a sales tax of 6 percent and also signs an installment contract for payment of the balance in 24 monthly payments,

a. What amount is being financed?

Price	1,150
Tax	69 (1,150 × 0.06)
Total	1,219
Down payment	250
Balance due	$969

b. Assuming a simple interest rate of 16 percent, what is the total amount of interest to be paid over the course of the loan?

$$Prt = I$$
$$969 \times 0.16 \times 24/12 = \$310.08$$

c. What are the monthly payments?

$$969.00 + 310.08 = 1,279.08$$
$$1,279.08 \div 24 = \$53.30$$

d. If the borrower pays off the loan immediately after making the 20th payment, how much interest will be saved under the Rule of 78?

$$310.08 \times \frac{1 + 2 + 3 + 4}{1 + 2 + 3 + 4 \ldots + 23 + 24} =$$

$$310.08 \times \frac{10}{300} = \$10.34$$

e. What is the payoff figure at that time?

Principal	$969.00
Interest	299.74 (310.08 − 10.34)
Due bank	$1,268.74
Paid	1,066.00 (53.30 × 20)
Balance	$202.74

As illustrated in Chapter 8, the equation or formula for calculating simple interest is relatively easy and straightforward. In contrast, as shown in this chapter, determination of the actual interest rate depends on the various methods of allocating funds between principal and interest.

EXERCISES (as assigned by your instructor)

9-1 How does a typical loan that is based on simple interest differ from a loan that has been discounted?

9-2 How do the proceeds of a straight loan differ from the proceeds of a discounted loan?

9-3 Precisely what amount of money will Garwood Corporation receive after a $50,000 loan for one year has been discounted at 15 percent?

9-4 If Proctor Land Corporation borrows $150,000 from American Trust Company for 60 days, to be discounted at a simple interest rate of 16-1/2 percent,

    a. What are the proceeds to the borrower?
    b. What amount of interest does the bank collect at maturity?
    c. What amount must the borrower repay at maturity?
    d. What effective rate of interest will the borrower have paid?

9-5 If Specialty Steel Corporation needs $100,000 for six months beginning October 3 and the current discount rate is 14-3/4 percent at First Security (where the company has established a line of credit),

a. What amount of money must be borrowed?
b. What is the maturity date of the loan?
c. What amount must be repaid at maturity?
d. What is the effective rate of interest?

9-6 Computer Leasing Corporation has received an invoice for equipment totaling $85,000 plus shipping charges of $760. The invoice calls for payment in full by August 20, after which time the invoice becomes delinquent. Because of a cash flow problem, company managers have decided to borrow for 30 days enough money to pay the invoice, the loan to be discounted at a simple interest rate of 17 percent.

a. How much money must the corporation borrow?
b. What are the proceeds?
c. What amount must the company pay the bank at maturity?
d. What is the effective rate of the loan?

9-7 What are the main elements of a promissory note?

9-8 In what type of situation would the payee prepare a promissory note?

9-9 Does the seller or the buyer normally prepare a draft? Explain.

9-10 What does the receiver of a time draft normally do to indicate acceptance of the stated terms?

9-11 If a note that is dated July 18 carries the term *at sight*, when is payment due?

9-12 If a bill of exchange that is dated January 23 reflects an acceptance date of January 27 and terms of "thirty days after sight," when is payment due?

9-13 Huntington Toy Corporation accepted a 30-day promissory note from a customer for $1,000. The note, which was dated April 2, was accepted on April 4.

a. If the toy company discounts the note on April 6 at a bank rate of 12 percent, what are the proceeds?
b. The bank will collect how much? from whom? on what date?
c. In effect, how much interest will the toy company have collected?
d. How much money will the toy company have lost on the deal?

9-14 If Jeannette Corporation issued a draft for $10,000 at 13 percent interest that is dated August 8, payable in 90 days after sight, and was accepted on August 11,

a. What are the proceeds if the corporation discounts the note on August 15 at a rate of 15 percent?

b. What are the proceeds if the draft were to be discounted at the end of 30 days instead?

c. What is the maturity date?

9-15 Define the acronym APR.

9-16 What is the main purpose of the APR requirement?

9-17 According to Regulation Z of the Truth in Lending Act, APR quotations must be within what degree of accuracy?

9-18 Find the APR for the following period rates:

a. 1.85% per month
b. 0.3% per week
c. 2.25% per month
d. 0.05% per day

9-19 Referring to the appropriate table, determine the APR for a $950 purchase on which the customer makes a down payment of $200 and pays the balance in six monthly payments of $133.75 each.

9-20 In Exercise 9-19, how does the APR compare with the simple interest rate that was applied to the contract?

9-21 Although an automobile salesman quotes a simple interest rate of 18 percent that was consistent with the rates being charged on credit sales at local department stores, what APR should be reflected in the contract for a three-year loan of $7,600?

9-22 A $3,600 motorcycle carries a minimum down payment of 25 percent, with the balance to be paid in monthly installments over a four-year period at 10 percent simple interest. What is the APR?

9-23 What is the justification for the application of Rule of 78 by some lending institutions?

9-24 If interest charges of $175 are to be paid over the life of a 12-month contract, how much interest under the Rule of 78 will the borrower save by paying three months early?

9-25 Compare the interest charge during the first month and twelfth month of a one-year contract for the purchase of a $1,500 home-entertainment system, assuming that the purchaser made a down payment of $350 and financed the balance at 14 percent interest under the Rule of 78.

9-26 For a 24-month loan of $1,500 at 12 percent per year, under the Rule of 78,

a. What are the monthly payments?
b. If the borrower pays off the loan ten months early, how much interest is saved?
c. What is the payoff figure after the 20th payment has been made (4 months early)?

10 Compound Interest

This chapter builds on the knowledge of simple interest that you acquired in the preceding two chapters, the mastery of which will enable you to

- explain the fundamental difference between simple interest and compound interest
- calculate compound interest either mathematically or with the use of a table and either with or without a calculator
- determine compound amount
- calculate interest that is compounded annually, semiannually, quarterly, and daily
- understand and explain the concept of present value
- determine the present value of compound amount

Compound interest is a better deal than simple interest for the people or institutions that are earning it, because they are earning interest on interest. Lending institutions generally offer compound interest to savers, regardless of whether deposits are of short- or long-term duration, as a way of enticing them to increase their deposits and maintain them for relatively long time periods. In this, the first of three chapters dealing with compound interest, we explore the basic concept of compounding and the processes for identifying the beginning and ending values of such transactions.

INTEREST ON THE INTEREST

When interest is compounded, it is computed not only on the principal of a deposit but also on any interest that has accrued. Rather than using the amount deposited as the principal each period, as with simple interest, we treat as the principal for each time period (year, quarter, month, day) the amount borrowed plus all accrued interest. Consider the following comparison of a four-year deposit of $5,000 at a rate of 12 percent — based on simple interest in the first computation and on interest compounded annually in the second computation.

Simple Interest

$$Prt = I$$

First year:	$5,000 \times 0.12 \times 1 =$	600
Second year:	$5,000 \times 0.12 \times 1 =$	600
Third year:	$5,000 \times 0.12 \times 1 =$	600
Fourth year:	$5,000 \times 0.12 \times 1 =$	600
		$2,400

Compounded Annually

First year: $5{,}000.00 \times 0.12 \times 1 = \qquad 600.00$
Second year: $5{,}600.00 \times 0.12 \times 1 = \qquad 672.00$
Third year: $6{,}272.00 \times 0.12 \times 1 = \qquad 752.64$
Fourth year: $7{,}024.64 \times 0.12 \times 1 = \underline{\qquad 842.96}$
$$\$2{,}867.60$$

Notice that simple interest is computed on the $5,000 principal each year, but that the principal under compound interest is increased each year by the amount of interest earned during the preceding period. As illustrated further in Figure 10.1, the principal for the second year includes the interest earned during the first period ($600), the principal for the third year includes the interest earned during the first and second periods ($600 + 672), and so forth. When interest is compounded, the lender receives $2,867.60 compared to $2,400.00 under simple interest, a difference of $467.60 for the four-year period.

COMPOUND AMOUNT As explained in Chapter 8, the amount of a loan is the sum of principal plus interest. Similarly, **compound amount** is principal plus interest — when the

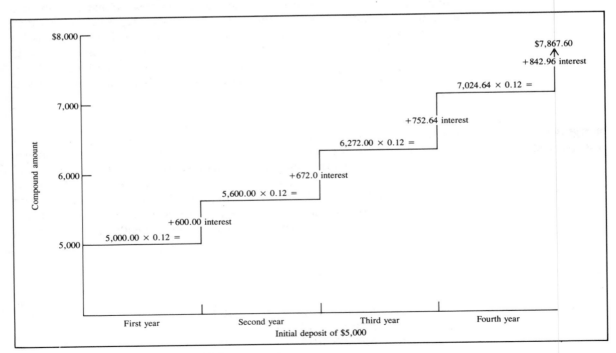

Figure 10.1
Compound Interest (a $5,000 deposit at 12 percent compounded annually)

Figure 10.2
The concept of *compound amount*

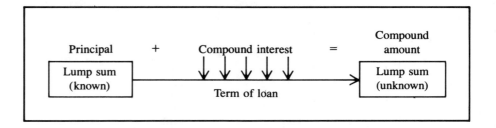

interest has been compounded. These relationships are illustrated in Figure 10.2. By depositing a lump sum (the principal) in a bank, for example, that figure, through periodic interest payments credited to the account, increases by the end of a term to a relatively large lump sum that is called *compound amount*. Using the same situation as in the preceding section, we have

Principal + Interest = Amount

or, more simply

$$P + I = A$$

$$5,000.00 + 2,867.60 = \$7,867.60$$

Rather than enduring the period-by-period computation of compound interest, we may use exponential notation (Chapter 3, page 59) to simplify our calculations, resulting in the following equation:

$$P(1 + \%)^n = A \leftarrow \text{the unknown}$$

$$5,000(1 + 0.12)^4 = A$$

$$5,000(1.12)^4 = A$$

$$5,000 \times 1.57351936 = \$7,867.60$$

Calculator	
Entries	**Display**
1 . 1 2	1.12
y^x	1.12
4	4.
×	1.57351936
5 0 0 0	5,000.
=	7,867.60

P is the \$5,000 principal; "1" is a constant, which has the effect of placing the principal in our answer rather than having to add it separately; 0.12 is our rate (%) of interest; and the exponential four (n) is the number of time periods (four years in this instance).

You will recall that the $(1.12)^4$ is actually $1.12 \times 1.12 \times 1.12 \times 1.12$. You may simplify this multiplication process with either the (y^x) key or, with some calculators, the (=) key. Restated, the equation is $5,000(1 + 0.12)^4$.

With a y^x key	
Entries	**Display**
1 . 1 2	1.12
y^x	1.12
4	4.
×	1.57351936
5 0 0 0	5,000.
=	7,867.5968

With an = key	
Entries	**Display**
1 . 1 2	1.12
×	1.12
1 . 1 2	1.12
=	1.2544
=	1.404928
=	1.57351936
×	1.57351936
5 0 0 0	5,000.
=	7,867.5968

Clearly, the (y^x) key is more efficient than use of an (=) key, provided that your calculator has such a capability, especially when dealing with more than just a few time periods. When using an (=) key in this manner, we are chain multiplying; having multiplied 1.12 by itself once, we simply press the (=) key for the second and third multiplications.

Recalling that we earlier computed compound interest on $5,000.00 to be $2,867.60, we may double-check our results.

$$P + Prt = A$$

5,000.00 + 2,867.60 = $7,867.60

Stated another way, **compound interest** is the difference between amount and principal.

Amount − Principal = Interest

7,867.60 − 5,000.00 = $2,867.60

Beginning with a principal of $5,000.00, the account will have accumulated interest of $2,867.60, for a total amount (principal plus interest) of $7,867.60.

APPLICATION 1. Compute manually the interest on a two-year loan of $3,500 at 15 percent compounded annually.

$$Prt = I$$

$$
\begin{aligned}
3{,}500 \times 0.15 \times 1 &= 525.00 \\
3{,}500 + 525 &= 4{,}025.00 \\
4{,}025 \times 0.15 \times 1 &= 603.75 \\
525.00 + 603.75 &= \$1{,}128.75
\end{aligned}
$$

APPLICATION 2. Using a calculator, determine the amount if the principal is $12,000, the term six years, and the rate 9 percent compounded annually.

$$P(1 + 0.09)^6 = A$$
$$12,000(1.09)^6 = A$$
$$12,000 \times 1.6771 = \$20,125.20$$

APPLICATION 3. In Application 2, how much interest was earned?

$$A - P = I$$
$$20,125.20 - 12,000.00 = \$8,125.20$$

APPLICATION 4. Find the compound amount for a 15-year loan of $25,000 at 11-1/2 percent compounded annually.

$$P(1 + 0.115)^{15} = A$$
$$25,000(1.115)^{15} = A$$
$$25,000 \times 5.118267862 = \$127,956.70$$

In the final example, if your calculator does not have a (y^x) key, you may derive the answer with some calculators by multiplying 1.115 by itself once, pressing the $(=)$ key 13 times, and multiplying the result by 25,000.

MULTIPLE COMPOUND PERIODS

When compounding annually, rate (r) remains unchanged and time (n) is the number of years. When compounding is *not* on an annual basis, we must adjust both rate and time. To compute compound amount on a four-year loan of $2,000 at 12 percent compounded semiannually, for example, rate becomes 6 percent and time becomes 8 periods.

12% paid semiannually

$$\% = 12 \div 2 = 6$$

$$n = 4 \times 2 = 8$$

When interest is compounded semiannually (twice a year), the annual rate of 12 percent must be halved and the four annual time periods must be doubled. When interest is compounded quarterly, we divide the rate by 4 and multiply time by 4, and so on. These relationships as they apply to a 12 percent, four-year loan are summarized below:

Compounded	12 percent	Four years
Annually	$\%^1 = 12 \div 1 = 12$	$n^2 = 4 \times 1 = 4$
Semiannually	$\% = 12 \div 2 = 6$	$n = 4 \times 2 = 8$
Quarterly	$\% = 12 \div 4 = 3$	$n = 4 \times 4 = 16$
Monthly	$\% = 12 \div 12 = 1$	$n = 4 \times 12 = 48$
Daily	$\% = 12 \div 365 = 0.0328767$	$n = 4 \times 365 = 1,460$

[1]$\% = $ Rate that has been adjusted for multiple compound periods.
[2]$n = $ Time (t) that has been adjusted for multiple compound periods.

If compounding is monthly, we are, in effect, computing interest during a four-year period at one percent every month for 48 months. For a principal of $5,000, the compound amount is $8,061.13:

$\% = 12 \div 12 = 1$

$n = 4 \times 12 = 48$

$$P(1 + \%)^n = A$$

$$5,000(1 + 0.01)^{48} = A$$

$5,000 \times 1.612226078 = \$8,061.13$

Calculator	
Entries	**Display**
1 . 0 1	1.01
y^x	1.01
4 8	48.
×	1.612226078
5 0 0 0	5,000.
=	8,061.13

Also consider the following problems.

APPLICATION 1. Convert percent and time to a quarterly basis for a compound interest rate of 15 percent for 5 years.

$\% = 15 \div 4 = 3\text{-}3/4 \qquad n = 5 \times 4 = 20$

APPLICATION 2. Find the compound amount for a three-year loan of $10,000 at 16 percent compounded quarterly.

$\% = 16 \div 4 = 4 \qquad n = 3 \times 4 = 12$

$$P(1 + \%)^n = A$$
$$10,000(1.04)^{12} = A$$
$$10,000 \times 1.601032219 = \$16,010.32$$

APPLICATION 3. What is the compound amount for a deposit of $8,500 ten years ago at 9 percent interest compounded monthly?

$\% = 9 \div 12 = 3/4 \qquad n = 10 \times 12 = 120$

$$P(1 + \%)^n = A$$
$$8,500(1 + 0.0075)^{120} = A$$
$$8,500 \times 2.451357078 = \$20,836.54$$

APPLICATION 4. If $500 is deposited today at 8 percent compounded daily, how much money will be in the account at the end of six years?

$\% = 8 \div 365 = 0.0219178 \qquad n = 6 \times 365 = 2,190$

$$P(1 + \%)^n = A$$
$$500(1 + 0.000219178)^{2,190} = A$$
$$500 \times 1.615989116 = \$807.99$$

Remember that the adjusted %, as a percent, must be divided by 100 (decimal point moved two places to the left) when applying it in the equation.

When compounding daily, some banks use a 360-day year in computing the adjusted rate (%) and a 365-day when figuring the adjusted time (*n*), resulting in a slightly higher interest payment.

**COMPOUND
AMOUNT TABLE**

People who deal regularly with compound interest occasionally use compound amount tables in their computations. Even though relying mainly on algebraic equations in computer and calculator applications, they find the tables handy for individual computations.

To use the table, however, we must first adjust the rate and time for multiple compound periods. We then rely on % to locate the appropriate page and *n* to locate the row. To compute interest on a five-year loan of $1,000 at 12 percent compounded quarterly, for instance, we refer to the 3% page in Table 10.1 (Appendix A). The principal becomes our multiplicand, and the figure in Column 1 at row 20 becomes the multiplier, resulting in a compound amount of $1,806.11.

$$\% = 12 \div 4 = 3 \qquad n = 5 \times 4 = 20$$

Principal × Table 10.1 figure = Amount

$$\$1,000.00 \times 1.80611123 = \$1,806.11$$

Even if your calculator accommodates the entire multiplier from the table, you may limit the number of digits used to the right of the decimal to the number of total digits in the principal (including all dollars and cents). For a principal of $1,000, you may disregard the last two digits in the figure from the table and still derive an accurate answer.

Number of significant digits in the principal	Number of digits to right of decimal in multiplier
$1,000.00	1.80611123
6 digits	6 digits

$$\$1,000 \times 1.806111 = \$1,806.11$$

Double-checking our results with use of the *compound amount* equation, we find that both answers are identical.

$$P(1 + \%)^n = A$$

$$1{,}000(1 + 0.03)^{20} = A$$

$$1{,}000(1.806111) = \$1{,}806.11$$

Notice also that the same equation was used to derive the entry in Table 10.1.

$$(1 + \%)^n = (1.03)^{20} = 1.80611123$$

The table doesn't reflect any figures that we cannot derive for ourselves, but it sometimes simplifies our calculations.

If a compound-interest problem goes beyond the number of rate periods given in a table, an extra calculation enables us to use tabled figures. For a thirty-year deposit of $5,000 that earns 8 percent interest compounded semiannually, for example, we have an adjusted rate of 4 percent ($\% = 8 \div 2 = 4$) and rate periods of $n = 60$ ($n = 30 \times 2 = 60$). After determining the compound amount for 50 rate periods, the limit of the table, we multiply it by the table figure for an additional ten rate periods.

$$P \times \text{Table 10.1 value} = A$$

(1) $5{,}000 \times 7.10668335 = 35{,}533.4168$

(2) $35{,}533.4169 \times 1.48024428 = \$52{,}598.14$

The more calculations involved, however, the greater the chance for error, which makes the compound-amount equation more convenient and more reliable in such circumstances.

$$P(1 + \%)^n = A$$

$$5{,}000(1.04)^{60} = \$52{,}598.14$$

The following examples will help to reinforce these concepts.

APPLICATION 1. Using Table 10.1, determine the compound amount for a two-year loan of $3,000 at 9 percent compounded annually.

$$\% = 9 \quad n = 2$$

Principal $\times$ Table 10.1 value = Amount
$$3{,}000 \times 1.1881 = \$3{,}564.30$$

APPLICATION 2. Using Table 10.1, determine the compound amount for a ten-year loan of $5,000 at 18 percent compounded quarterly.

$$\% = 18 \div 4 = 4\text{-}1/2 \qquad n = 10 \times 4 = 40$$

Principal × Table 10.1 value = Amount
$$\underbrace{5,000.00}_{6 \text{ digits}} \times \underbrace{5.816364}_{6 \text{ digits}} = \$29,081.82$$

APPLICATION 3. What amount of interest will accumulate in five years on an initial deposit of $1,000 at 16 percent compounded semiannually? Use Table 10.1.

$$\% = 16 \div 2 = 8 \qquad n = 5 \times 2 = 10$$

Principal × Table 10.1 value = Amount
1,000.00 × 2.158925 = 2,158.93
Amount − Principal = Interest
2,158.93 − 1,000.00 = $1,158.93

PRESENT VALUE OF COMPOUND AMOUNT

The term **present value**, as it pertains to financial transactions, is the quantity of money that is required at some starting date to equal a compound amount at some future date. These relationships are illustrated in Figure 10.3. Unlike *compound amount* (Figure 10.2) in which the end figure (amount) is unknown, in *present value of compound amount* (Figure 10.3) it is just the opposite, with the end value (compound amount) being known and the present value (principal) being unknown. With compound interest, therefore, the terms *principal* and *present value* are synonymous. If we know that the compound amount of an investment five years from now will be $10,000, for example, we may identify the present value of that amount. In so doing, we are determining the initial deposit that will be required, under current rates and terms of interest, to increase through interest payments to $10,000 at the end of five years.

To illustrate, the managers at Company Y may want to know the amount of money that must be deposited today to repay a $10,000 debt five years from today — at a bank that pays 12 percent interest compounded quarterly on five-year deposits. We use the same equation as when calculating compound amount, but identify the unknown principal (*P*).

Figure 10.3
The concept of *present value of compound amount*

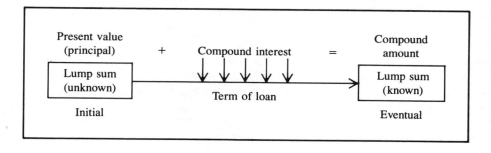

$$\% = 12 \div 4 = 3$$

$$n = 5 \times 4 = 20$$

$$P(1 + \%)^n = A$$

$$P(1 + 0.03)^{20} = 10,000$$

$$1.80611123P = 10,000$$

$$P = \$5,536.76$$

Calculator	
Entries	**Display**
$\boxed{1}\boxed{.}\boxed{0}\boxed{3}$	**1.03**
$\boxed{y^x}$	**1.03**
$\boxed{2}\boxed{0}$	**20.**
$\boxed{=}$	**1.80611123**
$\boxed{\text{STO}}$ or $\boxed{\text{M+}}$	**1.80611123**
$\boxed{1}\boxed{0}\boxed{0}\boxed{0}\boxed{0}$	**10,000.**
$\boxed{\div}$	**10,000.**
$\boxed{\text{RCL}}$ or $\boxed{\text{RM}}$	**1.80611123**
$\boxed{=}$	**5,536.757542**

At the prevailing rate of interest, the financial manager at Company Y may deposit $5,536.76 today and withdraw a compound amount (principal plus accrued interest) of $10,000 five years from today. Correspondingly, we refer to the lower of the two figures as being the present value of $10,000.

We may double-check our answer by plugging in the newly found principal and solving for compound amount.

$$P(1 + \%)^n = A$$
$$5,536.76(1 + 0.03)^{20} = A$$
$$5,536.76 \times 1.806111 = \$10,000.00$$

The following three examples provide interesting variations of the concept of *present value of compound amount*.

APPLICATION 1. What is the present value of $40,000 that is payable six years from now if the market value of money is presently 14-1/2 percent compound semiannually?

$$\% = 14\text{-}1/2 \div 2 = 7\text{-}1/4 \qquad n = 6 \times 2 = 12$$

$$P(1 + \%)^n = A$$
$$P(1 + 0.0725)^{12} = 40,000$$
$$2.316154951P = 40,000$$
$$P = \$17,270.00$$

APPLICATION 2. If a payment of $20,000 to you from a business associate is due three years from now, how much money would you be willing to settle for today, provided that the loan carries an interest rate of 14 percent compound annually? Current rates on this amount of money also approximate the 14 percent rate.

$$\% = 14 \qquad n = 3$$
$$P(1 + \%)^n = A$$
$$P(1 + 0.14)^3 = 20,000$$
$$1.481544P = 20,000$$
$$P = \$13,499.43$$

A principal of \$13,499.43 represents a break-even point, a point of in-difference, in that 13,499.43 deposited today under the prevailing rate of interest would total \$20,000 three years from now. At the end of the term the payee would possess a value of \$20,000 from the transaction — whether receiving the present value (\$13,499.43) today and reinvesting it or waiting three years to collect the full amount (\$20,000.00), including principal and accumulated interest.

APPLICATION 3. If Samuel Rutgers plans a European tour five years from now that will cost approximately \$7,000, how much must he deposit for that purpose in a bank today at 11 percent interest compounded daily?

$$\% = 11 \div 365 = 0.03013698 \qquad n = 5 \times 365 = 1,825$$

$$P(1 + \%)^n = A$$
$$P(1 + 0.0003013698)^{1.825} = 7,000$$
$$1.73310667P = 7,000$$
$$P = \$4,038.98$$

APPLICATION 4. In Application 3, how much interest will have accumulated over the five-year term of the deposit?

$$A - P = I$$
$$7,000.00 - 4,038.99 = \$2,961.01$$

PRESENT VALUE TABLE   As with finding *compound amount* in the first section of this chapter, we may also use a table to determine the *present value of compound amount*. We may use Table 10.2 in Appendix A, for example, to determine the present (begin-ning) value of \$100,000 five years from now at 10 percent compounded quarterly.

$$\% = 10 \div 4 = 2\text{-}1/2 \qquad n = 5 \times 4 = 20$$

Amount $\times$ Table 10.2 value = Principal (present value)

$$100,000.00 \times 0.61027094 = \$61,027.09$$

To realize a compound amount of \$100,000 (principal plus accumulated in-terest) five years from now at 10 percent compounded quarterly requires a principal (present value) of $61,027.09. To double-check our computation, we may determine the compound amount of that principal.

$$P(1 + \%)^n = A$$

$$61,027.09(1.025)^{20} = A$$

$$61,027.09 \times 1.63861644 = \$100,000$$

Because of the inability of most calculators to accommodate numbers as lengthy as this multiplier, the necessary rounding in this instance results in an insignificant difference of one cent. As before, the table does not represent any calculations that we ourselves cannot develop with the present value equation; it only makes the task a littler easier under some circumstances.

APPLICATION 1. Using Table 10.2, find the present value of a $50,000 payment eight years from today at an interest rate of 18 percent compound quarterly.

$\% = 18 \div 4 = 4\text{-}1/2$ $n = 8 \times 4 = 32$

Amount × Table 10.2 value = Principal (present value)
    $50,000.00 × 0.2444999 = $12,225.00

APPLICATION 2. What amount of money must be deposited today to result in a compound amount of $100,000 five years from now if interest of 7-1/2 percent compounded semiannually is to be realized on the deposit?

$\% = 7\text{-}1/2 \div 2 = 3\text{-}3/4$ $n = 5 \times 2 = 10$

Amount × Table 10.2 value = Principal (present value)
    $100,000.00 × 0.69202048 = $69,202.05

You will be introduced to four additional compound interest tables in Chapters 11 and 12, the applications of which are similar to tables in this chapter. Keep in mind that we have considered two concepts of compound interest thus far — *compound amount* and *present value of compound amount*. Although dealing with similar transactions in which compound interest is added to an initial deposit, in one situation we have the end amount (compound amount) as the unknown value and in the other situation we have the present (beginning) value as the unknown factor.

EXERCISES (as directed by your instructor)

10-1 What is the fundamental difference between simple interest and compound interest?

10-2 What do we call the sum of the principal and compound interest that is in an account at the end of a term?

10-3 What is "present value"?

10-4 Without the use of a calculator or a table, compute the interest on a $1,200 deposit for four years at 13 percent compound annually. (Show your computations.)

10-5 Without the use of a calculator or a table, determine the compound amount of a two-year deposit of $5,000 at 9 percent compounded semi-annually. (Show your computations.)

10-6 Determine % and n under the following terms:

	Rate/Term	Compounded
a.	16%, 6 years	Semiannually
b.	12%, 4 years	Quarterly
c.	8-1/2%, 2 years	Semiannually
d.	13%, 5 years	Annually
e.	12%, 5 years	Monthly
f.	8%, 1/2 year	Monthly
g.	14%, 5 years	Daily
h.	10%, 3 years	Quarterly

10-7 On a $2,500 deposit for two years, what is the difference between terms of 6 percent simple interest and 6 percent compounded daily?

10-8 Solve the following three problems *without* the use of a table:

a. Determine the compound amount at the end of five years of $8,500 deposited today at 10-1/2 percent compounded annually.
b. If $14,000 is placed in a bank account today at 6 percent compounded daily, what amount will be in the account at the end of four years?
c. How much interest will have accumulated at the end of a five-year period on a deposit today of $5,000 under terms of 7-1/2 percent compounded quarterly?

10-9 Solve the following three problems *with* the use of a table:

a. Determine the compound amount of $32,000 at the end of ten years at 11 percent compounded annually.
b. With a beginning principal of $6,500 and an interest rate of 15 percent compounded quarterly, what will be the compound amount at the end of eight years?
c. How much interest will accrue during a four-year period on a deposit of $7,000 at 18 percent compounded monthly?

10-10 Solve the following three problems *without* the use of a table:

    a. Determine the present value of $12,500 that is payable five years from now if the applicable rate of interest is 12-1/2 percent compounded annually.

    b. Determine the amount of interest that is included in a compound amount of $11,599.21 that has been accumulating interest over the past six years at a rate of 9 percent compounded quarterly.

    c. What amount of money in hand today is equivalent to $8,000 six years from now if the money could be invested to earn 11-1/4 percent interest compounded daily?

10-11 Use a table to solve the following three problems:

    a. What is the present value of $25,000 that is due five years from now if the applicable rate of interest is 16 percent compounded semi-annually?

    b. If the money could be invested at 16 percent compounded quarterly, how much money received today would be the equivalent of $6,000 received two years from now?

    c. How much money was deposited four years ago at 12 percent interest compounded monthly to have accumulated the current account balance of $1,209.17?

10-12 Solve the following problems with either the equation for *compound amount* or the equation for *present value of compound amount* and, where possible, double-check your answers through use of the applicable tables.

    a. What amount of money will have accumulated in a bank account at the end of five years on a deposit today of $9,000 at a rate of 18 percent compounded quarterly?

    b. At a rate of 16 percent compounded quarterly, how much interest will have accumulated three years from now on a $15,000 deposit today?

    c. What is the value today of $20,000 that is payable six years from now under terms of 18 percent compounded semiannually?

    d. What amount of interest will be earned over a five-year period on a deposit of $12,000 at 6 percent compounded daily?

    e. If $15,000.00 would accumulate to $17,547.88 under the current rates of interest during the next two years, what amount of money would you just as soon have today rather than waiting to collect at the end of the two-year term?

    f. If Company Y is to repay $20,000 to Company Z three years from now, how much money must Company Y deposit at this time in a bank that is paying 12 percent compounded quarterly in order to fulfill the obligation when it comes due?

    g. John Snyder opened a savings account five years ago, with an initial amount and no subsequent deposits. With an interest rate of 6 percent compounded daily, John now has $2,024.74 in the account. What was the initial sum deposited?

h. Two years ago Martha Dwyer placed $2,000 in a savings account at her credit union, where the money has earned interest of 6-1/2 percent compounded daily. How much money is she ahead by having patronized the credit union rather than a savings and loan company that pays only 6 percent compounded quarterly?

i. For an initial investment of $4,180, the City of Phoenix has just offered a bond that will mature thirty years from today. It is a zero-coupon bond, which means that it will pay all interest at the time of maturity. At a rate of 10-1/2 percent compounded semiannually, how much money (principal plus interest) may the bondholder expect to receive at maturity?

11 Ordinary Annuities

LEARNING OBJECTIVES

The materials in this second of three chapters on compound interest will enable you to

- define and describe the various types of annuities
- diagram the compound amount of periodic deposits
- apply the amount-of-an-annuity equation and table
- diagram the present value of periodic withdrawals
- apply the present-value-of-an-annuity equation and table
- solve a wide variety of related problems

In our initial discussion of compound interest in Chapter 10, we dealt with a lump sum of money at the beginning of a term (principal) and a lump sum at the end of a term (compound amount), with compound interest accumulating between two sets of dates. Annuities also involve compound interest; unlike the lump sums involved in compound amount calculations, however, annuities involve periodic deposits into accounts and periodic withdrawals from accounts.

TYPES OF ANNUITIES

An **annuity certain** has definite beginning and ending dates. On limited-payment life insurance policies, for example, policyholders know that they must pay premiums for a specified number of years before the policies are "paid up." A **contingent annuity** is just the opposite, in that either the beginning date is uncertain (benefits are to begin at death) or the ending date is uncertain (benefits are to continue until death).

Another factor that is important in the categorization of annuities is the time of payment. An **annuity due** exists when payments are made at the beginning of periods, such as payments by occupants at the beginning of the rental periods in which property is to be used. Conversely, **ordinary annuities** call for payments at the end of related periods, such as salaries paid following the periods during which they have been earned. As a practical matter, because a complete discussion of annuities would require an entire book, we will concern ourselves here with *ordinary annuities certain*.

AMOUNT OF AN ANNUITY

As previously defined, *ordinary annuities certain* involve periodic payments at the end of periods (usually monthly, quarterly, semiannually, or annually) between two known dates; and, as illustrated in Figure 11.1, interest is compounded periodically on the amount of money remaining in the account. Beginning with an initial deposit (payment) of $100 on March 31, at the end of

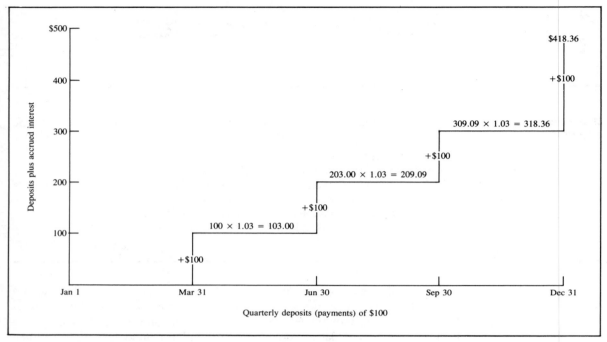

Figure 11.1
Amount of an annuity (one year at 12 percent compounded quarterly in which 12% ÷ 4 = 3%)

the first quarter (three-month period), identical deposits are made at the end of each quarter thereafter — four deposits in all, for a total of $400. During the second quarter, the first (March 31) deposit earns interest of $3.00. During the third quarter, interest is computed on the compound amount of $103.00 and the June 30 deposit (103.00 + 100.00 = 203.00). During the fourth quarter, interest is computed on the compound amount of $209.09, as well as the $100.00 deposited on September 30, to which the final deposit of $100 is added. Having deposited $100 at the end of each quarter, the investor has accumulated an *amount of an annuity* of $418.36 ($400.00 in deposits plus $18.36 in interest).

As with any compound interest problem, period-by-period calculations become very cumbersome when dealing with extended time periods. With only slight modifications, we may use the *compound-amount* equation [$P(1 + \%)^n = A$] to determine the amount of an annuity.

$$\text{Periodic} \atop \text{deposits} \quad \rightarrow \quad D \cdot \frac{(1 + \%)^n - 1}{\%} = An \quad \leftarrow \quad {\text{Amount of} \atop {\text{an annuity} \atop \text{(the unknown)}}}$$

We label the *periodic deposits* as "D" and use "An" to represent the *amount of an annuity*. The only difference between this equation and the one we used to calculate compound amount in Chapter 10 is that we subtract one (the number 1) from the numerator and divide the difference by the adjusted rate (%).

Continuing with the preceding example, in which $100 was deposited at the end of every quarter for one year, we may use the annuity equation to verify the compound amount of the annuity as $418.36.

$$12\% \div 4 = 3 \qquad n = 1 \times 4 = 4$$

$$D \cdot \frac{(1 + \%)^n - 1}{\%} = An$$

$$100 \cdot \frac{(1.03)^4 - 1}{0.03} = An$$

$$100 \cdot \frac{1.12550881 - 1}{0.03} = An$$

$$100 \cdot 4.183627 = \$418.36$$

Calculator	
Entries	**Display**
1 . 0 3	1.03
y^x	1.03
4	4.
−	1.12550881
1	1.
=	0.12550881
÷	0.12550881
. 0 3	0.03
×	4.183627
1 0 0	100.
=	418.3627

Using the (y^x) key to determine the 4th power of 1.03, we subtract 1, divide the difference by 0.03, and multiply the quotient by the size of the quarterly deposits ($100). Also consider the following examples:

APPLICATION 1. Without using the annuity equation, diagram the process and determine the amount in an account at the end of two years of an ordinary annuity that begins on January 1, ends December 31, and involves four semiannual deposits of $500 and interest of 10 percent compounded semiannually.

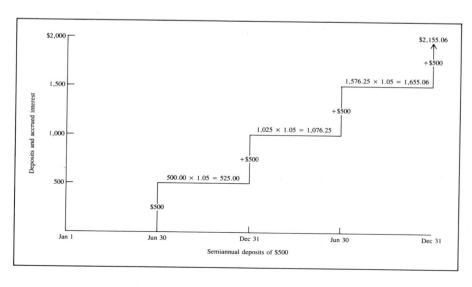

APPLICATION 2. Use the amount-of-an-annuity equation to double-check the answer in Application 1.

$$D \cdot \frac{(1 + \%)^n - 1}{\%} = An$$

$$500 \cdot \frac{(1.05)^4 - 1}{0.05} = An$$

$$500 \times 4.310125 = \$2,155.06$$

APPLICATION 3. How much interest will be earned on an ordinary annuity consisting of monthly deposits of $250 over a five-year period, provided that the interest earned is 12 percent compounded monthly?

$$12\% \div 12 = 1 \qquad n = 5 \times 12 = 60$$

$$D \cdot \frac{(1 + \%)^n - 1}{\%} = An$$

$$250 \cdot \frac{(1.01)^{60} - 1}{0.01} = An$$

$$250 \times 81.66966986 = \$20,417.42$$

Deposits $= 250 \times 60 = \$15,000$
Interest $= 20,417.42 - 15,000.00 = \$5,417.42$

AMOUNT-OF-AN-ANNUITY TABLE

As with other computations in which interest is compounded, we may use a table to compute the amount of an annuity. To solve the problem that was illustrated in Figure 11.1, for a one-year ordinary annuity of $100 deposited quarterly at 12 percent compounded quarterly, we may consult Appendix A, Table 11.1.

$$\% = 12 \div 4 = 3 \qquad n = 1 \times 4 = 4$$

$D \times$ Table 11.1 value $= An$

$$\$100 \times 4.183627 = \$418.36$$

The table, derived from the annuity formula, provides us with the amount of a one-dollar annuity.

$$D \cdot \frac{(1 + \%)^n - 1}{\%} = An$$

$$\$1 \cdot \frac{(1.03)^4 - 1}{0.03} = 4.183627 = \$4.18$$

Rather than solving the equation ourselves, however, we may simply multiply the table value by the size of our periodic deposits or payments ($100 in the preceding problem).

APPLICATION 1. If First National Bank pays depositors 10 percent interest compounded annually, how much money will be in an account in which $10,000 is deposited at the end of every year over a ten-year period?

$$\% = 10 \div 1 = 10 \qquad n = 10 \times 1 = 10$$

$D \times$ Table 11.1 value $= An$
$10,000 \times 15.9374246 = \$159,374.25$

APPLICATION 2. How much will a $200 monthly annuity total at the end of four years with a rate of 18 percent compounded monthly?

$$\% = 18 \div 12 = 1\text{-}1/2 \qquad n = 4 \times 12 = 48$$

$D \times$ Table 11.1 value $= An$
$200 \times 69.56521929 = \$13,913.04$

APPLICATION 3. Use the amount-of-an-annuity equation to double-check the answer in Application 2:

$$D \cdot \frac{(1 + \%)^n - 1}{\%} = An$$

$$200 \cdot \frac{(1.015)^{48} - 1}{0.015} = \$13,913.04$$

APPLICATION 4. Building on the situation in Application 2, how much interest was earned on the monthly deposits of $200?

Deposits: $200 \times 48 = \$9,600$
Interest: $\$13,913.04 - 9,600.00 = \$4,313.04$

PRESENT VALUE OF AN ANNUITY

The present value of an annuity is the lump sum of money that must be invested to provide a series of withdrawals over a prescribed time period. As illustrated in Figure 11.2, an initial investment of $371.71 provides four quarterly withdrawals of $100.00, assuming an interest rate of 12 percent compounded quarterly. Interest accrues on the $371.71 from January 1 to March 31, resulting

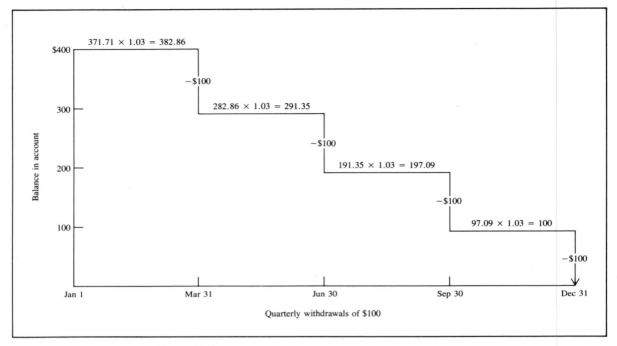

Figure 11.2
Present value of an annuity (for one year at 12 percent compounded quarterly in which 12% ÷ 4 = 3%)

in a balance of $382.86, from which the first $100 is withdrawn. Interest accrues on the balance of $282.86 (328.86 − 100.00 = 282.86) during the second quarter and so on, computing interest on the balance remaining after each withdrawal so that exactly $100 is in the account on December 31 to cover the fourth and final withdrawal.

The obvious challenge is to determine the unknown principal (present value) which, with interest accruing on any balance remaining in an account, will cover all withdrawals over a specified period of time. We may do so with only a slightly more detailed equation.

$$PV \text{ of } An = W \cdot \frac{1 - \dfrac{1}{(1 + \%)^n}}{\%}$$

Labeling present value as "*PV*" and periodic withdrawals as "*W*," we may confirm that $371.71 is truly the present value of four quarterly withdrawals of $100 over a one-year term, as illustrated in Figure 11.2, at a rate of 12 percent compounded quarterly.

$$Pv \text{ of } An = W \cdot \frac{1 - \dfrac{1}{(1 + \%)^n}}{\%}$$

$$= \$100 \cdot \frac{1 - \dfrac{1}{(1.03)^4}}{0.03}$$

$$= \$100 \cdot \frac{1 - 0.8884870479}{0.03}$$

$$= \$100 \cdot \frac{0.1115129521}{0.03}$$

$$= \$100 \cdot 3.717098403$$

$$= \$371.71$$

Calculator	
Entries	**Display**
1 . 0 3	1.03
y^x	1.03
4	4.
=	1.12550881
1/x	.8884870479
STO or M+	.8884870479
1	1.
−	1.
RCL or RM	.8884870479
=	.1115129521
÷	.1115129521
. 0 3	0.03
×	3.717098403
1 0 0	100.
=	371.7098403

Notice in the calculator application that 1/x (5th entry) effectively divides 1.12550881 (4th display) into the numerator one, with the quotient then being stored to be subtracted from one.

APPLICATION 1. How much money must be deposited today to provide monthly withdrawals of $250 for the next two years, assuming an interest rate of 12 percent compounded monthly?

$$\% = 12 \div 12 = 1 \qquad n = 2 \times 12 = 24$$

$$Pv \text{ of } An = W \cdot \frac{1 - \dfrac{1}{(1 + \%)^n}}{\%}$$

$$= 250 \cdot \frac{1 - \dfrac{1}{(1.01)^{24}}}{0.01}$$

$$= \$5,310.85$$

APPLICATION 2. How much interest was earned on the account in Application 1 during the two-year period?

Withdrawals: $250 \times 24 = 6,000$
Interest: $6,000.00 - 5,310.85 = \$689.15$

APPLICATION 3. If the state lottery commission is to pay a winner $10,000 on December 31 for each of the next ten years, how much money must the commission place in a trust today if the money will earn interest of 12 percent compounded annually?

$$\% = 12 \div 1 = 12 \qquad n = 10 \times 1 = 10$$

$$Pv \text{ of } An = W \cdot \frac{1 - \dfrac{1}{(1 + \%)^n}}{\%}$$

$$= 10,000 \cdot \frac{1 - \dfrac{1}{(1.12)^{10}}}{0.12}$$

$$= \$56,502.23$$

Although the individual in Application 3 is said to have won ten payments of $10,000, which would imply a total of $100,000, the lottery commission has a current outlay of only a little more than half that amount, with the future interest payments on the account balance to make up the difference.

PRESENT-VALUE-OF-AN-ANNUITY TABLE

The comparative complexity of computing the present value of an annuity makes the utility of an annuity table quite obvious. Assuming that the table includes the applicable percent (%) column and interest-period (n) row, we may simply multiply the periodic withdrawal figure by the value derived from the table. Using the situation in Figure 11.2, we may access the 3% page of Table 11.2 in Appendix A for time period (n) 4 and multiply the related value by the $100 withdrawals.

Withdrawals × Table 11.2 value = Pv of An

$$\$100 \times 3.71709840 = \$371.71$$

Figures in the table, which are based on withdrawals of one dollar, were derived through application of the equation presented in the preceding section of this chapter.

APPLICATION 1. What is the present value of yearly payments of $5,000 from an insurance account over the next five years if the account presently earns interest of 14 percent compounded annually?

$$\% = 14 \div 1 = 14 \qquad n = 5 \times 1 = 5$$

$$\text{Withdrawals} \times \text{Table 11.2 value} = \textit{PV of An}$$
$$5{,}000 \times 3.43308097 = \$17{,}165.40$$

APPLICATION 2. If the holder of an annuity is to receive \$400 per month for the next three years, how much money should the issuer place in an account today at 18 percent compounded monthly?

$$\% = 18 \div 12 = 1\text{-}1/2 \qquad n = 3 \times 12 = 36$$

$$\text{Withdrawals} \times \text{Table 11.2 value} = \textit{PV of An}$$
$$400 \times 27.66068431 = \$11{,}064.27$$

APPLICATION 3. Use the present-value-of-an-annuity equation to double-check the answer in Application 2.

$$\textit{PV of An} = W \cdot \frac{1 - \dfrac{1}{(1 + \%)^n}}{\%}$$

$$= 400 \cdot \frac{1 - \dfrac{1}{(1.015)^{36}}}{0.015}$$

$$= \$11{,}064.27$$

Although use of the table may be expedient, knowledge of the equation is essential when our adjusted percents and time periods exceed the scope of the table — as with selected problems in the following exercises. Also, the equation provides an excellent check on solutions derived from tables and on solutions produced with computers.

EXERCISES (as directed by your instructor)

11-1 Define the following terms:

   a. Annuity certain
   b. Contingent annuity
   c. Annuity due
   d. Ordinary annuity

11-2 Diagram the compound amount of an annuity for two semiannual deposits of \$1,000 at 16 percent compounded semiannually beginning January 1, showing the step-by-step computations that are required.

11-3 Use the amount-of-an-annuity equation to solve the following three problems:

a. What will be the end amount of deposits of $2,500 at the end of every three months for the next two years at a rate of 16 percent compounded quarterly?

b. What is the compound amount of $50 deposits at the end of every month for the next ten years if the rate of interest is 10-1/2 percent compounded monthly?

c. If the treasurer at Novar Corporation deposits $3,500 in a special account at the end of each quarter year for the next five years, how much interest will have accrued in the account at a rate of 7 percent compounded quarterly?

11-4 Use the appropriate table to solve the following three problems:

a. What is the total amount that will accrue from annual deposits of $1,200 over a 15-year period in a bank account that pays 13 percent compounded annually?

b. What will be the value two years from now of deposits of $700 at the end of each month for two years at a rate of 18 percent compounded monthly?

c. How much money will David Reuter have at the end of ten years if, beginning at the end of every three-month period, he deposits his quarterly bonuses of $750 in a bank account that pays 11 percent compounded quarterly?

11-5 Compute and diagram the present value of a one-year annuity beginning on January 1 and having withdrawals of $1,000 on June 30 and $1,000 on December 31 (resulting in a zero balance after the second withdrawal), assuming an interest rate of 12 percent compounded semiannually.

11-6 Use the present-value-of-compound-amount equation to solve the following three problems.

a. How much money would Janice Walker have to deposit this summer at 10-1/2 percent compounded annually to provide $1,000 withdrawals for each summer vacation during the next two summers?

b. What is the present value of monthly payments of $850 for ten years, assuming an interest rate of 8-1/2 percent compounded monthly?

c. The president of Ramco Corporation is using income averaging over the next three years to minimize his tax obligation on a $1 million bonus. If the resulting calculations call for annual payments to the Internal Revenue Service of approximately $100,000 for each of the next three years, how much money must be placed in an account today to cover these future payments as they come due if the deposit earns interest of 12 percent compounded annually?

11-7 Use the appropriate table to solve the following three problems.

a. What is the present value of six semiannual withdrawals of $1,200 each from a bank account that pays 7-1/2 percent compounded every six months?

b. James Spriggs, who is starting a new business, figures that he will need to withdraw $1,000 from a bank account at the end of every month for the next four years to cover current bills. How much money must he have in the account to begin with, assuming that the bank pays interest of 9 percent compounded monthly?

c. If Carla Hicks instructed her banker to make monthly rental payments of $850 to a mortgage company for the next three years, how much money would she have had to deposit in the bank to begin with, assuming that the bank pays interest of 6 percent compounded monthly?

11-8 Solve the following problems with use of the appropriate equation, and, where possible, double-check your answers through use of the applicable tables.

a. Upon early retirement at 55 years of age, Sylvia Roberts wishes to supplement her monthly pension checks with an ordinary annuity that pays $650 per month for the next ten years, until claiming Social Security payments. If her bank is paying 12 percent on a ten-year certificate of deposit, compounded monthly, how much money must she deposit at this time?

b. At the end of each month, Roger Marris receives a pension check for $550.50. Being able to manage without the money, he has instructed the trust company to deposit the checks directly to a special bank account in his name. At a current interest rate of 9 percent compounded monthly, how much money will Marris have in the account at the end of five years?

c. Upon the closure of one of its branch offices, Rutgers Manufacturing offered, as an incentive for employees to terminate their employment, five end-of-year payments of $1,000 or one payment of $3,000 at the time of departure. At a current interest rate of 13 percent compounded annually, which of the two options is preferable from the standpoint of the employee?

d. For 18 years Deborah Clyburn's company has made monthly payments of $50 into an annuity in her name. With the money having earned interest of 6 percent compounded monthly, what is the total amount of money in the account at this time?

e. If $650 is withdrawn from a bank account at the end of every six-month period for ten years, leaving a balance of zero, how much money was placed in the account to begin with, assuming that the money earned interest of 12 percent compounded semiannually until the time of withdrawal?

f. Find the present value of an ordinary annuity over a ten-year period with payments of $1,500 every three months and interest of 15 percent computed quarterly.

g. What amount of interest will accumulate in an account in which a small business owner deposits $300 at the end of every month for 15 years, assuming a 10-1/2 percent rate of interest on the savings — compounded monthly?

h. If you won a lottery prize of $100,000, to be paid in year-end installments of $10,000, over a ten-year period, how much cash would you be willing to settle for today in lieu of the future payments, assuming that you could invest the cash at 12-1/2 percent compounded annually?

12 Sinking Funds, Amortization — and a Summarization

LEARNING OBJECTIVES

This third and final chapter on compound interest not only explains the concepts and applications of sinking funds and amortization, but also provides a comparison of all six types of related problems. Upon its completion you will be able to

- explain the difference between a sinking fund and an amortized loan
- define and diagram the flow of deposits and interest that constitutes a sinking fund
- determine (through the use of a mathematical equation and a related table) the amount of money that must be deposited periodically to meet the monetary (future value) of sinking funds under varying circumstances
- interpret and prepare sinking-fund schedules
- define and diagram the flow of payments and earned interest that constitute what is commonly referred to as "amortization"
- determine (using a mathematical equation and a related table) the size of periodic payments required to pay current interest charges and reduce loans to zero within prescribed time periods
- interpret and prepare amortization schedules
- describe the fundamental similarities and differences of compound-interest problems: compound amount, present value of compound amount, amount of an annuity, present value of an annuity, sinking fund, and amortization

In the preceding chapter we were concerned with identifying either the beginning or ending value of a series of periodic deposits or withdrawals, with the size of the periodic payments being known and with either the beginning figure (present value of an annuity) or the ending value (amount of an annuity) being given. In a continuation of our study of compound interest, we now accept the challenge of determining the size of periodic deposits required to accumulate specified amounts of money within prescribed time frames (sinking funds) and the size of payments required to pay the interest and retire the principal of long-term loans (amortization). Subsequently, as a helpful summary, all six types of compound interest problems are contrasted and compared.

SINKING FUNDS

A **sinking fund** is an account that financial managers of businesses establish for the repayment of borrowed money through a series of periodic deposits that

Figure 12.1
The concept of *sinking
funds* (periodic
payments)

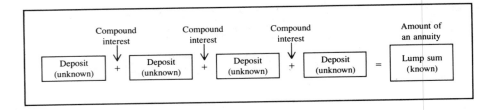

earn compound interest. Rather than waiting until a 30-year bond matures before arranging the repayment of millions of borrowed dollars to bondholders, for example, the borrowing company may be required to redeem (buy back) a certain number of bonds each year so that all of the money will have been repaid at the end of 30 years. More commonly, the contractual part of a bond requires the borrowing company to deposit a specified amount of money with a trustee (usually a bank) each year so that the deposits and the interest that accumulates on the invested deposits will total the principal of the loan at the date of repayment. This concept is illustrated in Figure 12.1. Knowing the end amount (that is, the amount that must be repaid), we must determine the size of the periodic deposits.

The end amount of a series of periodic deposits is the *amount of an annuity*, as you already know; now, however, the end value is known and it is the size of the periodic deposits that must be determined. We make this determination by using the reciprocal of the amount-of-an-annuity equation, that is, by dividing the earlier equation into one (the number "1").

$$D = \frac{\%}{(1 + \%)^n - 1} \cdot An$$

$\uparrow$
the
unknown

Assume, for example, that a corporation is issuing a $5 million bond that will mature in ten years. In addition to paying semiannual interest to bondholders for the use of their money, the corporation must place in a special fund each month enough money so that the deposits plus the compound interest earned on the deposits will equal $5 million at the end of the ten-year term. If the deposits earn an interest rate of 12 percent compounded monthly, the monthly sinking fund deposits will be calculated as follows:

$\% = 12 \div 12 = 1$

$n = 10 \times 12 = 120$

$$D = \frac{\%}{(1 + \%)^n - 1} \cdot An$$

$$D = \frac{0.01}{(1.01)^{120} - 1} \cdot 5{,}000{,}000$$

$$D = \$21{,}735.47$$

Calculator	
Entries	**Display**
$\boxed{1}\boxed{.}\boxed{0}\boxed{1}$	1.01
$\boxed{y^x}$	1.01
$\boxed{1}\boxed{2}\boxed{0}$	120.
$\boxed{-}$	3.300386895
$\boxed{1}$	1.
$\boxed{=}$	2.300386895
$\boxed{STO}$ or $\boxed{M+}$	2.300386895
$\boxed{.}\boxed{0}\boxed{1}$	0.01
$\boxed{\div}$	0.01
$\boxed{RCL}$ or $\boxed{MR}$	2.300386895
$\boxed{\times}$	.0043470948
$\boxed{5}\boxed{0}\boxed{0}\boxed{0}\boxed{0}\boxed{0}\boxed{0}$	5,000,000.
$\boxed{=}$	21,735.4742

Monthly deposits of \$21,735.47 will increase to \$5 million (principal plus interest) within ten years. We may use the amount-of-an-annuity equation to double check our answer.

$$D \cdot \frac{(1 - \%)^n - 1}{\%} = An$$

$$21{,}735.47 \cdot \frac{(1.01)^{120} - 1}{0.01} = \$4{,}999{,}999.03$$

The two answers differ by 97 cents because of rounding within the calculator, which, when dealing with large amounts of money over extensive periods, is insignificant. Also consider the varying circumstances in the following situations.

APPLICATION 1. If an accountant is to have \$15,000 in a special savings account six years from today, how much money must be deposited each month, assuming that the bank is paying 8-1/2 percent interest compounded monthly?

$$\% = 8\text{-}1/2 \div 12 = 0.70833333 \qquad n = 6 \times 12 = 72$$

$$D = \frac{\%}{(1 + \%)^n - 1} \cdot An$$

$$D = \frac{0.00708333}{(1.00708333)^{72} - 1} \cdot 15{,}000$$

$$D = \$160.43$$

APPLICATION 2. If a bond indenture stipulates that the bond issuer (a corporation) make annual contributions to a sinking fund of a sufficient size to equal $10 million at maturity 20 years from today, how much money must be set aside each year if a rate of 11 percent compounded annually may be expected on the deposits?

$$\% = 11 \qquad n = 20$$

$$D = \frac{\%}{(1 + \%)^n - 1} \cdot An$$

$$D = \frac{0.11}{(1.11)^{20} - 1} \cdot 10,000,000$$

$$D = \$155,756.37$$

APPLICATION 3. Use the amount-of-an-annuity equation to double-check the answer in Application 2.

$$D \cdot \frac{(1 + \%)^n - 1}{\%} = An$$

$$155,756.37 \cdot \frac{(1.11)^{20} - 1}{0.11} = \$10,000.000.08$$

As explained earlier, variations of only a few cents in long-term transactions are to be ignored.

SINKING-FUND TABLE　　　Because other people have used the sinking-fund equation to produce easy-to-use tables, we may sometimes simplify our calculations. We may, for example, refer to Table 12.1 in Appendix A to determine the amount that must be deposited each year to accumulate $20,000 in 16 years, assuming that the deposited money will realize a return of 12 percent interest compounded annually.

$$\% = 12 \qquad n = 16$$

$$D = \text{Table 12.1 value} \times An$$

$$D = 0.02339002 \times 20,000$$

$$D = \$467.80$$

Also consider the following two examples of similar applications.

APPLICATION 1. How much money would you need to place in a bank account each month for the next three years to provide $4,000 cash for a tour of Eastern Europe at that time, if the bank pays 12 percent interest compounded monthly?

$$\% = 12 \div 12 = 1 \qquad n = 3 \times 12 = 36$$

D = Table 12.1 value $\times$ An

D = 0.02321431 $\times$ 4,000

D = \$92.86

APPLICATION 2. What amount of money must a corporation invest each year for the next 25 years to repay a \$10 million bond that matures at that time, assuming that an average rate of 9 percent can be realized on the investments, compounded annually?

$$\% = 9 \qquad n = 25$$

D = Table 12.1 value $\times$ An

D = 0.01180625 $\times$ 10,000,000

D = \$118,062.50

**SINKING FUND
SCHEDULE**

A schedule that itemizes the transactions in a sinking fund proves very helpful to business managers — not only because it itemizes the interest that is earned and is taxable every year, but also because it provides a record of all transactions in the account. For simplicity, let's consider a five-year sinking fund for the repayment of \$10,000. If deposits in the fund may be expected to earn 12 percent interest compounded annually, the annual deposit would be \$1,574.10, and the schedule would appear as shown in Table 12.1. Treating the transactions as an ordinary annuity, the first deposit is made at the end of the first period (year), earns interest during the second period (\$1,574.10 $\times$ 0.12 = \$188.89), which is added with the first and second payments to total \$3,337.09. That amount becomes the principal for the third period, and so on, with the even annual payments increasing through compound interest to meet the \$10,000 objective at the end of the five-year term.

Table 12.1
Sinking-fund schedule
(\$10,000, five years, 12
percent, compounded
annually)

Period	(1) Principal	+	(2) Interest earned	+	(3) Periodic deposit	=	(1) + (2) + (3) Amount in account
1	zero		zero		1,574.10		1,574.10
2	1,574.10		188.89		1,574.10		3,337.09
3	3,337.09		400.45		1,574.10		5,311.64
4	5,311.64		637.40		1,574.10		7,523.14
5	7,523.14		902.78		1,574.10		10,000.02

APPLICATION 1. Record the first five deposits to a 20-year sinking fund of \$1 million, under terms of 8 percent interest compounded annually.

$$\% = 8 \quad n = 20 \quad D = 0.02185221 \times 1,000,000 = \$21,852.21$$

Period	Principal	Interest	Deposit	Amount
1	zero	zero	21,852.21	21,852.21
2	21,852.21	1,748.18	21,852.21	45,452.60
3	45,452.60	3,636.21	21,852.21	70,941.02
4	70,941.02	5,675.28	21,852.21	98,468.51
5	98,468.51	7,877.48	21,852.21	128,198.20

APPLICATION 2. At the end of the 20th period (20-year term), how much of the $1 million will consist of accumulated interest?

Periods × deposits = total deposited
20 × 21,852.21 = 437,044.20

Amount − deposits = interest
1,000,000 − 437,044.20 = $562,955.80

AMORTIZATION

Sinking-fund and amortization calculations have a mutual objective: a determination of the size of payments. Unlike sinking funds, wherein the accumulated amount is to be used to repay the principal of a loan, **amortization** involves a series of periodic payments (Py) that not only repay the principal but that also pay the interest as it is earned.

You will recall from the preceding examples that sinking funds were sometimes used to repay the face value of bonds, $5 million in one example and $10 million in another. The interest that the bond issuers (borrowing corporations) paid the bondholders (lenders) twice a year was a separate transaction. As illustrated in Figure 12.2 on the other hand, each payment to an amortized loan must be an amount that is large enough to cover current interest charges and to make a contribution to principal, so that the principal is reduced to zero at the end of the loan term.[1] Note also that interest charges are computed on the balance in the account at the end of the interest period — that figure in amortized loans being the unpaid balance.

Assuming that the diagram in Figure 12.2 represents a home loan, which is a common application of amortization, the relatively large shaded areas of the early payments denote large interest charges with relatively small portions of the payments (if any) being applied to reductions in the principal. As the payments continue, however, the declining principal results in progressively lower interest charges and correspondingly greater reductions in principal.

The challenge is to identify the size of the payments that, when divided between principal and interest, will reduce the principal to zero at the end of the loan term. Because amortization is the mirrored image of the *present value of an annuity*, we may simply invert and apply the present-value-of-an-annuity

---

[1] In some amortized loans, especially those for the purchase of residential property, all payments during the early years are to cover interest charges, with no money applied toward a reduction of the principal. Such agreements are designed to make property accessible to people with relatively low incomes on the premise that steadily rising incomes will enable higher future payments and eventual payment of the principal.

Figure 12.2
Concept of amortization.

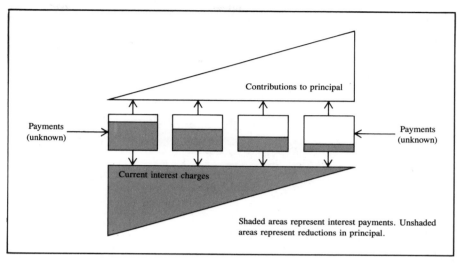

$\% = 9 \div 12$ monthly payments $= 0.75$

$n = 30 \times 12 = 360$

$$Py = P \cdot \frac{\%}{1 - \dfrac{1}{(1 + \%)^n}}$$
unknown

$$= 80,000 \cdot \frac{0.0075}{1 - \dfrac{1}{(1.0075)^{360}}}$$

$= \$643.70$

Calculator	
Entries	**Display**
1 . 0 0 7 5	1.0075
y^x	1.0075
3 6 0	360.
=	14.73057612
$1/x$	0.06788600
STO or M+	0.06788600
1	1.
−	1.
RCL or RM	.0678860074
=	.9321139926
STO or M+	.9321139926
. 0 0 7 5	0.0075
÷	0.0075
RCL or RM	.9321139926
=	.0080462261
×	.0080462261
8 0 0 0 0	80,000.
=	643.698094

We could double-check this answer with the present-value-of-an-annuity equation, of course, to determine that the present value of 360 future payments of \$643.70 is actually \$80,000. Also consider the following situations.

APPLICATION 1. You wish to finance over a five-year period a $150,000 combine that you have just sold to a farmer. After the farmer has made a 10 percent down payment, what will be the monthly payments at 18 percent per annum?

% = 18 ÷ 12 monthly payments = 1-1/2 $n = 5 \times 12 = 60$

Balance due = 150,000 − 15,000 = 135,000

$$Py = P \cdot \frac{\%}{1 - \frac{1}{(1 + \%)^n}}$$

$$= 135,000 \cdot \frac{0.015}{1 - \frac{1}{(1.015)^{60}}}$$

$$= \$3,428.11$$

APPLICATION 2. Marsha Dwyer financed a $9,000 automobile through her credit union, after having paid $2,000 down. If the loan manager grants her an amortized four-year loan at an annual rate of 14 percent, what will be her monthly payments?

% = 14 ÷ 12 monthly payments = 1.1666666667 $n = 4 \times 12 = 48$

$$Py = P \cdot \frac{\%}{1 - \frac{1}{(1 + \%)^n}}$$

$$= 7,000 \cdot \frac{0.0116666667}{1 - \frac{1}{(1.0116666667)^{48}}}$$

$$= \$191.29$$

APPLICATION 3. What are the monthly payments on an $85,000, 30-year home mortgage, assuming that the buyer makes a down payment of 10 percent of the purchase price and finances the balance at 15 percent? (Ignore property taxes and insurance.)

% = 15 ÷ 12 monthly payments = 1-1/4 $n = 30 \times 12 = 360$

Downpayment = 85,000 − 8,500 = 76,500

$$Py = P \cdot \frac{\%}{1 - \frac{1}{(1 + \%)^n}}$$

$$= 76{,}500 \cdot \frac{0.0125}{1 - \dfrac{1}{(1.0125)^{360}}}$$

$$= \$967.30$$

AMORTIZATION TABLE   The preceding equation has been used to derive the multipliers in Table 12.2
in Appendix A, which provides the combined principal and interest payments
for a principal of one dollar — at various interest rates and for different time
periods. To determine the payment on a ten-year loan of $50,000 at 16 percent
with quarterly payments, we turn to the 4% page of Table 12.2, proceed downward to the $n = 40$ column, and multiply the value there by the principal of
the loan.

$$\% = 16 \div 4 = 4 \qquad n = 10 \times 4 = 40$$

Payments = Principal $\times$ Table 12.2 value

$$= 50{,}000 \times 0.05052349$$

$$= \$2{,}526.17$$

Quarterly payments of $2,526.17 will, over the course of 10 years, simul-
taneously pay the interest as it is earned and progressively reduce the $50,000
principal to zero.

Now, rather than expending more time and energy in the manipulation of
figures from a table, which has probably become automatic for you at this
point, let's consider the procedure for preparing amortization schedules.

**AMORTIZATION
SCHEDULE**   For long-term loans, lenders commonly provide borrowers with amortization
schedules. For purposes of illustration, the annual payment and distribution
schedule in Table 12.2 is for a loan of $10,000 for just five years with interest
of 12 percent. The first step in developing this schedule is, of course, a determination that the annual payments are $2,774.10. Interest is computed on
the beginning principal at the end of the first period ($10,000 $\times$ 0.12 =
$1,200). Deducting that amount of interest from the $2,774.10 payment leaves
a remainder of $1,574.10 to apply to the principal. The reduced principal be-
comes the figure on which interest is computed for the second period, and so
on. In comparing sinking-fund schedules with amortization schedules, notice
that we begin sinking funds (Table 12.1 on page 215) with zero amounts and
build toward lump sums. Inversely, we begin amortization schedules with
lump-sum principals that are progressively reduced to zero balances. Also consider the following amortization problems.

Table 12.2 Amortization Schedule
($10,000, five years, 12 percent, with annual payments)

Period	(1) Principal	(2) Payment	(3) Interest charge	(4) = (2) − (3) Contribution to principal	(5) = (1) − (4) Balance owed
1	10,000.00	2,774.10	1,200.00	1,574.10	8,425.90
2	8,425.90	2,774.10	1,011.11	1,762.99	6,662.91
3	6,662.91	2,774.10	799.55	1,974.55	4,688.36
4	4,688.36	2,774.10	562.60	2,211.50	2,476.86
5	2,476.86	2,774.10	297.22	2,476.88	zero

APPLICATION 1. Prepare an amortization schedule for the first five monthly payments toward the retirement of a 20-year, $100,000 mortgage loan of 13-1/2 percent.

$$\% = 1.125 \qquad n = 240 \qquad \text{Payment} = \$1{,}207.37$$

Period	Principal	Payment	Interest	Cont. to principal	Balance
1	100,000.00	1,207.37	1,125.00	82.37	99,917.63
2	99,917.63	1,207.37	1,124.07	83.30	99,834.33
3	99,834.33	1,207.37	1,123.14	84.23	99,750.10
4	99,750.10	1,207.37	1,122.19	85.18	99,664.92
5	99,664.92	1,207.37	1,121.23	86.14	99,578.78
		6,036.85	5,615.63	421.22	

APPLICATION 2. Of the total amount of payments made thus far in Application 1, what percent has been applied to principal?

$$\text{Base} \times \text{Rate} = \text{Portion}$$
$$6{,}036.85\,R = 421.22$$
$$R = 7\%$$

A SUMMARIZATION   Table 12.3 presents a summary of the concepts presented in Chapters 10, 11, and 12 that serves not only as a handy reference source of processes and procedures, but also helps to reinforce your understanding of the ways in which these six categories of compound-interest problems are interrelated. *Compound amount* and *present value of compound amount* are identical in that each begins with a lump sum and increases with interest to a larger lump sum at the end of the term. The only difference depends on whether we know the beginning

Table 12.3 Summarization of Compound Interest Equations and Concepts

	Concept	Table, Appendix A	Equation	Principal (P) or present value (PV)	Periodic deposit (D) or payment (Py)	Periodic withdrawal (W)	Future value or amount (A)
Beginning of Term	Compound amount (A)	10.1	$P(1+\%)^n = A$?	lump sum (known)			lump sum (unknown)
	Present value of compound amount (P)	10.2	$P(1+\%)^n = A$?	lump sum (unknown)			lump sum (known)
	Amount of an annuity (An)	11.1	$D \cdot \dfrac{(1+\%)^n - 1}{\%} = An$?		(known)		lump sum (unknown)
End of Term	Present value of an annuity (PV An)	11.2	$Pv\,An = W \cdot \dfrac{1 - \dfrac{1}{(1+\%)^n}}{\%}$?	lump sum (unknown)		(known)	
	Sinking fund (D)	12.1	$D = \dfrac{\%}{(1+\%)^n - 1} \cdot An$?	zero	(unknown)		lump sum (known)
	Amortization payment (Py)	12.2	$Py = P \cdot \dfrac{\%}{1 - \dfrac{1}{(1+\%)^n}}$?	lump sum (known)	(unknown)		zero

figure and are identifying the end figure (compound amount) or know the end figure and are identifying the beginning amount (present value).

Amount of an annuity and *sinking fund* are identical in that both involve a series of deposits that (along with accumulated interest) become a lump sum at the end of a term. In the *amount of an annuity*, however, we are identifying the ending lump sum, and with a *sinking fund* we are identifying the size of the periodic deposits. The equation for either of these two types of problems is simply inverted for the other type of problem.

Both *present value of an annuity* and *amortization* involve lump sums at the beginning of the term, but in *present value* we are determining the size of a lump sum which will be sufficient to provide the series of withdrawals that are to follow. With *amortization*, on the other hand, the beginning lump sum is known, and it is the size of the periodic payments that must be identified. The equation for either of these two types of problems is simply inverted for the other type of problem. To comprehend fully the concept of compound interest, you must understand these relationships.

EXERCISES (as assigned by your instructor)

12-1 Define (verbally) and illustrate (graphically) the concept of a sinking fund.

12-2 Define (verbally) and illustrate (graphically) the concept of amortization.

12-3 What are the fundamental similarities and differences between sinking funds and amortized loans?

12-4 How does the application of compound interest differ between sinking funds and amortized loans?

12-5 Use the sinking-fund equation to solve the following three problems:

    a. If a corporation floats a bond issue for $50 million, how much money must be placed in a sinking-fund account each year to retire the bond at the end of 20 years, assuming that the deposits earn an average interest rate of 12 percent compounded annually?

    b. What amount of money must be deposited in a bank every month if the account is to grow from zero to $8,000 within four years, assuming an interest rate of 9 percent compounded monthly?

    c. If a sinking fund earns interest of 10-1/2 percent compounded semiannually, what amount of money must the financial manager of Argar Corporation place in the account every six months in order to repay a $100,000 loan when it comes due ten years from today?

12-6 Use the appropriate table to solve the following three problems:

    a. A city manager wishes to redeem (buy back) enough bonds each year for the next 30 years to retire $1 million of municipal bonds that were just issued. At an anticipated interest rate of 11 percent compounded annually, how much money must be used each year to buy back the bonds?

b. If a small-business owner wishes to construct a new storage facility five years from now costing $225,000, without having to finance any part of the cost, how much money must be placed in an account each year if interest earned on the deposits is 9-1/2 percent compounded annually?

c. The financial manager at Azore Corporation plans to replace one of the company cars every four years. Assuming that the next purchase will cost $14,000 after allowing for a trade-in of the old vehicle, how much money must be deposited in a sinking fund every month to cover the next purchase — assuming that the deposits will earn interest of 15 percent compounded monthly and that the car to be replaced was just purchased?

12-7 Prepare a sinking-fund schedule for yearly deposits (an ordinary annuity) that, with accumulated interest, will increase to $12,000 four years from now. The prevailing interest rate is 8 percent compounded annually.

12-8 Prepare a sinking-fund schedule that reflects the first five year-end deposits into a $10 million sinking fund that is to run 30 years with an interest rate of 9-1/4 percent compounded annually.

12-9 Use the amortization equation to solve the following problems:

a. If a member of a credit union receives $2,000 for a trade-in on a new car that is priced at $11,500, what will be the monthly payments over a five-year period if the credit union charges interest of 13-1/2 percent?

b. If the lowest-cost home in a new subdivision sells for $91,995 and the bank requires a down payment of 15 percent, what are the monthly payments for a 20-year loan at 9 percent?

c. The Ramco Corporation purchased a plot of land for $250,000 and gave title for the property to a bank to secure a ten-year mortgage loan at 9-1/2 percent interest. What is the annual (year-end) payment for each of the next ten years?

12-10 Use the appropriate table to solve the following three problems:

a. What is the monthly payment on a $150,000 computer system, assuming a down payment of 20 percent of the purchase price and a four-year loan on the balance at 12 percent?

b. If the financial manager at Rutgers Electric agrees to pay 5 percent down on a $23,000 photocopy machine and pay the balance in quarterly payments over the next five years, what is the size of the payments? The interest to be charged is 15 percent.

c. If an individual pays $250 down on an electronic typewriter that sells for $1,219 including sales tax, what are the monthly payments for the next two years if an annual interest rate of 18 percent is charged on the balance?

12-11 Prepare an amortization schedule for year-end payments (five of them) that will "pay off" a $50,000 obligation, assuming an interest rate of 13 percent.

12-12 Prepare an amortization schedule that reflects the first five end-of-year payments of a 30-year mortgage of $75,000 on which interest of 15 percent is to be paid.

12-13 Identify the type of compound-interest situation being described:

a. A series of payments (size unknown) leading to a lump sum (known) at the end of a term.
b. A lump sum principal (known), which is to be paid off by a series of payments (unknown).
c. A lump sum principal (known) increasing through accumulated interest to a lump sum (unknown) at the end of a term.
d. A lump-sum principal (unknown) from which a series of payments (known) is to be made.
e. A lump sum principal (unknown) increasing through accumulated interest to a lump sum (known) at the end of a term.
f. Periodic deposits (known) increasing to a lump sum (unknown) at the end of a term.

12-14 The following problems represent a mixture of compound-interest situations. Use the appropriate table where possible to solve the problems, reverting to the respective equations when the elements of a problem exceed the scope of the table.

a. How much money must be placed in an account today to increase to $7,000 five years from today under terms of 8 percent compounded quarterly?
b. If monthly deposits of $150 are placed in an account that earns 8-1/2 percent interest compounded monthly, how much money will be in the account at the end of three years?
c. A small business operator wishes to purchase a new facility six years from today that costs $510,000. If the business operator is to have that amount of money on hand to pay cash for the facility, how much money must be placed in an account each year, assuming that the deposits will earn interest of 11 percent compounded annually?
d. If the lottery commission is to pay $20,000 a year for life to a winner and the expected future life of the winner is 22 years, how much money must the commission set aside today at 10 percent interest compounded annually?
e. If $50,000 is deposited in a savings account at a savings-and-loan institution today, what will be the total amount in the account ten

years from today, assuming that interest of 8-1/2 percent is earned, compounded daily?

f. First Federal Savings is financing new homes in a tract where the prices range from a low of $225,000 to $375,000. Ignoring taxes, insurance, and closing costs, determine the monthly payments on one of the lowest-cost homes for a 30-year mortgage at interest of 15 percent. A down payment of 10 percent of the purchase price is required.

g. The financial manager at Nortex Industries must arrange payments into a special fund to repay a $25 million bond ten years from today. If the semiannual deposits may be expected to earn interest of 12 percent compounded semiannually, what size of deposit is required?

h. Rather than permitting a business customer to repay $10,000 three years from now, along with interest of 18 percent compounded monthly, how much cash would you accept today as payment in full?

i. If a customer plans to pay your company $125 per month during the next five years, how much cash would you be willing to settle for today in full payment of the obligation, assuming that the money received could be invested for a return of 10 percent compounded monthly?

j. If a bank customer deposits $100 every month for ten years, with earnings of 9 percent compounded monthly, how much money will have accumulated in the account at the end of ten years?

k. What are the monthly payments on a $12,000 automobile, assuming a down payment of $2,500, a four-year loan, and annual interest of 9 percent?

l. If an interest rate of 10-1/2 percent is compounded daily on a savings deposit of $2,000, how much money will be in an account five years from now?

m. If you wish to make 11 monthly deposits into what bankers refer to as a "goal account," beginning in January, so that in November you may withdraw $1,000 for Christmas shopping, how much money must you deposit each month — assuming an interest rate of 9 percent compounded monthly?

13 Bank Accounts

This chapter is designed for the practical application of much of the knowledge acquired in the preceding five chapters by enabling you to

- identify the unit cost of writing checks under a variety of plans
- minimize bank charges for check writing services
- compute bank charges on commercial accounts
- understand and describe the common elements of personal and business checks
- prepare checks correctly
- endorse checks properly under a variety of circumstances
- understand and describe the differences between regular checks, cashier's checks, and certified checks
- maintain check registers
- interpret bank statements
- reconcile check registers and bank statements
- compare savings plans
- compute interest on the basis of *average daily balance* and *lowest monthly reference*
- compare and contrast the provisions of certificates of deposit, money market funds, and individual retirement accounts

The word *bank*, as used here, has a very broad interpretation. As the federal government continues to loosen its regulatory hold on the banking industry, large banks are crossing state lines with their operations into the once protected markets of local banks. Americans are also witnessing widespread entry into full-service banking by such nontraditional companies as savings-and-loan institutions, credit unions, securities brokers, insurance companies, and retail chains. These firms offer a wide variety of services that, prior to the 1980s, were provided solely by commercial banks. The following references to banks, therefore, refer equally to all such lending and savings institutions.

When dealing with simple and compound interest in the preceding five chapters, we made frequent and general references to bank deposits. The terms that bankers offer depositors vary dramatically, and, unlike the required disclosure of *annual percentage rates* pertaining to loans (Chapter 9), consumers must assume responsibility for comparing the charges that bankers impose and the rates that bankers pay — on both checking and savings accounts.

CHECKING ACCOUNTS

Procedures for writing and recording personal and business checks are similar, but the terms that banks offer vary widely.

Personal Accounts   Bankers generally offer **special checking** accounts for individuals who write only a few checks each month. A nominal fee is collected for each check written, in addition to a monthly service charge. Assuming a per-check charge of 20 cents and a monthly maintenance fee of $1.50, a person writing 15 checks during a month would be charged $4.50 for an effective rate of 30 cents per check.

Check fees: $3.00 (15 × 0.20)
Monthly maintenance fee: 1.50
Total: $4.50
Unit cost: 4.50 ÷ 15 checks = 30¢ each

Under a plan that is sometimes termed **regular checking**, the customer may avoid any check writing charges if the account balance does not fall below a certain amount. Assuming a required minimum balance of $400 and also assuming that, as an alternative, the $400 could be placed in a savings account at an 8 percent rate of interest compounded monthly, the writer of 15 checks per month will pay almost 18 cents each.

Investment option: $Prt = I$

$$400 \times 0.08 \times 1/12 = \$2.67$$

Effective cost: $2.67 \div 15$ checks $= 17.8¢$ each

Under the assumed terms, the writer of 15 checks per month under *regular checking* is paying less than two thirds the cost of the per-unit cost and maintenance fee under the special checking plan — 17.8 cents each compared to 30 cents each. Once a depositor has agreed to such a minimum-balance plan, however, the banker will assess a penalty fee of several dollars if and when the depositor permits the balance to fall below the prescribed level.

Banks that offer **interest-earning accounts** not only provide free checking in connection with minimum balances, but also pay interest on the daily balance or on the lowest balance in checking accounts during the month. A bank might offer 5-1/4 percent interest on the lowest balance, for example, based on a minimum balance of $250. Assuming that the balance in an account ranges from $300 to $600 during a one-month period, interest will be computed on $300 — the lowest figure.

$$Prt = I$$

$$300 \times 0.0525 \times 1/12 = 1.3125 = \$1.31$$

Rather than paying a per-check charge and a monthly maintenance fee, the depositor collects $1.31 at the end of the month in the form of a bank credit to the checking account. Whether or not such an arrangement is best for the depositor depends on alternative investments, that is, on the amount of money that could be earned by placing the $250 in an investment other than a checking account.

To illustrate, let's assume that a depositor who writes an average of 25 checks per month keeps an extra $300 in a checking account as a way of avoiding a monthly charge of $1.50 and check-writing charges of 20 cents each. Assume further that the $300 either can be deposited in a checking account that pays 5 percent compounded monthly or can be placed along with other funds in a long-term investment that pays 8 percent interest compounded monthly.

Special checking

Check fee: $25 \times 0.20 = 5.00$

Maintenance fee: $\underline{1.50}$

6.50

Unit charge: $6.50 \div 25$ checks $= 26¢$ per check

Interest-earning account

Alternative investment: $\qquad Prt = I$

$300 \times 0.08 \times 1/12 = 2.00$ (long-term)

Interest earned: $300 \times 0.05 \times 1/12 = \underline{1.25}$ (checking)

Interest foregone: $\qquad 0.75$

Effective cost: $0.75 \div 25$ checks $= 0.03 = 3¢$ per check

If the alternative investment and checking account had been paying identical interest rates, it would have been a trade-off; that is, the investor's income would have remained unchanged and check writing would have been free. Because the alternative investment pays an interest rate that is 3 percent higher than that realized from keeping extra money in the checking account, however, the difference is attributable to the checking account as a charge for the privilege of writing checks without per-check charges or monthly maintenance fees. Stated another way, the interest that could be earned by investing the $300 elsewhere is partially offset by the interest being earned in the checking account, resulting in a per-check charge of only 3 cents per check — or 23 cents less per check than under the special checking plan. Although the savings may appear nominal when viewed on a monthly basis, the potential savings become compounded with the additional passage of time and with expanded transactions.

APPLICATION 1. First National Bank offers customer checking for which 25 cents is charged for each check written and a monthly fee of $5 is imposed.

Assuming that a depositor maintains from $300 to $650 in this type of account throughout March, during which time 13 checks are written, what is the effective charge per check?

Checks: 13 × 0.25 = 3.25
Monthly fee: 5.00
Total charges: 8.25

Unit charge: 8.25 ÷ 13 = 63-1/2¢ per check

APPLICATION 2. If the depositor in Application 1 has an opportunity to avoid all check-writing charges by maintaining a minimum balance of $500 in the account, should he invest $500 to maintain such an account or continue with the original plan and place the $500 in a certificate of deposit that pays interest of 9 percent compounded monthly?

Alternative investment: $Prt = I$
500 × 0.09 × 1/12 = 3.75

Unit cost: 3.75 ÷ 13 = 28.8¢ per check

Based on the writing of 13 checks per month, the interest lost by foregoing interest income on an alternative investment results in a significantly lower per-check cost (almost 29 cents each) than under the preceding plan (63-1/2 cents each).

APPLICATION 3. Assuming an alternative investment opportunity that pays 7-3/4 percent interest compounded monthly, what is the effective cost in April for each of 22 checks written on an account that involves no check-writing fees but which, instead, pays interest of 5-1/2 percent compounded monthly on the minimum monthly balance of $300. The balance in the account during April ranged from a low of $350.50 to a high of $925.10.

Alternative investment: $Prt = I$
300.00 × 0.0775 × 1/12 = 1.94

Interest earned: $Prt = I$
350.50 × 0.055 × 1/12 = 1.61
Interest foregone: 0.33

Unit cost: 0.33 ÷ 22 checks = 0.015 = 1-1/2¢ per check

The interest foregone in the missed investment in Application 3 exceeds the interest earned in the checking account by 1-1/2 cents per check. Depositors must also pay a nominal fee when ordering supplies of checks to help allay the cost of printing and mailing the checks. Note also that some banks provide discounted or "no charge" checking that is tied to minimum-balance requirements in savings accounts.

Business Accounts

Because the needs of businesses differ significantly from those of individual customers, bankers offer separate schedules of rates and charges for commercial accounts. The following terms are typical:

Schedule of charges	
Checks paid	10¢ per check
Deposits made	25¢ per deposit
Items deposited	4¢ per item
Maintenance fee	$4.00 per month
Earnings credit	3.75 percent per annum

The bank charges 10 cents for each check that is written, 25 cents for every deposit into the checking account (in addition to 4 cents for every check included in the deposits), and a $4 monthly maintenance fee. Then, as an incentive for business managers to maintain relatively high balances in their checking accounts, annual interest is paid each month on the average daily collected balance of the month. The word *collected* here refers to cash deposits and deposited checks written on other banks as credits are received.

To illustrate the application of these charges, let's assume that Smeltzer Electronics begins August with a checking account (collected) balance of $12,525.10, writes 65 checks (60 of which clear the bank during August), and makes eight separate deposits including a total of 415 customer checks. If the average daily collected balance in the account during the month is $11,200.20, what is the net cost of the bank account for August?

Bank charges

$$
\begin{aligned}
\text{Checks paid: } & 60 \times 0.10 = & 6.00 \\
\text{Deposits made: } & 8 \times 0.25 = & 2.00 \\
\text{Items deposited: } & 415 \times 0.04 = & 16.60 \\
\text{Maintenance fee: } & & \underline{4.00} \\
\text{Total charges: } & & \$28.60
\end{aligned}
$$

Interest earned

$$11{,}200.20 \times 0.0375 \times 1/12 = \$35.00$$

Net credit

$$35.00 - 28.60 = \$6.40$$

Interest earned exceeded monthly costs by $6.40, resulting in a net credit to the account. Also consider the following situations.

APPLICATION 1. Using the preceding schedule of charges, determine the net credit or debit to the account at the end of the month for 253 checks that cleared the bank during June, 20 deposits involving a total of 383 customer checks, and an average daily balance of $14,214.15.

Bank charges

Checks paid: 253 × 0.10 =   25.30
Deposits made: 20 × 0.25 =   5.00
Items deposited: 383 × 0.04 =   15.32
Maintenance fee: 4.00
    Total charges: $49.62

Interest earned

$$14,214.15 \times 0.0375 \times 1/12 = 44.42$$

Net debit

$$49.62 - 44.42 = \$5.20$$

APPLICATION 2. As a model of simplicity, one banks offers the following terms:

Earnings credit. Your account earns 25 cents per $100 on the average balance to offset (but not exceed) the activity charge.
Activity charge. The monthly charge includes a $4 maintenance fee, 25 cents for each deposit, and 9 cents for each check paid.
Note. If the activity charge exceeds the earnings credit, the account is charged only the difference, except that any net service charge of 50 cents or less is waived.
Under these conditions, what is the cost to a small corporation for 640 checks that cleared the bank during January, 22 deposits, and an *average daily balance* of $12,212.16 during the month?

Earnings credit

$$\frac{\text{Average daily balance}}{100} \times 0.25 =$$

$$\frac{12,212.16}{100} \times 0.25 = 30.53$$

Activity charge

Maintenance fee: 4.00
    Deposits: 22 × 0.25 =   5.50
    Checks: 640 × 0.09 = 57.60
                             67.10

Net debit

$$67.10 - 30.53 = \$36.57$$

Check Writing and Endorsements

Despite continuing predictions for drastic declines in the use of checks, individuals and businesses write more checks today than at any other time in history. Rather than making purchases or transacting business with large amounts of money, most people in industrialized societies use checks to transfer wealth among themselves. The checks that they (the writers) issue are actually orders to third parties (bankers) to withdraw money from their (the writers') accounts and give it to the bearers of checks — either in cash or through a transfer of funds from the writers' accounts to those of check recipients.

Checks written on personal or business accounts have common elements. As illustrated in the personal check in Figure 13.1, the writer (drawer) must enter the date, the amount of money (in figures and in words), and a signature. In addition, good practice dictates that the writer specify the purpose of each check. The names of the banks, the name or names of the writers, and the identification numbers are preprinted on checks.

Business checks differ from personal checks in that they normally have separate attachments that include details of transactions. A check to a vendor, for example, would include the vendor's invoice number, and a payroll check would include a job number and itemized deductions (current and year-to-date) for such items as taxes, Social Security contributions, union dues, and charitable donations. Recipients detach these perforated attachments before cashing the checks.

The **endorsement** (signing) of a check by a payee transfers the right to receive money. In signing his $500 paycheck and cashing it at a grocery store, for example, Ron Snyder is transferring to the grocery store his right to collect from the writer of the check. In stamping its identity on the back of the same check, in turn, the grocery store transfers to its bank the right to collect $500,

Figure 13.1
A personal check

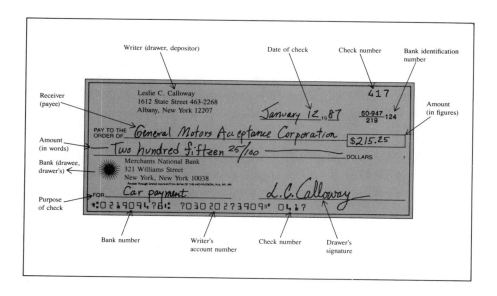

and so on. When cashing or depositing a check, the person to whom it is written must endorse it on the reverse side — in ink, exactly as the person's name appears on the face of the check.

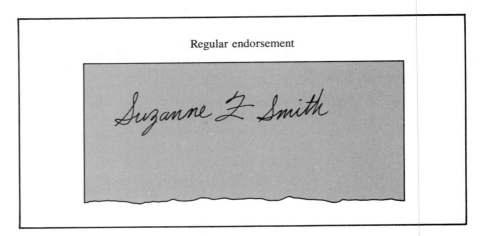

If the payee's name is misspelled on the face of the check, that person must sign the check as listed and write the correct signature immediately below the first one.

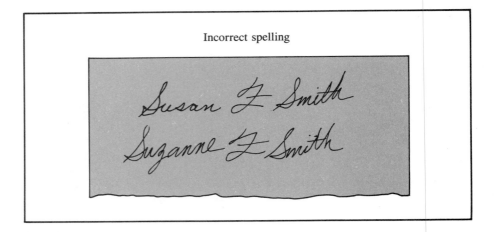

When mailing a check for deposit at a bank, a *deposit endorsement* prevents others from cashing it should it become lost or stolen.

Deposit endorsement

For deposit only
Suzanne Z. Smith

A *special (full) endorsement* enables the payee listed on the face of the check to transfer the right to receive payment to another person or company. The third party (Martin T. Farris, in this example) must also endorse the check when cashing or depositing it, making it a two-party check that most stores will not accept.

Special (full) endorsement

Pay to the order of
Martin T. Farris

Suzanne Z. Smith

When necessary, any individual or company may utilize a more secure method of transferring funds. A **cashier's check** is a negotiable instrument that is drawn on the bank's own funds. If you wish to send payment to someone in a distant city but have no checking account, for example, you may exchange the required amount of money at a bank for a cashier's check. In contrast, a **certified check** is your own check made out to a specific person or business that is certified (stamped and signed) by a bank officer as a guarantee to the recipient that a sufficient amount of money is in the issuer's checking account and will be held there until the check clears the bank. Under certain circumstances, individuals and companies accept only a cashier's check, certified check, money order, or cash — not wishing to assume the risk or inconvenience of having regular checks returned marked "INSUFFICIENT FUNDS."

Check Register

Although banks continue to offer checks attached to stubs for the recording of individual transactions, check registers like the one illustrated in Figure 13.2 are more popular by far. Check stubs must be checked individually, one transaction at a time, whereas check registers that are normally twice as long as the one illustrated here enable us to relate 12 transactions simultaneously. The transactions depicted in Figure 13.2 begin with a balance of $815.23. Because the checking plan involves a charge of 20 cents per check, the writer subtracts $67.70 ($67.50 + 0.20 = $67.70) for the first transaction. After writing two additional checks, this person deposits $450.00, bringing the account balance to $806.98. Notice that the writer has entered the check number, the date (including the year in the first entry), the payee's name, and the purpose of each payment. The check mark ($\sqrt{}$) flags the $450 deposit as an entry that is to be reflected on this person's next tax return. Complete information is required if a check register is to provide a useful record. Imagine the frustration at tax time, for example, of not being able to determine which entries represent deductible items and at some future date not being able to identify the year that certain checks were written. It is imperative, therefore, that we record complete information for each check — as we write it, when the details are fresh on our minds.

Check registers that accountants maintain for businesses normally include columns for debiting voucher accounts, a subject that is outside the scope of this book, and for recording cash discounts. Conceptually, however, they are the same as check registers used by individuals.

Figure 13.2
Check register

CHECK NO.	DATE	CHECKS ISSUED TO OR DESCRIPTION OF DEPOSIT	AMOUNT OF CHECK	CHECK FEE (if any)	√	AMOUNT OF DEPOSIT	BALANCE FORWARD 8 15 23
312	1/8	To Scott Automotive / For Repairs – Toyota	67 50	.20			Check or Dep. 67 70 / Bal. 747 53
313	1/12	To Central Services / For Electricty	225 15	.20			Check or Dep. 225 35 / Bal. 522 18
314	1/20	To City College / For Tuition	165 00	.20			Check or Dep. 165 20 / Bal. 356 98
	1/25	To NCVA Corporation / For Consulting fee			√	450 00	Check or Dep. 450 00 / Bal. 806 98
315	1/27	To First Federal / For Mortgage	420 71	.20			Check or Dep. 420 91 / Bal. 386 07
		To / For					Check or Dep. / Bal.

Bank Statements

Banks mail monthly statements to depositors, sometimes separate statements for checking and savings accounts and sometimes in single statements for both accounts. The statement in Figure 13.3 illustrates several types of entries that are typical in modern banking. The first entry reflects an **electronic funds transfer (EFT)** of $700, the depositor having authorized his or her employer (Randpar Corporation) to effect a transfer every payday from that company's computerized accounts to the bank's computerized accounts by way of a computer-to-computer telephone transmission. Also, as previously instructed by the depositor, the bank has credited a predetermined amount of the depositor's biweekly paycheck to this checking account and the balance to a savings account. An identical entry is shown for September 20.

Similarly, the September 13 entry records an electronic transfer of funds from the depositor's checking account to a bank account of the electric company. Items 620 through 626 are checks that the depositor had written prior to September 30 (the last day for which transactions are shown). (The checks are not in sequence because the entries show when they were received and processed by the bank rather than when they were issued.) The deposit on September 10 was a rebate check that the depositor had received from a manufacturer, and the deposit on the 21st reflects a transfer of funds ($200 from the depositor's savings account to this checking account. Two cash withdrawals were made on September 21. The final entry shows an interest payment based on an annual rate of 5-1/2 percent — compounded on the daily balance but paid quarterly.

During the one month represented by this particular bank statement, the de-

Figure 13.3
Monthly bank statement (individual checking account)

STATEMENTS OF ACCOUNT	PAGE NO. 01	SOCIAL SECURITY NUMBER 933 25 4033	STATEMENT PERIOD FROM 090186	TO 093086	ACCOUNT NUMBER 237915	PREVIOUS BALANCE $594.19
DATE	TRANSACTION DESCRIPTION				AMOUNT	BALANCE
0906	EFT DEPOSIT (PAYROLL) RANDPAR CORP				700 00	1294 19
0910	DEPOSIT				25 00	1319 19
0911	ITEM #621				27 03-	1292 16
0911	ITEM #623				31 80-	1260 36
0912	ITEM #624				100 00-	1160 36
0913	EFT WITHDRAWAL (CITIZENS POWER COMPANY)				92 00-	1068 36
0917	ITEM #620				30 00-	1038 36
0918	ITEM #626				59 00-	979 36
0920	EFT DEPOSIT (PAYROLL) RANDPAR CORP				700 00	1679 36
0921	ITEM #622				45 74-	1633 62
0921	DEPOSIT (TRANSFER)				200 00	1833 62
0921	WITHDRAWAL				770 00-	1063 62
0921	WITHDRAWAL				650 72-	412 90
0924	ITEM #625				271 01-	141 89
0928	DEPOSIT				900 00	1041 89
0930	INTEREST				11 96	1053 85

positor's employer avoided writing two checks, and the depositor avoided two trips to the bank to deposit them. Additionally, the depositor circumvented the task of writing and mailing a check to the electric company. EFTs are becoming commonplace as more employers use direct deposits and as more business managers (utilities, merchants, oil companies, and newspaper publishers, for example) arrange with bankers for the checkless collection of monthly bills. In some parts of the country, bank customers may use their personal computers and telephone lines to transfer funds between savings and checking accounts, and automatic teller machines (ATMs) are widely available for electronic deposits, transfers, and cash withdrawals. Obviously, the long-term impact of this rapidly emerging technology will be to lessen significantly our reliance on checks.

Reconciliations

Bank statements should be reconciled (balanced) with the check register (or stubs) as soon as possible after their receipt. Although depositors legally have 60 days to submit written questions concerning errors in bank statements, it is prudent to resolve any discrepancies at the earliest possible date and certainly before a statement is issued for the following month. Most bank statements provide guidelines for monthly reconciliations, but many, in an attempt to simplify the process, have neglected the check register. In many cases it is essential that end-of-month adjustments be made both to the bank statement and to the check register.

Bank statements must be adjusted to reflect any transactions that have taken place since they were issued:

```
  Statement balance
+ Unrecorded deposits
− Outstanding checks
= Adjusted balance
```

Beginning with the ending balance as shown on the statement, we add any deposits made after the closing date of the statement and subtract the amounts of any checks not listed in the statement.

Check registers must be adjusted to reflect any credits to the account that the bank may have made during the month and to deduct any charges that may have been imposed:

```
  Current checkbook balance
+ Bank credits
− Bank debits
= Adjusted balance
```

The quarterly interest entry in Figure 13.3 is an example of a credit that banks routinely make to checking accounts, and debits may include such items as

EFT withdrawals, charges for nonsufficient funds,[1] charges for an excessive number of cash withdrawals or transfers, and monthly maintenance fees. Upon completion of these adjustments, the register should include an entry for every transaction listed on the bank statement.

As the word *balance* suggests, these adjusted figures should be identical. When a variance occurs, the depositor should first check the register for errors in addition (deposits and transfers) and subtraction (checks, fees, and electronic transfers) and make certain that all credits and debits appearing on the bank statement have been accounted for in the register. If no error is found in the check register, the depositor should turn to the bank for assistance. Personnel there will help locate any errors and make any necessary corrections.

To illustrate the reconciliation process, let's compare the following entries from a check register and a bank statement.

Check Register

Date	Transaction	Amount	Balance
			1027.88
6/14	EFT ELECTRIC	92.00	935.88
6/15	DEPOSIT	124.51	1060.39
6/15	CASH WITHDRAWAL	200.00	860.39
6/15	CHECK 576	44.07	816.32
6/15	CHECK 577	24.68	791.64
6/15	CHECK 578	6.80	784.84
6/15	CHECK 579	61.84	723.00
6/15	CHECK 580	72.02	650.98
6/16	CHECK 581	39.37	611.61
6/16	CHECK 582	271.01	340.60
6/17	CHECK 583	107.54	233.06
6/20	CHECK 584	132.68	100.38
6/23	CHECK 585	VOID	
6/23	CHECK 586	24.00	76.38
6/25	EFT PAYROLL	700.00	776.38
6/27	CHECK 587	125.15	651.23
6/29	CHECK 588	27.13	624.10

Bank Statement

Date	Transaction	Amount	Balance
			1027.88
0614	EFT WITHDRAWAL	92.00−	935.88
0615	DEPOSIT	124.51	1060.39
0615	WITHDRAWAL	200.00−	860.39
0618	ITEM #577	24.68−	835.71
0618	ITEM #576	44.07−	791.64
0619	ITEM #578	6.80−	784.84
0619	ITEM #581	39.37−	745.47
0620	ITEM #579	61.48−	683.99
0620	ITEM #582	271.01−	412.98
0621	ITEM #580	72.02−	340.96
0621	ITEM #583	107.54−	233.42
0625	EFT DEPOSIT	700.00	933.42
0625	ITEM #584	132.68−	800.74
0626	ITEM #586	24.00−	776.74
0630	INTEREST	22.60	799.34

[1] Checks received by banks that are in excess of the account balances are said to "bounce," and bankers refer to such transactions as NSFs (nonsufficient funds) and penalize the writers by debiting their accounts at an established charge of ten dollars or more. Check writers may avoid the embarrassment of having checks returned to the payees marked "INSUFFICIENT FUNDS" by subscribing to a service that systematically transfers funds from savings accounts to checking accounts when necessary to prevent checks from bouncing. Most banks also offer *credit reserve* plans which enable their customers to "write their own loans." Under such plans, which must be arranged beforehand, customers whose checks exceed their checking account balances automatically receive bank loans (usually in multiples of $100) on which interest charges immediately begin to accrue.

Upon receipt of the bank statement a few days after the end of the month, the depositor must reconcile the bank balance of $799.34 with the checkbook balance of $624.10. Beginning with the bank statement, a comparison with the check register reveals that all *electronic funds transfers* are accounted for — the writer having recorded the EFT withdrawal on June 14 upon receipt of a mailed copy of the electric bill, as well as the EFTs on the regular paydays of June 15 and 25 upon the receipt of a check stub from the employer. The checks written on June 27 and June 29, however, are not listed. Adding the two *outstanding checks* to the statement balance results in an adjusted balance of $647.06.

Adjusted Statement Balance		Adjusted Register Balance	
Ending balance	799.34	Current balance	624.10
Unrecorded deposits		Bank credits	
Outstanding checks		Interest	22.60
No. 587 125.15		Bank debits	
No. 588 27.13	− 152.28		
	647.06		646.70

Turning to the checkbook (register) balance, the depositor finds no bank charges on the statement but notices one credit — the quarterly interest payment of $22.60. Adding this amount to the register balance results in an adjusted balance of $646.70 and a 36-cent variance with the statement balance ($647.06 − 646.70 = 36¢$). A quick check of calculations in the register verifies the final figure of $624.10, but a subsequent comparison of entries with those on the statement reveals that the depositor transposed the cents in Check 579; the $61.84 entry should read $61.48. The 36-cent difference, which understates the correct register balance, is corrected with the following register entry.

The record (register) having been altered, the statement and register are in balance.

When comparing the two documents initially, place the check marks on the statement behind each item that also appears on the register. Subsequently, every item shown on the statement but not on the register must be reflected in the adjusted register balance and every item listed in the register but not in the statement must be reflected in the adjusted statement balance. Any differences remaining between the adjusted figures are usually found in register mis-calculations.

Some banks return cancelled checks with the monthly statements, and some banks do not. Most would prefer to provide safekeeping for checks rather than pay the extra postage for returning them each month, and they provide copies of selected checks upon request — either for a nominal fee or, so long as the number of such requests is not excessive, without charge.

APPLICATION 1. Beginning in March with a register balance of $350.26, and allowing for a per-check fee of 20 cents, record the transactions that follow:

3/2	Check 112, Health Spa, 16.25	
3/3	Check 113, Electric Co., 95.13	
3/10	EFT Payroll Deposit, 812.00	
3/15	Check 114, Department Store, 121.16	
3/25	EFT Payroll Deposit, 812.00	
3/25	Check 115, Mortgage payment, 425.75	
3/27	Check 116, Telephone Company, 26.12	
3/20	Check 117, Cash, 300.00	

Check register:

	Balance		350.26
3/2	Check 112 Health Spa	16.25	16.45
	Balance		333.81
3/3	Check 113 Electric Co.	95.13	95.33
	Balance		238.48
3/10	Payroll deposit***	812.00	812.00
	Balance		1050.48
3/15	Check 114 Department Sto.	121.16	121.16
	Balance		929.32
3/25	Payroll Deposit***	812.00	812.00
	Balance		1741.32
3/25	Check 115 Mortgage pymnt	425.75	425.95
	Balance		1315.37
3/27	Check 116 Telephone Co.	26.12	26.32
	Balance		1289.05
3/30	Check 117 Cash	300.00	300.20
	Balance		988.85

APPLICATION 2. Reconcile the preceding register with the following bank statement:

Beginning balance					369.46
3/1	Check 111	19.00	0.20	19.20−	350.26
3/5	Check 112	16.25	0.20	16.45−	333.81
3/5	Check 113	95.13	0.20	95.33−	238.48
3/10	EFT Dep.	812.00		812.00	1050.48
3/19	Check 114	121.16	0.20	121.36−	929.12
3/25	EFT Dep.	812.00		812.00	1741.12
3/28	Check 115	425.75	0.20	425.95−	1315.17
3/30	Check 117	300.00	0.20	300.20−	1014.97
Monthly fee	4.00			4.00−	1010.97
Interest				241.58	1252.55

Adjusted Statement Balance		Adjusted Register Balance	
Ending balance	1252.55	Current balance	988.85
Unrecorded deposits		Bank credits	241.58
Outstanding checks	26.32	Bank debits	4.00−
	1226.23		1226.43

The two balances differ by 20 cents, which, upon checking the register entries, we find to be a missed service charge relating to Check 114. Check 111, which was written in February but not received at the bank until March, does not affect this reconciliation. Notice also that Check 117 appears on the bank statement although written three days later than Check 116 which did not reach the bank in March — only because the check writer wrote and cashed Check 117 at the bank to secure $200 cash. Check 116, on the other hand, was deposited at the bank used by the telephone company, processed at a clearing house, and charged against this account the following month.

APPLICATION 3. Beginning with the ending balance of $988.85 in Application 1, make the necessary adjustments to the check register based on the reconciliation in Application 2.

Balance		988.85
Monthly fee	4.00−	4.00
Balance		984.85
Interest	241.58	241.58
Balance		1226.43
Missed service charge Check 114	0.20−	0.20
Balance		1226.23

SAVINGS ACCOUNTS

Opening a savings account is almost as effortless as it ever was, but the simple passbook accounts that used to pay a stable interest rate of 3 percent compounded quarterly have become a historical concept. As is apparent in almost any current newspaper, potential depositors are confronted with a plethora of investment plans with respect to minimum deposits, fluctuating rates, and varying time periods. Unlike loans, which borrowers may rank through comparisons of *annual percentage rates*, savers are on their own when it comes to comparing regular savings accounts, certificates of deposit, and money market funds.

Regular Savings Accounts

The rates paid on regular accounts usually depend on the amount of money being deposited. At the time of this writing, for example, one bank is offering the following rates:

Account Balance	Rate of Interest (compounded daily)
$5 to $499	6%
$500 to $2,499	7%
$2,500 and over	8%

Interest is compounded daily and paid quarterly — not on the average balance in the account during the three-month period, but on the lowest balance at any time during the quarter. A depositor might have an average daily balance of over $1,000 but receive an interest credit on only $450, as in the following situation.

From	To	Days	×	Balance	=	Product
April 1–	April 20	20	×	1,200	=	24,000
April 21–	May 16	26	×	900	=	23,400
May 17–	May 25	9	×	450	=	4,050
May 26–	June 10	16	×	1,500	=	24,000
June 11–	June 30	20	×	1,250	=	25,000
		91				100,450

ADB: 100,450 ÷ 91 = $1,103.85

Computing the average daily balance (ADB), as we did with charge accounts in Chapter 8, results in a figure of $1,103.85 and interest of $19.43.

Interest of 7 percent is compounded daily on the *average daily balance* for April, May, and June.

$\% = 7 \div 365 = 0.01917808$
$n = 30 + 31 + 30 = 91$

$$P(1 + \%)^n = A$$
$$1{,}103.85(1.0001917808)^{91} = 1{,}123.28$$

Amount $-$ Principal $=$ Interest
$1{,}123.28 - 1{,}103.85 = \$19.43$

Calculator	
Entries	**Display**
. 0 7	0.07
$\div$	0.07
3 6 5	365.
$=$	0.0001917808
$+$	0.0001917808
1	1.
$=$	1.000191781
y^x	1.000191781
9 1	91.
$=$	1.017603529
$\times$	1.017603529
1 1 0 3 . 8 5	1103.85
$-$	1,123.281655
1 1 0 3 . 8 5	1103.85
$=$	19.431655

Keep in mind that the decimal in the adjusted percentage (0.01917808) must be moved two places to the left when used in the equation. Because some banks pay interest on the lowest balance (generally referred to as the "lowest reference"), a $450 principal in the preceding situation (May 17–25) results in the application of a 6 percent rate and interest for the quarter of only $6.78.

$\% = 6 \div 365 = 0.0164383562 \qquad n = 91$

$$P(1 + \%)^n = A$$

$$450(1.000164383562)^{91} = 456.78$$

$$A - P = I$$

$$456.78 - 450.00 = \$6.78$$

Using the *lowest balance* rather than the *average daily balance* results in a loss of $12.65 (19.43 − 6.78 = 12.65) to the customer and a corresponding gain to the bank. Such differences become more pronounced over the course of several years and with larger amounts of money. How may depositors avoid such losses? By carefully checking the terms offered by competing banks and choosing one that offers daily compounding on the average daily balance. Note also that some banks treat deposits made between the first and tenth of a month as though deposited on the first day, so that a deposit on December 10 or earlier would earn interest from December 1.

APPLICATION 1. Relating the following bank terms to the accompanying record of savings account balances, compute the quarterly interest payments based on daily compounding of the average daily balance.

Rate	Amount		Dates	Balance
5%	to $499		Jan 1–15	$1,200
5-1/4%	$500–1,000		Jan 16–31	1,420
5-1/2%	$1,000+		Feb 1–28	1,050
			Mar 1–10	1,050
			Mar 11–31	920

From	To	Days	×	Balance	=	Product
Jan 1	Jan 15	15	×	1,200		18,000
Jan 16	Jan 31	16	×	1,420		22,720
Feb 1	Mar 10	38	×	1,050		39,900
Mar 11	Mar 31	21	×	920		19,320
		90				99,940

ADB: 99,940 ÷ 90 = $1,110.44

$$\% = 5\text{-}1/2 \div 365 = 0.015068493 \qquad n = 90$$

$$P(1 + \%)^n = A$$
$$1,110.44(1.0001506849)^{90} = 1,125.60$$

$$A - P = I$$
$$1,125.60 - 1,110.44 = \$15.16$$

APPLICATION 2. Using the same sets of rates and balances, compute the quarterly interest payment on the lowest reference point.

$$\% = 5\text{-}1/4 \div 365 = 0.014383562 \qquad n = 90$$

$$P(1 + \%)^n = A$$
$$920(1.0001438356)^{90} = \$931.99$$

$$A - P = I$$
$$931.99 - 920.00 = \$11.99$$

APPLICATION 3. If a small-business owner opens a savings account on December 5 with a deposit of $10,000, how much interest will be credited to the account on December 31, assuming that (1) the money earns interest of

8-1/2 percent compounded daily and (2) the bank treats deposits made by the tenth of a month as though deposited on the first day?

$$\% = 8\text{-}1/2 \div 365 = 0.023287671 \qquad n = 31$$

$$P(1 + \%)^n = A$$
$$10,000(1.0002328767)^{31} = 10,072.44$$

$$A - P = I$$
$$10,072.44 - 10,000.00 = \$72.44$$

APPLICATION 4. If a depositor has an average daily balance of $1,523.16 during the quarter in a savings account that pays interest of 6-1/4 percent compounded quarterly, what credit does the account receive at the end of the quarter?

$$\% = 6\text{-}1/4 \div 4 = 1.5625 \qquad n = 1$$

$$P(1 + \%)^n = A$$
$$1,523.16(1.015625) = 1,546.96$$

$$A - P = I$$
$$1,546.96 - 1,523.16 = \$23.80$$

Reconciliations

Balancing savings accounts is usually a simple process. First, depositors should maintain personal records of deposits, transfers, and withdrawals, including those that are made electronically. Second, the ending balance of bank statements should be compared with balances in the personal records. Third, any discrepancies should be checked through a comparison of entries. A comparison of the depositor's personal savings account record with the bank statement in Figure 13.4 reveals, for example, a quarterly dividend (interest payment) of $201.53, which should also be entered in this depositor's personal record.

On December 12 the bank customer made two withdrawals: one a transfer of $300 from savings to checking and another for $200 cash. Two direct deposits were made by the depositor's employer to the savings account, with the balance being credited to the depositor's checking account. Notice also that,

Figure 13.4
Monthly bank statement (individual savings account)

TRANSACTION				
MONTH	DAY	TRANSACTION DESCRIPTION	AMOUNT	BALANCE
		PREVIOUS BALANCE		10566.65
12	12	WITHDRAWAL (TRANSFER)	300.00-	10266.65
12	12	WITHDRAWAL	200.00-	10066.65
12	13	EFT DEPOSIT (PAYROLL) RANDPAR CORP	545.70	10612.35
12	27	EFT DEPOSIT (PAYROLL) RANDPAR CORP	640.26	11252.61
12	31	DIVIDEND	201.53	11454.14
		DIVIDEND PAID YTD 667.85	NEW BALANCE	11454.14

in addition to the quarterly dividend (interest) entry, this end-of-year statement shows the total amount of taxable dividends (interest) paid into the account during the year (YTD = year to date) as being $667.85.

Certificates of Deposit

A **certificate of deposit (CD)** is an investment that, in exchange for a relatively high rate of interest compared to regular savings accounts, requires a minimum deposit for a prescribed time period — the higher the imposed minimum deposit and the longer the commitment, the higher the rate. Consider the following schedule of CD rates:

Fixed-Rate Certificates

Amount	3–6 mo	6 mo–12 mo	1–2 yr	2–3 yr	3–4 yr
$500–2,499	7.5%	9%	9.5%	9.75%	10.75%
$2,500 plus	8.75%	9.25%	9.75%	10.00%	11%

A two-year certificate for $1,000 would earn interest of 9-1/2 percent compounded daily, for example, whereas a deposit of $5,000 for four years would earn 11 percent.

As an alternative to *fixed rates*, which remain constant for the duration of a term, most banks also offer *variable rates* that are adjusted daily in relation to fluctuations in the interest rates that the federal government pays for newly issued securities. If investors believe that interest rates will decline, they may select fixed rates to "lock in" current yields for the duration of their investments. If they believe that interest rates are destined to rise, instead, they opt for variable rate CDs, hoping to benefit from progressively higher rates. Although some investors are better informed than others, no one knows for certain just which direction interest rates will take. The quantity of money that is made available, which has a direct effect on interest rates, and the rates themselves are subject to frequent adjustment by the Federal Reserve Board in response to changing economic conditions.

As a measure for discouraging investors from the frequent switching of money from one account to another in search of higher interest rates, bankers impose penalties for early withdrawals. The termination on August 15 of a one-year, $1,000 CD dated April 2, for example, might result in a penalty of 90 days' interest. Assuming a rate of 9 percent compounded daily, the proceeds would be $1,011.16.

Compound amount: $\% = 9 \div 365 = 0.024657534$
$n = 135$ (April 2 to August 15)

$$P(1 + \%)^n = A$$
$$1,000(1.00024657534)^{135} = 1,033.84$$

Penalty: $1{,}000(1.00024657534)^{90} = 1{,}022.44$
$$A - P = I$$
$$1{,}022.44 - 1{,}000.00 = 22.44$$

Proceeds: Compound amount $-$ penalty $=$ Proceeds
$$1{,}033.84 - 22.44 = \$1{,}011.40$$

The compound amount and the 90-day penalty are computed on the original principal of \$1,000. Common penalties for early withdrawals are the loss of interest for 30 days in connection with six-month certificates, 60 days for one-year certificates, and 180 days for certificates with terms of longer than one year. Penalties of as much as six month's interest are not uncommon, however, even in connection with maturities as short as three months (resulting in a loss not only of any interest earned but also a reduction of principal), which emphasizes the importance of comparing the essential provisions of any contract before entering into either short- or long-term commitments.

APPLICATION 1. If an accountant places \$10,000 in a three-year certificate on January 15 that pays 8 percent interest compounded daily, what would be the proceeds resulting from withdrawal just 95 days later, after allowing for a 180-day penalty for early withdrawal?

Interest $\% = 8 \div 365 = 0.021917808$ $\qquad n = 95$
earned: $P(1 + \%)^n = A$
$$10{,}000(1.00021917808)^{95} = 10{,}210.38$$

Penalty: $P(1 + \%)^n = A$
$$10{,}000(1.00021917808)^{180} = 10{,}402.36$$

Proceeds: Compound amount $-$ penalty $=$ Proceeds
$$10{,}210.38 - 402.36 = \$9{,}808.02$$

APPLICATION 2. If the accountant in Application 1 withdrew the money to invest it in a three-year CD paying 10.3 percent compounded daily, how much money would be gained or lost in the transaction by the time the first CD (if held) would have matured?

$\% = 10.3 \div 365 = 0.028219178$
$n = (3 \times 365) - 95 = 1{,}000$

New $\quad P(1 + \%)^n = A$
investment: $9{,}808.02(1.00028219178)^{1.000} = 13{,}005.24$

$$\text{First} \quad \% = 8 \div 365 = 0.021917808$$
$$\text{investment:} \quad n = 3 \times 365 = 1,095$$
$$10,000(1.00021917808)^{1.095} = 12,712.16$$

$$\text{Net} \quad \text{New} - \text{old} = \text{gain}$$
$$\text{gain:} \quad 13,005.24 - 12,712.16 = \$293.08$$

Computing interest on the new investment up to the date that the first invest-ment would have matured (1,000 days later) results in a compound amount of $13,005.24 as compared to $12,712.16 for the full 1,095 days of the first investment. The switch of investments was a wise one, and the investor will continue to earn the higher rate for the remainder of the three-year term of the second investment (an additional 95 days).

Money Market Funds

Money market funds represent a pool of deposits by individual investors in special (money market) accounts which bankers and securities brokers reinvest in short-term government securities that pay relatively high rates of interest. These government securities are of such large denominations (as much as $10,000 each) that most individuals could not otherwise participate in their purchase. Money market funds are similar to variable-rate CDs, in that the rate of interest being earned can fluctuate daily. They differ from CDs in that pe-riodic withdrawals may be made without the imposition of penalty charges. Minimum initial deposits range from $1,000 to $5,000, which need not be maintained thereafter.

Individual Retirement Accounts

Banks offer **Individual Retirement Accounts (IRAs)** which are personal re-tirement accounts that are available to all taxpayers, even those who are par-ticipating in separate pension plans at work. By following guidelines set forth by the federal government, individuals are exempt from paying tax each year on up to $2,000 (up to $4,000 for two working spouses or $2,250 for a taxpayer and nonworking spouse). The money must be placed in separate savings accounts, certificates of deposit, money market funds, stocks, or bonds. The government imposes a 10 percent penalty for funds withdrawn before age 59-1/2, but withdrawals must begin at a prescribed amount each year by age 70-1/2. Additionally, withdrawn amounts are reportable as taxable income regardless of age.

The taxpayers' objective is to report portions of present income as taxable income after retirement, with the expectation that income at that time and the percent of taxes imposed on the withdrawals will be substantially lower than during prime earning years. Investors may move IRA funds, including any earn-ings that have accumulated, from one account to another in pursuit of maxi-mum yields.

Taxpayers who make withdrawals within five years or so after the original investment may suffer a net loss, because the tax savings (assuming that the

IRA savings are invested immediately) will not have increased to a degree sufficient to offset the penalty that becomes payable at the time of early withdrawal.[2] The higher the individual's tax bracket, however, the shorter the time an IRA investment must be held before an early withdrawal results in a net gain compared to a non-IRA investment.

EXERCISES (as directed by your instructor)

13-1 Describe current trends away from what might be termed "traditional banking."

13-2 What is a monthly maintenance fee, and how may check writers avoid such charges?

13-3 If a person writes an average of 20 checks per month at a cost of 25 cents each and pays a monthly maintenance fee of $2.50, what is the per-check charge?

13-4 Would the person in No. 13-3 be better off to maintain a balance of $500 in the account as a way of avoiding the per-check charge and monthly maintenance fee — assuming that an alternative investment for the $500 would yield an annual rate of 8 percent compounded monthly?

13-5 In consideration of the following balances in a personal checking account, what is the end-of-quarter credit for interest of 5-1/2 percent that is paid on the average daily balance?

---

[2] Assume, for example, that a single taxpayer who is in the 25 percent tax bracket has options of (1) paying tax on $2,000 of earnings and placing the balance in a savings account that pays 8 percent compounded daily or (2) placing the entire $2,000 (tax deferred) in an IRA that pays the same rate. If the investor chooses the IRA and withdraws the accumulated amount (principal plus interest) at the end of five years, a net loss of $113.94 (compared to the non-IRA investment) results.

Option 1	$2,000 − 25% tax = $1,500	
(non-IRA):	1,500 at 8% compounded daily for 5 years = $2,237.64	
	Less 25% tax on the 737.64 interest	−184.41
		$2,053.23
Option 2		
(IRA):	$2,000 at 8% compounded daily for 5 years	$2,983.52
	Less 10% for early withdrawal penalty	−298.35
	Less 25% tax on $2,983.52	−745.88
		$1,939.29

Net loss: $2,053.23 (Option 1) − 1,939.39 (Option 2) = $113.94

Under these circumstances, the investor would have been better off to have paid income tax initially on the income and to have placed the remaining amount in a non-IRA investment.

April 1–April 20	$350
April 21–April 28	475
April 29–May 10	385
May 11–May 17	340
May 18–May 29	512
May 30–June 15	505
June 16–June 25	410
June 26–June 30	322

13-6 Again referring to the situation in No. 13-5,

    a. What would be the end-of-quarter credit for interest paid on the lowest reference within the three-month period?

    b. What is the difference in interest earned between *average daily balance* and the *lowest reference* point?

13-7 In consideration of the following schedule of bank charges for partnerships and corporations, what is the total bank charge for November for the 1,235 customer checks deposited, 225 company checks that were paid by the bank, and three customer checks returned because of nonsufficient funds? Additionally, company accountants deposited $5,025 in currency during the month and exchanged $200 in cash for 50 rolls of coins.

Activity Charges

Maintenance fee	$5.00/month
Items deposited	$0.035/item
Currency deposited	$0.90/$1,000
Checks paid	
for 1–10,000	$0.07/check
over 10,000	$0.065/check
Returned checks	$5.00/check
Currency furnished	$0.45/$1,000
Coin furnished	$0.05/roll
plus	$1.00/order

13-8 Use the following schedule of bank charges and credits for commercial accounts to determine the monthly charge to a corporation that wrote 2,125 checks (2,010 which cleared the bank during the month), made 15 deposits, and maintained an average balance in the account of $12,513.25.

    Earnings Credit: Your account earns 20 cents per $100 on the average balance to offset (but not exceed) the activity charge.

Activity Charge: The monthly charge includes a $5 maintenance fee, 25 cents for each deposit, and 10 cents for each check paid.

13-9 What are alternative designations for check writers and the receivers of checks?

13-10 What is the purpose of endorsing a check?

13-11 Where on a check should an endorsement appear?

13-12 How should a check be endorsed if the printed name of the payee differs slightly from the person's actual name?

13-13 What is the purpose of a deposit endorsement and how is it accomplished?

13-14 If the payee of a check wishes to transfer it to Ralph Sweringen, how should the endorsement read?

13-15 What is a cashier's check?

13-16 What is a certified check?

13-17 Assuming a prior balance of $312.90 in a checking account, record the following transactions:

January 3, Check 121 for $16.23
January 10, Deposit of $250.00
January 16, Check 122 for $115.15
January 23, Check 123 for $29.12

13-18 Referring to No. 13-17, record the same transactions to allow for a per-check charge of 20 cents.

13-19 What are EFTs and how are they used?

13-20 What are the inherent benefits of EFTs?

13-21 Cite the categories of possible adjustments to be made to bank statements when reconciling them with check registers.

13-22 Cite the categories of possible adjustments to check registers.

13-23 How may check writers avoid the possibility of paying a hefty bank charge for NSF checks?

13-24 Reconcile the bank statement with the check register, taking the following elements into consideration: ending statement balance, $407.71; current check register balance, $510.14; bank charge, $10.00; unrecorded deposit, $150.00; outstanding check, $44.45; and interest paid to the account, $13.12.

13-25 What procedure should be followed when the adjusted balances for the bank statement and check register do not agree?

13-26 Reconcile the following check register and bank statement:

	Check Register				Bank Statement		
	Previous balance		734.47		Previous balance		1005.48
12/01	656	100.00	634.47	1203	CK 656	100.00−	905.48
12/01	657	25.29	609.18	1204	CK 657	25.29−	880.19
12/02	658	30.00	579.18	1206	CK 654	271.01−	609.18
12/08	659	114.05	465.13	1211	CK 660	3.40−	605.78
12/08	660	4.30	460.83	1211	CK 662	26.66−	579.12
12/08	661	void	460.83	1211	CK 658	30.00−	549.12
12/08	662	26.66	434.17	1211	CK 663	33.66−	515.46
12/08	663	33.66	400.51	1211	CK 664	34.72−	480.74
12/08	664	34.72	365.79	1212	CK 659	114.05−	366.69
12/12	DEPOSIT (TRANSFER)	300.00	665.79	1212	DEPOSIT TFR	300.00	666.69
12/12	CASH WITHDRAWAL	100.73	565.06	1212	WITHDRAWAL	100.73−	565.96
12/13	EFT WITHDRAWAL	95.00	470.06	1213	EFT WITHDRAWAL	95.00−	470.96
12/13	EFT DEPOSIT	700.00	1170.06	1213	EFT DEPOSIT	700.00	1170.96
12/14	665	69.55	1100.51	1217	CK 666	54.49−	1116.47
12/14	666	54.49	1046.02	1217	CK 665	69.55−	1046.92
12/15	667	132.48	913.54	1218	CK 670	19.78−	1027.14
12/15	668	39.20	874.34	1219	CK 668	39.20−	987.94
12/15	669	400.00	474.34	1219	EFT DEPOSIT	700.00	1687.94
12/15	670	19.78	454.56	1221	CK 672	116.86−	1571.08
12/18	671	271.01	183.55	1221	CK 667	132.48−	1438.60
12/18	672	116.86	66.69	1221	WITHDRAWAL	400.00−	1038.60
12/19	EFT DEPOSIT	700.00	766.69	1226	CK 671	271.01−	767.59
12/21	CASH WITHDRAWAL	400.00	366.69	1226	CK 669	400.00−	367.59
12/25	673	21.85	344.84	1231	CK 673	21.85−	345.74
12/28	674	114.26	230.58	1231	INTEREST	9.48	355.22
1/2	DEPOSIT (TRANSFER)	200.00	430.58				
1/5	675	19.36	411.22				

13-27 Referring to the check register in No. 13-26, assume that today's date is January 8 of the current year and that no transactions have been recorded since Check 675. Make the necessary entries to bring the register into balance with the statement.

13-28 Reconcile the following check register and bank statement:

Bank Statement				Check Register			
	Previous balance		490.15		Previous balance		362.07
04 02	Item #531	6.80−	483.35	4/1	535	100.00	262.07
04 03	Item #533	14.28−	469.07	4/2	536	27.00	235.07
04 04	Item #535	100.00−	369.07	4/5	EFT DEPOSIT	700.00	935.07
04 05	EFT deposit	700.00	1069.07	4/5	537	35.00	900.07
04 06	Item #536	27.00−	1042.07	4/6	538	25.20	874.87
04 09	Item #537	35.00−	1007.07	4/7	539	393.59	481.28
04 12	Item #542	23.29−	983.78	4/7	540	20.00	461.28
04 12	Item #541	42.27−	941.51	4/7	541	42.27	419.01
04 12	DEPOSIT TRANSFER	600.00	1541.51	4/7	542	23.29	395.72
04 13	Item #540	20.00−	1521.51	4/8	543	50.00	345.72
04 13	Item #545	48.20−	1473.31	4/10	544	1.00	344.72
04 13	Item #543	50.00−	1423.31	4/10	545	48.20	296.52
04 13	Item #532	107.00−	1316.31	4/10	546	197.37	99.15
04 13	Item #546	197.37−	1118.94	4/12	DEPOSIT TRANSFER	600.00	699.15
04 13	EFT WITHDRAWAL	92.00−	1026.94	4/18	EFT DEPOSIT	700.00	1399.15
04 16	Item #544	1.00−	1025.94	4/20	547	100.00	1299.15
04 16	Item #539	393.59−	632.35	4/19	548	256.07	1043.08
04 18	EFT deposit	700.00	1332.35	4/19	549	271.01	772.07
04 23	DEPOSIT TRANSFER	900.00	2232.35	4/20	550	40.00	732.07
04 24	Item #551	132.45−	2099.90	4/20	551	132.45	599.62
04 24	Item #548	256.07−	1843.83	4/22	552	261.04	338.58
04 25	Item #554	50.00−	1793.83	4/22	553	100.00	238.58
04 25	Item #553	100.00−	1693.83	4/22	554	50.00	188.58
04 26	Item #557	871.45−	822.38	4/22	555	10.00	178.58
04 26	Item #556	72.16−	750.22	4/23	556	72.16	106.42
04 27	Item #550	40.00−	710.22	4/23	DEPOSIT TRANSFER	900.00	1006.42
04 27	Item #558	50.00−	660.22	4/23	557	871.45	134.97
04 27	Item #549	271.01−	389.21	4/24	558	50.00	84.97
04 30	Item #555	10.00−	379.21	4/27	559	65.00	19.97
	NEW BALANCE		379.21	4/29	DEPOSIT	600.00	619.97
				4/30	560	50.00	569.97
				5/1	561	69.82	500.15
				5/5	562	32.15	468.00

13-29 With reference to your computations for No. 13-28, make the required adjustments to the check register.

13-30 A savings account was opened with $2,710 on September 1. If a deposit of $1,500 was made on September 12 and a withdrawal of $750 on September 29, what is the monthly interest credit to the account based on 6-1/2 percent paid on the average daily balance — compounded daily and paid quarterly?

13-31 In consideration of the following interest rates and terms for a regular savings account, along with the record of beginning balance, deposits, and withdrawals, what is the interest credit at the end of the quarter based on daily compounding of the *average daily balance*?

Rate	Amount	Dates	Transactions	Amount
5-1/2%	to $499	April 1	Beginning balance	752.10
5-3/4%	$500 to 999	April 16	Deposit	350.00
6%	$1,000 plus	May 10	Deposit	350.00
		June 12	Deposit	350.00
		June 28	Withdrawal	150.00

13-32 In No. 13-31, what would be the quarterly interest credit if daily compounding was on the *lowest reference point*?

13-33 If the *average daily balance* in a savings account is $1,815 and the interest rate is 7-1/2 percent compounded and paid quarterly, what amount of interest is credited to the account at the end of the quarter?

13-34 If a savings account is opened with $5,000 on March 10 at interest of 10-1/4 percent compounded daily, how much money will be in the account at the end of the quarter (March 31), assuming that the bank treats all deposits by the tenth of the month as having been received on the first day of the month?

13-35 Why are reconciliations of savings accounts generally easier than those for checking accounts?

13-36 What is a CD?

13-37 Why do CDs normally pay higher rates of interest than paid to deposits in savings accounts?

13-38 What factors determine the rates of interest paid on CDs?

13-39 Under what conditions should investors opt for CDs with fixed rates? with variable rates?

13-40 What measures do banks take to discourage investors from switching from one CD offering to another?

13-41 If an investor has a one-year, $10,000 CD that pays 8 percent interest compounded daily, would it be economically advantageous to cancel the certificate at the end of 90 days (accepting a 60-day loss of interest) and switch to an alternative investment that pays 10 percent compounded daily?

13-42 How do *money market funds* usually differ from *certificates of deposit*?

13-43 What are IRAs and what is the rationale for their use?

14 Payroll Computations and Records

LEARNING OBJECTIVES

Whether you are preparing a payroll or simply checking the accuracy of a paycheck, the materials in this chapter will enable you to

- define and apply such terms as *gross pay, payroll deductions,* and *net pay,* as well as such acronyms as *FICA, FUT,* and *SUT*
- calculate gross pay for different time periods (weekly, biweekly, semiweekly, monthly) under a variety of systems (wages, salaries, piecework, differential piecework, production bonus, production premiums, and commissions)
- compute both regular and overtime pay under each system
- determine the amount of federal taxes to be withheld from different levels of gross pay, using either the wage-bracket tables or a percentage method of computation
- describe the primary elements of the Federal Insurance Contributions Act and determine the combined employer-employee contributions
- identify the amount of federal unemployment tax and state unemployment tax that employers must pay in relation to the gross pay of employees
- set up and maintain payroll records
- minimize the amount of money required to pay employees in cash rather than with checks

Company payrolls can range anywhere from a simple cash payment for only a few employees to the total involvement of entire departments of managerial and clerical personnel in the proration of salaries, the withholding and distribution of a wide variety of deductions, and the on-schedule issuance of thousands of payroll checks. A high degree of accuracy is required in payroll preparation, no matter how small or large the operation, in that errors which "shortchange" employees are detrimental to employee relations, often leaving them with the impression that management is uncaring, unappreciative, or even predisposed to cheating. Conversely, undetected overpayments to employees represent direct reductions in profitability and are, therefore, detrimental to the welfare of owners (proprietors, partners, or shareholders). Errors and inadequate records may also result in hefty financial penalties imposed by the Internal Revenue Service. To circumvent such adverse consequences, payroll personnel usually strive to achieve the highest possible degree of accuracy by following well-established policies and procedures and by applying a strict system of checks and double-checks.

GROSS PAY

Gross pay, which is the total amount of employee earnings before any deductions have been made by the employer, may be calculated in several ways. It may be based on either a salary or a wage, on either a time rate or a commission, or according to a combination of maintenance and incentive systems.

Salaries are either monthly or annual amounts that are paid employees. Most managerial personnel are paid salaries, as are many relatively low-level, non-union, white-collar workers. Nonmanagerial, blue-collar workers, on the other hand, especially those who belong to unions, are normally paid hourly wage rates. In preparing payrolls, we must prorate salaries to correspond with scheduled pay periods. If a company pays employees on a semimonthly basis (say the 10th and 25th of each month) and pays the accounting manager an annual salary of $42,000, we divide the salary by the number of pay periods to determine the manager's semimonthly gross pay.

$$\text{Months} \times \frac{\text{Monthly}}{\text{pay periods}} = \frac{\text{Number of}}{\text{semimonthly paydays}}$$

$$12 \times 2 = 24$$

$$\frac{\text{Annual}}{\text{salary}} \div \frac{\text{Number of}}{\text{paydays}} = \frac{\text{Gross pay per}}{\text{pay period}}$$

$$42,000 \div 24 = \$1,750$$

If, instead, the company schedules paydays for every other Friday throughout the year, we divide the salary by 26 (rather than 24) time periods.

$$\frac{\text{Number of weeks}}{\text{in a year}} \div \frac{\text{Number of weeks}}{\text{per pay period}} = \frac{\text{Number of biweekly}}{\text{pay periods}}$$

$$52 \div 2 = 26$$

$$\frac{\text{Annual}}{\text{salary}} \div \frac{\text{Number of}}{\text{paydays}} = \frac{\text{Gross pay}}{\text{per period}}$$

$$42,000 \div 26 = \$1,615.38$$

The difference in gross pay between semimonthly payments and biweekly payments arises because every month except February contains more than four weeks. When prorating salaries, therefore, we must make our calculations on the basis of 52 weeks in a year.

A **wage** is usually an hourly rate, with the specific rate depending on the importance and difficulty of the job, the availability of qualified applicants, the degree of responsibility that must be assumed, and the level of wages being paid for similar work at other companies. To compute gross pay based on an hourly wage, we simply multiply the number of regular hours worked by the rate, so that an employee who earns $4.45 per hour for a 40-hour week will gross $178.00.

Regular hours × Hourly rate = Gross pay

$$40 \times 4.45 = \$178.00$$

Employees who earn hourly wages — most supervisory personnel are not included in this category — are protected by the **Fair Labor Standards Act**. A main element of the Act provides that employers pay nonsupervisory employees time and one half the regular rate for overtime work; that is, for any hours worked in excess of 40 hours per week. Correspondingly, an employee who earns an hourly wage of $5.25 and who works a 48-1/2 hour week earns $7.875 (5.25 × 1.5 = 7.875) per overtime hour.

Regular pay: 40.0 × 5.25 =   210.00
Overtime pay: 8.5 × 7.875 =   66.94
  Gross pay: 48.5 $276.94

Overtime pay may begin with hours worked in excess of a 40-hour week, a 36-hour week, or whatever the standard workweek might be at a particular company, so long as employees receive at least the overtime rate for time worked in excess of 40 hours per week. Notice that having derived the overtime rate of $7.875 per hour, we do not discard the fractional cent. In fact, some agencies of the federal government carry hourly rates to four decimal places.

The word **piecework** applies to all arrangements in which an employer pays employees on the basis of the number of units (pieces) produced. For example, a worker may earn 30 cents for every shirt on which cuffs are sewn, so that an employee who attaches cuffs to 482 shirts within a 40-hour week will gross $144.60.

Units × Rate = Gross pay

482 × 0.30 = $144.60

Assuming that the employer is complying with the Fair Labor Standards Act, any employee engaging in piecework who works overtime must be paid one and one-half times the average hourly rate realized during the preceding 40-hour period. In the preceding example, the pieceworker who earned 30 cents per shirt would be paid a rate of $5.42-1/4 per hour for any overtime hours worked during that same week.

$$\frac{\text{Weekly}}{\text{piecework}} \div \frac{\text{Standards hours}}{\text{per week}} = \frac{\text{Hourly}}{\text{rate}}$$
earnings

144.60 ÷ 40 = $3.615

$$\begin{array}{c} \text{Hourly} \\ \text{rate} \end{array} \times \begin{array}{c} \text{Time and} \\ \text{one half} \end{array} = \begin{array}{c} \text{Overtime} \\ \text{rate} \end{array}$$

$$3.615 \times 1.5 = \$5.4225$$

Regardless of the number of units produced during the overtime period, the employee is entitled to the premium rate.

Employers may apply any of several such incentive plans with the objective of motivating employees to increase their productivity. Under what is called *differential piecework*, workers may earn different rates per unit, the rates applied depending on their individual level of output.

Units produced	Unit rate
Less than 120	33¢
120–139	37¢
140–160	43¢
More than 160	48¢

On the basis of this schedule of rates, a worker producing fewer than 120 units would earn 33 cents per unit or the prevailing minimum wage, whichever is higher. An employee producing 135 units in one eight-hour period would earn 37 cents each or $49.95 ($135 \times 0.37 = 49.95$). Many people, union leaders especially, consider differential piecework to be an unfair type of incentive system, reasoning that employees should receive equal pay for the initial units produced. They would argue in this situation, for instance, that the employee who produced 135 units should receive the same rate as anyone else for the first 120 units produced. As illustrated, however, the more productive employee earned 37 cents for each of the 135 units produced (not just for those in excess of 120), compared to 33 cents each for the slower worker.

Production bonuses are based on hourly wage rates, similar to the piecework differential, in that employees who reach or exceed prescribed levels of production are paid higher hourly rates for an entire shift than received by workers not reaching the targeted levels. If workers are earning a regular hourly rate of $6.50 per hour, for example, the employer may pay a 15 percent bonus to those people who produce at least 450 units in an eight-hour shift. If Janice Colby produces 425 units and Mark Steinhoff produces 452 units, the difference in pay for the one day is substantial.

Janice Colby: $425 < 450$

$$8 \text{ hours} \times 6.50 = \$52.00$$

Mark Steinhoff: 452 > 450

$$6.50 \times 1.15 = 7.475 \text{ per hour}$$

$$8 \text{ hours} \times 7.475 = \$59.80$$

For any overtime worked, Steinhoff would continue to benefit from the bonus rate.

Janice Colby: $6.50 \times 1\text{-}1/2 = \$9.75$ per hour

Mark Steinhoff: $7.475 \times 1\text{-}1/2 = \$11.2125$ per hour

The *production premium*, a third type of incentive system, rewards workers for producing the most units possible. Unlike the preceding bonus system, which fails to provide incentive for additional production once the targeted number of units is produced, production premiums enable workers to earn progressively higher hourly rates for every unit produced. If the standard production level is 85 units, for example, a worker who produces fewer units is paid at the standard hourly rate of $7.75. A worker who produces 94 units, on the other hand, earns 110.6 percent ($94 \div 85 = 110.6\%$) of the standard rate.

$$\frac{\text{Units produced}}{\text{Quota units}} \times \frac{\text{Standard}}{\text{pay}} = \frac{\text{Premium}}{\text{pay}}$$

$$\frac{94}{85} \times 7.75 = 8.57$$

$$\frac{\text{Hours}}{\text{worked}} \times \frac{\text{Hourly}}{\text{rate}} = \frac{\text{Gross}}{\text{daily pay}}$$

$$8 \times 8.57 = \$68.56$$

Calculator	
Entries	**Display**
9 4	94.
÷	94.
8 5	85.
×	1.105882353
7 . 7 5	7.75
×	8.570588236
8	8.
=	68.56470589

Every extra unit produced results in a higher hourly rate for the entire day, including any overtime that the employee may work.

Commission programs, under which employees receive a percentage of the price at which a product or service is sold, may consist of either a straight commission, a graduated commission, or a combination of a salary and a commission. An employee working under a *straight commission* of 6-1/2 percent, for example, would receive $1,209.98 on sales of $18,615.00.

$$\text{Sales} \times \text{Rate} = \text{Commission (gross pay)}$$

$$18,615 \times 0.065 = \$1,209.98$$

Under a *graduated commission* schedule, the employee might receive only 6 percent of the first $15,000 in sales and 6-1/2 percent of all sales in excess of that amount.

Sales × Rate = Commission

$$15,000 \times 0.06 = \quad 900.00$$
$$3,615 \times 0.065 = \underline{\quad 234.98}$$
$$\text{Gross pay} \quad \$1,134.98$$

Salary-commission combinations provide employees with the financial protection of a base salary and an opportunity to earn additional money as an incentive for generating extra sales. An employee might receive a base salary of $900 per month for the first $15,000 in sales, for instance, plus 7 percent of any sales beyond that amount, so that an employee with net sales of $18,615 would earn a gross monthly salary of $1,153.65.

	Sales	Rate	Gross pay
Salary	15,000	flat	900.00
Commission	3,615 × 0.07 =		253.05
	$18,615		$1,153.05

For a discussion of buying and selling commissions, see Chapter 6, page 110.

Tips received by employees are taxable and subject to payroll withholding. Those that are included in credit-card payments are easily determined, of course, and employees are required to report to their respective employers by the tenth of each month all cash tips received during the preceding month.

APPLICATION 1. What is the gross pay for a nonsupervisory employee who works a total of 46-1/2 hours during one week in a position that pays $6.15 per hour?

Hours × Rate = Gross pay

$$40.0 \times 6.15 = \quad 246.00$$
$$6.5 \times 9.225 = \underline{\quad 59.96}$$
$$\$305.96$$

APPLICATION 2. What is the gross pay of an employee who earns $5.115 per hour and works the following hours during a one-week period?

Days	Hours
Monday	8
Tuesday	6
Wednesday	8
Thursday	10
Friday	8

Hours × Rate = Gross pay
40 × 5.115 = $204.60

APPLICATION 3. What amount is earned by a postal employee who works ten hours on a given day if the regular rate for the job is $8.9096 and if double time is paid for time worked in excess of eight hours?

	Hours		Rate	Pay
Regular	8	×	8.9096	71.28
Overtime	2	×	17.8192	35.64
				$106.92

APPLICATION 4. For an employee who earns an annual salary of $22,500,

a. What is the semimonthly salary?

$$\frac{\text{Annual}}{\text{salary}} \div \frac{\text{Number of}}{\text{paydays}} = \frac{\text{Semimonthly}}{\text{salary}}$$

$$22,500 \div 24 = \$937.50$$

b. What is the biweekly salary?

$$\frac{\text{Annual}}{\text{salary}} \div \frac{\text{Number of}}{\text{paydays}} = \frac{\text{Biweekly}}{\text{salary}}$$

$$22,500 \div 26 = \$865.38$$

APPLICATION 5. If an employee earns $16,200 per year, what is the weekly salary?

$$\frac{\text{Annual}}{\text{salary}} \div \frac{\text{Number of}}{\text{weeks in year}} = \frac{\text{Weekly}}{\text{salary}}$$

$$16,200 \div 52 = \$311.54$$

APPLICATION 6. What is the biweekly pay of a nonmanagerial employee who produces 142 units during 40 hours of the first week and 156 units during

44 hours the second week (140 during the first 40 hours), assuming a piecework rate of $1.25 per unit?

$$\text{Overtime rate: } \frac{\text{Units} \times \text{Hourly rate}}{40 \text{ hours}} \cdot \frac{\text{Rate and}}{\text{one half}} = \frac{\text{Overtime}}{\text{rate}}$$

$$\frac{140 \times 1.25}{40} \cdot 1.5 = \$6.5625$$

	Hours × Rate		= Earnings
Regular time:	142 Units × 1.25	=	177.50 (first week)
Regular time:	140 Units × 1.25	=	175.00 (second week)
Overtime:	4 Hours × 6.5625	=	26.25 (second week)
			$378.75

APPLICATION 7. Under the following *differential piecework plan*, what is the monthly gross pay for an employee who produces 85 units?

Units produced	Unit rate
60 or less	$25.00
61 to 70	25.50
71 to 80	26.00
81 to 90	26.50
91 or more	27.00

Units × Rate = Gross pay
85 × 26.50 = $2,252.50

APPLICATION 8. Under a *production bonus program* that pays an additional 12 percent to employees who produce at least 650 units during 8 hours, what is the gross pay of an employee who receives a standard rate of $4.75 per hour and who produces 672 units during one eight-hour shift?

Rate × (1 + % bonus) × Hours = Gross pay
4.75 × 1.12 × 8 = $42.56

APPLICATION 9. Under a *production premium plan*, in which assembly line employees are paid $5.25 per hour for producing 1,760 units during an eight-hour shift, what is the hourly rate (rounded to 10ths of a cent) for one day in which they produced 2,116 units?

$$\frac{\text{Units produced}}{\text{Quota units}} \times \frac{\text{Standard}}{\text{pay}} = \frac{\text{Hourly}}{\text{rate}}$$

$$\frac{2,116}{1,760} \times 5.25 = \$6.312$$

APPLICATION 10. If a salesperson earns a monthly salary of $1,200 on the first $50,000 of sales and 3-1/2 percent of all sales in excess of that amount, how much money (gross) will a saleslady earn on $72,315.20 of sales during March?

Sales	Rate	Gross pay
50,000.00	flat	$1,200.00
22,315.20	0.035	781.03
$72,315.20		$1,981.03

PAYROLL DEDUCTIONS

Employees entering the job market are often startled to discover that their **net (take-home) pay** differs, sometimes drastically so, from their gross pay. Employers are normally forced to calculate and withhold (deduct) prescribed amounts of money for federal taxes, state taxes, Social Security contributions, and, in some cases, insurance premiums, charitable contributions, bond purchases, and union dues. Then, after matching certain employee contributions and calculating related payments of their own, employers are required to report and remit the accumulated amounts of money to the respective organizations and government agencies.

Federal taxes usually represent the most sizable payroll deduction, in connection with which employers must have every new employee complete a Form W-4 (Employee Withholding Allowance Certificate), making certain that the person already possesses or promptly secures a Social Security number. The amount of federal taxes to be withheld depends on the number of allowances claimed on Form W-4 and the amount of gross pay involved. In completing Form W-4, employees (usually those with part-time jobs) may request that no taxes be withheld from their wages during the current year if (1) they either had no taxes withheld the preceding year or received a full refund and (2) they do not expect to earn enough money during the current year to result in a tax obligation. Employees who qualify for such an exemption have the privilege of receiving every payday money that would otherwise have been withheld and sent to the IRS, and, of course, they need not file tax returns at the end of the tax year to claim refunds.

Employees must file W-4s each year that they seek exemptions from withholding or when they wish to change the number of allowances claimed. An employee with four dependents may list three or fewer (even zero) allowances on the W-4, for example, to assure a refund at the end of the year rather than a balance-due amount. Conversely, a person may specify allowances on the W-4 in excess of the actual number of exemptions — to reduce the amounts withheld every payday. An individual who has just signed a mortgage for a new house, for instance, can expect to pay several thousand dollars in interest payments — to be claimed as a tax-deductible expense which, in turn, reduces the person's tax obligation.

Rather than permitting the government to collect an excessive amount of taxes, money on which the government will not pay interest, the taxpayer may complete the worksheet on the back of Form W-4 to determine the number of allowances that may be used to compute the taxes withheld each payday. If the worksheet figures show that ten exemptions may be claimed, for example, the employer will withhold less tax on the basis of ten exemptions and the employee will report the actual number of exemptions on the end-of-year tax returns. In this manner, an end-of-year refund will be reduced significantly or completely avoided. Exemptions may include the taxpayer, the taxpayer's spouse, any dependent children (provided they are under 19 and earn less than $1,040 a year or are over 18 and attend school full time), and certain other relatives for whom the taxpayer provides support.

Employers may figure the amount of taxes to be withheld from employee paychecks with application of either wage-bracket tables or percentage tables. Selected *wage-bracket tables* are included in Appendix A, Table 14.1. Computing the biweekly tax withheld for a married person who lists three dependents and earns an annual salary of $32,000, for example, results in federal tax withholding of $180:

$$\frac{\text{Annual}}{\text{salary}} \div \frac{\text{Pay}}{\text{periods}} = \frac{\text{Gross}}{\text{pay}}$$

$$32,000 \div 26 = 1,230.77$$

Biweekly pay in Table 14.1 = Tax withheld

1,230.77 for three allowances = $180.00

Consulting Column 3 (number of withholding allowances claimed) in Table 14.1, we proceed downward to the row reading "At least 1,220 but less than 1,240."

Notice at the bottom of the same page that for people receiving biweekly pay greater than $2,220, employers must withhold a specified amount plus 37 percent of earnings in excess of that figure. If a married person with five allowances has a biweekly income of $2,700, for example, the employer must withhold $652.60.

Fixed amount	$475.00
0.37(2,700 − 2,220)	177.60
Tax withheld	$652.60

For persons claiming more than 10 allowances, employers must reduce the taxable income by the following amounts before consulting the table.

Payroll period	One allowance
Weekly	$20.00
Biweekly	40.00
Semimonthly	43.33
Monthly	86.67

To illustrate this procedure, let's assume that a married employee with semi-monthly earnings of $2,375 claims 12 allowances. We subtract from gross income $43.33 for each of the two extra ($12 - 10 = 2$) allowances and take the remainder to Column 10 of the tax for "MARRIED Persons — SEMIMONTHLY Payroll Period."

$$\frac{\text{One allowance}}{\text{semimonthly}} \times \frac{\text{Number of}}{\text{allowances} - 10} = \frac{\text{Income}}{\text{adjustment}}$$

$$43.33 \times (12 - 10) = 86.66$$

$$\frac{\text{Gross}}{\text{income}} - \text{Adjustment} = \frac{\text{Taxable}}{\text{income}}$$

$$2,375.00 - 86.66 = 2,288.34$$

$$\frac{\text{Taxable}}{\text{income}} \text{ to } \frac{\text{Table 14.1}}{\text{Column } n = 10} = \frac{\text{Tax}}{\text{Withheld}}$$

$$2,288.34 \quad \text{Row } 2,280\text{--}2,300 = \$395.00$$

Because the tax rates are subject to change from year to year, the most recently issued tables should be consulted for current figures.

The *percentage method*, which is especially applicable to computerized payroll computations, provides an alternative approach for determining the amount of federal tax to be withheld from an employee's gross pay. Using the *Percentage Method Withholding Schedules* in Table 14.2 of Appendix A, we (a) multiply the dollar amount by the number of allowances claimed, (b) subtract the resulting product from the employee's gross pay, and (c) apply the difference to the appropriate schedule. For a married employee who earns biweekly pay of $840 and reports three allowances the tax to be withheld is computed as follows:

(a) $\frac{\text{Number of}}{\text{allowances}} \times \frac{\text{One withholding}}{\text{allowance}} = \frac{\text{Total}}{\text{deduction}}$

$$3 \times 40.00 = 120.00$$

(b) Gross pay − Deduction = Taxable amount

$$840.00 - 120.00 = 720.00$$

(c) Table 14.2 Biweekly — MARRIED person

720.00 =	34.68
0.17(720.00 − 385.00) =	56.95
Tax withheld	$91.63

For wage-bracket and percentage-method tables pertaining to monthly, quarterly, and annual pay periods, you should secure from the Internal Revenue Service the current edition of *Circular E, Employer's Tax Guide.*

State income tax, in those states where they are collected, may be computed in a number of different ways, sometimes as a percentage of the federal tax and sometimes from a completely separate schedule. In Arizona, for example, an employer must withhold for state taxes either 10 or 15 percent of the amount of applicable federal tax — the percentage depending on the level of an employee's gross pay.

The **Federal Insurance Contributions Act (FICA)**, more commonly known as **Social Security**, provides retirement benefits to eligible people beginning at age 65 (or age 62 for reduced benefits), disability benefits to people under age 65 who are unable to work, survivor benefits to family members of deceased workers, and, through the Medicare program, health insurance to people over 65 years of age. To cover the costs of these programs, which are increasing steadily in correlation with the extended life spans of U.S. citizens, employers must not only withhold progressively higher percentages from the pay of employees, but must also match (with company funds) the amounts withheld.

To illustrate, an employer paying $2,125 to a middle manager for the current pay period must withhold 7.15 percent of the employee's gross pay and remit that amount to the federal government.

$$\frac{\text{Gross}}{\text{pay}} \times \frac{\text{Current}}{\text{FICA rate}} = \frac{\text{Employee}}{\text{contribution}}$$

$$2,125 \times 0.0715 = \$151.94$$

Employees earning less than $42,600 per year pay 7.15 percent on all income received during a tax year. For employees earning more than that amount, employers withhold contributions on only the first $42,600. If an employee receives gross pay of $1,730.77 on December 15, bringing year-to-date (YTD) income to $43,269.25, the FICA contribution is withheld on only $1,061.52 of the semimonthly gross pay.

$$\frac{\text{Gross}}{\text{pay (YTD)}} - \frac{\text{Withholding}}{\text{limit}} = \frac{\text{Nontaxable}}{\text{income}}$$

$$43,269.25 - 42,600.00 = 669.25$$

$$\frac{\text{Gross pay}}{\text{current period}} - \frac{\text{Nontaxable}}{\text{income}} = \frac{\text{Taxable}}{\text{income}}$$

$$1,730.77 - 669.25 = 1,061.52$$

$$\frac{\text{Taxable}}{\text{income}} \times \frac{\text{FICA}}{\text{rate}} = \frac{\text{FICA}}{\text{contribution}}$$

$$1,061.52 \times 0.0715 = \$75.90$$

Any additional income during the same tax year, moreover, would be free of FICA deductions.

In Appendix A, Table 14.3, the Social Security Employee Tax Table, provides an alternative method for computing FICA contributions that is especially useful for an employer with only a few employees. Because this table includes FICA amounts for only the first $100 of income, we must rely on the multiples at the bottom right corner of the second page. To compute FICA on weekly gross pay of $923.08, for example, we combine the taxes on $900 (amounts in multiples of $100) with the table figure for $23.08 (second column of wages on the first page between 23.05 and 23.20):

Gross pay	FICA
900.00	63.45
23.08	1.63
$923.08	$65.08

For gross pay in excess of $1,000 (say $1,515.25), we apply the $70.50 figure to the first $1,000 and compute the balance as previously illustrated.

Gross pay	FICA
1,000.00	70.50
500.00	35.25
15.25	1.08
$1,515.25	$106.83

Employers must match the FICA contributions that they withhold from the amounts earned by their employees, the details of which are discussed later in this same chapter.

FICA contributions apply to tips only if the amounts received are judged to include regular wages. For a person who reports a significant amount of tips in relation to a very low salary, for example, the employer must classify a portion of the person's total income (equivalent to the current minimum wage) as wages that are subject to FICA withholding. Self-employed persons, because there is no matching of funds, must make FICA contributions at the relatively high rate of 10 percent.

APPLICATION 1. Using the appropriate tax table, determine the amount of federal tax an employer should withhold from the biweekly gross pay of a married employee who earns an annual salary of $18,500 and claims five allowances.

$$\frac{\text{Annual}}{\text{salary}} \div \frac{\text{Pay}}{\text{periods}} = \frac{\text{Gross}}{\text{pay}}$$

$$18,500 \div 26 = 711.54$$

Biweekly pay in Table 14.1 = Tax withheld
711.54 for five allowances = $55

APPLICATION 2. With reference to the preceding example, what amount of federal taxes should be withheld if the employee, as a result of large interest payments on a newly acquired home, claims 13 allowances?

$$\frac{\text{One allowance}}{\text{biweekly}} \times \frac{\text{Number of}}{\text{allowances} - 10} = \frac{\text{Income}}{\text{adjustment}}$$

$$40 \times (13 - 10) = 120$$

$$\frac{\text{Gross}}{\text{income}} - \text{Adjustment} = \frac{\text{Taxable}}{\text{income}}$$

$$711.54 - 120.00 = 591.54$$

$$\frac{\text{Taxable}}{\text{income}} \text{ to Table 14.1} = \frac{\text{Tax}}{\text{withheld}}$$

$$591.54 \; \frac{\text{Column 10}}{\text{Row 580–600}} = \$10$$

APPLICATION 3. Using the percentage method, calculate the amount of federal income tax that an employer must withhold from the weekly gross pay of a single person who earns a weekly salary of $425 and claims five allowances.

(a) $$\frac{\text{Number of}}{\text{allowances}} \times \frac{\text{One withholding}}{\text{allowance}} = \frac{\text{Taxable}}{\text{deduction}}$$

$$5 \times 20 = 100$$

(b) Gross pay − Deduction = Taxable amount

$$425 - 100 = 325$$

(c) Table 14.2 Weekly-single person

$$325 = 42.32$$
$$0.25(325 - 292) = \underline{8.25}$$
$$\$50.57$$

APPLICATION 4. Using the percentage method and a rate of 7.15 percent, determine the amount of FICA contribution that an employer must withhold from an employee's gross pay of $1,850, which brings the employee's year-to-date gross to $42,550.

$$\frac{\text{Gross}}{\text{pay}} \times \frac{\text{FICA}}{\text{rate}} = \frac{\text{FICA}}{\text{withheld}}$$

$$1,850 \times 0.0715 = \$132.28$$

APPLICATION 5. Building on the preceding example, recalling that the maximum taxable income is $42,600 and assuming an identical amount of gross pay each payday, what amount of FICA contributions must the employer withhold the following payday?

$$\frac{\text{Maximum}}{\text{taxable}} - \frac{\text{YTD earnings}}{\text{previous}} = \frac{\text{Taxable}}{\text{amount}}$$
$$\text{amount} \qquad \text{paycheck} \qquad \text{remaining}$$

$$42,600 - 42,550 = 50$$

$$\frac{\text{Taxable}}{\text{amount}} \times \frac{\text{FICA}}{\text{rate}} = \frac{\text{FICA}}{\text{withheld}}$$

$$50 \times 0.0715 = \$3.58$$

Net income is the balance due the employee after all deductions have been made, an amount commonly referred to as an employee's "take-home pay." Employers usually provide employees with detailed information on paycheck stubs regarding current and year-to-date figures, and they are required by law to present employees with W-2 statements of earnings and deductions by January 31 of the following year.

EMPLOYER CONTRIBUTIONS

The gross pay of employees represents the biggest payroll outlay for employers, of course, but the obligation does not end there. Employers must match the amounts withheld for FICA contributions, and they must pay unemployment taxes.

The **FICA contributions of employers** are identical to those of employees. If an employee earns a gross income of $625.30, for example, the total FICA payment to the government is $89.42.

$$\frac{\text{Gross}}{\text{pay}} \times \frac{\text{FICA}}{\text{rate}} = \frac{\text{FICA}}{\text{contribution}}$$

$$
\begin{aligned}
625.30 \times 0.0715 &= \ \ 44.71 \ \text{(employee)} \\
\text{Matching funds} &= \ \ \underline{44.71} \ \text{(employer)} \\
&\quad \ \ \$89.42
\end{aligned}
$$

The maximum amount of FICA contribution for any employee during a one-year period, therefore, is $6,091.80.

$$\frac{\substack{\text{Maximum} \\ \text{taxable} \\ \text{income}}}{} \times \frac{\text{FICA}}{\text{rate}} = \frac{\text{FICA}}{\text{contribution}}$$

$$
\begin{aligned}
42,600 \times 0.0715 &= \ 3{,}045.90 \ \text{(employee)} \\
\text{Matching funds} &= \ \underline{3{,}045.90} \ \text{(employer)} \\
&\quad \ \$6{,}091.80
\end{aligned}
$$

The rate of increase in the steadily climbing FICA percents will depend primarily on the reduced number of people entering the system each year as contrasted with the expanding number of participants becoming eligible for benefits.

Additionally, businesses must pay **federal unemployment taxes (FUT)** and **state unemployment taxes (SUT)**. The FUT rate at the time of the preparation of this book is 6.2 percent of the first $7,000 of an employee's gross pay. Because the federal government permits employers to reduce this rate by a state unemployment tax rate of up to 5.4 percent, however, the effective FUT is 0.8 percent.

$$
\begin{aligned}
\text{Federal Unemployment Tax (FUT)} &\quad 6.2\% \\
\text{State Unemployment Tax (SUT)} &\ \underline{-5.4\%} \\
\text{Effective FUT} &\quad 0.8\%
\end{aligned}
$$

For an employee earning gross pay of $1,220 in January, for example, the unemployment taxes are

$$
\begin{aligned}
\text{FUT: } 1{,}220 \times 0.008 &= \ \ \ 9.76 \\
\text{SUT: } 1{,}220 \times 0.054 &= \ \underline{65.88} \\
&\quad \ \$75.64
\end{aligned}
$$

If, instead, an employee received $1,220 on the second payday in April, bringing the year-to-date earnings to $7,320, both FUT and SUT would be payable by the employer on only $900 of that amount.

$$\frac{\text{Gross pay}}{\text{(YTD)}} - \frac{\text{Withholding}}{\text{limit}} = \frac{\text{Nontaxable}}{\text{income}}$$

$$7,320 - 7,000 = 320$$

$$\frac{\text{Gross pay}}{\text{current period}} - \frac{\text{Nontaxable}}{\text{income}} = \frac{\text{Taxable}}{\text{income}}$$

$$1,220 - 320 = 900$$

$$\frac{\text{Taxable}}{\text{income}} \times \frac{\text{Applicable}}{\text{rate}} = \frac{\text{Tax}}{\text{amount}}$$

FUT: $900 \times 0.008 =$ 7.20
SUT: $900 \times 0.054 =$ <u>48.60</u>
$55.80

Although no FUT or SUT is withheld from employee paychecks, employers naturally attribute such outlays to the total cost of wages and salaries.

APPLICATION 1. Using the percentage method for computing FICA, determine the total employee-employer contribution for gross pay of $225.15.

$$\frac{\text{Gross}}{\text{pay}} \times \frac{\text{FICA}}{\text{rate}} = \frac{\text{FICA}}{\text{contribution}}$$

$225.15 \times 0.0715 =$ 16.10 (employee)
Matching funds = <u>16.10</u> (employer)
$32.20

APPLICATION 2. Using the FICA table, determine the total employee-employer contribution for gross pay of $417.24.

Table 14.3 for $400.00 = $28.20
for <u>17.24</u> = <u>1.22</u>
$417.24 $29.42

APPLICATION 3. What amount of FUT and SUT must an employer pay on an employee's gross earnings of $115?

SUT: $115 \times 0.054 =$ 6.21
FUT: $115 \times 0.008 =$ <u>.92</u>
$7.13

APPLICATION 4. Keeping the $7,000 maximum taxable income limit in mind, determine the FUT and SUT obligation for an employer with gross pay of

$245.92, which brings the individual's gross year-to-date earnings to $7,101.20.

$$\frac{\text{Gross}}{\text{pay}} - (\text{YTD} - 7,000) = \frac{\text{Taxable}}{\text{amount}}$$

$$245.92 - (7,101.20 - 7,000.) = 144.72$$

$$\frac{\text{Taxable}}{\text{amount}} \times \text{Rate} = \text{Tax}$$

SUT: $144.72 \times 0.054 = 7.81$
FUT: $144.72 \times 0.008 = \underline{1.16}$
$\$8.97$

Employers must deposit at banks that have been designated by the federal government to be official depositories all taxes that are withheld and all matching funds. Deposits may range from as frequently as every fourth day to as infrequently as every three months — depending on the amounts of money involved. (See *Circular E, Employer's Tax Guide*.)

PAYROLL RECORDS

When preparing a payroll for several employees, we bring all of the related information together on a record similar to the one illustrated in Figure 14–1. Whether processing payroll manually or with a computer, the totals should be double-checked to assure accuracy. Subtract from total gross pay the totals at the bottom of the deduction columns and compare the difference with total net pay.

Gross pay	1,089.96
Federal taxes	−86.00
State taxes	−8.60
FICA Contribution	−77.75
Other	−12.50
Net pay	$905.11

Also double-check to make certain that the sum of total regular pay and total overtime pay equal total gross pay.

Regular wages:	948.80
Overtime wages:	141.16
Gross wages:	$1,089.96

The total amount of FICA due the government from this one pay period is $155.50, double the amount withheld from employee wages because the employer's contribution must be included.

Employee name	Hours worked								Regular time			Overtime			Gross pay	Deductions				Net pay
	M	T	W	T	F	S	S	Tot	Hours	Rate	Wages	Hours	Rate	Wages		F. tax	State	FICA	Other	
Elbert T. Davis	8	8	8	8	8			40	40	4.15	166.00				166.00	16.00	1.60	12.16		136.24
J. Mark Glasser	8	9	8	7	8	3		43	40	3.95	158.00	3	5.925	17.78	175.78	10.00	1.00	12.84	2.50	149.44
Susan L. Johns	8	10	9	10	8			45	40	5.15	206.00	5	7.725	38.63	244.63	29.00	2.90	17.25	5.00	190.48
Rudy S. Oliver	9	8	9	10	10			46	40	4.15	166.00	6	6.225	37.35	203.35	11.00	1.10	14.34	2.50	174.41
John F. Peters	10	8	11	8	9	2		48	40	3.95	158.00	8	5.925	47.40	205.40	14.00	1.40	14.48	2.50	173.02
Ruth J. Simmons	8	10	6					24	24	3.95	94.80				94.80	6.00	0.60	6.68		81.52
Totals											948.80			141.16	1089.96	86.00	8.60	77.75	12.50	905.11

Figure 14.1
Payroll Record

Figure 14.2
Change Tally

Employee	Net pay	$100	$50	$20	$10	$5	$1	50c	25c	10c	5c	1c
Elbert T. Davis	136.24	1		1	1	1	1			2		4
J. Mark Glasser	149.44	1		2		1	4		1	1	1	4
Susan L. Johns	190.48	1	1	2					1	2		3
Rudy S. Oliver	174.41	1	1	1			4		1	1	1	1
John F. Peters	173.02	1	1	1			3					2
Ruth J. Simmons	81.52		1	1	1		1	1				2
Totals	905.11	5	4	8	2	2	13	1	3	6	2	16

CASH PAYMENTS

Some companies, ranging in size from a fishing boat owner to the giant K Mart Corporation and military establishments, pay their employees in cash. Also, in what is termed the "underground economy," many billions of dollars are paid in cash each year as a way of avoiding detection of taxable income by the IRS and as a way of avoiding detection by the FBI of illegal transactions. Whatever the situation, the cash payment of employee wages requires the development of change tallies and change slips.

A **change tally**, as illustrated in Figure 14.2, divides net pay into the highest possible denominations of money; for example, two tens are never substituted for a twenty dollar bill, and five ones are never substituted for a five dollar bill. If the system is to work most efficiently, the "breaking" of large bills into relatively small ones must be refused or accomplished from a separate money source.

A **change slip** is then prepared, as illustrated in Figure 14.3, by transferring from the change tally the total number of bills and coins that are required and by computing the total values involved.

Figure 14.3
Change slip

Denomination	Number	Amount
100.00	5	500.00
50.00	4	200.00
20.00	8	160.00
10.00	2	20.00
5.00	2	10.00
1.00	13	13.00
50¢	1	.50
25¢	3	.75
10¢	6	.60
5¢	2	.10
1¢	16	.16
Total		905.11

To double-check the accuracy of these figures, we compare the total net pay as shown in the change tally with the total value of money required as shown in the change slip.

$1,611.71 = $1,611.71

Having balanced these two worksheets, the employer may approach payday with only $1,611.71 in cash, rather than having to maintain a much larger reserve to make certain that all payments can be made.

EXERCISES (as directed by your instructor)

14-1 Define the following terms:

  a. Gross pay
  b. Net pay
  c. FICA
  d. FUT
  e. SUT

14-2 If an employee who is protected by the Fair Labor Standards Act works 45 hours during a one-week period at a regular rate of $4.25 per hour, what is the person's gross pay?

14-3 What is the difference between a wage and a salary?

14-4 How many paydays are there each year when employees are paid

  a. Monthly?
  b. Semimonthly?
  c. Biweekly?

14-5 What is the biweekly gross pay of an employee who earns $32,500 per year?

14-6 What is the semimonthly gross pay of an employee who earns $27,125 per year?

14-7 If an employee is paid 15-1/2 cents for each unit produced, what will be the person's gross pay for a 40-hour week in which 1,064 units are produced?

14-8 What is the overtime rate for an employee who produces 1,250 units during a 40-hour week at a per-unit rate of 16 cents?

14-9 Assuming a minimum-wage requirement of $3.35 per hour under the Fair Labor Standards Act, what is the gross pay of a person who produces 531 units during a 40-hour week at a piecework rate of 25 cents per unit?

14-10 Under the following *differential piecework* rates, what is the daily gross pay earned by a worker who produces (a) 600 units? (b) 491 units? (c) 540 units?

Units produced	Unit rate
Less than 500	3-1/2¢
501–550	3-3/4¢
551–600	4¢
More than 600	4-1/4¢

14-11 Referring to the same schedule of *differential piecework* rates, and assuming that the minimum wage is ignored, what is the gross pay of an employee who produces 502 units during an eight-hour shift and then produces 55 units during the ninth hour?

14-12 Under a *production bonus plan*, employees earn a standard rate of $5.25 per hour plus an 8 percent bonus if they produce at least 315 units during any eight-hour shift. What is the gross pay for this one day for the following three employees?

a. Marty Robinson, 299 units
b. Rhonda Van Patten, 300 units
c. Leslie R. Stokes, 325 units

14-13 If an employer offers a *production premium* for all units produced during an eight-hour shift in excess of 105 units, what is the gross pay of the following five employees?

Employee	Hourly rate	Units produced
a. Ralph Sweringen	$4.25	112
b. Donald C. Cooper	4.15-1/2	121
c. Elizabeth J. Rogers	4.15-1/2	123
d. Joyce C. Missura	4.25	101
e. Mario D. Campagna	4.25	132

14-14 At a commission rate of 6-1/4 percent, what is the gross pay of an employee with monthly sales of $35,200?

14-15 If an employee has gross pay of $22,000 annually, plus a commission of 2 percent on all monthly sales in excess of $75,000, what is the person's gross pay for February on $86,110 in sales?

14-16 If an employee with biweekly gross pay of $711.54 has net pay of $391.35, what is the total amount of deductions?

14-17 Using the applicable wage-bracket tax table for four allowances, compute the federal tax that is to be withheld from a married person's weekly gross pay of $425.

14-18 Using the percentage method of computation, determine the amount of federal tax to be withheld from a single employee's semimonthly gross pay of $860 — assuming that only one allowance is claimed.

14-19 Under what circumstances may an employee with four exemptions claim more than that number of allowances when computing the amount of federal tax to be withheld?

14-20 Under what circumstances might an employee wish to claim fewer allowances for federal payroll tax purposes than the actual number of exemptions claimed on the end-of-year tax return?

14-21 What amount of federal tax must an employer withhold from a married employee's biweekly gross pay of $1,423.08, assuming that the employee has filed a W-4 calling for 13 allowances? (Use Table 14.1, rather than the percentage method.)

14-22 If a married person with weekly gross pay of $461.54 claims six allowances on a W-4, what amount of federal tax must be withheld?

14-23 Assuming a current FICA rate of 7.15 percent, what contribution should be withheld from the biweekly gross pay of $875.12?

14-24 If an employee earns gross pay of $750.75, bringing the year-to-date earnings to $42,810.80, what amount of FICA should be withheld?

14-25 If, prior to the current pay period, an employee had YTD earnings of $45,000, what amount of FICA must be withheld from gross earnings of $1,225 in the current (December 1 through 15) pay period?

14-26 Using the applicable table, determine the amount of FICA to be withheld on biweekly gross pay of $628.30.

14-27 If a person receives $225 in tips during a 40-hour week, combined with a weekly salary of $70, what amount of FICA should be withheld, assuming a legal minimum wage of $3.35 per hour?

14-28 Using the appropriate table, determine the amount of FICA contribution that an employer must deduct from an employee's gross pay of $395.20, an amount that brings YTD earnings to $42,350.75.

14-29 Building on the situation in the preceding problem, use the table to determine the amount of FICA to be withheld from this employee's gross pay of $395.20 the following payday.

14-30 If an employee earns $1,350.12 of semimonthly pay, bringing the individual's YTD earnings to $3,395.15, what is the total employer-employee FICA contribution this pay period for the one employee?

14-31 What is the total employer-employee FUT and SUT on an employee's gross income of $335.65, an amount that brings the person's YTD earnings to $4,210.19?

14-32 What FUT and SUT must an employer pay on an employee's gross earnings of $235.18, an amount that brings the person's YTD earnings to $7,125.16?

14-33 Complete the weekly payroll record below. Double-check the totals.

	Employee	Days of Week							Total hours	Regular		
		M	T	W	T	F	S	S		Hours	Rate	Wages
1	Robert D. Ball	8	8	8	8	8					5.75	
2	Walter A. Edwards	8	10	9	10	8					5.50	
3	Ernest J. Nestor	8	9	8	7	8	3				5.255	
4	Louis D. Slayton	10	8	11	8	9	2				6.05	
5	Greg R. Whittier	8	8	8	8	8					6.15	
6	Janet J. Ziegler	9	8	9	10	10					5.75	
	Totals											

	Overtime		Wages	Gross pay	Fed. tax	State tax	FICA	Other	Net pay
	Hours	Rate							
1						3.24			
2						2.76		11.00	
3						2.16			
4						3.36			
5						3.12		16.10	
6						3.12			
	Totals								

Ball is single; Edwards, Nestor, and Zeigler are married with two dependents each; Slayton is married with three dependents; and Whittier is single with two dependents.

14-34 Complete the following weekly payroll record and double-check the results.

	Employee	Gross sales	Returns	Net sales	Commission rate	Gross income
1	Brenda S. Abbott	4,131.21	212.00		3%	
2	Joseph L. Jarvis	4,980.00			4%	
3	L. James Rush	5,165.70	37.95		4%	
4	Randy C. Scott	4,742.23	16.48		4%	
5	Barbara L. Smith	5,738.00			5%	
6	Constance Thomas	5,160.00	112.50		4%	
	Totals					

	Fed. tax	State tax	FICA cont.	Other	Net income
1		0.90			
2		1.95			
3		2.10		18.75	
4		2.85			
5		3.90		25.50	
6		1.35			
Totals					

Abbott and Scott are both single; Jarvis, Rush, and Smith are married, and each has two exemptions; and Thomas is married with four exemptions.

14-35 Complete the following change talley and change slip and double-check the totals.

Change Talley

Employee	Net pay	$100	$50	$20	$10	$5	$1	50¢	25¢	10¢	5¢	1¢
Carla S. Cohen	188.92											
Samual Gomez	189.85											
Susan L. Lashyn	211.08											
Joyce L. Maldin	167.39											
Jane M. Muncie	192.75											
Richard M. Price	189.16											
Ralph T. Snyder	201.12											
Calvin S. Taylor	175.45											
Totals												

Change slip

Denomination	Number	Amount
100.00		
50.00		
20.00		
10.00		
5.00		
1.00		
0.50		
0.25		
0.10		
0.05		
0.01		
Total		

15   Inventory Valuation

LEARNING OBJECTIVES

As preparation for the discussion of financial statements presented in subsequent chapters, the materials here will enable you to

- describe the three common categories of inventories
- maintain and interpret inventory records
- make a distinction between perpetual and periodic inventory records
- determine the value of ending inventories on the basis of either *cost* or the *lower of cost or market*
- apply specific identity, average cost, FIFO, and LIFO in the valuation of ending inventories
- estimate the value of ending inventories

The word **inventory** may relate to any of the following categories:

1. Raw materials — materials that are to be used in a manufacturing process.
2. Goods in process — materials presently being used to manufacture products.
3. Finished goods — products that are complete and ready for sale.

Although accountants may identify the value of the first two groups by simply checking the amounts paid for the materials, a determination of the value of finished products presents them with several options: Are the products to be valued at cost or market? Should valuation be on the basis of specific identity? a weighted average? first-in, first out? last-in, first out? Whatever the approach, the objective of inventory valuation is to assign a dollar value to finished products, products that a business has either manufactured for sale or has purchased from other companies for resale.

INVENTORY CONTROL

People within an inventory-control department perform the essential function of keeping track of a company's products — those products that are sold immediately upon their completion and those that are placed in inventory for later sale. Most companies maintain inventories of finished products for two reasons. First, a business must have products available when customers want them or risk losing sales to competitors who do have stock on hand. Second, business managers may assure a stable work force by producing to inventory during slack periods; that is, by producing and storing products for which orders have not yet been received as an alternative to furloughing workers and attempting to recall them when business improves.

Perpetual inventory records provide current information at all times regarding product availability. For example, an employee in the distribution department of Valley Canning Company may determine immediately whether 2,500 cases of 48/1 Diet Rite cling peaches are available for shipment to Safeway Stores in Oakland, California. If that number of cases is available, the employee reserves them for Safeway Stores and effectively reduces the number of available cases by 2,500.

Periodic inventory control systems are those in which employees rely on an actual count of products on hand — on either a daily, weekly, monthly, or yearly basis or a combination of time intervals. For example, an employee at an oil refinery might be charged with recording the daily readings of gauges that measure the quantities of fuel remaining in a series of storage tanks. Then, as a double check, a different employee may be required to climb to the top of each tank periodically to determine firsthand whether the actual amounts of fuel on hand are identical to those recorded remotely by the first employee.

Most businesses now rely on computers for the maintenance of perpetual inventory records and on physical counts of inventory for auditing purposes. Whether using computers or making manual entries, the concept is the same as illustrated in Figure 15.1. The number of finished products received into inventory is added to the preceding balance, and the number of products sold is subtracted.

The recording of its own purchase order number indicates that this company is purchasing thermostats from suppliers (rather than manufacturing them) for eventual resale to customers. Notice also that the time period was started with a 73-unit balance, in that the January 12 purchase of 140 units resulted in an

Figure 15.1

Perpetual inventory record

PRODUCT			WAREHOUSE		
NUMBER	DESCRIPTION		NUMBER	LOCATION	
A19FBC-1	DUAL BULB THERMO		G-12	OAK BROOK IL	
DATE OF TRANSACTION	PURCHASE ORDER NO.	QUANTITY RECEIVED	SHIPPING ORDER NO.	QUANTITY SHIPPED	INVENTORY BALANCE
01-12-86	H-23109	140			213
02-05-86			T-1625	50	163
03-15-86			T-1697	65	98
04-12-86	H-23211	100			198
06-05-86			T-1758	40	158
08-15-86			T-1785	50	108
10-04-86			T-1811	60	48
10-25-86	H-2532	150			198
11-15-86			T-1902	50	148

inventory balance of 213 units (73 + 140 = 213). Knowing the number of units remaining is only part of the process, however; we must also determine the value of the stock on hand at the end of every accounting period.

COST OR MARKET

Referring to Figure 15.1 and assuming that the 50-unit sale on November 15 was the last transaction during the year at a retailing establishment, the retailer may value each of the 148 units remaining at either (1) cost or (2) the lower of cost or market. A new business may use either of the two methods but may not switch from one method to the other without prior permission from the Internal Revenue Service. The *cost* is the price that the retailer paid for each unit, after any discounts were allowed, whereas *market* is the current or replacement price of the thermostats.

If all three purchases of thermostats listed in Figure 15.1 were from a manufacturer at $42.65 each, for example, compared to a current (replacement) price of $44.25, the retailer would value the remaining 148 cases at the lower of the two figures.

Unsold units	Cost	Market	Value
148	$42.65	$44.25	$6,312.20

In some businesses, accountants may also use market prices for inventory valuation. For instance, stockbrokers may value stocks, bonds, and other securities that they hold at the end of an accounting period by either cost, market, or the lower of cost or market. As discussed later in this chapter, however, we may not use market (current) prices in all situations.

APPLICATION 1. On the basis of the lower of cost or market, determine the value of the following items remaining in inventory at the end of the month.

Code	Size	Weight	Quantity	Cost	Market	Value
S158	6/10	45	115	15.00	14.30	1,644.50
S159	6/10	45	205	14.80	14.30	2,931.50
S1034	12/5	45	110	13.75	14.25	1,512.50
S166	12/50	43	315	15.70	16.40	4,945.50
C1903	12/50	43	90	11.00	11.30	990.00
Totals			835			12,024.00

APPLICATION 2. Using the inventory records in Application 1, determine the end-of-month value of the 835 cases of foodstuffs on the basis of cost.

Quantity		Cost		Value
115	×	15.00	=	1,725.00
205	×	14.80	=	3,034.00
110	×	13.75	=	1,512.50
315	×	15.70	=	4,945.50
90	×	11.00	=	990.00
835				12,207.00

SPECIFIC IDENTITY

Specific identity, as the term denotes, identifies each item as opposed to categorizing inventory items and averaging their costs or prices. Accountants normally use a specific identity approach to inventory valuation for large-ticket items; that is, for products that carry relatively high prices. An automobile dealer would value the end-of-period inventory by using the exact cost or market (price) figures for each automobile, for example, rather than grouping each class of car and estimating their collective value. Whether *cost* or the *lower of cost or market* is used would depend, as previously mentioned, on whichever method the dealer selected to begin with or on the particular method selected and approved by the Internal Revenue Service. Inventory valuation by *specific identity* is practical only when the identity of products can be maintained such as with automobiles, refrigerators, and computers — all of which carry identifying serial numbers.

AVERAGE COST

The average-cost method of inventory valuation bases the cost of inventories by an average of the cost for producing them or of the prices paid for purchasing them. Rather than trying to maintain the specific identity of batches of thermostats, for example, a manufacturer or retailer may simply average their costs. Assuming the costs for each purchase of thermostats illustrated in Figure 15.1, we may determine the average cost.

Purchase date	Number of units		Unit cost		Total value
01-12-86	140	×	39.95	=	5,593.00
04-12-86	100	×	41.50	=	4,150.00
10-25-86	150	×	42.65	=	6,397.50
	390				16,140.50

Total value ÷ Units = Average cost

$16,140.50 ÷ 390 = $41.39

Further assuming an end-of-year count of 148 units, we have

$$\frac{\text{Inventory}}{\text{balance}} \times \frac{\text{Average}}{\text{cost}} = \frac{\text{Inventory}}{\text{value}}$$

$$148 \quad \times \quad 41.39 \quad = \$6,125.72$$

After deriving the average cost per unit by dividing total value by the number of units purchased, we multiply the number of units remaining unsold at the end of the accounting period (148) by the average cost per unit ($41.39), giving us the value (based on average cost) of the inventoried (stored) thermostats. The average-cost approach to inventory valuation is applicable to relatively inexpensive products such as cases of canned goods, boxes of typewriter ribbons and computer diskettes, and crates of apples and oranges.

APPLICATION 1. Compute the average cost of the following product that was purchased on five separate orders placed by a wholesaler during June of the current year.

Date	Units		Cost		Total
June 6	1,000	×	3.25	=	3,250.00
June 13	1,200	×	2.96	=	3,552.00
June 18	1,000	×	3.10	=	3,100.00
June 25	1,500	×	3.19	=	4,785.00
June 28	750	×	3.31	=	2,482.50
	5,450				17,169.50

$$\frac{\text{Total}}{\text{value}} \div \frac{\text{Units}}{} = \frac{\text{Average}}{\text{cost}}$$

$$17,169.50 \div 5,450 = \$3.15$$

APPLICATION 2. Continuing with the situation in Application 1, what would be the value of an ending inventory of 1,910 units?

$$\frac{\text{Inventory}}{\text{balance}} \times \frac{\text{Average}}{\text{cost}} = \frac{\text{Inventory}}{\text{value}}$$

$$1,910 \quad \times \quad 3.15 \quad \times \$6,016.50$$

FIRST-IN, FIRST-OUT (FIFO)

First-in, first-out (FIFO) assumes, in a logical manner, that the first items received by a company (first in) are the first ones sold (first out). To do otherwise would result in the seller's eventually getting stuck with relatively old and unsalable merchandise. Correspondingly, any items remaining unsold at the end of an accounting period are considered to be from the most recent items received. Consider the following purchases of merchandise by a retailer, as related to 1,400 items remaining at the end of the accounting period.

Date	Units	Cost
April 10	850	22.20
April 16	1,125	23.15
April 23	910	24.12
April 28	1,050	24.95
April 30	1,200	25.35

$$\frac{\text{Inventory}}{\text{balance}} \times \frac{\text{Most recent}}{\text{cost}} = \frac{\text{Inventory}}{\text{value}}$$

$$
\begin{array}{rcl}
1,200 \times 25.35 & = & 30,420.00 \\
\underline{200} \times 24.95 & = & \underline{4,990.00} \\
1,400 & & \$35,410.00
\end{array}
$$

If the first items received were the first to be sold, the 1,400 units remaining at the end of the month are from the most recent order or orders received. Because the 1,400-unit balance exceeds the number of units received on April 30, we assume that only 1,200 of the 1,400 units are from that order and that the remaining 200 units are from the April 28 order, the next-to-last order received.

APPLICATION 1. Using the following record of orders received by the Englehart Corporation, use the FIFO method to determine the end-of-month value of 1,200 units remaining in stock.

Date	Quantity	Price
Oct 3	2,000	21.50
Oct 8	1,500	21.50
Oct 17	1,000	21.75
Oct 24	1,600	21.25
Oct 29	1,900	21.00

$$\frac{\text{Inventory}}{\text{balance}} \times \frac{\text{Most recent}}{\text{cost}} = \frac{\text{Inventory}}{\text{value}}$$

$$1,200 \times 21.00 = \$25,200$$

APPLICATION 2. Referring to the situation in Example 1, determine the FIFO value of an inventory balance of 2,040 units.

$$\frac{\text{Inventory}}{\text{balance}} \times \frac{\text{Most recent}}{\text{cost}} = \frac{\text{Inventory}}{\text{value}}$$

$$
\begin{array}{rcl}
1,900 \times & 21.00 & = & 39,900 \\
\underline{140} \times & 21.25 & = & \underline{2,975} \\
2,040 & & & \$42,875
\end{array}
$$

LAST-IN, FIRST-OUT (LIFO)

The last-in, first-out (LIFO) method of inventory valuation assumes a perspective just the opposite of that of first-in, first-out (FIFO), in that we make our calculations as though the most recently received shipments (last in) were sold first (first out). Business people do not actually handle their inventories in such a manner, because to do so would eventually result in obsolescent or (in some cases) spoiled stock. They process their inventories on a FIFO basis but value them on a LIFO basis. To illustrate this concept, let's assume that 1,000 units from the following orders remain unsold at the end of the month.

Date	Quantity	Price
May 6	1,600	18.75
May 13	2,100	19.50
May 18	1,900	19.95
May 24	2,000	20.45
May 29	1,500	20.95

$$\frac{\text{Inventory}}{\text{balance}} \times \frac{\text{Earliest}}{\text{cost}} = \frac{\text{Inventory}}{\text{value}}$$

$$1,000 \times 18.75 = \$18,750$$

Treating the most recently received shipments as though they have already been sold, we pretend further that the 1,000 units remaining in stock are part of the earlier shipment or shipments received. Rather than using the unit price of $20.95, as we would do under a FIFO arrangement, we apply the cost figure of $18.75.

Using the same inventory record, assume instead that the end-of-month inventory is 1,800 units.

$$\frac{\text{Inventory}}{\text{balance}} \times \frac{\text{Earliest}}{\text{cost}} = \frac{\text{Inventory}}{\text{value}}$$

$$
\begin{array}{rcl}
1,600 \times 18.75 &=& 30,000.00 \\
\underline{200} \times 19.50 &=& \underline{3,900.00} \\
1,800 & & \$33,900.00
\end{array}
$$

Because the inventory balance of 1,800 units exceeds the 1,600 units of the May 6 order by 200 units, we value 1,600 units at $18.75 each and the remaining 200 units from the next-earliest shipment at $19.50 per unit.

Why do some business people apply the LIFO method when they are actually rotating their stocks on the FIFO method? They do so because the LIFO approach results in lower tax obligations during periods of inflation. In the preceding inventory record, for instance, the prices paid by the company became progressively higher during the month. By claiming that the remaining stock was from earlier orders, therefore, the value of the ending stock is understated compared to the average-cost or FIFO methods of inventory valuation. This lower figure, in turn, enables the company to show a higher cost for the goods actually sold and a lower taxable profit.

APPLICATION 1. Using the following record of orders received by Carlton Distributing Company, use the LIFO method to determine the end-of-month value of 500 units remaining in stock.

Date	Quantity	Price
July 3	800	27.00
July 11	750	27.50
July 29	500	27.50
July 23	1,000	28.00
July 25	800	28.00
July 28	300	28.00

$$\frac{\text{Inventory}}{\text{balance}} \times \frac{\text{Earliest}}{\text{cost}} = \frac{\text{Inventory}}{\text{value}}$$

$$500 \times 27.00 = \$13,500$$

APPLICATION 2. Again using the LIFO method of inventory valuation and the inventory record in Application 1, determine the value of an end-of-month inventory balance of 1,000 units

$$\frac{\text{Inventory}}{\text{balance}} \times \frac{\text{Earliest}}{\text{cost}} = \frac{\text{Inventory}}{\text{value}}$$

800	× 27.00 =	21,600.00
200	× 27.50	5,500.00
1,000		$27,100.00

A COMPARISON

To assure understanding of these four methods of inventory valuation, let's determine the value of 1,200 of the following units remaining unsold at the end of June.

Date	Quantity	Price
June 1	1,000	7.85
June 8	1,100	7.95
June 12	950	8.10
June 19	1,225	8.10
June 23	1,050	8.25
June 27	975	8.32

a. Assume that 500 of the remaining units were from the June 27 order and that 700 units were part of the June 19 order.

$$\frac{\text{Inventory}}{\text{balance}} \times \frac{\text{Specific}}{\text{identity}} = \frac{\text{Inventory}}{\text{value}}$$

500	× 8.32 =	4,160.00
700	× 8.10 =	5,670.00
1,200		$9,830.00

b. Assume that the average-cost method of valuation is applied.

UNITS	×	COST	=	TOTAL
1,000	×	7.85	=	7,850.00
1,100	×	7.95	=	8,745.00
950	×	8.10	=	7,695.00
1,225	×	8.10	=	9,922.50
1,050	×	8.25	=	8,662.50
975	×	8.32	=	8,112.00
6,300				$50,987.00

$$\text{Total} \quad \div \quad \text{Units} \quad = \quad \text{Average cost}$$

$$50,987.00 \div 6,300 = \quad \$8.09$$

$$\frac{\text{Inventory}}{\text{balance}} \times \frac{\text{Average}}{\text{cost}} = \frac{\text{Inventory}}{\text{value}}$$

$$1,200 \quad \times \quad 8.09 \quad = \$9,708.00$$

c. Assume that the FIFO method is used.

$$\frac{\text{Inventory}}{\text{balance}} \times \frac{\text{Recent}}{\text{cost}} = \frac{\text{Inventory}}{\text{value}}$$

$$
\begin{array}{rcrcr}
975 & \times & 8.32 & = & 8,112.00 \\
\underline{225} & \times & 8.25 & = & \underline{1,856.25} \\
1,200 & & & & \$9,968.25
\end{array}
$$

d. Assume that the LIFO method is used.

$$\frac{\text{Inventory}}{\text{balance}} \times \frac{\text{Earliest}}{\text{cost}} = \frac{\text{Inventory}}{\text{value}}$$

$$
\begin{array}{rcrcr}
1,000 & \times & 7.85 & = & 7,850.00 \\
\underline{200} & \times & 7.95 & = & \underline{1,590.00} \\
1,200 & & & & \$9,440.00
\end{array}
$$

The results of these separate calculations may be compared in the following table:

Table 15.1
A comparison of the results of inventory-valuation methods

Valuation method	Inventory value
Specific identity	$9,830.00
Average cost	9,708.00
First-in, first-out	9,968.25
Last-in, first-out	9,440.00

INVENTORY-VALUE ESTIMATION

In the preceding situations, we knew the exact number of units remaining in stock at the end of the accounting periods, either through perpetual inventory records or by actual count — or both. Occasionally, as in the case of missing records or destroyed products, we may need to estimate the value of all or part of our inventories.

To illustrate this procedure, let's assume that we had a beginning inventory of truck tires valued at a cost of $35,000 and that an additional $50,000 worth were purchased during the current accounting period. Assume further that the item normally includes a markup on price of 30 percent and that retail sales of the item during the accounting period totaled $72,000. Restating the retail sales figure on a cost basis, we can estimate the ending inventory.

Beginning inventory	$35,000
+Goods purchased	50,000
=Goods available for sale	$85,000
−Sales at cost	50,400 (72,000 × 0.70 = 50,400)
=Ending inventory	$34,600 (estimate)

If the figure for total sales at the retail price includes a 30 percent markup on price, it follows that 70 percent (100% − 30% = 70%) of that amount is cost.

APPLICATION 1. Amerace Corporation began the current accounting period with inventory valued at cost totaling $40,000 and purchased during the period additional merchandise valued at $111,000 — all to be resold at a markup on price of 32 percent. If retail sales totaled $121,000, what is the value of the remaining inventory?

Beginning inventory	$40,000
+Goods purchased	111,000
=Goods available for sale	$151,000
−Sales at cost	82,280 (121,000 × 0.68)
=Ending inventory (estimated)	$68,720

APPLICATION 2. Champion Chemical Supply had a total of $320,610 in chemical products available for sale during June, including beginning inventory, and experienced retail sales of $211,200 prior to June 25, at which time the remaining chemicals were lost in a fire. What was the cost of the lost chemicals, assuming that the selling price included a markup on price of 28 percent?

Goods available for sale	$320,610
−Sales at cost	152,064 (211,200 × 0.72)
Cost of lost chemicals	$168,546 (estimate)

EXERCISES (as directed by your instructor)

15-1 Define the following terms:

    a. Raw materials
    b. Goods in process
    c. Finished goods

15-2 What is the primary function of personnel in an inventory-control department of a company?

15-3 If perpetual inventory systems are maintained so that employees have a current record of all inventory balances, are periodic, physical checks ever necessary?

15-4 What is the difference between perpetual and periodic inventory records?

15-5 Prepare an inventory record for the following transactions involving 48/2 COS CHUNK LIGHT TUNA (Product Code L-2128A) at the Terminal Island, California, plant (Warehouse TI-3) of Van Camp Sea Food Company.

Date	Transaction	Warehouse receipt	Shipping order number
May 1	Beginning balance of 210,320 cases		
May 5	Produced 60,000 cases	B-1738	
May 6	Shipped 12,000 cases		P-26138
May 8	Shipped 15,500 cases		P-26159
May 10	Shipped 25,605 cases		P-26231
May 12	Produced 10,000 cases	B-1756	
May 15	Shipped 5,550 cases		P-27158
May 17	Shipped 42,820 cases		P-27214
May 21	Shipped 36,910 cases		P-27381
May 24	Shipped 12,750 cases		P-27412
May 25	Produced 22,000 cases	B-1783	
May 28	Shipped 38,665 cases		P-27516

15-6 A retailer paid $16.50 each for an item last month that is being sold currently at $21.95 each. Using the *lower of cost or market*, determine the end-of-period value of 2,100 of the items that remain in inventory unsold.

15-7 Determine the total value of the following products on the basis of cost or market — whichever is lower.

Product	Quantity	Cost	Market
L212	2,350	4.16	4.25
L221	756	5.23	4.95
L225	1,110	3.23	4.10
L336	529	6.16	6.15
L352	1,995	7.12	7.00
L363	215	5.55	5.72
L376	565	16.12	16.88

15-8 Describe the concept of "specific identity."

15-9 What methods of inventory valuation may be considered as alternatives to *specific identification*?

15-10 The inventory records below are related to the five questions that follow:

Purchase date	Units purchased	Unit price
August 12	215	35.12
August 19	320	35.42
August 23	250	35.40
August 28	200	35.73

a. Using the *average cost* method of inventory valuation, what is the end-of-month value of 160 units that remain in inventory?

b. What is the value of the 160 units in inventory under the FIFO method of inventory valuation?

c. What is the value of the 160 units remaining in inventory under the LIFO method?

d. If 210 items remain in inventory instead, what is their value under the FIFO method of inventory valuation?

e. What value would be attached to the 210 items that are under the LIFO method?

15-11 The purchases and sales below are related to the six exercises that follow:

Purchases			Sales	
Date	Units	Cost	Date	Units
May 3	750	33.10	May 3	250
May 12	1,000	33.90	May 4	300
May 20	800	34.28	May 8	175
May 26	625	34.28	May 10	350
May 29	850	34.85	May 10	200
			May 11	310
			May 13	400
			May 15	350
			May 18	210
			May 22	375
			May 24	250
			May 24	200
			May 28	500
			May 28	250
			May 30	500

a. Assuming an inventory balance of 1,653 units on May 1, record all purchases and sales — in chronological order and in good form.
b. What is the value of ending inventory on the basis of *specific identification*?
c. Using the average-cost method of inventory valuation, determine the value of the end-of-month inventory.
d. Determine the value of the end-of-month inventory using the *first-in, first-out* method of valuation.
e. Make the same determination using the LIFO method of inventory valuation.
f. What is the benefit to be derived by using the ending inventory value based on LIFO as compared with the *average cost* and FIFO methods?

15-12 If the beginning stock of universal joints in August was valued at $312,607, if an additional $514,836 worth was purchased during the month, if this product normally includes a markup in price of 22 percent, and if a total of $725,540 worth of stock (at retail) was sold during the period, what is the estimated value of the end-of-month inventory (at cost)? (Round answer to even dollars.)

15-13 Saiger Distributors lost most of a warehouse and the total supply of paint brushes within the warehouse during a three-alarm fire on October 15. Paint brushes valued at $41,250 (at cost) were on hand October 1 and the purchasing department has a warehouse receipt dated October 12 for an additional supply of brushes received the preceding day at a total cost of $12,500. If retail sales (based on a 33 percent markup on price) during the 15-day period totaled $36,470.58, determine the cost to the company of the destroyed paint brushes.

16 Depreciation Methods and Investment Credits

LEARNING OBJECTIVES

Following a study of inventory valuation in Chapter 15, this chapter expands upon the various methods of determining the values of a wide range of business properties that are needed in the production of goods and services, in further preparation for an analysis of financial statements in Chapter 17. Upon mastery of these materials, you will be able to

- define the word "asset" as it pertains to business administration and explain why some assets may be expensed while others must be depreciated
- explain the rationale for depreciation allowances
- compute depreciation and compile depreciation schedules under the straight-line (including units-of-production and hours-of-service), sum-of-the years' digits, and declining-balance methods
- prorate depreciation expenses in accordance with varying purchase dates
- apply the relatively new cost-recovery tables for both personal property and real property
- explain and apply the concept of "half-year convention"
- calculate the investment tax credit as it applies to different classes of business assets

One definition of the word **asset** encompasses all items, ranging from product inventories to office supplies, from buildings to robots, and from patents to trademarks, items that are used in a business to create income. As one might imagine, the Internal Revenue Service permits businesses to deduct from taxable income the cost of producing the goods or services that they market. Businesses may also deduct from taxable income any related expenses, such as administrative salaries and advertising — all expenditures, in fact, that are directly related to business income in the current year.

Payments for **fixed assets** such as office equipment and machinery, assets that have useful economic lives of longer than one year, must be prorated and deducted from taxable income over the course of several years. If a newly purchased computer system has an expected useful life of five years, for example, its cost is related to business income not for just the year of purchase, but also for the four years following. The term for such an adjustment is **depreciation**, which is, in essence, yearly reductions in the value of business assets in the form of tax-free income. Depreciation is not a recovery from the government of actual money, therefore, but is instead a related exemption of profits from taxation.

The value of a business asset may decline through progressive wear, such as a delivery truck that is being driven an average of 50,000 miles a year; or an asset may become technologically obsolete, such as a computer becoming progressively outdated as more sophisticated systems are introduced to the marketplace. In many instances, assets may be depreciated on a yearly basis even when the actual market value is increasing. Business managers may have been depreciating the $250,000 cost of a warehouse for several years, for example, even though the market value of the building during that time has doubled; and they may continue to claim depreciation allowances for the "useful economic life" of the building — as defined by the Internal Revenue Service, not as reflected by the actual condition or value of the asset. Over the years, in fact, Congress has abandoned depreciation schedules that approximated the expected lives of assets in exchange for schedules that are more in the form of tax incentives to businesses, as tools for accelerating the national economy through incentives to business owners to increase their investments in "job producing" assets.

A two-tier system of depreciation has resulted. Assets placed into service prior to 1981 are subject to one set of rules, which we may label "traditional methods," with those entering service in 1981 or later being subject to a significantly different arrangement officially labeled "cost recovery."

TRADITIONAL METHODS

With traditional schedules being more closely attuned to the actual longevity of assets than under the cost recovery system, many companies continue to rely on them in their internal records as relatively accurate measurements of the current value of assets. Also, businesses continue to depreciate according to the traditional methods all existing assets that were placed in service prior to 1981, some of which have many useful years remaining. A final reason for studying the traditional methods of depreciation is that much of the acquired knowledge is applicable to the newer "cost recovery" system. The three methods are straight line, some-of-the-years' digits, and declining balance. Included also are the service-hours and units-of-production methods.

Straight-Line Depreciation

The straight-line method of depreciation represents the simplest and most logical approach to depreciation, as reflected in the following equation.

$$D_{SL} = \frac{c - s}{n}$$

in which

D_{SL} = annual depreciation expense under the straight-line method

c = adjusted cost of the asset

s = resale or salvage value at the end of the useful economic life of the asset

n = number of years that the asset is expected to remain economically useful

The adjusted cost of an asset includes the purchase price plus any related transportation or installation costs that may be incurred by a business. If the purchasing manager at Nortex Corporation issued a purchase order in January 1980 for a $50,000 lathe and arranged installation at an additional $2,000, the adjusted cost of the asset is $52,000. Assuming that the IRS publications suggested a useful life for such an asset to be five years and that at the end of the period the asset would have an estimated salvage value of approximately $5,000, the accountants at Nortex Corporation would have claimed a depreciation expense of $9,400 for the year of purchase and $9,400 for each of the following four years.

$$D_{SL} = \frac{c - s}{n} = \frac{(50,000 + 2,000) - 5,000}{5} = \$9,400$$

Once the lathe had been purchased and placed in service, moreover, the accountants would have prepared a depreciation schedule similar to the one illustrated in Table 16.1. Beginning with the adjusted cost of the lathe (c), depreciation (D) is subtracted from the adjusted cost to derive book value. For tax purposes, therefore, the **book value** of an asset is the value remaining after the scheduled depreciation has been deducted. Note especially that depreciation for the first year is subtracted from the adjusted cost; that is, from the cost of an asset without any reduction for salvage value. Beginning with a book value of $52,000 the asset is depreciated to $5,000, its salvage value. To assure accuracy of computation, the preparer should always make certain that total accumulated depreciation and the ending book value equal the beginning book value (47,000 + 5,000 = 52,000).

Table 16.1
Straight-line depreciation schedule
(c = $52,000, s = $5,000, n = 5)

Year	Annual depreciation (D)	Accumulated depreciation (ΣD)	Book value ($c - D$)
0	—	—	52,000
1980	9,400	9,400	42,600
1981	9,400	18,800	33,200
1982	9,400	28,200	23,800
1983	9,400	37,600	14,400
1984	9,400	47,000	5,000

Accumulated depreciation, as the term denotes, is the sum of annual depreciation claimed for the current year and for any preceding years, the application of which is explained in Chapter 17. Having completed such a depreciation schedule, the accountants at Nortex Corporation could use figures from the schedule rather than undertake annual calculations for each of the five years.

Unless, under the pre-1981 rules, an asset were purchased during the period January 1 through January 15, the annual depreciation expense must be prorated. Assume, for instance, that the people at Nortex placed the lathe into service on March 25 rather than early January. Because the depreciation schedule begins during the last half of March rather than on the 15th or earlier, March is ignored and depreciation is claimed for only three fourths (April through December) of 1981 and depreciation is claimed as follows:

Year	Annual depreciation	Book value
—	—	52,000
1980	7,050	44,950
1981	9,400	35,550
1982	9,400	26,150
1983	9,400	16,750
1984	9,400	7,350
1985	2,350	5,000

Only $7,050 (three fourths of 9,400) is claimed the first year, $9,400 for each of the following four years, and $2,350 (one fourth of 9,400) the sixth year. Because of the carryover of $2,350 from the first year, the five-year schedule is expanded to six years.

Under the **units-of-production method**, a business claims annual depreciation on the basis of the number of units produced by a particular piece of equipment rather than on the simple passage of time. The equation is

$$D_{UP} = (c - s)R$$

As before, "c" represents the adjusted cost of an asset, and "s" represents its salvage value. Additionally,

D_{UP} = annual depreciation under the units-of-production method

R = rate (as in $BR = P$), the number of units produced during the year as a percentage of the total number of units the asset may be expected to produce during its entire economic life.

Assume, for example, that the lathe discussed earlier may be expected to produce 1,575,000 machine parts before wearing out. Assume further that the lathe is used to produce 345,651 parts during the current tax year. Under the units-of-production method, depreciation for the current year will be $10,293.

$$R = \frac{P}{B} = \frac{345,651}{1,575,000} = 21.9\%$$

$$D_{UP} = (c - s)R$$

$$= (52,000 - 5,000)0.219$$

$$= \$10,293$$

Similarly, depreciation for preceding and subsequent years of service depends on the number of units produced each year.

The **service-hours methods of depreciation**, identified as D_{SH}, bases annual depreciation on the number of hours that an asset is operational in the production process. The symbol "R" in this calculation represents the hours of operation during the current period as a percentage of the total hours that the asset is expected to operate during its economic life. Assuming that the owners of the $52,000 lathe anticipate 20,000 total hours of service and that the unit was operated 3,620 hours during the current tax year, they have an annual depreciation expense of $8,507.

$$R = \frac{\text{Hours operated current year}}{\text{Total hours expected to operate}} = \frac{3,620}{20,000} = 18.1\%$$

$$D_{SH} = (c - s)R$$

$$= (52,000 - 5,000)0.181$$

$$= \$8,507$$

Because the units-of-production and hours-of-service methods are based on criteria other than the passage of time, no prorating is required to adjust for differing dates that assets are placed in service.

APPLICATION 1. If a company purchases a computer for $250,000, including the cost of installation in early January 1980, and estimates its resale value at the end of six years to be $15,000,

    a. What amount of straight-line depreciation may the company claim for the first year of ownership?

$$D_{SL} = \frac{c - s}{n} = \frac{250,000 - 15,000}{6} = \$39,166.67$$

b. What is the annual depreciation for the second year?

$39,166.67

APPLICATION 2. Assuming instead that the computer in Application 1 was purchased on August 10, 1980, what is the annual depreciation expense, accumulated depreciation, and book value for the year of purchase and for each of the remaining years?

Year	Depreciation expense	Accumulated depreciation	Book value
	—	—	250,000.00
1980	16,319.45	16,319.45	233,680.55
1981	39,166.67	55,486.12	194,513.88
1982	39,166.67	94,652.79	155,347.21
1983	39,166.67	133,819.46	116,180.54
1984	39,166.67	172,986.13	77,013.87
1985	39,166.67	212,152.80	37,847.20
1986	22,847.20[1]	235,000.00	15,000.00

1980:   39,166.67 × 5/12 = 16,319.45
1986:   39,166.67 × 7/12 = 22,847.22

[1]Reduced by 2 cents to avoid reduction in book value below $15,000 salvage value.

APPLICATION 3. If a manufacturer paid $153,000, plus an installation charge of $2,000, for a robot that was placed into service on June 10, 1978, what is the annual depreciation expense for 1985 under the units-of-production method? Assume that the robot has a salvage value of only $1,000 and is expected to remain operational for a total of 2,500,000 units, and that 312,500 units were processed during 1985.

$$R = \frac{\text{Units produced}}{\text{Total units expected}} = \frac{312,500}{2,500,000} = 12.5\%$$

$$
\begin{aligned}
D_{UP} &= (c - s)R \\
&= (155,000 - 1,000)0.125 \\
&= \$19,250
\end{aligned}
$$

APPLICATION 4. Assume instead that the robot in Application 3 is depreciated by the hours-of-service method and that the unit was operated 3,990 hours during 1985 as related to an anticipated total of 28,000 hours during the economic life of the asset.

$$R = \frac{\text{Hours operated}}{\text{Total hours expected}} = \frac{3,990}{28,000} = 14.25\%$$

$$\begin{aligned} D_{HS} &= (c - s)R \\ &= (155,000 - 1,000)0.1425 \\ &= \$21,945 \end{aligned}$$

Sum-of-the-Years' Digits

The **sum-of-the-years'-digits method** (**SYD**), as the term suggests, is based on the total number of years (n) in the economic life of an asset. The equation is the same as for straight-line depreciation, except for a determination of rate (R).

$$D_{SYD} = (c - s)R$$

The rate (R), which is always expressed in fractions, is found by using the sum of the years as the denominator and the year of ownership (in reverse order) as the numerator. For the same lathe as in the earlier examples, in which the purchase price was $50,000, installation $2,000, and salvage value $5,000, we take the sum of five years ($1 + 2 + 3 + 4 + 5 = 15$) as our denominator and take the individual years (reversing their order) as our numerators (5/15 for the first year of service), a procedure that is identical to the Rule of 78 in Chapter 9.

$$D_{SYD} = (c - s)R$$

$$= (52,000 - 5,000)5/15$$

$$= \$15,666.67$$

Multiplying $47,000 by 5/15 results in first-year depreciation of $15,666.67. Keeping $47,000 as a constant multiplicand, we use 4/15 as a multiplier for the second year, 3/15 for the third year, and so on, resulting in the depreciation schedule presented in Table 16.2.

As with straight-line depreciation, we subtract annual depreciation from the adjusted cost (c), lowering book value to the equivalent of salvage value by the end of five years. Unlike the straight-line method, however, sum-of-the-years' digits permits the owners of assets to claim a higher depreciation expense in the early years of ownership and a progressively lower expense in each succeeding year. The benefit of this accelerated form of depreciation lies in the time value of money. The higher the depreciation, the lower the reportable

Table 16.2
Sum-of-the-years' digits
depreciation schedule
(c = $52,000, s =
$5,000, n = 5 years)

Year	Annual depreciation (D)	Accumulated depreciation (ΣD)	Book value ($c - D$)
	—	—	52,000.00
1980	15,666.67	15,666.67	36,333.33
1981	12,533.33	28,200.00	23,800.00
1982	9,400.00	37,600.00	14,400.00
1983	6,266.67	43,866.67	8,133.33
1984	3,133.33	47,000.00	5,000.00

Rather than multiplying 47,000 (the after-salvage value) by 5 and then dividing by 15, it is easier to divide 47,000 by 15 and then multiply the dividend by 5, 4, 3, 2, and 1. The rationale for this procedure is explained in the footnote on page 74.

Calculator	
Entries	**Display**
4 7 0 0 0	47,000.
÷	47,000.
1 5	15.
×	3,133.333333
5	5.
=	15,666.66667
4	4.
=	12,533.33333
and so on	

income on which taxes are assessed; and, as explained in earlier discussions of compound interest, a tax dollar saved today is more valuable than a dollar saved at some future date, because it can be "put to work" to earn interest or profits that would not otherwise be realized.

APPLICATION 1. If a drilling rig costing a coal company $110,000 has an estimated salvage value of $10,000 at the end of six years, using *SYD* depreciation,

a. What is the depreciation expense for the first year of ownership?

$$R = 1 + 2 + 3 + 4 + 5 + 6 = 21$$

(or)

$$\frac{n(n + 1)}{2} = \frac{6(6 + 1)}{2} = \frac{42}{2} = 21$$

$$\begin{aligned} D_{SYD} &= (c - s)R \\ &= (110,000 - 10,000)6/21 \\ &= \$28,571.43 \end{aligned}$$

b. What is the depreciation expense for the second year? $100,000 \times 5/21$ = \$23,809.52

c. What is the depreciation expense for the sixth year? $100,000 \times 1/21$ = \$4,761.90

APPLICATION 2. If the drilling rig in Application 1 was purchased on August 18,

a. What amount of depreciation may be claimed for the first year of ownership?

$28,571.43 \times 4/12 = \$9,523.81$

b. What amount may be claimed for the second year of ownership?

$$
\begin{aligned}
28{,}571.43 \times 8/12 &= 19{,}047.62 \\
23{,}809.52 \times 4/12 &= \underline{7{,}936.51} \\
&\$26{,}984.13
\end{aligned}
$$

Declining Balance

The declining-balance (D_{DB}) method also provides accelerated depreciation by permitting businesses to claim a relatively high portion of a total depreciation expense during the early years of ownership. The equation is

$$D_{DB} = c \times R$$

The symbol "c" is for the adjusted cost of an asset, as before, and "R," although computed differently, is for rate, as in the units-of-production, hours-of-service, and sum-of-digits methods.

For double-declining balance, rate (R) is determined by calculating the reciprocal of the number of years (n) (dividing the number one by the number of years) and multiplying by 2. Using the earlier example of a lathe with an adjusted cost of \$52,000 and an expected economic life of five years, we have

$$R = \frac{1}{n} \times 2$$

$$= \frac{1}{5} \times 2$$

$$= 40\%$$

The 2 is for 200 percent, which is routinely referred to as *double-declining balance*. For used (secondhand) assets, the rate is more commonly 1.5 (150 percent). Noting that the \$5,000 salvage is not included in the computation, we determine the amount of depreciation that may be claimed for the first year of ownership.

Table 16.3

Double-declining-balance depreciation schedule ($c = \$52,000$, $s = \$5,000$, $n = 5$)

Year	Annual depreciation (D)	Accumulated depreciation (ΣD)	Book value ($c - D$)
	—	—	52,000.00
1980	20,800.00	20,800.00	31,200.00
1981	12,480.00	33,280.00	18,720.00
1982	7,488.00	40,768.00	11,232.00
1983	4,492.80	45,260.80	6,739.20
1984	1,739.20	47,000.00	5,000.00

$$D_{DB} = c \times R$$

$$= 52,000 \times 0.4$$

$$= \$20,800$$

We subtract the annual depreciation (D_{DB}) from cost (c) to determine book value, use the book value as cost (c) in our equation for the second year, and so on, resulting in a depreciation schedule as illustrated in Table 16.3. Rather than claim depreciation the last year of $2,695.68 ($6,739.20 \times 0.4 = 2,695.68$), which would reduce the book value to lower than the salvage value of $5,000, we claim only $1,739.20, which is the difference between book value the preceding year and salvage value ($6,739.20 - 5,000.00 = 1,739.20$).

APPLICATION 1. On November 12, 1979, Ajax Corporation purchased a stamping machine costing $210,000. The unit was installed on January 20 the following year for additional cost of $5,000. Assuming that the machine has a useful economic life of ten years and an estimated salvage value of $10,000,

a. What amount of depreciation can the company claim for 1980?

$$R = \frac{1}{n} \times 2 = \frac{1}{10} \times 2 = 20\%$$
$$D_{DB} = c \times R$$
$$= 215,000 \times 0.2$$
$$= 43,000$$

Prorated: $43,000 \times 11/12 = \$39,416.67$

b. What amount of depreciation could the company claim for 1981?

$$\text{Cost} - D_{DB} \text{ first year} = \text{book value} \times \text{rate} = D_{DB} \text{ second year}$$
$$215,000 - 43,000 = 172,000 \times 0.2 \quad = 34,400$$

$$1981: 43,000 \times 1/12 \ = \ \ \ 3,583.33$$
$$34,400 \times 11/12 = \ \underline{31,533.33}$$
$$\$35,116.66$$

APPLICATION 2. If in early January 1980, Rutgers Electric purchased a warehouse costing \$200,000 (excluding the value of the land) that had a life expectancy of 20 years and salvage value of \$20,000, what is the first year's depreciation expense using the 150 percent declining-balance method?

$$R = \frac{1}{n} \times 1.5 = \frac{1}{20} \times 1.5 = 7\text{-}1/2\%$$

$$
\begin{aligned}
D_{DB} &= c \times r \\
&= 200,000 \times 0.075 \\
&= \$15,000
\end{aligned}
$$

To minimize the calculations under any of the depreciation methods in this chapter, similar assets bought at the same time may be grouped and depreciated as single entities.

COST RECOVERY

Beginning with assets placed in service in 1981, the Internal Revenue Service implemented **Accelerated Cost Recovery System (ACRS)**. The procedure not only simplifies the concept of depreciation, but also offers businesses greater incentive for increased investment through the application of more highly accelerated schedules than could be realized from either the sum-of-digits or declining-balance methods. Procedures vary with ACRS, however, with respect to whether an asset is categorized as personal or real property.

Personal Property

Personal property, so far as taxation is concerned, includes all business assets other than real estate; and, as shown in Table 16.4, four recovery periods or classifications apply to all types of personal property. Once the assets are classified, the percents listed in Table 16.5 are applied to the adjusted cost (c) without considering salvage value. Under what is termed **half-year convention**, ACRS is based on the assumption that an asset was purchased in the middle of a year, which makes unnecessary any of the tedious prorating associated with the traditional methods of depreciation. To illustrate the application of ACRS, assume that the owners of a small business purchased a new delivery truck on March 6, 1986, for a total price of \$17,500. Depreciation (tax-free cost recovery) would be calculated as follows.

$$
\begin{array}{llll}
1986: & \$17,500 \times 0.25 = & \$4,375 \\
1987: & 17,500 \times 0.38 = & 6,650 \\
1988: & 17,500 \times \underline{0.37} = & \underline{6,475} \\
& 1.00 & \$17,500
\end{array}
$$

Table 16.4

Recovery periods for personal property

Class	Types of assets
3-year	Autos Light duty trucks Other short-lived personal property Research-and-development equipment
5-year	All personal property not included in the three-year category, such as office equipment and heavy machinery
10-year	Certain public utility personal property Amusement parks Mobile homes Railroad tank cars
15-year	Longer-lived public utility property

Table 16.5

Accelerated cost recovery for personal property (percents)

Year of ownership	Class of Investment			
	3-year	5-year	10-year	15-year
1	25	15	8	5
2	38	22	14	10
3	37	21	12	9
4		21	10	8
5		21	10	7
6			10	7
7			9	6
8			9	6
9			9	6
10			9	6
11				6
12				6
13				6
14				6
15				6
Total	100	100	100	100

Because of the half-year convention, the lowest depreciation on this three-year class asset comes in the first year.

Optional recovery periods are available to businesses, as shown in Table 16.6, as options to the four property classes in accelerated cost recovery. Because the $17,500 delivery truck falls within the 3-year class (Table 16.4), the owner may apply straight-line depreciation over a 3-, 5-, or 12-year period

Table 16.6
Optional recovery
periods — personal
property

Property class	Extended periods
3-year	3, 5, or 12 years
5-year	5, 12, or 25 years
10-year	10, 25, or 35 years
15-year	15, 35, or 45 years

Table 16.7
Depreciation schedule
under five-year option

Year	Annual depreciation (D)	Accumulated depreciation (ΣD)	Book value (c − D)
	—	—	17,500
1986	1,750	1,750	15,750
1987	3,500	5,250	12,250
1988	3,500	8,750	8,750
1989	3,500	12,250	5,250
1990	3,500	15,750	1,750
1991	1,750	17,500	zero

(Table 16.6). Choice of the five-year option would result in a first- and sixth-year depreciation expense of $1,750, as illustrated in Table 16.7.

Because of the half-year convention, under which we assume that assets are acquired at midyear regardless of the date placed into service, only one half ($1,750) of the annual depreciation may be claimed the first year. Full annual depreciation is claimed in each of the following four years, with the carryover ($1,750) from the first year being claimed in the sixth year. As a consequence of the half-year convention, therefore, a five-year depreciation schedule is expanded to six years. As with all ACRS computations, book value is reduced to zero with no consideration for any salvage value that may exist.

Investment Tax Credit

The acquisition of most personal property also entitles business purchasers to **investment tax credits**, which is an added incentive to business owners to create jobs through increased investments. Unlike depreciation or cost recovery, which represents reductions in taxable income, tax credits are direct reductions in taxes at the rates shown in Table 16.8.

Table 16.8
Investment tax credit

Class of investment	Percent credit
3-year	6
5-, 10-, 15-year	10

The purchaser of the previously mentioned delivery truck, in addition to "writing off" (depreciating) the entire purchase price over a three-year period of cost recovery, may claim a tax credit of $1,050 in the year of purchase.

$17,500 \times 0.06 = \$1,050$

Keep in mind, however, that the investment tax credit applies only to personal property, not to real estate.

Real Property

The term **real property**, for purposes of depreciation, includes buildings and properties (such as air conditioners and lighting fixtures) that are attached to buildings. Any land, including the land upon which buildings are constructed, is not included in this definition because land cannot be depreciated for tax purposes. Compared to the traditional methods discussed earlier, the depreciation of real property is greatly simplified through application of Table 16.9.

For example, a business owner who purchased a building in February 1986 for $225,000 (not including the value of the land) may claim a depreciation expense of $24,750 in 1986 ($225,000 \times 0.11 = 24,750$), a depreciation expense of $22,500 in 1987 ($225,000 \times 0.10 = 22,500$), and so on. As with ACRS for personal property, the potential salvage value of real estate has no influence under ACRS.

APPLICATION 1. In May 1986 Oceanside Thrill Park installed a new roller-coaster ride costing $150,000.

a. What is the appropriate ACRS class for this asset?

10-year class for amusement parks

b. What tax benefits may the company claim for the first year of ownership?

Cost recovery (reduction in taxable income) of $12,000
$150,000 \times 0.08 = \$12,000$

Plus an investment tax credit of $15,000
$150,000 \times 0.10 = \$15,000$

APPLICATION 2. If instead of using accelerated depreciation, the amusement park owners decided to use straight-line depreciation,

a. From what different time periods may they choose?

10, 25, or 35 years (Table 16.6 for 10-year class)

b. If the owners opt for the 25-year option, what amount of depreciation (cost recovery) may be claimed for the first year of ownership?

$$\frac{150,000}{25} \times \frac{1}{2} = \$3,000$$
(Half-year convention applies)

Table 16.9 Accelerated cost recovery for real property (percents)

Year of Ownership	Month asset placed in service											
	JAN	FEB	MAR	APR	MAY	JUN	JUL	AUG	SEP	OCT	NOV	DEC
1	12	11	10	9	8	7	6	5	4	3	2	1
2	10	10	11	11	11	11	11	11	11	11	11	12
3	9	9	9	9	10	10	10	10	10	10	10	10
4	8	8	8	8	8	8	9	9	9	9	9	9
5	7	7	7	7	7	7	8	8	8	8	8	8
6	6	6	6	6	7	7	7	7	7	7	7	7
7	6	6	6	6	6	6	6	6	6	6	6	6
8	6	6	6	6	6	6	5	6	6	6	6	6
9	6	6	6	6	5	6	5	5	5	6	6	6
10	5	6	5	6	5	5	5	5	5	5	6	5
11	5	5	5	5	5	5	5	5	5	5	5	5
12	5	5	5	5	5	5	5	5	5	5	5	5
13	5	5	5	5	5	5	5	5	5	5	5	5
14	5	5	5	5	5	5	5	5	5	5	5	5
15	5	5	5	5	5	5	5	5	5	5	5	5
16			1	1	2	2	3	3	4	4	4	5
Total	100	100	100	100	100	100	100	100	100	100	100	100

APPLICATION 3. If Zephr Plastics finished construction of a new factory building in August 1986 that had a value of $750,000 (including the land which was appraised at $100,000),

a. What amount of depreciation (cost recovery) may the firm claim for the first year of ownership?

750,000 − 100,000 = 650,000
650,000 × 0.05 = $32,500

b. For the second year of ownership?

650,000 × 0.11 = $71,500

c. For the tenth year of ownership?

650,000 × 0.05 = $32,500

Note: The cost recovery tables in this chapter are also presented in Appendix A for use during examinations.

EXERCISES (as assigned by your instructor)

16-1 For tax purposes, in what way are expenses (such as office supplies) treated differently from fixed assets (such as machinery)?

16-2 In what ways may assets actually depreciate?

16-3 What is the rationale for deducting depreciation expenses from income that would otherwise be taxable?

16-4 Must the value of an asset actually decline in order for the business to be entitled to a depreciation expense? Explain.

16-5 What is the government's primary objective in offering accelerated depreciation schedules and investment tax credits?

16-6 Briefly explain the two-tier system of depreciation.

16-7 A business firm purchased a grinding machine and placed it in service on January 8, 1980, at a cost of $85,000 plus $1,500 for installation. Assuming that the unit has a useful economic life of eight years and an estimated salvage value of $1,000,

a. What is the first-year depreciation under the straight-line method?
b. What is the first year's depreciation under the units-of-production method, assuming that from a projected total of 3,500,000 units the machine is used to produce 436,500 units during the second year?

c. What is the second year's depreciation under the hours of service method, assuming that from a total of 35,000 hours of useful service the machine is operated 4,150 hours the second year?

16-8 On November 12, 1980, Comstat Computer Systems installed a $450,000 computer system at Ellis Distributors. The system, which has a useful economic life of six years and an estimated salvage value of $15,000, also carried an installation charge of $10,000.

   a. What is the first-year depreciation under the straight-line method of computation?
   b. If the unit is judged capable of producing a total of 4,000,000 units during its useful economic life and was used to produce 87,500 units during the remainder of November and all of December, what is the depreciation expense for 1980 under the units-of-production method?
   c. If the unit is judged to have a total of 25,000 operating hours during its estimated lifetime, what is the depreciation expense for 1980 based on the 208 hours it was operated in November and the 352 hours in December — using the hours-of-service method?

16-9 Scott Pharmaceuticals had a $320,000 sealing machine installed on January 10, 1980. Taking into account a delivery and installation cost of $4,050, an estimated useful life of ten years, and an estimated salvage value of $5,000,

   a. Prepare a straight-line depreciation schedule.
   b. Prepare a sum-of-the-years' digits depreciation schedule.

16-10 Norman Cosmetics, Inc. purchased a new robot on November 11, 1979, and placed it in service on February 18, 1980, which automatically retrieves inventoried items sixteen hours each workday. The truck-like machine cost $125,000 (including delivery), has an estimated useful life of five years, and has an estimated scrap value at the end of that time of $1,000.

   a. Prepare a straight-line depreciation schedule.
   b. Prepare a sum-of-the-years' digits schedule.

16-11 Arthur Kerr and Associates, Inc. had a new computer delivered and placed in service on January 5, 1980. The cost was $42,000, including installation, and the unit was judged to have a useful economic life of five years with an estimated sales value at the end of five years of $5,000. Prepare a depreciation schedule using the double-declining balance method.

16-12 Roadrunner Tire Service began using a new balancing machine on June 12, 1980, a unit that cost $7,500 plus an installation charge of $450. Estimating the useful life of the machine to be four years, with a salvage value of $500, prepare a depreciation schedule based on the double-declining-balance method.

16-13 Using 150 percent declining balance, determine the first year's depreciation expense for a $50,000 asset (including delivery and installation on January 10, 1980) that has an estimated useful life of ten years and salvage value of $5,000.

16-14 Richard's Auto Mart purchased a used storage building for $125,000 (excluding the value of the land) and began using it on October 3, 1980. Using a ten-year depreciation schedule and the 150 percent declining balance method,

a. Determine the depreciation expense for 1980.
b. Determine the depreciation expense for 1981.

16-15 To what assets must businesses apply the Accelerated Cost Recovery System (ACRS)?

16-16 In what class do we place research-and-development equipment?

16-17 In what class do we place mobile homes?

16-18 Five Star Enterprises purchased ten new electronic typewriters at $1,275 each. The price included delivery, which was made on March 19, 1986. Prepare a depreciation schedule for this group of assets.

16-19 In Exercise 16-18, what optional recovery periods are available to this company?

16-20 Still referring to Exercise 16-18, prepare a depreciation schedule using a five-year optional recovery period.

16-21 On January 12, 1987, Flores Financial Group purchased for $3,750 a new postage machine that automatically seals and stamps standard-sized business envelopes. Prepare a depreciation schedule for this business asset.

16-22 In Exercise 16-21, what optional recovery periods are available to this company?

16-23 Still referring to Exercise 16-21, prepare a depreciation schedule using a twelve-year optional recovery period.

16-24 Associated Towing, Inc. took delivery of a new tow truck on April 4, 1986. The unit cost $65,000, including destination charges and taxes. Prepare a depreciation schedule for this light-duty vehicle.

16-25 Garrett Construction Company took delivery of five mobile homes during May 1986, to be used as on-site field offices. Each unit cost $18,500, including delivery costs and taxes. Prepare a depreciation schedule for this group of assets.

16-26 The owner of Fowler Insurance Group bought a new company car on July 17, 1986, for $12,315. By how much were the taxes of this company reduced that year by claiming a tax credit?

16-27 Northwest Insurance Agency had a computer installed during January 1987 at an adjusted cost (price plus installation) of $125,000. What reduction in federal taxes was realized through a tax credit?

16-28 What is the rationale for offering investment tax credits to businesses?

16-29 Is an investment credit of $10,000 more or less valuable to a business than a reduction in taxable income of $10,000? Explain.

16-30 Midwest Airlines purchased an office building in Indianapolis during September 1985 for a total price of $750,000. What is the annual depreciation for the first five years of ownership, assuming that a recent appraisal placed the value of the land on which the building rests at $90,000?

16-31 Regarding the building in Exercise 16-30, what is the last year of the depreciation schedule and what is the annual depreciation expense that year?

16-32 Brad and Margaret Anderson paid $85,000 for a used home in April 1986 that they have rented to another family ever since. With the value of the land itself being estimated at $15,000, what annual depreciation are they entitled to during the first five years of ownership?

16-33 With reference to Exercise 16-32, what is the last year for which depreciation may be claimed, assuming that they claim such an expense every preceding year, and how much is the depreciation expense for that final year?

17 Financial Statements and Income Distribution

LEARNING OBJECTIVES

Mastery of the materials in this chapter will help you combine much of the earlier concepts into a more coherent whole, through analysis of the two most important financial statements in business administration — the income statement and the balance sheet — following which you will be able to

- explain the three major categories of business organization — sole proprietorships, partnerships, and corporations
- calculate net sales, cost of goods sold, gross profit, and net income
- compute federal taxes on corporate income
- identify, define, and place in correct order the major segments of income statements and balance sheets
- present data in the form of income statements and balance sheets
- prepare consolidated income statements and balance sheets
- conduct vertical and horizontal analysis of financial statements
- distribute corporate income among the holders of both common and preferred stock

Sole proprietorships are businesses that are owned by one person, and **partnerships** are those that are owned by two or more people. The owners of either of these two types of unincorporated organizations are themselves the legal entities. Checking accounts, savings accounts, and contracts are in the names of the owners rather than that of their companies. Similarly, it is the sole proprietors and the partners who pay taxes and who may sue or be sued, not the companies.

A company becomes a **corporation** upon the application for and the receipt of a charter from any of the 50 states, and, once incorporated, the company has the same legal rights and responsibilities of any citizen. Corporate employees establish bank accounts in the corporate name and regularly commit the companies to contractual arrangements. Corporations must pay federal, state, and local taxes; and it is the corporation that may sue or be sued, rather than its owners.

Whatever the form of organization, business people must, for tax purposes at least, keep records of all business transactions. Even if the Internal Revenue Service and local tax agencies did not require the maintenance of such records, most business owners and managers would prepare them religiously — as indicators of profit or loss, as evidence of credit worthiness, as measures of operational efficiency, and as indicators of earnings potential.

Records are maintained through a series of reports, ranging from just a few reports in small businesses to thousands in large corporations. Reports are prepared on such detailed transactions as hours worked, wages earned, and employee productivity; the number of units produced of every product, as well as the number inventoried and sold; the prices charged, the money received, the balance owned; and so on, seemingly without end. These reports are condensed as they are submitted to progressively higher management, until the results of all transactions are culminated into two financial statements: the income statement and the balance sheet.

INCOME STATEMENT

An **income statement** is a report of profits and losses and is, therefore, commonly referred to as a "profit-and-loss" statement. Income statements summarize revenues from the sale of products or services, as well as all related costs and expenses, for a period of time — monthly and yearly in most companies, and also on a weekly or even a daily basis in others.

Major Segments

The major segments of an income statement comprise the following equation:

Revenues − cost of goods sold − expenses = income (profit or loss)

These elements are illustrated in the condensed income statement in Figure 17.1, in which we have

Revenues (sales)	$970,162
− Cost of goods sold	738,642
= Gross profit	$231,520
− Expenses	77,566
= Net income	$153,954

Notice that the net income (profit) for the year is almost $154 million, with all entries being stated in thousands of dollars (as noted).

    Revenues consist of income realized through the sale of either products or services. **Gross sales** (not shown) consist of a total of all sales income, whereas **net sales** are the dollar amounts remaining after deductions have been made for returns and allowances.

Gross sales − Returns and allowances = Net sales

$$998,511 - 36,281 = 962,230$$

Some individual consumers and business customers invariably return all or part of the merchandise purchased — for a variety of reasons, ranging from the wrong items being ordered or shipped to quality control problems. Also, as

Figure 17.1
Income statement
(condensed)

Commodore Manufacturing, Inc.
Income Statement (in thousands of dollars)
for year ending December 31, 1986

Revenue:		
Net sales	$962,230	
Other income	7,932	$970,162
Cost of goods sold		738,642
Gross profit		$231,520
Expenses:		
Operating	$ 59,246	
General	18,320	77,566
Net income		$153,954
Provision for income taxes		70,799
Net income after taxes		$ 83,155

---

you will recall from Chapter 5, many manufacturers offer cash discounts. If a manufacturer bills a retailer for $10,000 worth of merchandise at terms of 2/10, *n*/30, for example, an allowance of $200 is subtracted from gross sales to derive net sales of $9,800.

Other income may represent incoming dollars from any of several sources, such as interest received on securities held by the corporation or the sale of unneeded real estate; that is, from some source other than routine business transactions. This income is combined with net sales to derive a total revenue figure of $970,162.

The **cost of goods sold** (COGS) during an accounting period is determined by adding to beginning inventory the value of all goods purchased or manufactured during the current accounting period. From this figure, which is termed "goods available," we subtract the value of ending inventory. Using the COGS amount in Figure 17.1 to illustrate the computation, we have

Beginning inventory	$ 98,605
+ Goods purchased	752,350
= Goods available	$850,955
− Ending inventory	112,313
= Cost of goods sold	$738,642

Beginning with inventory left over from the preceding accounting period valued at $98,605, additional merchandise of $752,350 was manufactured, making available for sale during the period (a year in this instance) a total inventory valued at $850,955. Not all items were sold during the period, which, when

Table 17.1
Corporate tax rates

Taxable income	Rate	Computation	Tax
$0 to $25,000	15%	25,000 × 0.15	$3,750
$25,000 to $50,000	18%	25,000 × 0.18	4,500
$50,000 to $75,000	30%	25,000 × 0.30	7,500
$75,000 to $100,000	40%	25,000 × 0.40	10,000
		$100,000	$25,750
Over $100,000	46%		

subtracted from goods available, resulted in an ending inventory of $112,313 and a cost of goods sold of $738,642. (The various methods for determining the values of inventories are presented in Chapter 15.)

Gross profit, frequently referred to as "margin," is the balance of income remaining after subtracting the cost of goods sold from the total revenue received. Gross profit must exceed expenses if net income (profit) is to be realized.

Expenses are generally divided into two or more categories. The income statement in Figure 17.1 includes **operating expenses** (such as sales salaries, showroom rental, advertising outlays, and freight charges) and **general expenses** (such as office salaries, office rental, and related depreciation).

The **net income** figure is the profit (or loss) that has resulted from transactions during the accounting period. The owners of unincorporated businesses enter this figure (sole proprietors) or a portion of this figure (partners) on their individual tax returns (Form 1040s) and pay taxes on the basis of their individual incomes from all sources. The managers of corporations, on the other hand, submit special tax returns and pay taxes on the basis of the **corporate tax rates** in Table 17.1.

The federal tax paid by Commodore Manufacturing (Figure 17.1 on page 321) was computed as follows:

$$\$153,954 + 000 = 153,954,000$$
$$\frac{100,000 =}{153,854,000 \times 0.46 =} \quad \begin{array}{r} 25,750 \\ 70,772,840 \\ \hline \$70,798,590 \end{array}$$

Tax on the first $100,000 is $25,750, as shown in Table 17.1, with the balance of $153,854,000 being taxed at the 46 percent rate and rounded to thousands of dollars.

Comparative Statements

Consolidated statements are those that include figures for two or more consecutive years, as illustrated in Figure 17.2. Consolidated statements in the annual reports of corporations typically include income figures for from two to five years. **Comparative statements** are financial reports, such as the in-

Figure 17.2
Consolidated income statement of earnings (in thousands of dollars)

	Year ended December 31	
Revenue:	1986	1985
Net sales	$962,230	$701,803
Other income	7,932	5,807
Total revenue	$970,162	$707,610
Cost of goods sold	738,642	567,920
Gross profit	$231,520	$139,690
Expenses:		
Operating	59,246	44,831
General	18,320	19,923
Total expenses	$ 77,566	$ 64,754
Net income	153,954	74,936
Income taxes	70,799	34,450
Net income after taxes	$ 83,155	$ 40,486

come statement and the balance sheet, in which individual entries are compared from one time period to another.

Percentage comparisons provide analysts with still clearer pictures of trends in business transactions. In what is termed **vertical analysis**, every entry in an income statement is computed as a percentage of net sales. As illustrated in Figure 17.3, net sales for 1986 ($962,230) divided by itself equals 100 percent; *other income* ($7,932) divided by *net sales* equals 0.8 percent, and so on.

The most significant information to be derived from this particular comparison is that the *cost of goods sold* in 1986 decreased, which exerted a positive effect on gross profit and net income in that year.

Figure 17.3
Vertical analysis of income statement (in thousands of dollars)

	1986 Amount	Percent of net sales	1985 Amount	Percent of net sales
Revenue:				
Net sales	962,230	100.0	701,803	100.0
Other income	7,932	0.8	5,807	0.8
Total revenue	970,162	100.8	707,610	100.8
Cost of goods sold	738,642	76.8	567,920	80.9
Gross profit	231,520	24.1	139,690	19.9
Expenses:				
Operating	59,246	6.2	44,831	6.4
General	18,320	1.9	19,923	2.8
Total expenses	77,566	8.1	64,754	9.2
Net income	153,954	16.0	74,936	10.7
Income taxes	70,799	7.4	34,450	4.9
Income after taxes	83,155	8.6	40,486	5.8

Calculations may be simplified with use of chain division. If your calculator will not perform the functions as illustrated, use the storage (M+ or STO) key in conjunction with the recall (MR or RCL) key. A % key, if your calculator has one, may be used in place of the = key to further simplify the calculations.

Calculator	
Entries	**Display**
7 9 3 2	7,932.
÷	7,932.
9 6 2 2 3 0	962,230.
=	.0082433513
9 7 0 1 6 2	970,162.
=	1.008243351
7 3 8 6 4 2	738,642.
=	.7676355965
and so on	

Horizontal analysis, like that illustrated in Figure 17.4, also provides a useful comparison of the two sets of data by identifying the percent of increase or decrease in each entry from one year to the next. From net sales for the current year (1986) we subtract net sales for the earlier year (1985) and divide the difference by the earlier (1985) figure, revealing an increase of 37.1 percent.

$$\frac{\text{Most recent year} - \text{preceding year}}{\text{Preceding year}} = \frac{962{,}230 - 701{,}803}{701{,}803} = 37.1\%$$

These comparisons make it obvious that while revenues for 1986 increased more than 37 percent over those for 1985, the smaller increases in *cost of goods*

Figure 17.4
Horizontal analysis of income statements (in thousands of dollars)

Revenue:	1986	1985	Increase or decrease Amount	Percent
Net sales	962,230	701,803	260,427	37.1
Other income	7,932	5,807	2,125	36.6
Total revenue	970,162	707,610	262,552	37.1
Cost of goods sold	738,642	567,920	170,722	30.1
Gross profit	231,520	139,690	91,830	65.7
Expenses:				
Operating	59,246	44,831	14,415	32.2
General	18,320	19,923	(1,603)	(8.0)
Total expenses	77,566	64,754	12,812	19.8
Net income	153,954	74,936	79,018	105.4
Income taxes	70,799	34,450	36,349	105.5
Income after taxes	83,155	40,486	42,669	105.4

These calculations may be simplified with use of the storage key.

Calculator	
Entries	**Display**
9 6 2 2 3 0	962,230.
−	962,230.
7 0 1 8 0 3	701,803.
M+ or STO	701,803.
=	260,427.
÷	260,427.
MR or RCL	701,803.
=	.3710827682

sold and in *expenses* resulted in a more than doubling of *net income*. Notice that parentheses are used to indicate a decrease.

Distribution of Income

Only corporations may sell **stock**, which is actually the sale of ownership in a company. **Common stock** entitles the owners to receive **dividends** (distributions of profits) and usually entitles them to one vote in company affairs for every share held. In contrast, most **preferred stock** confines owners to a fixed dividend and leaves them without voting rights. As the word *preferred* denotes, however, these owners have preference to dividends relative to the owners of common stock and, in case of the complete failure of a company, they have preference over the owners of common stock to any money realized from the sale of company assets.

The directors of corporations are under no legal obligation to declare dividends. Once on record as having done so, however, they are required by law to follow through with the scheduled payment in the form of checks mailed to stockholders. Because preferred shareholders usually have preference to dividends, they are paid first, and the holders of common stock receive what is left. If, for example, the directors of Amax Corporation allocate $500,000 from net income for the payment of dividends, the holders of 2,500 shares of $100 par value,[1] 6 percent preferred stock will receive a dividend of $6.00 per share, and the holders of 303,125 shares of common stock will receive $1.60 per share.

$$\text{Preferred dividend} = \text{Par value} \times \text{rate}$$

$$= \$100 \times 0.06 = \$6.00 \text{ per share}$$

[1] **Par value** is the dollar value placed on stock when it is first sold — a value on which preferred dividends are computed but a value that usually has no long-term relationship to the market price of the stock. (Reasons for the fluctuations in prices of preferred stock are similar to those for fluctuations in bond prices, as explained on page 370).

$$\frac{\text{Amount}}{\text{received}} = \frac{\text{Number}}{\text{of shares}} \times \frac{\text{Dividend}}{\text{per share}}$$

$$= 2{,}500 \times 6 = \$15{,}000$$

$$\frac{\text{Common}}{\text{dividend}} = \frac{\text{Dollars available}}{\text{Shares outstanding}}$$

$$= \frac{500{,}000 - 15{,}000}{303{,}125}$$

$$= \$1.60 \text{ per share}$$

Dividends paid to the holders of common stock may be either higher or lower than those paid to preferred stockholders, depending on the amount of earnings to be distributed. During periods of increasing profitability, company directors may elect to increase the rate of dividends paid to common stock, whereas, as stated earlier, preferred dividends are generally a fixed percentage of par value.

When stock is designated as being **cumulative preferred**, company directors must pay to preferred shareholders any missed dividends before paying current dividends to the holders of common stock. If, for instance, a downturn in business had caused the directors at Amax Corporation to skip all dividend payments during the preceding year, the distribution of dividends for the current year would be as follows:

Preferred:	Preceding year	$15,000
	Current year	15,000
		$30,000

$$\text{Common:} \quad \frac{\text{Dollars}}{\text{shares}} = \frac{500{,}000 - 30{,}000}{303{,}125} = \$1.55 \text{ per share}$$

The preferred shareholders receive payment for both years, which reduces by $30,000 the amount currently available for common-stock dividends.

The annual dividend payments discussed here would normally be mailed to stockholders on a quarterly basis (shortly after the end of the third month, shortly after the end of the sixth month, etc.). Also, it is quite common for corporate directors to declare an extra dividend for the final quarter, as a way of sharing with common stockholders extraordinary profits realized during the year without officially increasing the established rate of payout.

APPLICATION 1. Anamar Drilling Corporation had gross sales of $2,137,441 and returns of $115,430. Cost of goods sold totaled $1,110,739 and expenses (general and administrative) were $654,807. What is the net income before taxes?

Gross sales	$2,137,441
Returns	115,430
Net sales	2,022,011
Cost of goods	1,110,739
Expenses	654,807
Net income	$ 256,465

APPLICATION 2. What was the federal tax (rounded to dollars) on the net income in Application 1?

$256,465

$\dfrac{100,000 =}{156,465 \times 0.46 =}$ $\quad$ $\dfrac{\$25,750 \text{ (Table 17.1, page 322)}}{71,974}$

$\quad\quad\quad\quad\quad\quad\quad\quad$ $97,724

APPLICATION 3. What is the federal tax (rounded to dollars) on net income of $216,512 as reported on a corporate income statement in thousands of dollars?

216,512 + 000 = 216,512,000
216,512,000

$\dfrac{100,000 =}{216,412,000 \times 0.46 =}$ $\quad\quad\quad$ $\dfrac{25,750 \text{ (Table 17.1)}}{99,549,520}$

$\quad\quad\quad\quad\quad\quad\quad\quad\quad$ $99,575,270

APPLICATION 4. If beginning inventory was $88,516; ending inventory, $79,412; and goods purchased, $216,509; what is the cost of goods sold?

Beginning inventory	$ 88,516
Goods purchased	216,509
Goods available	$305,025
Ending inventory	79,412
Cost of goods sold	$225,613

APPLICATION 5. Using the following data:

	Millions of dollars	
	1986	1985
Gross sales	7,690	7,132
Returns and allowances	90	96
Net sales	7,600	7,036
Cost of goods sold	5,708	5,100
Expenses	1,134	998
Net income	758	938

a. Prepare a vertical analysis based on net sales.

	1986	1985
Gross sales	101.2	101.4
Returns and allowances	1.2	1.4
Net sales	100.0	100.0
Cost of goods sold	75.1	72.5
Expenses	14.9	14.2
Net income	10.0	13.3

b. Prepare a horizontal analysis.

	Amount	Percent
Gross sales	558	7.8
Returns and allowances	(6)	(6.3)
Net sales	564	8.0
Cost of goods sold	608	11.9
Expenses	136	13.6
Net income	(180)	(19.2)

Notice in the vertical analysis that the sum of the percents for cost of goods sold, expenses, and net income totals 100 percent (of net sales). Because the percents in the horizontal analysis are calculated on separate bases (not just as a percent of net sales), no such relationship exists.

APPLICATION 6. If the annual dividend rate for common stock is $2.80 per share, what quarterly dividend will be received by a stockholder who owns 100 shares?

$$\frac{\text{Annual dividend}}{\text{Quarters}} = \frac{2.80}{4} = 0.70 \times 100 \text{ shares} = \$70.00$$

APPLICATION 7. What will be the amount of a quarterly dividend check mailed to the owner of 200 shares of 7-1/2 percent preferred stock that has a par value of $10?

$$\frac{\text{Par value} \times \text{rate}}{\text{Quarters}} \times 200 \text{ shares} = 0.1875 \times 200 = \$37.50$$

APPLICATION 8. The directors at Corporation B have decided to pay end-of-quarter (March 31) dividends of $400,000. Assuming that the owners of 20,000 shares of cumulative preferred stock (with a par value of $100 and a fixed dividend of 6 percent) have not received any dividends for the two preceding years and that 200,000 shares of common stock are outstanding, how much money will a stockholder receive who owns 100 shares of common?

Preferred: Par value × rate × shares = $\dfrac{\text{Annual}}{\text{Payment}}$

$$\$100 \times 0.06 \times 20{,}000 = \$120{,}000$$

Year before last	$120,000
Last year	120,000
Current quarter	30,000
	$270,000

Common: Total − preferred = common

$$400{,}000 - 270{,}000 = \$130{,}000$$

$$\frac{\text{Dollars available}}{\text{Shares outstanding}} \times \frac{\text{Shares}}{\text{owned}} = \frac{\text{Amount}}{\text{received}}$$

$$\frac{130{,}000}{200{,}000} \times 100 = \$65$$

Owners of preferred stock receive payment for the two years of dividends that were in arrears and payment for the first quarter of the current year, leaving just $130,000 to be divided among the owners of common stock.

BALANCE SHEET

A balance sheet is a statement of a company's financial position that reveals the value of company assets and details the claims of creditors and owners on those assets. Accountants sometimes describe balance sheets as "snapshots" of companies because, unlike the varying time spans of income statements, a balance sheet applies to one specific date. The income statement in Figure 17.1 (page 321) was for the year ending December 31, 1986, whereas the balance sheet for the same company in Figure 17.5 (page 330) is for December 31, 1986 — the one day, rather than a week, a month, a quarter, or a year. The elements that comprise a balance sheet are in a constant state of flux; as business transactions take place, so too do elements in the balance sheet undergo change.

The Balance Sheet Equation

The **balance-sheet equation** is as follows:

Assets = liabilities + owners' equity

Figure 17.5
Balance sheet
(condensed)

Commodore Manufacturing, Inc.
Balance sheet (in thousands of dollars)
December 31, 1986

Current assets	$297,628	Current liabilities	$164,816
Fixed assets	348,110	Long-term liabilities	93,479
Total assets	$645,738	Total liabilities	$258,295
		Owners' equity	387,443
		Total liabilities and equity	$645,738

Assets, as defined earlier, consist of the buildings, machinery, vehicles, office equipment, supplies, cash, and all other items of monetary value that are used to operate a business. The dollar value of assets is, therefore, the dollar value of a company.

On the other side of the equation are liabilities and equity. **Liabilities** consist of all outstanding debts and **owners' equity** represents the value of the owners' investment in a company. Restating the balance-sheet equation for Commodore Manufacturing (Figure 17.5), we have

Assets   = liabilities + owners' equity

645,738 = 258,295 + 387,443

645,738 = 645,738

In theory at least, these figures must always balance. One side of the equation identifies the value of the company, with figures on the other side specifying (1) the claims of creditors on those assets and (2) the extent of owner investment.

Further Categorization

Assets and liabilities are further categorized according to the time elements involved, and owners' equity may be labeled in any of a number of ways, depending mainly on the manner in which a company has been organized. **Current assets** include the cash that a business has on hand (including money in checking accounts) and such near-cash items as merchandise inventories and accounts receivable. Inventories, which were defined at length in Chapter 15, are classified as current assets on the assumption that they will be converted to (sold for) cash within a one-year period from the date of the balance sheet. **Accounts receivable** represent money that consumers and business customers owe the company. Businesses regularly sell to consumers on credit, of course; and you will recall from Chapter 5 that producers regularly sell to wholesalers and to retailers on credit, either offering them cash discounts for prompt payment or imposing extended charges for late payment. These outstanding bills are classified as current assets on the assumption that they will be collected well within a one-year period.

Fixed assets consist of relatively long-lived items such as office equipment, machinery, buildings, and land. **Intangible assets**, as the adjective "intangible" denotes, consist of such nonphysical items as patents and goodwill. A patent that is readily marketable is definitely an asset, and, because of the extent of its expected useful life, it is also classified as a fixed asset. The word **goodwill**, as it is used in business, is defined as the difference between the market value of the assets of a business and the book value of company assets. A janitorial company might be priced at $100,000, for example, even though its tangible assets (trucks, equipment, supplies) may have a market value of only $60,000. The $40,000 dollar spread between the market value of the assets and the selling price of the company reflects the value of an on-going business. In recognizing the value of a reputable company name, an established clientele, and an efficient operation, a buyer may knowingly pay a premium for such intangibles — intangibles that are reflected on balance sheets as "goodwill."

Current liabilities consist of outstanding debts that are payable within a one-year period, and they include such obligations as accounts payable and accrued wages and taxes. **Accounts payable** are the payments that a company owes other companies for products bought on credit. When a vendor delivers supplies to Commodore International, for example, the bill eventually received from the supplier becomes part of Commodore's accounts payable and a current liability. Wages may have been earned by employees, but, because payday has not yet arrived, the amounts that remain unpaid are a current liability. Similarly, provisions made for the payment of taxes before the official due date are reflected on the balance sheet as a current liability.

Long-term liabilities are company debts that will not be paid in their entirety within one year. Examples of such obligations are a five-year bank loan and a thirty-year mortgage, items that will be entered on the balance sheet for relatively long periods.

The term **owners' equity** is redundant in that the word *equity* is synonymous with "ownership." The term is used in business, nevertheless, when referring to the value of an owner's investment in a company. In sole proprietorships and partnerships, the dollar amount of the owner's investment is listed on the balance sheet as "Jim Smith capital," for example, or as "Joan Nelson capital." In contrast, owners' equity is listed on corporate balance sheets as "stockholders' equity," which is the sum of the dollar amounts of common stock and preferred stock outstanding (to reflect the amounts that shareholders have invested), along with retained earnings (the earnings that have been retained for reinvestment in the business).

Comparative Statements

Consolidated balance sheets, like the one illustrated in Figure 17.6, include asset-liability-equity data for two or more months, quarters, or years.

Figure 17.6
Consolidated balance sheet (in thousands of dollars)

	12/31/86	12/31/85
Current assets	$297,628	$249,418
Fixed assets	348,110	246,728
Total assets	$645,738	$496,146
Current liabilities	$164,816	$137,610
Long-term liabilities	93,479	80,172
Total liabilities	$258,295	$217,782
Owners' equity	387,443	278,364
Total liabilities and equity	$645,738	$496,146

As with income statements, percentage comparisons of balance-sheet entries are helpful in gaining insight into the relationships of dollar amounts. In the **vertical analysis** of a balance sheet, total assets serve as the base figure. As illustrated in Figure 17.7, current assets are divided by total assets, fixed assets are divided by total assets, and so on. These comparisons make fluctuating relationships more identifiable. A decline of about 4 percent in current assets, as a percent of total assets, has resulted in a corresponding increase in fixed assets. Current liabilities declined a little more than 2 percent and long-term liabilities declined almost 2 percent, resulting in a decline in total liabilities of nearly 4 percent and a corresponding increase in owners' equity.

Horizontal analysis of the entries, as presented in Figure 17.8 provides still further clarification of these relationships. For a company with a 37 percent increase in net sales (see Figure 17.4 on page 324), we would expect a parallel increase in assets, as reflected here (30.2 percent). The most significant increases were in fixed assets and in owners' equity, with the smallest increases being in current assets and in liabilities.

Figure 17.7
Vertical analysis of a balance sheet (in thousands of dollars)

	1986 Amounts	Percent of assets	1985 Amount	Percent of assets
Current assets	297,628	46.1	249,418	50.3
Fixed assets	348,110	53.9	246,728	49.7
Total assets	645,738	100.0	496,146	100.0
Current liabilities	164,816	25.5	137,610	27.7
Long-term liabilities	93,479	14.5	80,172	16.2
Total liabilities	258,295	40.0	217,782	43.9
Owners' equity	387,443	60.0	278,364	56.1
Liabilities and equity	645,738	100.0	496,146	100.0

Figure 17.8
Horizontal analysis of a balance sheet (in thousands of dollars)

	1986	1985	Increase or decrease Amount	Percent
Current assets	297,628	249,418	48,210	19.3
Fixed assets	348,110	246,728	101,382	41.1
Total assets	645,738	496,146	149,592	30.2
Current liabilities	164,816	137,610	27,206	19.8
Long-term liabilities	93,479	80,172	13,307	16.6
Total liabilities	258,295	217,782	40,513	18.6
Owners' equity	387,443	278,364	109,079	39.2
Liabilities and equity	645,738	496,146	149,592	30.2

APPLICATION 1. Arrange the following data to derive the appropriate balance.

Current liabilities	$93,615	Long-term liabilities	$375,500
Current assets	118,340	Fixed assets	514,903

Current assets	$118,340	Current liabilities	$ 93,615
Fixed assets	514,903	Long-term liabilities	375,500
Total assets	$633,243	Total liabilities	$469,115
		Owners' equity	164,128
		Liabilities and equity	$633,243

Total assets = total liabilities + equity
  (so that, algebraically)
Owners' equity = total assets − total liabilities

APPLICATION 2. Using the following consolidated balance sheet,

	(in thousands of dollars)	
	12/31/86	12/31/85
Current assets	$1,553,606	$1,151,957
Fixed assets	1,632,728	1,419,561
Total assets	$3,186,334	$2,571,518
Current liabilities	$1,303,104	$ 862,759
Long-term liabilities	806,716	578,056
Total liabilities	$2,109,820	$1,440,815
Owners' equity	1,076,514	1,130,703
Liabilities and equity	$3,186,334	$2,571,518

a. Prepare a vertical analysis.

	1986 Amount	Percent of assets	1985 Amount	Percent of assets
Current assets	1,553,606	48.8	1,151,957	44.8
Fixed assets	1,632,728	51.2	1,419,561	55.2
Total assets	3,186,334	100.0	2,571,518	100.0
Current liabilities	1,303,104	40.9	862,759	33.6
Long-term liabilities	806,716	25.3	578,056	22.5
Total liabilities	2,109,820	66.2	1,440,815	56.0
Owners' equity	1,076,514	33.8	1,130,703	44.0
Liabilities-equity	3,186,334	100.0	2,571,518	100.0

b. Prepare a horizontal analysis.

			Increase or decrease	
	1986	1985	Amount	Percent
Current assets	1,553,606	1,151,957	401,649	34.9
Fixed assets	1,632,728	1,419,561	213,167	15.0
Total assets	3,186,334	2,571,518	614,816	23.9
Current liabilities	1,303,104	862,759	440,345	51.0
Long-term liabilities	806,716	578,056	228,660	39.6
Total liabilities	2,109,820	1,440,815	669,005	46.4
Owners' equity	1,076,514	1,130,703	(54,189)	(4.8)
Liabilities-equity	3,186,334	2,571,518	614,816	23.9

APPLICATION 3. What conclusions appear obvious in Application 2?

As a percent of total assets (vertical analysis), current liabilities have increased by more than 7 points. That increase, coupled with a more modest increase in long-term liabilities, resulted in a 10 percent increase in total liabilities. In an inverse relationship, owners' equity slipped from 44 to less than 34 percent of total assets.

Correspondingly, the percents in the horizontal analysis that are prominent are for current and total liabilities, with owners' equity reflecting a nearly 5 percent decrease from the preceding year.

Additional methods of financial analysis are presented in the following chapter, for comparisons of income-statement entries to those on balance sheets as they relate to specific areas of decision making in business.

EXERCISES (as assigned by your instructor)

17-1 How does an unincorporated business become incorporated?

17-2 As legal entities, how do sole proprietorships and partnerships differ from corporations?

17-3 What is an income statement?

17-4 What happens to any after-tax income that is reflected on corporate income statements?

17-5 If gross revenue is $316,912.50 and returns and allowances are $9,631.25, what is the amount of net sales?

17-6 If gross sales are $1,543,120 and net sales are $1,115,160, what was the amount of returns and allowances?

17-7 If beginning inventory was $176,318 and goods purchased totaled $985,986, and ending inventory was $129,875, what is the cost of goods sold?

17-8 If beginning inventory was $239,192; goods available, $2,986,153; and ending inventory, $286,212,

a. What was the value of goods purchased?
b. What was the cost of goods sold?

17-9 If cost of goods sold was $382,161; goods available, $463,483; and goods purchased, $364,520,

a. What was the value of beginning inventory?
b. What was the value of ending inventory?

17-10 What is the federal tax obligation of a corporation that had net income of $65,000?

17-11 What is the federal tax obligation of a corporation with net income of $90,315?

17-12 Rounded to whole numbers, what is the federal tax obligation of a corporation with net income of $259,812?

17-13 Rounded to whole dollars, what is the federal tax obligation of a corporation with net income of $2,961,591?

17-14 What is the federal tax obligation of a sole proprietorship with pre-tax income of $122,612?

17-15 What is the federal tax obligation of a partnership with taxable income of $313,166?

17-16 What is the federal tax obligation (rounded to whole dollars) on income of $325,616 as stated on a corporate income statement in thousands of dollars?

17-17 What is a consolidated income statement?

17-18 How does the vertical analysis of an income statement differ from a horizontal analysis?

17-19 Using the following data,

	1986	1985
Revenue:		
Net sales	2,199,220	2,110,051
Other income	316,512	412,890
Total revenue	2,515,732	2,522,941
Cost of goods sold	1,743,002	1,649,249
Gross profit	772,730	873,692
Expenses:		
Operating	111,901	112,320
General	113,293	110,968
Total expenses	245,194	223,288
Net income	527,536	650,404
Income taxes	222,417	278,936
After-tax income	305,119	371,468

a. Prepare a vertical analysis.
b. Prepare a horizontal analysis.
c. Identify any obvious changes that have occurred.

17-20 Using the following data,

	1986	1985
Revenue:		
Net sales	872,249	645,268
Other income	8,839	9,052
Total revenue	881,088	654,320
Cost of goods sold	579,817	428,545
Gross profit	301,271	225,775
Expenses:		
Operating	163,510	112,498
General	39,633	34,374
Total expenses	203,143	146,872
Net income	98,128	78,903
Income taxes	25,001	17,311
After-tax income	73,127	61,592

a. Prepare a vertical analysis.
b. Prepare a horizontal analysis.
c. Identify any obvious changes that have occurred.

17-21 Which type of stock usually has the most stable rate of dividends? Explain.

17-22 What amount of dividends will a corporation pay to a stockholder who owns 50 shares of 5.7 percent preferred stock that has a market value of 95-3/4 and a par value of $100?

17-23 What sized dividend check may a stockholder expect to receive on 100 shares of 12 percent preferred stock that has a par value of $64 and a market price of $66?

17-24 If a company has $332,000 to distribute as dividends among 200,000 outstanding shares of common stock, what amount of money will be paid to the owner of 200 shares?

17-25 If the directors of a corporation decide to distribute $650,000 in dividends for the current year, what amount will be paid to owners of 60,000 shares of outstanding 6-1/2 percent preferred (par value $100) stock and what amount will be paid to each of the 315,000 shares of common stock?

17-26 If a corporation has been in arrears on the payment of dividends to the owners of 7 percent preferred (par value $100) for the past three years, what amount of the $3,000,000 to be distributed on March 31 of this year will go to the owners of 25,500 shares of preferred stock; in addition, how much money will be paid to the owners of 275,000 shares of common?

17-27 If the annual dividend rate for common stock is $7.48, what is the quarterly dividend?

17-28 What is a balance sheet?

17-29 Cite and explain the balance-sheet equation.

17-30 What is the distinction between current and fixed assets?

17-31 Provide at least two examples of intangible assets.

17-32 What is the distinction between current and long-term liabilities?

17-33 XYZ Corporation has current assets of $625,000 and fixed assets totaling $1,033,000. In consideration of current liabilities of $266,070 and long-term liabilities of $655,430, derive a balance.

17-34 Arrange the following data to derive the appropriate balance: Current assets, $48,210; total assets, $415,610; long-term liabilities, $112,113; total liabilities, $123,516.

17-35 Using the following entries,

	12/31/86	12/31/85
Current assets	821,517	757,924
Fixed assets	880,168	827,903
Total assets	1,701,685	1,585,827
Current liabilities	380,033	322,227
Long-term liabilities	366,125	392,137
Total liabilities	746,158	714,364
Owners' equity	955,527	871,463
Total liabilities-equity	1,701,685	1,585,827

a. Prepare a vertical analysis.
b. Prepare a horizontal analysis.
c. Identify any obvious changes that have occurred.

17-36 Using the following entries,

	12/31/86	12/31/85
Current assets	526,636	453,942
Fixed assets	192,172	125,253
Total assets	718,808	579,195
Current liabilities	344,191	248,947
Long-term liabilities	89,753	88,007
Total liabilities	433,944	336,954
Owners' equity	284,864	242,241
Total liabilities-equity	718,808	579,195

a. Prepare a vertical analysis.
b. Prepare a horizontal analysis.
c. Identify any obvious changes that have occurred.

18 Financial Ratios

The analysis of financial statements in Chapter 17 is continued in this chapter as we focus on specific segments of income statements and balance sheets as they relate to bankers, customers, governments, investors, suppliers, and other groups that are concerned with the financial condition of a company. Upon completion of the chapter, you will be able to

- explain the concept and purpose of ratios
- analyze income statements and balance sheets for financial decision making
- measure the liquidity of business organizations through computation and interpretation of the current ratio, quick ratio, and working capital
- assess the financial leverage (borrowing power) of firms as measured by the debt-equity, debt-to-total-assets, and times-interest-earned ratios
- evaluate the efficiency with which inventory is maintained and rotated (through use of the inventory-turnover computation) and the efficiency of the credit department in the collection of accounts receivable (through use of the receivables-turnover equation and an aging of accounts)
- compare with alternative investments the profitability of businesses through the application of sales margin and return on investment

A **ratio** is the relationship in the amount, quantity, or size of two or more things. For ease of comparison, we form ratios by placing two numbers side by side and reducing them to lowest terms. If, for example, American East Airlines in June sold 110,784 full-fare tickets and 276,960 discount tickets, we have

Full fare : discounted

110,784 : 276,960

To reduce the two numbers to lowest terms, we divide both by the lower of the two numbers. Any number divided by itself has a quotient of one, of course, which means that we need only divide the largest number by the smallest.

$$\frac{\text{Larger number}}{\text{Smaller number}} = \frac{276{,}960}{110{,}784} = 2.5 \text{ to } 1.0$$

For the company to report that two and one-half times as many (2-1/2 : 1)

Figure 18.1
Income statement for a
manufacturer of farm
machinery

Commodore Manufacturing, Inc.
Income statement (in thousands of dollars)
for year ending December 31, 1986

REVENUE:

Gross sales		$998,511
Returns and allowances		36,281
Net sales		$962,230
Other income		7,932
Total revenue		$970,162

COST OF GOODS SOLD:

Inventory January 1	$ 98,605	
Goods manufactured	752,350	
Goods available	$850,955	
Inventory December 31	112,313	
Cost of goods sold		738,642
Gross profit		$231,520

EXPENSES:

Selling expenses			
Sales salaries	$21,306		
Rent — sales space	11,112		
Advertising	6,910		
Samples	7,918	47,246	
General expenses			
Office salaries	$ 2,118		
Rent — office space	2,693		
Office supplies	363		
Depreciation	3,126		
Interest	22,020	30,320	
Total expenses			77,566
NET INCOME			$153,954
Tax payments			70,845
Net income after taxes			$ 83,109

Figure 18.2
Balance sheet for a
manufacturer of farm
machinery

Commodore Manufacturing, Inc.
Balance sheet (in thousands of dollars)
December 31, 1986

CURRENT ASSETS:

Cash	$ 41,915	
Accounts receivable	143,192	
Merchandise inventory	112,313	
Prepaid insurance	208	
Total current assets		$297,628

FIXED ASSETS:

Plant facilities	$225,600		
Accumulated depreciation	45,112	$180,488	
Office buildings	$ 98,600		
Accumulated depreciation	12,410	86,190	
Land		80,767	
Office equipment	$ 912		
Accumulated depreciation	247	665	
Total fixed assets			348,110
Total assets			$645,738

CURRENT LIABILITIES:

Accounts payable	$ 85,912	
Notes payable	45,865	
Accrued wages	15,539	
Tax obligations	17,500	
Total current liabilities		$164,816

LONG-TERM
    LIABILITIES:

Mortgage payable	$ 52,005	
Notes payable	41,474	
Total long-term liabilities		93,479
Total liabilities		$258,295

OWNERS' EQUITY:

Common stock	$311,895	
Retained earnings	75,548	
Total owners' equity		387,443
Total liabilities and equity		$645,738

discounted tickets were sold as full-fare tickets is much more effective than a listing of the actual figures.

A limited number of business ratios are presented in this chapter, having been selected on the basis of their relative importance; and, rather than deal with them randomly, the ratios are categorized as pertaining either to liquidity, activity, leverage, or profitability. Each ratio is related to either the income statement in Figure 18.1, the balance sheet in Figure 18.2, or both.

LIQUIDITY RATIOS

The word **liquidity**, in financial applications, refers to cash and near-cash items such as accounts receivable and merchandise inventories, items that we would expect to be converted to cash within a relatively short time. Any measure of liquidity is, therefore, a measure of the capability of a firm to pay current debts as they come due. Before extending credit terms to Commodore Manufacturing, for instance, a supplier would consider the company's current ratio, quick ratio, and working capital.

Current Ratio

The **current ratio** reduces to lowest terms current assets and current liabilities, resulting in a ratio of 1.8 to 1.0 for Commodore Manufacturing (Figure 18.2).

Current ratio = current assets : current liabilities

$$297,628 : 164,816$$

which gives us

$$\frac{297,628}{164,816} = 1.8 \text{ to } 1.0$$

The company has approximately $1.80 in current assets for every $1.00 of current liabilities. To have any meaning, however, this relationship must be compared with the norm for the industry. Assuming that Commodore Manufacturing produces agricultural machinery, an industry in which a current ratio of about 2.6 is considered typical, a ratio of 1.8 must be considered significantly below normal, and a supplier might be reluctant to sell to the company on credit.

Quick Ratio

The **quick ratio**, sometimes referred to as the "acid test," includes only those current assets that can be converted to cash within a very short time period. The computation is the same as for the current ratio except for the exclusion of Commodore's inventory (which may take several months or even years to sell) and prepaid insurance (which, although classified as a current asset, will never be converted to cash).

$$\frac{\text{Quick}}{\text{ratio}} = \frac{\text{current}}{\text{assets}} - \frac{\text{merchandise}}{\text{inventory}} - \frac{\text{prepaid}}{\text{insurance}} : \frac{\text{current}}{\text{liabilities}}$$

$$= 297,628 - 112,313 - 208 : 164,816$$
$$185,107 : 164,816$$

which gives us

$$\frac{185,107}{164,816} = 1.1 \text{ to } 1.0$$

The company has $1.10 (roughly speaking, having rounded to tenths) in quick assets for every $1.00 of short-term bills (current liabilities). The industry norm for the quick ratio is 1.0 meaning that potential creditors expect their business customers to have at least one dollar of quick assets for every one dollar of current liabilities. A ratio of 1.1 is a positive factor in extending credit terms to Commodore, therefore, helping to offset the relatively low current ratio.

Working Capital

Working capital, which is the difference between current assets and current liabilities, is another factor to consider when attempting to judge the capacity of a company to pay its current debts on time.

Working capital = current assets − current liabilities

$$= 297,628 - 164,816$$

$$= \$132,812$$

Working capital, as the term denotes, is the money that a company has to work with in the short term. When working capital is low or nonexistent, a liquidity problem (or crisis) is said to exist.

When liquidity ratios are disproportionately high, on the other hand, it is an indication that too much money is tied up in current assets. Under such circumstances, the financial manager should evaluate the level of inventories being maintained and the level of accounts receivable outstanding, as discussed in the following section, as well as the level of cash being kept in relatively low yielding checking and savings accounts.

APPLICATION 1. In consideration of the following balance-sheet entries,

CURRENT ASSETS:		CURRENT LIABILITIES:	
Cash	$ 79,183	Accounts payable	$ 52,017
Accounts receivable	141,216	Notes payable	175,000
Merchandise inventory	250,720	Accrued wages	62,112
Total	$471,119		$289,129

a. Determine the current ratio:

$$\frac{\text{Current assets}}{\text{Current liabilities}} = \frac{471{,}119}{289{,}129} = 1.6$$

b. Assuming that a current ratio of 2.0 is typical for the industry in which this company exists, would you be willing to offer credit terms for supplies purchased from the company for which you work?

Because of the wide disparity between the current ratio and the industry norm, we would probably ask the business customer for permission to forward any merchandise ordered on a C.O.D. basis, with payment for the value of the merchandise being made at the time of delivery.

APPLICATION 2. Continuing with the entries in Application 1,

a. Calculate the quick ratio.

$$\frac{\begin{array}{c}\text{Current} \; - \; \text{merchandise}\\ \text{assets} \quad\;\; \text{inventories}\end{array}}{\text{Current liabilities}} = \frac{471{,}119 - 250{,}720}{289{,}129} = 0.76$$

b. If a quick ratio of 1.0 is typical for the industry, is a ratio of 0.76 a positive or a negative factor in a decision on whether to sell to the company on credit?

A negative factor, in that the company has only 76 cents in quick assets for every dollar of current liabilities.

c. Determine the amount of working capital available.

$$\frac{\text{Working}}{\text{capital}} = \frac{\text{current}}{\text{assets}} - \frac{\text{current}}{\text{liabilities}}$$

$$= 471{,}119 - 289{,}129$$

$$= \$181{,}990$$

LEVERAGE RATIOS

Leverage ratios relate the debt obligations of companies to the extent of owners' investment — as measures of borrowing power. Before lending money to a corporation, for instance, a lending officer at a bank would consider the debt-equity, debt-to-total-assets, and times-interest-earned measures.

Debt-Equity Ratio

The **debt-equity ratio**, as the term denotes, compares total liabilities with owners' equity, so that for Commodore Manufacturing in Figure 18.2 we have

Figure 18.3
Debt-equity ratio

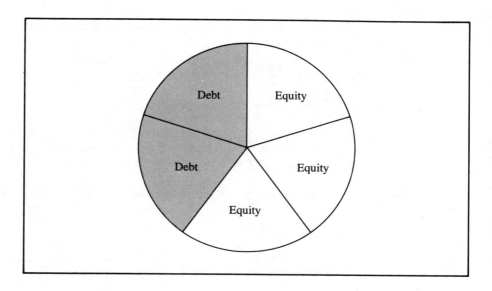

Debt-equity ratio = debt : equity

258,295 : 387,443

which we reduce to lowest terms through division

$$\frac{258,295}{258,295} : \frac{387,443}{258,295} = 1.0 \text{ to } 1.5$$

For every \$1.00 of debt (liabilities) the owners have \$1.50 invested in the corporation.

Viewing the company as a pie in Figure 18.3, the creditors have claim to two pieces (40 percent), with shareholders owning the remaining three pieces (60 percent).

1.0 + 1.5 = 2.5

$$\frac{1.0}{2.5} = 40\% \quad \frac{1.5}{2.5} = 60\%$$

Debt-to-Total-Assets Ratio

The **debt-to-total-assets ratio,** although labeled as a ratio, states total debt as a percent of total assets.

$$\text{Debt-to-total assets} = \frac{\text{Total liabilities}}{\text{Total assets}} = \frac{258,295}{645,738} = 40\%$$

With debt constituting 40 percent of total assets, we may deduce that owners' equity represents 60 percent.

100% − debt = equity

100% − 40% = 60%

The creditors' holding claim to 40 percent of company assets does not compare well with an industry average of 30-35 percent, suggesting that Commodore Manufacturing is slightly overextended with debt.

TIMES-INTEREST-EARNED EQUATION

Potential lenders to businesses also consider the **times-interest-earned equation** to be an indicator of a borrowers' capacity for generating sufficient profits to service company debts.

$$\text{Times-interest-earned equation} = \frac{\text{Profit before taxes} + \text{interest charges}}{\text{Interest charges}}$$

$$= \frac{153,954 + 22,020}{22,020} = 8 \text{ times}$$

As with the preceding ratio, pretax profits of 8.0 times the amount of interest currently being paid falls a little short of an industry average of 8.5 times. On the basis of the information generated from these three measurements, the company is not a prime candidate at present for additional long-term borrowing. If one or more officers of the corporation have acceptable personal credit ratings, a banker might approve a loan application if they (the officers) are willing to endorse the transaction — effectively transferring the responsibility for repayment from the corporation to the individual officers.

APPLICATION 1. On the basis of the following income statement and balance sheet information,

Interest expense	$ 929,612
Total liabilities	36,120,519
Pretax income	13,594,974
Owners' equity	68,645,228
Total assets	104,004,182

a. Compute the debt-equity ratio (industry average = 2).

$$\text{Debt} : \text{Equity}$$
$$\frac{36,120,519}{36,120,519} : \frac{68,645,228}{36,120,519}$$
$$1.0 : 1.9$$

b. Compute the debt-to-total assets ratio (industry average = 40%).

$$\frac{\text{Total liabilities}}{\text{Total assets}} = \frac{36,120,519}{104,004,182} = 34.7\%$$

c. Compute the percent of total assets to which the creditors have claim.

Same answer as in "b," 34.7%

d. Compute the times-interest-earned equation (industry average = 16).

$$\frac{\text{Profit before taxes + interest charges}}{\text{Interest charges}} =$$

$$\frac{13,594,974 + 929,612}{929,612} = 15.6 \text{ times}$$

APPLICATION 2. Interpret the findings in Application 1 as they relate to the accompanying industry averages.

The company's debt load, as revealed by all three measures, is very close to the industry norm. A common procedure when the capacity of a company to absorb additional debt (borrow additional funds) is limited, is for the owner or officer of the borrowing firm to assume personal responsibility for repaying a loan.

ACTIVITY RATIOS

The two main activity ratios are inventory turnover and receivables turnover, which provide indications as to how efficiently two very important business activities are being managed — inventory control and accounts receivable.

Inventory-Turnover

Inventory turnover reveals the number of times within a one-year period that inventories are sold and replenished, and it is computed by dividing cost of goods sold by average inventory.

$$\frac{\text{Cost of goods sold}}{\text{Average inventory}} = \frac{738,642}{\dfrac{98,605 + 112,213}{2}} = \frac{738,642}{105,409} = 7 \text{ times}$$

Having only two inventory figures to average (beginning and ending inventory from the income statement in Figure 18.1), we add them and divide by 2. If we also had a midyear figure, we would add the three numbers and divide by 3. If we had monthly inventory figures, we would add them and divide by 12. The more numbers we average, the more representative the average will be.

Compared to an industry average in manufacturing of 9 times, this turnover rate of 7 times is significantly low. Company managers should either reduce production, increase sales, or both. The implications of a low rate of turnover are higher than necessary costs for storage, insurance, and handling. The implications of a disproportionately high turnover rate, on the other hand, are inventory shortages, lost sales, and alienated customers. A primary objective of most companies with respect to inventory turnover, therefore, is to approximate the industry averages.[1]

An inventory turnover of 7 indicates that average (not total) inventory is being sold and replenished about every 50 days (365 days ÷ 7 times = 52.1 days). Some items will be moved directly from production lines into trucks and railcars, while other products may be stored for a year or longer before being sold. Slow-moving stocks represent a problem that must be dealt with continually at most companies, regardless of the turnover rate, in order to minimize storage costs and to sell merchandise before it becomes spoiled or obsolete.

Receivables Turnover

The **accounts-receivable turnover** provides an approximation of the number of times that accounts receivable (money due a company from credit sales to consumers and business customers) are collected each year — on the average. Assuming that 95 percent of all sales at Commodore Manufacturing are credit sales, we have

$$\text{Receivables turnover} = \frac{\text{Net sales} \times \text{percent of sales made on credit}}{\text{Average accounts receivable}}$$

$$= \frac{962,230 \times 0.95}{\dfrac{162,312 + 143,192}{2}}$$

$$= \frac{914,118.5}{152,752}$$

$$= 6.0$$

The income statement in Figure 18.1 lists nets sales of $962,230, and the balance sheet in Figure 18.2 lists accounts receivable of $143,192 as of the close of business on December 31. Assuming that accounts receivable were $162,312 on January 1 of that year (December 31 of the preceding year), we have an average of $152,752 which, when divided into 95 percent of net sales for the year, results in a turnover of 6 times.

---

[1] This statement is not intended to suggest that businesses should always carry enough inventory to avoid occasional shortages. The cost of ordering products for resale or arranging special production runs should be related to the cost of carrying inventory, in an effort to replenish inventories strategically. **Economic order quantity (EOQ)** models are available for minimizing costs associated with order quantities and order dates, a presentation of which is beyond the scope of this book.

Aging Receivables

The **average age of accounts receivable** may then be computed as follows:

$$\frac{\text{Average age}}{\text{of receivables}} = \frac{\text{Number of days in a year}}{\text{Receivables turnover}} = \frac{365}{6} = 60.8 = 61 \text{ days}$$

Compared to an industry average of 40 days or 9 times (360 ÷ 40 = 9), a turnover rate of 6.0 and an average collection period of 61 days deviate somewhat from the industry norm, suggesting that Commodore Manufacturing is offering extended payment terms to customers as a way of increasing sales.

Turnover rates that are extraordinarily low, coupled with an average age of receivables that is inversely high, means that customers are using money that, unless special terms have been offered, rightfully belongs to the manufacturer. Conversely, a turnover rate that is comparatively high, coupled with an average age of receivables that is low, may indicate that sales are lower than necessary as the result of a tight credit policy.

APPLICATION 1. The accompanying income statement entries pertain to the questions that follow.

Net sales		$4,357,285
Beginning inventory	$610,461	
Goods purchased	3,623,635	
Goods available	$4,234,096	
Ending inventory	554,376	
Cost of goods sold		3,679,720
Total expenses		314,948
Net income		$362,617

a. Determine the inventory turnover ratio.

$$\frac{\text{Inventory}}{\text{turnover}} = \frac{\text{Cost of goods sold}}{\text{Average inventory}}$$

$$= \frac{3,679,720}{\dfrac{610,461 + 554,376}{2}}$$

$$= 6.3 \text{ times}$$

b. What are the possible implications of this ratio as compared to an average industry ratio of 5.1?

An above average turnover of inventory suggests that the company could be experiencing recurring shortages of product, resulting in lost orders and, possibly, lost future business.

APPLICATION 2. Still referring to the data in Application 1, calculate the accounts receivable turnover on the assumption that customer credit is extended on 75 percent of all sales and that accounts receivable were $112,459 on January 1, $142,271 on June 30, and $153,762 on December 31.

$$\frac{\text{Receivables}}{\text{turnover}} = \frac{\text{Net sales} \times \text{percent of sales made on credit}}{\text{Average accounts receivable}}$$

$$= \frac{4,357,285 \times 0.75}{\dfrac{112,459 + 142,271 + 153,762}{3}}$$

$$= \frac{3,267,963.75}{136,164}$$

$$= 24 \text{ times}$$

APPLICATION 3. Determine the average age of the accounts receivable.

$$\frac{\text{Age of}}{\text{receivables}} = \frac{\text{Number of days in year}}{\text{Receivables turnover}}$$

$$= \frac{365}{24}$$

$$= 15.2 \text{ days}$$

APPLICATION 4. How do the answers in Applications 2 and 3 compare to an industry average receivables turnover of 20 and an average collection period of 18 days?

Personnel in the accounts receivable department are apparently being cautious with credit approvals and diligent in their collection efforts. Controls that are exceptionally tight, however, invariably result in lost sales.

PROFITABILITY RATIOS   Many groups of people have an inherent interest in profitability ratios. The degree of profit realized is the measure of managerial success or failure, which is of special interest to stockholders, potential investors, creditors, and the managers themselves; and the primary measures of profitability are sales margin and return on investment.

Sales Margin   **Sales margin** reveals the percent or number of cents from each dollar of sales revenue that are retained as profit after having accounted for all costs and expenses. For Commodore Manufacturing, Inc., we derive *net income after taxes* and *net sales* from the income statement in Figure 18.1 (page 342), giving us

$$\text{Sales margin} = \frac{\text{Net income after taxes}}{\text{Net sales}} = \frac{83,109}{962,230} = 8.6\% \text{ (or } 8.6\text{¢)}$$

A little more than 8.6 percent of every dollar of net sales is realized in profits. Stated another way, the company earned a profit of about 8.6 cents from every one dollar of net sales, with the balance being used to pay for cost of goods sold and related expenses. Assuming an industry average of 6 percent, a sales margin of 8.6 percent appears impressive.

Return on Investment

Return on investment is a measurement with which most people are familiar. If a deposit in a bank is earning 7-1/2 percent, for example, the depositor is receiving a return on investment at that rate; if an investor buys a $1,000 bond that pays 11 percent interest, the person is receiving a return on investment at that rate; and so on. Similarly, the stockholders at Commodore Manufacturing are receiving a return on investment of 21-1/2 percent on their investment in the corporation.

$$\frac{\text{Net income after taxes}}{\text{Owners' equity}} = \frac{83,109}{387,443} = 21.5\%$$

We take the net income shown in Figure 18.1, as we did when computing sales margin, and take owners' equity from the balance sheet in Figure 18.2. The resulting 21.5 percent is extraordinarily high when compared to an industry average of 12.5 percent.

Opportunity Costs

Opportunity costs, which are the returns that could be realized through alternative investments, must be considered when evaluating the return on investment. The shareholders and potential investors in Commodore Manufacturing might be able to earn a still higher return from some other investment with an equal or lower risk. Because the after-tax profits of corporations are still subject to taxation when received by shareholders in the form of dividends, we use after-tax profits for comparisons with alternative investments. To do otherwise would be tantamount to an attempted comparison of apples with oranges.

Also keep in mind that the ratios presented in this chapter tend to differ from one industry to another. A manufacturer of heavy machinery might be justifiably pleased with an inventory turnover of one half (every two years), while the owners of a chain of apparel stores would find a turnover ratio of less than ten to be totally unacceptable. Similarly, a one-to-one debt-equity ratio might be standard for trucking companies with hundreds of thousands of dollars invested in rolling stock, compared to a ratio of as high as four-to-one for an airline with many millions of dollars invested in highly sophisticated aircraft. Rather than judging any one element of a company in isolation, therefore, all financial analyses should be as broadly based as possible.

APPLICATION 1. Using the accompanying entries from an income statement and a balance sheet, respond to the questions that follow.

Net sales	$4,357,285
Net profit	362,617
Taxes	146,554
Income after taxes	216,063
Owners' equity	3,095,519

a. Compute the sales margin.

$$\text{Sales margin} = \frac{\text{Net income after taxes}}{\text{Net sales}} = \frac{216,063}{4,357,285} = 5\%$$

b. Interpret the sales margin as compared with an industry average of 7 percent.

The owners of this company are benefiting from only 5 cents of profit from each dollar of net sales, as opposed to 7 cents as an average profit for companies within this industry.

APPLICATION 2. Again referring to the entries in Application 1,

a. Determine the shareholders' return on investment.

$$\text{ROI} = \frac{\text{Net income after taxes}}{\text{Owners' equity}} = \frac{216,063}{3,095,519} = 7\%$$

b. Interpret the return on investment as compared with an industry average of 10 percent.

A return of 7 percent appears low in relation to an industry average of 10 percent, but an evaluation should include a comparison of this rate with rates that could be earned from alternative investments with equal or lesser risk. If an investor could purchase risk-free government securities with a yield of at least 7 percent, for instance, it would be prudent to switch investments — unless, of course, potential earnings of the company are especially promising.

EXERCISES (as assigned by your instructor)

18-1 What are the liquidity ratios presented here, and what is their purpose?

18-2 What are the leverage ratios presented here, and what is their purpose?

18-3 What are the two main activity ratios, and for what purpose are they applied?

18-4 What profitability ratios are presented here, and how are they interpreted?

18-5 What are opportunity costs?

18-6 If beginning inventory is $79,182; midyear inventory, $101,618; and ending inventory, $85,109; what is the average inventory?

The accompanying income statement and balance sheet entries (stated in thousands of dollars) are related to the exercises that follow. (Round answers to tenths.)

INCOME:		CURRENT ASSETS:	
Sales	$669,769	Cash and equivalents	$ 25,305
Returns	6,853	Receivables	61,978
Net sales	$662,916	Inventories	166,987
COST OF GOODS SOLD:		Other	12,362
Beginning inventory	$ 65,300	Total	$266,632
Goods manufactured	544,132	FIXED ASSETS:	
Goods available	$609,432	Plant and equipment	$106,301
Ending inventory	72,985	Patents at cost	3,894
Total cost	$536,447	Securities	14,612
SELLING EXPENSES:		Total	$124,807
Sales salaries	$ 8,815	CURRENT LIABILITIES:	
Selling space	9,206	Accounts payable	$ 41,110
Advertising	14,033	Taxes payable	15,856
Deliveries	2,781	Current portion of	
Total	$ 34,835	long-term debt	4,661
GENERAL EXPENSES:		Total	$ 61,627
Office salaries	$ 38,372	LONG-TERM LIABILITIES:	
Office space	3,414	Mortgages	$138,313
Office supplies	785	Deferred taxes	25,545
Total	$ 42,571	Other	10,339
TOTAL EXPENSES:	$ 77,406	Total	$174,197
NET INCOME:		OWNERS' EQUITY:	
		Preferred stock	$ 680
Pre-tax income	$ 49,063	Common stock	104,612
Federal tax	22,549	Retained earnings	50,323
After-tax income	$ 26,514	Total	$155,615

18-7 Liquidity ratios:

    a. Determine the current ratio (industry average is 2.5).
    b. Determine the quick ratio, excluding "other" income from the equation (industry average is 1.5).
    c. What is the extent of the firm's working capital?
    d. What are the implications of the findings in a, b, and c?

18-8 Leverage ratios:

    a. Calculate the debt-equity ratio (industry average is 1 to 1).
    b. Compute the debt-to-total-assets relationship (industry average is 50 percent).
    c. In what way are the debt-equity ratio and the debt-to-total assets ratio related?
    d. Assuming an annual interest expense of \$22,163, determine the times-interest-earned equation (industry average is 5).
    e. On the basis of your answers to the preceding exercises, how do you assess the borrowing power of this company?
    f. As a bank loan officer who is analyzing this company's application for a long-term loan, what alternative might you offer?

18-9 Activity ratios:

    a. Compute inventory turnover (industry average is 6 times).
    b. Interpret the inventory-turnover figure that you computed in the preceding exercise.
    c. Assuming that accounts receivable on January 1 was \$72,586 and that credit terms are extended on 72 percent of net sales, compute the receivables-turnover ratio (industry average is 9).
    d. Determine the average age of the accounts receivable (industry average is 42 days).
    e. Considering your findings in c and d, do you conclude that the personnel in accounts receivable are doing a commendable job?

18-10 Profitability ratios:

    a. Determine sales margin (industry average is 5 percent).
    b. Interpret the sales margin figure that you derived in the preceding question.
    c. What return on investment did the owners realize during the one-year period?
    d. On the basis of the return-on-investment figure, would you consider buying stock in this company?

The accompanying income statement and balance sheet entries (stated in thousands of dollars) are related to the exercises that follow.
(Round answers to tenths.)

INCOME:

Sales	$1,301,797
Returns	50,069
Net sales	$1,251,728

COST OF GOODS SOLD:

Beginning inventory	$ 101,285
Goods purchased	933,246
Goods available	$1,034,531
Ending inventory	121,251
Total cost	$ 913,280

GROSS PROFIT: $ 338,448

OPERATING EXPENSES:

Salaries	$ 51,095
Advertising	57,428
Utilities	28,942
Depreciation	60,531
Property tax	1,566
Interest	18,312
Total	$ 217,874

NET INCOME:

Income before taxes	$ 120,574
Federal taxes	55,444
Income after taxes	$ 65,130

CURRENT ASSETS:

Cash	$ 13,378
Accounts receivable	173,467
Inventory	186,866
Prepaid expenses	59,358
Short-term investments	181,682
Total	$614,751

FIXED ASSETS:

Property, plant and equipment	$891,200
Less depreciation	488,958
Net property account	$402,242
Other companies	180,997
Other investments	7,889
Goodwill	8,899
Total	$600,027

CURRENT LIABILITIES:

Accounts payable	$ 80,087
Accrued income taxes	36,576
Accrued wages	9,553
Advanced payments on contracts	76,155
Total	$202,371

LONG-TERM LIABILITIES:

Long-term debt	$163,398
Unfunded pensions	43,523
Accrued salaries	63,769
Total	$270,690

OWNERS' EQUITY:

Common stock	$100,281
Retained earnings	641,436
Total	$741,717

18-11 What percent of sales is the after-tax income?

18-12 Would the purchase of stock in this company be a viable alternative to the purchase of government securities that pay annual interest of 11-1/2 percent?

18-13 What percent of total assets is represented by debt?

18-14 What is the debt-equity ratio?

18-15 What is the rate of inventory turnover in terms of number of days?

18-16 How does the inventory turnover compare with an industry average of ten times, and what are the implications involved?

18-17 As a supplier, would you want to offer your standard terms of "2/10, n/30" to this customer on an order for $50,000 of merchandise?

18-18 As a banker, would you consider this company to be a likely candidate for a long-term loan, assuming that the average company within the same industry is leveraged 50 percent?

18-19 How much working capital is available?

18-20 What is the times-interest-earned ratio?

19 Securities Analysis and Transactions

New businesses need money for getting started — for constructing or acquiring buildings, for purchasing equipment and supplies, for advertising their products and services, for meeting payrolls and paying taxes. Once established, businesses have recurring needs for capital investment — for developing new product lines, for expanding production facilities, for acquiring other companies, and for a host of other business ventures. For most such investments, the financial managers at established companies rely on internally generated funds, by using for expansion all or part of the profits that are realized from the sale of products and services. When capital expenditures exceed available investment funds, however, financial managers may turn to either of two other basic sources of money: the sale of stocks or bonds.

STOCK ISSUES

As explained in Chapter 17, the sale of stock is tantamount to a sale of ownership in a company. A **stock exchange** is a place where the buying and selling needs of investors are identified and paired in a bidding process that may result in a slightly higher or lower price than initially offered. For example, an investor in Milwaukee may wish to sell 100 shares of International Business Machines (IBM), and an investor in Atlanta may wish to buy 100 shares of IBM. When representatives of the Milwaukee and Atlanta investors meet at a place on the exchange floor where transactions in IBM shares are conducted, an offered price of $120.50 and a bid price of $120.00 may be reconciled at an exchange price of $120.25.[1] Such a transaction may take place on the floor of the New York Stock Exchange (NYSE), American Stock Exchange (Amex), or any of several exchanges throughout the country or around the world — wherever IBM stock is listed (traded).

Stock Quotations

Any number of factors may influence the prices of stock, ranging from company operations and profitability to economic conditions and political events, but the only reason that can be stated with certainty concerning fluctuations in stock prices is that the price rises when the demand for a stock increases and the price declines in response to decreased demand. Details of stock prices, dividends, earnings, and trading volume are routinely reported in newspapers and on the radio, with the quotations in Table 19.1 being representative of the nearly 2,000 companies that are listed on the New York Stock Exchange as reported daily in *The Wall Street Journal* and in most city newspapers.

52-Weeks. The highest and lowest prices at which the stock was sold during the preceding 52 weeks — including the current trading week except for the current trading day. Abbott Laboratories (the first listed) sold during that period for as high as $58.00 and as low as $36.75, whereas Continental Telecom (second listed) sold for as high as $24.75 and as low as $18.875.

Table 19.1 Selected stock quotations from the New York Stock Exchange

52 Weeks				Yld	P-E	Sales				Net
High	Low	Stock	Div.	%	Ratio	100s	High	Low	Close	Chg.
58	$36^3/_4$	AbtLab	1.40	2.4	17	1667	$u58^3/_8$	$57^3/_4$	$57^7/_8$	$+^1/_8$
$24^3/_4$	$18^7/_8$	ConTel	1.80	7.8	9	1514	$23^1/_8$	$23^1/_8$	$23^1/_8$	$-^1/_4$
$138^1/_4$	$102^3/_4$	IBM	4.40	3.6	12	17530	$123^3/_8$	$121^3/_8$	122	$+1^1/_8$
$3^1/_8$	$1^7/_8$	MaseyF		..	..	523	$2^1/_8$	$1^7/_8$	2	....
$29^3/_4$	22	USSteel	1	3.6	19	2405	$27^3/_4$	$27^1/_4$	$27^5/_8$	$+^3/_8$
30	$22^7/_8$	USSteel	pf2.25	7.9	..	162	$28^7/_8$	$28^3/_8$	$28^5/_8$	$+^1/_8$
$23^3/_8$	$16^3/_8$	Wynns	.60	3.8	6	1372	$16^5/_8$	$d15^1/_2$	$15^7/_8$	$-1^1/_8$

[1] A type of auction takes place in which representatives bid against one another to secure the lowest possible price (purchase) or the highest possible price (sale). So-called *security specialists* create markets in the absence of either a bid or an offer by making bids or offers from their own accounts.

Stock. Abbreviations of corporate names: Abbott Laboratories, Continental Telecom, International Business Machines, Massey Ferguson, United States Steel, and Wynns International.

Dividend. The annual dividend (distribution of profits among shareholders) based on the most recent payment. For example, a quarterly dividend of 35 cents per share by Abbott Laboratories represents an annual dividend (payout) of $1.40 per share (0.35 × 4 = 1.40). The "pf" designation in the second entry for U.S. Steel specifies that the quotation is for preferred stock as opposed to common.

Yield. The rate of return realized by relating the annual dividend to the closing price for the day. If an investor buys shares of IBM at the closing price of $122.00, for example, an annual dividend of $4.40 would represent a return on investment of 3.6 percent.

$$\text{Yield} = \frac{\text{Annual dividend}}{\text{Closing price}} = \frac{4.40}{122.00} = 0.036 = 3.6\%$$

Why would anyone buy a stock that provides a return on investment of only 3.6 percent? They would do so with expectation that dividends would eventually improve or, relatedly, that the stock would appreciate in value so that they could at some future date sell it for a profit. Many investors, especially those in high tax brackets, prefer to purchase stock on which little or no taxable dividends are paid.

P-E Ratio. The price-earnings ratio is the relationship of the current (closing) price of a stock to company earnings. After determining from separate sources that the earnings per share of all outstanding common stock at Abbott Laboratories is $3.40, for instance, we may determine that the company's stock is presently selling for 17 times that amount — as quoted.

$$\text{P-E ratio} = \frac{\text{Closing price}}{\text{Earnings per share}} = \frac{57.875}{3.40} = 17$$

Companies with P-E ratios that are substantially below ten are considered to be undervalued with respect to company earnings, and companies with ratios significantly above ten are considered to be overpriced. Conversely, some investors view high P-E ratios as a positive factor, believing that high ratios reflect investor confidence in the profit potential of companies. No P-E ratio is shown for preferred stock, as in the second listing for U.S. Steel, nor for Massey Ferguson, because the company showed a loss rather than a profit for the most recent reporting period. Notice also that P-E ratios are listed in whole numbers, with fractional amounts being disregarded.

Sales 100s. The listed figure plus two zeros denotes the number of shares of stock that exchanged ownership on the one trading day. For instance, shares of Abbott Laboratories that were bought and sold on this date totaled 166,700 (1,667 + 00). This figure provides information concerning investor activity in a particular stock.

High and low. The high and low prices at the right of the listings are for the one trading day. For example, Abbott Laboratories sold during the day for as high as $58.375 and for as low as $57.75. The "u" indicates that the price of $58.375 is a new high, the highest price for which this stock has sold during the past 52 weeks. Conversely, the "d" preceding the low price of the day for Wynns International (last listed) indicates a decline, specifying that $15.50 is the lowest price at which this stock has sold during the 52-week period.

Close. The price of the last sale of the day. The final sale of Wynns, for example, was consummated at $15.875.

Net Chg. The net change is the difference between the closing price for the day and the closing price of the same stock the preceding day. The price for Abbott Laboratories increased 1/8 of a point ($0.125) "on the day," as stockbrokers say, whereas the price of Wynns decreased by 1-1/8 points ($1.125). Notice that the close for Massey Ferguson stock is unchanged from the preceding day.

Stock transactions, as reported in newspapers, are accompanied with legends that explain all entries and define all symbols.

APPLICATION 1. Referring to the entries in Table 19.1, respond to the following questions:

a. What is the highest price of the year (in dollars and cents) for International Business Machines?

138-1/4 = $138.25

b. Identify and explain the price-earnings ratio for U.S. Steel common.

The P-E ratio of 19 means that the current closing price of $27.625 is 19 times the most recently reported earnings per share, which is a relatively high ratio.

c. What quarterly dividend have the owners of U.S. Steel common been receiving?

$$\text{Quarterly dividend} = \frac{\text{Annual dividend}}{4} = \frac{\$1.00}{4} = 25\cent$$

d. What was the lowest price that U.S. Steel common sold for on this one trading day?

27-1/4 = $27.25

e. What was the closing price of U.S. Steel common the preceding trading day?

27-5/8 − 3/8 = 27-2/8 = 27-1/4

f. How many shares of U.S. Steel preferred exchanged hands on this one trading day?

162 + 00 = 16,200

APPLICATION 2. If a stock with a closing price of 27-5/8 pays an annual dividend of $2.35, what is the present yield?

27-5/8 = 27.625

$$\text{Yield} = \frac{\text{Dividend}}{\text{Price}} = \frac{2.35}{27.625} = 8.5\%$$

APPLICATION 3. What is the P-E ratio for preferred stock that has a closing price of $18.75, provided that the most recently reported company earnings were $1.15 per share?

No P-E ratio is computed for preferred stock.

Stock Transactions   Once an investor has opened an account at a brokerage office by sharing with an account executive (sales person) certain financial information and investment objectives, an order may be placed. A **market order** would authorize the broker's representative to purchase the stock for whatever the amount the issue is selling at the time of the transaction, which might be slightly higher or slightly lower than the price of the most recently reported transactions. In contrast, a **limit order** would limit the purchase to a specific price, such as authorizing the representative to purchase the stock only if it can be secured at a price of $57.50 or lower. The investor may place a **day order** (to be in effect for only the current trading day), a *week order* (valid for only one week), or a *GTC* (good till canceled) order.

Upon the *purchase of stock*, the investor receives from the broker within the following day or two a statement (bill) for the value of the stock plus related costs.

Purchase of stock:

Stock value + commissions + taxes and fees = Amount due

The purchase of 400 shares of ConTel at a price of 23-1/2 might be billed as follows:

Stock value	$9,400 (400 shares × $23.50 each)
Commission	188
Taxes and fees	2
Total due	$9,590

Commission rates vary considerably from one stock to another and among brokers. Rates for **round lots** (multiples of 100 shares) are lower than for **odd lots** (other than 100 shares). **Volume**, the dollar amount of a transaction, is the main factor in the broker's assessment of a commission, with large orders being rated at as low as 1-1/2 percent and small orders as high as 4 or 5 percent of that value. Transactions involving $100,000 or more may be negotiated, with investors often paying only a fraction of 1 percent. Although most commission rates are unpublished, **full-service brokers**, who provide a limited amount of financial counseling, generally charge the highest rates, and **discount brokers**, who offer virtually no advice, charge the lowest rates. Statements mailed by brokers, which may also include fees and taxes as imposed by federal and local governments, are payable upon receipt but no later than five business days following a transaction date.

Upon the *sale of stock*, on the other hand, the commission rate and any fees or taxes are subtracted from the proceeds.

Sale of stock:

Stock value − commissions − fees and taxes = proceeds

Assume that the same investor who purchased 400 shares of ConTel at 23-1/2 later sold the entire lot at 25-1/4, with only slightly higher commissions, taxes, and fees.

Stock value	$10,100 (400 shares × $25.25 each)
Commission	−202
Taxes and fees	−3
Proceeds	$ 9,895

The investor paid total buying and selling commissions of $390 (188 + 202) and total taxes and fees of $5 (2 + 3), resulting in a net gain of only $305 (9,895 − 9,590).

APPLICATION 1. If an investor purchases 150 shares, is the transaction a round lot or an odd lot?

The transaction consists of one round lot (100 shares) and one odd lot (50 shares), the latter of which would be subject to a relatively high commission through what is called an "odd lot differential."

APPLICATION 2. If an investor purchases 300 shares of Amalgamated Steel at 94-1/8, subject to a commission of 1-3/4 percent of the stock value and taxes and fees totaling $10, what will be the amount due on the broker's statement?

Total value	$28,237.50 (300 shares × $94.125)
Commission	494.16 (28,237.50 × 0.0175)
Taxes and Fees	10.00
Amount due	$28,741.66

APPLICATION 3. If an investor sells 500 shares of Rutgers Electric for 23-5/8, with a commission rate of 2 percent of the stock value and taxes and fees totaling $10, what are the proceeds?

Total value	$11,812.50 (500 shares × 23.625)
Commission	−236.25 (11,812.50 × 0.02)
Taxes and fees	−10.00
Proceeds	$11,566.25

Whether the investor requests that a **stock certificate** (written proof of ownership) be provided depends on several factors. Stock certificates enable investors to sell stock at any brokerage office, whereas the absence of a certificate ties them to a particular broker. Investors may also use stock certificates as collateral in the securance of lower-cost (secured) loans. Certificates are negotiable instruments, on the other hand, which must be protected like money, and investors must take or mail (certified) them to brokers at the time of sale.

CORPORATE BONDS

Unlike stock, which is the sale of ownership in a corporation, **bonds** are debt securities from which investors receive interest rather than dividends. Instead of securing direct loans from banks or from other companies, corporate managers may issue bonds as a way of borrowing millions of dollars from a variety of sources — from individual investors, from other corporations, from institutions that manage money for individuals (such as pension funds and insurance companies), and from state, local, and foreign governments.

Secured bonds are backed by collateral (buildings and equipment, for example) which may be sold in order to repay bondholders in the case of default (failure to repay a loan or to pay interest as scheduled). **Debentures**, on the other hand, are bonds that are sold strictly on the financial and operational reputations of corporations, with no collateral whatsoever behind them.

The **indenture** (contractual segments) of bonds may include any number of **covenants** (promises by corporate borrowers), ranging from interest rates to be paid to repayment schedules, from provisions for exchanging the bonds for stock to rights of the issuing corporations to redeem the bonds. Because of the complexity of such provisions, and because of the wide dispersion of bond-holders that normally exists, the borrowing companies must appoint and pay a **trustee** (usually a bank) to protect the rights of bondholders.

Convertible Bonds

If the sale of a bond issue is to be completed successfully, it must compete with other corporate issues — as well as with **municipal bonds** (tax-exempt bonds issued by state and city governments) and a wide array of bonds issued by the federal government. As a "sweetener," corporations often include a **conversion privilege** in a bond indenture entitling bondholders to convert their bonds to common stock at a prescribed price. In 1984, for example, a hospital supply company raised $75 million by selling 5-3/4 percent $1,000 convertible debentures that mature (become payable) in 1999 — a conversion from debt (bonds) to equity (stock) being permitted at a price of $29.50. If a conversion were eventually made at a time when the stock was selling at $39.50 per share, the highest price of the stock since the bonds were issued, the investor could have sold the stock for a gain (profit) of $339.05 on the conversion.

Stock purchase: $\dfrac{\text{Bond}}{\text{value}} \div \dfrac{\text{conversion}}{\text{price}} = \dfrac{\text{number of}}{\text{shares}}$

$$1,000 \div 29.50 = 33.9$$

Stock sale: $\dfrac{\text{Number of}}{\text{shares}} \times \dfrac{\text{market}}{\text{price}} = \dfrac{\text{market}}{\text{value}}$

$$33.9 \times 39.50 = \$1,339.05$$

Gain on transaction: $\dfrac{\text{Market}}{\text{value}} - \dfrac{\text{bond}}{\text{value}} = \text{gain}$

$$1,339.05 - 1,000.00 = \$339.05$$

Rather than converting the value of a bond to an unspecified number of shares of common stock at a specified price, some bond issues provide for an exchange of a bond for a specified number of shares at an unspecified price. In the preceding situation, for example, the indenture might have stated that one bond could be exchanged at any time for 34 shares of common stock.

Call Provision

Corporate financial managers must also include in bond indentures provisions that protect their companies. During times of relatively high interest rates, for example, it is imperative that they include a **call provision** to entitle the issuing corporation to recall (redeem) the bonds in order to **refund** (reissue) the bonds at lower rates. The dates and redemption percents in Table 19.2 are typical. If

Table 19.2
Redemption rates for
Convertible Debentures
due 2009

1984	105.750%	1994	102.875%
1985	105.463	1995	102.588
1986	105.175	1996	102.300
1987	104.888	1997	102.013
1988	104.600	1998	101.725
1989	104.313	1999	101.438
1990	104.25	2000	104.150
1991	103.738	2001	100.863
1992	103.450	2002	100.575
1993	103.163	2003	100.288

the company were to redeem these $1,000 bonds in 1990, it would have to pay bondholders $1,042.50 for each bond ($1,000 × 1.0425 = $1,042.50). Redemption at any time after the year 2003 would be at the face value of $1,000 each. Corporate managers would pay such a premium and undertake the considerable expense of redeeming a bond and issuing a new one, of course, only if current interest rates were significantly lower than the contractual rate on the bond; that is, only if it were profitable for them to replace a high-cost loan with one that is less costly.

Bond Quotations

Bond transactions are reported in *The Wall Street Journal*, *Barron's*, and most city newspapers, with those in Table 19.3 having been selected from listings on the New York Exchange.

Table 19.3
Selected bond
quotations from the New
York Stock Exchange

Bonds	Cur Yld	Vol	High	Low	Close	Net Chg.
AAirl $4^1/_4$92	6.3	1	67	67	67	$+^1/_2$
BurlInd $11^1/_4$90	11.	30	$100^7/_8$	$100^7/_8$	$100^7/_8$	$+^1/_8$
CitSvc zr89	..	58	$63^3/_8$	$62^1/_2$	$62^1/_2$	....
ConEd $4^1/_4$86	4.5	32	$94^3/_4$	$94^3/_8$	$94^1/_2$	$+^1/_8$
CnPw $6^7/_8$98	11.	16	62	61	62	$-1^1/_2$
Dow $8^7/_8$2000	11.	2	83	83	83	$+^1/_2$
Dow 7.4s02	10.	2	72	72	72	$-^1/_2$
Dow $8^5/_8$08	11.	2	$77^3/_8$	$77^3/_8$	$77^3/_8$	$-^7/_8$
Dow $11^1/_4$10	12.	3	94	94	94	$-4^1/_2$
FrdC 8.85s86	8.9	1	100	100	100	....
GMills $8^7/_8$95	10.	5	89	89	89	-2
PhilP $14^3/_4$00	14	272	$106^1/_2$	$106^1/_4$	$106^1/_4$	$-^5/_8$
WstgE 9s09	cv	63	$124^1/_2$	$124^1/_4$	$124^1/_4$	$+1$
XeroxCr 16s91	14.	10	117	117	117	$-^7/_8$

Bonds. This first column includes four or five items of information:

1. The name of the company (American Airlines, Burlington Industries, Cities Service, Consolidated Edison).
2. The annual rate of interest (American Airlines, 4-1/4 percent; Burlington Industries, 11-1/4 percent, Consolidated Edison, 4-1/4 percent, etc.). Bond issuers may pay interest on January 15 and July 15, February 1 and August 1, June 1 and December 1 — whatever dates are stated in the bond indenture. **Bearer bonds** entitle their possessors (bearers), who are unknown to the issuing company, to remove coupons (called "clipping coupons") on the dates that interest payments are due and to cash them at authorized banks. **Registered bonds**, which are the dominant form among current issues, are registered by the issuing company in the names of purchasers, and interest checks are mailed directly to owners on prescribed payment dates.
3. The year of maturity (American Airlines, 1992; Burlington Industries, 1990; Cities Service, 1989; etc.).
4. The "s" in several of the listings serves only to separate the numerical entries. This letter, which may be thought of as representing a space, is unneeded when the interest rate includes a fractional value.
5. The "zr" notation for the Cities Service entry denotes a **zero-coupon bond** on which interest, rather than being paid periodically, is allowed to accumulate until the bond matures. An investor purchasing this bond today at a price of $621.20, for example, would receive $1,000 (the face value of the bond) upon maturity of the bond in 1989.

Cur Yld. The **current yield** is the rate of return that would be realized by an investor who purchased a bond at the closing price, and it is computed by dividing the annual interest payment by the current (closing) price. An investor purchasing an American Airlines bond for $670, for example, would be receiving a return on investment (yield) of 6.3 percent.

$$\text{Yield} = \frac{\text{Annual interest}}{\text{Closing price}}$$

$$= \frac{1,000 \times 0.0425}{670} = \frac{42.50}{670} = 0.063 = 6.3\%$$

In buying a $1,000 bond for only $670, the investor would receive an effective interest rate of 6.3 percent as opposed to the quoted rate of 4-1/2 percent. Notice that the Westinghouse Electric (next-to-last) entry substitutes a "cv" notation for the yield percent, denoting that this is a convertible bond.

Vol. The **volume** of transactions for the day is stated in thousands of dollars. Because most bonds are issued in $1,000 denominations, this figure typically indicates the actual number of bonds that investors have bought and sold. Volume for the American Airlines listing consisted of only one bond; Burlington Industries, 30 bonds; Cities Service, 58 bonds.

High, Low, Close. These columns list the prices for the day — the highest and lowest prices and the closing prices. They are stated as a percent of maturity value, indicating that the American Airlines issue closed at $670 ($1,000 × 0.67 = $670) and that the Burlington Industries bond closed at $1,008.75 ($1,000 × 1.00875 = $1,008.75).

Net Chg. As with bond prices, the net change in the closing price of a bond from its closing price the preceding day is stated as a percent. For example, the American Airlines bond gained $5 on the day ($1,000 × 0.005 = 5) and the Burlington Industries issue gained $1.25 ($1,000 × 0.00125 = $1.25).

Interest rates vary in correlation with the financial conditions of companies and the probability of their being able to meet the obligations of paying interest as it comes due and repaying the bonds when they mature. To assist investors in their selection and sale of bonds, two financial services rate the financial conditions of issuing companies: Moody's Investors Service and Standard & Poor's Corporation. Although the two services use varying letter combinations, the ratings are similar.

Moodys: Aaa, Aa, A, Baa, Ba, B, Ccc

S & P: AAA, AA, A, BBB, BB, B, CCC

Bond issues by companies with Aaa and AAA ratings represent a lower risk to investors than companies with Aa and AA ratings; those with Aa and AA are superior in this respect to companies with ratings of A; and so on, with each such move to the right of the two scales representing progressively higher risks that, if the bonds are to be purchased by investors, must be accompanied by correspondingly high interest rates. No rational investor would purchase a corporate bond from a company with a rating of Baa or BBB in lieu of a government security, for instance, unless the corporate issue carried an interest rate significantly higher than that offered in the government security.

APPLICATION 1. As listed in Table 19.3, what would be the amount of semiannual interest received by a holder of ten General Mills bonds?

$$\frac{\text{Maturity}}{\text{value}} \times \text{Rate} = \text{Interest}$$
$$1,000 \times 0.08875 \times 1/2 = 44.38$$

$$\text{Interest} \times \frac{\text{number}}{\text{of bonds}} = \frac{\text{Total}}{\text{interest}}$$
$$44.38 \times 10 = \$443.80$$

APPLICATION 2. In what year does the General Mills bond mature?

1995

APPLICATION 3. At the closing price (excluding any commissions, taxes, or fees), what is the value of 20 Westinghouse Electric bonds?

$$\frac{\text{Maturity}}{\text{value}} \times \text{Close} = \frac{\text{Closing}}{\text{price}}$$
$$1{,}000 \times 1.2425 = 1{,}242.50$$

$$\frac{\text{Closing}}{\text{price}} \times \frac{\text{Number}}{\text{of bonds}} = \frac{\text{Total}}{\text{value}}$$
$$1{,}242.50 \times 20 = \$24{,}850$$

APPLICATION 4. What was the market value of all General Mills bonds that exchanged hands on this one trading day?

$$\frac{\text{Maturity}}{\text{value}} \times \text{High-low-close} = \text{Price}$$
$$1{,}000 \times 0.89 = \$890$$

$$\text{Price} \times \frac{\text{Number}}{\text{of bonds}} = \frac{\text{Market}}{\text{value}}$$
$$890 \times 5 = \$4{,}450$$

APPLICATION 5. In dollars and cents, what was the loss of value for the Xerox bond on this one trading day?

$$\frac{\text{Maturity}}{\text{value}} \times \frac{\text{Net}}{\text{change}} = \frac{\text{Decline in}}{\text{value}}$$
$$1{,}000 \times (-0.00875) = (\$8.75)$$

APPLICATION 6. If a $1,000 bond pays an annual interest rate of 12 percent and closes at 85, what is the yield?

$$\text{Yield} = \frac{\text{Annual interest}}{\text{Current price}}$$
$$= \frac{1{,}000 \times 0.12}{1{,}000 \times 0.85} = \frac{120}{850} = 14.1\%$$

Price Fluctuations. Most bonds sell at or near their face value during only two periods: at the time of issue and near the maturity date. Varying interest rates represent the major factor in causing the prices of bonds (and preferred stock) to fluctuate, with increasing market rates causing prices to fall and decreasing rates causing bond prices to rise. Notice in Table 19.3, for example, that the

American Airlines bond carried an interest rate of only 4-1/4 percent at a time (1986) when current bond rates hovered around 12 percent. As a consequence, investors would purchase these bonds from other investors only at a discount; that is, only if the asking price were at a point where the sum of the discount and the interest yet to be collected would approximate the prevailing (market) rate of interest. **Yield to maturity** is used to measure this combination. For an investor buying the American Airlines stock in 1986, the yield to maturity would be 11.7 percent.

Yield to Maturity for a Discounted Bond

$$\text{Yield to maturity} = \frac{\text{Annual interest} + \text{prorated discount}}{\text{Average investment}}$$

$$\text{Annual interest} = \text{Prt} = 1{,}000 \times 0.0425 \times 1 = \$45.50$$

$$\text{Prorated discount} = \frac{\text{Face value} - \text{price}}{\text{Years remaining}} = \frac{1{,}000 - 670}{1992 - 1986} = \frac{330}{6} = \$55$$

$$\text{Average investment} = \frac{\text{Face value} + \text{current price}}{2} = \frac{1{,}000 + 670}{2} = \$835$$

$$\text{which gives us} \quad \frac{42.50 + 55.00}{835} = \frac{97.50}{835} = 11.7\%$$

The 4-1/4 percent annual interest payment, when combined with the extra $55 each year (prorated discount), provides the 1986 purchaser of this bond with the market rate of interest (11.7%) for the remainder of the term (six years).

Sellers of bonds that carry a higher than market rate of interest, on the other hand, may expect to receive **premiums** in the form of prices that exceed face value. Phillips Petroleum, as listed in Table 19.3, carried a relatively high 14-3/4 percent and a 6-1/4 percent premium (106-1/4% − 100% = 6-1/4%). Correspondingly, a purchaser of this bond in 1986 at 106-1/4 would realize a *yield to maturity* of 13.9 percent. To make this determination, we alter the preceding formula by subtracting the prorated premium in the numerator rather than adding the annual gain.

Yield to Maturity for a Premium Bond

$$\text{Yield to maturity} = \frac{\text{Annual interest} - \text{prorated premium}}{\text{Average investment}}$$

$$\text{Annual interest} = \text{Prt} = 1{,}000 \times 0.1475 \times 1 = 147.50$$

$$\text{Prorated premium} = \frac{\text{Price} - \text{face value}}{\text{Years remaining}}$$

$$= \frac{1,062.50 - 1,000.00}{2000 - 1986}$$

$$= \frac{62.50}{14}$$

$$= \$4.46$$

$$\text{Average investment} = \frac{\text{Face value} + \text{current price}}{2}$$

$$= \frac{1,000.00 + 1,062.50}{2}$$

$$= 1,031.25$$

$$\text{which gives us} \quad \frac{147.50 - 4.46}{1,031.25} = \frac{143.04}{1,031.25} = 13.9\%$$

An investor in the Phillips Petroleum bonds in 1986 will receive during the ensuing 14 years a return on investment of approximately 14 percent, which compares favorably with the market rate at that time (around 12 percent), with the $62.50 premium serving to reward the seller for having originally purchased the bond at a relatively high rate of interest.

Notice in Table 19.3 that both Burlington Industries and Frederick Cooper (FrdC) were selling near their face value in 1986 — Burlington because it carried a near market rate of 11-1/4 percent and Frederick because it was close to maturity. As bonds approach maturity, their prices gravitate to their face value; in this case, toward the $1,000 that the company was to repay the current owner of the bond. Convertible bonds differ in this respect. When the price of the issuing company's common stock increases, the real or perceived increase in the value of the bond is reflected in the price of the bond.

APPLICATION 1. With reference to Table 19.3, why do you imagine the 2008 (3rd listed) bond for Dow Chemical carried a bigger discount than the 2010 (4th listed) bond?

Because the 2008 bond reflects interest of only 8-5/8 percent compared to 11-1/4 percent for the 2010 bond.

APPLICATION 2. Based on the 1986 listing in Table 19.3, what is the *yield to maturity* for the Continental Power (CnPw) bond?

$$\text{Yield to maturity} = \frac{\text{Annual interest} + \text{prorated discount}}{\text{Average investment}}$$

$$\text{Annual interest} + \text{Prt} = 1{,}000 \times 0.06875 \times 1 = 68.75$$

$$\text{Prorated discount} = \frac{\text{Face value} - \text{price}}{\text{Years remaining}} = \frac{1{,}000 - 620}{1998 - 1986} = \frac{380}{12} = 31.67$$

$$\text{Average investment} = \frac{\text{Face value} + \text{current price}}{2} = \frac{1{,}000 + 620}{2} = 810$$

$$\text{which gives us} \quad \frac{68.75 + 31.67}{810} = \frac{100.42}{810} = 12.4\%$$

APPLICATION 3. In view of the 1986 listing in Table 19.3, what is the *yield to maturity* for the Xerox bond?

$$\text{Yield to maturity} = \frac{\text{Annual interest} - \text{prorated premium}}{\text{Average investment}}$$

$$\text{Annual interest} = \text{Prt} = 1{,}000 \times 0.16 \times 1 = 160.00$$

$$\text{Prorated premium} = \frac{\text{Price} - \text{face value}}{\text{Years remaining}}$$

$$= \frac{1{,}170.00 - 1{,}000.00}{1991 - 1986}$$

$$= \frac{170}{5}$$

$$= 34$$

$$\text{Average investment} = \frac{\text{Face value} + \text{current price}}{2}$$

$$= \frac{1{,}000.00 + 1{,}170.00}{2}$$

$$= 1{,}085.00$$

$$\text{which gives us} \quad \frac{160 - 34}{1{,}085} = = 11.6\%$$

Bond Transactions   The purchase or sale of bonds is similar to that of stock, with one major exception: The interest must be prorated. If, for example, a $1,000 bond pays interest on January 15 (for the six-month term July 1 through December 31 of the preceding year) and on July 15 (for the six-month term January 1 through June 30 of the current year), a settlement date of February 11 would entitle the bond seller to 41 days' interest. Assuming further that the bond pays annual interest of 8 percent and that the transaction price is at 72, the buyer pays $739.11 and the seller receives $719.11.

Term: Jan 1–31 = 31
$\qquad$ Feb 1–10 = <u>10</u> (settlement date not included)
$\qquad\qquad\qquad$ 41

Buyer pays: Market value $\qquad$ 1,000 × 0.72 = $720.00
$\qquad\qquad$ Interest 1,000 × 0.08 × 41/360 = $\qquad$ 9.11
$\qquad\qquad$ Commission $\qquad\qquad\qquad\qquad\qquad$ <u>10.00</u>
$\qquad\qquad$ Total cost $\qquad\qquad\qquad\qquad\qquad$ $739.11

Seller receives: Market value $\qquad\qquad\qquad$ $720.00
$\qquad\qquad$ Interest $\qquad\qquad\qquad\qquad\qquad$ 9.11
$\qquad\qquad$ Commission $\qquad\qquad\qquad\qquad$ <u>−10.00</u>
$\qquad\qquad$ Net proceeds $\qquad\qquad\qquad\qquad$ $719.11

Notice that these interest calculations are based on a 360-day year. Having paid interest of $9.11, the buyer loses the use of that amount of money until receipt of the July 15 interest payment which will include the 41 days' interest paid to the seller. Conversely, the seller receives interest of $9.11 more than five months before the next scheduled payment (July 15), during which time the money can be earning interest. The importance of such detail becomes more pronounced, of course, when dealing with more than one bond.

Although the commission on bonds varies among brokers, a charge of $10 per bond is typical. Some brokers limit this charge to $20 or $30 for the purchase or sale of as many as ten bonds in a single transaction.

APPLICATION 1. A $1,000 bond with a market quotation of 85 carries an annual interest rate of 11-1/2 percent — payable on June 1 (for the term December 1 of the preceding year to May 31 of the current year) and on December 1 (for the term June 1 through November 30 of the current year). With a broker's commission of $25 and a settlement date of March 15, what amount of money must the buyer remit to the broker?

Dec 1–31 = $\;$ 31
Jan 1–31 = $\;$ 31
Feb 1–28 = $\;$ 28
Mar 1–14 = $\;$ <u>14</u> (settlement date not included)
$\qquad\qquad\quad$ 104 days

Market value = 1,000 × 0.85 = $850.00
Interest = 1,000 × 0.115 × 104/360 =   33.22
Commission   25.00
Total cost $908.22

APPLICATION 2. Continuing with the transaction in the preceding application, what amount of money may the seller expect to receive from the broker?

Market value $850.00
Interest   33.22
Commission   −25.00
Net proceeds $858.22

Keep in mind that the interest-earned figure is added in each computation but that the broker's commission is added to the buyer's cost and subtracted from the seller's proceeds.

CAPITAL GAINS PROVISION

Capital assets include such items as buildings, machinery, vehicles, and securities. Correspondingly, **capital gains** include any profits realized from the sale of capital assets. When investors purchase bonds at discounted prices, therefore, they realize capital gains at maturity. An investor who purchases an American Airlines bond at $670 and holds it to maturity, for example, will realize a capital gain of $330.

Selling price − original cost = capital gain

$$\$1,000 - 670 = \$330$$

A **long-term capital gain** is realized when and if an investor owns a capital asset for longer than six months (that is, for at least six months and one day), and the capital gains provision of the federal tax law comes into play. **Short-term capital gains** (asset held six months or less) are reported to the Internal Revenue Service as regular income and taxed at a rate based on total income. Long-term capital gains, on the other hand, are discounted at the current rate of 60 percent, so that on a $330 long-term gain an investor in the 30 percent tax bracket would pay taxes of $39.60.

$$\frac{\text{Long-term}}{\text{gain}} \times (100\% - 60\%) = \frac{\text{Taxable}}{\text{gain}}$$

$$330 \times 0.40 = 132$$

$$\frac{\text{Taxable}}{\text{gain}} \times \frac{\text{Tax}}{\text{rate}} = \text{Tax}$$

$$132.00 \times 0.30 = \$39.60$$

or, more simply,

$$330 \times 0.40 \times 0.30 = \$39.60$$

The **maximum rate** that any taxpayer can be made to pay on a capital gain, therefore, is 20 percent. For example, a taxpayer in the highest tax bracket (currently 50 percent) will pay a tax rate of only 20 percent on a long-term capital gain of $1,000.

$$\frac{\text{Long-term}}{\text{gain}} \times (100\% - 60\%) = \text{Taxable gain}$$

$$1,000 \times 0.40 = 400$$

$$\frac{\text{Taxable}}{\text{gain}} \times \frac{\text{Tax}}{\text{rate}} = \text{Tax}$$

$$400 \times 0.50 = 200$$

$$BR = P$$

$$1,000R = 200$$

$$R = 20\%$$

Investors who purchase bonds at a premium, on the other hand, may reduce their tax obligations by claiming capital losses at maturity — but only after having reduced the loss by 60 percent. An investor purchasing a Westinghouse bond at $1,240.50, for example, can upon receiving payment at maturity of only $1,000.00, claim a long-term capital loss of $240.50.[2]

---

[2] In reporting capital gains and losses at the end of a tax year, investors may use short-term losses to offset any short-term gains to determine the net short-term capital gain or loss. Similarly, they may use long-term losses to offset long-term gains to determine the net long-term capital gain or loss. Subsequently, they subtract net short-term totals and net long-term totals from each other to determine the overall net gain or loss. A net gain (if any) is included in taxable income, and a net loss (if any) may be used to reduce ordinary income — up to a maximum of $3,000 for any one tax year, with the balance (if any) being carried forward to following tax years until fully claimed.

$$\frac{\text{Purchase}}{\text{price}} - \frac{\text{Maturity}}{\text{payment}} = \frac{\text{Long-term}}{\text{loss}}$$

$$1,240.50 - 1,000.00 = 240.50$$

$$\frac{\text{Capital}}{\text{loss}} \times (100\% - 60\%) = \frac{\text{Applicable}}{\text{loss}}$$

$$240.50 \times 0.40 = \$96.20$$

Obviously, the capital gains provision provides investors with a useful method of reducing their tax obligations.

APPLICATION 1. If an investor in the 35 percent tax bracket buys a $1,000 bond at a discounted price of $890, how much of the long-term gain realized at maturity (two years later) will be paid in federal taxes?

$$\frac{\text{Maturity}}{\text{value}} - \frac{\text{Purchase}}{\text{price}} = \frac{\text{Long-term}}{\text{gain}}$$
$$1,000 - 890 = 110$$

$$\frac{\text{Long-term}}{\text{gain}} \times (100\% - 60\%) = \frac{\text{Taxable}}{\text{income}}$$
$$110 \times 0.40 = 44$$

$$\frac{\text{Taxable}}{\text{income}} \times \frac{\text{Tax}}{\text{rate}} = \text{Tax}$$
$$44.00 \times 0.35 = \$15.40$$

APPLICATION 2. By what amount of money is a taxpayer's taxable income reduced at maturity on a $1,000 bond that was purchased for $1,250, assuming that the taxpayer had held the bond for longer than six months?

$$\frac{\text{Purchase}}{\text{price}} - \frac{\text{Maturity}}{\text{value}} = \frac{\text{Long-term}}{\text{loss}}$$
$$1,250 - 1,000 = 250$$

$$\frac{\text{Long-term}}{\text{loss}} \times (100\% - 60\%) = \frac{\text{Applicable}}{\text{loss}}$$
$$250 \times 0.40 = \$100$$

APPLICATION 3. What is the maximum tax rate that an investor who is in the 35 percent tax bracket pays on net long-term capital gains?

$$(100\% - 60\%) \times 0.35 = \text{maximum tax rate}$$
$$0.40 \times 0.35 = 14\%$$

GOVERNMENT SECURITIES

Securities issued by the federal government are considered by most investors to be virtually risk free. **U.S. bonds**, which are available in varying denominations and maturities, cannot be traded among investors but can be redeemed at any time. **Treasury bills** normally have a term of only three months and are sold in minimum denominations of $10,000. Both bonds and bills are discounted, with the discount depending on the market value of money (prevailing interest rates) at the time of issue.

U.S. Treasury notes have maturities ranging from one to ten years and, rather than being discounted, entitle investors to semiannual interest payments. They may be purchased in denominations ranging from $500 to more than $10,000. **Treasury bonds**, which may be either bearer or registered, have durations of longer than ten years and they are callable. Government securities provide an informal floor or lower limit for interest rates on new issues of corporate bonds, in that no rational investor would pay a higher price (or even the same price) for corporate issues as for a virtually risk free government security.

MUTUAL FUNDS

Mutual funds are investment companies that sell shares in their own organizations, usually to relatively small investors, using the investors' money to purchase government securities and the stocks and bonds of selected corporations. In **open-end funds**, the number of shares is unlimited, whereas in **closed-end funds** limited memberships require that investors buy into the funds by purchasing shares from existing members who wish to sell their shares. **Front-end-load funds** charge investors for both buying and selling fees at the time of purchase. **No-load funds** do not assess such charges; neither do they employ sales staff, which makes it necessary for investors to contact the investment companies directly. Mutual funds offer investment expertise and diversification through the investors' indirect participation in the ownership of a broad array of securities.

EXERCISES (as assigned by your instructor)

19-1 Define the term *capital investment*.

19-2 What is the major distinction between stocks and bonds?

19-3 What types of business organizations are empowered to sell stock?

19-4 The following seven questions pertain to this recent quotation for American Express common stock:

$$48^7/_8 \quad 25 \quad \text{AmExp} \quad 1.28 \quad 2.6 \quad 17 \quad 16886 \quad u49^3/_8 \quad 48^1/_8 \quad 48^3/_8 \quad +^1/_8$$

a. What does the letter *u* designate?

b. By what amount of money did the price of this stock increase or decrease from the closing price of the preceding trading day?

c. What was the lowest price of this stock during the last 52 weeks?

d. How many shares of American Express stock changed hands on this one trading day?

e. What quarterly dividend is specified?

f. What is meant by the "2.6" entry?

g. Identify and explain the P-E ratio for this stock.

19-5 What factors govern the price levels of common stock?

19-6 If the closing price of General Products Corporation is 22-7/8 and the annual dividend per share is 80 cents, what is the yield?

19-7 If Mariott Motors has 250,000 shares of common stock outstanding and earnings of $687,500, what are the company's earnings per share?

19-8 If Jackson Apparel Manufacturing stock closed today at 12-3/4 and if company earnings were last reported at $2.12 per share, what is the P-E ratio?

19-9 Under what circumstances would no P-E ratio be reported in a stock quotation?

19-10 What is the usual title for a person in a stockbroker's office who transacts business with individual investors?

19-11 What is a market order?

19-12 What is a limit order?

19-13 Define a "round lot" and explain why investors prefer to deal in them.

19-14 If an investor purchases 100 shares of stock at a quotation of 23-7/8, on which a commission of $42 is charged and taxes and fees of $13 assessed, what amount must the investor pay the broker?

19-15 Assuming that the investor in Exercise 19-14 sells the 100 shares two years later at 30-1/8 with commissions of $49.50 and taxes and fees of $15.00,

a. What are the proceeds to the investor?

b. What capital gain was realized from the related transactions?

c. What amount of the capital gain is subject to federal income tax?

d. If the investor is in the 35 percent tax bracket, what amount of tax should be paid on the gain?

19-16 An investor purchased 300 shares of common stock at a quotation of 11-1/4 (plus commissions of $67.50 and taxes and fees of $15.00). Just three months and five days later the investor sold the 300 shares at 12-1/2 (plus commissions of $75.00 and taxes and fees of $15.50). What amount of gain is taxable?

19-17 In Exercise 19-16, what amount of gain would have been taxable if the investor had held (owned) the stock for longer than six months before selling at 12-1/2?

19-18 An investor bought 100 shares of common stock at 47-1/2 (plus commissions of $89.30 and taxes and fees of $17.25), held the round lot for a little over a year, and sold all 100 shares at 39-1/8 (commissions of $72.15 and taxes and fees of $16.10). What amount of loss can the investor report as a way of reducing his tax obligation on other income?

19-19 What are the benefits of requesting a stock certificate?

19-20 What are the disadvantages of holding a stock certificate?

19-21 Stockholders share in corporate earnings upon the receipt of _____ _____, whereas bondholders receive _____ payments.

19-22 Define the following terms:
   a. Secured bond
   b. Debenture
   c. Indenture
   d. Covenant

19-23 Who appoints a trustee, and what is the function of the trustee?

19-24 Why is a conversion privilege sometimes called a "sweetener"?

19-25 Under what conditions may a conversion privilege be exercised?

19-26 Why do the prices of convertible bonds tend to fluctuate more widely than the prices of regular bonds?

19-27 Why would the financial managers of corporations include conversion privileges in bonds?

19-28 Under what circumstances would a conversion privilege of a bond become worthless to the bondholder?

19-29 With reference to Table 19.2 on page 367, what amount of money would the owner of ten bonds receive if the bond issue were to be redeemed in 1995?

19-30 The following seven questions pertain to this recent quotation on a bond issue of the Exxon Corporation:

Exxon	6s97	8.8	84	$68^1/_2$	$68^1/_4$	$68^1/_4$	$-^3/_4$

   a. What does the letter *s* designate?
   b. What is the semiannual interest payment on one $1,000 bond?
   c. What is the year of maturity?

d. What was the closing price (in dollars and cents) of this $1,000 bond?
e. What was yesterday's closing price (in dollars and cents)?
f. Compute the yield for this bond based on the close for the day.
g. How many $1,000 bonds exchanged hands on this one trading day?

19-31 What would be the implication of Moody's Investors Service changing the bond rating of a corporation from A to Baa?

19-32 Why do the rates on securities sold by the federal government represent an unofficial floor below which corporate bonds may not be rated?

19-33 If current interest rates are high in relation to the rate being paid on a previously issued bond, how will the price of the bond be affected?

19-34 What does *yield to maturity* measure?

19-35 If a bond issued by The Greyhound Corporation matures in 2001, carries an interest rate of 9-3/8, and has a market quotation of 84-7/8 in 1988, what is the 1988 yield to maturity?

19-36 If a Western Airlines bond that matures in 1998 carries an interest rate of 10-3/4 and has a market quotation of 127-1/2 in 1988, what is the 1988 yield to maturity?

19-37 A $1,000, 8-1/4 percent bond that is quoted at 87-1/2 pays interest on January 1 (for the term July 1 through December 31) and on July 1 (for the term January 1 through June 30). Assuming that the broker's commission is $10 per bond, with a maximum charge of $35 for up to ten bonds per transaction,

a. How much money must the buyer of ten bonds invest for a settlement date of August 10?
b. What will be the proceeds to the seller?
c. When will the buyer be reimbursed for the interest paid to the seller?

19-38 The Ford Motor Company has a bond issue that pays an annual rate of 14-1/4 percent on January 15 (for the last six months of the preceding year) and on July 15 (for the first six months of the current year). The year of maturity is 1990, the settlement date for the exchange of five bonds is March 14, and the broker's commission is $7.50 per bond (maximum charge of $45 for as many as ten bonds in a single transaction).

a. What amount will the buyer be billed at a quotation of 108-5/8?
b. What will be the seller's proceeds?
c. Which party benefits from the premium and to what degree?

19-39 If the seller of the five bonds in Application 19-38 had owned the five bonds for longer than six months before selling them, what amount of the transaction would be taxed as a capital gain?

19-40 If an investor purchases common stock for a total of $8,275.15 (including commissions and fees) and sells the stock three months later for net proceeds of $9,116.20, how much of the gain is taxable?

19-41 In Exercise 19-40, how much of the gain would be taxable if the investor had held (owned) the stocks for longer than six months before selling them?

19-42 An investor purchases 200 shares of common stock at 14-1/2 per share (with commissions of $29 and taxes and fees of $5) and sells them over a year later at 16-1/8 (plus commissions of $32 and taxes and fees of $6). If the investor is in the 30 percent tax bracket, what will be his or her tax obligation on the transaction?

19-43 In Exercise 19-42, what is the effective (actual) tax rate on the gain?

19-44 If an investor, after having held 100 shares of common stock for over three years, sells all 100 shares at a net loss of $2,230, how much of the loss may be used to reduce the investor's taxable income — assuming that no other losses (or gains) are reported the same year?

19-45 Define the following terms:

a. Mutual fund
b. Open-end fund
c. Closed-end fund

19-46 What is the difference between a front-end-load and a no-load fund?

19-47 What is the main attraction of small investors to mutual funds?

20 Tables and Graphs

LEARNING OBJECTIVES

The communication and interpretation of data is becoming progressively more important in our rapidly evolving "information society." Accordingly, the materials in this chapter will enable you to

- prepare unlabeled and labeled tables, including the phrasing of introductory statements and the tabulation of data
- understand and apply the variant procedures for creating tables and figures
- present a wide variety of data in single-line and cumulative-line graphs
- avoid potential distortions in the preparation of line graphs and recognize distortions when they exist in graphs prepared by others
- prepare single-bar, multiple-bar, and component-bar graphs
- construct circle graphs, with and without the use of a protractor
- select the most effective form of table or graph, based on their respective strengths and constraints
- interpret graphic data in any of these several forms

The verbal presentation of information, especially of quantitative data, is often inadequate, leaving readers or listeners confused and uninterested. A corporate accountant might explain trends in profitability with some success, but simultaneous references to sales, costs, and expense figures would result in an almost complete breakdown in communications. To convey such materials effectively, we must supplement our words with graphic illustrations such as tables, line graphs, bar graphs, and circle graphs. Pictorial graphs, flowcharts, organizational charts, and maps, although not directly related to this coverage of business mathematics, can also prove useful.

Except for relatively simple tabulations, all columns, rows, and graphs that are set apart from the regular text in letters, pamphlets, reports, magazines, and books should be properly labeled. We use the word **table** for data that are listed in rows and columns, and the word **figure** for formatted data and drawings. In addition to identifications such as *Table 3* (meaning the third table in a document) or *Figure 3.1* (meaning the first figure in Chapter 3), all tables and figures should have descriptive labeling, column headings, and source identification, so that readers may interpret graphic information even when they do not take the time to read accompanying explanations.

The following types of statements are included within the written text to introduce readers to tables and figures:

1. As illustrated in Table 2.3, sales figures for the five-year period have remained fairly stable.
2. Table 2.7 provides a comparison of current sales periods with those for the preceding year.
3. These concepts are illustrated in Figure 3 on page 79.
4. Please see Figure 7.1 for a comparison of departmental totals.

When possible, we should avoid surprises by providing readers with such introductions before they actually encounter tabulated or graphic materials.

TABLES

Rather than only speaking or writing about complex numerical relationships, we can more effectively communicate with and maintain the interest of other people (business associates, customers, employees) by including properly prepared charts and tables. The degree of formality involved depends on the importance and extensiveness of our data.

Unlabeled Tables

Unlabeled tables consist of data that are easier to interpret when set apart from the regular text but too limited in scope to require special labeling. As in the following example, we use verbal explanations to introduce readers to such materials.

We began 1986 ten points lower than in 1985, as illustrated in the accompanying table, but enjoyed a price range in the fourth quarter that was about fourteen points higher than for the preceding year.

	1986 High	1986 Low	1985 High	1985 Low
First quarter	33-1/2	24-1/8	46-1/8	33-1/2
Second quarter	38-1/4	27-1/8	36-3/8	30
Third quarter	38-1/8	31-7/8	32-1/8	22-3/8
Fourth quarter	37-7/8	33-7/8	24-1/4	20-5/8

An unlabeled table is especially appropriate when no other graphic data are to be used in the same document. If, in this situation, additional graphics were present and this were the third of several tables, we would label it "Table 3," add ruled lines as illustrated in Table 20.1, and identify it as "Price Range of Common Stock." Because stock prices would have been taken from the records of the company for which the writer is employed, rather than from some outside publication, no source need be cited.

Labeled Tables

As already mentioned, an expedient method for identifying numerical relationships is to place the data in columns and rows, where readers can readily interpret their meanings; and, except for relatively simple tabulations, as discussed and illustrated in the preceding section, we use table numbers and de-

Table 20.1
Annual sales by
division — 1980 through
1986

	Consumer	Chain store	Institutional	Government	Total
1980	5,321,268	4,090,820	2,532,412	2,288,912	14,233,412
1981	5,401,376	4,207,632	2,551,616	2,727,495	14,888,119
1982	6,550,771	4,929,268	3,078,277	3,561,144	18,119,460
1983	6,679,245	5,127,690	3,257,344	3,950,842	19,015,121
1984	7,069,978	5,976,695	3,867,274	5,198,218	22,112,165
1985	7,376,338	6,700,349	4,419,380	6,016,058	24,512,125
1986	7,937,539	6,950,972	4,623,908	6,709,199	26,221,618

scriptive labeling. Instead of conveying product sales information in paragraph form, for example, we may construct the table above, showing time (years) at the left and categories (product groups) at the top. The table represents an orderly presentation of data that enables readers to readily identify the extent of growth that has been realized in each of the product areas during the past seven years. Notice also that horizontal lines are added to labeled tables. Dates may be placed at the left, and the data placed in columns (as shown here) or vice versa, depending on which pattern is judged most appropriate for the situation.

APPLICATION 1. On October 1 the Bureau of the Census reported that the median gross income of Americans increased from $16,000 in 1975 to nearly $31,000 in 1985, whereas the median gross rent (including utilities) increased from $133 per month to $315 per month. Place this information in an unlabeled table immediately following an introductory statement.

According to recently issued figures by the Census Bureau, increases in rental payments have significantly exceeded increases in income.

	Median gross rent	Median gross income
1975	$133	$16,000
1985	315	31,000

APPLICATION 2. The Big T Gas & Oil Corporation reported net income for 1982 through 1986 for three product divisions — reading from past to present. Natural gas: $5,512,109, $5,610,013, $11,251,398, $7,216,512, and $9,205,618. Petroleum: $79,599,450, $73,522,131, $30,612,810, $35,529,951, $47,516,908. Chemicals: $1,912,654, $2,003,029, $2,105,823, $2,111,916, $2,115,590. Arrange these figures, along with

totals for each category and for each of the five years, in rows and columns labeled "Table 6."

Table 6. Net income by product division 1982–1986

	Natural gas	Petroleum	Chemicals	Totals
1982	$ 5,512,109	$ 79,599,450	$ 1,912,654	$ 87,024,213
1983	5,610,013	73,522,131	2,003,029	81,135,173
1984	11,251,398	30,612,810	2,105,823	43,970,031
1985	7,216,512	35,529,951	2,111,916	44,858,379
1986	9,205,618	47,516,908	2,115,590	58,838,116
	$38,795,650	$266,781,250	$10,249,012	$315,825,912

LINE GRAPHS

In discussing graphic illustrations, we are, in essence, considering the presentation of data in pictorial form, and line graphs help us paint a much clearer picture than can be realized with tables. As shown in Figure 20.1, line graphs consist of two axes, an *x* (horizontal) axis and a *y* (vertical) axis, that may be combined to form four quadrants.

Figure 20.1
Two axes form four quadrants

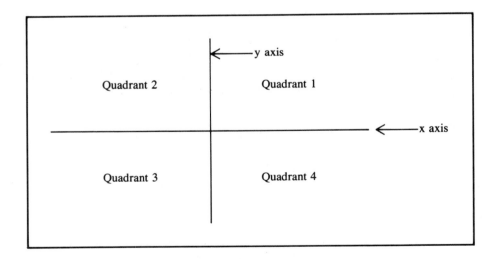

Business people rely primarily on Quadrant 1 when presenting data, but must also use Quadrant 4 when including negative numbers.

Single-Line Graphs

To create a single-line graph for the data in Table 20.1 on page 385, we draw Quadrant 1 as shown in Figure 20.2, placing time (years) on the *x*-axis and money (in millions of dollars) on the *y*-axis. Then, beginning with 1980, we move up the *y*-axis and place a dot at approximately 5 1/3 (million), a second dot at 5.4 above 1981, a third dot a little higher than 6.5 above 1982, and so on for each category, resulting in four separate (single) lines. Although the dots are prominent in Figure 20.2, for illustrative purposes, we usually make them just dark enough to be able to connect them with lines but light enough to remain unnoticeable to readers. Having subsequently entered dots and connecting lines for the other four product divisions, it is obvious that sales volume has increased in all four areas — with less dramatic increases being reflected in the final year for sales to chain stores and institutional customers.

Notice in Figure 20.2 that the lines for government and institutional sales intersect during the first period. When several such intersections exist, we may maintain the identity of individual lines by using a different color (pencil or pen) for each line or by replacing solid lines with lines of small x's, dots, dashes, or different combinations of dots and dashes. Grid lines (as shown) ease the entry of data and improve accuracy, but their use is optional.

As mentioned earlier, **negative data** may be plotted by displaying Quadrant 1 and Quadrant 4 simultaneously, as depicted in Figure 20.3.

Figure 20.2
Annual sales by division

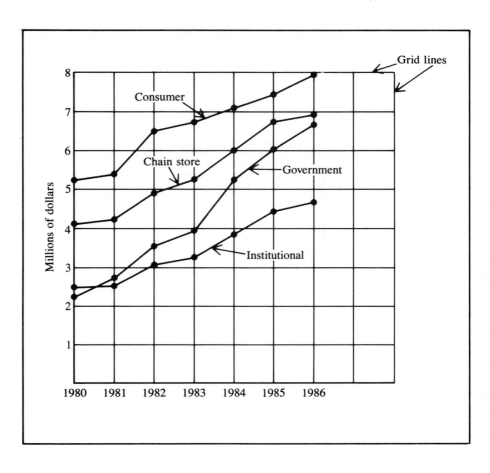

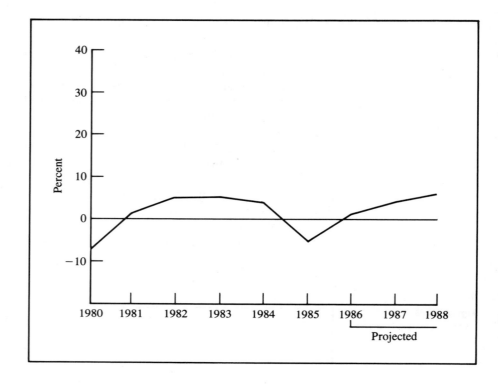

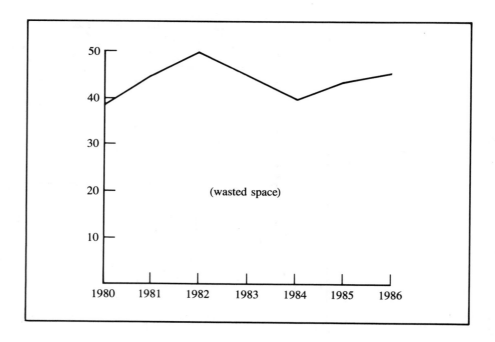

Following a negative sales margin in 1980, this measurement of profitability is shown to have remained positive in all of the following years except for 1985.

Although the *y*-axis should always begin with zero, we may **break the vertical line** when necessary to avoid large amounts of unused space at the lower part of a graph. This approach is illustrated in Figures 20.4 and 20.5.

Figure 20.5
Broken *y*-axis

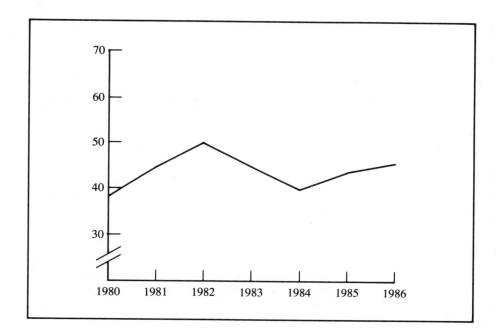

Figure 20.6
Disproportional spacing

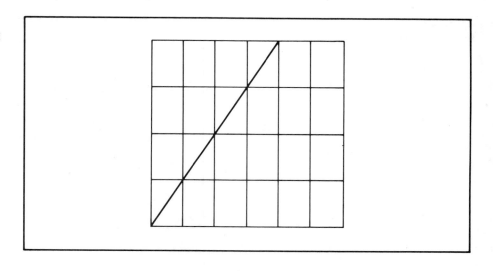

Figure 20.7
Disproportional spacing

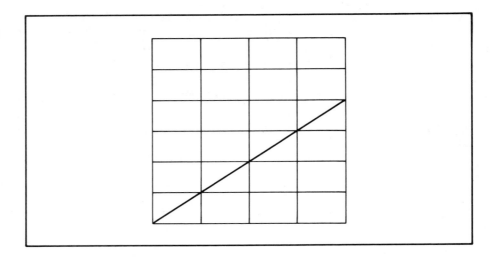

Finally, we should avoid distortions in line graphs by maintaining proportional spacing of our measurements on both axes. Because the spacing in Figure 20.6 on page 389 is scrunched on the *x*-axis compared to that on the *y*-axis, the upward slant of the data line is exaggerated. Conversely, the crowded spacing of measurements on the *y*-axis in Figure 20.7, compared to that on the *x*-axis, results in a data line that is inordinately flat. By comparison, the well-balanced measurements on both axes in Figure 20.8 result in a more accurate data line. The squares produced by the grid lines in Figure 20.8 are indicative of consistent relationships, as opposed to the rectangles in the accompanying figures.

Figure 20.8
Proportional spacing

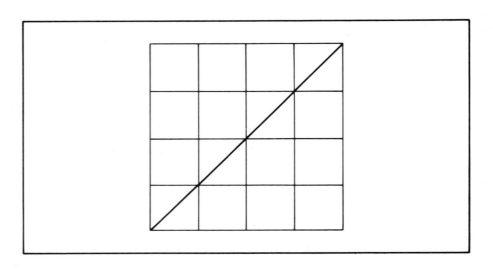

Figure 20.9
Total operating and non-
operating income
(Cumulative-Line Graph)

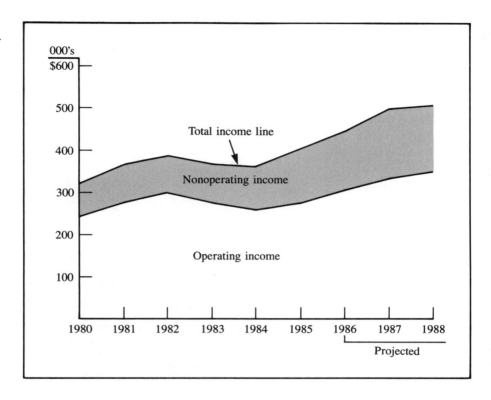

**Cumulative-Line
Graphs**

Unlike the line graph in Figure 20.2, where each line was plotted independently of the others, we can sometimes make a clearer presentation by combining our data. In Figure 20.9 we first plot operating income at $240,000. Then, rather than plotting nonoperating income for the beginning year as $80,000, we combine it with operating income of $240,000, resulting in total income of $320,000.

In contrast to single-line graphs, the *y*-axis of a cumulative-line graph should not be broken. To do so would be to understate the bottom entity (operating income in Figure 20.9) in the comparisons for which cumulative graphs are designed. The word projected at the bottom of the graph specifies that the data entries for the last three years were based on estimates rather than on actual data. Notice also that the three zeros (000's) at the top of the *y*-axis, in conjunction with the dollar sign, indicate that the related figures are in thousands of dollars — $600,000, $500,000, etc.

As illustrated in Figure 20.10, cumulative-line graphs are equally appropriate for as many as three or four divisions. Cost of goods sold is plotted at the bottom, and we build upon that line for expenses and add a third segment for

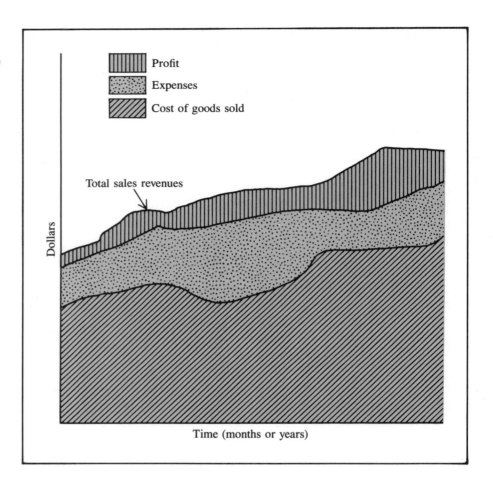

profits. The top line in Figure 20.10 represents sales revenues, which is the sum of all three components (costs + expenses + profits). When such identification marks as dots, stripes, and shading are used, a **legend** like the one in Figure 20.10 is required to define each segment.

APPLICATION 1. Prepare a single-line graph (including the appropriate labeling) in order to present annual sales data for the following three product groups.

	Group A	Group B	Group C
1980	$37,500	$45,610	$40,269
1981	40,100	47,500	50,750
1982	32,009	45,995	55,122
1983	35,010	48,211	62,198
1984	30,250	50,119	75,996
1985	31,510	51,001	77,500
1986	32,011	55,119	78,213

APPLICATION 2. Interpret the sales data in the graph for Application 1.

An increase in sales for Group A was followed by a serious decline the following year before stabilizing at slightly above the $30,000 level. Group B sales, except for one year, have increased slowly but steadily. Sales for Group C increased dramatically through 1984, with only moderate increases thereafter.

Annual sales by product group 1980–1986

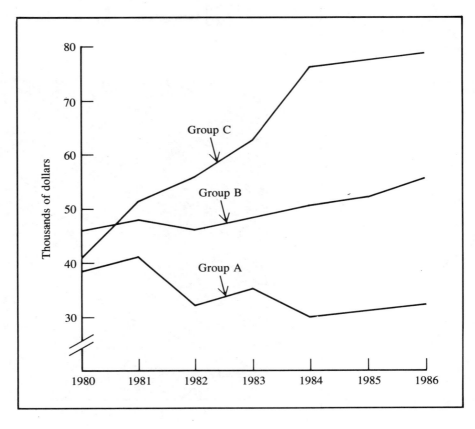

APPLICATION 3. Present the following data for net sales in a cumulative-line graph. Include the proper labeling, showing the graph to be Figure 2, and include a legend.

Domestic sales		Foreign sales	
1981 —	$305,010	1981 —	$213,512
1982 —	330,516	1982 —	232,361
1983 —	329,217	1983 —	228,452
1984 —	372,739	1984 —	195,122
1985 —	359,610	1985 —	198,746
1986 —	385,125	1986 —	191,074

APPLICATION 4. Provide a brief interpretation of the graph in Application 3.
   Both foreign and domestic sales are on a steadily upward tilt, except for a slight one-year decline in 1985.

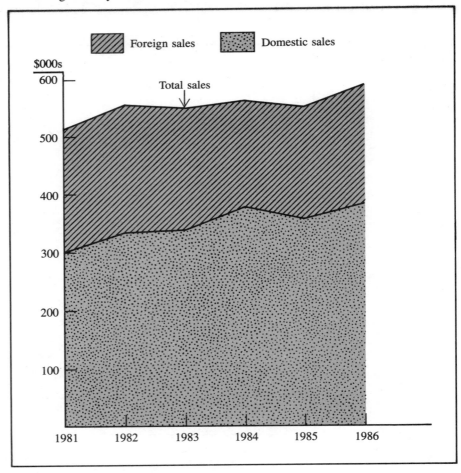

Figure 2. Annual net sales (1981–86)

APPLICATION 5. Why wasn't the *y*-axis broken to reduce the empty space at the lower part of the graph?

Because to break the *y*-axis would distort the comparison, causing the casual observer to view international sales as having exceeded domestic sales.

APPLICATION 6. Without including any labeling other than dollars and years, use a single-line graph to illustrate the following data.

1982	$59,750
1983	58,345
1984	56,225
1985	27,772
1986	(10,223)
1987	18,522 (projected)
1988	27,156 (projected)

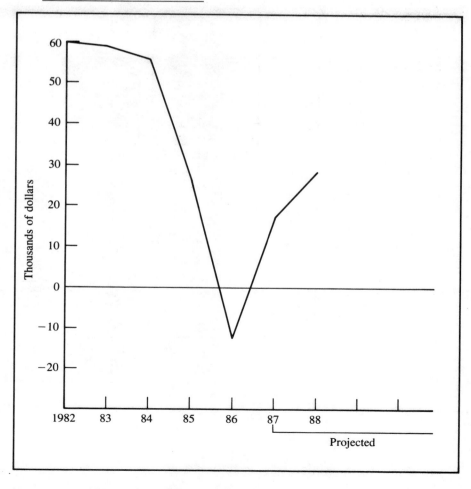

BAR GRAPHS

Bar graphs consist of boxed areas that extend to varying degrees either upward (positive data) or downward (negative data) from the *x*-axis. When only positive data are presented, we have the alternative of using the *y*-axis as a base and extending bars horizontally to the right. Bar graphs vary in their complexity, depending on whether we are using single, multiple, or component bars; but whatever type of bar chart is being used, neither axis should ever be split.

Single-Bar Graphs

Graphs that are composed of single bars are relatively limited in scope. We may present data for several entities for a single time period, as illustrated in Figure 20.11, or we may present data for a single entity for several time periods, as shown in Figure 20.12.

Figure 20.11
Divisional sales for 1986
(Vertical-Bar Graph)

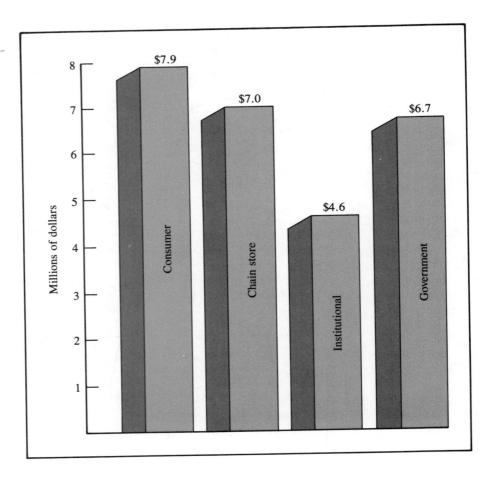

Figure 20.12

Annual sales CONSUMER
DIVISION — 1981
through 1986
(Vertical-Bar Graph)

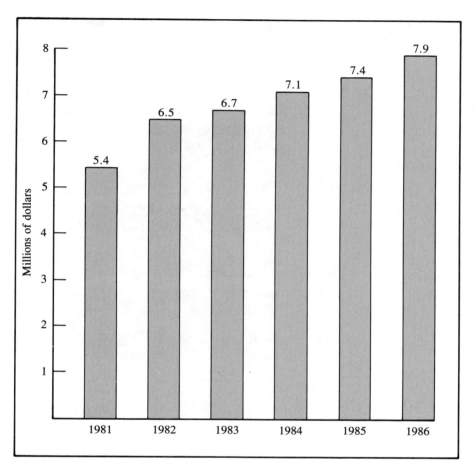

Time is not shown on the *x*-axis in Figure 20.11 because the data pertain to just one year; and, rather than trying to squeeze the names of the individual divisions into the small area at the bottom of each bar, we simply label the bars themselves as "consumer," "chain store," "institutional," and "government." Time is shown on the *x*-axis in Figure 20.12, on the other hand, because the data pertain to a single entity (consumer division) over the course of several years. Notice also that the two figures differ in another respect, in that shaded areas have been added to Figure 20.11 to provide a three-dimensional effect.

A negative feature of the vertical-bar graph in Figure 20.11 is that the division names must be read sideways. This deficiency may be overcome with

Figure 20.13
Divisional sales for 1986
(Horizontal-Bar Graph)

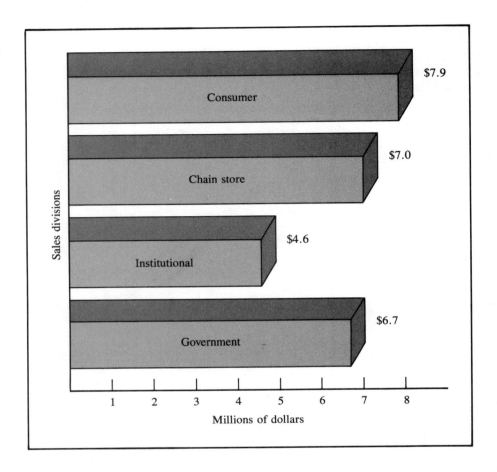

the use of a horizontal-bar graph as illustrated in Figure 20.13.

Notice that with either form, a vertical-bar or a horizontal-bar graph, we may, when practical, assist the reader by noting the dollar amounts at the top of each bar (vertical-bar graph) or at the right end of each bar (horizontal-bar graph), rounded either to whole numbers or, as in this instance, to the tenths position.

Multiple-Bar Graphs

Multiple-bar graphs, which employ several bars for each entity or for each time period, may be used to overcome the previously mentioned constraints in single-bar graphs. To illustrate, all four products in Table 20.1 (page 385) are

Figure 20.14
Annual sales by division
(1982–1986)
(Multiple-Bar Graph)

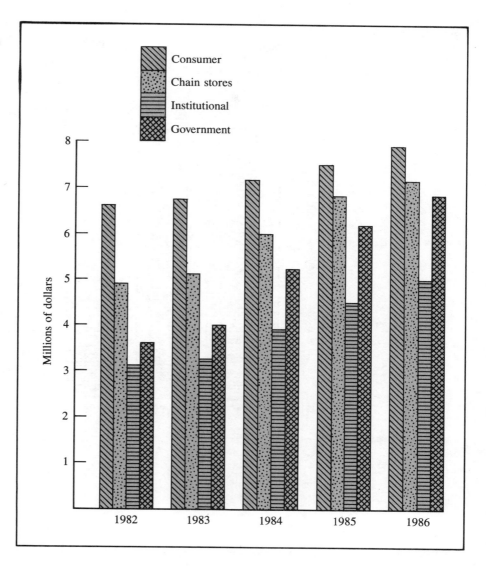

presented in Figure 20.14 for multiple time periods. Multiple-bar graphs are useful for illustrating as many as three or four entities, but any greater number tends to result in more confusion than clarity. Also, because individual labeling would be cumbersome, a legend is needed.

Figure 20.15
Annual product sales
(1982–1986)
(Component-Bar Graph)

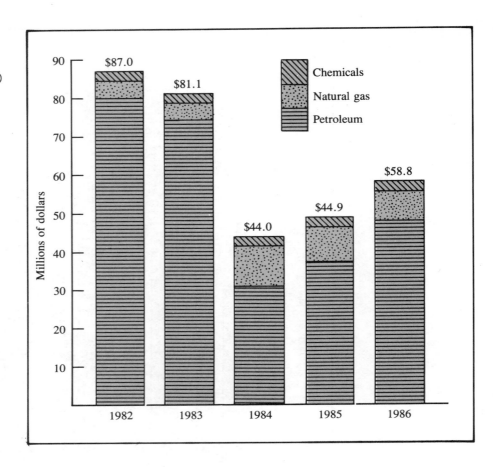

Component-Bar Graphs

Component-bar graphs, as with component-line graphs, enable us to illustrate the relationships of two or more entities that are combined to form a whole. In Figure 20.15, for example, the annual revenues from natural gas, petroleum, and chemicals are combined to form component bars for each of the five years that are included.

As the component bars clearly indicate, the dominant petroleum revenues declined drastically in 1984 and 1985 and recovered only slightly in 1986. Revenues from the sale of natural gas increased significantly in 1984 and remained close to the new level throughout 1985 and 1986. Sales of chemicals, on the other hand, remained relatively constant throughout the five-year period.

APPLICATION 1. Prepare a vertical-bar graph to reflect the following net income (loss) figures, labeling the presentation as Figure 3.

1981	$25 million
1982	15 million
1983	11 million (loss)
1984	15 million (loss)
1985	21 million
1986	26 million

Rather than add a second quadrant (as shown) to illustrate negative data, you may elect to omit the downward bars and rely instead on the paren-**thetical notations**.

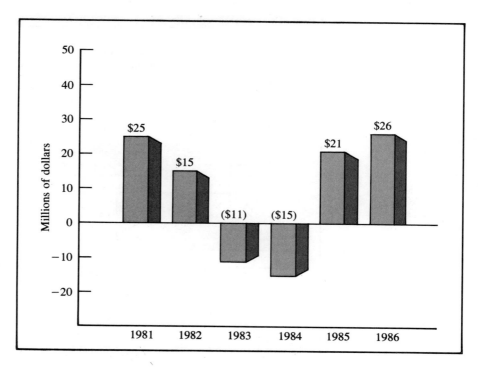

Figure 3
Net income for 1981–86

APPLICATION 2. Use a horizontal-bar graph to illustrate the following sales data for January 1986, using the label, "Figure 12."

Division	Amount
Eastern	$525,011
Southern	473,214
Midwest	452,920
Mountain	318,215
Western	550,670

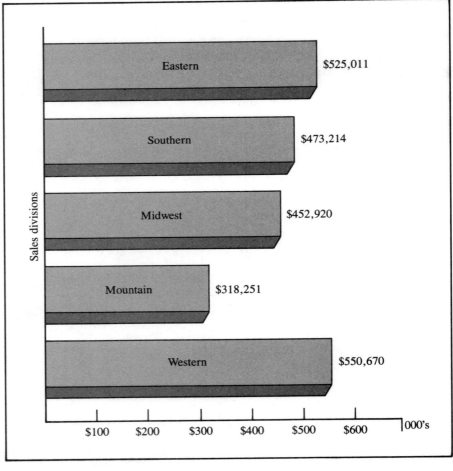

Figure 12
Divisional sales for January 1986

APPLICATION 3. Construct a multiple-bar graph (label it Figure 3.2) to present in pictorial form the number of units sold.

	1983	1984	1985	1986
Product A	5,010	5,998	6,115	6,501
Product B	8,911	8,752	8,825	9,215
Product C	8,519	8,006	7,512	6,201

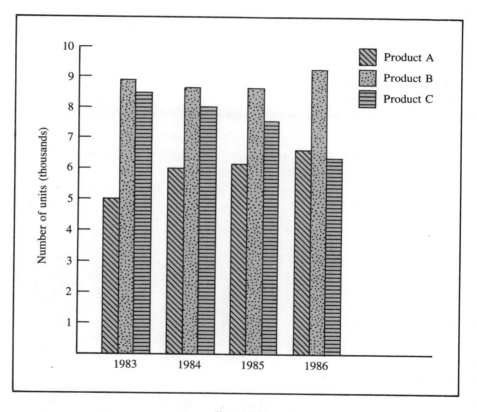

Figure 3.2
Product sales, 1983–1984

APPLICATION 4. Interpret the data in Application 3.

With sales of Product B holding fairly constant, the volume of Product A has increased and that of Product C has decreased to where both products are almost tied for second place.

APPLICATION 5. Prepare a component-bar graph (label it Figure 2) to illustrate the dollar amount and percent of earnings being "paid out" in dividends each year.

	Per share	
	Earnings	Dividends
1981	$3.75	$1.15
1982	3.85	1.15
1983	4.15	1.45
1984	4.28	1.50
1985	4.53	1.50
1986	4.93	1.60

APPLICATION 6. Interpret the data in Application 5.

With steadily increasing earnings, the payout of dividends as a percent of earnings per share peaked in 1983 and 1984 at approximately 35 percent.

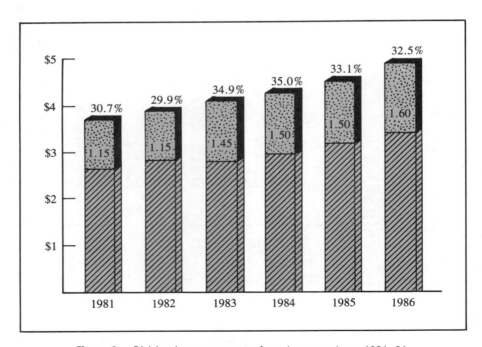

Figure 2. Dividends as a percent of earnings per share, 1981–86

Despite a 10-cent increase in the annual dividend for 1986, the ratio of dividends to earnings declined in both 1985 and 1986.

CIRCLE GRAPHS

Circle graphs enable us to present data as though they were divisions of a pie; consequently, some people refer to them as "pie graphs." Circle graphs are limited (unless two or more graphs are presented simultaneously) in that they may be used to compare numerical relationships for only one time period. Circle graphs can be very powerful, nevertheless, because they represent more of a pictorial presentation than either line or bar graphs.

Four-Step Procedure

The following procedure is applicable whatever the size of graph desired — ranging from a very small circle to one that would be appropriate for a poster to be viewed from the back of a fairly good-sized room. Using the following cost and expense data for 1986, we execute four basic steps.

Cost of goods sold	$235,375
Administrative expenses	60,730
Operating expenses	146,750
Other	31,845
Total	$474,700

Step 1. Determine the percent that each entity is of the total.

$$\frac{\text{Individual}}{\text{amount}} \div \frac{\text{Total}}{\text{amount}} = \frac{\text{Percent}}{\text{of total}}$$

$$235,375 \div 474,700 = 0.496$$
$$60,730 \div 474,700 = 0.128$$
$$146,750 \div 474,700 = 0.309$$
$$31,845 \div 474,700 = 0.067$$

474,700	1.000

Step 2. Determine the number of degrees in a circle that are to represent each category by multiplying the percents by the number of degrees in a circle.

$$\text{Percent} \times \text{Circle} = \text{Degrees}$$
$$0.496 \times 360 = 179$$
$$0.128 \times 360 = 46$$
$$0.309 \times 360 = 111$$
$$0.067 \times 360 = 24$$
$$360$$

Step 3. After drawing a circle with a compass (Figure 20.16), draw a straight
line from the top to the center of the circle (as marked by the perforation
left by the point of the compass). Place the flat part of a protractor (Figure
20.17) on the line, with the rounded part to the right of the circle.

Then, reading from the left (zero side) of the scale, place a mark at 179
(the largest segment to be plotted) and draw an aligned line from the edge
of the circle to its center. Label that section "Cost of goods sold."

Proceed by placing the flat part of the protractor on the newly drawn line,
marking "111" (the second largest segment) and drawing an aligned line
from the edge to the center. Label this section "Operating expenses."

Place the protractor on the newly drawn line, mark "46," draw a line, and
label the section "Administrative expenses." The remaining section should

Figure 20.16
Compass

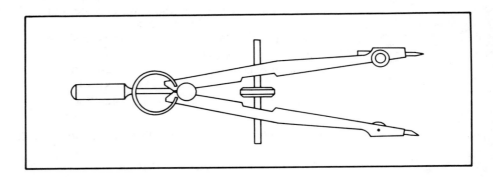

Figure 20.17
Protractor

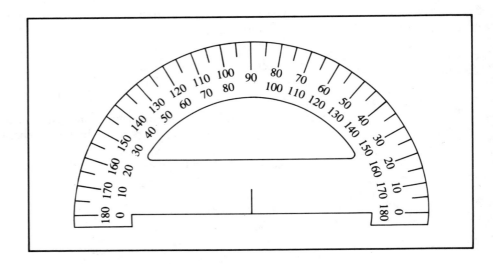

Figure 20.18
Cost and expense data
for 1986 (Circle Graph)

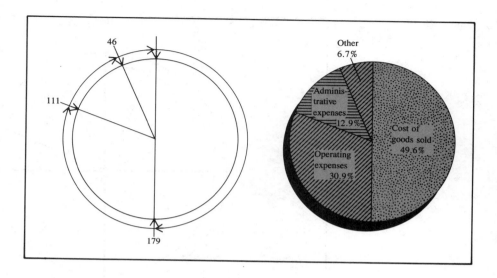

segment next, and so on, with an "other" category, when there is one, plotted last (just to the left of top center).

Step 4. Finally, and also as illustrated in Figure 20.18, labeling must be added to identify the general categories and the applicable term (year, quarter, month).

In what might be considered a nonessential final step in the preparation of the circle graph in Figure 20.18, we add a little shading at the lower edge of the otherwise completed graph to gain a three-dimensional effect.

Alternative Method

Approximations are sometimes practical when preparing circle graphs, especially if a protractor is not readily available. Whether the lines are absolutely accurate in Figure 20.18, for instance, is not crucial to interpretation of the data, especially since the percent that each segment is of the total is reflected in the graph.

First, divide a circle into fourths, as shown in Figure 20.19, and then divide each fourth into fourths again, resulting in 16 divisions. Each division of the circle is valued at 22.5 degrees (360 degrees ÷ 16 sections = 22.5 degrees). Then, using the figures generated in Step 2 for creation of the first circle, we determine the number of sections required to complete each segment in this second circle.

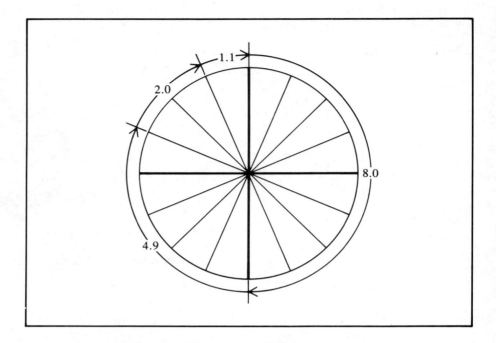

	Degrees of a circle	÷	Degrees in each segment	=	Sections per segment
Cost of goods sold	179	÷	22.5	=	8.0
Administrative expenses	46	÷	22.5	=	2.0
Operating expenses	111	÷	22.5	=	4.9
Other	24	÷	22.5	=	1.1
	360				16.0

Making certain that the sum of the segments is 16, we place a mark at the top of the circle, count eight segments to the right, and place a mark. We count beyond that point for 4.9 segments, for 2.0 segments, and so on. We may then erase the section lines within the circle, assuming that we have penciled them in lightly, and add heavy lines for the four segments as marked.

APPLICATION 1. With the use of a protractor, prepare a circle graph for the following ton-miles of freight that were handled in 1986 — as reported in the *Yearbook of Facts*, Association of American Railroads, 1986.

Mode	Ton miles (millions)
Railroads	$926,410
Trucks	565,383
Barge lines	410,948
Pipelines	553,321
Air	4,710

Step 1.

$$
\begin{array}{rcll}
\text{Ton miles} & \div & \text{Total} & = \text{Rate} \\
926{,}410 & \div & 2{,}460{,}772 & = 0.376 \\
565{,}383 & \div & 2{,}460{,}772 & = 0.230 \\
410{,}948 & \div & 2{,}460{,}772 & = 0.167 \\
553{,}321 & \div & 2{,}460{,}772 & = 0.225 \\
\underline{\quad 4{,}710} & \div & 2{,}460{,}772 & = \underline{0.002} \\
2{,}460{,}772 & & & 1.000
\end{array}
$$

Step 2.

$$
\begin{array}{rcl}
\text{Percent} \times 360 & = & \text{Degrees} \\
0.376 \times 360 & = & 135.4 \\
0.230 \times 360 & = & 82.8 \\
0.167 \times 360 & = & 60.1 \\
0.225 \times 360 & = & 81.0 \\
0.002 \times 360 & = & \underline{0.7} \\
& & 360.0
\end{array}
$$

Rounding to the tenths position (rather than to whole numbers) is necessary here in order to avoid excluding completely the smallest of the five segments.

Step 3.

We approximate a little by drawing a very small section for air freight, even though less than one percent of air freight is virtually impossible to plot.

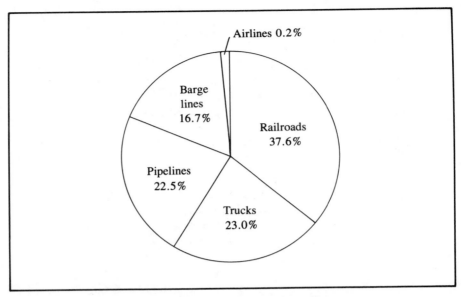

Source: *Yearbook of Facts*, Association of American Railroads, 1986

Figure 5
Ton miles of freight hauled — 1986

APPLICATION 2. Using the alternative method, identify the segments of a circle graph for the following data:

Product A $130,000
Product B   123,000
Product C   118,000

Step 1.

130,000 + 123,000 + 118,000 = 371,000

$$130,000 \div 371,000 = 0.350$$
$$123,000 \div 371,000 = 0.332$$
$$\underline{118,000} \div 371,000 = \underline{0.318}$$
371,000   1.000

Step 2.

$$0.35 \times 360 = 126$$
$$0.332 \times 360 = 120$$
$$0.318 \times 360 = \underline{114}$$
360

Step 3.

$$126 \div 22.5 = 5.6$$
$$120 \div 22.5 = 5.3$$
$$114 \div 22.5 = \underline{5.1}$$
$$16.0$$

Step 4.

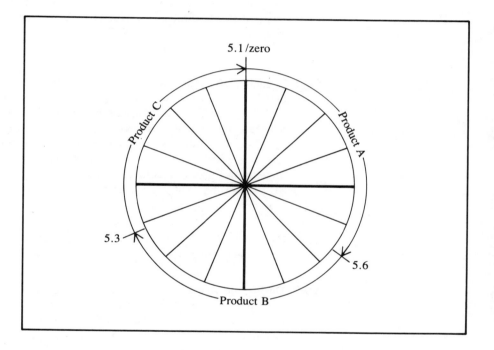

The absence of questions calling for interpretation of these graphs is not an oversight. Because the scope of circle graphs is limited to just one time period, comparisons are, in essence, one dimensional and very obvious.

EXERCISES (as directed by your instructor)

20-1 In what ways do tables differ from figures?

20-2 How does the labeling of tables vary from that for figures?

20-3 How and at what point in written communications should readers be introduced to graphic materials?

20-4 Under what circumstance might an unlabeled table be more appropriate than a table that is labeled?

20-5 Prepare an introductory statement and an unlabeled table showing that of all blue collar workers employed, 1,325 (58.3%) are male and 948 (41.7%) are female, and that of total white collar employees, 54 (31.8%) are male and 116 (68.2%) are female.

20-6 Prepare an introductory statement and an unlabeled table for the following information taken from a recent edition of *Business World* magazine. In 1986 the average salary offered by business firms was $19,213 for graduating students with bachelor's degrees in business administration and $29,150 for those with M.B.A. degrees. In contrast, graduates with bachelor's degrees in 1987 were offered $18,350 while those with M.B.A. degrees received offers of $28,275.

20-7 In each of the years 1982 through 1986, a business firm had total assets of $161,235, $203,023, $269,224, $351,021, and $808,294, respectively. Working capital during the same periods was $46,712, $48,442, $75,164, $111,808, and $232,812. Long-term debt was $31,451, $30,096, $24,688, $20,175, and $105,374. Common stockholders' equity was $65,399, $73,603, $97,824, $138,611, and $188,926. Tabulate these figures to form a financial summary in a table (label it Table 6), placing the 1986 figures in the left column, the 1985 figures in the next column, and so on.

20-8 From the table that you prepared in Exercise 20-7, interpret any trends that appear prominent.

20-9 During the five-year period 1982 through 1986, a manufacturing firm had operating profits in government aerospace (reading from present to past in thousands of dollars) of $62,209, $57,377, $46,208, $24,921, and $12,742. Profits in Commercial Aerospace during the same period were $32,042, $30,616, $19,336, $11,267, and $7,523. Profits for Aerospace Fasteners and Plastic Tooling for 1986 (the first year of production) were $5,740 and $1,839, respectively. Profits in General Industries (still reading from 1986 back to 1982) were $4,935, $2,939, $2,510, $2,904, and $1,819. Prepare a table (label it Table 3.1) to include total sales for each of the five years.

20-10 In interpretation of the table prepared in Exercise 20-9,

    a. What was total net profit for 1985 as stated in millions of dollars rounded to the tenths position?
    b. What was the net profit in commercial aerospace for 1985?

20-11 Assume that the following data for the average prices of cars (including optional equipment) were taken from the January 7, 1987, issue of a magazine titled *Automotive Technology* and prepare a single-line graph to reflect the prices in thousands of dollars. Use the label, "Figure 8."

	1986	1985	1984	1983	1982	1981
Compacts	$8,261	$8,010	$7,875	$7,695	$7,326	$7,101
Intermediates	11,150	11,118	10,648	10,520	10,012	9,865
Full-sized	14,210	14,150	13,892	13,416	12,990	12,510

20-12 Interpret the graph that you prepared in 20-11.

20-13 Prepare a single-line graph (label it Figure 3.2) to illustrate the net profit (or loss) from each of the product categories for each of the six months in 1986.

	Jan	Feb	Mar	Apr	May	Jun
Groceries	$42,316	$45,112	$45,016	$47,309	$48,621	$52,912
Produce	6,612	(11,093)	(4,001)	1,229	4,122	3,280
Frozen	12,113	10,005	16,211	18,908	17,162	19,252
Meat	9,229	12,614	10,923	13,612	14,801	14,982
Dairy	3,515	3,750	3,690	3,989	4,610	4,721

20-14 Illustrate the following debt-equity figures with a cumulative-line graph.

	1981	1982	1983	1984	1985
Debt	$105,374	$112,502	$120,610	$145,300	$162,812
Equity	188,926	195,313	215,189	245,180	260,591

20-15 Interpret the data illustrated in the graph prepared for Exercise 20-14.

20-16 What is the primary limitation of single-bar graphs?

20-17 How can this limitation be overcome?

20-18 Why are horizontal-bar graphs sometimes superior to vertical-bar graphs?

20-19 Prepare a vertical-bar graph (labeled Figure 16) showing the following net income amounts in millions of dollars.

1980 $5,532,638
1981   5,593,119
1982   11,213,193
1983   7,249,916
1984   9,193,167
1985   10,621,513
1986   11,515,918

20-20 Prepare a horizontal-bar graph (labeled Figure 3) to illustrate the following operating profits for 1986.

Natural gas $52,209,320
Liquid fuels   32,042,610
Solid fuels   15,740,118
Petrochemicals   24,935,912

20-21 Prepare a bar graph (label it Figure 9) to encompass 1986 results from the following profitability centers at a publishing company.

Universities and colleges $345,009
High schools   276,991
Business and vocational   326,807
Book stores and clubs   (26,918)
General interest   176,512

20-22 Present the following divisional sales data, which are expressed in millions of dollars, in a multiple-bar chart labeled "Figure 3-2."

	1986	1985	1984	1983	1982
Households	$9,416	$9,212	$9,150	$7,981	$7,490
Commercial	4,615	3,985	3,250	2,190	1,585
Leasing	2,815	2,788	2,312	2,914	2,163
Equipment	2,638	1,919	1,511	752	335

20-23 Interpret the graph that you developed in Exercise 20-22.

20-24 Midwest Airlines had the following passenger revenues for the first half of the current year. Present these data in a cumulative-line graph (labeled Figure 2) to illustrate the percent that revenues from discount fares are of total fares.

	Full fares	Discount fares	Total fares
Jan	$344,076	$516,139	$860,215
Feb	353,445	541,667	895,112
Mar	387,244	525,866	913,110
Apr	338,636	512,954	851,590
May	405,928	609,392	1,015,320
Jun	500,065	750,096	1,250,161

20-25 Interpret the graph that you developed in Exercise 20-24.

20-26 Showing all calculations involved, prepare a circle graph (labeled Figure 3) to illustrate the following "Sales mix" for 1986.

Consumer products	$1,172,962.77
Industrial products	545,411.26
Electronic technology	995,539.83
Graphic technology	571,696.14

20-27 If, in preparing the circle graph for Exercise 20-26, you had used the alternative method, how many of the 16 parts would you have assigned to be plotted for each segment?

20-28 Prepare a circle graph (label it Figure 2.5) to compare employee take-home (net) pay in 1986 with the individual deductions.

Gross pay	$3,276,520
Social Security	214,509
Federal taxes	819,130
State tax	129,605
Other	88,913
Net pay	$2,024,363

20-29 Use the following data for a comparison of units of production with units of sales (labeled Figure 4), to prepare a (a) line graph, (b) bar graph, (c) circle graph.

(1986)	Jan	Feb	Mar	Apr	May	Jun
Production	2,000	4,000	3,900	4,250	5,000	6,600
Sales	2,500	3,100	4,200	3,150	3,750	4,900

21   Basic Statistics

LEARNING OBJECTIVES

The art of statistical analysis has progressed far beyond simple comparisons of trans-actional data into a field of mathematics commonly referred to as "statistics." As an introduction to this relatively new field of study as it affects today's business enter-prise, the materials in this chapter will enable you to

- place data in arrangements that are conducive to detailed analysis
- classify data when dealing with large numbers of responses or observations
- calculate and describe the arithmetic mean (including its variations), the median, and the mode — with both grouped and ungrouped data
- explain the concept of dispersion and normal distribution
- measure dispersion through application of the standard deviation

In its broadest meaning, the word **statistics** includes the collection, analysis, interpretation, and presentation of data. By this definition, the field of statistics encompasses a wide variety of business activities. In a narrower sense which relates more specifically to the materials in this chapter, statistics embodies a branch of mathematics that prepares and interprets averages — averages that have an existing or potential impact on the decision-making process.

In today's so-called "information age," business managers are confronted with reams of data — some internally generated (such as recorded sales, pro-jected costs, and budgeted expenses) and some from external sources (such as government-prepared population forecasts, inflation measurements, and per capita income). Correspondingly, managers must arrange for the skillful col-lection, processing, and interpretation of a wide variety of data if they are to make informed business decisions.

Obviously, the field of statistical analysis represents an essential analytical tool which helps modern business managers fulfill their informational needs among a rising tide of data. Rather than addressing statistics as a whole, how-ever, an endeavor that could consume several volumes of printed text, the ma-terials in this chapter are designed to introduce you to the principal methods of analyzing quantitative data — arranging numbers, deriving central tenden-cies, and measuring degrees of dispersion.

ORDERING OF DATA

In statistics the word **value** refers to numerical quantity (number of units, num-ber of defects, number of responses, etc.), and a meaningful analysis of values can be difficult, even impossible, if not arranged in some orderly fashion. An **array** exists when values are placed in a logical order such as from smallest to largest or vice versa. For example, the following set of data, representing the number of defective welds per day during a ten-day period, may easily be rearranged so that certain features of the set become more apparent.

Set   12, 13, 12, 11, 14, 11, 10, 12, 7, 16

Array: 7, 10, 11, 11, 12, 12, 12, 13, 14, 16

From the array, we may identify the **range** (the difference between the highest and lowest values) to be nine.

Range: $16 - 7 = 9$

Arrays are generally suitable for small sets of numbers, but they can be cumbersome and ineffective with relatively large sets.

Frequency Distribution

Instead of dealing with individual values, as we did with the preceding array, we may rely on frequency distribution by relating to the total number of times that each value appears in a large set of numbers. Consider the following set of values, each of which represents the number of defective welds per day over a 20-day period.

Defective welds per day

1st week	12	13	9	11	14
2nd week	11	13	12	8	16
3rd week	13	12	15	12	11
4th week	12	14	10	12	11

Upon ordering each value (x) from the lowest to highest in Table 21.1, we enter a mark (tally) every time the value appears in the preceding list of de-

Table 21.1
A frequency distribution (without grouping)

Value (x)	Tally	Frequency (f)	x times f
16	I	1	16
15	I	1	15
14	II	2	28
13	III	3	39
12	JHT I	6	72
11	IIII	4	44
10	I	1	10
9	I	1	9
8	I	1	8
Totals		20	241

fective welds. A total of the tally represents the frequency (f) of the value, which, when multiplied by the value (f times x), results in the total of each value. There was only one tally each for 8, 9, and 10, so that their total values remain unchanged ($8 \times 1 = 8$, $9 \times 1 = 9$, $10 \times 1 = 10$). The four 11's result in 44 ($4 \times 11 = 44$), the six 12's result in 72 ($6 \times 12 = 72$), and so on. Finally, we total the frequencies (20) and the values (241). The total number of frequencies in Table 21.1 is small, relatively speaking, in that most business transactions to which statistical analysis is applicable entail thousands of values. For expediency when dealing with large sets of numbers (values), we place the values into **classes** (groups of similar values). To illustrate this procedure, let's assume that a sales manager in an insurance agency wants to analyze the following set of ages of insured customers.

Age of policy holders (at time policies issued)

45	33	56	55	30
35	29	51	46	40
32	57	47	38	39
44	52	59	46	43
45	40	41	53	42
50	46	42	38	47
43	36	38	52	39
41	27	44	37	43

The ages vary from a low of 27 to a high of 59, so that the range of 35 (25 to 60) would include all of the values and also provide a number that is easily divisible.

Class Intervals

Then, arbitrarily deciding on seven classes, we have a **class interval** (the size of each class) of five.

$$\text{Range} \div \frac{\text{Number of}}{\text{classes}} = \frac{\text{Class}}{\text{interval}}$$

$$35 \div 7 = 5$$

If we were instead to divide the range into five classes, we would have a class interval of 7 ($35 \div 5 = 7$). The number of classes (groups) that are generally used ranges from 5 to 15. Fewer than five may conceal important characteristics of the data, whereas too large a number may create sudden dips and peaks of frequencies that would obscure general patterns. The relationships of range, classes, and class intervals are further clarified in Figure 21.1

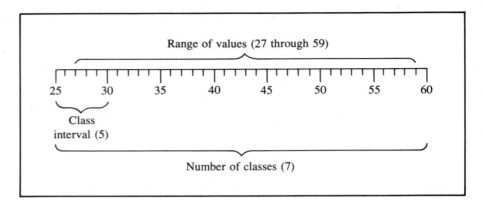

Class Limits and Midpoints

Two additional terms should be defined. **Class limits** are the lowest and highest values of each class. In Figure 21.1 the class limits are 25–29, 30–34, 35–39, and so on, with 5 points in each. The **midpoint** is the central value of a class, which is determined by averaging the class limits. In Figure 21.1, for example, the midpoint between the class limits of 25 and 29 is 27.

$$\text{Midpoint} = \frac{\text{Sum of class limits}}{2} = \frac{25 + 29}{2} = 27$$

These figures are brought together in Table 21.2. The class interval of 25–29, for instance, shows that two values (tallies) from our original set of numbers (page 419) fall within that class, resulting in a frequency (f) of 2. We then multiply the frequency (f) by the midpoint (x) to derive the class value (fx).

$$f \times x = fx$$

$$2 \times 27 = 54$$

We then multiply 3×32, 8×37, and so on.

Table 21.2
A frequency distribution
(with class intervals)

Class	Tally	Frequency (f)		Midpoint (x)		Class value (fx)
55–59	IIII	4	×	57	=	228
50–54	JHT	5	×	52	=	260
45–49	JHT II	7	×	47	=	329
40–44	JHT JHT I	11	×	42	=	462
35–39	JHT III	8	×	37	=	296
30–34	III	3	×	32	=	96
25–29	II	2	×	27	=	54
Totals		40				1,725

Although the figures in the final (fx) column are very close estimates, they are estimates nevertheless, in that each tally in a class is given equal weight, with that weight or value being the class midpoint. The greater the set of numbers, however, the more accurate the approximations. Finally, for purposes to be explained later in this chapter, we total the f and fx columns, resulting in sums of 40 and 1,725 respectively.

APPLICATION 1. Tally the following set of numbers, using ten classes with class intervals of ten.

48	71	39	77	0	84	73	86
73	17	64	60	63	61	68	33
51	57	31	44	58	33	65	59
29	51	52	75	57	23	59	80
44	70	43	49	54	96	54	55
63	42	89	50	46	55	70	49

90–99	|	40–49	ﬀ |||
80–89	||||	30–39	||||
70–79	ﬀ ||	20–29	||
60–69	ﬀ ||	10–19	|
50–59	ﬀ ﬀ |||	0–9	|

APPLICATION 2. Continuing with the data in Application 1, complete a table (label it "Table 12, A Frequency Distribution"), showing the frequency (f), midpoint (x), total value (fx) for each class, and the totals of the f and fx columns.

Table 12, A Frequency Distribution

Class	Frequency (f)		Midpoint (x)		Class value (fx)
90–99	1	×	94.5	=	94.5
80–89	4	×	84.5	=	338.0
70–79	7	×	74.5	=	521.5
60–69	7	×	64.5	=	451.5
50–59	13	×	54.5	=	708.5
40–49	8	×	44.5	=	356.0
30–39	4	×	34.5	=	138.0
20–29	2	×	24.5	=	49.0
10–19	1	×	14.5	=	14.5
0–9	1	×	4.5	=	4.5
Totals	48				2,676.0

COMMONLY USED
AVERAGES

After data have been collected, classified, and tabulated, as discussed and illustrated in the preceding section, we may consider useful applications of the resulting information. Most useful, perhaps, are the three basic averages of central tendency — the mean, the median, and the mode.

Arithmetic Mean

When people use the word *average* to refer to such measurements as average income, average sales, average prices, average height, or average speed, they are, knowingly or unknowingly, referring to the arithmetic mean. When computing unclassified (ungrouped) data, the following equation is applicable.

$$\text{Arithmetic mean (ungrouped data)} = \bar{X} = \frac{\Sigma x}{n}$$

$\bar{X}$ (read "X bar") is the symbol for the arithmetic mean, x (lower case) represents the variables (the values to be averaged), Σ (the Greek letter sigma) is the summation or total of the values being averaged, and n represents the total number of values being averaged. As an illustration, suppose that a homeowner decides to accept a budget payment plan offered by the local utility company. Rather than having to pay relatively high bills during periods of heavy power usage, as opposed to low bills during the remainder of the year, the homeowner will make monthly payments based on an average (the mean) of the 12 preceding monthly bills.

Jan $90.80	Apr $60.95	Jul $155.60	Oct $95.90
Feb 82.00	May 67.38	Aug 145.48	Nov 60.55
Mar 82.44	Jun 73.50	Sep 138.40	Dec 77.60

The monthly payments under the budget plan will be $94.22, the average (arithmetic mean) of the 12 monthly bills:

$$\bar{X} = \frac{\Sigma x}{n}$$

$$= \frac{90.80 + 82.00 \ldots + 77.60}{12}$$

$$= \frac{1,130.60}{12}$$

$$= \$94.22$$

In averaging 12 figures, we have added the figures and divided the sum by 12.

When averaging six numbers, we divide their sum by six, when averaging four numbers we divide their sum by 4, and so on.

As you already know, however, we switch to a shortcut method when dealing with numerous values; rather than add them individually, we classify (tally) the values (giving us the frequency) and multiply the frequency by the midpoint of the class. The following figures are the result of our earlier calculations in Table 21.2.

Frequency (f)		Midpoint (x)		Product of fx
4	×	57	=	228
5	×	52	=	260
7	×	47	=	329
11	×	42	=	462
8	×	37	=	296
3	×	32	=	96
2	×	27	=	54
$n = 40$		Σfx	=	1,725

Placing the totals in the following equation, we derive a mean of 43.125.

$$\text{Arithmetic mean} \atop \text{(grouped data)} : \bar{X} = \frac{\Sigma fx}{n} = \frac{1,725}{40} = 43.125$$

Recalling that the data in Table 21.2 concern the ages of people, we have found the average (mean) age to be 43-1/8 years. The only difference between this formula and the preceding one is that we have multiplied the midpoint of each class by the frequency (the number of times a value appears in the class interval). We have used a short-cut method rather than adding the numbers individually.

Modified Mean

A common criticism of the arithmetic mean is that extreme values, both high and low, often result in distorted or unrealistic figures. Correspondingly, a **modified mean** is a mean that has been calculated after extreme values have been removed from the data being averaged. To average the following ages of employees, in consideration of issuing a group health policy, the one extreme age (62) has a significant impact on the mean age.

Array: 21, 23, 23, 29, 32, 35, 37, 62

$$\text{Mean:} \frac{21 + 23 \ldots + 62}{8} = \frac{262}{8} = 32.75 \text{ years}$$

By removing the extreme age and recalculating, we derive a mean age that is more representative of the employee group.

$$\text{Modified mean} = \frac{21 + 23 \ldots + 37}{7} = \frac{200}{7} = 28.6 \text{ years}$$

The median sometimes represents a more accurate average than either the arithmetic mean or the modified mean, as explained later in this same section.

Weighted Mean

Theoretically, at least, arithmetic means are weighted. All of the values in the unweighted means discussed this far have been assigned equal weights of one. A **weighted mean**, as more commonly defined, is obtained from values that are assigned relative weights based on their varying degrees of importance. The average daily balance on which credit purchases are financed is a weighted mean, in that the number of days is weighted by the amount of money owed. A weighted mean with which students are even more familiar is the cumulative grade-point average. The number of credit hours for each subject is based on its degree of difficulty, such as Calculus I being weighted more heavily than Introductory Algebra, and the letter grades are assigned points.

Grade	Points
A	4
B	3
C	2
D	1
F	0

Assume, for example, that a student takes the classes and earns the grades reflected in Table 21.3. After multiplying the credit hours (weight factor) by the grade points earned, to derive the relative importance of each grade, we calculate the weighted mean by dividing the total relative importance by the

Table 21.3
Weighted mean
(cumulative grade-point
average)

Subject	Credit hours (weight)	Letter grade	Grade points	Relative importance
BA 201	3	A	4	12
MA 121	5	A	4	20
EC 201	3	B	3	9
DP 100	2	C	2	4
Totals	13			45

Grade point average: 45/13 = 3.4615 = 3.46

total credit hours taken. Because a mean of 3.50 or higher is defined as an "A average," a 3.46 average is a B+.

A simple average of the grade points (4, 4, 3, 2) is 3.25. The weighted mean is 0.21 points higher, reflecting the fact that the student earned relatively high grades in the more difficult (more heavily weighted) courses. If the situation were reversed, with low grades being earned in the high credited courses and high grades in the low credit courses, the weighted average would be lower than the simple average.

The Median

The **median**, another widely used measure of central tendency, is the value that divides a set of data into two equal parts, so that half of the data are higher than the average and half are lower. Unlike the mean, the median is unaffected by extreme values, causing it to be viewed in many situations as a superior measure of central tendency. To cite the mean annual income of Americans, for example, would be to include salaries of over $1 million per year, resulting in a mean that would suggest that the average citizens are better off than they actually are. A figure for the median annual income of Americans, on the other hand, indicates that one half of the population is receiving incomes higher than the average and one half is receiving lower incomes.

Consider, for example, the annual salaries for five employees in a small accounting firm: $15,000, $15,500, $16,000, $17,000, and $30,000.

$$\text{Mean: } \frac{15,000 + 15,500 + 16,000 + 17,000 + 30,000}{5} = \frac{93,500}{5} = \$18,700$$

Median: 15,000, 15,500, 16,000, 17,000, 30,000

To derive the mean, we add the five figures and divide the sum by 5; for the median we order the values into an array and identify the middle value. The median of $16,000 is considerably lower than the $18,700 mean, because the mean is affected significantly by the extreme salary at the upper end of the income scale.

Ungrouped Data. The first step in determining the median in an ungrouped set of values, as already mentioned, is to arrange the values in an array, as in the following rates of personal savings in the United States during a five-year period.

Unordered values: 5.6, 7.7, 8.1, 6.4, 4.9

An array: 4.9, 5.6, 6.4, 7.7, 8.1

The median (arrow) is easily identified in the *odd number of values* as being the middle value, with one half of the values being higher than 6.4 percent and one half being lower.

When an *even number of values* exists, there is no middle figure, making it necessary to derive the median (M_d) by averaging the two middle values. Consider the following six figures.

Array: 4.7, 4.9, 5.6, 6.4, 7.7, 8.1

$$\underbrace{\qquad\qquad}$$

two middle
values

$$M_d = \frac{5.6 + 6.4}{2} = 6.0 = 6\%$$

The median is exactly between the two middle values, with three values being higher than 6 percent and three values being lower.

The equation for identifying the *location of the median*, when the number of values is either odd or even, is

$$\text{Location of median: } \frac{n + 1}{2}$$

In our array of five numbers, we locate the median as the third number; in the array of six numbers, we move into the array three and one-half values.

Odd array

Five values $\begin{cases} 8.1 \\ \\ 7.7 \\ \\ 6.4 \leftarrow \\ \\ 5.6 \\ \\ 4.9 \end{cases}$

up 3

$$\text{Location} = \frac{n + 1}{2}$$

$$= \frac{5 + 1}{2}$$

$$= 3$$

Even array

$$
\text{Six values} \left\{ \begin{array}{l} 8.1 \\[10pt] 7.7 \\[10pt] 6.4 \\[10pt] 5.6 \\[10pt] 5.9 \\[10pt] 4.7 \end{array} \right.
$$

up 3-1/2

$$
\begin{aligned}
\text{Location} &= \frac{n+1}{2} \\[10pt]
&= \frac{6+1}{2} \\[10pt]
&= 3.5
\end{aligned}
$$

In the odd array, the median is 6.4, three numbers from the low or high end of values. In the even array, the median is located three and one-half numbers from either end, somewhere between 5.6 and 6.4 (which we have already determined to be 6 percent). The equation for finding the location of the median is especially helpful when dealing with large sets of grouped data

Grouped (Classified) Data. A determination of the median of values that have been classified involves several steps. Data with which you are already familiar (Table 21.2) are restated on page 428 to illustrate the procedure.[1]

STEP 1. Determine the number of values that we must cumulate in order to locate the median position.

$$
\text{Median position: } \frac{n+1}{2} = \frac{40+1}{2} = \frac{41}{2} = 20.5
$$

As illustrated with the arrow in the table, we begin at the bottom (lowest

---

[1] Although more than one approach may be used to identify the median value of grouped data, for consistency of procedure it is advisable to arrange the data as shown in Table 21.2 with the lower values at the bottom of the class column and the higher values at the top.

Table 21.2
(restated with
modifications) A
frequency distribution

Class	Tally	Frequency (f)		Midpoint (x)		Product of fx
55–59	IIII	4	×	57	=	228
50–54	JHT	5	×	52	=	260
45–49	JHT II	7	×	47	=	329
40–44	JHT JHT I ← →	11	×	42	=	462
35–39	JHT III	8	×	37	=	296
30–34	III	3	×	32	=	96
25–29	II	2	×	27	=	54
Totals		$n = 40$		Σfx	=	1,725

up 20-1/2

value) and count upward through the first three classes, which total 13
frequencies ($2 + 3 + 8 = 13$), which takes us 7-1/2 frequencies into
Class 40–44 ($20.5 - 13 = 7.5$).

STEP 2. Find the value of each frequency within the median class. Since each
class interval is 5 and there are 11 frequencies (tallies) in the median (40–
44) class, we divide 5 by 11.

$$\frac{\text{Class}}{\text{interval}} \div \frac{\text{Frequencies}}{\text{(tallies)}} = \frac{\text{Value of each}}{\text{frequency}}$$

$$5 \div 11 = 0.4545$$

STEP 3. Determine the value of the 7-1/2 frequencies into the median (40–44)
class that must be made to reach the median, by multiplying the value of
each frequency within the class by 7.5.

$$\begin{array}{c}\text{Value of}\\\text{each frequency} \times\\\text{in Class 40–44}\end{array} \begin{array}{c}\text{Frequencies into}\\\text{Class 40–44}\\\text{(Step 1)}\end{array} = \begin{array}{c}\text{Required value}\\\text{from Class 40–44}\end{array}$$

$$0.4545 \times 7.5 = 3.4$$

STEP 4. Determine the median by adding the value from Class 40–44 to an average of the lower limit of Class 40–44 and the value of the upper limit
of the preceding (lower valued) class.[2]

---

[2] Although some authors would recommend adding 3.4 to 40.0 (the lower limit of Class 40–44),
rather than taking the time to average the lower limit of that class with the upper limit of the
preceding class, such a shortcut results in a less accurate average and sometimes (as it would in
Application 2 on page 342) results in answers that are obviously erroneous.

$$\frac{\text{Upper limit} \quad \text{Lower limit}}{\begin{array}{c}\text{preceding class} + \text{median class}\\ 2\end{array}} = \frac{39 + 40}{2} = 39.5$$

$$\begin{aligned}\text{Median} &= 39.5 + 3.4\\ &= 42.9\end{aligned}$$

The median of the values in Table 21.2 is 42.9, which, as explained earlier, is a close estimate of the real median. Also as already explained, the greater the number of values being averaged, the more accurate the average will be.

As an alternative to the four-step procedure, we may use the following **formula to determine the median**.

$$M_d = L + \frac{\left(\dfrac{n+1}{2} - F\right)i}{f}$$

The symbol L represents an average of the lower limit of the median class and the upper limit of the preceding class, giving us

$$L = \frac{40 + 39}{2} = 39.5$$

The median-position equation, with which you are also familiar, is

$$\frac{n+1}{2} = \frac{40+1}{2} = \frac{41}{2} = 20.5$$

The symbol F (uppercase) represents the cumulative frequency up to but not including the median class.

$$F = 2 + 3 + 8 = 13$$

The symbol i (lowercase) is the class interval, that is, the number of values represented in each class (group).

$$i = 25 \text{ through } 29 = 5$$

Finally, the symbol f (lowercase) is the number of frequencies (tallies) in the median class,

$$f = \text{⌿⊬⊤ ⌿⊬⊤ |} = 11$$

which gives us

$$M_d = L + \frac{\left(\dfrac{n+1}{2} - F\right)i}{f}$$

$$= 39.5 + \frac{(20.5 - 13)5}{11}$$

$$= 39.5 + \frac{(7.5)5}{11}$$

$$= 39.5 + \frac{37.5}{11}$$

$$= 39.5 + 3.4$$

$$= 42.9$$

Either approach (the step-by-step descriptive method or the equation) derives the median for classified (grouped) data.

The Mode

In ungrouped data, the **mode** is the value that has the greatest frequency. The value nine is the mode in the following array.

Single Mode: 3, 8, 9, 9, 9, 11, 13, 16

mode

Sometimes a set of numbers may contain no mode because no two values are identical.

No mode: 4, 5, 7, 8, 9, 10

The following array is bimodal because it has two modes.

Bimodal: 20, 22, 22, 22, 23, 24, 24, 24, 25, 26

mode   mode

The mode is easy to identify, but it is the least reliable and least useful of the three averages. Its main applications are for identifying the dominant segments of markets as measured in surveys and for determining the most popular characteristics of products such as size, color, and fabric.

APPLICATION 1. In the array 6, 8, 12, 18, 22, 22, 22, 24, 28, 59, what is the

    a. Arithmetic mean?

$$\bar{X} = \frac{x}{n} = \frac{6 + 8 + 12 + 18 + 22 + 22 + 22 + 24 + 28 + 59}{10}$$
$$= \frac{221}{10}$$
$$= 22.1$$

    b. Modified mean?

$$\frac{221 - 59}{9} = \frac{162}{9} = 18$$

    c. Mode?

      22

APPLICATION 2. The following groupings were developed in applications earlier in this chapter (Applications 1 and 2, page 421).

Class	Tally	Frequency (f)		Midpoint (x)		Class value (fx)
90–99	I	1	×	94.5	=	94.5
80–89	IIII	4	×	84.5	=	338.0
70–79	JHT II	7	×	74.5	=	521.5
60–69	JHT II	7	×	64.5	=	451.5
50–59	JHT JHT III	13	×	54.5	=	708.5
40–49	JHT III	8	×	44.5	=	356.0
30–39	IIII	4	×	34.5	=	138.0
20–29	II	2	×	24.5	=	49.0
10–19	I	1	×	14.5	=	14.5
0–9	I	1	×	4.5	=	4.5
Totals		$n = 48$		$\Sigma fx =$		2,676.0

    a. What is the arithmetic mean?

$$\bar{X} = \frac{\Sigma fx}{n} = \frac{2,676}{48} = 55.8$$

    b. What is the modal class?

      50 through 59 = 13 frequencies

c. What is the median?

Step 1: Number of values into the median (50–59) class

$$\frac{n+1}{2} = \frac{48+1}{2} = 24.5$$
$$1 + 1 + 2 + 4 + 8 = 16$$
$$24.5 - 16 = 8.5$$

Step 2: Value of each frequency in the median class

$$\frac{\text{Class interval}}{\text{Frequency}} = \frac{10}{13} = 0.769$$

Step 3: Value of 8.5 frequencies into median class

$$0.769 \times 8.5 = 6.5$$

Step 4: Determine median

$$\frac{\text{Upper limit} + \text{lower limit}}{2} = \frac{49+50}{2} = 49.5$$
$$49.5 + 6.5 = 56$$

Formula approach: $M_d = L + \dfrac{\left(\dfrac{n+1}{2} - F\right)i}{f}$

$$= 49.5 + \frac{\left(\dfrac{48+1}{2} - 16\right)10}{13}$$

$$= 49.5 + \frac{(8.5)(10)}{13}$$

$$= 49.5 + 6.5$$

$$= 56$$

APPLICATION 3. The accompanying chart shows the number of economy cars that were sold by an automobile dealership during the past year. Using these data, determine (a) the average price per car and (b) the average price per car sold.

Model	Number sold	Price per car	Total sales
Runabouts	85	$6,000	$510,000
Hatchbacks	60	7,000	420,000
Sedans	40	8,000	320,000
	185		$1,250,000

a. Simple mean: $\dfrac{6,000 + 7,000 + 8,000}{3} = \$7,000$

b. Weighted mean: $\dfrac{1,250,000}{185} = 6,756.76$

Because more than twice as many runabouts were sold than the more expensive sedans, the average price per car sold is $243.24 less than the average price (simple average) of all three models.

STANDARD DEVIATION

The **standard deviation** is a mathematical equation that is used to measure the **dispersion** (variation from the mean) of a relatively large set of numbers. Although there are other measures of dispersion, the standard deviation is the most widely accepted measurement because it is more stable than other measures of dispersion and because it is more adaptable to advanced methods of statistical analysis. Before working with the standard deviation equation, however, let's explore the concept of dispersion.

Dispersion

The word **population**, as used in statistics, refers to the whole of whatever is being analyzed — all prices charged for a particular item, all weights of a product, all views on a topic. Because it would be impractical in many instances to study each element of an entire population, statisticians take a **sample** (study a representative few) of a population and, on the basis of statistical analysis, estimate with a high degree of confidence the characteristics of an entire population.

To identify important characteristics of a population, we must, in addition to considering the measures of central tendency (mean, median, and mode), analyze the amount of dispersion or scattering (also termed "variability") of a sample of a population. The basic purpose of measuring dispersion is to estimate the reliability of averages; that is, to determine the degree to which the sample values vary from the average and, relatedly, to determine whether the average is representative of an entire population.

For analysis of dispersion, as illustrated in Figure 21.2, we may plot all values on the x-axis of a graph, which has the effect of simply turning the tallies sideways.

Figure 21.2
Tally column turned
sideways

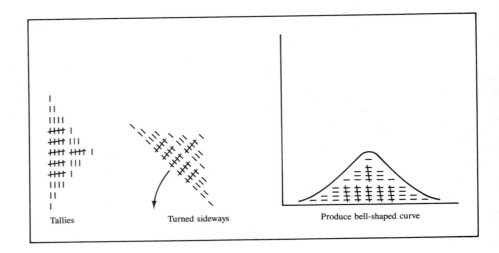

Tallies   Turned sideways   Produce bell-shaped curve

Figure 21.3
Values negatively skewed

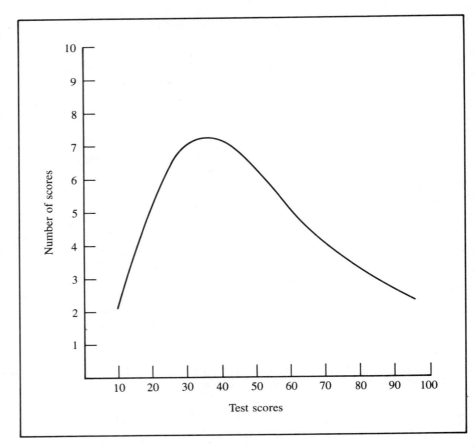

Figure 21.4
Values positively skewed

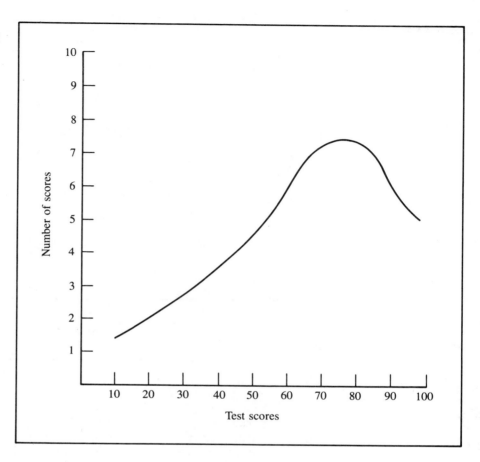

The drawing of a curved line to represent the number of responses (tallies) serves further to illustrate a normal (bell-shaped) curve — with a dominating central tendency (most of the responses concentrated near the middle) and with progressively fewer responses recorded as we read either to the left or to the right of center.

When dealing with relatively few values, the plotted values sometimes produce skewed results, being either negatively skewed (an inordinate number of low values) or positively skewed (an inordinate number of high values). Such patterns are illustrated as test scores in Figures 21.3 and 21.4. As depicted in the two graphs, educators may record a disproportionate number of either high or low test scores when analyzing the performance of a small body of students. When plotting the scores of hundreds of students, on the other hand, a central tendency becomes apparent (as shown earlier in Figure 21.2), with most of the scores falling in the middle range of the scale and a fairly even distribution (tapering) of scores to either side. To achieve a normal (symmetrical) distribution of values, therefore, statisticians generally deal in samples of several

Figure 21.5
One standard deviation

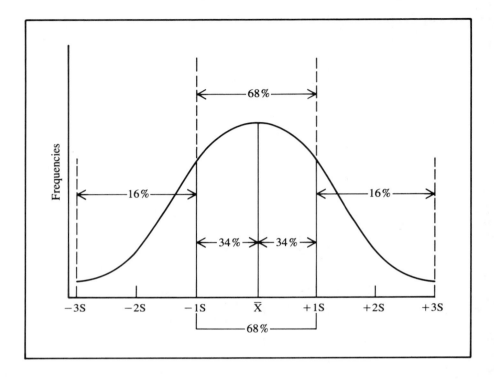

hundred, a thousand, or more.[3]

The two main characteristics of a normal distribution are that (1) the recorded values are distributed symmetrically about the mean and (2) the mean, median, and mode all have the same value — that value on the x-axis that corresponds to the highest point on the curve. This symmetry enables us to predict with some precision the number of values of a total population that will fall within a prescribed area of a curve: Approximately 68 percent of all values of a given population may be expected to fall within one standard deviation (Figure 21.5), approximately 95 percent within two standard deviations (Figure 21.6), and approximately 100 percent within three standard deviations (Figure 21.7). The word "approximate" is used here because the percents have been rounded to whole numbers (68.27 to 68, 95.45 to 95, and 99.73 to 100).

Now, assuming that an analysis of values produces a mean ($\bar{X}$) of 42 and a standard deviation (S) of 4, we may expect approximately 68 percent of the entire population of values to fall within the range of 38 to 46 (Figure 21.8), 95 percent to fall within a range of 34 to 50 (Figure 21.9), and nearly 100 percent within a range of 30 to 54 (Figure 21.10).

[3] Equations are available for determining the appropriate size of samples, as indicated from the results of preliminary data, a discussion of which is beyond the scope of this presentation.

Figure 21.6
Two standard deviations

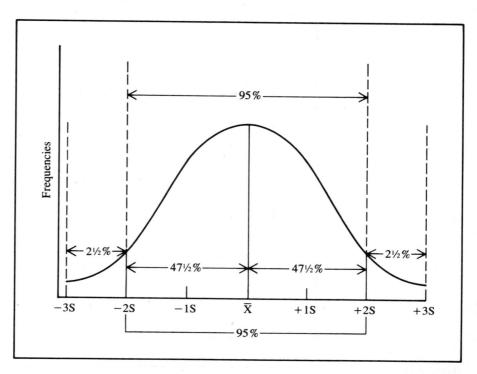

Figure 21.7
Three standard
deviations

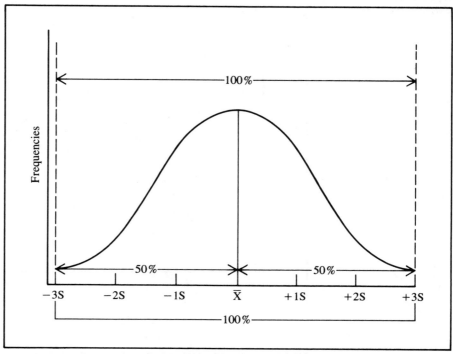

Figure 21.8
One standard deviation
(±4)

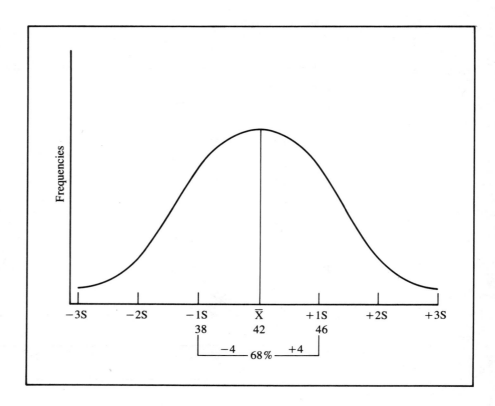

Figure 21.9
Two standard deviations
(±8)

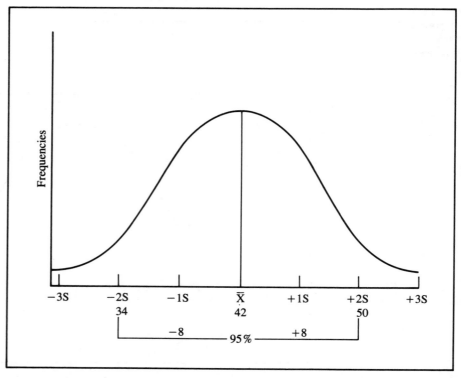

Figure 21.10
Three standard deviations (±12)

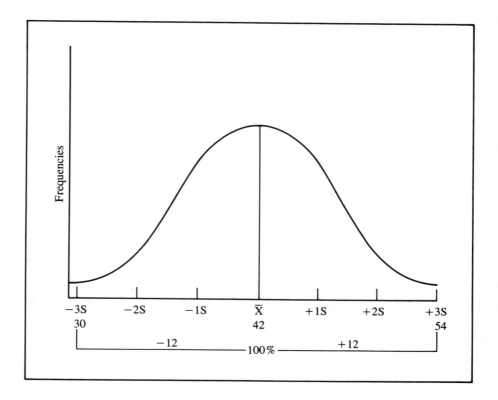

One standard deviation (±S) of four results in a range of four on both sides of the mean, two standard deviations (±2S) results in a range of eight (2 × 4 = 8) on both sides of the mean, and a standard deviation of three (±3S) results in a range of twelve (3 × 4 = 12) on both sides of the mean. Note that the scale used in marking each standard deviation on the x-axis is equal, even though the area under the curve represented by each standard deviation is unequal.

The Equation

Since the mean represents the central value, those values not located at the mean are said to deviate from the mean. To determine the degree that each value may deviate from the mean, we rely on the standard deviation (S or σ). The standard deviation is an average, essentially, an average of all the individual deviations from the mean that is used to measure the dispersion of values. It is the amount of dispersion that is important, not the direction of variance from the mean, because a squaring of deviations in the standard deviation equation has the effect of making all values positive.

The basic equation for determining the **standard deviation of ungrouped data** is

$$S = \sqrt{\frac{\Sigma d^2}{n}} \text{ (ungrouped data)}$$

The symbol Σ, you will recall, specifies the sum of something; in this case, the sum of d^2. The symbol d^2 represents deviations from a mean that have been squared. The symbol n, you will also recall, represents the number of values being analyzed.

Assume, for example, that a manufacturer of ties has taken a small sample of retail prices — $7, $13, $15, $17, and $28, resulting in a mean of 16.

$$X = \frac{x}{n} = \frac{7 + 13 + 15 + 17 + 28}{5} = 16$$

Then, as illustrated in Table 21.3, we subtract the mean from the value (price) of each tie (x), to determine the deviation from the mean, and derive d^2 by squaring the deviations.

Table 21.3
Standard deviation
(ungrouped data)

Value (x)	Deviation from the mean $(x - \bar{X} = d)$	Deviation squared (d^2)
28 ⎫	28 − 16 = +12	12 × 12 = 144
17 ⎪	17 − 16 = +1	1 × 1 = 1
15 ⎬ $n = 5$	15 − 16 = −1	−1 × −1 = 1
13 ⎪	13 − 16 = −3	−3 × −3 = 9
7 ⎭	7 − 16 = −9	−9 × −9 = 81
		$\Sigma d^2 = 236$

Plugging these figures into the equation gives us

$$S = \sqrt{\frac{\Sigma d^2}{n}}$$

$$= \sqrt{\frac{236}{5}}$$

$$= \sqrt{47.2}$$

$$= 6.87$$

Calculator	
Entries	**Display**
2 3 6	236.
÷	236.
5	5.
=	47.2
√x̄	6.8702256

We solve the equation beneath the radical sign and, as shown in the calculator application, extract the square root of 47.2 with the $(\sqrt{x})$ key.

Rounding the standard deviation of 6.87 to a whole number, we may expect that, of all ties being sold, 68 percent of them are priced within a range of $9 to $23, that 95 percent are within a range of $2 to $30, and that 100 percent are within a range of a zero to $37.

$$\bar{X}$$

$$1S = \qquad 9 \xleftarrow{\quad -7 \quad} 16 \xrightarrow{\quad +7 \quad} 23$$

$$2S = \qquad 2 \xleftarrow{\quad -14 \quad} 16 \xrightarrow{\quad +14 \quad} 30$$

$$3S = \qquad 0 \xleftarrow{\quad -16 \quad} 16 \xrightarrow{\quad +21 \quad} 37$$

To subtract three standard deviations ($3 \times 7 = 21$) from the mean of 16 would suggest that retailers are paying customers to take ties. We place the lower end of the range at zero, instead, meaning that about 100 percent of all ties are priced somewhere between zero and $37. To have any statistical significance, of course, such calculations must be based on a relatively large sample of existing prices.

Procedures for calculating the **standard deviation for grouped data** are the same as for ungrouped data, with one exception; we must multiply the squared deviations by the number of frequencies (f) in each class.[4] Adding this extra step to our equation, we have

$$S = \sqrt{\frac{\Sigma fd^2}{n}} \text{ (grouped data)}$$

[4] Because this presentation is in the form of an introduction to statistics, the equation has been simplified slightly to exclude a compensation for the error in the mean resulting from grouping. This exclusion produces only a small variation in answers, however.

Number of particles per million (class)	Frequency (f)	Midpoint of class (x)	Class value (fx)	Deviation from mean (d)	Deviation squared (d²)	Product of (f)(d²)
41–45	1	43	43	+16	256	256
36–40	4	38	152	+11	121	484
31–35	10	33	330	+6	36	360
26–30	15	28	420	+1	1	15
21–25	12	23	276	−4	16	192
16–20	5	18	90	−9	81	405
11–15	3	13	39	−14	196	588
	$n = 50$		$\Sigma fx = 1,350$			$\Sigma fd^2 = 2,300$

Table 21.4 Standard deviations (grouped data)

The application of this equation is illustrated in Table 21.4, which is based on sample data for the number of lead particles per million parts of petroleum. The first four columns are familiar, in that they represent part of the solution in determining averages for frequency distributions when dealing with class intervals. We must compute the mean, of course, before we can calculate deviations from the mean.

$$\bar{X} = \frac{\Sigma fx}{n} = \frac{1,350}{50} = 27$$

After entering the deviations between the midpoints and the mean, we square the deviations and multiply the squared values (d^2) by the frequencies (f).

From information developed in Table 21.4, we find the standard deviation to be 6.78.

$$S = \sqrt{\frac{\Sigma fd^2}{n}} = \sqrt{\frac{2,300}{50}} = \sqrt{46} = 6.78$$

Because the set of values approximates a normal distribution, we may expect about 68 percent of the total population to fall within a range of 20.22 to 33.78 lead particles per million parts of petroleum (±6.78 points from the mean of 27), about 95 percent within a range of 13.44 to 40.56 (±13.56 points from the mean), and nearly 100 percent within a range of 6.66 to 47.34 (±20.34 points from the mean).

Figure 21.11
Small standard deviation
relative to the mean

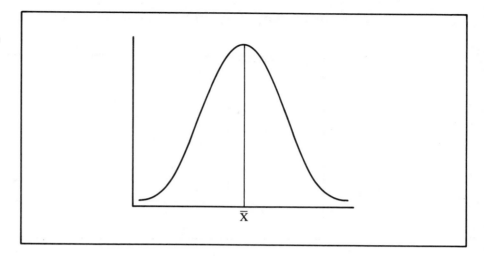

A small standard deviation in relation to the mean indicates that the values are clustered near the mean (Figure 21.11), whereas a relatively large standard deviation discloses that the data are widely dispersed from the mean (Figure 21.12).

The standard deviation of 6.78 that relates to a wide range in values (Table 21.4, page 442) is significantly lower than the nearly identical standard deviation of 6.87 in relation to a smaller range in values (Table 21.3, page 440). In other words, the values in Table 21.4 are more heavily concentrated about the mean than are those in Table 21.3

Figure 21.12
Large standard deviation
relative to the mean

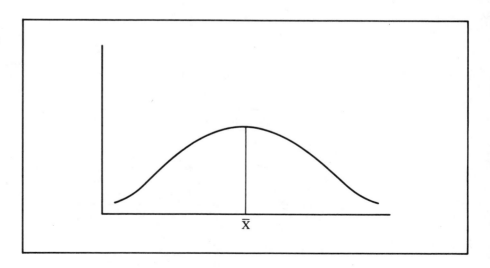

APPLICATION 1. Consider the following distribution.

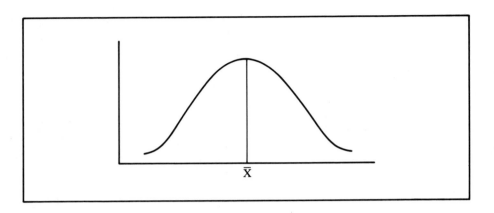

a. If the mean is 64 and the standard deviation is 5, what is the range within which we may expect about 68 percent of the population to fall?

$$\frac{-1S \quad \bar{X} \quad +1S}{59 \quad 64 \quad 69}$$
$$\llcorner 68\% \lrcorner$$

b. What percent of values may be expected to be within a range of 64 to 69?

$$\frac{68}{2} = 34\%$$

APPLICATION 2. Consider the following array of ungrouped values.

24	26	28	28	29	32	32	33	38

a. What is the mean?

$$\bar{X} = \frac{\Sigma x}{n} = \frac{24 + 26 + 28 + 28 + 29 + 32 + 32 + 33 + 38}{9}$$
$$= \frac{270}{9}$$
$$= 30$$

b. What is the standard deviation?

Value (x)	Deviation from the mean $(x - \bar{X} = d)$	Deviation squared (d^2)
38	+8	64
33	+3	9
32	+2	4
32	+2	4
29	−1	1
28	−2	4
28	−2	4
26	−4	16
24	−6	36
		$\Sigma d^2 = 142$

$$S = \sqrt{\frac{\Sigma d^2}{n}} = \sqrt{\frac{142}{9}} = \sqrt{15.78} = 3.97$$

c. What is the range for one standard deviation? for two standard deviations? for three standard deviations?

$1S = 30 \pm 3.97 = 26.03$ to 33.97
$2S = 30 \pm 7.94 = 22.06$ to 37.94
$3S = 30 \pm 11.91 = 18.09$ to 41.91

APPLICATION 3. Consider the following distribution of data.

Class	Tally	Frequency (x)
500–599	JHT II	7
400–499	JHT JHT II	12
300–399	JHT JHT JHT	15
200–299	JHT JHT I	11
100–199	JHT I	6

a. What is the mean?

Frequency (f)	Midpoint (x)	Class value (f)(x)
7	549.5	3,846.5
12	449.5	5,394.0
15	349.5	5,242.5
11	249.5	2,744.5
6	149.5	897.0
51		18,124.5

$$\bar{X} = \frac{\Sigma fx}{n} = \frac{18,124.5}{51} = 355.38$$

b. What is the standard deviation?

Deviation from mean	Deviation squared	Product of (f)(d^2)
194.12	37,682.57	263,777.99
94.12	8,858.57	106,302.84
−5.88	34.57	518.55
−105.88	11,210.57	123,316.27
−205.88	42,386.57	254,319.42
		$\Sigma fd^2 = 748,235.07$

$$S = \sqrt{\frac{\Sigma fd^2}{n}} = \sqrt{\frac{748,235.07}{51}} = \sqrt{14,671.28} = 121.13$$

c. What is the range for one standard deviation? two standard deviations? three standard deviations?

$$1S = 234.25 \xleftarrow{-121.13} 355.38 \xrightarrow{+121.13} 476.51$$

$$2S = 113.12 \xleftarrow{-242.26} 355.38 \xrightarrow{+242.26} 597.64$$

$$3S = \text{zero} \xleftarrow{-355.38} 355.38 \xrightarrow{+363.39} 718.77$$

EXERCISES (as assigned by your instructor)

21-1 Determine from the following set of numbers (to the tenths position)

    a. The arithmetic mean   25, 28, 35, 40, 30, 25, 27, 28, 29,
    b. The median   21, 17, and 24
    c. The mode

21-2 The workers at Artistry Glass Designs specialize in stained and leaded glass works. During one month, they produced the following number of pieces: 2, 4, 10, 8, 6, 7, 5, 9, and 12. Find (a) the arithmetic mean, (b) the median, and (c) the mode. (Round answers to tenths.)

21-3 Salespeople at Zaffel's Wholesalers, Inc. submitted the following expense accounts for June: $78.00, $95.50, $89.75, $67.40, $72.25, $92.80, $72.60, $90.10, $66.70, and $83.50. Find the (a) arithmetic mean, (b) median, and (c) mode of this set of numbers. (Round answers to tenths.)

21-4 Prescription sales at Johnson's Drugs varied widely throughout the week. Daily sales figures were $218.10, $557.30, $751.23, $340.50, $278.85, $492.50, and $263.48. Compute the daily mean for these sales.

21-5 Commissions paid to five brokers were $99.50, $199.65, $125.00, $155.00, and $175.00. What is the mean commission?

21-6 Gentry Apparel sold 12 men's suits on the first day of their spring sale. Prices varied considerably: $75, $95, $105, $210, $95, $175, $105, $190, $95, $105, $95, $75. What was the

    a. Mean price of the 12 suits?
    b. Median price?
    c. Most popular suit sold in terms of price?

21-7 The sales staff at Hadley's Department Store sold 15 quality dresses within a few hours of the start of the fall sale. Prices were $55, $105, $65, $115, $125, $65, $80, $95, $65, $115, $140, $160, $115, $190, $55.

    a. What was the mean price?
    b. What was the median price?
    c. What dress was the most popular in terms of price?

21-8 The annual salaries of ten administrative personnel at Glenview Hospital were $65,000, $18,000, $13,000, $15,000, $45,000, $20,000, $15,000, $15,000, $16,000, and $14,000. Which average would you use as the most representative of the salaries? What is that figure?

21-9 Janice and Hans could process 21 and 20 batches of data, whereas the other word processors could manage only 8, 14, 10, 11, 9, 9, 13, and 10 batches each. Which average is the most typical of the number of batches processed by the workers? What is the average?

21-10 Which average would a production manager of automobiles use to determine which color car the company should produce the most of?

21-11 Which average should be used to determine the most popular size of clothing to manufacture such as dresses, shoes, suits, and hats?

21-12 Jaison's Appliance Center is currently offering five different brands of stereo systems — Toshiba equipment sells for $600; JVC, $1,200; Fisher, $1,100; Sanyo, $700; and Panasonic, $900. The manager knew the average cost of these five brands to be $900 per system, but needed to know the average price of all systems that were sold during the past year. Upon checking the records, the manager's assistant made the following list of sales. Determine the average cost of all systems that were sold during the year.

Brand	Units sold
Toshiba	24
JVC	6
Fisher	7
Sanyo	20
Panasonic	10
Total	67

21-13 During a recent sales promotion, the luggage department reported the following sales:

Brand	Price	Sets sold
Oleg Cassini	$224	5
Jordache	211	4
Beach & Racquet Club	142	10
Enrico	70	13
Sassoon	67	15

What is the difference between the average price of a set of luggage, compared with the average price of those sets sold during the promotion?

21-14 As of July 1, the balance in Susan Boon's account with a local department store is $135. She charged several items amounting to $96 on July 10, made a payment of $125 on July 21, and then charged another $76 on July 25. What is her average daily balance for the month of July?

21-15 Gary Feldstein deposited $1,700 in a money market access account with a local savings and loan association on May 1. He deposited another $600 on June 1, withdrew $300 on June 11, and made two more deposits of $500 each on July 1 and July 15. What is Feldstein's average daily investment during the 90-day period beginning May 1 and ending July 29?

21-16 Sort the following data into a frequency distribution using intervals of 20 (0–19, 20–39, etc.) to determine (a) the arithmetic mean, (b) the median, and (c) the modal class.

63	19	51	10	47	85
36	55	77	25	29	14
59	56	39	51	66	68
38	92	75	28	26	21
44	74	40	56	43	70

21-17 Using intervals of 50 (0–49, 50–99, etc.), sort the following set of data into a frequency distribution to determine (a) the arithmetic mean, (b) the median, and (c) the modal class.

101	25	80	93	155	19
15	89	130	41	99	58
86	28	85	175	44	249
32	51	72	148	69	36
190	120	37	68	135	55

21-18 A large producer of salad oil shipped 500 cases, each case containing 12 bottles. The net and mean weight of each bottle of salad oil is 24 ounces with a standard deviation of 0.2 ounces, as shown in the following diagram.

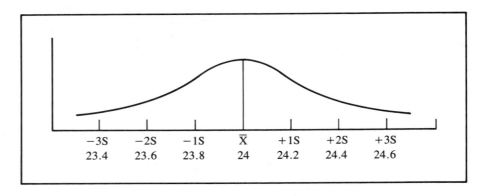

a. What percent of the bottles contain 24 ounces or more?
b. What percent contain from 24 to 24.2 ounces?
c. What percent contain from 23.8 to 24.2 ounces?
d. What percent weigh 23.8 ounces or more?
e. How many bottles weigh 23.8 ounces or more?
f. What percent weigh less than 23.8 ounces?
g. What percent weight more than 24.4 ounces?
h. What percent weigh less than or more than two standard deviations from the mean?
i. How many bottles contain from 23.6 to 24.4 ounces?

21-19 A producer packed 5,000 cans of ground coffee with a mean weight of 13 ounces and a standard deviation of 0.1 ounce, as shown in the diagram.

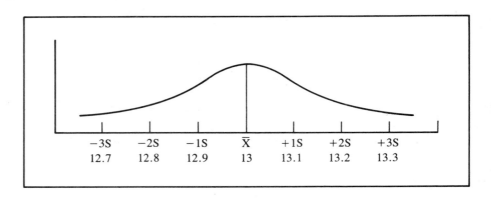

a. What percent of the cans contain 13 ounces or less?
b. What percent contain from 12.9 to 13 ounces?
c. What percent contain from 12.9 to 13.1 ounces?
d. What percent weigh 13.1 ounces or less?
e. How many cans weigh 13.1 ounces or less?
f. What percent weigh more than 13.1 ounces?
g. What percent weigh less than 12.8 ounces?
h. What percent weigh less or more than two standard deviations from the mean?
i. How many cans weigh from 12.8 to 13.2 ounces?

21-20 A manufacturer produces stainless steel products according to buyer specifications. Samples from a production run of 20,000 bearings reveal a mean diameter of one inch with a standard deviation of 0.001 inch.

a. Draw a normal distribution curve showing the values associated with one, two, and three standard deviations from the mean.
b. How many of the 20,000 bearings may we expect to have diameters measuring from 0.999 to 1.001 inches?
c. If customers will not accept bearings with tolerances outside the range of 0.998 to 1.002, how many of the 20,000 bearings may we expect to discard?

21-21 The specifications for a custom designed cylinder that is to be a part of a precision instrument is for a width of 2 centimeters with a standard deviation of no more than 0.0001 centimeters.

a. Prepare a normal distribution curve showing the values associated with one, two, and three standard deviations from the mean.
b. Of 1,000 units produced, how many units may we expect to meet the buyer's stringent specifications?
c. If the buyer changes the acceptable tolerance to 0.0002 centimeters, how many of the 1,000 units may we expect to qualify?
d. If cylinders with widths beyond a range of 1.9998 to 2.0002 are unsalable, how many of the 1,000 units may we expect to scrap?

21-22 Analyze the following ungrouped data and compute the

25	22	27	30	28	20	24

a. Arithmetic mean
b. Standard deviation

21-23 Analyze the following data and calculate the

Class	Frequency (f)
80–99	8
60–79	11
40–59	20
20–39	12
0–19	9

a. Arithmetic mean
b. Standard deviation

English and Metric Measurements

Most U.S. citizens are familiar with measurements commonly used in the English system such as inches, feet, yards, ounces, pounds, pints, and quarts. Relatively few people could define a rod, furlong, bushel, or peck, on the other hand, which are also integral elements of our English system of weights and measures. The majority of Americans are even more deficient in their knowledge of metric measurements, even though this system is used throughout the world and even though our competitiveness in international trade is currently in jeopardy. Through a very brief summary of the English system and a comparative analysis of the metric system, concepts presented in this chapter will enable you to

- describe and apply units of measurement under both the English and the metric systems
- calculate linear measurements (including those of squares, rectangles, triangles, pyramids, cylinders, and cones), capacity measurements, and weight measurements
- solve business problems using both English and metric measurements
- apply the proper form when working with metric symbols
- convert English measurements to metric and vice versa

During the medieval period and early modern times, measurements of length, weight, and capacity were selected arbitrarily, usually in relation to some part of the human anatomy such as the length of a person's foot or width of the palm. The yard was first based on the girth of (distance around) the king's waist and later changed to the distance from the tip of the king's nose to the end of the thumb on his outstretched hand. But as trade increased among people of different areas and of different countries, such "rule of thumb" guidelines were replaced with standardized units of measurements. Two predominant systems evolved: the English system and the international metric system.

THE ENGLISH SYSTEM

Until recently (nearly two decades or so) common units of measurements throughout the English-speaking world included the ounce, pound, quart, foot, yard, and other elements of what is called the English system. Currently, however, the United States is the only major country relying on this antiquated structure; even the leaders in Great Britain, where the system originated, have replaced it with the metric system.

The English system, the most common units of which are summarized in Table 22.1, is cumbersome. Comparatively speaking, it requires excessive mathematical operations when converting measurements to equivalent units within the same group of measures — such as relating inches to feet and feet to miles, ounces to pints and gallons, ounces to pounds, and pounds to tons.

The mathematical operations of addition, subtraction, multiplication, and division under the English system are even more laborious. To determine the amount remaining after subtracting a 3-foot 7-inch piece of steel from a rod measuring 8 feet 3 inches, for example, we must place the smallest unit to the right and, if necessary, borrow from the larger unit at left.

$$
\begin{array}{lrl}
\text{Length of steel rod:} & 8 \text{ ft } 3 \text{ in} = & 7 \text{ ft } 15 \text{ in} \\
\text{Less piece:} & 3 \text{ ft } 7 \text{ in} = & \underline{3 \text{ ft } \quad 7 \text{ in}} \\
\text{Length of remaining piece:} & & 4 \text{ ft } \quad 8 \text{ in}
\end{array}
$$

Division, a more complex operation than subtraction, becomes especially unwieldy, as demonstrated later in this chapter when operations under the English system are compared with those that utilize metric.

THE METRIC SYSTEM

The following statement might seem appropriate for a proclamation under Ripley's "Believe It or Not" format: Although officials of the U.S. government adopted the metric system in 1893 (yes, nearly 100 years ago), and even though President Gerald R. Ford signed the Metric Conversion Act on December 23, 1975, the metric system has yet to be widely embraced by Americans. In the absence of an official timetable for conversion, U.S. citizens, including most

Table 22.1

Common units of measure in the English system

LINEAR	CAPACITY (LIQUID)
12 inches (in or ″) = 1 foot	16 fluid ounces (fl oz) = 1 pint (pt)
3 feet (ft or ′) = 1 yard	2 pints = 1 quart (qt)
5.5 yards (yd) = 1 rod	4 quarts = 1 gallon (gal)
40 rods (rd) = 1 furlong	
8 furlongs (fur) = 1 mile (mi)	
1,760 yards = 1 mile	
5,280 feet = 1 mile	

WEIGHT	CAPACITY (DRY)
16 ounces (oz) = 1 pound (lb)	2 pints = 1 quart (qt)
100 pounds = 1 hundredweight (cwt)	8 quarts = 1 peck (pk)
20 hundredweights = 1 short ton (T)	4 pecks = 1 bushel (bu)
2,000 pounds = 1 short ton	
2,240 pounds = 1 long ton	

leaders within the business community, have shunned the relatively efficient metric system in favor of the status quo.

The use of metric within the country *is* increasing, nevertheless, as American scientists and engineers express their measurements in metric terms and as many businesses, especially those involved in foreign trade, adapt to the world order. Some products, such as beverages, are labeled solely in liters, and many canned and bottled products are labeled in both English and metric measurements.

During the final decade of the eighteenth century, the French government commissioned a group of scientists to develop a comprehensive system of weights and measures. The system that evolved from this endeavor became known as the "metric system," which has since become the scientific and international standard of measure, replacing nearly all other national units of weights and measures.

The metric system is based on a single element — the meter — which was originally defined as one ten-millionth of the distance from the equator to the North Pole. Upon discovery that the earth is not a perfect sphere, scientists reexamined the meter several times to redefine it most recently in terms of the wavelength of a special type of light.

Logical Structure

The metric system has two important features. First, it is a coherent system in which the basic units of measurement (meter, kilogram, and liter) are integrated. The **meter** is the basic unit for measuring length or distance. The **kilogram**, which is a measure of mass or weight, was originally defined in terms of the meter; that is, the kilogram was defined as the weight of one cubic decimeter (1/10 of a meter) of water at the temperature of its highest density (4.00 Celsius or 39.20 Fahrenheit). A **liter**, the unit for measuring capacity, was also defined in terms of the meter; as illustrated in Figure 22.1, a liter is the amount of fluid that can be held in a container with dimensions on all sides of one decimeter. These units have since been redefined for improved accuracy.

Figure 22.1
Container measuring one cubic decimeter

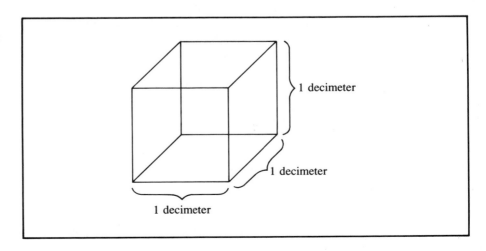

1 decimeter

1 decimeter

1 decimeter

Table 22.2
Commonly used prefixes
in the Metric System

Prefix	Symbol	Value	Multiplication factor
giga	G	one billion	$1,000,000,000 = 10^9$
mega	M	one million	$1,000,000 = 10^6$
kilo	k	one thousand	$1,000 = 10^3$
hecto	h	one hundred	$100 = 10^2$
deka	da	ten	$10 = 10^1$
BASE UNIT			$1 = 10^0$
deci	d	one tenth	$0.1 = 10^{-1}$
centi	c	one hundredth	$0.01 = 10^{-2}$
milli	m	one thousandth	$0.001 = 10^{-3}$
micro	u	one millionth	$0.000\ 001 = 10^{-6}$
nano	n	one billionth	$0.000\ 000\ 001 = 10^{-9}$

The second important feature of the metric system is that it is ordered. As shown in Table 22.2, units greater than and less than the base unit are expressed as products and ratios of the base, with each unit of measure being either ten times greater or ten times smaller than the units next to it.

Metric Prefixes:

Greek prefixes are used to express multiples of ten that are greater than the base unit, and Latin prefixes represent by a factor of ten those values that are less than the base. Because the prefixes are symbols, rather than abbreviations, they do not require periods. Note that lowercase and uppercase letters are used in some instances, to distinguish milli (m) from mega (M). Also, two-letter symbols are used selectively to distinguish such prefixes as deka (da) from deci (d). The prefixes of each unit of measurement indicate the number: *deci* meaning one-tenth; *centi*, one one-hundredth; *deka*, ten; *hecto*, 100; and *kilo*, 1,000.

Because the middle six prefixes (unshaded area in Table 22.2) are the most frequently used, we should memorize the related symbols and values. We are familiar with most of these prefixes, however, so that only a few must be memorized. **Deci** is part of the word *decimal*, for instance, which refers to the value 10. **Centi** is similar to our word *cents*, meaning 1/100. **Mill**, derived from *milli*, is an amount of money (1/10 of a cent or 1/1,000 of $1.00) that has long been used in property-tax computations. The prefixes **deka** and **deca** are synonymous, being part of the word *decade*, meaning a period of ten years. Only two prefixes are left to memorize: **hecto**, meaning 100, and **kilo**, meaning 1,000.

Basic Units of Measurement

As already mentioned, the basic units of metric measurements are the meter, the liter, and the kilogram.

The meter. (m) may be expressed in English units as a little longer than one yard (1.1 yards) or approximately 39.37 inches. Table 22.3 displays the six

Table 22.3
The meter
(with multiples
and submultiples)

1 kilometer (km) = 1,000 meters	1 meter = 0.001 kilometer
1 hectometer (hm) = 100 meters	1 meter = 0.01 hectometer
1 dekameter (dam) = 10 meters	1 meter = 0.1 dekameter
1 meter (m) = BASIC UNIT OF LENGTH	
1 decimeter (dm) = 0.1 meter	1 meter = 10 decimeters
1 centimeter (cm) = 0.01 meter	1 meter = 100 centimeters
1 millimeter (mm) = 0.001 meter	1 meter = 1,000 millimeters

most commonly used prefixes as related to the meter, along with each of the measurements defined in terms of one meter. The **kilometer** (km) is used to measure long distances, such as the distance between cities and the speed of a vehicle in terms of the number of kilometers per hour. The **centimeter (cm)**, because of established practices, is retained for body measurements and clothing production, and the **millimeter** is used extensively to measure miniscule lengths as in the design and production of computer chips.

The liter. (1), as the basic unit of capacity, is roughly equivalent to the English quart. Correspondingly, the **deciliter** is used to measure units of capacity of about one third of a cup and smaller. The **centiliter** and **milliliter**, in turn, are useful in securing precise measurements of very small quantities. The liter and its multiples are presented in Table 22.4. Interestingly, bottles in the United States that contain less than one liter of fluid have the contents labeled in milliliters, which has the effect of reflecting whole numbers rather than fractional amounts. For example, a 0.75 liter bottle is labeled "750 milliliters."

The kilogram. (km) is used as the basic unit of weight. Because the **gram** (g) weighs only 0.035 ounces (35/1,000ths of one ounce), it is impractical for most applications. As a consequence, the **kilogram** (kg) (approximately 2.2 pounds) has been embraced as the basic metric unit for measuring weight. The kilogram is, therefore, the only base unit that includes a prefix as part of its identification. Nevertheless, as illustrated in Table 22.5, the gram serves as the base unit from which numerical values are determined.

Table 22.4
The liter (with multiples
and submultiples)

1 kiloliter (kl) = 1,000 liters	1 liter = 0.001 kiloliter
1 hectoliter (hl) = 100 liters	1 liter = 0.01 hectoliter
1 dekaliter (dal) = 10 liters	1 liter = 0.1 dekaliter
1 liter (l) = BASIC UNIT OF LENGTH	
1 deciliter (dl) = 0.1 liter	1 liter = 10 deciliters
1 centiliter (cl) = 0.01 liter	1 liter = 100 centiliters
1 milliliter (ml) = 0.001 liter	1 liter = 1,000 milliliters

Table 22.5
The gram (with multiples and submultiples)

1 kilogram (kg) = 1,000 grams	1 gram = 0.001 kilograms
1 hectogram (hg) = 100 grams	1 gram = 0.01 hectograms
1 dekagram (dag) = 10 grams	1 gram = 0.1 dekagram
1 gram (g) = ORIGINAL BASIC UNIT OF WEIGHT	
1 decigram (dg) = 0.1 gram	1 gram = 10 decigrams
1 centigram (cg) = 0.01 gram	1 gram = 100 centigrams
1 milligram (mg) = 0.001 gram	1 gram = 1,000 milligrams

The **metric ton**, although not shown in Table 22.5, parallels the kilogram as one of the most important units for measuring weights. The metric ton is 1,000 kilograms, which is equivalent to about 2,240 pounds.

Easy Conversions

A main advantage of the metric system is the ease with which arithmetic operations may be performed when changing to higher or lower units. To convert one unit to a higher unit, we need only divide by 10 (move the decimal one place to the left); to convert one unit to a second higher unit, we divide by 100 (move the decimal two places to the left); and so on.

Converting from lower to higher units

22.48 meters
= 2.248 dekameters
= 0.02248 kilometers

5.3 centiliters
= 0.53 deciliters
= 0.053 liters

750 milligrams
= 0.0075 hectograms

To convert one unit to a lower unit, we need only multiply by 10 (move the decimal one place to the right); to convert one unit to a second lower unit, we multiply by 100 (move the decimal two places to the right); and so on.

Converting from higher to lower units

1.75 kilograms
= 175 dekagrams
= 1750 grams

8.75 kilometers
= 8,750 meters
= 87,500 decimeters

1.35 liters
= 135 centiliters
= 1,350 milliliters

With only minimal application and practice, we may convert values up and down the metric scale with relative ease.

Proper Form

The following list pertains to the recommended form for writing metric terms.

1. Unit names are in lower case letters
   10 kilograms (not 10 Kilograms)
   3 meters (not 3 Meters)
2. Metric symbols, because they are not abbreviations, are written without periods, unless the sentence is ended with a metric symbol.
   9 ml (not 9 ml.)
   12 hm (not 12 hm.)
3. Metric symbols represent both singular and plural forms so that no added "s" is required.
   44 cm (not 44 cms)
   150 mg (not 150 mgs)
4. Only exponents are used to express power greater than one.
   3 m^2 (not 3 sq m)
   8 dm^3 (not 8 cu dm)
5. Only decimal notation is used to denote parts or quantities less than one.
   1.75 l (not 1-3/4 l)
   0.5 g (not 1/2 g)
6. A zero is placed before the decimal point for numbers less than one.
   0.7 km (not .7 km)
   0.25 mg (not .25 mg)

Adherence to these few rules will enable you to express yourself correctly in metric — not only in solving the problems in the following section, but also when engaging in business transactions involving metric measurements.

COMPARATIVE APPLICATIONS

Mathematical problems, whether using English or metric, are solved in the same conceptual manner, which makes it convenient to demonstrate the application of both systems when discussing linear, capacity, and weight measurements.

Linear Measurements

A **line** is defined as having length but no width or depth. A **plane** is a flat, two-dimensional figure that has length and width; whereas a **solid** is a three-dimensional figure that has length, width, and height. When measuring perimeters and areas, therefore, we are working with plane figures.

A *perimeter* is the boundary of a closed plane figure, except that the word **circumference** is used when referring to the perimeter of a circle. Formulas for deriving perimeters are relatively simple and logical.

To determine the distance or length of the **perimeter of a rectangle and a square**, the equation is

Perimeter of a rectangle: $P = 2(l + w)$

where P is perimeter, l is length, and w is width. Because all sides of a square are equal, the equation for determining the perimeter may be simplified to read

Perimeter of a square: $P = 4l$

To find the perimeter of a rectangle measuring 4 feet 5 inches by 3 feet 9 inches, for example, we have

$P = 2(l + w)$

$\quad = 2(4 \text{ ft } 5 \text{ in} + 3 \text{ ft } 9 \text{ in})$

$\quad = 2(7 \text{ ft } 14 \text{ in})$

$\quad = 2(8 \text{ ft } 2 \text{ in})$

$\quad = 16 \text{ ft } 4 \text{ in}$

To find the perimeter of a rectangle that is 0.45 meters in length and 3.25 decimeters wide, we have

$0.45 \text{ m} = 4.5 \text{ dm}$

$P = 2(l + w)$

$\quad = 2(4.5 + 3.25)$

$\quad = 2(7.75)$

$\quad = 15.5 \text{ dm or } 1.55 \text{ m}$

The **perimeter of a triangle** with sides a, b, and c is the sum of all three sides.

Perimeter of a triangle: $P = a + b + c$

For a triangle measuring 1-1/2 by 3-5/8 and 2-1/4 inches, we have

$P = a + b + c$

$\quad = 1\text{-}1/2 + 3\text{-}5/8 + 2\text{-}1/4$

$\quad = 1\text{-}4/8 + 3\text{-}5/8 + 2\text{-}2/8$

$\quad = 6\text{-}11/8 \text{ or } 7\text{-}3/8 \text{ in}$

In metric, the perimeter of a triangle that measures 2.25 decimeters, 3.15 decimeters, and 25 centimeters is

25 cm = 2.5 dm

$$P = a + b + c$$

$$= 2.25 + 3.15 + 2.5$$

$$= 7.9 \text{ dm}$$

Regardless of the size of a circle, the ratio of the circumference to the diameter remains constant. This constant, called pi (π), has a value of $\frac{22}{7}$, which is generally rounded to 3.14. The formula for calculating the **circumference of a circle** is the diameter (d) × 3.14.

Circumference of a circle
when diameter is known: $C = \pi d$

where C is the circumference and d is the diameter.

Because the radius (r) of a circle is one half the diameter, the formula may also be expressed as

Circumference of a circle
when radius is known: $C = 2\pi r$

To determine the circumference of a circle that has a diameter of 4-5/8 inches, we have

4-5/8 = 4.625

$$C = \pi d$$

$$= (3.14)(4.625)$$

$$= 14.52 \text{ in}$$

To find the circumference of a circle with a radius of 3.5 centimeters, we multiply as follows:

$$C = 2\pi r$$

$$= (2)(3.14)(3.5)$$

$$= 21.98 \text{ cm}$$

APPLICATION 1. As specified in the contract, a landscaper is required to enclose with a wooden border a rectangular flower bed measuring 9 yards 9 inches long and 5 yards 7 inches wide. How many yards of border will be required?

9 yd 9 in = 9-9/36 = 333/36 yd
5 yd 7 in = 5-7/36 = 187/36 yd

$$P = \frac{2(l + w)}{36}$$

$$= \frac{2(333 + 187)}{36}$$

$$= 28.89 \text{ yd}$$

APPLICATION 2. A mason constructed a block wall around three sides of a yard, leaving open one width on the north side. The yard measures 32.25 meters long and 2.4 dekameters wide. How long is the block wall as expressed in meters?

2.4 dam = 24 m

Length of wall = $2l + w$
$\qquad\qquad\quad$ = 2(32.25) + 24
$\qquad\qquad\quad$ = 88.5 m

APPLICATION 3. A white border trim is to be sewn on a pennant measuring 10 inches on one side and 22 inches each on the other two sides. How much trim is required for 2 dozen pennants?

$P = a + b + c$
$\quad$ = 10 + 22 + 22
$\quad$ = 54 in or 1.5 yd

Amount: 1.5 × 24 = 36 yd

APPLICATION 4. A designer of women's costumes requires triangular strips of narrow rickrack to be sewn just above the hem of a skirt. One skirt requires 15 triangles measuring 5 centimeters on each side. If an order is for 20 skirts, how many meters of rickrack are required?

One skirt: 15(5 + 5 + 5) = 225 cm
20 skirts: 225 cm × 20 = 4,500 cm

4,500 cm = 45.0 m

APPLICATION 5. The price of a 3-inch wide fringe that is used by a manufacturer of plastic tablecloths for patio furniture has increased by 75 cents a yard. If a production run includes 500 forty-inch (diameter), round tablecloths and 1,000 forty-eight-inch (diameter), round tablecloths, how much more must the manufacturer pay for the fringe because of the price increase?

40-inch tablecloth: $C = \pi d = (3.14)(40) = 125.6$ in
48-inch tablecloth: $C = \pi d = (3.14)(48) = 150.72$ in

500 tablecloths =	(125.6)(500) =	62,800 in
1,000 tablecloths =	(150.72)(1,000) =	150,720 in
Total		213,520 in

Yards: $213,520 \div 36 = 5,931.11$
Increase: $(5,931.11)(0.75) = \$4,448.33$

APPLICATION 6. Three large circular flower beds in a city garden are to be enclosed with bender board. If each bed has a radius of 2.5 meters and if the price of a 2-meter precut board is $3.00, how much will it cost to enclose the flower beds?

One flower bed:	$C = 2\pi r = 2(3.14)(2.5) = 15.7$ m
Three flower beds:	$1.57 \times 3 = 47.1$ m
Board required:	47.1 m $\div 2 = 23.55$ or 24
Price:	$24 \times 3.00 = \$72.00$

Area is the measurement of the surface of a plane figure, and it is measured in square units. The equation for finding the **area of a rectangle** is

Area of a rectangle: $A = lw$

Because all sides of a square are equal, the **area of a square** may also be stated as

Area of a square: $A = l^2$

To find the area in square feet of a square measuring one yard long, for example, we have

1 yd = 3 ft

$A = l^2$

$= 3^2$

$= 9$ sq ft

Just as the multiplication of English linear measurements results in answers (products) that are squared (such as 10 ft × 10 ft = 100 sq ft), so, too, does the multiplication of two metric linear measurements result in squared products. Similarly, the multiplication of three measurements results in an answer that is cubed (10 ft × 10 ft × 10 ft = 1,000 cu ft). Because we are dealing with multiples of ten in the metric system, when converting *squared values* to the next highest multiple, we divide by 100; when converting *cubed values* to one higher value, we divide by 1,000, and so on. Remember that multiplying by 0.01 is the same as dividing by 100 and that multiplying by 0.001 is the same as dividing by 1,000.

Example: $500 \text{ dm}^2 \times 0.01 = 5 \text{ m}^2$

Example: $500 \text{ dm}^3 \times 0.001 = 0.5 \text{ m}^3$

When converting squared values to the next lowest multiple, we multiply by 100 (move the decimal two places to the right, rather than one); when converting cubed values to one lower value, we multiply by 1,000 (move the decimal three places to the right, rather than one); and so on.

Example: $5 \text{ m}^2 \times 100 = 500 \text{ dm}^2$

Example: $5 \text{ m}^3 \times 1,000 = 5,000 \text{ dm}^3$

As a helpful hint, we always multiply by fractional numbers (0.1, 0.01, 0.001, etc.) to change to larger metric units, and we multiply by whole numbers (10, 100, 1,000, etc.) to change to smaller metric units.

To find the area in decimeters of a rectangle measuring 1 meter long and 0.75 meters wide, we have

$A = lw$

$= 1 \times 0.75$

$= 0.75 \text{ m}^2$

$0.75 \text{ m}^2 \times 100 = 75 \text{ dm}^2$

(or)

$1 \text{ m} = 10 \text{ dm}$

$0.75 \text{ m} = 7.5 \text{ dm}$

$A = 10 \times 7.5 = 75 \text{ dm}^2$

Figure 22.2
Area of a triangle

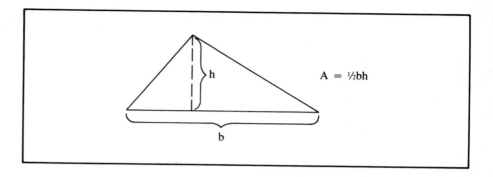

Compare this system to the English method, in which to change from square inches to square feet we must divide by 144 (12 in × 12 in = 144 in). To convert square yards to square feet, we must multiply by 9 (3 ft × 3 ft = 9 sq ft). The calculations become even more extensive when changing cubic units to either a higher or lower order. To convert cubic yards to cubic feet, for instance, we must multiply by 27 (3 ft × 3 ft × 3 ft = 27 cu ft = 1 sq yd). Inversely, we change cubic feet to cubic yards by using 27 as a divisor.

The **area of a triangle** is equal to one half of the product of its base times its height. In Figure 22.2, *b* is the base and *h* is the height. Note, however, that any side of a triangle may be defined as the base. To determine the area of a triangle with a base of 6 inches and a height of 8-3/4 inches, we have

$$A = \frac{1}{2} bh$$

$$= 0.5 \times 6 \times 8.75$$

$$= 26.25 \text{ sq in}$$

Using metric, we determine the area of a triangle measuring 6.5 centimeters long and 5.25 centimeters high in the same manner.

$$A = \frac{1}{2} bh$$

$$= 0.5 \times 6.5 \times 5.25$$

$$= 17.06 \text{ cm}^2$$

The equation for finding the **area of a circle** is

Area of a circle: $A = \pi r^2$

To find the area of a circle with a diameter of 10 inches, we have

$r = d \div 2$

$\quad = 10 \div 2$

$\quad = 5$

$A = \pi r^2$

$\quad = 3.14 \times 5^2$

$\quad = 78.5 \text{ sq in}$

In metric, the area (in square meters) of a circle that has a radius of 8 decimeters is

$A = \pi r^2$

$\quad = 3.14 \times 8^2$

$\quad = 200.96 \; dm^2$

$200.96 \; dm^2 \times 0.01 = 2.01 \; m^2$

APPLICATION 1. A room measures 20 feet long and 18 feet wide. How much will it cost to carpet the area at a price of $17.95 per square yard?

$A = lw$

$\quad = 20 \times 18$

$\quad = 360 \text{ sq ft}$

Sq yd: $360 \div 9 = 40 \text{ sq yd}$
Cost: $40 \times 17.95 = \$718.00$

APPLICATION 2. A patio measures 1.25 dekameters long and 0.2 dekameters wide. If outdoor carpeting is priced at $6.95 per square meter, how much will it cost to carpet the patio?

$A = lw$

$\quad = 1.25 \times 0.2$

$\quad = 0.25 \; dam^2$

$0.25 \; dam^2 \times 100 = 25 \; m^2$

Cost: $25 \times 6.95 = \$173.75$

APPLICATION 3. Because a triangular section of a roof in Tucson, Arizona, receives the most sun, it alone needs to be reroofed. The section measures 68 ft 4 in at the edge and 26 ft 7 in from the edge to the peak. Stated in square feet, how much roofing material is needed?

68 ft 4 in = (68 × 12) + 4 = 820 in
26 ft 7 in = (26 × 12) + 7 = 319 in

$A = \dfrac{1}{2} bh$
$= 0.5 \times 820 \times 319$
$= 130{,}790$ sq in

Amount: 130,790 ÷ 144 = 908.26 sq ft

APPLICATION 4. A floor design for a large hotel lobby stipulates that 12 triangular-shaped pieces of marble, each measuring 6.25 decimeters at the base with a height of 4.3 decimeters, be incorporated into the pattern. Stated in square meters, how much marble is required?

$A = \dfrac{1}{2} bh$
$= 0.5 \times 6.25 \times 4.3$
$= 13.437$ dm^2

13.437 dm^2 × 0.01 = 0.134 m^2

Marble needed: 0.134 m^2 × 12 = 1.608 m^2

APPLICATION 5. A wool frieze rug sells for $28.95 a square yard. How much will it cost for a round rug measuring 5 feet across?

$r = d \div 2$
$= 5 \div 2$
$= 2.5$

$A = \pi r^2$
$= 3.14 \times (2.5)^2$
$= 19.625$ sq ft

19.625 ÷ 9 = 2.18 sq yd

Cost: 2.18 × 28.95 = $63.11

APPLICATION 6. How many square meters of extra heavy material are required to construct 12 round trampolines that each measures 45 decimeters across?

$$r = d \div 2$$
$$= 45 \div 2$$
$$= 22.5$$

$$A = \pi r^2$$
$$= (3.14)(22.5)^2$$
$$= 1,589.625 \text{ dm}^2$$

$$1,589.625 \text{ dm}^2 \times 0.01 = 15.9 \text{ m}^2$$

$$15.9 \text{ m}^2 \times 12 = 190.8 \text{ m}^2$$

Volume may be defined as the space occupied by a three-dimensional figure. Volume measurements pertain to such solid objects as blocks of wood, bars of soap, and cubes of water — objects that can be measured in terms of length, width, and height. Volume measurements also include the capacity of containers such as cartons, storage areas, and transport vehicles. Figure 22.3 illustrates four shapes that are frequently used in business.

The **volume of a cube or any type of rectangular prism** is the product of its length, width, and height, as expressed in the following equation.

Volume of a cube or rectangle: $V = lwh$

Figure 22.3
Diagrams of three-dimensional figures

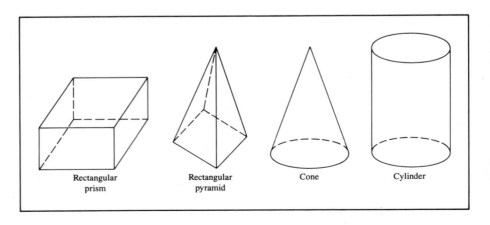

Rectangular prism   Rectangular pyramid   Cone   Cylinder

To find the volume of a brick measuring 7 inches long, 5 inches wide, and 3 inches high, for example, we have

$$V = lwh$$

$$= 7 \times 5 \times 3$$

$$= 105 \text{ cu in}$$

To determine the capacity of a square container measuring 5 decimeters, we have

$$V = lwh$$

$$= 5^3$$

$$= 125 \text{ dm}^3$$

The **volume of pyramids and cones** is found by (1) calculating the area of the base and (2) taking one third of the area times the height.

Volume of pyramids and cones: $V = \dfrac{1}{3} Bh$

where B is the area of the base and h is the height.

If the base is square or rectangular, you will recall that we determine its area by multiplying the length times the width. Replacing B (base) with ($l \times w$), therefore, gives us

$$V = \frac{1}{3} lwh$$

To illustrate, let's determine the volume of a rectangular pyramid measuring 8.2 decimeters by 5.34 decimeters at the base with a height of 10.75 decimeters.

$$V = \left(\frac{1}{3} \right)(lwh)$$

$$= \frac{1}{3}(8.2 \times 5.34 \times 10.75)$$

$$= 156.91 \text{ dm}^3$$

For a cone-shaped figure, we determine the area of the base with the familiar πr^2 (area of a circle), so that we may restate the volume equation as

$$V = \frac{1}{3}\pi r^2 h$$

To find the volume of a cone with a diameter of 3 inches and a height of 5-3/4 inches, we have

$$r = d \div 2$$

$$= 3 \div 2$$

$$= 1.5 \text{ in}$$

$$V = \frac{1}{3}\pi r^2 h$$

$$= \frac{1}{3}(3.14)(1.5)^2(5.75)$$

$$= 13.54 \text{ cu in}$$

The cylinder, along with the rectangular prism, is one of the most applicable shapes as containers and storage tanks. The equation for deriving **the volume of a cylinder** is similar to that of a cone.

Volume of a cylinder: $V = Bh$

where B is the area of the base and h is the height. As with the equation for a cone, the area of the base of a cylinder may be restated so that the equation reads

$$V = \pi r^2 h$$

To determine in cubic feet the capacity of a cylinder with a diameter of 10 inches and a height of 14 inches, we have

$$r = d \div 2$$

$$= 10 \div 2$$

$$= 5$$

$$V = \pi r^2 h$$

$$= (3.14)(5)^2(14)$$

$$= 1,099 \text{ cu in}$$

Number of cubic inches in one cubic foot: $12 \times 12 \times 12 = 1,728$

Number of cubic feet: $1,099 \div 1,728 = 0.64$

Working with cubic meters, instead, the capacity of a barrel measuring 50 centimeters wide and 120 centimeters high is

$$r = d \div 2$$

$$= 50 \div 2$$

$$= 25 \text{ cm}$$

$$V = \pi r^2 h$$

$$= (3.14)(25)^2(120)$$

$$= 235,500 \text{ cm}^3$$

Number of cubic centimeters in a cubic meter: $0.01 \times 0.01 \times 0.01 = 0.000001$

$$235,500 \text{ cm}^3 \times 0.000001 = 0.2355 \text{ m}^3$$

APPLICATION 1. How many boxes (each measuring 10 inches long, 6 inches wide, and 4 inches high) can be shipped in a crate that is 9 feet long, 4 feet wide, and 3 feet high?

One box: $V = lwh$
$$= 10 \times 6 \times 4$$
$$= 240 \text{ cu in}$$

One crate: $V = lwh$
$$= 9 \times 4 \times 3$$
$$= 108 \text{ cu ft}$$

Number of cu in in one cu ft: $12 \times 12 \times 12 = 1,728$
Capacity of crate in cu in: $108 \times 1,728 = 186,624$
Number of boxes shipped: $186,624 \div 240 = 777.6 = 777$

APPLICATION 2. A metal reinforced container measures 3.6 meters long, 2.8 meters wide, and 4 meters high. How many packages with dimensions of 8 by 6 by 5 decimeters each can be placed in the container?

Volume of container: $V = lwh$
$$= 3.6 \times 2.8 \times 4$$
$$= 40.32 \text{ m}^3$$

Volume of package: $V = lwh$
$$= 8 \times 6 \times 5$$
$$= 240 \text{ dm}^3$$

Number of cubic decimeters in a cubic meter: $10 \times 10 \times 10 = 1,000$
$40.32 \text{ m}^3 \times 1,000 = 40,320 \text{ dm}^3$
Number of packages: $40,320 \div 240 = 168$

APPLICATION 3. A cement railcar contains 4 cone-shaped containers, each measuring 8 feet across and 12 feet 4 inches high. In cubic yards determine the capacity of the cement railcar.

$r = d \div 2$
$ = 8 \div 2$
$ = 4$

Volume of a cone: $V = \dfrac{1}{3} \pi r^2 h$

$$= \frac{1}{3}(3.14)(4)^2(12.3)$$
$$= 205.984 \text{ cu ft}$$

Four cones: $205.984 \times 4 = 823.936$ cu ft
$823.936 \div 27 = 30.52$ cu yd

APPLICATION 4. Find the amount of cement in cubic meters that is required to form 5 rectangular pyramids, each measuring 4.25 dekameters long, 2.66 dekameters wide, and 10.5 dekameters high.

Volume of a rectangular pyramid:

$V = \dfrac{1}{3} lwh$

$$= \frac{1}{3} \times 4.25 \times 2.66 \times 10.5$$
$$= 39.57 \; dam^3$$

Five pyramids: $39.57 \times 5 = 197.85 \; dam^3$
$197.85 \; dam^3 \times 1,000 = 197,850 \text{ m}^3$

APPLICATION 5. If one cubic foot equals almost 7.5 U.S. gallons, what is the capacity of a water tank measuring 25 feet in diameter and 70 feet high?

$r = d \div 2$
$\quad = 25 \div 2$
$\quad = 12.5$ ft

Volume of a cylinder: $V = \pi r^2 h$
$\qquad\qquad\qquad = (3.14)(12.5)^2(70)$
$\qquad\qquad\qquad = 34{,}343.75$ cu ft

Gallons: $34{,}343.75$ cu ft $\times$ 7.5 gal/cu ft $= 257{,}578.125$

APPLICATION 6. The interior dimensions of a storage tank at a gasoline station are a 12-meter diameter and a 34-meter height. If one kiloliter equals one cubic meter, what is the capacity of the storage tank in kiloliters?

$r = d \div 2$
$\quad = 12 \div 2$
$\quad = 6$ m

Volume of a cylinder: $V = \pi r^2 h$
$\qquad\qquad\qquad = (3.14)(6)^2(34)$
$\qquad\qquad\qquad = 3{,}843.36$ m^3

$1\ m^3 = 1$ kl, so that
$3{,}843.36$ m$^3 = 3{,}843.36$ kl

Only the most commonly used planes and solids have been used to illustrate arithmetic problems pertaining to linear measurement. Similarly, only the most frequently used units for measuring capacity and weight are presented in the following section.

Capacity and Weight   In addition to linear measurement, which includes perimeter, area, and volume, we also have need to measure capacity and weight.

Capacity is the measurement of the contents of containers. English measures of capacity are categorized in Table 22.1 on page 454, as units for measuring capacity for liquid or dry ingredients. We differentiate the two by adding the word "fluid" for liquid capacity.

Dry capacity: pints, quarts, pecks, bushels

Liquid capacity: *fluid* ounces, pints, quarts, gallons

Liquid capacity pertains to such items as water, milk, juice, and toothpaste, whereas dry capacity measures such products as fruits, vegetables, and grains.

To determine the number of ounces in a can of tomato juice that contains 1.5 quarts, we have

$$1 \text{ pt} = 16 \text{ oz}$$

$$2 \text{ pt} = 32 \text{ oz} = 1 \text{ qt}$$

$$1.5 \text{ qt} \times 32 \text{ oz/qt} = 48 \text{ oz}$$

In contrast to the dual-category approach of the English method, the metric system relies on only one basic unit for measuring capacity — the liter. If the label on a bottle of grape juice shows 1,250 milliliters, we can determine the contents in terms of liters through simple division by 1,000 or multiplying by 0.001.

$$1,250 \text{ ml} \div 1,000 = 1.25 \ l$$

$$1,250 \times 0.001 = 1.25 \ l$$

Weight measurements under the English system utilize the pound as the basic unit. If a package shows 64 ounces on its label, for example, we may determine the weight in terms of pounds.

$$1 \text{ lb} = 16 \text{ oz}$$

$$64 \text{ oz} \div 16 \text{ oz/lb} = 4 \text{ lb}$$

As explained earlier, users of the metric system have embraced the kilogram (as opposed to the miniscule gram) as the basic unit for measuring weight. To determine the number of kilograms in a 538-gram can of coffee, for instance, we simply multiply by 0.001.

$$538 \text{ g} \times 0.001 = 0.538 \text{ kg}$$

APPLICATION 1. A two-gallon cleaning solution contains one pint of ammonia. If the price of ammonia is 75 cents per quart, how much will it cost to produce 100 gallons of the cleaning solution?

Ammonia: $100 \div 2 = 50$ pints
Number of quarts: $50 \div 2 = 25$
Cost: $25 \times 0.75 = \$18.75$

APPLICATION 2. A large bakery uses 12 dekaliters of milk to make a basic sweet dough of one hectoliter. If the wholesale price of milk is 35 cents per liter, how much is the cost of milk for 5 hectoliters of batter?

Milk: 12 dal × 5 = 60 *dal*
60 dal × 10 = 600 *l*
Cost: 600 × 0.35 = $210.00

APPLICATION 3. The price of a box of laundry soap weighing 9 pounds 13 ounces is $7.49; for a box weighing 6 pounds 4 ounces, the price is $5.79. What is the difference in price per ounce?

Large box: (9 × 16) + 13 = 157 oz
Price per ounce: 7.49 ÷ 157 = $0.048

Small box: (6 × 16) + 4 = 100 oz
Price per ounce: 5.79 ÷ 100 = $0.058

Difference: 0.058 − 0.048 = $0.01 per oz

APPLICATION 4. Each tablet of calcium supplement contains 600 milligrams of calcium. If a bottle of 150 tablets costs $9.50, what is the cost per gram?

One tablet: 600 mg × 0.001 = 0.6 g
150 tablets: 0.6 × 150 = 90 g
Price per gram: $9.50 ÷ 90 = 0.105 = $0.11

SELECTED CONVERSIONS

Even though the United States remains committed to the English system, business people involved in international trade must become sufficiently conversant with metric to be able to convert measurements from one system to the other. As international trade continues to expand, moreover, and as more imported products become available, the ability to compare products in terms of metric units becomes progressively more important to consumers.

Efficiency with metric operations requires considerable exposure to the system, but its use becomes much easier as people begin thinking in terms of meters, liters, and kilograms. The major difficulty arises when they must switch back and forth, using metric units in rote fashion while visualizing the English equivalents.

Linear, Capacity, and Weight Conversions

So long as U.S. citizens must cope with both systems, charts such as the one in Table 22.6 are very useful.

To determine the number of meters in 15 yards, for example, we multiply the number of yards by the metric equivalent.

1 yd = 0.9 m

15 yd = 15 × 0.9

= 13.5 m

Table 22.6
Conversion chart
(approximate
equivalents)

English to Metric	Metric to English
LINEAR MEASUREMENTS	LINEAR MEASUREMENTS
Length:	*Length:*
1 inch = 2.5 centimeters	1 centimeter = 0.4 inch
1 foot = 0.3 decimeter	1 meter = 39.37 inches
1 yard = 0.9 meter	1 meter = 1.1 yards
1 mile = 1.6 kilometers	1 kilometer = 0.6 mile
Area:	*Area:*
1 square inch = 6.5 square centimeters	1 square centimeter = 0.16 square inch
1 square foot = 0.09 square meter	1 square meter = 1.2 square yards
1 square yard = 0.8 square meter	1 square kilometer = 0.4 square mile
1 square mile = 2.6 square kilometers	
Volume:	*Volume:*
1 cubic inch = 16.4 cubic centimeters	1 cubic centimeter = 0.06 cubic inch
1 cubic foot = 0.03 cubic meter	1 cubic meter = 35 cubic feet
1 cubic yard = 0.76 cubic meter	1 cubic meter = 1.3 cubic yards
CAPACITY MEASUREMENTS (LIQUID)	CAPACITY MEASUREMENTS (LIQUID)
1 pint = 0.47 liter	1 liter = 2.1 pints
1 quart = 0.95 liter	1 liter = 1.06 quarts
1 gallon = 3.8 liters	1 liter = 0.26 gallon
WEIGHT MEASUREMENTS	WEIGHT MEASUREMENTS
1 ounce = 28 grams	1 gram = 0.035 ounce
1 pound = 0.45 kilogram	1 kilogram = 2.2 pounds
1 short ton = 0.9 tons	1 ton = 1.1 short tons

Inversely, to determine the number of quarts represented by 4 liters, we multiply the number of liters by the English equivalent.

$$1l = 1.06 \text{ qt}$$

$$4l = 4 \times 1.06$$

$$= 4.24 \text{ qt}$$

APPLICATION 1. How many liters are there in 3.5 gallons?

$$1 \text{ gal} = 3.8l$$
$$3.5 \text{ gal} = 3.5 \times 3.8$$
$$= 13.3l$$

APPLICATION 2. How many cubic yards are there in 2 cubic meters?

$$1 \text{ m}^3 = 1.3 \text{ cu yd}$$
$$2 \text{ m}^3 = 2 \times 1.3$$
$$= 2.6 \text{ cu yd}$$

APPLICATION 3. The distance between Los Angeles and Phoenix is 380 miles. How many kilometers are there in this distance?

$$1 \text{ mi} = 1.6 \text{ km}$$
$$\text{Distance} = 380 \times 1.6$$
$$= 608 \text{ km}$$

APPLICATION 4. The Soviet Union purchased from the United States 250,000 metric tons of wheat and 125,000 metric tons of corn. As expressed in short tons, what is the total quantity purchased?

$$250,000 \times 1.1 = \quad 275,000$$
$$125,000 \times 1.1 = \quad \underline{137,500}$$
$$\text{Total short tons} = \quad 412,500$$

Temperature Conversions

Although the Celsius system of temperature measurements is not part of the metric system, the adoption of it usually accompanies that of metric. The basic unit of temperature under the English system is the degree Fahrenheit (°F); under the newer system, it is the degree Celsius (°C). Both symbols are capitalized, you will notice, because the measurements were named after the persons who developed them.

Although both systems are based on the freezing and boiling points of water, the Fahrenheit system defines freezing at 32 degrees and boiling at 212 degrees. The Celsius system is based on a 100-degree range, with freezing at zero degrees and boiling at 100 degrees. The Celsius system, because of the 100-degree range, was formerly called centrigrade, and is still defined in terms of the decimal system but with subunits.

The difference between freezing and boiling points in the Celsius system is 100 degrees; in the Fahrenheit system it is 180 degrees. The ratio of the Celsius scale to the Fahrenheit scale, therefore, is 100 to 180, or 5 to 9, so that a Fahrenheit reading may be converted to Celsius by first subtracting 32 degrees from the Fahrenheit reading and then multiplying the difference by 5/9, resulting in the following equation.

Fahrenheit to Celsius: $°C = 5/9(°F - 32)$

To convert a reading of 68 degrees Fahrenheit to Celsius, we have

$°C = 5/9(°F - 32)$

$= 5/9(68 - 32)$

$= 20$

Conversion from Celsius to Fahrenheit is the inverse operation, the ratio becoming 180 to 100, or 9 to 5, making it necessary to multiply the Celsius reading by 9/5 and to then add 32 degrees.

Celsius to Fahrenheit: $°F = 9/5 °C + 32$

To determine the Fahrenheit reading that is equivalent to 12 degrees Celsius, for example, we have

$$°F = 9/5 °C + 32$$

$$= 9/5(12) + 32$$

$$= 21.6 + 32$$

$$= 53.6$$

APPLICATION 1. A comfortable indoor temperature is around 75° F. What would the temperature read on a Celsius scale?

$°C = 5/9(°F - 32)$
$= 5/9(75 - 32)$
$= 23.9$

APPLICATION 2. A recipe states that a roast should be baked at a temperature of about 165° C. At what Fahrenheit temperature should the oven be set?

$°F = 9/5 °C + 32$
$= 9/5(165) + 32$
$= 297 + 32$
$= 329$

EXERCISES (as assigned by your instructor)

22-1 How many yards long is a steel beam that measures 10 feet 8 inches from one end to the other?

22-2 A plank is 9.65 meters long. Express its length in

a. dekameters.
b. decimeters.

22-3 How many square inches are in 15 square feet?

22-4 How many cubic yards are in 360 cubic feet?

22-5 How many square meters are in 7.64 square dekameters?

22-6 Indicate the multiple of each given unit for

3.22 meters = ____ centimeters   6,000 grams = ____ kilograms

100 dekagrams = ____ grams   1 kiloliter = ____ liters

155 milliliters = ____ liters   0.75 kilometers = ____ meters

22-7 The piping (cordlike border) on a bedspread follows the dimensions of a mattress on three sides of a bed. No piping is sewn on one end where the headboard is located. If the mattress measures 84 inches long and 60 inches wide, how much piping is required to make 500 bedspreads? (Piping is always sold by the yard.)

22-8 If fencing materials cost $3.95 per meter, how much will it cost the owner of a ranch to enclose property measuring 5 kilometers on each of the four sides?

22-9 In decimeters, what is the perimeter of a triangular design measuring 55 by 48 by 32 centimeters?

22-10 Triangular pieces of stained glass are to be surrounded by silver metal strips. If the stained glass pieces each measure 9 by 7 by 5 inches and if there are 18 pieces, how much will it cost to enclose the pieces at a price of $4.50 per foot?

22-11 A circle measures 9.75 centimeters across. What is the circumference?

22-12 The top and bottom borders of a lampshade are to be trimmed in gold braid. The diameter measures 12 inches at the top and 16 inches at the bottom of the shade. Expressed in yards, how much trim is needed to produce 1,000 lamp shades?

22-13 How much will it cost to carpet a living room measuring 20 feet by 18 feet 6 inches and a dining room measuring 16 by 16 feet if the desired carpeting is priced at $19.95 per square yard?

22-14 New linoleum that costs $8.95 per square meter is to be laid in a recreation building with interior dimensions of 32.5 meters long and 25.8 meters wide. Excluding an area consumed by a counter measuring 6.5 meters long and 1 meter wide, what is the total cost of the linoleum?

22-15 A triangle measures 15 decimeters at the base, 12 decimeters on each of the other two sides, and 9 decimeters high. Determine the area of the triangle.

22-16 The preliminary sketch of a mural contains two large triangular sections to be painted blue. Each measures 3.25 meters at the base with a height of 4.5 meters. If a one-liter can of paint covers about 20 square meters, how much paint will be used to cover these two triangular sections?

22-17 Determine in square meters the area of half a circle that has a radius of 122 centimeters.

22-18 If a pound of fertilizer covers 25 square feet, how many pounds will be required to fertilize a semicircular patch that has a diameter at the base of 7 yards?

22-19 How many cubic centimeters are there in 5 cubic decimeters?

22-20 Piggyback containers to be transported on a ship each measure 10 meters long, 2 meters wide, and 5.5 meters high. If two such containers can be stacked on top of each other and if the available area in the ship measures 40 meters by 25 meters, how many containers may be loaded?

22-21 The interior dimensions of a refrigerator-freezer are 16.5 by 6.1 by 7.75 decimeters for the refrigerator section and 16.5 by 3.5 by 7.75 decimeters for the freezer compartment. What is the total capacity in cubic meters of this refrigerator-freezer combination?

22-22 In cubic centimeters, what is the volume of a cone that measures 48 millimeters across and 85 millimeters high?

22-23 A funnel-shaped device releases one drop of liquid at a time. The device measures 8 inches across the top and 14 inches deep. If 57.75 cubic inches contains one quart, how many quarts of liquid can the device hold?

22-24 The diameter of a cylindrical shaped gas can measures 14 inches across and 20 inches high. If one cubic foot holds almost 7.5 U.S. gallons, what is the capacity of the can?

22-25 What is the capacity in cubic meters of a washing machine if the drum measures 8 decimeters across and 20.2 decimeters high?

22-26 If a restaurant sells nearly 70 eight-ounce glasses of milk a day, about how many gallons will the manager need to order?

22-27 How many one-liter bottles of champagne should a caterer provide for a wedding party of 75 people if it is expected that the average guest will consume about 300 milliliters?

22-28 If a particular brand of dog food costs $500 per metric ton to produce, and if the final product is distributed in 5 kilogram packages priced at $5.95 each, what is the producer's profit per ton?

22-29 If a can of pineapple weighs 20 ounces, how much will it cost to ship 200 twelve-can cartons of pineapple at the rate of $2.65 per hundred weight? Add 4 ounces for each cardboard carton used.

22-30 The distance between New York and Chicago is 810 miles. What is the distance in kilometers?

22-31 An American tourist in Windsor, Ontario, Canada, filled his car with 55.8 liters of gasoline and 3.8 liters of oil. What is the equivalent amount of

a. Gasoline in U.S. gallons?
b. Oil in U.S. quarts?

22-32 If you noticed in the newspaper that the temperature in London, England, is 22 degrees Celsius, would most citizens there be wearing overcoats? Explain.

22-33 If, when flying over Kansas City, Missouri, you heard the pilot announce that the temperature there is 92 degrees Fahrenheit, what would be the equivalent reading on a Celsius scale?

A   Selected Tables

Table 8.1. The Number of Each Day of the Year

Day of month	Jan	Feb	Mar	Apr	May	June	July	Aug	Sept	Oct	Nov	Dec	Day of month
1	1	32	60	91	121	152	182	213	244	274	305	335	1
2	2	33	61	92	122	153	183	214	245	275	306	336	2
3	3	34	62	93	123	154	184	215	246	276	307	337	3
4	4	35	63	94	124	155	185	216	247	277	308	338	4
5	5	36	64	95	125	156	186	217	248	278	309	339	5
6	6	37	65	96	126	157	187	218	249	279	310	340	6
7	7	38	66	97	127	158	188	219	250	280	311	241	7
8	8	39	67	98	128	159	189	220	251	281	312	342	8
9	9	40	68	99	129	160	190	221	252	282	313	343	9
10	10	41	69	100	130	161	191	222	253	283	314	344	10
11	11	42	70	101	131	162	192	223	254	284	315	345	11
12	12	43	71	102	132	163	193	224	255	285	316	346	12
13	13	44	72	103	133	164	194	225	256	286	317	347	13
14	14	45	73	104	134	165	195	226	257	287	318	348	14
15	15	46	74	105	135	166	196	227	258	288	319	349	15
16	16	47	75	106	136	167	197	228	259	289	320	350	16
17	17	48	76	107	137	168	198	229	260	290	321	351	17
18	18	49	77	108	138	169	199	230	261	291	322	352	18
19	19	50	78	109	139	170	200	231	262	292	323	353	19
20	20	51	79	110	140	171	201	232	263	293	324	354	20
21	21	52	80	111	141	172	202	233	264	294	325	355	21
22	22	53	81	112	142	173	203	234	265	295	326	356	22
23	23	54	82	113	143	174	204	235	266	296	327	357	23
24	24	55	83	114	144	175	205	236	267	297	328	358	24
25	25	56	84	115	145	176	206	237	268	298	329	359	25
26	26	57	85	116	146	177	207	238	269	299	330	360	26
27	27	58	86	117	147	178	208	239	270	300	331	361	27
28	28	59	87	118	148	179	209	240	271	301	332	362	28
29	29	[1]	88	119	149	180	210	241	272	302	333	363	29
30	30	—	89	120	150	181	211	242	273	303	334	364	30
31	31	—	90	—	151	—	212	243	—	304	—	365	31

[1]In Leap (presidential election years in the United States), add one day if February 29 falls between the beginning and ending dates.

Table 9.1. Annual Percentage Rate: Finance Charge per $100 of Amount Financed

Number of Payments	10%	10¼%	10½%	10¾%	11%	11¼%	11½%	11¾%	12%	12¼%	12½%	12¾%	13%	13¼%
1	0.83	0.85	0.88	0.90	0.92	0.94	0.96	0.98	1.00	1.02	1.04	1.06	1.08	1.10
2	1.25	1.28	1.31	1.35	1.38	1.41	1.44	1.47	1.50	1.53	1.57	1.60	1.63	1.66
3	1.67	1.71	1.76	1.80	1.84	1.88	1.92	1.96	2.01	2.05	2.09	2.13	2.17	2.22
4	2.09	2.14	2.20	2.25	2.30	2.35	2.41	2.46	2.51	2.57	2.62	2.67	2.72	2.78
5	2.51	2.58	2.64	2.70	2.77	2.83	2.89	2.96	3.02	3.08	3.15	3.21	3.27	3.34
6	2.94	3.01	3.08	3.16	3.23	3.31	3.38	3.45	3.53	3.60	3.68	3.75	3.83	3.90
7	3.36	3.45	3.53	3.62	3.70	3.78	3.87	3.95	4.04	4.12	4.21	4.29	4.38	4.47
8	3.79	3.88	3.98	4.07	4.17	4.26	4.36	4.46	4.55	4.65	4.74	4.84	4.94	5.03
9	4.21	4.32	4.43	4.53	4.64	4.75	4.85	4.96	5.07	5.17	5.28	5.39	5.49	5.60
10	4.64	4.76	4.88	4.99	5.11	5.23	5.35	5.46	5.58	5.70	5.82	5.94	6.05	6.17
11	5.07	5.20	5.33	5.45	5.58	5.71	5.84	5.97	6.10	6.23	6.36	6.49	6.62	6.75
12	5.50	5.64	5.78	5.92	6.06	6.20	6.34	6.48	6.62	6.76	6.90	7.04	7.18	7.32
13	5.93	6.08	6.23	6.38	6.53	6.68	6.84	6.99	7.14	7.29	7.44	7.59	7.75	7.90
14	6.36	6.52	6.69	6.85	7.01	7.17	7.34	7.50	7.66	7.82	7.99	8.15	8.31	8.48
15	6.80	6.97	7.14	7.32	7.49	7.66	7.84	8.01	8.19	8.36	8.53	8.71	8.88	9.06
16	7.23	7.41	7.60	7.78	7.97	8.15	8.34	8.53	8.71	8.90	9.08	9.27	9.46	9.64
17	7.67	7.86	8.06	8.25	8.45	8.65	8.84	9.04	9.24	9.44	9.63	9.83	10.03	10.23
18	8.10	8.31	8.52	8.73	8.93	9.14	9.35	9.56	9.77	9.98	10.19	10.40	10.61	10.82
19	8.54	8.76	8.98	9.20	9.42	9.64	9.86	10.08	10.30	10.52	10.74	10.96	11.18	11.41
20	8.98	9.21	9.44	9.67	9.90	10.13	10.37	10.60	10.83	11.06	11.30	11.53	11.76	12.00
21	9.42	9.66	9.90	10.15	10.39	10.63	10.88	11.12	11.36	11.61	11.85	12.10	12.34	12.59
22	9.86	10.12	10.37	10.62	10.88	11.13	11.39	11.64	11.90	12.16	12.41	12.67	12.93	13.19
23	10.30	10.57	10.84	11.10	11.37	11.63	11.90	12.17	12.44	12.71	12.97	13.24	13.51	13.78
24	10.75	11.02	11.30	11.58	11.86	12.14	12.42	12.70	12.98	13.26	13.54	13.82	14.10	14.38
25	11.19	11.48	11.77	12.06	12.35	12.64	12.93	13.22	13.52	13.81	14.10	14.40	14.69	14.98
26	11.64	11.94	12.24	12.54	12.85	13.15	13.45	13.75	14.06	14.36	14.67	14.97	15.28	15.59
27	12.09	12.40	12.71	13.03	13.34	13.66	13.97	14.29	14.60	14.92	15.24	15.56	15.87	16.19
28	12.53	12.86	13.18	13.51	13.84	14.16	14.49	14.82	15.15	15.48	15.81	16.14	16.47	16.80
29	12.98	13.32	13.66	14.00	14.33	14.67	15.01	15.35	15.70	16.04	16.38	16.72	17.07	17.41
30	13.43	13.78	14.13	14.48	14.83	15.19	15.54	15.89	16.24	16.60	16.95	17.31	17.66	18.02
31	13.89	14.25	14.61	14.97	15.33	15.70	16.06	16.43	16.79	17.16	17.53	17.90	18.27	18.63
32	14.34	14.71	15.09	15.46	15.84	16.21	16.59	16.97	17.35	17.73	18.11	18.49	18.87	19.25
33	14.79	15.18	15.57	15.95	16.34	16.73	17.12	17.51	17.90	18.29	18.69	19.08	19.47	19.87
34	15.25	15.65	16.05	16.44	16.85	17.25	17.65	18.05	18.46	18.86	19.27	19.67	20.08	20.49
35	15.70	16.11	16.53	16.94	17.35	17.77	18.18	18.60	19.01	19.43	19.85	20.27	20.69	21.11
36	16.16	16.58	17.01	17.43	17.86	18.29	18.71	19.14	19.57	20.00	20.43	20.87	21.30	21.73
37	16.62	17.06	17.49	17.93	18.37	18.81	19.25	19.69	20.13	20.58	21.02	21.46	21.91	22.36
38	17.08	17.53	17.98	18.43	18.88	19.33	19.78	20.24	20.69	21.15	21.61	22.07	22.52	22.99
39	17.54	18.00	18.46	18.93	19.39	19.86	20.32	20.79	21.26	21.73	22.20	22.67	23.14	23.61
40	18.00	18.48	18.95	19.43	19.90	20.38	20.86	21.34	21.82	22.30	22.79	23.27	23.76	24.25
41	18.47	18.95	19.44	19.93	20.42	20.91	21.40	21.89	22.39	22.88	23.38	23.88	24.38	24.88
42	18.93	19.43	19.93	20.43	20.93	21.44	21.94	22.45	22.96	23.47	23.98	24.49	25.00	25.51
43	19.40	19.91	20.42	20.94	21.45	21.97	22.49	23.01	23.53	24.05	24.57	25.10	25.62	26.15
44	19.86	20.39	20.91	21.44	21.97	22.50	23.03	23.57	24.10	24.64	25.17	25.71	26.25	26.79
45	20.33	20.87	21.41	21.95	22.49	23.03	23.58	24.12	24.67	25.22	25.77	26.32	26.88	27.43
46	20.80	21.35	21.90	22.46	23.01	23.57	24.13	24.69	25.25	25.81	26.37	26.94	27.51	28.08
47	21.27	21.83	22.40	22.97	23.53	24.10	24.68	25.25	25.82	26.40	26.98	27.56	28.14	28.72
48	21.74	22.32	22.90	23.48	24.06	24.64	25.23	25.81	26.40	26.99	27.58	28.18	28.77	29.37
49	22.21	22.80	23.39	23.99	24.58	25.18	25.78	26.38	26.99	27.59	28.19	28.80	29.41	30.02
50	22.69	23.29	23.89	24.50	25.11	25.72	26.33	26.95	27.56	28.18	28.80	29.42	30.04	30.67
51	23.16	23.78	24.40	25.02	25.64	26.26	26.89	27.52	28.15	28.78	29.41	30.05	30.68	31.32
52	23.64	24.27	24.90	25.53	26.17	26.81	27.45	28.09	28.73	29.38	30.02	30.67	31.32	31.98
53	24.11	24.76	25.40	26.05	26.70	27.35	28.00	28.66	29.32	29.98	30.64	31.30	31.97	32.63
54	24.59	25.25	25.91	26.57	27.23	27.90	28.56	29.23	29.91	30.58	31.25	31.93	32.61	33.29
55	25.07	25.74	26.41	27.09	27.77	28.44	29.13	29.81	30.50	31.18	31.87	32.56	33.26	33.95
56	25.55	26.23	26.92	27.61	28.30	28.99	29.69	30.39	31.09	31.79	32.49	33.20	33.91	34.62
57	26.03	26.73	27.43	28.13	28.84	29.54	30.25	30.97	31.68	32.39	33.11	33.83	34.56	35.28
58	26.51	27.23	27.94	28.66	29.37	30.10	30.82	31.55	32.27	33.00	33.74	34.47	35.21	35.95
59	27.00	27.72	28.45	29.18	29.91	30.65	31.39	32.13	32.87	33.61	34.36	35.11	35.86	36.62
60	27.48	28.22	28.96	29.71	30.45	31.20	31.96	32.71	33.47	34.23	34.99	35.75	36.52	37.29

Table 9.1 (continued). Annual Percentage Rate: Finance Charge per $100 of Amount Financed

Number of Payments	$13^{1}/_{2}\%$	$13^{3}/_{4}\%$	14%	$14^{1}/_{4}\%$	$14^{1}/_{2}\%$	$14^{3}/_{4}\%$	15%	$15^{1}/_{4}\%$	$15^{1}/_{2}\%$	$15^{3}/_{4}\%$	16%	$16^{1}/_{4}\%$	$16^{1}/_{2}\%$	$16^{3}/_{4}\%$
1	1.13	1.15	1.17	1.19	1.21	1.23	1.25	1.27	1.29	1.31	1.33	1.35	1.38	1.40
2	1.69	1.72	1.75	1.78	1.82	1.85	1.88	1.91	1.94	1.97	2.00	2.04	2.07	2.10
3	2.26	2.30	2.34	2.38	2.43	2.47	2.51	2.55	2.59	2.64	2.68	2.72	2.76	2.80
4	2.83	2.88	2.93	2.99	3.04	3.09	3.14	3.20	3.25	3.30	3.36	3.41	3.46	3.51
5	3.40	3.46	3.53	3.59	3.65	3.72	3.78	3.84	3.91	3.97	4.04	4.10	4.16	4.23
6	3.97	4.05	4.12	4.20	4.27	4.35	4.42	4.49	4.57	4.64	4.72	4.79	4.87	4.94
7	4.55	4.64	4.72	4.81	4.89	4.98	5.06	5.15	5.23	5.32	5.40	5.49	5.58	5.66
8	5.13	5.22	5.32	5.42	5.51	5.61	5.71	5.80	5.90	6.00	6.09	6.19	6.29	6.38
9	5.71	5.82	5.92	6.03	6.14	6.25	6.35	6.46	6.57	6.68	6.78	6.89	7.00	7.11
10	6.29	6.41	6.53	6.65	6.77	6.88	7.00	7.12	7.24	·7.36	7.48	7.60	7.72	7.84
11	6.88	7.01	7.14	7.27	7.40	7.53	7.66	7.79	7.92	8.05	8.18	8.31	8.44	8.57
12	7.46	7.60	7.74	7.89	8.03	8.17	8.31	8.45	8.59	8.74	8.88	9.02	9.16	9.30
13	8.05	8.20	8.36	8.51	8.66	8.81	8.97	9.12	9.27	9.43	9.58	9.73	9.89	10.04
14	8.64	8.81	8.97	9.13	9.30	9.46	9.63	9.79	9.96	10.12	10.29	10.45	10.62	10.78
15	9.23	9.41	9.59	9.76	9.94	10.11	10.29	10.47	10.64	10.82	11.00	11.17	11.35	11.53
16	9.83	10.02	10.20	10.39	10.58	10.77	10.95	11.14	11.33	11.52	11.71	11.90	12.09	12.28
17	10.43	10.63	10.82	11.02	11.22	11.42	11.62	11.82	12.02	12.22	12.42	12.62	12.83	13.03
18	11.03	11.24	11.45	11.66	11.87	12.08	12.29	12.50	12.72	12.93	13.14	13.35	13.57	13.78
19	11.63	11.85	12.07	12.30	12.52	12.74	12.97	13.19	13.41	13.64	13.86	14.09	14.31	14.54
20	12.23	12.46	12.70	12.93	13.17	13.41	13.64	13.88	14.11	14.35	14.59	14.82	15.06	15.30
21	12.84	13.08	13.33	13.58	13.82	14.07	14.32	14.57	14.82	15.06	15.31	15.56	15.81	16.06
22	13.44	13.70	13.96	14.22	14.48	14.74	15.00	15.26	15.52	15.78	16.04	16.30	16.57	16.83
23	14.05	14.32	14.59	14.87	15.14	15.41	15.68	15.96	16.23	16.50	16.78	17.05	17.32	17.60
24	14.66	14.95	15.23	15.51	15.80	16.08	16.37	16.65	16.94	17.22	17.51	17.80	18.09	18.37
25	15.28	15.57	15.87	16.17	16.46	16.76	17.06	17.35	17.65	17.95	18.25	18.55	18.85	19.15
26	15.89	16.20	16.51	16.82	17.13	17.44	17.75	18.06	18.37	18.68	18.99	19.30	19.62	19.93
27	16.51	16.83	17.15	17.47	17.80	18.12	18.44	18.76	19.09	19.41	19.74	20.06	20.39	20.71
28	17.13	17.46	17.80	18.13	18.47	18.80	19.14	19.47	19.81	20.15	20.48	20.82	21.16	21.50
29	17.75	18.10	18.45	18.79	19.14	19.49	19.83	20.18	20.53	20.88	21.23	21.58	21.94	22.29
30	18.38	18.74	19.10	19.45	19.81	20.17	20.54	20.90	21.26	21.62	21.99	22.35	22.72	23.08
31	19.00	19.38	19.75	20.12	20.49	20.87	21.24	21.61	21.99	22.37	22.74	23.12	23.50	23.88
32	19.63	20.02	20.40	20.79	21.17	21.56	21.95	22.33	22.72	23.11	23.50	23.89	24.28	24.68
33	20.26	20.66	21.06	21.46	21.85	22.25	22.65	23.06	23.46	23.86	24.26	24.67	25.07	25.48
34	20.90	21.31	21.72	22.13	22.54	22.95	23.37	23.78	24.19	24.61	25.03	25.44	25.86	26.28
35	21.53	21.95	22.38	22.80	23.23	23.23	24.08	24.51	24.94	25.36	25.79	26.23	26.66	27.09
36	22.17	22.60	23.04	23.48	23.92	24.35	24.80	25.24	25.68	26.12	26.57	27.01	27.46	27.90
37	22.81	23.25	23.70	24.16	24.61	25.06	25.51	25.97	26.42	26.88	27.34	27.80	28.26	28.72
38	23.45	23.91	24.37	24.84	25.30	25.77	26.24	26.70	27.17	27.64	28.11	28.59	29.06	29.53
39	24.09	24.56	25.04	25.52	26.00	26.48	26.96	27.44	27.92	28.41	28.89	29.38	29.87	30.36
40	24.73	25.22	25.71	26.20	26.70	27.19	27.69	28.18	28.68	29.18	29.68	30.18	30.68	31.18
41	25.38	25.88	26.39	26.89	27.40	27.91	28.41	28.92	29.44	29.95	30.46	30.97	31.49	32.01
42	26.03	26.55	27.06	27.58	28.10	28.62	29.15	29.67	30.19	30.72	31.25	31.78	32.31	32.84
43	26.68	27.21	27.74	28.27	28.81	29.34	29.88	30.42	30.96	31.50	32.04	32.58	33.13	33.67
44	27.33	27.88	28.42	28.97	29.52	30.07	30.62	31.17	31.72	32.28	32.83	33.39	33.95	34.51
45	27.99	28.55	29.11	29.67	30.23	30.79	31.36	31.92	32.49	33.06	33.63	34.20	34.77	35.35
46	28.65	29.22	29.79	30.36	30.94	31.52	32.10	32.68	33.26	33.84	34.43	35.01	35.60	36.19
47	29.31	29.89	30.48	31.07	31.66	32.25	32.84	33.44	34.03	34.63	35.23	35.83	36.43	37.04
48	29.97	30.57	31.17	31.77	32.37	32.98	33.59	34.20	34.81	35.42	36.03	36.65	37.27	37.88
49	30.63	31.24	31.86	32.48	33.09	33.71	34.34	34.96	35.59	36.21	36.84	37.47	38.10	38.74
50	31.29	31.92	32.55	33.18	33.82	34.45	35.09	35.73	36.37	37.01	37.65	38.30	38.94	39.59
51	31.96	32.60	33.25	33.89	34.54	35.19	35.84	36.50	37.15	37.81	38.46	39.12	39.79	40.45
52	32.63	33.29	33.95	34.61	35.27	35.93	36.60	37.27	37.94	38.61	39.28	39.96	40.63	41.31
53	33.30	33.97	34.65	35.32	36.00	36.68	37.36	38.04	38.72	39.41	40.10	40.79	41.48	42.17
54	33.98	34.66	35.35	36.04	36.73	37.42	38.12	38.82	39.52	40.22	40.92	41.63	42.33	43.04
55	34.65	35.35	36.05	36.76	37.46	38.17	38.88	39.60	40.31	41.03	41.74	42.47	43.19	43.91
56	35.33	36.04	36.76	37.48	38.20	38.92	39.65	40.38	41.11	41.84	42.57	43.31	44.05	44.79
57	36.01	36.74	37.47	38.20	38.94	39.68	40.42	41.16	41.91	42.65	43.40	44.15	44.91	45.66
58	36.69	37.43	38.18	38.93	39.68	40.43	41.19	41.95	42.71	43.47	44.23	45.00	45.77	46.54
59	37.37	38.13	38.89	39.66	40.42	41.19	41.96	42.74	43.51	44.29	45.07	45.85	46.64	47.42
60	38.06	38.83	39.61	40.39	41.17	41.95	42.74	43.53	44.32	45.11	45.91	46.71	47.51	48.31

Table 9.1 (continued). Annual Percentage Rate: Finance Charge per $100 of Amount Financed

Number of Payments	17%	17¼%	17½%	17¾%	18%	18¼%	18½%	18¾%	19%	19¼%	19½%	19¾%	20%	20¼%
1	1.42	1.44	1.46	1.48	1.50	1.52	1.54	1.56	1.58	1.60	1.63	1.65	1.67	1.69
2	2.13	2.16	2.19	2.22	2.26	2.29	2.32	2.35	2.38	2.41	2.44	2.48	2.51	2.54
3	2.85	2.89	2.93	2.97	3.01	3.06	3.10	3.14	3.18	3.23	3.27	3.31	3.35	3.39
4	3.57	3.62	3.67	3.73	3.78	3.83	3.88	3.94	3.99	4.04	4.10	4.15	4.20	4.25
5	4.29	4.35	4.42	4.48	4.54	4.61	4.67	4.74	4.80	4.86	4.93	4.99	5.06	5.12
6	5.02	5.09	5.17	5.24	5.32	5.39	5.46	5.54	5.61	5.69	5.76	5.84	5.91	5.99
7	5.75	5.83	5.92	6.00	6.09	6.18	6.26	6.35	6.43	6.52	6.60	6.69	6.78	6.86
8	6.48	6.58	6.67	6.77	6.87	6.96	7.06	7.16	7.26	7.35	7.45	7.55	7.64	7.74
9	7.22	7.32	7.43	7.54	7.65	7.76	7.87	7.97	8.08	8.19	8.30	8.41	8.52	8.63
10	7.96	8.08	8.19	8.31	8.43	8.55	8.67	8.79	8.91	9.03	9.15	9.27	9.39	9.51
11	8.70	8.83	8.96	9.09	9.22	9.35	9.49	9.62	9.75	9.88	10.01	10.14	10.28	10.41
12	9.45	9.59	9.73	9.87	10.02	10.16	10.30	10.44	10.59	10.73	10.87	11.02	11.16	11.31
13	10.20	10.35	10.50	10.66	10.81	10.97	11.12	11.28	11.43	11.59	11.74	11.90	12.05	12.21
14	10.95	11.11	11.28	11.45	11.61	11.78	11.95	12.11	12.28	12.45	12.61	12.78	12.95	13.11
15	11.71	11.88	12.06	12.24	12.42	12.59	12.77	12.95	13.13	13.31	13.49	13.67	13.85	14.03
16	12.46	12.65	12.84	13.03	13.22	13.41	13.60	13.80	13.99	14.18	14.37	14.56	14.75	14.94
17	13.23	13.43	13.63	13.83	14.04	14.24	14.44	14.64	14.85	15.05	15.25	15.46	15.66	15.86
18	13.99	14.21	14.42	14.64	14.85	15.07	15.28	15.49	15.71	15.93	16.14	16.36	16.57	16.79
19	14.76	14.99	15.22	15.44	15.67	15.90	16.12	16.35	16.58	16.81	17.03	17.26	17.49	17.72
20	15.54	15.78	16.01	16.25	16.49	16.73	16.97	17.21	17.45	17.69	17.93	18.17	18.41	18.66
21	16.31	16.56	16.81	17.07	17.32	17.57	17.82	18.07	18.33	18.58	18.83	19.09	19.34	19.60
22	17.09	17.36	17.62	17.88	18.15	18.41	18.68	18.94	19.21	19.47	19.74	20.01	20.27	20.54
23	17.88	18.15	18.43	18.70	18.98	19.26	19.54	19.81	20.09	20.37	20.65	20.93	21.21	21.49
24	18.66	18.95	19.24	19.53	19.82	20.11	20.40	20.69	20.98	21.27	21.56	21.86	22.15	22.44
25	19.45	19.75	20.05	20.36	20.66	20.96	21.27	21.57	21.87	22.18	22.48	22.79	23.10	23.40
26	20.24	20.56	20.87	21.19	21.50	21.82	22.14	22.45	22.77	23.09	23.41	23.73	24.04	24.36
27	21.04	21.37	21.69	22.02	22.35	22.68	23.01	23.34	23.67	24.00	24.33	24.67	25.00	25.33
28	21.84	22.18	22.52	22.86	23.20	23.55	23.89	24.23	24.58	24.92	25.27	25.61	25.96	26.30
29	22.64	22.99	23.35	23.70	24.06	24.41	24.77	25.13	25.49	25.84	26.20	26.56	26.92	27.28
30	23.45	23.81	24.18	24.55	24.92	25.29	25.66	26.03	26.40	26.77	27.14	27.52	27.89	28.26
31	24.26	24.64	25.02	25.40	25.78	26.16	26.55	26.93	27.32	27.70	28.09	28.47	28.86	29.25
32	25.07	25.46	25.86	26.25	26.65	27.04	27.44	27.84	28.24	28.64	29.04	29.44	29.84	30.24
33	25.88	26.29	26.70	27.11	27.52	27.93	28.34	28.75	29.16	29.57	29.99	30.40	30.82	31.23
34	26.70	27.12	27.54	27.97	28.39	28.81	29.24	29.66	30.09	30.52	30.95	31.37	31.80	32.23
35	27.52	27.96	28.39	28.83	29.27	29.71	30.14	30.58	31.02	31.47	31.91	32.35	32.79	33.24
36	28.35	28.80	29.25	29.70	30.15	30.60	31.05	31.51	31.96	32.42	32.87	33.33	33.79	34.25
37	29.18	29.64	30.10	30.57	31.03	31.50	31.97	32.43	32.90	33.37	33.84	34.32	34.79	35.26
38	30.0ı	30.49	30.96	31.44	31.92	32.40	32.88	33.37	33.85	34.33	34.82	35.30	35.79	36.28
39	30.85	31.34	31.83	32.32	32.81	33.31	33.80	34.30	34.80	35.30	35.80	36.30	36.80	37.30
40	31.68	32.19	32.69	33.20	33.71	34.22	34.73	35.24	35.75	36.26	36.78	37.29	37.81	38.33
41	32.52	33.04	33.56	34.08	34.61	35.13	35.66	36.18	36.71	37.24	37.77	38.30	38.83	39.36
42	33.37	33.90	34.44	34.97	35.51	36.05	36.59	37.13	37.67	38.21	38.76	39.30	39.85	40.40
43	34.22	34.76	35.31	35.86	36.42	36.97	37.52	38.08	38.63	39.19	39.75	40.31	40.87	41.44
44	35.07	35.63	36.19	36.76	37.33	37.89	38.46	39.03	39.60	40.18	40.75	41.33	41.90	42.48
45	35.92	36.50	37.08	37.66	38.24	38.82	39.41	39.99	40.58	41.17	41.75	42.35	42.94	43.53
46	36.78	37.37	37.96	38.56	39.16	39.75	40.35	40.95	41.55	42.16	42.76	43.37	43.98	44.58
47	37.64	38.25	38.86	39.46	40.08	40.69	41.30	41.92	42.54	43.15	43.77	44.40	45.02	45.64
48	38.50	39.13	39.75	40.37	41.00	41.63	42.26	42.89	43.52	44.15	44.79	45.43	46.07	46.71
49	39.37	40.01	40.65	41.29	41.93	42.57	43.22	43.86	44.51	45.16	45.81	46.46	47.12	47.77
50	40.24	40.89	41.55	42.20	42.86	43.52	44.18	44.84	45.50	46.17	46.83	47.50	48.17	48.84
51	41.11	41.78	42.45	43.12	43.79	44.47	45.14	45.82	46.50	47.18	47.86	48.55	49.23	49.92
52	41.99	42.67	43.36	44.04	44.73	45.42	46.11	46.80	47.50	48.20	48.89	49.59	50.30	51.00
53	42.87	43.57	44.27	44.97	45.67	46.38	47.08	47.79	48.50	49.22	49.93	50.65	51.37	52.09
54	43.75	44.47	45.18	45.90	46.62	47.34	48.06	48.79	49.51	50.24	50.97	51.70	52.44	53.17
55	44.64	45.37	46.10	46.83	47.57	48.30	49.04	49.78	50.52	51.27	52.02	52.76	53.52	54.27
56	45.53	46.27	47.02	47.77	48.52	49.27	50.03	50.78	51.54	52.30	53.06	53.83	54.60	55.37
57	46.42	47.18	47.94	48.71	49.47	50.24	51.01	51.79	52.56	53.34	54.12	54.90	55.68	56.47
58	47.32	48.09	48.87	49.65	50.43	51.22	52.00	52.79	53.58	54.38	55.17	55.97	56.77	57.57
59	48.21	49.01	49.80	50.60	51.39	52.20	53.00	53.80	54.61	55.42	56.23	57.05	57.87	58.68
60	49.12	49.92	50.73	51.55	52.36	53.18	54.00	54.82	55.64	56.47	57.30	58.13	58.96	59.80

Table 9.1 (continued). Annual Percentage Rate: Finance Charge per $100 of Amount Financed

Number of Payments	20½%	20¾%	21%	21¼%	21½%	21¾%	22%	22¼%	22½%	22¾%	23%	23¼%	23½%	23¾%
1	1.71	1.73	1.75	1.77	1.79	1.81	1.83	1.85	1.88	1.90	1.92	1.94	1.96	1.98
2	2.57	2.60	2.63	2.66	2.70	2.73	2.76	2.79	2.82	2.85	2.88	2.92	2.95	2.98
3	3.44	3.48	3.52	3.56	3.60	3.65	3.69	3.73	3.77	3.82	3.86	3.90	3.94	3.98
4	4.31	4.36	4.41	4.47	4.52	4.57	4.62	4.68	4.73	4.78	4.84	4.89	4.94	5.00
5	5.18	5.25	5.31	5.37	5.44	5.50	5.57	5.63	5.69	5.76	5.82	5.89	5.95	6.02
6	6.06	6.14	6.21	6.29	6.36	6.44	6.51	6.59	6.66	6.74	6.81	6.89	6.96	7.04
7	6.95	7.04	7.12	7.21	7.29	7.38	7.47	7.55	7.64	7.73	7.81	7.90	7.99	8.07
8	7.84	7.94	8.03	8.13	8.23	8.33	8.42	8.52	8.62	8.72	8.82	8.91	9.01	9.11
9	8.73	8.84	8.95	9.06	9.17	9.28	9.39	9.50	9.61	9.72	9.83	9.94	10.04	10.15
10	9.63	9.75	9.88	10.00	10.12	10.24	10.36	10.48	10.60	10.72	10.84	10.96	11.08	11.21
11	10.54	10.67	10.80	10.94	11.07	11.20	11.33	11.47	11.60	11.73	11.86	12.00	12.13	12.26
12	11.45	11.59	11.74	11.88	12.02	12.17	12.31	12.46	12.60	12.75	12.89	13.04	13.18	13.33
13	12.36	12.52	12.67	12.83	12.99	13.14	13.30	13.46	13.61	13.77	13.93	14.08	14.24	14.40
14	13.28	13.45	13.62	13.79	13.95	14.12	14.29	14.46	14.63	14.80	14.97	15.13	15.30	15.47
15	14.21	14.39	14.57	14.75	14.93	15.11	15.29	15.47	15.65	15.83	16.01	16.19	16.37	16.56
16	15.14	15.33	15.52	15.71	15.90	16.10	16.29	16.48	16.68	16.87	17.06	17.26	17.45	17.65
17	16.07	16.27	16.48	16.68	16.89	17.09	17.30	17.50	17.71	17.92	18.12	18.33	18.53	18.74
18	17.01	17.22	17.44	17.66	17.88	18.09	18.31	18.53	18.75	18.97	19.19	19.41	19.62	19.84
19	17.95	18.18	18.41	18.64	18.87	19.10	19.33	19.56	19.79	20.02	20.26	20.49	20.72	20.95
20	18.90	19.14	19.38	19.63	19.87	20.11	20.36	20.60	20.84	21.09	21.33	21.58	21.82	22.07
21	19.85	20.11	20.36	20.62	20.87	21.13	21.38	21.64	21.90	22.16	22.41	22.67	22.93	23.19
22	20.81	21.08	21.34	21.61	21.88	22.15	22.42	22.69	22.96	23.23	23.50	23.77	24.04	24.32
23	21.77	22.05	22.33	22.61	22.90	23.18	23.46	23.74	24.03	24.31	24.60	24.88	25.17	25.45
24	22.74	23.03	23.33	23.62	23.92	24.21	24.51	24.80	25.10	25.40	25.70	25.99	26.29	26.59
25	23.71	24.02	24.32	24.63	24.94	25.25	25.56	25.87	26.18	26.49	26.80	27.11	27.43	27.74
26	24.68	25.01	25.33	25.65	25.97	26.29	26.62	26.94	27.26	27.59	27.91	28.24	28.56	28.89
27	25.67	26.00	26.34	26.67	27.01	27.34	27.68	28.02	28.35	28.69	29.03	29.37	29.71	30.05
28	26.65	27.00	27.35	27.70	28.05	28.40	28.75	29.10	29.45	29.80	30.15	30.51	30.86	31.22
29	27.64	28.00	28.37	28.73	29.09	29.46	29.82	30.19	30.55	30.92	31.28	31.65	32.02	32.39
30	28.64	29.01	29.39	29.77	30.14	30.52	30.90	31.28	31.66	32.04	32.42	32.80	33.18	33.57
31	29.64	30.03	30.42	30.81	31.20	31.59	31.98	32.38	32.77	33.17	33.56	33.96	34.35	34.75
32	30.64	31.05	31.45	31.85	32.26	32.67	33.07	33.48	33.89	34.30	34.71	35.12	35.53	35.94
33	31.65	32.07	32.49	32.91	33.33	33.75	34.17	34.59	35.01	35.44	35.86	36.29	36.71	37.14
34	32.67	33.10	33.53	33.96	34.40	34.83	35.27	35.71	36.14	36.58	37.02	37.46	37.90	38.34
35	33.68	34.13	34.58	35.03	35.47	35.92	36.37	36.83	37.28	37.73	38.18	38.64	39.09	39.55
36	34.71	35.17	35.63	36.09	36.56	37.02	37.49	37.95	38.42	38.89	39.35	39.82	40.29	40.77
37	35.74	36.21	36.69	37.16	37.64	38.12	38.60	39.08	39.56	40.05	40.53	41.02	41.50	41.99
38	36.77	37.26	37.75	38.24	38.73	39.23	39.72	40.22	40.72	41.21	41.71	42.21	42.71	43.22
39	37.81	38.31	38.82	39.32	39.83	40.34	40.85	41.36	41.87	42.39	42.90	43.42	43.93	44.45
40	38.85	39.37	39.89	40.41	40.93	41.46	41.98	42.51	43.04	43.56	44.09	44.62	45.16	45.69
41	39.89	40.43	40.96	41.50	42.04	42.58	43.12	43.66	44.20	44.75	45.29	45.84	46.39	46.94
42	40.95	41.50	42.05	42.60	43.15	43.71	44.26	44.82	45.38	45.94	46.50	47.06	47.62	48.19
43	42.00	42.57	43.13	43.70	44.27	44.84	45.41	45.98	46.56	47.13	47.71	48.29	48.87	49.45
44	43.06	43.64	44.22	44.81	45.39	45.98	46.56	47.15	47.74	48.33	48.93	49.52	50.11	50.71
45	44.13	44.72	45.32	45.92	46.52	47.12	47.72	48.33	48.93	49.54	50.15	50.76	51.37	51.98
46	45.20	45.81	46.42	47.03	47.65	48.27	48.89	49.51	50.13	50.75	51.38	52.00	52.63	53.26
47	46.27	46.90	47.53	48.16	48.79	49.42	50.06	50.69	51.33	51.97	52.61	53.25	53.89	54.54
48	47.35	47.99	48.64	49.28	49.93	50.58	51.23	51.88	52.54	53.19	53.85	54.51	55.16	55.83
49	48.43	49.09	49.75	50.41	51.08	51.74	52.41	53.08	53.75	54.42	55.09	55.77	56.44	57.12
50	49.52	50.19	50.87	51.55	52.23	52.91	53.59	54.28	54.96	55.65	56.34	57.03	57.73	58.42
51	50.61	51.30	51.99	52.69	53.38	54.08	54.78	55.48	56.19	56.89	57.60	58.30	59.01	59.73
52	51.71	52.41	53.12	53.83	54.55	55.26	55.98	56.69	57.41	58.13	58.86	59.58	60.31	61.04
53	52.81	53.53	54.26	54.98	55.71	56.44	57.18	57.91	58.65	59.38	60.12	60.87	61.61	62.35
54	53.91	54.65	55.39	56.14	56.88	57.63	58.38	59.13	59.88	60.64	61.40	62.16	62.92	63.68
55	55.02	55.78	56.54	57.30	58.06	58.82	59.59	60.36	61.13	61.90	62.67	63.45	64.23	65.01
56	56.14	56.91	57.68	58.46	59.24	60.02	60.80	61.59	62.38	63.17	63.96	64.75	65.54	66.34
57	57.26	58.04	58.84	59.63	60.43	61.22	62.02	62.83	63.63	64.44	65.25	66.06	66.87	67.68
58	58.38	59.18	59.99	60.80	61.62	62.43	63.25	64.07	64.89	65.71	66.54	67.37	68.20	69.03
59	59.51	60.33	61.15	61.98	62.81	63.64	64.48	65.32	66.15	67.00	67.84	68.68	69.53	70.38
60	60.64	61.48	62.32	63.17	64.01	64.86	65.71	66.57	67.42	68.28	69.14	70.01	70.87	71.74

Table 9.1 (continued). Annual Percentage Rate: Finance Charge per $100 of Amount Financed

Number of Payments	24%	24¹/₄%	24¹/₂%	24³/₄%	25%	25¹/₄%	25¹/₂%	25³/₄%	26%	26¹/₄%	26¹/₂%	26³/₄%	27%	27¹/₄%
1	2.00	2.02	2.04	2.06	2.08	2.10	2.12	2.15	2.17	2.19	2.21	2.23	2.25	2.27
2	3.01	3.04	3.07	3.10	3.14	3.17	3.20	3.23	3.26	3.29	3.32	3.36	3.39	3.42
3	4.03	4.07	4.11	4.15	4.20	4.24	4.28	4.32	4.36	4.41	4.45	4.49	4.53	4.58
4	5.05	5.10	5.16	5.21	5.26	5.32	5.37	5.42	5.47	5.53	5.58	5.63	5.69	5.74
5	6.08	6.14	6.21	6.27	6.34	6.40	6.46	6.53	6.59	6.66	6.72	6.79	6.85	6.91
6	7.12	7.19	7.27	7.34	7.42	7.49	7.57	7.64	7.72	7.79	7.87	7.95	8.02	8.10
7	8.16	8.25	8.33	8.42	8.51	8.59	8.68	8.77	8.85	8.94	9.03	9.11	9.20	9.29
8	9.21	9.31	9.40	9.50	9.60	9.70	9.80	9.90	9.99	10.09	10.19	10.29	10.39	10.49
9	10.26	10.37	10.48	10.59	10.70	10.81	10.92	11.03	11.14	11.25	11.36	11.47	11.58	11.69
10	11.33	11.45	11.57	11.69	11.81	11.93	12.06	12.18	12.30	12.42	12.54	12.67	12.79	12.91
11	12.40	12.53	12.66	12.80	12.93	13.06	13.20	13.33	13.46	13.60	13.73	13.87	14.00	14.13
12	13.47	13.62	13.76	13.91	14.05	14.20	14.34	14.49	14.64	14.78	14.93	15.07	15.22	15.37
13	14.55	14.71	14.87	15.03	15.18	15.34	15.50	15.66	15.82	15.97	16.13	16.29	16.45	16.61
14	15.64	15.81	15.98	16.16	16.32	16.49	16.66	16.83	17.00	17.17	17.35	17.52	17.69	17.86
15	16.74	16.92	17.10	17.28	17.47	17.65	17.83	18.02	18.20	18.38	18.57	18.75	18.93	19.12
16	17.84	18.03	18.23	18.42	18.62	18.81	19.01	19.21	19.40	19.60	19.79	19.99	20.19	20.38
17	18.95	19.16	19.36	19.57	19.78	19.99	20.20	20.40	20.61	20.82	21.03	21.24	21.45	21.66
18	20.06	20.28	20.50	20.72	20.95	21.17	21.39	21.61	21.83	22.05	22.27	22.50	22.72	22.94
19	21.19	21.42	21.65	21.89	22.12	22.35	22.59	22.82	23.06	23.29	23.53	23.76	24.00	24.23
20	22.31	22.56	22.81	23.05	23.30	23.55	23.79	24.04	24.29	24.54	24.79	25.04	25.28	25.53
21	23.45	23.71	23.97	24.23	24.49	24.75	25.01	25.27	25.53	25.79	26.05	26.32	26.58	26.84
22	24.59	24.86	25.13	25.41	25.68	25.96	26.23	26.50	26.78	27.05	27.33	27.61	27.88	28.16
23	25.74	26.02	26.31	26.60	26.88	27.17	27.46	27.75	28.04	28.32	28.61	28.90	29.19	29.48
24	26.89	27.19	27.49	27.79	28.09	28.39	28.69	29.00	29.30	29.60	29.90	30.21	30.51	30.82
25	28.05	28.36	28.68	28.99	29.31	29.62	29.94	30.25	30.57	30.89	31.20	31.52	31.84	32.16
26	29.22	29.55	29.87	30.20	30.53	30.86	31.19	31.52	31.85	32.18	32.51	32.84	33.18	33.51
27	30.39	30.73	31.07	31.42	31.76	32.10	32.45	32.79	33.14	33.48	33.83	34.17	34.52	34.87
28	31.57	31.93	32.28	32.64	33.00	33.35	33.71	34.07	34.43	34.79	35.15	35.51	35.87	36.23
29	32.76	33.13	33.50	33.87	34.24	34.61	34.98	35.36	35.73	36.10	36.48	36.85	37.23	37.61
30	33.95	34.33	34.72	35.10	35.49	35.88	36.26	36.65	37.04	37.43	37.82	38.21	38.60	38.99
31	35.15	35.55	35.95	36.35	36.75	37.15	37.55	37.95	38.36	38.76	39.16	39.57	39.97	40.38
32	36.35	36.77	37.18	37.60	38.01	38.43	38.84	39.26	39.68	40.10	40.52	40.94	41.36	41.78
33	37.57	37.99	38.42	38.85	39.28	39.71	40.14	40.58	41.01	41.44	41.88	42.31	42.75	43.19
34	38.78	39.23	39.67	40.11	40.56	41.01	41.45	41.90	42.35	42.80	43.25	43.70	44.15	44.60
35	40.01	40.47	40.92	41.38	41.84	42.31	42.77	43.23	43.69	44.16	44.62	45.09	45.56	46.02
36	41.24	41.71	42.19	42.66	43.14	43.61	44.09	44.57	45.05	45.53	46.01	46.49	46.97	47.45
37	42.48	42.96	43.45	43.94	44.43	44.93	45.42	45.91	46.41	46.90	47.40	47.90	48.39	48.89
38	43.72	44.22	44.73	45.23	45.74	46.25	46.75	47.26	47.77	48.29	48.80	49.31	49.82	50.34
39	44.97	45.49	46.01	46.53	47.05	47.57	48.10	48.62	49.15	49.68	50.20	50.73	51.26	51.79
40	46.22	46.76	47.29	47.83	48.37	48.91	49.45	49.99	50.53	51.07	51.62	52.16	52.71	53.26
41	47.48	48.04	48.59	49.14	49.69	50.25	50.80	51.36	51.92	52.48	53.04	53.60	54.16	54.73
42	48.75	49.32	49.89	50.46	51.03	51.60	52.17	52.74	53.32	53.89	54.47	55.05	55.63	56.21
43	50.03	50.61	51.19	51.78	52.36	52.95	53.54	54.13	54.72	55.31	55.90	56.50	57.09	57.69
44	51.31	51.91	52.51	53.11	53.71	54.31	54.92	55.52	56.13	56.74	57.35	57.96	58.57	59.19
45	52.59	53.21	53.82	54.44	55.06	55.68	56.30	56.92	57.55	58.17	58.80	59.43	60.06	60.69
46	53.89	54.52	55.15	55.78	56.42	57.05	57.69	58.33	58.97	59.61	60.26	60.90	61.55	62.20
47	55.18	55.83	56.48	57.13	57.78	58.44	59.09	59.75	60.40	61.06	61.72	62.39	63.05	63.71
48	56.49	57.15	57.82	58.49	59.15	59.82	60.50	61.17	61.84	62.52	63.20	63.87	64.56	65.24
49	57.80	58.48	59.16	59.85	60.53	61.22	61.91	62.60	63.29	63.98	64.68	65.37	66.07	66.77
50	59.12	59.81	60.51	61.21	61.92	62.62	63.33	64.03	64.74	65.45	66.16	66.88	67.59	68.31
51	60.44	61.15	61.87	62.59	63.31	64.03	64.75	65.48	66.20	66.93	67.66	68.39	69.12	69.86
52	61.77	62.50	63.23	63.97	64.70	65.44	66.18	66.92	67.67	68.41	69.16	69.91	70.66	71.41
53	63.10	63.85	64.60	65.35	66.11	66.86	67.62	68.38	69.14	69.90	70.67	71.43	72.20	72.97
54	64.44	65.21	65.98	66.75	67.52	68.29	69.07	69.84	70.62	71.40	72.18	72.97	73.75	74.54
55	65.79	66.57	67.36	68.14	68.93	69.72	70.52	71.31	72.11	72.91	73.71	74.51	75.31	76.12
56	67.14	67.94	68.74	69.55	70.36	71.16	71.97	72.79	73.60	74.42	75.24	76.06	76.88	77.70
57	68.50	69.32	70.14	70.96	71.78	72.61	73.44	74.27	75.10	75.94	76.77	77.61	78.45	79.29
58	69.86	70.70	71.54	72.38	73.22	74.06	74.91	75.76	76.61	77.46	78.32	79.17	80.03	80.89
59	71.23	72.09	72.94	73.80	74.66	75.52	76.39	77.25	78.12	78.99	79.87	80.74	81.62	82.50
60	72.61	73.48	74.35	75.23	76.11	76.99	77.87	78.76	79.64	80.53	81.42	82.32	83.21	84.11

Table 9.1 (continued). Annual Percentage Rate: Finance Charge per $100 of Amount Financed

Number of Payments	27½%	27¾%	28%	28¼%	28½%	28¾%	29%	29¼%	29½%	29¾%	30%	30¼%	30½%	30¾%
1	2.29	2.31	2.33	2.35	2.37	2.40	2.42	2.44	2.46	2.48	2.50	2.52	2.54	2.56
2	3.45	3.48	3.51	3.54	3.58	3.61	3.64	3.67	3.70	3.73	3.77	3.80	3.83	3.86
3	4.62	4.66	4.70	4.74	4.79	4.83	4.87	4.91	4.96	5.00	5.04	5.08	5.13	5.17
4	5.79	5.85	5.90	5.95	6.01	6.06	6.11	6.17	6.22	6.27	6.33	6.38	6.43	6.49
5	6.98	7.04	7.11	7.17	7.24	7.30	7.37	7.43	7.49	7.56	7.62	7.69	7.75	7.82
6	8.17	8.25	8.32	8.40	8.48	8.55	8.63	8.70	8.78	8.85	8.93	9.01	9.08	9.16
7	9.37	9.46	9.55	9.64	9.72	9.81	9.90	9.98	10.07	10.16	10.25	10.33	10.42	10.51
8	10.58	10.68	10.78	10.88	10.98	11.08	11.18	11.28	11.38	11.47	11.57	11.67	11.77	11.87
9	11.80	11.91	12.03	12.14	12.25	12.36	12.47	12.58	12.69	12.80	12.91	13.02	13.13	13.24
10	13.03	13.15	13.28	13.40	13.52	13.64	13.77	13.89	14.01	14.14	14.26	14.38	14.50	14.63
11	14.27	14.40	14.54	14.67	14.81	14.94	15.08	15.21	15.35	15.48	15.62	15.75	15.89	16.02
12	15.51	15.66	15.81	15.95	16.10	16.25	16.40	16.54	16.69	16.84	16.98	17.13	17.28	17.43
13	16.77	16.93	17.09	17.24	17.40	17.56	17.72	17.88	18.04	18.20	18.36	18.52	18.68	18.84
14	18.03	18.20	18.37	18.54	18.72	18.89	19.06	19.23	19.41	19.58	19.75	19.92	20.10	20.27
15	19.30	19.48	19.67	19.85	20.04	20.22	20.41	20.59	20.78	20.96	21.15	21.34	21.52	21.71
16	20.58	20.78	20.97	21.17	21.37	21.57	21.76	21.96	22.16	22.36	22.56	22.76	22.96	23.16
17	21.87	22.08	22.29	22.50	22.71	22.92	23.13	23.34	23.55	23.77	23.98	24.19	24.40	24.61
18	23.16	23.39	23.61	23.83	24.06	24.28	24.51	24.73	24.96	25.18	25.41	25.63	25.86	26.08
19	24.47	24.71	24.94	25.18	25.42	25.65	25.89	26.13	26.37	26.61	26.85	27.08	27.32	27.56
20	25.78	26.03	26.28	26.53	26.78	27.04	27.29	27.54	27.79	28.04	28.29	28.55	28.80	29.05
21	27.11	27.37	27.63	27.90	28.16	28.43	28.69	28.96	29.22	29.49	29.75	30.02	30.29	30.55
22	28.44	28.71	28.99	29.27	29.55	29.82	30.10	30.38	30.66	30.94	31.22	31.50	31.78	32.07
23	29.77	30.07	30.36	30.65	30.94	31.23	31.53	31.82	32.11	32.41	32.70	33.00	33.29	33.59
24	31.12	31.43	31.73	32.04	32.34	32.65	32.96	33.27	33.57	33.88	34.19	34.50	34.81	35.12
25	32.48	32.80	33.12	33.44	33.76	34.08	34.40	34.72	35.04	35.37	35.69	36.01	36.34	36.66
26	33.84	34.18	34.51	34.84	35.18	35.51	35.85	36.19	36.52	36.86	37.20	37.54	37.88	38.21
27	35.21	35.56	35.91	36.26	36.61	36.96	37.31	37.66	38.01	38.36	38.72	39.07	39.42	39.78
28	36.59	36.96	37.32	37.68	38.05	38.41	38.78	39.15	39.51	39.88	40.25	40.61	40.98	41.35
29	37.98	38.36	38.74	39.12	39.50	39.88	40.26	40.64	41.02	41.40	41.78	42.17	42.55	42.94
30	39.38	39.77	40.17	40.56	40.95	41.35	41.75	42.14	42.54	42.94	43.33	43.73	44.13	44.53
31	40.79	41.19	41.60	42.01	42.42	42.83	43.24	43.65	44.07	44.48	44.89	45.30	45.72	46.13
32	42.20	42.62	43.05	43.47	43.90	44.32	44.75	45.17	45.60	46.03	46.46	46.89	47.32	47.75
33	43.62	44.06	44.50	44.94	45.38	45.82	46.26	46.70	47.15	47.59	48.04	48.48	48.93	49.37
34	45.05	45.51	45.96	46.42	46.87	47.33	47.79	48.24	48.70	49.16	49.62	50.08	50.55	51.01
35	46.49	46.96	47.43	47.90	48.37	48.85	49.32	49.79	50.27	50.74	51.22	51.70	52.17	52.65
36	47.94	48.42	48.91	49.40	49.88	50.37	50.86	51.35	51.84	52.33	52.83	53.32	53.81	54.31
37	49.39	49.89	50.40	50.90	51.40	51.91	52.41	52.92	53.42	53.93	54.44	54.95	55.46	55.97
38	50.86	51.37	51.89	52.41	52.93	53.45	53.97	54.49	55.02	55.54	56.07	56.59	57.12	57.65
39	52.33	52.86	53.39	53.93	54.46	55.00	55.54	56.08	56.62	57.16	57.70	58.24	58.79	59.33
40	53.81	54.35	54.90	55.46	56.01	56.56	57.12	57.67	58.23	58.79	59.34	59.90	60.47	61.03
41	55.29	55.86	56.42	56.99	57.56	58.13	58.70	59.28	59.85	60.42	61.00	61.57	62.15	62.73
42	56.79	57.37	57.95	58.54	59.12	59.71	60.30	60.89	61.48	62.07	62.66	63.25	63.85	64.44
43	58.29	58.89	59.49	60.09	60.69	61.30	61.90	62.51	63.11	63.72	64.33	64.94	65.56	66.17
44	59.80	60.42	61.03	61.65	62.27	62.89	63.51	64.14	64.76	65.39	66.01	66.64	67.27	67.90
45	61.32	61.95	62.59	63.22	63.86	64.50	65.13	65.77	66.42	67.06	67.70	68.35	69.00	69.64
46	62.84	63.49	64.15	64.80	65.45	66.11	66.76	67.42	68.08	68.74	69.40	70.07	70.73	71.40
47	64.38	65.05	65.71	66.38	67.06	67.73	68.40	69.08	69.75	70.43	71.11	71.79	72.47	73.16
48	65.92	66.60	67.29	67.98	68.67	69.36	70.05	70.74	71.44	72.13	72.83	73.53	74.23	74.93
49	67.47	68.17	68.87	69.58	70.29	70.99	71.70	72.41	73.13	73.84	74.56	75.27	75.99	76.71
50	69.03	69.75	70.47	71.19	71.91	72.64	73.37	74.10	74.83	75.56	76.29	77.02	77.76	78.50
51	70.59	71.33	72.07	72.81	73.55	74.29	75.04	75.78	76.53	77.28	78.03	78.79	79.54	80.30
52	72.16	72.92	73.67	74.43	75.19	75.95	76.72	77.48	78.25	79.02	79.79	80.56	81.33	82.11
53	73.74	74.52	75.29	76.07	76.85	77.62	78.41	79.19	79.97	80.76	81.55	82.34	83.13	83.92
54	75.33	76.12	76.91	77.71	78.50	79.30	80.10	80.90	81.71	82.51	83.32	84.13	84.94	85.75
55	76.92	77.73	78.55	79.36	80.17	80.99	81.81	82.63	83.45	84.27	85.10	85.93	86.75	87.58
56	78.53	79.35	80.18	81.02	81.85	82.68	83.52	84.36	85.20	86.04	86.89	87.73	88.58	89.43
57	80.14	80.98	81.83	82.68	83.53	84.39	85.24	86.10	86.96	87.82	88.68	89.55	90.41	91.28
58	81.75	82.62	83.48	84.35	85.22	86.10	86.97	87.85	88.72	89.60	90.49	91.37	92.26	93.14
59	83.38	84.26	85.15	86.03	86.92	87.81	88.71	89.60	90.50	91.40	92.30	93.20	94.11	95.01
60	85.01	85.91	86.81	87.72	88.63	89.54	90.45	91.37	92.28	93.20	94.12	95.04	95.97	96.89

Table 9.1 (continued). Annual Percentage Rate: Finance Charge per $100 of Amount Financed

Number of Payments	31%	31¼%	31½%	31¾%	32%	32¼%	32½%	32¾%	33%	33¼%	33½%	33¾%	34%	34¼%
1	2.58	2.60	2.63	2.65	2.67	2.69	2.71	2.73	2.75	2.77	2.79	2.81	2.83	2.85
2	3.89	3.92	3.95	3.99	4.02	4.05	4.08	4.11	4.14	4.18	4.21	4.24	4.27	4.30
3	5.21	5.25	5.30	5.34	5.38	5.42	5.46	5.51	5.55	5.59	5.63	5.68	5.72	5.76
4	6.54	6.59	6.65	6.70	6.75	6.81	6.86	6.91	6.97	7.02	7.08	7.13	7.18	7.24
5	7.88	7.95	8.01	8.08	8.14	8.21	8.27	8.33	8.40	8.46	8.53	8.59	8.66	8.72
6	9.23	9.31	9.39	9.46	9.54	9.61	9.69	9.77	9.84	9.92	9.99	10.07	10.15	10.22
7	10.60	10.68	10.77	10.86	10.95	11.03	11.12	11.21	11.30	11.39	11.47	11.56	11.65	11.74
8	11.97	12.07	12.17	12.27	12.37	12.47	12.57	12.67	12.77	12.87	12.97	13.07	13.17	13.27
9	13.36	13.47	13.58	13.69	13.80	13.91	14.02	14.14	14.25	14.36	14.47	14.58	14.69	14.81
10	14.75	14.87	15.00	15.12	15.24	15.37	15.49	15.62	15.74	15.86	15.99	16.11	16.24	16.36
11	16.16	16.29	16.43	16.56	16.70	16.84	16.97	17.11	17.24	17.38	17.52	17.65	17.79	17.93
12	17.58	17.72	17.87	18.02	18.17	18.32	18.47	18.61	18.76	18.91	19.06	19.21	19.36	19.51
13	19.00	19.16	19.33	19.49	19.65	19.81	19.97	20.13	20.29	20.45	20.62	20.78	20.94	21.10
14	20.44	20.62	20.79	20.96	21.14	21.31	21.49	21.66	21.83	22.01	22.18	22.36	22.53	22.71
15	21.89	22.08	22.27	22.45	22.64	22.83	23.01	23.20	23.39	23.58	23.76	23.95	24.14	24.33
16	23.35	23.55	23.75	23.95	24.15	24.35	24.55	24.75	24.96	25.16	25.36	25.56	25.76	25.96
17	24.83	25.04	25.25	25.47	25.68	25.89	26.11	26.32	26.53	26.75	26.96	27.18	27.39	27.61
18	26.31	26.54	26.76	26.99	27.22	27.44	27.67	27.90	28.13	28.35	28.58	28.81	29.04	29.27
19	27.80	28.04	28.28	28.52	28.76	29.00	29.25	29.49	29.73	29.97	30.21	30.45	30.70	30.94
20	29.31	29.56	29.81	30.07	30.32	30.58	30.83	31.09	31.34	31.60	31.86	32.11	32.37	32.63
21	30.82	31.09	31.36	31.62	31.89	32.16	32.43	32.70	32.97	33.24	33.51	33.78	34.05	34.32
22	32.35	32.63	32.91	33.19	33.48	33.76	34.04	34.33	34.61	34.89	35.18	35.46	35.75	36.04
23	33.88	34.18	34.48	34.77	35.07	35.37	35.66	35.96	36.26	36.56	36.86	37.16	37.46	37.76
24	35.43	35.74	36.05	36.36	36.67	36.99	37.30	37.61	37.92	38.24	38.55	38.87	39.18	39.50
25	36.99	37.31	37.64	37.96	38.29	38.62	38.94	39.27	39.60	39.93	40.26	40.59	40.92	41.25
26	38.55	38.89	39.23	39.58	39.92	40.26	40.60	40.94	41.29	41.63	41.97	42.32	42.66	43.01
27	40.13	40.49	40.84	41.20	41.56	41.91	42.27	42.63	42.99	43.34	43.70	44.06	44.42	44.78
28	41.72	42.09	42.46	42.83	43.20	43.58	43.95	44.32	44.70	45.07	45.45	45.82	46.20	46.57
29	43.32	43.71	44.09	44.48	44.87	45.25	45.64	46.03	46.42	46.81	47.20	47.59	47.98	48.37
30	44.93	45.33	45.73	46.13	46.54	46.94	47.34	47.75	48.15	48.56	48.96	49.37	49.78	50.19
31	46.55	46.97	47.38	47.80	48.22	48.64	49.06	49.48	49.90	50.32	50.74	51.17	51.59	52.01
32	48.18	48.61	49.05	49.48	49.91	50.35	50.78	51.22	51.66	52.09	52.53	52.97	53.41	53.85
33	49.82	50.27	50.72	51.17	51.62	52.07	52.52	52.97	53.43	53.88	54.33	54.79	55.24	55.70
34	51.47	51.94	52.40	52.87	53.33	53.80	54.27	54.74	55.21	55.68	56.15	56.62	57.09	57.56
35	53.13	53.61	54.09	54.58	55.06	55.54	56.03	56.51	57.00	57.48	57.97	58.46	58.95	59.44
36	54.80	55.30	55.80	56.30	56.80	57.30	57.80	58.30	58.80	59.30	59.81	60.31	60.82	61.33
37	56.49	57.00	57.51	58.03	58.54	59.06	59.58	60.10	60.62	61.14	61.66	62.18	62.70	63.22
38	58.18	58.71	59.24	59.77	60.30	60.84	61.37	61.90	62.44	62.98	63.52	64.06	64.59	65.14
39	59.88	60.42	60.97	61.52	62.07	62.62	63.17	63.72	64.28	64.83	65.39	65.94	66.50	67.06
40	61.59	62.15	62.72	63.28	63.85	64.42	64.99	65.56	66.13	66.70	67.27	67.84	68.42	68.99
41	63.31	63.89	64.47	65.06	65.64	66.22	66.81	67.40	67.99	68.57	69.16	69.76	70.35	70.94
42	65.04	65.64	66.24	66.84	67.44	68.04	68.65	69.25	69.86	70.46	71.07	71.68	72.29	72.90
43	66.78	67.40	68.01	68.63	69.25	69.87	70.49	71.11	71.74	72.36	72.99	73.61	74.24	74.87
44	68.53	69.17	69.80	70.43	71.07	71.71	72.35	72.99	73.63	74.27	74.91	75.56	76.20	76.85
45	70.29	70.94	71.60	72.25	72.90	73.56	74.21	74.87	75.53	76.19	76.85	77.52	78.18	78.84
46	72.06	72.73	73.40	74.07	74.74	75.42	76.09	76.77	77.44	78.12	78.80	79.48	80.17	80.85
47	73.84	74.53	75.22	75.91	76.60	77.29	77.98	78.67	79.37	80.07	80.76	81.46	82.16	82.87
48	75.63	76.34	77.04	77.75	78.46	79.17	79.88	80.59	81.30	82.02	82.74	83.45	84.17	84.89
49	77.43	78.15	78.88	79.60	80.33	81.06	81.79	82.52	83.25	83.98	84.72	85.45	86.19	86.93
50	79.24	79.98	80.72	81.46	82.21	82.96	83.70	84.45	85.20	85.96	86.71	87.47	88.22	88.98
51	81.06	81.81	82.58	83.34	84.10	84.87	85.63	86.40	87.17	87.94	88.71	89.49	90.26	91.04
52	82.88	83.66	84.44	85.22	86.00	86.79	87.57	88.36	89.15	89.94	90.73	91.52	92.32	93.11
53	84.72	85.51	86.31	87.11	87.91	88.72	89.52	90.33	91.13	91.94	92.75	93.57	94.38	95.20
54	86.56	87.38	88.19	89.01	89.83	90.66	91.48	92.30	93.13	93.96	94.79	95.62	96.45	97.29
55	88.42	89.25	90.09	90.92	91.76	92.60	93.45	94.29	95.14	95.99	96.83	97.69	98.54	99.39
56	90.28	91.13	91.99	92.84	93.70	94.56	95.43	96.29	97.15	98.02	98.89	99.76	100.63	101.51
57	92.15	93.02	93.90	94.77	95.65	96.53	97.41	98.30	99.18	100.07	100.96	101.85	102.74	103.63
58	94.03	94.92	95.82	96.71	97.61	98.51	99.41	100.31	101.22	102.12	103.03	103.94	104.85	105.77
59	95.92	96.83	97.75	98.66	99.58	100.50	101.42	102.34	103.26	104.19	105.12	106.05	106.98	107.91
60	97.82	98.75	99.68	100.62	101.56	102.49	103.43	104.38	105.32	106.27	107.21	108.16	109.12	110.07

Table 9.1 (continued). Annual Percentage Rate: Finance Charge per $100 of Amount Financed

Number of Payments	34¹/₂%	34³/₄%	35%	35¹/₄%	35¹/₂%	35³/₄%	36%	36¹/₄%	36¹/₂%	36³/₄%	37%	37¹/₄%	37¹/₂%	37³/₄%
1	2.87	2.90	2.92	2.94	2.96	2.98	3.00	3.02	3.04	3.06	3.08	3.10	3.12	3.15
2	4.33	4.36	4.40	4.43	4.46	4.49	4.52	4.55	4.59	4.62	4.65	4.68	4.71	4.74
3	5.80	5.85	5.89	5.93	5.97	6.02	6.06	6.10	6.14	6.19	6.23	6.27	6.31	6.36
4	7.29	7.34	7.40	7.45	7.50	7.56	7.61	7.66	7.72	7.77	7.83	7.88	7.93	7.99
5	8.79	8.85	8.92	8.98	9.05	9.11	9.18	9.24	9.31	9.37	9.44	9.50	9.57	9.63
6	10.30	10.38	10.45	10.53	10.61	10.68	10.76	10.83	10.91	10.99	11.06	11.14	11.22	11.29
7	11.83	11.91	12.00	12.09	12.18	12.27	12.35	12.44	12.53	12.62	12.71	12.80	12.88	12.97
8	13.36	13.46	13.56	13.66	13.76	13.86	13.97	14.07	14.17	14.27	14.37	14.47	14.57	14.67
9	14.92	15.03	15.14	15.25	15.37	15.48	15.59	15.70	15.82	15.93	16.04	16.15	16.27	16.38
10	16.48	16.61	16.73	16.86	16.98	17.11	17.23	17.36	17.48	17.60	17.73	17.85	17.98	18.10
11	18.06	18.20	18.34	18.47	18.61	18.75	18.89	19.02	19.16	19.30	19.43	19.57	19.71	19.85
12	19.66	19.81	19.96	20.11	20.25	20.40	20.55	20.70	20.85	21.00	21.15	21.31	21.46	21.61
13	21.26	21.43	21.59	21.75	21.91	22.08	22.24	22.40	22.56	22.73	22.89	23.05	23.22	23.38
14	22.88	23.06	23.23	23.41	23.59	23.76	23.94	24.11	24.29	24.47	24.64	24.82	25.00	25.17
15	24.52	24.71	24.89	25.08	25.27	25.46	25.65	25.84	26.03	26.22	26.41	26.60	26.79	26.98
16	26.16	26.37	26.57	26.77	26.97	27.17	27.38	27.58	27.78	27.99	28.19	28.39	28.60	28.80
17	27.82	28.04	28.25	28.47	28.69	28.90	29.12	29.34	29.55	29.77	29.99	30.20	30.42	30.64
18	29.50	29.73	29.96	30.19	30.42	30.65	30.88	31.11	31.34	31.57	31.80	32.03	32.26	32.49
19	31.18	31.43	31.67	31.91	32.16	32.40	32.65	32.89	33.14	33.38	33.63	33.87	34.12	34.36
20	32.88	33.14	33.40	33.66	33.91	34.17	34.43	34.69	34.95	35.21	35.47	35.73	35.99	36.25
21	34.60	34.87	35.14	35.41	35.68	35.96	36.23	36.50	36.78	37.05	37.33	37.60	37.88	38.15
22	36.32	36.61	36.89	37.18	37.47	37.76	38.04	38.33	38.62	38.91	39.20	39.49	39.78	40.07
23	38.06	38.36	38.66	38.96	39.27	39.57	39.87	40.18	40.48	40.78	41.09	41.39	41.70	42.00
24	39.81	40.13	40.44	40.76	41.08	41.40	41.71	42.03	42.35	42.67	42.99	43.31	43.63	43.95
25	41.58	41.91	42.24	42.57	42.90	43.24	43.57	43.90	44.24	44.57	44.91	45.24	45.58	45.91
26	43.36	43.70	44.05	44.40	44.74	45.09	45.44	45.79	46.14	46.49	46.84	47.19	47.54	47.89
27	45.15	45.51	45.87	46.23	46.60	46.96	47.32	47.69	48.05	48.42	48.78	49.15	49.52	49.89
28	46.95	47.33	47.70	48.08	48.46	48.84	49.22	49.60	49.98	50.36	50.75	51.13	51.51	51.89
29	48.77	49.16	49.55	49.95	50.34	50.74	51.13	51.53	51.92	52.32	52.72	53.12	53.52	53.92
30	50.60	51.00	51.41	51.82	52.23	52.65	53.06	53.47	53.88	54.30	54.71	55.13	55.54	55.96
31	52.44	52.86	53.29	53.71	54.14	54.57	55.00	55.43	55.85	56.28	56.72	57.15	57.58	58.01
32	54.29	54.73	55.17	55.62	56.06	56.50	56.95	57.39	57.84	58.29	58.73	59.18	59.63	60.08
33	56.16	56.62	57.07	57.53	57.99	58.45	58.92	59.38	59.84	60.30	60.77	61.23	61.70	62.16
34	58.04	58.51	58.99	59.46	59.94	60.42	60.89	61.37	61.85	62.33	62.81	63.30	63.78	64.26
35	59.93	60.42	60.91	61.40	61.90	62.39	62.89	63.38	63.88	64.38	64.88	65.37	65.87	66.37
36	61.83	62.34	62.85	63.36	63.87	64.38	64.89	65.41	65.92	66.44	66.95	67.47	67.98	68.50
37	63.75	64.27	64.80	65.33	65.85	66.38	66.91	67.44	67.97	68.51	69.04	69.57	70.11	70.64
38	65.68	66.22	66.76	67.31	67.85	68.40	68.95	69.49	70.04	70.59	71.14	71.69	72.25	72.80
39	67.62	68.18	68.74	69.30	69.86	70.43	70.99	71.56	72.12	72.69	73.26	73.83	74.40	74.97
40	69.57	70.15	70.73	71.31	71.89	72.47	73.05	73.63	74.22	74.80	75.39	75.98	76.56	77.15
41	71.53	72.13	72.73	73.32	73.92	74.52	75.12	75.72	76.32	76.93	77.53	78.14	78.74	79.35
42	73.51	74.12	74.74	75.35	75.97	76.59	77.21	77.82	78.44	79.07	79.69	80.31	80.94	81.56
43	75.50	76.13	76.76	77.40	78.03	78.67	79.30	79.94	80.58	81.22	81.86	82.50	83.14	83.79
44	77.50	78.15	78.80	79.45	80.10	80.76	81.41	82.07	82.72	83.38	84.04	84.70	85.36	86.03
45	79.51	80.18	80.85	81.52	82.19	82.86	83.53	84.21	84.88	85.56	86.24	86.92	87.60	88.28
46	81.53	82.22	82.91	83.60	84.28	84.98	85.67	86.36	87.06	87.75	88.45	89.15	89.85	90.55
47	83.57	84.27	84.98	85.69	86.39	87.10	87.81	88.53	89.24	89.95	90.67	91.39	92.11	92.83
48	85.61	86.34	87.06	87.79	88.52	89.24	89.97	90.70	91.44	92.17	92.91	93.64	94.38	95.12
49	87.67	88.41	89.16	89.90	90.65	91.40	92.14	92.89	93.65	94.40	95.15	95.91	96.67	97.42
50	89.74	90.50	91.26	92.03	92.79	93.56	94.33	95.10	95.87	96.64	97.41	98.19	98.96	99.74
51	91.82	92.60	93.38	94.16	94.95	95.74	96.52	97.31	98.10	98.89	99.69	100.48	101.28	102.07
52	93.91	94.71	95.51	96.31	97.12	97.92	98.73	99.54	100.35	101.16	101.97	102.79	103.60	104.42
53	96.01	96.83	97.65	98.47	99.30	100.12	100.95	101.78	102.61	103.44	104.27	105.10	105.94	106.78
54	98.13	98.96	99.80	100.64	101.49	102.33	103.18	104.03	104.88	105.73	106.58	107.43	108.29	109.14
55	00.25	101.11	101.97	102.83	103.69	104.55	105.42	106.29	107.16	108.03	108.90	109.77	110.65	111.53
56	02.38	103.26	104.14	105.02	105.90	106.79	107.67	108.56	109.45	110.34	111.23	112.13	113.02	113.92
57	04.53	105.43	106.32	107.22	108.13	109.03	109.94	110.85	111.75	112.67	113.58	114.49	115.41	116.33
58	06.68	107.60	108.52	109.44	110.36	111.29	112.21	113.14	114.07	115.00	115.93	116.87	117.81	118.74
59	08.85	109.79	110.73	111.67	112.61	113.55	114.50	115.45	116.40	117.35	118.30	119.26	120.22	121.17
60	11.03	111.98	112.94	113.90	114.87	115.83	116.80	117.77	118.74	119.71	120.68	121.66	122.64	123.62

Table 9.1 (continued). Annual Percentage Rate: Finance Charge per $100 of Amount Financed

Number of Payments	38%	38¹/₄%	38¹/₂%	38³/₄%	39%	39¹/₄%	39¹/₂%	39³/₄%	40%	40¹/₄%	40¹/₂%	40³/₄%	41%	41¹/₄%	41¹/₂%	41³/₄%
1	3.17	3.19	3.21	3.23	3.25	3.27	3.29	3.31	3.33	3.35	3.37	3.40	3.42	3.44	3.46	3.48
2	4.77	4.81	4.84	4.87	4.90	4.93	4.96	5.00	5.03	5.06	5.09	5.12	5.15	5.19	5.22	5.25
3	6.40	6.44	6.48	6.53	6.57	6.61	6.65	6.70	6.74	6.78	6.82	6.87	6.91	6.95	7.00	7.04
4	8.04	8.09	8.15	8.20	8.25	8.31	8.36	8.42	8.47	8.52	8.58	8.63	8.69	8.74	8.79	8.85
5	9.70	9.76	9.83	9.89	9.96	10.02	10.09	10.15	10.22	10.28	10.35	10.41	10.48	10.54	10.61	10.68
6	11.37	11.45	11.52	11.60	11.68	11.75	11.83	11.91	11.99	12.06	12.14	12.22	12.29	12.37	12.45	12.52
7	13.06	13.15	13.24	13.33	13.42	13.50	13.59	13.68	13.77	13.86	13.95	14.04	14.13	14.21	14.30	14.39
8	14.77	14.87	14.97	15.07	15.17	15.27	15.37	15.47	15.57	15.67	15.77	15.88	15.98	16.08	16.18	16.28
9	16.49	16.60	16.72	16.83	16.94	17.05	17.17	17.28	17.39	17.51	17.62	17.73	17.85	17.96	18.07	18.19
10	18.23	18.35	18.48	18.61	18.73	18.86	18.98	19.11	19.23	19.36	19.48	19.61	19.74	19.86	19.99	20.12
11	19.99	20.12	20.26	20.40	20.54	20.68	20.81	20.95	21.09	21.23	21.37	21.51	21.65	21.78	21.92	22.06
12	21.76	21.91	22.06	22.21	22.36	22.51	22.66	22.81	22.97	23.12	23.27	23.42	23.57	23.72	23.88	24.03
13	23.54	23.71	23.87	24.04	24.20	24.37	24.53	24.69	24.86	25.02	25.19	25.35	25.52	25.68	25.85	26.01
14	25.35	25.53	25.70	25.88	26.06	26.24	26.41	26.59	26.77	26.95	27.13	27.30	27.48	27.66	27.84	28.02
15	27.17	27.36	27.55	27.74	27.93	28.12	28.32	28.51	28.70	28.89	29.08	29.27	29.47	29.66	29.85	30.04
16	29.01	29.21	29.41	29.62	29.82	30.03	30.23	30.44	30.65	30.85	31.06	31.26	31.47	31.68	31.88	32.09
17	30.86	31.08	31.29	31.51	31.73	31.95	32.17	32.39	32.61	32.83	33.05	33.27	33.49	33.71	33.93	34.15
18	32.73	32.96	33.19	33.42	33.66	33.89	34.12	34.36	34.59	34.83	35.06	35.29	35.53	35.76	36.00	36.23
19	34.61	34.86	35.10	35.35	35.60	35.85	36.09	36.34	36.59	36.84	37.09	37.34	37.59	37.84	38.09	38.34
20	36.51	36.77	37.03	37.30	37.56	37.82	38.08	38.35	38.61	38.87	39.14	39.40	39.66	39.93	40.19	40.46
21	38.43	38.70	38.98	39.26	39.53	39.81	40.09	40.36	40.64	40.92	41.20	41.48	41.76	42.04	42.32	42.60
22	40.36	40.65	40.94	41.23	41.52	41.82	42.11	42.40	42.69	42.99	43.28	43.58	43.87	44.16	44.46	44.75
23	42.31	42.61	42.92	43.23	43.53	43.84	44.15	44.46	44.76	45.07	45.38	45.69	46.00	46.31	46.62	46.93
24	44.27	44.59	44.91	45.23	45.56	45.88	46.20	46.53	46.85	47.17	47.50	47.82	48.15	48.48	48.80	49.13
25	46.25	46.59	46.92	47.26	47.60	47.94	48.28	48.61	48.95	49.29	49.63	49.98	50.32	50.66	51.00	51.34
26	48.24	48.60	48.95	49.30	49.66	50.01	50.36	50.72	51.07	51.43	51.79	52.14	52.50	52.86	53.22	53.58
27	50.25	50.62	50.99	51.36	51.73	52.10	52.47	52.84	53.21	53.58	53.96	54.33	54.70	55.08	55.45	55.83
28	52.28	52.66	53.05	53.43	53.82	54.20	54.59	54.98	55.37	55.76	56.14	56.53	56.92	57.31	57.70	58.10
29	54.32	54.72	55.12	55.52	55.92	56.33	56.73	57.13	57.54	57.94	58.35	58.75	59.16	59.57	59.97	60.38
30	56.37	56.79	57.21	57.63	58.05	58.46	58.88	59.30	59.73	60.15	60.57	60.99	61.42	61.84	62.26	62.69
31	58.44	58.88	59.31	59.75	60.18	60.62	61.05	61.49	61.93	62.37	62.81	63.25	63.69	64.13	64.57	65.01
32	60.53	60.98	61.43	61.88	62.34	62.79	63.24	63.70	64.15	64.61	65.06	65.52	65.98	66.43	66.89	67.35
33	62.63	63.10	63.57	64.03	64.50	64.97	65.44	65.92	66.39	66.86	67.33	67.81	68.28	68.76	69.23	69.71
34	64.75	65.23	65.72	66.20	66.69	67.18	67.66	68.15	68.64	69.13	69.62	70.11	70.61	71.10	71.59	72.09
35	66.88	67.38	67.88	68.38	68.89	69.39	69.90	70.40	70.91	71.42	71.93	72.44	72.95	73.46	73.97	74.48
36	69.02	69.54	70.06	70.58	71.10	71.62	72.15	72.67	73.20	73.72	74.25	74.78	75.30	75.83	76.36	76.89
37	71.18	71.72	72.25	72.79	73.33	73.87	74.41	74.96	75.50	76.04	76.59	77.13	77.68	78.22	78.77	79.32
38	73.35	73.91	74.46	75.02	75.58	76.14	76.69	77.25	77.81	78.38	78.94	79.50	80.07	80.63	81.20	81.76
39	75.54	76.11	76.69	77.26	77.84	78.41	78.99	79.57	80.15	80.73	81.31	81.89	82.47	83.06	83.64	84.23
40	77.74	78.33	78.93	79.52	80.11	80.71	81.30	81.90	82.50	83.09	83.69	84.29	84.90	85.50	86.10	86.70
41	79.96	80.57	81.18	81.79	82.40	83.01	83.63	84.24	84.86	85.48	86.09	86.71	87.33	87.95	88.58	89.20
42	82.19	82.82	83.45	84.07	84.71	85.34	85.97	86.60	87.24	87.87	88.51	89.15	89.79	90.43	91.07	91.71
43	84.43	85.08	85.73	86.37	87.02	87.67	88.33	88.98	89.63	90.29	90.94	91.60	92.26	92.92	93.58	94.24
44	86.69	87.36	88.02	88.69	89.36	90.03	90.70	91.37	92.04	92.72	93.39	94.07	94.74	95.42	96.10	96.78
45	88.96	89.65	90.33	91.02	91.70	92.39	93.08	93.77	94.47	95.16	95.85	96.55	97.24	97.94	98.64	99.34
46	91.25	91.95	92.65	93.36	94.07	94.77	95.48	96.19	96.90	97.62	98.33	99.04	99.76	100.48	101.20	101.91
47	93.55	94.27	94.99	95.72	96.44	97.17	97.90	98.63	99.36	100.09	100.82	101.56	102.29	103.03	103.77	104.50
48	95.86	96.60	97.34	98.09	98.83	99.58	100.33	101.07	101.82	102.58	103.33	104.08	104.84	105.59	106.35	107.11
49	98.18	98.94	99.71	100.47	101.23	102.00	102.77	103.54	104.31	105.08	105.85	106.62	107.40	108.18	108.95	109.73
50	100.52	101.30	102.08	102.87	103.65	104.44	105.22	106.01	106.80	107.59	108.39	109.18	109.98	110.77	111.57	112.37
51	102.87	103.67	104.47	105.28	106.08	106.89	107.69	108.50	109.31	110.12	110.94	111.75	112.57	113.38	114.20	115.02
52	105.24	106.06	106.88	107.70	108.53	109.35	110.18	111.01	111.84	112.67	113.50	114.33	115.17	116.01	116.85	117.69
53	107.61	108.45	109.29	110.14	110.98	111.83	112.68	113.52	114.37	115.23	116.08	116.93	117.79	118.65	119.51	120.37
54	110.00	110.86	111.72	112.59	113.45	114.32	115.19	116.05	116.93	117.80	118.67	119.55	120.42	121.30	122.18	123.06
55	112.40	113.28	114.17	115.05	115.94	116.82	117.71	118.60	119.49	120.38	121.28	122.17	123.07	123.97	124.87	125.77
56	114.82	115.72	116.62	117.53	118.43	119.34	120.25	121.16	122.07	122.98	123.90	124.81	125.73	126.65	127.57	128.49
57	117.25	118.17	119.09	120.01	120.94	121.87	122.80	123.73	124.66	125.59	126.53	127.47	128.40	129.34	130.29	131.23
58	119.68	120.63	121.57	122.51	123.46	124.41	125.36	126.31	127.26	128.22	129.17	130.13	131.09	132.05	133.02	133.98
59	122.13	123.10	124.06	125.03	125.99	126.96	127.93	128.91	129.88	130.86	131.83	132.81	133.79	134.78	135.76	136.75
60	124.60	125.58	126.56	127.55	128.54	129.53	130.52	131.51	132.51	133.51	134.51	135.51	136.51	137.51	138.52	139.52

Table 9.1 (continued). Annual Percentage Rate: Finance Charge per $100 of Amount Financed

Number of Payments	42%	42¼%	42½%	42¾%	43%	43¼%	43½%	43¾%	44%	44¼%	44½%	44¾%	45%	45¼%	45½%	45¾%
1	3.50	3.52	3.54	3.56	3.58	3.60	3.62	3.65	3.67	3.69	3.71	3.73	3.75	3.77	3.79	3.81
2	5.28	5.31	5.34	5.37	5.41	5.44	5.47	5.50	5.53	5.56	5.60	5.63	5.66	5.69	5.72	5.75
3	7.08	7.12	7.17	7.21	7.25	7.29	7.34	7.38	7.42	7.46	7.51	7.55	7.59	7.63	7.68	7.72
4	8.90	8.95	9.01	9.06	9.12	9.17	9.22	9.28	9.33	9.39	9.44	9.49	9.55	9.60	9.66	9.71
5	10.74	10.81	10.87	10.94	11.00	11.07	11.13	11.20	11.26	11.33	11.39	11.46	11.53	11.59	11.66	11.72
6	12.60	12.68	12.76	12.83	12.91	12.99	13.06	13.14	13.22	13.30	13.37	13.45	13.53	13.60	13.68	13.76
7	14.48	14.57	14.66	14.75	14.84	14.93	15.02	15.10	15.19	15.28	15.37	15.46	15.55	15.64	15.73	15.82
8	16.38	16.48	16.58	16.69	16.79	16.89	16.99	17.09	17.19	17.29	17.40	17.50	17.60	17.70	17.80	17.90
9	18.30	18.42	18.53	18.64	18.76	18.87	18.98	19.10	19.21	19.33	19.44	19.55	19.67	19.78	19.90	20.01
10	20.24	20.37	20.49	20.62	20.75	20.87	21.00	21.13	21.25	21.38	21.51	21.63	21.76	21.89	22.02	22.14
11	22.20	22.34	22.48	22.62	22.76	22.90	23.04	23.18	23.32	23.46	23.60	23.74	23.88	24.02	24.16	24.30
12	24.18	24.33	24.49	24.64	24.79	24.94	25.10	25.25	25.40	25.55	25.71	25.86	26.01	26.17	26.32	26.48
13	26.18	26.35	26.51	26.68	26.84	27.01	27.18	27.34	27.51	27.67	27.84	28.01	28.18	28.34	28.51	28.68
14	28.20	28.38	28.56	28.74	28.92	29.10	29.28	29.46	29.64	29.82	30.00	30.18	30.36	30.54	30.72	30.90
15	30.24	30.43	30.62	30.82	31.01	31.20	31.40	31.59	31.79	31.98	32.17	32.37	32.56	32.76	32.95	33.15
16	32.30	32.50	32.71	32.92	33.12	33.33	33.54	33.75	33.96	34.17	34.37	34.58	34.79	35.00	35.21	35.42
17	34.37	34.59	34.82	35.04	35.26	35.48	35.70	35.93	36.15	36.37	36.60	36.82	37.04	37.27	37.49	37.71
18	36.47	36.71	36.94	37.18	37.41	37.65	37.89	38.13	38.36	38.60	38.84	39.08	39.31	39.55	39.79	40.03
19	38.59	38.84	39.09	39.34	39.59	39.84	40.09	40.34	40.60	40.85	41.10	41.35	41.61	41.86	42.11	42.37
20	40.72	40.99	41.25	41.52	41.79	42.05	42.32	42.59	42.85	43.12	43.39	43.66	43.92	44.19	44.46	44.73
21	42.88	43.16	43.44	43.72	44.00	44.28	44.56	44.85	45.13	45.41	45.69	45.98	46.26	46.55	46.83	47.11
22	45.05	45.35	45.64	45.94	46.24	46.53	46.83	47.13	47.43	47.72	48.02	48.32	48.62	48.92	49.22	49.52
23	47.24	47.55	47.87	48.18	48.49	48.80	49.12	49.43	49.74	50.06	50.37	50.69	51.00	51.32	51.63	51.95
24	49.45	49.78	50.11	50.44	50.77	51.09	51.42	51.75	52.08	52.41	52.74	53.07	53.41	53.74	54.07	54.40
25	51.69	52.03	52.37	52.72	53.06	53.40	53.75	54.10	54.44	54.79	55.13	55.48	55.83	56.18	56.53	56.87
26	53.93	54.29	54.65	55.01	55.37	55.73	56.10	56.46	56.82	57.18	57.55	57.91	58.27	58.64	59.00	59.37
27	56.20	56.58	56.95	57.33	57.71	58.08	58.46	58.84	59.22	59.60	59.98	60.36	60.74	61.12	61.50	61.89
28	58.49	58.88	59.27	59.67	60.06	60.45	60.85	61.24	61.64	62.04	62.43	62.83	63.23	63.63	64.02	64.42
29	60.79	61.20	61.61	62.02	62.43	62.84	63.25	63.67	64.08	64.49	64.91	65.32	65.73	66.15	66.57	66.98
30	63.11	63.54	63.97	64.39	64.82	65.25	65.68	66.11	66.54	66.97	67.40	67.83	68.26	68.70	69.13	69.56
31	65.45	65.90	66.34	66.79	67.23	67.68	68.12	68.57	69.02	69.46	69.91	70.36	70.81	71.26	71.71	72.16
32	67.81	68.27	68.73	69.20	69.66	70.12	70.59	71.05	71.51	71.98	72.45	72.91	73.38	73.85	74.32	74.79
33	70.19	70.67	71.15	71.63	72.11	72.59	73.07	73.55	74.03	74.52	75.00	75.48	75.97	76.45	76.94	77.43
34	72.58	73.08	73.58	74.07	74.57	75.07	75.57	76.07	76.57	77.07	77.57	78.07	78.58	79.08	79.59	80.09
35	74.99	75.51	76.02	76.54	77.05	77.57	78.09	78.61	79.12	79.64	80.16	80.68	81.21	81.73	82.25	82.78
36	77.42	77.95	78.49	79.02	79.55	80.09	80.62	81.16	81.70	82.24	82.77	83.31	83.85	84.39	84.94	85.48
37	79.87	80.42	80.97	81.52	82.07	82.63	83.18	83.74	84.29	84.85	85.40	85.96	86.52	87.08	87.64	88.20
38	82.33	82.90	83.47	84.04	84.61	85.18	85.76	86.33	86.90	87.48	88.05	88.63	89.21	89.79	90.37	90.95
39	84.81	85.40	85.99	86.58	87.17	87.76	88.35	88.94	89.53	90.13	90.72	91.32	91.91	92.51	93.11	93.71
40	87.31	87.91	88.52	89.13	89.74	90.35	90.96	91.57	92.18	92.79	93.41	94.02	94.64	95.25	95.87	96.49
41	89.82	90.45	91.07	91.70	92.33	92.96	93.58	94.22	94.85	95.48	96.11	96.75	97.38	98.02	98.65	99.29
42	92.35	93.00	93.64	94.29	94.93	95.58	96.23	96.88	97.53	98.18	98.83	99.49	100.14	100.80	101.45	102.11
43	94.90	95.56	96.23	96.89	97.56	98.22	98.89	99.56	100.23	100.90	101.57	102.25	102.92	103.60	104.27	104.95
44	97.46	98.14	98.83	99.51	100.20	100.88	101.57	102.26	102.95	103.64	104.33	105.03	105.72	106.41	107.11	107.81
45	100.04	100.74	101.45	102.15	102.85	103.56	104.27	104.98	105.69	106.40	107.11	107.82	108.53	109.25	109.96	110.68
46	102.63	103.36	104.08	104.80	105.53	106.25	106.98	107.71	108.44	109.17	109.90	110.63	111.37	112.10	112.84	113.58
47	105.25	105.99	106.73	107.47	108.22	108.96	109.71	110.46	111.21	111.96	112.71	113.46	114.22	114.97	115.73	116.49
48	107.87	108.63	109.39	110.16	110.92	111.69	112.46	113.23	113.99	114.77	115.54	116.31	117.09	117.86	118.64	119.42
49	110.51	111.29	112.08	112.86	113.64	114.43	115.22	116.01	116.80	117.59	118.38	119.17	119.97	120.77	121.56	122.36
50	113.17	113.97	114.77	115.58	116.38	117.19	118.00	118.81	119.62	120.43	121.24	122.06	122.87	123.69	124.51	125.32
51	115.84	116.66	117.48	118.31	119.14	119.96	120.79	121.62	122.45	123.28	124.12	124.95	125.79	126.63	127.46	128.30
52	118.53	119.37	120.21	121.06	121.90	122.75	123.60	124.45	125.30	126.16	127.01	127.87	128.72	129.58	130.44	131.30
53	121.23	122.09	122.95	123.82	124.69	125.56	126.43	127.30	128.17	129.04	129.92	130.80	131.67	132.55	133.43	134.32
54	123.94	124.83	125.71	126.60	127.49	128.38	129.27	130.16	131.05	131.95	132.84	133.74	134.64	135.54	136.44	137.35
55	126.67	127.58	128.48	129.39	130.30	131.21	132.12	133.03	133.95	134.87	135.78	136.70	137.62	138.54	139.47	140.39
56	129.42	130.34	131.27	132.20	133.13	134.06	134.99	135.93	136.86	137.80	138.74	139.68	140.62	141.56	142.51	143.45
57	132.17	133.12	134.07	135.02	135.97	136.92	137.88	138.83	139.79	140.75	141.71	142.67	143.63	144.60	145.56	146.53
58	134.95	135.91	136.88	137.85	138.83	139.80	140.78	141.75	142.73	143.71	144.69	145.68	146.66	147.65	148.63	149.62
59	137.73	138.72	139.71	140.70	141.70	142.69	143.69	144.69	145.69	146.69	147.69	148.70	149.70	150.71	151.72	152.73
60	140.53	141.54	142.55	143.57	144.58	145.60	146.62	147.64	148.66	149.68	150.71	151.73	152.76	153.79	154.82	155.85

Tables 10 Through 12. Compound Interest

1/4%	Table 10.1. Compound amount	Table 10.2. Present value	Table 11.1. Amount of annuity	Table 11.2. Present value of annuity	Table 12.1. Sinking fund	Table 12.2. Amortization	1/4%
n							n
1	1.00250000	0.99750623	1.00000000	0.99750623	1.00000000	1.00250000	1
2	1.00500625	0.99501869	2.00250000	1.99252492	0.49937578	0.50187578	2
3	1.00751877	0.99253734	3.00750625	2.98506227	0.33250139	0.33500139	3
4	1.01003756	0.99006219	4.01502502	3.97512446	0.24906445	0.25156445	4
5	1.01256266	0.98759321	5.02506258	4.96271766	0.19900250	0.20150250	5
6	1.01509406	0.98513038	6.03762523	5.94784804	0.16562803	0.16812803	6
7	1.01763180	0.98267370	7.05271930	6.93052174	0.14178928	0.14428928	7
8	1.02017588	0.98022314	8.07035110	7.91074487	0.12391035	0.12641035	8
9	1.02272632	0.97777869	9.09052697	8.88852357	0.11000462	0.11250462	9
10	1.02528313	0.97534034	10.11325329	9.86386391	0.09888015	0.10138015	10
11	1.02784634	0.97290807	11.13853642	10.83677198	0.08977840	0.09227840	11
12	1.03041596	0.97048187	12.16638277	11.80725384	0.08219370	0.08469370	12
13	1.03299200	0.96806171	13.19679872	12.77531555	0.07577595	0.07827595	13
14	1.03557448	0.96564759	14.22979072	13.74096314	0.07027510	0.07277510	14
15	1.03816341	0.96323949	15.26536520	14.70420264	0.06550777	0.06800777	15
16	1.04075882	0.96083740	16.30352861	15.66504004	0.06133642	0.06383642	16
17	1.04336072	0.95844130	17.34428743	16.62348133	0.05765587	0.06015587	17
18	1.04596912	0.95605117	18.38764815	17.57953250	0.05438433	0.05688433	18
19	1.04858404	0.95366700	19.43361727	18.53319950	0.05145722	0.05395722	19
20	1.05120550	0.95128878	20.48220131	19.48448828	0.04882288	0.05132288	20
21	1.05383352	0.94891649	21.53340682	20.43340477	0.04643947	0.04893947	21
22	1.05646810	0.94655011	22.58724033	21.37995488	0.04427278	0.04677278	22
23	1.05910927	0.94418964	23.64370843	22.32414452	0.04229455	0.04479455	23
24	1.06175704	0.94183505	24.70281770	23.26597957	0.04048121	0.04298121	24
25	1.06441144	0.93948634	25.76457475	24.20546591	0.03881298	0.04131298	25
26	1.06707247	0.93714348	26.82898619	25.14260939	0.03727312	0.03977312	26
27	1.06974015	0.93480646	27.89605865	26.07741585	0.03584736	0.03834736	27
28	1.07241450	0.93247527	28.96579880	27.00989112	0.03452347	0.03702347	28
29	1.07509553	0.93014990	30.03821330	27.94004102	0.03329093	0.03579093	29
30	1.07778327	0.92783032	31.11330883	28.86787134	0.03214059	0.03464059	30
31	1.08047773	0.92551653	32.19109210	29.79338787	0.03106449	0.03356449	31
32	1.08317892	0.92320851	33.27156983	30.71659638	0.03005569	0.03255569	32
33	1.08588687	0.92090624	34.35474876	31.63750262	0.02910806	0.03160806	33
34	1.08860159	0.91860972	35.44063563	32.55611234	0.02821620	0.03071620	34
35	1.09132309	0.91631892	36.52923722	33.47243126	0.02737533	0.02987533	35
36	1.09405140	0.91403384	37.62056031	34.38646510	0.02658121	0.02908121	36
37	1.09678653	0.91175445	38.71461171	35.29821955	0.02583004	0.02833004	37
38	1.09952850	0.90948075	39.81139824	36.20770030	0.02511843	0.02761843	38
39	1.10227732	0.90721272	40.91092673	37.11491302	0.02444335	0.02694335	39
40	1.10503301	0.90495034	42.01320405	38.01986336	0.02380204	0.02630204	40
41	1.10779559	0.90269361	43.11823706	38.92255697	0.02319204	0.02569204	41
42	1.11056508	0.90044250	44.22603265	39.82299947	0.02261112	0.02511112	42
43	1.11334149	0.89819701	45.33659774	40.72119648	0.02205724	0.02455724	43
44	1.11612485	0.89595712	46.44993923	41.61715359	0.02152855	0.02402855	44
45	1.11891516	0.89372281	47.56606408	42.51087640	0.02102339	0.02352339	45
46	1.12171245	0.89149407	48.68497924	43.40237047	0.02054022	0.02304022	46
47	1.12451673	0.88927090	49.80669169	44.29164137	0.02007762	0.02257762	47
48	1.12732802	0.88705326	50.93120842	45.17869463	0.01963433	0.02213433	48
49	1.13014634	0.88484116	52.05853644	46.06353580	0.01920915	0.02170915	49
50	1.13297171	0.88263457	53.18868278	46.94617037	0.01880099	0.02130099	50

Tables 10 Through 12 (continued). Compound Interest

$1/2\%$ n	Table 10.1. Compound amount	Table 10.2. Present value	Table 11.1. Amount of annuity	Table 11.2. Present value of annuity	Table 12.1. Sinking fund	Table 12.2. Amortization	$1/2\%$ n
1	1.00500000	0.99502488	1.00000000	0.99502488	1.00000000	1.00500000	1
2	1.01002500	0.99007450	2.00500000	1.98509938	0.49875312	0.50375312	2
3	1.01507513	0.98514876	3.01502500	2.97024814	0.33167221	0.33667221	3
4	1.02015050	0.98024752	4.03010013	3.95049566	0.24813279	0.25313279	4
5	1.02525125	0.97537067	5.05025063	4.92586633	0.19800997	0.20300997	5
6	1.03037751	0.97051808	6.07550188	5.89638441	0.16459546	0.16959546	6
7	1.03552940	0.96568963	7.10587939	6.86207404	0.14072854	0.14572854	7
8	1.04070704	0.96088520	8.14140879	7.82295924	0.12282886	0.12782886	8
9	1.04591058	0.95610468	9.18211583	8.77906392	0.10890736	0.11390736	9
10	1.05114013	0.95134794	10.22802641	9.73041186	0.09777057	0.10277057	10
11	1.05639583	0.94661487	11.27916654	10.67702673	0.08865903	0.09365903	11
12	1.06167781	0.94190534	12.33556237	11.61893207	0.08106643	0.08606643	12
13	1.06698620	0.93721924	13.39724018	12.55615131	0.07464224	0.07964224	13
14	1.07232113	0.93255646	14.46422639	13.48870777	0.06913609	0.07413609	14
15	1.07768274	0.92791688	15.53654752	14.41662465	0.06436436	0.06936436	15
16	1.08307115	0.92330037	16.61423026	15.33992502	0.06018937	0.06518937	16
17	1.08848651	0.91870684	17.69730141	16.25863186	0.05650579	0.06150579	17
18	1.09392894	0.91413616	18.78578791	17.17276802	0.05323173	0.05823173	18
19	1.09939858	0.90958822	19.87971685	18.08235624	0.05030253	0.05530253	19
20	1.10489558	0.90506290	20.97911544	18.98741915	0.04766645	0.05266645	20
21	1.11042006	0.90056010	22.08401101	19.88797925	0.04528163	0.05028163	21
22	1.11597216	0.89607971	23.19443107	20.78405896	0.04311380	0.04811380	22
23	1.12155202	0.89162160	24.31040322	21.67568055	0.04113465	0.04613465	23
24	1.12715978	0.88718567	25.43195524	22.56286622	0.03932061	0.04432061	24
25	1.13279558	0.88277181	26.55911502	23.44563803	0.03765186	0.04265186	25
26	1.13845955	0.87837991	27.69191059	24.32401794	0.03611163	0.04111163	26
27	1.14415185	0.87400986	28.83037015	25.19802780	0.03468565	0.03968565	27
28	1.14987261	0.86966155	29.97452200	26.06768936	0.03336167	0.03836167	28
29	1.15562197	0.86533488	31.12439461	26.93302423	0.03212914	0.03712914	29
30	1.16140008	0.86102973	32.28001658	27.79405397	0.03097892	0.03597892	30
31	1.16720708	0.85674600	33.44141666	28.65079997	0.02990304	0.03490304	31
32	1.17304312	0.85248358	34.60862375	29.50328355	0.02889453	0.03389453	32
33	1.17890833	0.84824237	35.78166686	30.35152592	0.02794727	0.03294727	33
34	1.18480288	0.84402226	36.96057520	31.19554818	0.02705586	0.03205586	34
35	1.19072689	0.83982314	38.14537807	32.03537132	0.02621550	0.03121550	35
36	1.19668052	0.83564492	39.33610496	32.87101624	0.02542194	0.03042194	36
37	1.20266393	0.83148748	40.53278549	33.70250372	0.02467139	0.02967139	37
38	1.20867725	0.82735073	41.73544942	34.52985445	0.02396045	0.02896045	38
39	1.21472063	0.82323455	42.94412666	35.35308900	0.02328607	0.02828607	39
40	1.22079424	0.81913886	44.15884730	36.17222786	0.02264552	0.02764552	40
41	1.22689821	0.81506354	45.37964153	36.98729141	0.02203631	0.02703631	41
42	1.23303270	0.81100850	46.60653974	37.79829991	0.02145622	0.02645622	42
43	1.23919786	0.80697363	47.83957244	38.60527354	0.02090320	0.02590320	43
44	1.24539385	0.80295884	49.07877030	39.40823238	0.02037541	0.02537541	44
45	1.25162082	0.79896402	50.32416415	40.20719640	0.01987117	0.02487117	45
46	1.25787892	0.79498907	51.57578497	41.00218547	0.01938894	0.02438894	46
47	1.26416832	0.79103390	52.83366390	41.79321937	0.01892733	0.02392733	47
48	1.27048916	0.78709841	54.09783222	42.58031778	0.01848503	0.02348503	48
49	1.27684161	0.78318250	55.36832138	43.36350028	0.01806087	0.02306087	49
50	1.28322581	0.77928607	56.64516299	44.14278635	0.01765376	0.02265376	50

Tables 10 Through 12 (continued). Compound Interest

3/4%	Table 10.1. Compound amount	Table 10.2. Present value	Table 11.1. Amount of annuity	Table 11.2. Present value of annuity	Table 12.1. Sinking fund	Table 12.2. Amortization	3/4%
1	1.00750000	0.99255583	1.00000000	0.99255583	1.00000000	1.00750000	1
2	1.01505625	0.98516708	2.00750000	1.97772291	0.49813200	0.50563200	2
3	1.02266917	0.97783333	3.02255625	2.95555624	0.33084579	0.33834579	3
4	1.03033919	0.97055417	4.04522542	3.92611041	0.24720501	0.25470501	4
5	1.03806673	0.96332920	5.07556461	4.88943961	0.19702242	0.20452242	5
6	1.04585224	0.95615802	6.11363135	5.84559763	0.16356891	0.17106891	6
7	1.05369613	0.94904022	7.15948358	6.79463785	0.13967488	0.14717488	7
8	1.06159885	0.94197540	8.21317971	7.73661325	0.12175552	0.12925552	8
9	1.06956084	0.93496318	9.27477856	8.67157642	0.10781929	0.11531929	9
10	1.07758255	0.92800315	10.34433940	9.59957958	0.09667123	0.10417123	10
11	1.08566441	0.92109494	11.42192194	10.52067452	0.08755094	0.09505094	11
12	1.09380690	0.91423815	12.50758636	11.43491267	0.07995148	0.08745148	12
13	1.10201045	0.90743241	13.60139325	12.34234508	0.07352188	0.08102188	13
14	1.11027553	0.90067733	14.70340370	13.24302242	0.06801146	0.07551146	14
15	1.11860259	0.89397254	15.81367923	14.13699495	0.06323639	0.07073639	15
16	1.12699211	0.88731766	16.93228183	15.02431261	0.05905879	0.06655879	16
17	1.13544455	0.88071231	18.05927394	15.90502492	0.05537321	0.06287321	17
18	1.14396039	0.87415614	19.19471849	16.77918107	0.05209766	0.05959766	18
19	1.15254009	0.86764878	20.33867888	17.64682984	0.04916740	0.05666740	19
20	1.16118414	0.86118985	21.49121897	18.50801969	0.04653063	0.05403063	20
21	1.16989302	0.85477901	22.65240312	19.36279870	0.04414543	0.05164543	21
22	1.17866722	0.84841589	23.82229614	20.21121459	0.04197748	0.04947748	22
23	1.18750723	0.84210014	25.00096336	21.05331473	0.03999846	0.04749846	23
24	1.19641353	0.83583140	26.18847059	21.88914614	0.03818474	0.04568474	24
25	1.20538663	0.82960933	27.38488412	22.71875547	0.03651650	0.04401650	25
26	1.21442703	0.82343358	28.59027075	23.54218905	0.03497693	0.04247693	26
27	1.22353523	0.81730380	29.80469778	24.35949286	0.03355176	0.04105176	27
28	1.23271175	0.81121966	31.02823301	25.17071251	0.03222871	0.03972871	28
29	1.24195709	0.80518080	32.26094476	25.97589331	0.03099723	0.03849723	29
30	1.25127176	0.79918690	33.50290184	26.77508021	0.02984816	0.03734816	30
31	1.26065630	0.79323762	34.75417361	27.56831783	0.02877352	0.03627352	31
32	1.27011122	0.78733262	36.01482991	28.35565045	0.02776634	0.03526634	32
33	1.27963706	0.78147158	37.28494113	29.13712203	0.02682048	0.03432048	33
34	1.28923434	0.77565418	38.56457819	29.91277621	0.02593053	0.03343053	34
35	1.29890359	0.76988008	39.85381253	30.68265629	0.02509170	0.03259170	35
36	1.30864537	0.76414896	41.15271612	31.44680525	0.02429973	0.03179973	36
37	1.31846021	0.75846051	42.46136149	32.20526576	0.02355082	0.03105082	37
38	1.32834866	0.75281440	43.77982170	32.95808016	0.02284157	0.03034157	38
39	1.33831128	0.74721032	45.10817037	33.70529048	0.02216893	0.02966893	39
40	1.34834861	0.74164796	46.44648164	34.44693844	0.02153016	0.02903016	40
41	1.35846123	0.73612701	47.79483026	35.18306545	0.02092276	0.02842276	41
42	1.36864969	0.73064716	49.15329148	35.91371260	0.02034452	0.02784452	42
43	1.37891456	0.72520809	50.52194117	36.63892070	0.01979338	0.02729338	43
44	1.38925642	0.71980952	51.90085573	37.35873022	0.01926751	0.02676751	44
45	1.39967584	0.71445114	53.29011215	38.07318136	0.01876521	0.02626521	45
46	1.41017341	0.70913264	54.68978799	38.78231401	0.01828495	0.02578495	46
47	1.42074971	0.70385374	56.09996140	39.48616775	0.01782532	0.02532532	47
48	1.43140533	0.69861414	57.52071111	40.18478189	0.01738504	0.02488504	48
49	1.44214087	0.69341353	58.95211644	40.87819542	0.01696292	0.02446292	49
50	1.45295693	0.68825165	60.39425732	41.56644707	0.01555787	0.02405787	50

Tables 10 Through 12 (continued). Compound Interest

1%	Table 10.1. Compound amount	Table 10.2. Present value	Table 11.1. Amount of annuity	Table 11.2. Present value of annuity	Table 12.1. Sinking fund	Table 12.2. Amortization	1%
n							n
1	1.01000000	0.99009901	1.00000000	0.99009901	1.00000000	1.01000000	1
2	1.02010000	0.98029605	2.01000000	1.97039506	0.49751244	0.50751244	2
3	1.03030100	0.97059015	3.03010000	2.94098521	0.33002211	0.34002211	3
4	1.04060401	0.96098034	4.06040100	3.90196555	0.24628109	0.25628109	4
5	1.05101005	0.95146569	5.10100501	4.85343124	0.19603980	0.20603980	5
6	1.06152015	0.94204524	6.15201506	5.79547647	0.16254837	0.17254837	6
7	1.07213535	0.93271805	7.21353521	6.72819453	0.13862828	0.14862828	7
8	1.08285671	0.92348322	8.28567056	7.65167775	0.12069029	0.13069029	8
9	1.09368527	0.91433982	9.36852727	8.56601758	0.10674036	0.11674036	9
10	1.10462213	0.90528695	10.46221254	9.47130453	0.09558208	0.10558208	10
11	1.11566835	0.89632372	11.56683467	10.36762825	0.08645408	0.09645408	11
12	1.12682503	0.88744923	12.68250301	11.25507747	0.07884879	0.08884879	12
13	1.13809328	0.87866260	13.80932804	12.13374007	0.07241482	0.08241482	13
14	1.14947421	0.86996297	14.94742132	13.00370304	0.06690117	0.07690117	14
15	1.16096896	0.86134947	16.09689554	13.86505252	0.06212378	0.07212378	15
16	1.17257864	0.85282126	17.25786449	14.71787378	0.05794460	0.06794460	16
17	1.18430443	0.84437749	18.43044314	15.56225127	0.05425806	0.06425806	17
18	1.19614748	0.83601731	19.61474757	16.39826858	0.05098205	0.06098205	18
19	1.20810895	0.82773992	20.81089504	17.22600850	0.04805175	0.05805175	19
20	1.22019004	0.81954447	22.01900399	18.04555297	0.04541531	0.05541531	20
21	1.23239194	0.81143017	23.23919403	18.85698313	0.04303075	0.05303075	21
22	1.24471586	0.80339621	24.47158598	19.66037934	0.04086372	0.05086372	22
23	1.25716302	0.79544179	25.71630183	20.45582113	0.03888584	0.04888584	23
24	1.26973465	0.78756613	26.97346485	21.24338726	0.03707347	0.04707347	24
25	1.28243200	0.77976844	28.24319950	22.02315570	0.03540675	0.04540675	25
26	1.29525631	0.77204796	29.52563150	22.79520366	0.03386888	0.04386888	26
27	1.30820888	0.76440392	30.82088781	23.55960759	0.03244553	0.04244553	27
28	1.32129097	0.75683557	32.12909669	24.31644316	0.03112444	0.04112444	28
29	1.33450388	0.74934215	33.45038766	25.06578530	0.02989502	0.03989502	29
30	1.34784892	0.74192292	34.78489153	25.80770822	0.02874811	0.03874811	30
31	1.36132740	0.73457715	36.13274045	26.54228537	0.02767573	0.03767573	31
32	1.37494068	0.72730411	37.49406785	27.26958947	0.02667089	0.03667089	32
33	1.38869009	0.72010307	38.86900853	27.98969255	0.02572744	0.03572744	33
34	1.40257699	0.71297334	40.25769862	28.70266589	0.02483997	0.03483997	34
35	1.41660276	0.70591420	41.66027560	29.40858009	0.02400368	0.03400368	35
36	1.43076878	0.69892495	43.07687836	30.10750504	0.02321431	0.03321431	36
37	1.44507647	0.69200490	44.50764714	30.79950994	0.02246805	0.03246805	37
38	1.45952724	0.68515337	45.95272361	31.48466330	0.02176150	0.03176150	38
39	1.47412251	0.67836967	47.41225085	32.16303298	0.02109160	0.03109160	39
40	1.48886373	0.67165314	48.88637336	32.83468611	0.02045560	0.03045560	40
41	1.50375237	0.66500311	50.37523709	33.49968922	0.01985102	0.02985102	41
42	1.51878989	0.65841892	51.87898946	34.15810814	0.01927563	0.02927563	42
43	1.53397779	0.65189992	53.39777936	34.81000806	0.01872737	0.02872737	43
44	1.54931757	0.64544546	54.93175715	35.45545352	0.01820441	0.02820441	44
45	1.56481075	0.63905492	56.48107472	36.09450844	0.01770505	0.02770505	45
46	1.58045885	0.63272764	58.04588547	36.72723608	0.01722775	0.02722775	46
47	1.59626344	0.62646301	59.62634432	37.35369909	0.01677111	0.02677111	47
48	1.61222608	0.62026041	61.22260777	37.97395949	0.01633384	0.02633384	48
49	1.62834834	0.61411921	62.83483385	38.58807871	0.01591474	0.02591474	49
50	1.64463182	0.60803882	64.46318218	39.19611753	0.01551273	0.02551273	50

Tables 10 Through 12 (continued). Compound Interest

1¹/₄% n	Table 10.1. Compound amount	Table 10.2. Present value	Table 11.1. Amount of annuity	Table 11.2. Present value of annuity	Table 12.1. Sinking fund	Table 12.2. Amortization	1¹/₄% n
1	1.01250000	0.98765432	1.00000000	0.98765432	1.00000000	1.01250000	1
2	1.02515625	0.97546106	2.01250000	1.96311538	0.49689441	0.50939441	2
3	1.03797070	0.96341833	3.03765625	2.92653371	0.32920117	0.34170117	3
4	1.05094534	0.95152428	4.07562695	3.87805798	0.24536102	0.25786102	4
5	1.06408215	0.93977706	5.12657229	4.81783504	0.19506211	0.20756211	5
6	1.07738318	0.92817488	6.19065444	5.74600992	0.16153381	0.17403381	6
7	1.09085047	0.91671593	7.26803762	6.66272585	0.13758872	0.15008872	7
8	1.10448610	0.90539845	8.35888809	7.56812429	0.11963314	0.13213314	8
9	1.11829218	0.89422069	9.46337420	8.46234498	0.10567055	0.11817055	9
10	1.13227083	0.88318093	10.58166637	9.34552591	0.09450307	0.10700307	10
11	1.14642422	0.87227746	11.71393720	10.21780337	0.08536839	0.09786839	11
12	1.16075452	0.86150860	12.86036142	11.07931197	0.07775831	0.09025831	12
13	1.17526395	0.85087269	14.02111594	11.93018466	0.07132100	0.08382100	13
14	1.18995475	0.84036809	15.19637988	12.77055275	0.06580515	0.07830515	14
15	1.20482918	0.82999318	16.38633463	13.60054592	0.06102646	0.07352646	15
16	1.21988955	0.81974635	17.59116382	14.42029227	0.05684672	0.06934672	16
17	1.23513817	0.80962602	18.81105336	15.22991829	0.05316023	0.06566023	17
18	1.25057739	0.79963064	20.04619153	16.02954893	0.04988479	0.06238479	18
19	1.26620961	0.78975866	21.29676893	16.81930759	0.04695548	0.05945548	19
20	1.28203723	0.78000855	22.56297854	17.59931613	0.04432039	0.05682039	20
21	1.29806270	0.77037881	23.84501577	18.36969495	0.04193749	0.05443749	21
22	1.31428848	0.76086796	25.14307847	19.13056291	0.03977238	0.05227238	22
23	1.33071709	0.75147453	26.45736695	19.88203744	0.03779666	0.05029666	23
24	1.34735105	0.74219707	27.78808403	20.62423451	0.03598665	0.04848665	24
25	1.36419294	0.73303414	29.13543508	21.35726865	0.03432247	0.04682247	25
26	1.38124535	0.72398434	30.49962802	22.08125299	0.03278729	0.04528729	26
27	1.39851092	0.71504626	31.88087337	22.79629925	0.03136677	0.04386677	27
28	1.41599230	0.70621853	33.27938429	23.50251778	0.03004863	0.04254863	28
29	1.43369221	0.69749978	34.69537659	24.20001756	0.02882228	0.04132228	29
30	1.45161336	0.68888867	36.12906880	24.88890623	0.02767854	0.04017854	30
31	1.46975853	0.68038387	37.58068216	25.56929010	0.02660942	0.03910942	31
32	1.48813051	0.67198407	39.05044069	26.24127418	0.02560791	0.03810791	32
33	1.50673214	0.66368797	40.53857120	26.90496215	0.02466786	0.03716786	33
34	1.52556629	0.65549429	42.04530334	27.56045644	0.02378387	0.03628387	34
35	1.54463587	0.64740177	43.57086963	28.20785822	0.02295111	0.03545111	35
36	1.56394382	0.63940916	45.11550550	28.84726737	0.02216533	0.03466533	36
37	1.58349312	0.63151522	46.67944932	29.47878259	0.02142270	0.03392270	37
38	1.60328678	0.62371873	48.26294243	30.10250133	0.02071983	0.03321983	38
39	1.62332787	0.61601850	49.86622921	30.71851983	0.02005365	0.03255365	39
40	1.64361946	0.60841334	51.48955708	31.32693316	0.01942141	0.03192141	40
41	1.66416471	0.60090206	53.13317654	31.92783522	0.01882063	0.03132063	41
42	1.68496677	0.59348352	54.79734125	32.52131874	0.01824906	0.03074906	42
43	1.70602885	0.58615656	56.48230801	33.10747530	0.01770466	0.03020466	43
44	1.72735421	0.57892006	58.18833687	33.68639536	0.01718557	0.02968557	44
45	1.74894614	0.57177290	59.91569108	34.25816825	0.01669012	0.02919012	45
46	1.77080797	0.56471397	61.66463721	34.82288222	0.01621675	0.02871675	46
47	1.79294306	0.55774219	63.43544518	35.38062442	0.01576406	0.02826406	47
48	1.81535485	0.55085649	65.22838824	35.93148091	0.01533075	0.02783075	48
49	1.83804679	0.54405579	67.04374310	36.47553670	0.01491563	0.02741563	49
50	1.86102237	0.53733905	68.88178989	37.01287575	0.01451763	0.02701763	50

Tables 10 Through 12 (continued). Compound Interest

1½%	Table 10.1. Compound amount	Table 10.2. Present value	Table 11.1. Amount of annuity	Table 11.2. Present value of annuity	Table 12.1. Sinking fund	Table 12.2. Amortization	1½%
n							n
1	1.01500000	0.98522167	1.00000000	0.98522167	1.00000000	1.01500000	1
2	1.03022500	0.97066175	2.01500000	1.95588342	0.49627792	0.51127792	2
3	1.04567837	0.95631699	3.04522500	2.91220042	0.32838296	0.34338296	3
4	1.06136355	0.94218423	4.09090338	3.85438465	0.24444479	0.25944479	4
5	1.07728400	0.92826033	5.15226693	4.78264497	0.19408932	0.20908932	5
6	1.09344326	0.91454219	6.22955093	5.69718717	0.16052521	0.17552521	6
7	1.10984491	0.90102679	7.32299419	6.59821396	0.13655616	0.15155616	7
8	1.12649259	0.88771112	8.43283911	7.48592508	0.11858402	0.13358402	8
9	1.14338998	0.87459224	9.55933169	8.36051732	0.10460982	0.11960982	9
10	1.16054083	0.86166723	10.70272167	9.22218455	0.09343418	0.10843418	10
11	1.17794894	0.84893323	11.86326249	10.07111779	0.08429384	0.09929384	11
12	1.19561817	0.83638742	13.04121143	10.90750521	0.07667999	0.09167999	12
13	1.21355244	0.82402702	14.23682960	11.73153222	0.07024036	0.08524036	13
14	1.23175573	0.81184928	15.45038205	12.54338150	0.06472332	0.07972332	14
15	1.25023207	0.79985150	16.68213778	13.34323301	0.05994436	0.07494436	15
16	1.26898555	0.78803104	17.93236984	14.13126405	0.05576508	0.07076508	16
17	1.28802033	0.77638526	19.20135539	14.90764931	0.05207966	0.06707966	17
18	1.30734064	0.76491159	20.48937572	15.67256089	0.04880578	0.06380578	18
19	1.32695075	0.75360747	21.79671636	16.42616837	0.04587847	0.06087847	19
20	1.34685501	0.74247042	23.12366710	17.16863879	0.04324574	0.05824574	20
21	1.36705783	0.73149795	24.47052211	17.90013673	0.04086550	0.05586550	21
22	1.38756370	0.72068763	25.83757994	18.62082437	0.03870332	0.05370332	22
23	1.40837715	0.71003708	27.22514364	19.33086145	0.03673075	0.05173075	23
24	1.42950281	0.69954392	28.63352080	20.03040537	0.03492410	0.04992410	24
25	1.45094535	0.68920583	30.06302361	20.71961120	0.03326345	0.04826345	25
26	1.47270953	0.67902052	31.51396896	21.39863172	0.03173196	0.04673196	26
27	1.49480018	0.66898574	32.98667850	22.06761746	0.03031527	0.04531527	27
28	1.51722218	0.65909069	34.48147867	22.72671671	0.02900108	0.04400108	28
29	1.53998051	0.64935887	35.99870085	23.37607558	0.02777878	0.04277878	29
30	1.56308022	0.63976243	37.53868137	24.01583801	0.02663919	0.04163919	30
31	1.58652642	0.63030781	39.10176159	24.64614582	0.02557430	0.04057430	31
32	1.61032432	0.62099292	40.68828801	25.26713874	0.02457710	0.03957710	32
33	1.63447918	0.61181568	42.29861233	25.87895442	0.02364144	0.03864144	33
34	1.65899637	0.60277407	43.93309152	26.48172849	0.02276189	0.03776189	34
35	1.68388132	0.59386608	45.59208789	27.07559458	0.02193363	0.03693363	35
36	1.70913954	0.58508974	47.27596921	27.66068431	0.02115240	0.03615240	36
37	1.73477663	0.57644309	48.98510874	28.23712740	0.02041437	0.03541437	37
38	1.76079828	0.56792423	50.71988538	28.80505163	0.01971613	0.03471613	38
39	1.78721025	0.55953126	52.48068366	29.36458288	0.01905463	0.03405463	39
40	1.81401841	0.55126232	54.26789391	29.91584520	0.01842710	0.03342710	40
41	1.84122868	0.54311559	56.08191232	30.45896079	0.01783106	0.03283106	41
42	1.86884712	0.53508925	57.92314100	30.99405004	0.01726426	0.03226426	42
43	1.89687982	0.52718153	59.79198812	31.52123157	0.01672465	0.03172465	43
44	1.92533302	0.51939067	61.68886794	32.04062223	0.01621038	0.03121038	44
45	1.95421301	0.51171494	63.61420096	32.55233718	0.01571976	0.03071976	45
46	1.98352621	0.50415265	65.56841398	33.05648983	0.01525125	0.03025125	46
47	2.01327910	0.49670212	67.55194018	33.55319195	0.01480342	0.02980342	47
48	2.04347829	0.48936170	69.56521929	34.04255365	0.01437500	0.02937500	48
49	2.07413046	0.48212975	71.60869758	34.52468339	0.01396478	0.02896478	49
50	2.10524242	0.47500468	73.68282804	34.99968807	0.01357168	0.02857168	50

Tables 10 Through 12 (continued). Compound Interest

1³/₄%	Table 10.1. Compound amount	Table 10.2. Present value	Table 11.1. Amount of annuity	Table 11.2. Present value of annuity	Table 12.1. Sinking fund	Table 12.2. Amortization	1³/₄%
n							n
1	1.01750000	0.98280098	1.00000000	0.98280098	1.00000000	1.01750000	1
2	1.03530625	0.96589777	2.01750000	1.94869875	0.49566295	0.51316295	2
3	1.05342411	0.94928528	3.05280625	2.89798403	0.32756746	0.34506746	3
4	1.07185903	0.93295851	4.10623036	3.83094254	0.24353237	0.26103237	4
5	1.09061656	0.91691254	5.17808939	4.74785508	0.19312142	0.21062142	5
6	1.10970235	0.90114254	6.26870596	5.64899762	0.15952256	0.17702256	6
7	1.12912215	0.88564378	7.37840831	6.53464139	0.13553059	0.15303059	7
8	1.14888178	0.87041157	8.50753045	7.40505297	0.11754292	0.13504292	8
9	1.16898721	0.85544135	9.65641224	8.26049432	0.10355813	0.12105813	9
10	1.18944449	0.84072860	10.82539945	9.10122291	0.09237534	0.10987534	10
11	1.21025977	0.82626889	12.01484394	9.92749181	0.08323038	0.10073038	11
12	1.23143931	0.81205788	13.22510371	10.73954969	0.07561377	0.09311377	12
13	1.25298950	0.79809128	14.45654303	11.53764097	0.06917283	0.08667283	13
14	1.27491682	0.78436490	15.70953253	12.32200587	0.06365562	0.08115562	14
15	1.29722786	0.77087459	16.98444935	13.09288046	0.05887739	0.07637739	15
16	1.31992935	0.75761631	18.28167721	13.85049677	0.05469958	0.07219958	16
17	1.34302811	0.74458605	19.60160656	14.59508282	0.05101623	0.06851623	17
18	1.36653111	0.73177990	20.94463468	15.32686272	0.04774492	0.06524492	18
19	1.39044540	0.71919401	22.31116578	16.04605673	0.04482061	0.06232061	19
20	1.41477820	0.70682458	23.70161119	16.75288130	0.04219122	0.05969122	20
21	1.43953681	0.69466789	25.11638938	17.44754919	0.03981464	0.05731464	21
22	1.46472871	0.68272028	26.55592620	18.13026948	0.03765638	0.05515638	22
23	1.49036146	0.67097817	28.02065490	18.80124764	0.03568796	0.05318796	23
24	1.51644279	0.65943800	29.51101637	19.46068565	0.03388565	0.05138565	24
25	1.54298054	0.64809632	31.02745915	20.10878196	0.03222952	0.04972952	25
26	1.56998269	0.63694970	32.57043969	20.74573166	0.03070269	0.04820269	26
27	1.59745739	0.62599479	34.14042238	21.37172644	0.02929079	0.04679079	27
28	1.62541290	0.61522829	35.73787977	21.98695474	0.02798151	0.04548151	28
29	1.65385762	0.60464697	37.36329267	22.59160171	0.02676424	0.04426424	29
30	1.68280013	0.59424764	39.01715029	23.18584934	0.02562975	0.04312975	30
31	1.71224913	0.58402716	40.69995042	23.76987650	0.02457005	0.04207005	31
32	1.74221349	0.57398247	42.41219955	24.34385897	0.02357812	0.04107812	32
33	1.77270223	0.56411053	44.15441305	24.90796951	0.02264779	0.04014779	33
34	1.80372452	0.55440839	45.92711527	25.46237789	0.02177363	0.03927363	34
35	1.83528970	0.54487311	47.73083979	26.00725100	0.02095082	0.03845082	35
36	1.86740727	0.53550183	49.56612949	26.54275283	0.02017507	0.03767507	36
37	1.90008689	0.52629172	51.43353675	27.06904455	0.01944257	0.03694257	37
38	1.93333841	0.51724002	53.33362365	27.58628457	0.01874990	0.03624990	38
39	1.96717184	0.50834400	55.26696206	28.09462857	0.01809399	0.03559399	39
40	2.00159734	0.49960098	57.23413390	28.59422955	0.01747209	0.03497209	40
41	2.03662530	0.49100834	59.23573124	29.08523789	0.01688170	0.03438170	41
42	2.07226624	0.48256348	61.27235654	29.56780136	0.01632057	0.03382057	42
43	2.10853090	0.47426386	63.34462278	30.04206522	0.01578666	0.03328666	43
44	2.14543019	0.46610699	65.45315367	30.50817221	0.01527810	0.03277810	44
45	2.18297522	0.45809040	67.59858386	30.96626261	0.01479321	0.03229321	45
46	2.22117728	0.45021170	69.78155908	31.41647431	0.01433043	0.03183043	46
47	2.26004789	0.44246850	72.00273637	31.85894281	0.01388836	0.03138836	47
48	2.29959872	0.43485848	74.26278425	32.29380129	0.01346569	0.03096569	48
49	2.33984170	0.42737934	76.56238298	32.72118063	0.01306124	0.03056124	49
50	2.38078893	0.42002883	78.90222468	33.14120946	0.01267391	0.03017391	50

Tables 10 Through 12 (continued). Compound Interest

2%	Table 10.1. Compound amount	Table 10.2. Present value	Table 11.1. Amount of annuity	Table 11.2. Present value of annuity	Table 12.1. Sinking fund	Table 12.2. Amortization	2%
n							n
1	1.02000000	0.98039216	1.00000000	0.98039216	1.00000000	1.02000000	1
2	1.04040000	0.96116878	2.02000000	1.94156094	0.49504950	0.51504950	2
3	1.06120800	0.94232233	3.06040000	2.88388327	0.32675467	0.34675467	3
4	1.08243216	0.92384543	4.12160800	3.80772870	0.24262375	0.26262375	4
5	1.10408080	0.90573081	5.20404016	4.71345951	0.19215839	0.21215839	5
6	1.12616242	0.88797138	6.30812096	5.60143089	0.15852581	0.17852581	6
7	1.14868567	0.87056018	7.43428338	6.47199107	0.13451196	0.15451196	7
8	1.17165938	0.85349037	8.58296905	7.32548144	0.11650980	0.13650980	8
9	1.19509257	0.83675527	9.75462843	8.16223671	0.10251544	0.12251544	9
10	1.21899442	0.82034830	10.94972100	8.98258501	0.09132653	0.11132653	10
11	1.24337431	0.80426304	12.16871542	9.78684805	0.08217794	0.10217794	11
12	1.26824179	0.78849318	13.41208973	10.57534122	0.07455960	0.09455960	12
13	1.29360663	0.77303253	14.68033152	11.34837375	0.06811835	0.08811835	13
14	1.31947876	0.75787502	15.97393815	12.10624877	0.06260197	0.08260197	14
15	1.34586834	0.74301473	17.29341692	12.84926350	0.05782547	0.07782547	15
16	1.37278571	0.72844581	18.63928525	13.57770931	0.05365013	0.07365013	16
17	1.40024142	0.71416256	20.01207096	14.29187188	0.04996984	0.06996984	17
18	1.42824625	0.70015937	21.41231238	14.99203125	0.04670210	0.06670210	18
19	1.45681117	0.68643076	22.84055863	15.67846201	0.04378177	0.06378177	19
20	1.48594740	0.67297133	24.29736980	16.35143334	0.04115672	0.06115672	20
21	1.51566634	0.65977582	25.78331719	17.01120916	0.03878477	0.05878477	21
22	1.54597967	0.64683904	27.29898354	17.65804820	0.03663140	0.05663140	22
23	1.57689926	0.63415592	28.84496321	18.29220412	0.03466810	0.05466810	23
24	1.60843725	0.62172149	30.42186247	18.91392560	0.03287110	0.05287110	24
25	1.64060599	0.60953087	32.03029972	19.52345647	0.03122044	0.05122044	25
26	1.67341811	0.59757928	33.67090572	20.12103576	0.02969923	0.04969923	26
27	1.70688648	0.58586204	35.34432383	20.70689780	0.02829309	0.04829309	27
28	1.74102421	0.57437455	37.05121031	21.28127236	0.02698967	0.04698967	28
29	1.77584469	0.56311231	38.79223451	21.84438466	0.02577836	0.04577836	29
30	1.81136158	0.55207089	40.56807921	22.39645555	0.02464992	0.04464992	30
31	1.84758882	0.54124597	42.37944079	22.93770152	0.02359635	0.04359635	31
32	1.88454059	0.53063330	44.22702961	23.46833482	0.02261061	0.04261061	32
33	1.92223140	0.52022873	46.11157020	23.98856355	0.02168653	0.04168653	33
34	1.96067603	0.51002817	48.03380160	24.49859172	0.02081867	0.04081867	34
35	1.99988955	0.50002761	49.99447763	24.99861933	0.02000221	0.04000221	35
36	2.03988734	0.49022315	51.99436719	25.48884248	0.01923285	0.03923285	36
37	2.08068509	0.48061093	54.03425453	25.96945341	0.01850678	0.03850678	37
38	2.12229879	0.47118719	56.11493962	26.44064060	0.01782057	0.03782057	38
39	2.16474477	0.46194822	58.23723841	26.90258883	0.01717114	0.03717114	39
40	2.20803966	0.45289042	60.40198318	27.35547924	0.01655575	0.03655575	40
41	2.25220046	0.44401021	62.61002284	27.79948945	0.01597188	0.03597188	41
42	2.29724447	0.43530413	64.86222330	28.23479358	0.01541729	0.03541729	42
43	2.34318936	0.42676875	67.15946777	28.66156233	0.01488993	0.03488993	43
44	2.39005314	0.41840074	69.50265712	29.07996307	0.01438794	0.03438794	44
45	2.43785421	0.41019680	71.89271027	29.49015987	0.01390962	0.03390962	45
46	2.48661129	0.40215373	74.33056447	29.89231360	0.01345342	0.03345342	46
47	2.53634352	0.39426836	76.81717576	30.28658196	0.01301792	0.03301792	47
48	2.58707039	0.38653761	79.35351927	30.67311957	0.01260184	0.03260184	48
49	2.63881179	0.37895844	81.94058966	31.05207801	0.01220396	0.03220396	49
50	2.69158803	0.37152788	84.57940145	31.42360589	0.01182321	0.03182321	50

Tables 10 Through 12 (continued). Compound Interest

$2\frac{1}{4}\%$	Table 10.1. Compound amount	Table 10.2. Present value	Table 11.1. Amount of annuity	Table 11.2. Present value of annuity	Table 12.1. Sinking fund	Table 12.2. Amortization	$2\frac{1}{4}\%$
n							n
1	1.02250000	0.97799511	1.00000000	0.97799511	1.00000000	1.02250000	1
2	1.04550625	0.95647444	2.02250000	1.93446955	0.49443758	0.51693758	2
3	1.06903014	0.93542732	3.06800625	2.86989687	0.32594458	0.34844458	3
4	1.09308332	0.91484335	4.13703639	3.78474021	0.24171893	0.26421893	4
5	1.11767769	0.89471232	5.23011971	4.67945253	0.19120021	0.21370021	5
6	1.14282544	0.87502427	6.34779740	5.55447680	0.15753496	0.18003496	6
7	1.16853901	0.85576946	7.49062284	6.41024626	0.13350025	0.15600025	7
8	1.19483114	0.83693835	8.65916186	7.24718461	0.11548462	0.13798462	8
9	1.22171484	0.81852161	9.85399300	8.06570622	0.10148170	0.12398170	9
10	1.24920343	0.80051013	11.07570784	8.86621635	0.09028768	0.11278768	10
11	1.27731050	0.78289499	12.32491127	9.64911134	0.08113649	0.10363649	11
12	1.30604999	0.76566748	13.60222177	10.41477882	0.07351740	0.09601740	12
13	1.33543611	0.74881905	14.90827176	11.16359787	0.06707686	0.08957686	13
14	1.36548343	0.73234137	16.24370788	11.89593924	0.06156230	0.08406230	14
15	1.39620680	0.71622628	17.60919130	12.61216551	0.05678852	0.07928852	15
16	1.42762146	0.70046580	19.00539811	13.31263131	0.05261663	0.07511663	16
17	1.45974294	0.68505212	20.43301957	13.99768343	0.04894039	0.07144039	17
18	1.49258716	0.66997763	21.89276251	14.66766106	0.04567720	0.06817720	18
19	1.52617037	0.65523484	23.38534966	15.32289590	0.04276182	0.06526182	19
20	1.56050920	0.64081647	24.91152003	15.96371237	0.04014207	0.06264207	20
21	1.59562066	0.62671538	26.47202923	16.59042775	0.03777572	0.06027572	21
22	1.63152212	0.61292457	28.06764989	17.20335232	0.03562821	0.05812821	22
23	1.66823137	0.59943724	29.69917201	17.80278955	0.03367097	0.05617097	23
24	1.70576658	0.58624668	31.36740338	18.38903624	0.03188023	0.05438023	24
25	1.74414632	0.57334639	33.07316996	18.96238263	0.03023599	0.05273599	25
26	1.78338962	0.56072997	34.81731628	19.52311260	0.02872134	0.05122134	26
27	1.82351588	0.54839117	36.60070590	20.07150376	0.02732188	0.04982188	27
28	1.86454499	0.53632388	38.42422178	20.60782764	0.02602525	0.04852525	28
29	1.90649725	0.52452213	40.28876677	21.13234977	0.02482081	0.04732081	29
30	1.94939344	0.51298008	42.19526402	21.64532985	0.02369934	0.04619934	30
31	1.99325479	0.50169201	44.14465746	22.14702186	0.02265280	0.04515280	31
32	2.03810303	0.49065233	46.13791226	22.63767419	0.02167415	0.04417415	32
33	2.08396034	0.47985558	48.17601528	23.11752977	0.02075722	0.04325722	33
34	2.13084945	0.46929641	50.25997563	23.58682618	0.01989655	0.04239655	34
35	2.17879356	0.45896960	52.39082508	24.04579577	0.01908731	0.04158731	35
36	2.22781642	0.44887002	54.56961864	24.49466579	0.01832522	0.04082522	36
37	2.27794229	0.43899268	56.79743506	24.93365848	0.01760643	0.04010643	37
38	2.32919599	0.42933270	59.07537735	25.36299118	0.01692753	0.03942753	38
39	2.38160290	0.41988528	61.40457334	25.78287646	0.01628543	0.03878543	39
40	2.43518897	0.41064575	63.78617624	26.19352221	0.01567738	0.03817738	40
41	2.48998072	0.40160954	66.22136521	26.59513174	0.01510087	0.03760087	41
42	2.54600528	0.39277216	68.71134592	26.98790390	0.01455364	0.03705364	42
43	2.60329040	0.38412925	71.25735121	27.37203316	0.01403364	0.03653364	43
44	2.66186444	0.37567653	73.86064161	27.74770969	0.01353901	0.03603901	44
45	2.72175639	0.36740981	76.52250605	28.11511950	0.01306805	0.03556805	45
46	2.78299590	0.35932500	79.24426243	28.47444450	0.01261921	0.03511921	46
47	2.84561331	0.35141809	82.02725834	28.82586259	0.01219107	0.03469107	47
48	2.90963961	0.34368518	84.87287165	29.16954777	0.01178233	0.03428233	48
49	2.97510650	0.33612242	87.78251126	29.50567019	0.01139179	0.03389179	49
50	3.04204640	0.32872608	90.75761776	29.83439627	0.01101836	0.03351836	50

Tables 10 Through 12 (continued). Compound Interest

2½%	Table 10.1. Compound amount	Table 10.2. Present value	Table 11.1. Amount of annuity	Table 11.2. Present value of annuity	Table 12.1. Sinking fund	Table 12.2. Amortization	2½%
n							n
1	1.02500000	0.97560976	1.00000000	0.97560976	1.00000000	1.02500000	1
2	1.05062500	0.95181440	2.02500000	1.92742415	0.49382716	0.51882716	2
3	1.07689062	0.92859941	3.07562500	2.85602356	0.32513717	0.35013717	3
4	1.10381289	0.90595064	4.15251563	3.76197421	0.24081788	0.26581788	4
5	1.13140821	0.88385429	5.25632852	4.64582850	0.19024686	0.21524686	5
6	1.15969342	0.86229687	6.38773673	5.50812536	0.15654997	0.18154997	6
7	1.18868575	0.84126524	7.54743015	6.34939060	0.13249543	0.15749543	7
8	1.21840290	0.82074657	8.73611590	7.17013717	0.11446735	0.13946735	8
9	1.24886297	0.80072836	9.95451880	7.97086553	0.10045689	0.12545689	9
10	1.28008454	0.78119840	11.20338177	8.75206393	0.08925876	0.11425876	10
11	1.31208666	0.76214478	12.48346631	9.51420871	0.08010596	0.10510596	11
12	1.34488882	0.74355589	13.79555297	10.25776460	0.07248713	0.09748713	12
13	1.37851104	0.72542038	15.14044179	10.98318497	0.06604827	0.09104827	13
14	1.41297382	0.70772720	16.51895284	11.69091217	0.06053652	0.08553652	14
15	1.44829817	0.69046556	17.93192666	12.38137773	0.05576646	0.08076646	15
16	1.48450562	0.67362493	19.38022483	13.05500266	0.05159899	0.07659899	16
17	1.52161826	0.65719506	20.86473045	13.71219772	0.04792777	0.07292777	17
18	1.55965872	0.64116591	22.38634871	14.35336363	0.04467008	0.06967008	18
19	1.59865019	0.62552772	23.94600743	14.97889134	0.04176062	0.06676062	19
20	1.63861644	0.61027094	25.54465761	15.58916229	0.03914713	0.06414713	20
21	1.67958185	0.59538629	27.18327405	16.18454857	0.03678733	0.06178733	21
22	1.72157140	0.58086467	28.86285590	16.76541324	0.03464661	0.05964661	22
23	1.76461068	0.56669724	30.58442730	17.33211048	0.03269638	0.05769638	23
24	1.80872595	0.55287535	32.34903798	17.88498583	0.03091282	0.05591282	24
25	1.85394410	0.53939059	34.15776393	18.42437642	0.02927592	0.05427592	25
26	1.90029270	0.52623472	36.01170803	18.95061114	0.02776875	0.05276875	26
27	1.94780002	0.51339973	37.91200073	19.46401087	0.02637687	0.05137687	27
28	1.99649502	0.50087778	39.85980075	19.96488866	0.02508793	0.05008793	28
29	2.04640739	0.48866125	41.85629577	20.45354991	0.02389127	0.04889127	29
30	2.09756758	0.47674269	43.90270316	20.93029259	0.02277764	0.04777764	30
31	2.15000677	0.46511481	46.00027074	21.39540741	0.02173900	0.04673900	31
32	2.20375694	0.45377055	48.15027751	21.84917796	0.02076831	0.04576831	32
33	2.25885086	0.44270298	50.35403445	22.29188094	0.01985938	0.04485938	33
34	2.31532213	0.43190534	52.61288531	22.72378628	0.01900675	0.04400675	34
35	2.37320519	0.42137107	54.92820744	23.14515734	0.01820558	0.04320558	35
36	2.43253532	0.41109372	57.30141263	23.55625107	0.01745158	0.04245158	36
37	2.49334870	0.40106705	59.73394794	23.95731812	0.01674090	0.04174090	37
38	2.55568242	0.39128492	62.22729664	24.34860304	0.01607012	0.04107012	38
39	2.61957448	0.38174139	64.78297906	24.73034443	0.01543615	0.04043615	39
40	2.68506384	0.37243062	67.40255354	25.10277505	0.01483623	0.03983623	40
41	2.75219043	0.36334695	70.08761737	25.46612200	0.01426786	0.03926786	41
42	2.82099520	0.35448483	72.83980781	25.82060683	0.01372876	0.03872876	42
43	2.89152008	0.34583886	75.66080300	26.16644569	0.01321688	0.03821688	43
44	2.96380808	0.33740376	78.55232308	26.50384945	0.01273037	0.03773037	44
45	3.03790328	0.32917440	81.51613116	26.83302386	0.01226751	0.03726751	45
46	3.11385086	0.32114576	84.55403443	27.15416962	0.01182676	0.03682676	46
47	3.19169713	0.31331294	87.66788530	27.46748255	0.01140669	0.03640669	47
48	3.27148956	0.30567116	90.85958243	27.77315371	0.01100599	0.03600599	48
49	3.35327680	0.29821576	94.13107199	28.07136947	0.01062348	0.03562348	49
50	3.43710872	0.29094221	97.48434879	28.36231168	0.01025806	0.03525806	50

Tables 10 Through 12 (continued). Compound Interest

2³/₄%	Table 10.1. Compound amount	Table 10.2. Present value	Table 11.1. Amount of annuity	Table 11.2. Present value of annuity	Table 12.1. Sinking fund	Table 12.2. Amortization	2³/₄%
n							n
1	1.02750000	0.97323601	1.00000000	0.97323601	1.00000000	1.02750000	1
2	1.05575625	0.94718833	2.02750000	1.92042434	0.49321825	0.52071825	2
3	1.08478955	0.92183779	3.08325625	2.84226213	0.32433243	0.35183243	3
4	1.11462126	0.89716573	4.16804580	3.73942787	0.23992059	0.26742059	4
5	1.14527334	0.87315400	5.28266706	4.61258186	0.18929832	0.21679832	5
6	1.17676836	0.84978491	6.42794040	5.46236678	0.15557083	0.18307083	6
7	1.20912949	0.82704128	7.60470876	6.28940806	0.13149747	0.15899747	7
8	1.24238055	0.80490635	8.81383825	7.09431441	0.11345795	0.14095795	8
9	1.27654602	0.78336385	10.05621880	7.87767826	0.09944095	0.12694095	9
10	1.31165103	0.76239791	11.33276482	8.64007616	0.08823972	0.11573972	10
11	1.34772144	0.74199310	12.64441585	9.38206926	0.07908629	0.10658629	11
12	1.38478378	0.72213440	13.99213729	10.10420366	0.07146871	0.09896871	12
13	1.42286533	0.70280720	15.37692107	10.80701086	0.06503252	0.09253252	13
14	1.46199413	0.68399728	16.79978639	11.49100814	0.05952457	0.08702457	14
15	1.50219896	0.66569078	18.26178052	12.15669892	0.05475917	0.08225917	15
16	1.54350944	0.64787424	19.76397948	12.80457315	0.05059710	0.07809710	16
17	1.58595595	0.63053454	21.30748892	13.43510769	0.04693186	0.07443186	17
18	1.62956973	0.61365892	22.89344487	14.04876661	0.04368063	0.07118063	18
19	1.67438290	0.59723496	24.52301460	14.64600157	0.04077802	0.06827802	19
20	1.72042843	0.58125057	26.19739750	15.22725213	0.03817173	0.06567173	20
21	1.76774021	0.56569398	27.91782593	15.79294612	0.03581941	0.06331941	21
22	1.81635307	0.55055375	29.68556615	16.34349987	0.03368640	0.06118640	22
23	1.86630278	0.53581874	31.50191921	16.87931861	0.03174410	0.05924410	23
24	1.91762610	0.52147809	33.36822199	17.40079670	0.02996863	0.05746863	24
25	1.97036082	0.50752126	35.28584810	17.90831795	0.02833997	0.05583997	25
26	2.02454575	0.49393796	37.25620892	18.40225592	0.02684116	0.05434116	26
27	2.08022075	0.48071821	39.28075467	18.88297413	0.02545776	0.05295776	27
28	2.13742682	0.46785227	41.36097542	19.35082640	0.02417738	0.05167738	28
29	2.19620606	0.45533068	43.49840224	19.80615708	0.02298935	0.05048935	29
30	2.25660173	0.44314421	45.69460831	20.24930130	0.02188442	0.04938442	30
31	2.31865828	0.43128391	47.95121003	20.68058520	0.02085453	0.04835453	31
32	2.38242138	0.41974103	50.26986831	21.10032623	0.01989263	0.04739263	32
33	2.44793797	0.40850708	52.65228969	21.50883332	0.01899253	0.04649253	33
34	2.51525626	0.39757380	55.10022765	21.90640712	0.01814875	0.04564875	34
35	2.58442581	0.38693314	57.61548391	22.29334026	0.01735645	0.04485645	35
36	2.65549752	0.37657727	60.19990972	22.66991753	0.01661132	0.04411132	36
37	2.72852370	0.36649856	62.85540724	23.03641609	0.01590953	0.04340953	37
38	2.80355810	0.35668959	65.58393094	23.39310568	0.01524764	0.04274764	38
39	2.88065595	0.34714316	68.38748904	23.74024884	0.01462256	0.04212256	39
40	2.95987399	0.33785222	71.26814499	24.07810106	0.01403151	0.04153151	40
41	3.04127052	0.32880995	74.22801898	24.40691101	0.01347200	0.04097200	41
42	3.12490546	0.32000968	77.26928950	24.72692069	0.01294175	0.04044175	42
43	3.21084036	0.31144495	80.39419496	25.03836563	0.01243871	0.03993871	43
44	3.29913847	0.30310944	83.60503532	25.34147507	0.01196100	0.03946100	44
45	3.38986478	0.29499702	86.90417379	25.63647209	0.01150693	0.03900693	45
46	3.48308606	0.28710172	90.29403857	25.92357381	0.01107493	0.03857493	46
47	3.57887093	0.27941773	93.77712463	26.20299154	0.01066358	0.03816358	47
48	3.67728988	0.27193940	97.35599556	26.47493094	0.01027158	0.03777158	48
49	3.77841535	0.26466122	101.03328544	26.73959215	0.00989773	0.03739773	49
50	3.88232177	0.25757783	104.81170079	26.99716998	0.00954092	0.03704092	50

Tables 10 Through 12 (continued). Compound Interest

3%	Table 10.1. Compound amount	Table 10.2. Present value	Table 11.1. Amount of annuity	Table 11.2. Present value of annuity	Table 12.1. Sinking fund	Table 12.2. Amortization	3%
n							n
1	1.03000000	0.97087379	1.00000000	0.97087379	1.00000000	1.03000000	1
2	1.06090000	0.94259591	2.03000000	1.91346970	0.49261084	0.52261084	2
3	1.09272700	0.91514166	3.09090000	2.82861135	0.32353036	0.35353036	3
4	1.12550881	0.88848705	4.18362700	3.71709840	0.23902705	0.26902705	4
5	1.15927407	0.86260878	5.30913581	4.57970719	0.18835457	0.21835457	5
6	1.19405230	0.83748426	6.46840988	5.41719144	0.15459750	0.18459750	6
7	1.22987387	0.81309151	7.66246218	6.23028296	0.13050635	0.16050635	7
8	1.26677008	0.78940923	8.89233605	7.01969219	0.11245639	0.14245639	8
9	1.30477318	0.76641673	10.15910613	7.78610892	0.09843386	0.12843386	9
10	1.34391638	0.74409391	11.46387931	8.53020284	0.08723051	0.11723051	10
11	1.38423387	0.72242128	12.80779569	9.25262411	0.07807745	0.10807745	11
12	1.42576089	0.70137988	14.19202956	9.95400399	0.07046209	0.10046209	12
13	1.46853371	0.68095134	15.61779045	10.63495533	0.06402954	0.09402954	13
14	1.51258972	0.66111781	17.08632416	11.29607314	0.05852634	0.08852634	14
15	1.55796742	0.64186195	18.59891389	11.93793509	0.05376658	0.08376658	15
16	1.60470644	0.62316694	20.15688130	12.56110203	0.04961085	0.07961085	16
17	1.65284763	0.60501645	21.76158774	13.16611847	0.04595253	0.07595253	17
18	1.70243306	0.58739461	23.41443537	13.75351308	0.04270870	0.07270870	18
19	1.75350605	0.57028603	25.11686844	14.32379911	0.03981388	0.06981388	19
20	1.80611123	0.55367575	26.87037449	14.87747486	0.03721571	0.06721571	20
21	1.86029457	0.53754928	28.67648572	15.41502414	0.03487178	0.06487178	21
22	1.91610341	0.52189250	30.53678030	15.93691664	0.03274739	0.06274739	22
23	1.97358651	0.50669175	32.45288370	16.44360839	0.03081390	0.06081390	23
24	2.03279411	0.49193374	34.42647022	16.93554212	0.02904742	0.05904742	24
25	2.09377793	0.47760557	36.45926432	17.41314769	0.02742787	0.05742787	25
26	2.15659127	0.46369473	38.55304225	17.87684242	0.02593829	0.05593829	26
27	2.22128901	0.45018906	40.70963352	18.32703147	0.02456421	0.05456421	27
28	2.28792768	0.43707675	42.93092252	18.76410823	0.02329323	0.05329323	28
29	2.35656551	0.42434636	45.21885020	19.18845459	0.02211467	0.05211467	29
30	2.42726247	0.41198846	47.57541571	19.60044135	0.02101926	0.05101926	30
31	2.50008035	0.39998715	50.00267818	20.00042849	0.01999893	0.04999893	31
32	2.57508276	0.38833703	52.50275852	20.38876553	0.01904662	0.04904662	32
33	2.65233524	0.37702625	55.07784128	20.76579178	0.01815612	0.04815612	33
34	2.73190530	0.36604490	57.73017652	21.13183668	0.01732196	0.04732196	34
35	2.81386245	0.35538340	60.46208181	21.48722007	0.01653929	0.04653929	35
36	2.89827833	0.34503243	63.27594427	21.83225250	0.01580379	0.04580379	36
37	2.98522668	0.33498294	66.17422259	22.16723544	0.01511162	0.04511162	37
38	3.07478348	0.32522615	69.15944927	22.49246159	0.01445934	0.04445934	38
39	3.16702698	0.31575355	72.23423275	22.80821513	0.01384385	0.04384385	39
40	3.26203779	0.30655684	75.40125973	23.11477197	0.01326238	0.04326238	40
41	3.35989893	0.29762800	78.66329753	23.41239997	0.01271241	0.04271241	41
42	3.46069589	0.28895922	82.02319645	23.70135920	0.01219167	0.04219167	42
43	3.56451677	0.28054294	85.48389234	23.98190213	0.01169811	0.04169811	43
44	3.67145227	0.27237178	89.04840911	24.25427392	0.01122985	0.04122985	44
45	3.78159584	0.26443862	92.71986139	24.51871254	0.01078518	0.04078518	45
46	3.89504372	0.25673653	96.50145723	24.77544907	0.01036254	0.04036254	46
47	4.01189503	0.24925876	100.39650095	25.02470783	0.00996051	0.03996051	47
48	4.13225188	0.24199880	104.40839598	25.26670664	0.00957777	0.03957777	48
49	4.25621944	0.23495029	108.54064785	25.50165693	0.00921314	0.03921314	49
50	4.38390602	0.22810708	112.79686729	25.72976401	0.00886549	0.03886549	50

Tables 10 Through 12 (continued). Compound Interest

3¹/₄%	Table 10.1. Compound amount	Table 10.2. Present value	Table 11.1. Amount of annuity	Table 11.2. Present value of annuity	Table 12.1. Sinking fund	Table 12.2. Amortization	3¹/₄%
n							n
1	1.03250000	0.96852300	1.00000000	0.96852300	1.00000000	1.03250000	1
2	1.06605625	0.93803681	2.03250000	1.90655981	0.49200492	0.52450492	2
3	1.10070308	0.90851022	3.09855625	2.81507003	0.32273095	0.35523095	3
4	1.13647593	0.87991305	4.19925933	3.69498308	0.23813723	0.27063723	4
5	1.17341140	0.85221603	5.33573526	4.54719911	0.18741560	0.21991560	5
6	1.21154727	0.82539083	6.50914665	5.37258994	0.15362997	0.18612997	6
7	1.25092255	0.79941000	7.72069392	6.17199994	0.12952204	0.16202204	7
8	1.29157754	0.77424698	8.97161647	6.94624692	0.11146263	0.14396263	8
9	1.33355381	0.74987601	10.26319401	7.69612292	0.09743555	0.12993555	9
10	1.37689430	0.72627216	11.59674781	8.42239508	0.08623107	0.11873107	10
11	1.42164337	0.70341129	12.97364212	9.12580637	0.07707936	0.10957936	11
12	1.46784678	0.68127002	14.39528548	9.80707639	0.06946719	0.10196719	12
13	1.51555180	0.65982568	15.86313226	10.46690207	0.06303925	0.09553925	13
14	1.56480723	0.63905635	17.37868406	11.10595842	0.05754176	0.09004176	14
15	1.61566347	0.61894078	18.94349129	11.72489920	0.05278858	0.08528858	15
16	1.66817253	0.59945838	20.55915476	12.32435758	0.04864013	0.08114013	16
17	1.72238814	0.58058923	22.22732729	12.90494681	0.04498966	0.07748966	17
18	1.77836575	0.56231402	23.94971543	13.46726083	0.04175415	0.07425415	18
19	1.83616264	0.54461407	25.72808118	14.01187490	0.03886804	0.07136804	19
20	1.89583792	0.52747125	27.56424382	14.53934615	0.03627888	0.06877888	20
21	1.95745266	0.51086804	29.46008174	15.05021419	0.03394424	0.06644424	21
22	2.02106987	0.49478745	31.41753440	15.54500163	0.03182936	0.06432936	22
23	2.08675464	0.47921302	33.43860426	16.02421466	0.02990555	0.06240555	23
24	2.15457416	0.46412884	35.52535890	16.48834349	0.02814891	0.06064891	24
25	2.22459782	0.44951945	37.67993307	16.93786295	0.02653933	0.05903933	25
26	2.29689725	0.43536993	39.90453089	17.37323288	0.02505981	0.05755981	26
27	2.37154641	0.42166579	42.20142815	17.79489867	0.02369588	0.05619588	27
28	2.44862167	0.40839302	44.57297456	18.20329169	0.02243512	0.05493512	28
29	2.52820188	0.39553803	47.02159623	18.59882973	0.02126682	0.05376682	29
30	2.61036844	0.38308768	49.54979811	18.98191741	0.02018172	0.05268172	30
31	2.69520541	0.37102923	52.16016655	19.35294664	0.01917172	0.05167172	31
32	2.78279959	0.35935035	54.85537196	19.71229699	0.01822976	0.05072976	32
33	2.87324058	0.34803908	57.63817155	20.06033607	0.01734961	0.04984961	33
34	2.96662089	0.33708385	60.51141213	20.39741992	0.01652581	0.04902581	34
35	3.06303607	0.32647346	63.47803302	20.72389339	0.01575348	0.04825348	35
36	3.16258475	0.31619706	66.54106909	21.04009045	0.01502831	0.04752831	36
37	3.26536875	0.30624413	69.70365384	21.34633457	0.01434645	0.04684645	37
38	3.37149323	0.29660448	72.96902259	21.64293905	0.01370445	0.04620445	38
39	3.48106676	0.28726826	76.34051582	21.93020732	0.01309920	0.04559920	39
40	3.59420143	0.27822592	79.82158259	22.20843324	0.01252794	0.04502794	40
41	3.71101298	0.26946820	83.41578402	22.47790144	0.01198814	0.04448814	41
42	3.83162090	0.26098615	87.12679700	22.73888759	0.01147753	0.04397753	42
43	3.95614858	0.25277109	90.95841791	22.99165869	0.01099403	0.04349403	43
44	4.08472341	0.24481462	94.91456649	23.23647330	0.01053579	0.04303579	44
45	4.21747692	0.23710859	98.99928990	23.47358189	0.01010108	0.04260108	45
46	4.35454492	0.22964512	103.21676682	23.70322701	0.00968835	0.04218835	46
47	4.49606763	0.22241658	107.57131174	23.92564360	0.00929616	0.04179616	47
48	4.64218983	0.21541558	112.06737937	24.14105917	0.00892320	0.04142320	48
49	4.79306100	0.20863494	116.70956920	24.34969412	0.00856828	0.04106828	49
50	4.94883548	0.20206774	121.50263020	24.55176185	0.00823027	0.04073027	50

Tables 10 Through 12 (continued). Compound Interest

3¹/₂%	Table 10.1. Compound amount	Table 10.2. Present value	Table 11.1. Amount of annuity	Table 11.2. Present value of annuity	Table 12.1. Sinking fund	Table 12.2. Amortization	3¹/₂%
n							n
1	1.03500000	0.96618357	1.00000000	0.96618357	1.00000000	1.03500000	1
2	1.07122500	0.93351070	2.03500000	1.89969428	0.49140049	0.52640049	2
3	1.10871788	0.90194271	3.10622500	2.80163698	0.32193418	0.35693418	3
4	1.14752300	0.87144223	4.21494287	3.67307921	0.23725114	0.27225114	4
5	1.18768631	0.84197317	5.36246588	4.51505238	0.18648137	0.22148137	5
6	1.22925533	0.81350064	6.55015218	5.32855302	0.15266821	0.18766821	6
7	1.27227926	0.78599096	7.77940751	6.11454398	0.12854449	0.16354449	7
8	1.31680904	0.75941156	9.05168677	6.87395554	0.11047665	0.14547665	8
9	1.36289735	0.73373097	10.36849581	7.60768651	0.09644601	0.13144601	9
10	1.41059876	0.70891881	11.73139316	8.31660532	0.08524137	0.12024137	10
11	1.45996972	0.68494571	13.14199192	9.00155104	0.07609197	0.11109197	11
12	1.51106866	0.66178330	14.60196164	9.66333433	0.06848395	0.10348395	12
13	1.56395606	0.63940415	16.11303030	10.30273849	0.06206157	0.09706157	13
14	1.61869452	0.61778179	17.67698636	10.92052028	0.05657073	0.09157073	14
15	1.67534883	0.59689062	19.29568088	11.51741090	0.05182507	0.08682507	15
16	1.73398604	0.57670591	20.97102971	12.09411681	0.04768483	0.08268483	16
17	1.79467555	0.55720378	22.70501575	12.65132059	0.04404313	0.07904313	17
18	1.85748920	0.53836114	24.49969130	13.18968173	0.04081684	0.07581684	18
19	1.92250132	0.52015569	26.35718050	13.70983742	0.03794033	0.07294033	19
20	1.98978886	0.50256588	28.27968181	14.21240330	0.03536108	0.07036108	20
21	2.05943147	0.48557090	30.26947068	14.69797420	0.03303659	0.06803659	21
22	2.13151158	0.46915063	32.32890215	15.16712484	0.03093207	0.06593207	22
23	2.20611448	0.45328563	34.46041373	15.62041047	0.02901880	0.06401880	23
24	2.28332849	0.43795713	36.66652821	16.05836760	0.02727283	0.06227283	24
25	2.36324498	0.42314699	38.94985669	16.48151459	0.02567404	0.06067404	25
26	2.44595856	0.40883767	41.31310168	16.89035226	0.02420540	0.05920540	26
27	2.53156711	0.39501224	43.75906024	17.28536451	0.02285241	0.05785241	27
28	2.62017196	0.38165434	46.29062734	17.66701885	0.02160265	0.05660265	28
29	2.71187798	0.36874815	48.91079930	18.03576700	0.02044538	0.05544538	29
30	2.80679370	0.35627841	51.62267728	18.39204541	0.01937133	0.05437133	30
31	2.90503148	0.34423035	54.42947098	18.73627576	0.01837240	0.05337240	31
32	3.00670759	0.33258971	57.33450247	19.06886547	0.01744150	0.05244150	32
33	3.11194235	0.32134271	60.34121005	19.39020818	0.01657242	0.05157242	33
34	3.22086033	0.31047605	63.45315240	19.70068423	0.01575966	0.05075966	34
35	3.33359045	0.29997686	66.67401274	20.00066110	0.01499835	0.04999835	35
36	3.45026611	0.28983272	70.00760318	20.29049381	0.01428416	0.04928416	36
37	3.57102543	0.28003161	73.45786930	20.57052542	0.01361325	0.04861325	37
38	3.69601132	0.27056194	77.02889472	20.84108736	0.01298214	0.04798214	38
39	3.82537171	0.26141250	80.72490604	21.10249987	0.01238775	0.04738775	39
40	3.95925972	0.25257247	84.55027775	21.35507234	0.01182728	0.04682728	40
41	4.09783381	0.24403137	88.50953747	21.59910371	0.01129822	0.04629822	41
42	4.24125799	0.23577910	92.60737128	21.83488281	0.01079828	0.04579828	42
43	4.38970202	0.22780590	96.84862928	22.06268870	0.01032539	0.04532539	43
44	4.54334160	0.22010231	101.23833130	22.28279102	0.00987768	0.04487768	44
45	4.70235855	0.21265924	105.78167290	22.49545026	0.00945343	0.04445343	45
46	4.86694110	0.20546787	110.48403145	22.70091813	0.00905108	0.04405108	46
47	5.03728404	0.19851968	115.35097255	22.89943780	0.00866919	0.04366919	47
48	5.21358898	0.19180645	120.38825659	23.09124425	0.00830646	0.04330646	48
49	5.39606459	0.18532024	125.60184557	23.27656450	0.00796167	0.04296167	49
50	5.58492686	0.17905337	130.99791016	23.45561787	0.00763371	0.04263371	50

Tables 10 Through 12 (continued). Compound Interest

3³/₄%	Table 10.1. Compound	Table 10.2. Present	Table 11.1. Amount of	Table 11.2. Present value	Table 12.1. Sinking	Table 12.2.	3³/₄%
n	amount	value	annuity	of annuity	fund	Amortization	n
1	1.03750000	0.96385542	1.00000000	0.96385542	1.00000000	1.03750000	1
2	1.07640625	0.92901727	2.03750000	1.89287270	0.49079755	0.52829755	2
3	1.11677148	0.89543834	3.11390625	2.78831103	0.32114005	0.35864005	3
4	1.15865042	0.86307310	4.23067773	3.65138413	0.23636875	0.27386875	4
5	1.20209981	0.83187768	5.38932815	4.48326181	0.18555189	0.22305189	5
6	1.24717855	0.80180981	6.59142796	5.28507162	0.15171219	0.18921219	6
7	1.29394774	0.77282874	7.83860650	6.05790036	0.12757370	0.16507370	7
8	1.34247078	0.74489517	9.13255425	6.80279553	0.10949839	0.14699839	8
9	1.39281344	0.71797125	10.47502503	7.52076677	0.09546517	0.13296517	9
10	1.44504394	0.69202048	11.86783847	8.21278725	0.08426134	0.12176134	10
11	1.49923309	0.66700769	13.31288241	8.87979494	0.07511521	0.11261521	11
12	1.55545433	0.64289898	14.81211550	9.52269392	0.06751230	0.10501230	12
13	1.61378387	0.61966167	16.36756983	10.14235558	0.06109642	0.09859642	13
14	1.67430076	0.59726426	17.98135370	10.73961984	0.05561317	0.09311317	14
15	1.73708704	0.57567639	19.65565447	11.31529623	0.05087595	0.08837595	15
16	1.80222781	0.55486881	21.39274151	11.87016504	0.04674483	0.08424483	16
17	1.86981135	0.53481331	23.19496932	12.40497835	0.04311280	0.08061280	17
18	1.93992927	0.51548271	25.06478067	12.92046106	0.03989662	0.07739662	18
19	2.01267662	0.49685080	27.00470994	13.41731187	0.03703058	0.07453058	19
20	2.08815200	0.47889234	29.01738656	13.89620421	0.03446210	0.07196210	20
21	2.16645770	0.46158298	31.10553856	14.35778719	0.03214862	0.06964862	21
22	2.24769986	0.44489926	33.27199626	14.80268645	0.03005531	0.06755531	22
23	2.33198860	0.42881856	35.51969612	15.23150501	0.02815339	0.06565339	23
24	2.41943818	0.41331910	37.85168472	15.64482411	0.02641890	0.06391890	24
25	2.51016711	0.39837985	40.27112290	16.04320396	0.02483169	0.06233169	25
26	2.60429838	0.38398058	42.78129001	16.42718454	0.02337470	0.06087470	26
27	2.70195956	0.37010176	45.38558838	16.79728630	0.02203343	0.05953343	27
28	2.80328305	0.35672459	48.08754794	17.15401089	0.02079540	0.05829540	28
29	2.90840616	0.34383093	50.89083099	17.49784183	0.01964991	0.05714991	29
30	3.01747139	0.33140331	53.79923715	17.82924513	0.01858762	0.05608762	30
31	3.13062657	0.31942487	56.81670855	18.14867001	0.01760046	0.05510046	31
32	3.24802507	0.30787940	59.94733512	18.45654941	0.01668131	0.05418131	32
33	3.36982601	0.29675123	63.19536019	18.75330063	0.01582395	0.05332395	33
34	3.49619448	0.28602528	66.56518619	19.03932591	0.01502287	0.05252287	34
35	3.62730178	0.27568702	70.06138067	19.31501293	0.01427320	0.05177320	35
36	3.76332559	0.26572242	73.68868245	19.58073535	0.01357060	0.05107060	36
37	3.90445030	0.25611800	77.45200804	19.83685335	0.01291122	0.05041122	37
38	4.05086719	0.24686072	81.35645834	20.08371407	0.01229159	0.04979159	38
39	4.20277471	0.23793805	85.40732553	20.32165212	0.01170860	0.04920860	39
40	4.36037876	0.22933788	89.61010024	20.55098999	0.01115946	0.04865946	40
41	4.52389296	0.22104855	93.97047900	20.77203855	0.01064164	0.04814164	41
42	4.69353895	0.21305885	98.49437196	20.98509739	0.01015286	0.04765286	42
43	4.86954666	0.20535793	103.18791091	21.19045532	0.00969106	0.04719106	43
44	5.05215466	0.19793535	108.05745757	21.38839067	0.00925434	0.04675434	44
45	5.24161046	0.19078106	113.10961223	21.57917173	0.00884098	0.04634098	45
46	5.43817085	0.18388536	118.35122269	21.76305709	0.00844943	0.04594943	46
47	5.64210226	0.17723890	123.78939354	21.94029599	0.00807824	0.04557824	47
48	5.85368109	0.17083268	129.43149579	22.11112866	0.00772609	0.04522609	48
49	6.07319413	0.16465800	135.28517689	22.27578666	0.00739179	0.04489179	49
50	6.30093891	0.15870651	141.35837102	22.43449317	0.00707422	0.04457422	50

Tables 10 Through 12 (continued). Compound Interest

4% n	Table 10.1. Compound amount	Table 10.2. Present value	Table 11.1. Amount of annuity	Table 11.2. Present value of annuity	Table 12.1. Sinking fund	Table 12.2. Amortization	4% n
1	1.04000000	0.96153846	1.00000000	0.96153846	1.00000000	1.04000000	1
2	1.08160000	0.92455621	2.04000000	1.88609467	0.49019608	0.53019608	2
3	1.12486400	0.88899636	3.12160000	2.77509103	0.32034854	0.36034854	3
4	1.16985856	0.85480419	4.24646400	3.62989522	0.23549005	0.27549005	4
5	1.21665290	0.82192711	5.41632256	4.45182233	0.18462711	0.22462711	5
6	1.26531902	0.79031453	6.63297546	5.24213686	0.15076190	0.19076190	6
7	1.31593178	0.75991781	7.89829448	6.00205467	0.12660961	0.16660961	7
8	1.36856905	0.73069021	9.21422626	6.73274487	0.10852783	0.14852783	8
9	1.42331181	0.70258674	10.58279531	7.43533161	0.09449299	0.13449299	9
10	1.48024428	0.67556417	12.00610712	8.11089578	0.08329094	0.12329094	10
11	1.53945406	0.64958093	13.48635141	8.76047671	0.07414904	0.11414904	11
12	1.60103222	0.62459705	15.02580546	9.38507376	0.06655217	0.10655217	12
13	1.66507351	0.60057409	16.62683768	9.98564785	0.06014373	0.10014373	13
14	1.73167645	0.57747508	18.29191119	10.56312293	0.05466897	0.09466897	14
15	1.80094351	0.55526450	20.02358764	11.11838743	0.04994110	0.08994110	15
16	1.87298125	0.53390818	21.82453114	11.65229561	0.04582000	0.08582000	16
17	1.94790050	0.51337325	23.69751239	12.16566885	0.04219852	0.08219852	17
18	2.02581652	0.49362812	25.64541288	12.65929697	0.03899333	0.07899333	18
19	2.10684918	0.47464242	27.67122940	13.13393940	0.03613862	0.07613862	19
20	2.19112314	0.45638695	29.77807858	13.59032634	0.03358175	0.07358175	20
21	2.27876807	0.43883360	31.96920172	14.02915995	0.03128011	0.07128011	21
22	2.36991879	0.42195539	34.24796979	14.45111533	0.02919881	0.06919881	22
23	2.46471554	0.40572633	36.61788858	14.85684167	0.02730906	0.06730906	23
24	2.56330416	0.39012147	39.08260412	15.24696314	0.02558683	0.06558683	24
25	2.66583633	0.37511680	41.64590829	15.62207994	0.02401196	0.06401196	25
26	2.77246978	0.36068923	44.31174462	15.98276918	0.02256738	0.06256738	26
27	2.88336858	0.34681657	47.08421440	16.32958575	0.02123854	0.06123854	27
28	2.99870332	0.33347747	49.96758298	16.66306322	0.02001298	0.06001298	28
29	3.11865145	0.32065141	52.96628630	16.98371463	0.01887993	0.05887993	29
30	3.24339751	0.30831867	56.08493775	17.29203330	0.01783010	0.05783010	30
31	3.37313341	0.29646026	59.32833526	17.58849356	0.01685535	0.05685535	31
32	3.50805875	0.28505794	62.70146867	17.87355150	0.01594859	0.05594859	32
33	3.64838110	0.27409417	66.20952742	18.14764567	0.01510357	0.05510357	33
34	3.79431634	0.26355209	69.85790851	18.41119776	0.01431477	0.05431477	34
35	3.94608899	0.25341547	73.65222486	18.66461323	0.01357732	0.05357732	35
36	4.10393255	0.24366872	77.59831385	18.90828195	0.01288688	0.05288688	36
37	4.26808986	0.23429685	81.70224640	19.14257880	0.01223957	0.05223957	37
38	4.43881345	0.22528543	85.97033626	19.36786423	0.01163192	0.05163192	38
39	4.61636599	0.21662061	90.40914971	19.58448484	0.01106083	0.05106083	39
40	4.80102063	0.20828904	95.02551570	19.79277388	0.01052349	0.05052349	40
41	4.99306145	0.20027793	99.82653633	19.99305181	0.01001738	0.05001738	41
42	5.19278391	0.19257493	104.81959778	20.18562674	0.00954020	0.04954020	42
43	5.40049527	0.18516820	110.01238169	20.37079494	0.00908989	0.04908989	43
44	5.61651508	0.17804635	115.41287696	20.54884129	0.00866454	0.04866454	44
45	5.84117568	0.17119841	121.02939204	20.72003970	0.00826246	0.04826246	45
46	6.07482271	0.16461386	126.87056772	20.88465356	0.00788205	0.04788205	46
47	6.31781562	0.15828256	132.94539043	21.04293612	0.00752189	0.04752189	47
48	6.57052824	0.15219476	139.26320604	21.19513088	0.00718065	0.04718065	48
49	6.83334937	0.14634112	145.83373429	21.34147200	0.00685712	0.04685712	49
50	7.10668335	0.14071262	152.66708366	21.48218462	0.00655020	0.04655020	50

Tables 10 Through 12 (continued). Compound Interest

$4^1/_2\%$ n	Table 10.1. Compound amount	Table 10.2. Present value	Table 11.1. Amount of annuity	Table 11.2. Present value of annuity	Table 12.1. Sinking fund	Table 12.2. Amortization	$4^1/_2\%$ n
1	1.04500000	0.95693780	1.00000000	0.95693780	1.00000000	1.04500000	1
2	1.09202500	0.91572995	2.04500000	1.87266775	0.48899756	0.53399756	2
3	1.14116612	0.87629660	3.13702500	2.74896435	0.31877336	0.36377336	3
4	1.19251860	0.83856134	4.27819112	3.58752570	0.23374365	0.27874365	4
5	1.24618194	0.80245105	5.47070973	4.38997674	0.18279164	0.22779164	5
6	1.30226012	0.76789574	6.71689166	5.15787248	0.14887839	0.19387839	6
7	1.36086183	0.73482846	8.01915179	5.89270094	0.12470147	0.16970147	7
8	1.42210061	0.70318513	9.38001362	6.59588607	0.10660965	0.15160965	8
9	1.48609514	0.67290443	10.80211423	7.26879050	0.09257447	0.13757447	9
10	1.55296942	0.64392768	12.28820937	7.91271818	0.08137882	0.12637882	10
11	1.62285305	0.61619874	13.84117879	8.52891692	0.07224818	0.11724818	11
12	1.69588143	0.58966386	15.46403184	9.11858078	0.06466619	0.10966619	12
13	1.77219610	0.56427164	17.15991327	9.68285242	0.05827535	0.10327535	13
14	1.85194492	0.53997286	18.93210937	10.22282528	0.05282032	0.09782032	14
15	1.93528244	0.51672044	20.78405429	10.73954573	0.04811381	0.09311381	15
16	2.02237015	0.49446932	22.71933673	11.23401505	0.04401537	0.08901537	16
17	2.11337681	0.47317639	24.74170689	11.70719143	0.04041758	0.08541758	17
18	2.20847877	0.45280037	26.85508370	12.15999180	0.03723690	0.08223690	18
19	2.30786031	0.43330179	29.06356246	12.59329359	0.03440734	0.07940734	19
20	2.41171402	0.41464286	31.37142277	13.00793645	0.03187614	0.07687614	20
21	2.52024116	0.39678743	33.78313680	13.40472388	0.02960057	0.07460057	21
22	2.63365201	0.37970089	36.30337795	13.78442476	0.02754565	0.07254565	22
23	2.75216635	0.36335013	38.93702996	14.14777489	0.02568249	0.07068249	23
24	2.87601383	0.34770347	41.68919631	14.49547837	0.02398703	0.06898703	24
25	3.00543446	0.33273060	44.56521015	14.82820896	0.02243903	0.06743903	25
26	3.14067901	0.31840248	47.57064460	15.14661145	0.02102137	0.06602137	26
27	3.28200956	0.30469137	50.71132361	15.45130282	0.01971946	0.06471946	27
28	3.42969999	0.29157069	53.99333317	15.74287351	0.01852081	0.06352081	28
29	3.58403649	0.27901502	57.42303316	16.02188853	0.01741461	0.06241461	29
30	3.74531813	0.26700002	61.00706966	16.28888854	0.01639154	0.06139154	30
31	3.91385745	0.25550241	64.75238779	16.54439095	0.01544345	0.06044345	31
32	4.08998104	0.24449991	68.66624524	16.78889086	0.01456320	0.05956320	32
33	4.27403018	0.23397121	72.75622628	17.02286207	0.01374453	0.05874453	33
34	4.46636154	0.22389589	77.03025646	17.24675796	0.01298191	0.05798191	34
35	4.66734781	0.21425444	81.49661800	17.46101240	0.01227045	0.05727045	35
36	4.87737846	0.20502817	86.16396581	17.66604058	0.01160578	0.05660578	36
37	5.09686049	0.19619921	91.04134427	17.86223979	0.01098402	0.05598402	37
38	5.32621921	0.18775044	96.13820476	18.04999023	0.01040169	0.05540169	38
39	5.56589908	0.17966549	101.46442398	18.22965572	0.00985567	0.05485567	39
40	5.81636454	0.17192870	107.03032306	18.40158442	0.00934315	0.05434315	40
41	6.07810094	0.16452507	112.84668760	18.56610949	0.00886158	0.05386158	41
42	6.35161548	0.15744026	118.92478854	18.72354975	0.00840868	0.05340868	42
43	6.63743818	0.15066054	125.27640402	18.87421029	0.00798235	0.05298235	43
44	6.93612290	0.14417276	131.91384220	19.01838305	0.00758071	0.05258071	44
45	7.24824843	0.13796437	138.84996510	19.15634742	0.00720202	0.05220202	45
46	7.57441961	0.13202332	146.09821353	19.28837074	0.00684471	0.05184471	46
47	7.91526849	0.12633810	153.67263314	19.41470884	0.00650734	0.05150734	47
48	8.27145557	0.12089771	161.58790163	19.53560654	0.00618858	0.05118858	48
49	8.64367107	0.11569158	169.85935720	19.65129813	0.00588722	0.05088722	49
50	9.03263627	0.11070965	178.50302828	19.76200778	0.00560215	0.05060215	50

Tables 10 Through 12 (continued). Compound Interest

5% n	Table 10.1. Compound amount	Table 10.2. Present value	Table 11.1. Amount of annuity	Table 11.2. Present value of annuity	Table 12.1. Sinking fund	Table 12.2. Amortization	5% n
1	1.05000000	0.95238095	1.00000000	0.95238095	1.00000000	1.05000000	1
2	1.10250000	0.90702948	2.05000000	1.85941043	0.48780488	0.53780488	2
3	1.15762500	0.86383760	3.15250000	2.72324803	0.31720856	0.36720856	3
4	1.21550625	0.82270247	4.31012500	3.54595050	0.23201183	0.28201183	4
5	1.27628156	0.78352617	5.52563125	4.32947667	0.18097480	0.23097480	5
6	1.34009564	0.74621540	6.80191281	5.07569207	0.14701747	0.19701747	6
7	1.40710042	0.71068133	8.14200845	5.78637340	0.12281982	0.17281982	7
8	1.47745544	0.67683936	9.54910888	6.46321276	0.10472181	0.15472181	8
9	1.55132822	0.64460892	11.02656432	7.10782168	0.09069008	0.14069008	9
10	1.62889463	0.61391325	12.57789254	7.72173493	0.07950457	0.12950457	10
11	1.71033936	0.58467929	14.20678716	8.30641422	0.07038889	0.12038889	11
12	1.79585633	0.55683742	15.91712652	8.86325164	0.06282541	0.11282541	12
13	1.88564914	0.53032135	17.71298285	9.39357299	0.05645577	0.10645577	13
14	1.97993160	0.50506795	19.59863199	9.89864094	0.05102397	0.10102397	14
15	2.07892818	0.48101710	21.57856359	10.37965804	0.04634229	0.09634229	15
16	2.18287459	0.45811152	23.65749177	10.83776956	0.04226991	0.09226991	16
17	2.29201832	0.43629669	25.84036636	11.27406625	0.03869914	0.08869914	17
18	2.40661923	0.41552065	28.13238467	11.68958690	0.03554622	0.08554622	18
19	2.52695020	0.39573396	30.53900391	12.08532086	0.03274501	0.08274501	19
20	2.65329771	0.37688948	33.06595410	12.46221034	0.03024259	0.08024259	20
21	2.78596259	0.35894236	35.71925181	12.82115271	0.02799611	0.07799611	21
22	2.92526072	0.34184987	38.50521440	13.16300258	0.02597051	0.07597051	22
23	3.07152376	0.32557131	41.43047512	13.48857388	0.02413682	0.07413682	23
24	3.22509994	0.31006791	44.50199887	13.79864179	0.02247090	0.07247090	24
25	3.38635494	0.29530277	47.72709882	14.09394457	0.02095246	0.07095246	25
26	3.55567269	0.28124073	51.11345376	14.37518530	0.01956432	0.06956432	26
27	3.73345632	0.26784832	54.66912645	14.64303362	0.01829186	0.06829186	27
28	3.92012914	0.25509364	58.40258277	14.89812726	0.01712253	0.06712253	28
29	4.11613560	0.24294632	62.32271191	15.14107358	0.01604551	0.06604551	29
30	4.32194238	0.23137745	66.43884750	15.37245103	0.01505144	0.06505144	30
31	4.53803949	0.22035947	70.76078988	15.59281050	0.01413212	0.06413212	31
32	4.76494147	0.20986617	75.29882937	15.80267667	0.01328042	0.06328042	32
33	5.00318854	0.19987254	80.06377084	16.00254921	0.01249004	0.06249004	33
34	5.25334797	0.19035480	85.06695938	16.19290401	0.01175545	0.06175545	34
35	5.51601537	0.18129029	90.32030735	16.37419429	0.01107171	0.06107171	35
36	5.79181614	0.17265741	95.83632272	16.54685171	0.01043446	0.06043446	36
37	6.08140694	0.16443563	101.62813886	16.71128734	0.00983979	0.05983979	37
38	6.38547729	0.15660536	107.70954580	16.86789271	0.00928423	0.05928423	38
39	6.70475115	0.14914797	114.09502309	17.01704067	0.00876462	0.05876462	39
40	7.03998871	0.14204568	120.79977424	17.15908635	0.00827816	0.05827816	40
41	7.39198815	0.13528160	127.83976295	17.29436796	0.00782229	0.05782229	41
42	7.76158756	0.12883962	135.23175110	17.42320758	0.00739471	0.05739471	42
43	8.14966693	0.12270440	142.99333866	17.54591198	0.00699333	0.05699333	43
44	8.55715028	0.11686133	151.14300559	17.66277331	0.00661625	0.05661625	44
45	8.98500779	0.11129651	159.70015587	17.77406982	0.00626173	0.05626173	45
46	9.43425818	0.10599668	168.68516366	17.88006650	0.00592820	0.05592820	46
47	9.90597109	0.10094921	178.11942185	17.98101571	0.00561421	0.05561421	47
48	10.40126965	0.09614211	188.02539294	18.07715782	0.00531843	0.05531843	48
49	10.92133313	0.09156391	198.42666259	18.16872173	0.00503965	0.05503965	49
50	11.46739979	0.08720373	209.34799572	18.25592546	0.00477674	0.05477674	50

Tables 10 Through 12 (continued). Compound Interest

5¹/₂% n	Table 10.1. Compound amount	Table 10.2. Present value	Table 11.1. Amount of annuity	Table 11.2. Present value of annuity	Table 12.1. Sinking fund	Table 12.2. Amortization	5¹/₂% n
1	1.05500000	0.94786730	1.00000000	0.94786730	1.00000000	1.05500000	1
2	1.11302500	0.89845242	2.05500000	1.84631971	0.48661800	0.54161800	2
3	1.17424137	0.85161366	3.16802500	2.69793338	0.31565407	0.37065407	3
4	1.23882465	0.80721674	4.34226638	3.50515012	0.23029449	0.28529449	4
5	1.30696001	0.76513435	5.58109103	4.27028448	0.17917644	0.23417644	5
6	1.37884281	0.72524583	6.88805103	4.99553031	0.14517895	0.20017895	6
7	1.45467916	0.68743681	8.26689384	5.68296712	0.12096442	0.17596442	7
8	1.53468651	0.65159887	9.72157300	6.33456599	0.10286401	0.15786401	8
9	1.61909427	0.61762926	11.25625951	6.95219525	0.08883946	0.14383946	9
10	1.70814446	0.58543058	12.87535379	7.53762583	0.07766777	0.13266777	10
11	1.80209240	0.55491050	14.58349825	8.09253633	0.06857065	0.12357065	11
12	1.90120749	0.52598152	16.38559065	8.61851785	0.06102923	0.11602923	12
13	2.00577390	0.49856068	18.28679814	9.11707853	0.05468426	0.10968426	13
14	2.11609146	0.47256937	20.29257203	9.58964790	0.04927912	0.10427912	14
15	2.23247649	0.44793305	22.40866350	10.03758094	0.04462560	0.09962560	15
16	2.35526270	0.42458109	24.64113999	10.46216203	0.04058254	0.09558254	16
17	2.48480215	0.40244653	26.99640269	10.86460856	0.03704197	0.09204197	17
18	2.62146627	0.38146590	29.48120483	11.24607447	0.03391992	0.08891992	18
19	2.76564691	0.36157906	32.10267110	11.60765352	0.03115006	0.08615006	19
20	2.91775749	0.34272896	34.86831801	11.95038248	0.02867933	0.08367933	20
21	3.07823415	0.32486158	37.78607550	12.27524406	0.02646478	0.08146478	21
22	3.24753703	0.30792567	40.86430965	12.58316973	0.02447123	0.07947123	22
23	3.42615157	0.29187267	44.11184669	12.87504239	0.02266965	0.07766965	23
24	3.61458990	0.27665656	47.53799825	13.15169895	0.02103580	0.07603580	24
25	3.81339235	0.26223370	51.15258816	13.41393266	0.01954935	0.07454935	25
26	4.02312893	0.24856275	54.96598051	13.66249541	0.01819307	0.07319307	26
27	4.24440102	0.23560450	58.98910943	13.89809991	0.01695228	0.07195228	27
28	4.47784307	0.22332181	63.23351045	14.12142172	0.01581440	0.07081440	28
29	4.72412444	0.21167944	67.71135353	14.33310116	0.01476857	0.06976857	29
30	4.98395129	0.20064402	72.43547797	14.53374517	0.01380539	0.06880539	30
31	5.25806861	0.19018390	77.41942926	14.72392907	0.01291665	0.06791665	31
32	5.54726238	0.18026910	82.67749787	14.90419817	0.01209519	0.06709519	32
33	5.85236181	0.17087119	88.22476025	15.07506936	0.01133469	0.06633469	33
34	6.17424171	0.16196321	94.07712207	15.23703257	0.01062958	0.06562958	34
35	6.51382501	0.15351963	100.25136378	15.39055220	0.00997493	0.06497493	35
36	6.87208538	0.14551624	106.76518879	15.53606843	0.00936635	0.06436635	36
37	7.25005008	0.13793008	113.63727417	15.67399851	0.00879993	0.06379993	37
38	7.64880283	0.13073941	120.88732425	15.80473793	0.00827217	0.06327217	38
39	8.06948699	0.12392362	128.53612708	15.92866154	0.00777991	0.06277991	39
40	8.51330877	0.11746314	136.60561407	16.04612469	0.00732034	0.06232034	40
41	8.98154076	0.11133947	145.11892285	16.15746416	0.00689090	0.06189090	41
42	9.47552550	0.10553504	154.10046360	16.26299920	0.00648927	0.06148927	42
43	9.99667940	0.10003322	163.57598910	16.36303242	0.00611337	0.06111337	43
44	10.54649677	0.09481822	173.57266850	16.45785063	0.00576128	0.06076128	44
45	11.12655409	0.08987509	184.11916527	16.54772572	0.00543127	0.06043127	45
46	11.73851456	0.08518965	195.24571936	16.63291537	0.00512175	0.06012175	46
47	12.38413287	0.08074849	206.98423392	16.71366386	0.00483129	0.05983129	47
48	13.06526017	0.07653885	219.36836679	16.79020271	0.00455854	0.05955854	48
49	13.78384948	0.07254867	232.43362696	16.86275139	0.00430230	0.05930230	49
50	14.54196120	0.06876652	246.21747645	16.93151790	0.00406145	0.05906145	50

Tables 10 Through 12 (continued). Compound Interest

6%	Table 10.1. Compound amount	Table 10.2. Present value	Table 11.1. Amount of annuity	Table 11.2. Present value of annuity	Table 12.1. Sinking fund	Table 12.2. Amortization	6%
n							n
1	1.06000000	0.94339623	1.00000000	0.94339623	1.00000000	1.06000000	1
2	1.12360000	0.88999644	2.06000000	1.83339267	0.48543689	0.54543689	2
3	1.19101600	0.83961928	3.18360000	2.67301195	0.31410981	0.37410981	3
4	1.26247696	0.79209366	4.37461600	3.46510561	0.22859149	0.28859149	4
5	1.33822558	0.74725817	5.63709296	4.21236379	0.17739640	0.23739640	5
6	1.41851911	0.70496054	6.97531854	4.91732433	0.14336263	0.20336263	6
7	1.50363026	0.66505711	8.39383765	5.58238144	0.11913502	0.17913502	7
8	1.59384807	0.62741237	9.89746791	6.20979381	0.10103594	0.16103594	8
9	1.68947896	0.59189846	11.49131598	6.80169227	0.08702224	0.14702224	9
10	1.79084770	0.55839478	13.18079494	7.36008705	0.07586796	0.13586796	10
11	1.89829856	0.52678753	14.97164264	7.88687458	0.06679294	0.12679294	11
12	2.01219647	0.49696936	16.86994120	8.38384394	0.05927703	0.11927703	12
13	2.13292826	0.46883902	18.88213767	8.85268296	0.05296011	0.11296011	13
14	2.26090396	0.44230096	21.01506593	9.29498393	0.04758491	0.10758491	14
15	2.39655819	0.41726506	23.27596988	9.71224899	0.04296276	0.10296276	15
16	2.54035168	0.39364628	25.67252808	10.10589527	0.03895214	0.09895214	16
17	2.69277279	0.37136442	28.21287976	10.47725969	0.03544480	0.09544480	17
18	2.85433915	0.35034379	30.90565255	10.82760348	0.03235654	0.09235654	18
19	3.02559950	0.33051301	33.75999170	11.15811649	0.02962086	0.08962086	19
20	3.20713547	0.31180473	36.78559120	11.46992122	0.02718456	0.08718456	20
21	3.39956360	0.29415540	39.99272668	11.76407662	0.02500455	0.08500455	21
22	3.60353742	0.27750510	43.39229028	12.04158172	0.02304457	0.08304457	22
23	3.81974966	0.26179726	46.99582769	12.30337898	0.02127848	0.08127848	23
24	4.04893464	0.24697855	50.81557735	12.55035753	0.01967900	0.07967900	24
25	4.29187072	0.23299863	54.86451200	12.78335616	0.01822672	0.07822672	25
26	4.54938296	0.21981003	59.15638272	13.00316619	0.01690435	0.07690435	26
27	4.82234594	0.20736795	63.70576568	13.21053414	0.01569717	0.07569717	27
28	5.11168670	0.19563014	68.52811162	13.40616428	0.01459255	0.07459255	28
29	5.41838790	0.18455674	73.63979832	13.59072102	0.01357961	0.07357961	29
30	5.74349117	0.17411013	79.05818622	13.76483115	0.01264891	0.07264891	30
31	6.08810064	0.16425484	84.80167739	13.92908599	0.01179222	0.07179222	31
32	6.45338668	0.15495740	90.88977803	14.08404339	0.01100234	0.07100234	32
33	6.84058988	0.14618622	97.34316471	14.23022961	0.01027293	0.07027293	33
34	7.25102528	0.13791153	104.18375460	14.36814114	0.00959843	0.06959843	34
35	7.68608679	0.13010522	111.43477987	14.49824636	0.00897386	0.06897386	35
36	8.14725200	0.12274077	119.12086666	14.62098713	0.00839483	0.06839483	36
37	8.63608712	0.11579318	127.26811866	14.73678031	0.00785743	0.06785743	37
38	9.15425235	0.10923885	135.90420578	14.84601916	0.00735812	0.06735812	38
39	9.70350749	0.10305552	145.05845813	14.94907468	0.00689377	0.06689377	39
40	10.28571794	0.09722219	154.76196562	15.04629687	0.00646154	0.06646154	40
41	10.90286101	0.09171905	165.04768356	15.13801592	0.00605886	0.06605886	41
42	11.55703267	0.08652740	175.95054457	15.22454332	0.00568342	0.06568342	42
43	12.25045463	0.08162962	187.50757724	15.30617294	0.00533312	0.06533312	43
44	12.98548191	0.07700908	199.75803188	15.38318202	0.00500606	0.06500606	44
45	13.76461083	0.07265007	212.74351379	15.45583209	0.00470050	0.06470050	45
46	14.59048748	0.06853781	226.50812462	15.52436990	0.00441485	0.06441485	46
47	15.46591673	0.06465831	241.09861210	15.58902821	0.00414768	0.06414768	47
48	16.39387173	0.06099840	256.56452882	15.65002661	0.00389765	0.06389765	48
49	17.37750403	0.05754566	272.95840055	15.70757227	0.00366356	0.06366356	49
50	18.42015427	0.05428836	290.33590458	15.76186064	0.00344429	0.06344429	50

Tables 10 Through 12 (continued). Compound Interest

6½%	Table 10.1. Compound amount	Table 10.2. Present value	Table 11.1. Amount of annuity	Table 11.2. Present value of annuity	Table 12.1. Sinking fund	Table 12.2. Amortization	6½%
n							n
1	1.06500000	0.93896714	1.00000000	0.93896714	1.00000000	1.06500000	1
2	1.13422500	0.88165928	2.06500000	1.82062642	0.48426150	0.54926150	2
3	1.20794963	0.82784909	3.19922500	2.64847551	0.31257570	0.37757570	3
4	1.28646635	0.77732309	4.40717463	3.42579860	0.22690274	0.29190274	4
5	1.37008666	0.72988084	5.69364098	4.15567944	0.17563454	0.24063454	5
6	1.45914230	0.68533412	7.06372764	4.84101356	0.14156831	0.20656831	6
7	1.55398655	0.64350621	8.52286994	5.48451977	0.11733137	0.18233137	7
8	1.65499567	0.60423119	10.07685648	6.08875096	0.09923730	0.16423730	8
9	1.76257039	0.56735323	11.73185215	6.65610419	0.08523803	0.15023803	9
10	1.87713747	0.53272604	13.49442254	7.18883022	0.07410469	0.13910469	10
11	1.99915140	0.50021224	15.37156001	7.68904246	0.06505521	0.13005521	11
12	2.12909624	0.46968285	17.37071141	8.15872532	0.05756817	0.12256817	12
13	2.26748750	0.44101676	19.49980765	8.59974208	0.05128256	0.11628256	13
14	2.41487418	0.41410025	21.76729515	9.01384233	0.04594048	0.11094048	14
15	2.57184101	0.38882652	24.18216933	9.40266885	0.04135278	0.10635278	15
16	2.73901067	0.36509533	26.75401034	9.76776418	0.03737757	0.10237757	16
17	2.91704637	0.34281251	29.49302101	10.11057670	0.03390633	0.09890633	17
18	3.10665438	0.32188969	32.41006738	10.43246638	0.03085461	0.09585461	18
19	3.30858691	0.30224384	35.51672176	10.73471022	0.02815575	0.09315575	19
20	3.52364506	0.28379703	38.82530867	11.01850725	0.02575640	0.09075640	20
21	3.75268199	0.26647608	42.34895373	11.28498333	0.02361333	0.08861333	21
22	3.99660632	0.25021228	46.10163573	11.53519562	0.02169120	0.08669120	22
23	4.25638573	0.23494111	50.09824205	11.77013673	0.01996078	0.08496078	23
24	4.53305081	0.22060198	54.35462778	11.99073871	0.01839770	0.08339770	24
25	4.82769911	0.20713801	58.88767859	12.19787673	0.01698148	0.08198148	25
26	5.14149955	0.19449579	63.71537769	12.39237251	0.01569480	0.08069480	26
27	5.47569702	0.18262515	68.85687725	12.57499766	0.01452288	0.07952288	27
28	5.83161733	0.17147902	74.33257427	12.74647668	0.01345305	0.07845305	28
29	6.21067245	0.16101316	80.16419159	12.90748984	0.01247440	0.07747440	29
30	6.61436616	0.15118607	86.37486405	13.05867591	0.01157744	0.07657744	30
31	7.04429996	0.14195875	92.98923021	13.20063465	0.01075393	0.07575393	31
32	7.50217946	0.13329460	100.03353017	13.33392925	0.00999665	0.07499665	32
33	7.98982113	0.12515925	107.53570963	13.45908850	0.00929924	0.07429924	33
34	8.50915950	0.11752042	115.52553076	13.57660892	0.00865610	0.07365610	34
35	9.06225487	0.11034781	124.03469026	13.68695673	0.00806226	0.07306226	35
36	9.65130143	0.10361297	133.09694513	13.79056970	0.00751332	0.07251332	36
37	10.27863603	0.09728917	142.74824656	13.88785867	0.00700534	0.07200534	37
38	10.94674737	0.09135134	153.02688259	13.97921021	0.00653480	0.07153480	38
39	11.65828595	0.08577590	163.97362996	14.06498611	0.00609854	0.07109854	39
40	12.41607453	0.08054075	175.63191590	14.14552687	0.00569373	0.07069373	40
41	13.22311938	0.07562512	188.04799044	14.22115199	0.00531779	0.07031779	41
42	14.08262214	0.07100950	201.27110981	14.29216149	0.00496842	0.06996842	42
43	14.99799258	0.06667559	215.35373195	14.35883708	0.00464352	0.06964352	43
44	15.97286209	0.06260619	230.35172453	14.42144327	0.00434119	0.06934119	44
45	17.01109813	0.05878515	246.32458662	14.48022842	0.00405968	0.06905968	45
46	18.11681951	0.05519733	263.33568475	14.53542575	0.00379743	0.06879743	46
47	19.29441278	0.05182848	281.45250426	14.58725422	0.00355300	0.06855300	47
48	20.54854961	0.04866524	300.74691704	14.63591946	0.00332505	0.06832505	48
49	21.88420533	0.04569506	321.29546665	14.68161451	0.00311240	0.06811240	49
50	23.30667868	0.04290616	343.17967198	14.72452067	0.00291393	0.06791393	50

Tables 10 Through 12 (continued). Compound Interest

7%	Table 10.1. Compound	Table 10.2. Present	Table 11.1. Amount of	Table 11.2. Present value	Table 12.1. Sinking	Table 12.2.	7%
n	amount	value	annuity	of annuity	fund	Amortization	n
1	1.07000000	0.93457944	1.00000000	0.93457944	1.00000000	1.07000000	1
2	1.14490000	0.87343873	2.07000000	1.80801817	0.48309179	0.55309179	2
3	1.22504300	0.81629788	3.21490000	2.62431604	0.31105167	0.38105167	3
4	1.31079601	0.76289521	4.43994300	3.38721126	0.22522812	0.29522812	4
5	1.40255173	0.71298618	5.75073901	4.10019744	0.17389069	0.24389069	5
6	1.50073035	0.66634222	7.15329074	4.76653966	0.13979580	0.20979580	6
7	1.60578148	0.62274974	8.65402109	5.38928940	0.11555322	0.18555322	7
8	1.71818618	0.58200910	10.25980257	5.97129851	0.09746776	0.16746776	8
9	1.83845921	0.54393374	11.97798875	6.51523225	0.08348647	0.15348647	9
10	1.96715136	0.50834929	13.81644796	7.02358154	0.07237750	0.14237750	10
11	2.10485195	0.47509280	15.78359932	7.49867434	0.06335690	0.13335690	11
12	2.25219159	0.44401196	17.88845127	7.94268630	0.05590199	0.12590199	12
13	2.40984500	0.41496445	20.14064286	8.35765074	0.04965085	0.11965085	13
14	2.57853415	0.38781724	22.55048786	8.74546799	0.04434494	0.11434494	14
15	2.75903154	0.36244602	25.12902201	9.10791401	0.03979462	0.10979462	15
16	2.95216375	0.33873460	27.88805355	9.44664860	0.03585765	0.10585765	16
17	3.15881521	0.31657439	30.84021730	9.76322299	0.03242519	0.10242519	17
18	3.37993228	0.29586392	33.99903251	10.05908691	0.02941260	0.09941260	18
19	3.61652754	0.27650833	37.37896479	10.33559524	0.02675301	0.09675301	19
20	3.86968446	0.25841900	40.99549232	10.59401425	0.02439293	0.09439293	20
21	4.14056237	0.24151309	44.86517678	10.83552733	0.02228900	0.09228900	21
22	4.43040174	0.22571317	49.00573916	11.06124050	0.02040577	0.09040577	22
23	4.74052986	0.21094688	53.43614090	11.27218738	0.01871393	0.08871393	23
24	5.07236695	0.19714662	58.17667076	11.46933400	0.01718902	0.08718902	24
25	5.42743264	0.18424918	63.24903772	11.65358318	0.01581052	0.08581052	25
26	5.80735292	0.17219549	68.67647036	11.82577867	0.01456103	0.08456103	26
27	6.21386763	0.16093037	74.48382328	11.98670904	0.01342573	0.08342573	27
28	6.64883836	0.15040221	80.69769091	12.13711125	0.01239193	0.08239193	28
29	7.11425705	0.14056282	87.34652927	12.27767407	0.01144865	0.08144865	29
30	7.61225504	0.13136712	94.46078632	12.40904118	0.01058640	0.08058640	30
31	8.14511290	0.12277301	102.07304137	12.53181419	0.00979691	0.07979691	31
32	8.71527080	0.11474113	110.21815426	12.64655532	0.00907292	0.07907292	32
33	9.32533975	0.10723470	118.93342506	12.75379002	0.00840807	0.07840807	33
34	9.97811354	0.10021934	128.25876481	12.85400936	0.00779674	0.07779674	34
35	10.67658148	0.09366294	138.23687835	12.94767230	0.00723396	0.07723396	35
36	11.42394219	0.08753546	148.91345984	13.03520776	0.00671531	0.07671531	36
37	12.22361814	0.08180884	160.33740202	13.11701660	0.00623685	0.07623685	37
38	13.07927141	0.07645686	172.56102017	13.19347345	0.00579505	0.07579505	38
39	13.99482041	0.07145501	185.64029158	13.26492846	0.00538676	0.07538676	39
40	14.97445784	0.06678038	199.63511199	13.33170884	0.00500914	0.07500914	40
41	16.02266989	0.06241157	214.60956983	13.39412041	0.00465962	0.07465962	41
42	17.14425678	0.05832857	230.63223972	13.45244898	0.00433591	0.07433591	42
43	18.34435475	0.05451268	247.77649650	13.50696167	0.00403590	0.07403590	43
44	19.62845959	0.05094643	266.12085125	13.55790810	0.00375769	0.07375769	44
45	21.00245176	0.04761349	285.74931084	13.60552159	0.00349957	0.07349957	45
46	22.47262338	0.04449859	306.75176260	13.65002018	0.00325996	0.07325996	46
47	24.04570702	0.04158747	329.22438598	13.69160764	0.00303744	0.07303744	47
48	25.72890651	0.03886679	353.27009300	13.73047443	0.00283070	0.07283070	48
49	27.52992997	0.03632410	378.99899951	13.76679853	0.00263853	0.07263853	49
50	29.45702506	0.03394776	406.52892947	13.80074629	0.00245985	0.07245985	50

Tables 10 Through 12 (continued). Compound Interest

$7^1/_2\%$ n	Table 10.1. Compound amount	Table 10.2. Present value	Table 11.1. Amount of annuity	Table 11.2. Present value of annuity	Table 12.1. Sinking fund	Table 12.2. Amortization	$7^1/_2\%$ n
1	1.07500000	0.93023256	1.00000000	0.93023256	1.00000000	1.07500000	1
2	1.15562500	0.86533261	2.07500000	1.79556517	0.48192771	0.55692771	2
3	1.24229688	0.80496057	3.23062500	2.60052574	0.30953763	0.38453763	3
4	1.33546914	0.74880053	4.47292188	3.34932627	0.22356751	0.29856751	4
5	1.43562933	0.69655863	5.80839102	4.04588490	0.17216472	0.24716472	5
6	1.54330153	0.64796152	7.24402034	4.69384642	0.13804489	0.21304489	6
7	1.65904914	0.60275490	8.78732187	5.29660132	0.11380032	0.18880032	7
8	1.78347783	0.56070223	10.44637101	5.85730355	0.09572702	0.17072702	8
9	1.91723866	0.52158347	12.22984883	6.37888703	0.08176716	0.15676716	9
10	2.06103156	0.48519393	14.14708750	6.86408096	0.07068593	0.14568593	10
11	2.21560893	0.45134319	16.20811906	7.31542415	0.06169747	0.13669747	11
12	2.38177960	0.41985413	18.42372799	7.73527827	0.05427783	0.12927783	12
13	2.56041307	0.39056198	20.80550759	8.12584026	0.04806420	0.12306420	13
14	2.75244405	0.36331347	23.36592066	8.48915373	0.04279737	0.11779737	14
15	2.95887735	0.33796602	26.11836470	8.82711975	0.03828724	0.11328724	15
16	3.18079315	0.31438699	29.07724206	9.14150674	0.03439116	0.10939116	16
17	3.41935264	0.29245302	32.25803521	9.43395976	0.03100003	0.10600003	17
18	3.67580409	0.27204932	35.67738785	9.70600908	0.02802896	0.10302896	18
19	3.95148940	0.25306913	39.35319194	9.95907821	0.02541090	0.10041090	19
20	4.24785110	0.23541315	43.30468134	10.19449136	0.02309219	0.09809219	20
21	4.56643993	0.21898897	47.55253244	10.41348033	0.02102937	0.09602937	21
22	4.90892293	0.20371067	52.11897237	10.61719101	0.01918687	0.09418687	22
23	5.27709215	0.18949830	57.02789530	10.80668931	0.01753528	0.09253528	23
24	5.67287406	0.17627749	62.30498744	10.98296680	0.01605008	0.09105008	24
25	6.09833961	0.16397906	67.97786150	11.14694586	0.01471067	0.08971067	25
26	6.55571508	0.15253866	74.07620112	11.29948452	0.01349961	0.08849961	26
27	7.04739371	0.14189643	80.63191620	11.44138095	0.01240204	0.08740204	27
28	7.57594824	0.13199668	87.67930991	11.57337763	0.01140520	0.08640520	28
29	8.14414436	0.12278761	95.25525816	11.69616524	0.01049811	0.08549811	29
30	8.75495519	0.11422103	103.39940252	11.81038627	0.00967124	0.08467124	30
31	9.41157683	0.10625212	112.15435771	11.91663839	0.00891628	0.08391628	31
32	10.11744509	0.09883918	121.56593454	12.01547757	0.00822599	0.08322599	32
33	10.87625347	0.09194343	131.68337963	12.10742099	0.00759397	0.08259397	33
34	11.69197248	0.08552877	142.55963310	12.19294976	0.00701461	0.08201461	34
35	12.56887042	0.07956164	154.25160558	12.27251141	0.00648291	0.08148291	35
36	13.51153570	0.07401083	166.82047600	12.34652224	0.00599447	0.08099447	36
37	14.52490088	0.06884729	180.33201170	12.41536952	0.00554533	0.08054533	37
38	15.61426844	0.06404209	194.85691258	12.47941351	0.00513197	0.08013197	38
39	16.78533858	0.05957580	210.47118102	12.53898931	0.00475124	0.07975124	39
40	18.04423897	0.05541935	227.25651960	12.59440866	0.00440031	0.07940031	40
41	19.39755689	0.05155288	245.30075857	12.64596155	0.00407663	0.07907663	41
42	20.85237366	0.04795617	264.69831546	12.69391772	0.00377789	0.07877789	42
43	22.41630168	0.04461039	285.55068912	12.73852811	0.00350201	0.07850201	43
44	24.09752431	0.04149804	307.96699080	12.78002615	0.00324710	0.07824710	44
45	25.90483863	0.03860283	332.06451511	12.81862898	0.00301146	0.07801146	45
46	27.84770153	0.03590961	357.96935375	12.85453858	0.00279354	0.07779354	46
47	29.93627915	0.03340428	385.81705528	12.88794287	0.00259190	0.07759190	47
48	32.18150008	0.03107375	415.75333442	12.91901662	0.00240527	0.07740527	48
49	34.59511259	0.02890582	447.93483451	12.94792244	0.00223247	0.07723247	49
50	37.18974603	0.02688913	482.52994709	12.97481157	0.00207241	0.07707241	50

Tables 10 Through 12 (continued). Compound Interest

8% n	Table 10.1. Compound amount	Table 10.2. Present value	Table 11.1. Amount of annuity	Table 11.2. Present value of annuity	Table 12.1. Sinking fund	Table 12.2. Amortization	8% n
1	1.08000000	0.92592593	1.00000000	0.92592593	1.00000000	1.08000000	1
2	1.16640000	0.85733882	2.08000000	1.78326475	0.48076923	0.56076923	2
3	1.25971200	0.79383224	3.24640000	2.57709699	0.30803351	0.38803351	3
4	1.36048896	0.73502985	4.50611200	3.31212684	0.22192080	0.30192080	4
5	1.46932808	0.68058320	5.86660096	3.99271004	0.17045645	0.25045645	5
6	1.58687432	0.63016963	7.33592904	4.62287966	0.13631539	0.21631539	6
7	1.71382427	0.58349040	8.92280336	5.20637006	0.11207240	0.19207240	7
8	1.85093021	0.54026888	10.63662763	5.74663894	0.09401476	0.17401476	8
9	1.99900463	0.50024897	12.48755784	6.24688791	0.08007971	0.16007971	9
10	2.15892500	0.46319349	14.48656247	6.71008140	0.06902949	0.14902949	10
11	2.33163900	0.42888286	16.64548746	7.13896426	0.06007634	0.14007634	11
12	2.51817012	0.39711376	18.97712646	7.53607802	0.05269502	0.13269502	12
13	2.71962373	0.36769792	21.49529658	7.90377594	0.04652181	0.12652181	13
14	2.93719362	0.34046104	24.21492030	8.24423698	0.04129685	0.12129685	14
15	3.17216911	0.31524170	27.15211393	8.55947869	0.03682954	0.11682954	15
16	3.42594264	0.29189047	30.32428304	8.85136916	0.03297687	0.11297687	16
17	3.70001805	0.27026895	33.75022569	9.12163811	0.02962943	0.10962943	17
18	3.99601950	0.25024903	37.45024374	9.37188714	0.02670210	0.10670210	18
19	4.31570106	0.23171206	41.44626324	9.60359920	0.02412763	0.10412763	19
20	4.66095714	0.21454821	45.76196430	9.81814741	0.02185221	0.10185221	20
21	5.03383372	0.19865575	50.42292144	10.01680316	0.01983225	0.09983225	21
22	5.43654041	0.18394051	55.45675516	10.20074366	0.01803207	0.09803207	22
23	5.87146365	0.17031528	60.89329557	10.37105895	0.01642217	0.09642217	23
24	6.34118074	0.15769934	66.76475922	10.52875828	0.01497796	0.09497796	24
25	6.84847520	0.14601790	73.10593995	10.67477619	0.01367878	0.09367878	25
26	7.39635321	0.13520176	79.95441515	10.80997795	0.01250713	0.09250713	26
27	7.98806147	0.12518682	87.35076836	10.93516477	0.01144810	0.09144810	27
28	8.62710639	0.11591372	95.33882983	11.05107849	0.01048891	0.09048891	28
29	9.31727490	0.10732752	103.96593622	11.15840601	0.00961854	0.08961854	29
30	10.06265689	0.09937733	113.28321111	11.25778334	0.00882743	0.08882743	30
31	10.86766944	0.09201605	123.34586800	11.34979939	0.00810728	0.08810728	31
32	11.73708300	0.08520005	134.21353744	11.43499944	0.00745081	0.08745081	32
33	12.67604964	0.07888893	145.95062044	11.51388837	0.00685163	0.08685163	33
34	13.69013361	0.07304531	158.62667007	11.58693367	0.00630411	0.08630411	34
35	14.78534429	0.06763454	172.31680368	11.65456822	0.00580326	0.08580326	35
36	15.96817184	0.06262458	187.10214797	11.71719279	0.00534467	0.08534467	36
37	17.24562558	0.05798572	203.07031981	11.77517851	0.00492440	0.08492440	37
38	18.62527563	0.05369048	220.31594540	11.82886899	0.00453894	0.08453894	38
39	20.11529768	0.04971341	238.94122103	11.87858240	0.00418513	0.08418513	39
40	21.72452150	0.04603093	259.05651871	11.92461333	0.00386016	0.08386016	40
41	23.46248322	0.04262123	280.78104021	11.96723457	0.00356149	0.08356149	41
42	25.33948187	0.03946411	304.24352342	12.00669867	0.00328684	0.08328684	42
43	27.36664042	0.03654084	329.58300530	12.04323951	0.00303414	0.08303414	43
44	29.55597166	0.03383411	356.94964572	12.07707362	0.00280152	0.08280152	44
45	31.92044939	0.03132788	386.50561738	12.10840150	0.00258728	0.08258728	45
46	34.47408534	0.02900730	418.42606677	12.13740880	0.00238991	0.08238991	46
47	37.23201217	0.02685861	452.90015211	12.16426741	0.00220799	0.08220799	47
48	40.21057314	0.02486908	490.13216428	12.18913649	0.00204027	0.08204027	48
49	43.42741899	0.02302693	530.34273742	12.21216341	0.00188557	0.08188557	49
50	46.90161251	0.02132123	573.77015642	12.23348464	0.00174286	0.08174286	50

Tables 10 Through 12 (continued). Compound Interest

8¹/₂% n	Table 10.1. Compound amount	Table 10.2. Present value	Table 11.1. Amount of annuity	Table 11.2. Present value of annuity	Table 12.1. Sinking fund	Table 12.2. Amortization	8¹/₂% n
1	1.08500000	0.92165899	1.00000000	0.92165899	1.00000000	1.08500000	1
2	1.17722500	0.84945529	2.08500000	1.77111427	0.47961631	0.56461631	2
3	1.27728913	0.78290810	3.26222500	2.55402237	0.30653925	0.39153925	3
4	1.38585870	0.72157428	4.53951413	3.27559666	0.22028789	0.30528789	4
5	1.50365669	0.66504542	5.92537283	3.94064208	0.16876575	0.25376575	5
6	1.63146751	0.61294509	7.42902952	4.55358717	0.13460708	0.21960708	6
7	1.77014225	0.56492635	9.06049702	5.11851352	0.11036922	0.19536922	7
8	1.92060434	0.52066945	10.83063927	5.63918297	0.09233065	0.17733065	8
9	2.08385571	0.47987968	12.75124361	6.11906264	0.07842372	0.16342372	9
10	2.26098344	0.44228542	14.83509932	6.56134806	0.06740771	0.15240771	10
11	2.45316703	0.40763633	17.09608276	6.96898439	0.05849293	0.14349293	11
12	2.66168623	0.37570168	19.54924979	7.34468607	0.05115286	0.13615286	12
13	2.88792956	0.34626883	22.21093603	7.69095490	0.04502287	0.13002287	13
14	3.13340357	0.31914178	25.09886559	8.01009668	0.03984244	0.12484244	14
15	3.39974288	0.29413989	28.23226916	8.30423658	0.03542046	0.12042046	15
16	3.68872102	0.27109667	31.63201204	8.57533325	0.03161354	0.11661354	16
17	4.00226231	0.24985869	35.32073306	8.82519194	0.02831198	0.11331198	17
18	4.34245461	0.23028450	39.32299538	9.05547644	0.02543041	0.11043041	18
19	4.71156325	0.21224378	43.66544998	9.26772022	0.02290140	0.10790140	19
20	5.11204612	0.19561639	48.37701323	9.46333661	0.02067097	0.10567097	20
21	5.54657005	0.18029160	53.48905936	9.64362821	0.01869541	0.10369541	21
22	6.01802850	0.16616738	59.03562940	9.80979559	0.01693892	0.10193892	22
23	6.52956092	0.15314965	65.05365790	9.96294524	0.01537193	0.10037193	23
24	7.08457360	0.14115176	71.58321882	10.10409700	0.01396975	0.09896975	24
25	7.68676236	0.13009378	78.66779242	10.23419078	0.01271168	0.09771168	25
26	8.34013716	0.11990210	86.35455478	10.35409288	0.01158017	0.09658017	26
27	9.04904881	0.11050885	94.69469193	10.46460174	0.01056025	0.09556025	27
28	9.81821796	0.10185148	103.74374075	10.56645321	0.00963914	0.09463914	28
29	10.65276649	0.09387233	113.56195871	10.66032554	0.00880577	0.09380577	29
30	11.55825164	0.08651828	124.21472520	10.74684382	0.00805058	0.09305058	30
31	12.54070303	0.07974035	135.77297684	10.82658416	0.00736524	0.09236524	31
32	13.60666279	0.07349341	148.31367987	10.90007757	0.00674247	0.09174247	32
33	14.76322913	0.06773586	161.92034266	10.96781343	0.00617588	0.09117588	33
34	16.01810360	0.06242936	176.68357179	11.03024279	0.00565984	0.09065984	34
35	17.37964241	0.05753858	192.70167539	11.08778137	0.00518937	0.09018937	35
36	18.85691201	0.05303095	210.08131780	11.14081233	0.00476006	0.08976006	36
37	20.45974953	0.04887645	228.93822981	11.18968878	0.00436799	0.08936799	37
38	22.19882824	0.04504042	249.39797935	11.23473620	0.00400966	0.08900966	38
39	24.08572865	0.04151836	271.59680759	11.27625457	0.00368193	0.08868193	39
40	26.13301558	0.03826577	295.68253624	11.31452034	0.00338201	0.08838201	40
41	28.35432190	0.03526799	321.81555182	11.34978833	0.00310737	0.08810737	41
42	30.76443927	0.03250506	350.16987372	11.38229339	0.00285576	0.08785576	42
43	33.37941660	0.02995858	380.93431299	11.41225197	0.00262512	0.08762512	43
44	36.21666702	0.02761160	414.31372959	11.43986357	0.00241363	0.08741363	44
45	39.29508371	0.02544848	450.53039661	11.46531205	0.00221961	0.08721961	45
46	42.63516583	0.02345482	489.82548032	11.48876686	0.00204154	0.08704154	46
47	46.25915492	0.02161734	532.46064615	11.51038420	0.00187807	0.08687807	47
48	50.19118309	0.01992382	578.71980107	11.53030802	0.00172795	0.08672795	48
49	54.45743365	0.01836297	628.91098416	11.54867099	0.00159005	0.08659005	49
50	59.08631551	0.01692439	683.36841782	11.56559538	0.00146334	0.08646334	50

Tables 10 Through 12 (continued). Compound Interest

9% n	Table 10.1. Compound amount	Table 10.2. Present value	Table 11.1. Amount of annuity	Table 11.2. Present value of annuity	Table 12.1. Sinking fund	Table 12.2. Amortization	9% n
1	1.09000000	0.91743119	1.00000000	0.91743119	1.00000000	1.09000000	1
2	1.18810000	0.84167999	2.09000000	1.75911119	0.47846890	0.56846890	2
3	1.29502900	0.77218348	3.27810000	2.53129467	0.30505476	0.39505476	3
4	1.41158161	0.70842521	4.57312900	3.23971988	0.21866866	0.30866866	4
5	1.53862395	0.64993139	5.98471061	3.88965126	0.16709246	0.25709246	5
6	1.67710011	0.59626733	7.52333456	4.48591859	0.13291978	0.22291978	6
7	1.82803912	0.54703424	9.20043468	5.03295284	0.10869052	0.19869052	7
8	1.99256264	0.50186628	11.02847380	5.53481911	0.09067438	0.18067438	8
9	2.17189328	0.46042778	13.02103644	5.99524689	0.07679880	0.16679880	9
10	2.36736367	0.42241081	15.19292972	6.41765770	0.06582009	0.15582009	10
11	2.58042641	0.38753285	17.56029339	6.80519055	0.05694666	0.14694666	11
12	2.81266478	0.35553473	20.14071980	7.16072528	0.04965066	0.13965066	12
13	3.06580461	0.32617865	22.95338458	7.48690392	0.04356656	0.13356656	13
14	3.34172703	0.29924647	26.01918919	7.78615039	0.03843317	0.12843317	14
15	3.64248246	0.27453804	29.36091622	8.06068843	0.03405888	0.12405888	15
16	3.97030588	0.25186976	33.00339868	8.31255819	0.03029991	0.12029991	16
17	4.32763341	0.23107318	36.97370456	8.54363137	0.02704625	0.11704625	17
18	4.71712042	0.21199374	41.30133797	8.75562511	0.02421229	0.11421229	18
19	5.14166125	0.19448967	46.01845839	8.95011478	0.02173041	0.11173041	19
20	5.60441077	0.17843089	51.16011964	9.12854567	0.01954648	0.10954648	20
21	6.10880774	0.16369806	56.76453041	9.29224373	0.01761663	0.10761663	21
22	6.65860043	0.15018171	62.87333815	9.44242544	0.01590499	0.10590499	22
23	7.25787447	0.13778139	69.53193858	9.58020683	0.01438188	0.10438188	23
24	7.91108317	0.12640494	76.78981305	9.70661177	0.01302256	0.10302256	24
25	8.62308066	0.11596784	84.70089623	9.82257960	0.01180625	0.10180625	25
26	9.39915792	0.10639251	93.32397689	9.92897211	0.01071536	0.10071536	26
27	10.24508213	0.09760781	102.72313481	10.02657992	0.00973491	0.09973491	27
28	11.16713952	0.08954845	112.96821694	10.11612837	0.00885205	0.09885205	28
29	12.17218208	0.08215454	124.13535646	10.19828291	0.00805572	0.09805572	29
30	13.26767847	0.07537114	136.30753855	10.27365404	0.00733635	0.09733635	30
31	14.46176953	0.06914783	149.57521702	10.34280187	0.00668560	0.09668560	31
32	15.76332879	0.06343838	164.03698655	10.40624025	0.00609619	0.09609619	32
33	17.18202838	0.05820035	179.80031534	10.46444060	0.00556173	0.09556173	33
34	18.72841093	0.05339481	196.98234372	10.51783541	0.00507660	0.09507660	34
35	20.41396792	0.04898607	215.71075465	10.56682148	0.00463584	0.09463584	35
36	22.25122503	0.04494135	236.12472257	10.61176282	0.00423505	0.09423505	36
37	24.25383528	0.04123059	258.37594760	10.65299342	0.00387033	0.09387033	37
38	26.43668046	0.03782623	282.62978288	10.69081965	0.00353820	0.09353820	38
39	28.81598170	0.03470296	309.06646334	10.72552261	0.00323555	0.09323555	39
40	31.40942005	0.03183758	337.88244504	10.75736020	0.00295961	0.09295961	40
41	34.23626786	0.02920879	369.29186510	10.78656899	0.00270789	0.09270789	41
42	37.31753197	0.02679706	403.52813296	10.81336604	0.00247814	0.09247814	42
43	40.67610984	0.02458446	440.84566492	10.83795050	0.00226837	0.09226837	43
44	44.33695973	0.02255455	481.52177477	10.86050504	0.00207675	0.09207675	44
45	48.32286610	0.02069224	525.85873450	10.88119729	0.00190165	0.09190165	45
46	52.67674185	0.01898371	574.18602060	10.90018100	0.00174160	0.09174160	46
47	57.41764862	0.01741625	626.86276245	10.91759725	0.00159525	0.09159525	47
48	62.58523700	0.01597821	684.28041107	10.93357546	0.00146139	0.09146139	48
49	68.21790833	0.01465891	746.86564807	10.94823436	0.00133893	0.09133893	49
50	74.35752008	0.01344854	815.08355640	10.96168290	0.00122687	0.09122687	50

Tables 10 Through 12 (continued). Compound Interest

9¹/₂% n	Table 10.1. Compound amount	Table 10.2. Present value	Table 11.1. Amount of annuity	Table 11.2. Present value of annuity	Table 12.1. Sinking fund	Table 12.2. Amortization	9¹/₂% n
1	1.09500000	0.91324201	1.00000000	0.91324201	1.00000000	1.09500000	1
2	1.19902500	0.83401097	2.09500000	1.74725298	0.47732697	0.57232697	2
3	1.31293237	0.76165385	3.29402500	2.50890683	0.30357997	0.39857997	3
4	1.43766095	0.69557429	4.60695737	3.20448112	0.21706300	0.31206300	4
5	1.57423874	0.63522767	6.04461833	3.83970879	0.16543642	0.26043642	5
6	1.72379142	0.58011659	7.61885707	4.41982538	0.13125328	0.22625328	6
7	1.88755161	0.52978684	9.34264849	4.94961222	0.10703603	0.20203603	7
8	2.06686901	0.48382360	11.23020009	5.43343581	0.08904561	0.18404561	8
9	2.26322156	0.44184803	13.29706910	5.87528385	0.07520454	0.17020454	9
10	2.47822761	0.40351419	15.56029067	6.27879803	0.06426615	0.15926615	10
11	2.71365924	0.36850611	18.03851828	6.64730414	0.05543693	0.15043693	11
12	2.97145686	0.33653526	20.75217752	6.98383940	0.04818771	0.14318771	12
13	3.25374527	0.30733813	23.72363438	7.29117753	0.04215206	0.13715206	13
14	3.56285107	0.28067410	26.97737965	7.57185163	0.03706809	0.13206809	14
15	3.90132192	0.25623337	30.54023072	7.82817500	0.03274370	0.12774370	15
16	4.27194750	0.23408527	34.44155263	8.06226028	0.02903470	0.12403470	16
17	4.67778251	0.21377651	38.71350013	8.27603678	0.02583078	0.12083078	17
18	5.12217185	0.19522969	43.39128265	8.47126647	0.02304610	0.11804610	18
19	5.60877818	0.17829195	48.51345450	8.64955842	0.02061284	0.11561284	19
20	6.14161210	0.16282370	54.12223267	8.81238212	0.01847670	0.11347670	20
21	6.72506525	0.14869744	60.26384478	8.96107956	0.01659370	0.11159370	21
22	7.36394645	0.13579675	66.98891003	9.09687631	0.01492784	0.10992784	22
23	8.06352137	0.12401530	74.35285649	9.22089161	0.01344938	0.10844938	23
24	8.82955590	0.11325598	82.41637785	9.33414759	0.01213351	0.10713351	24
25	9.66836371	0.10343012	91.24593375	9.43757770	0.01095939	0.10595939	25
26	10.58685826	0.09445673	100.91429745	9.53203443	0.00990940	0.10490940	26
27	11.59260979	0.08626185	111.50115571	9.61829629	0.00896852	0.10396852	27
28	12.69390772	0.07877795	123.09376551	9.69707423	0.00812389	0.10312389	28
29	13.89982896	0.07194303	135.78767323	9.76901756	0.00736444	0.10236444	29
30	15.22031271	0.06570167	149.68750218	9.83471924	0.00668058	0.10168058	30
31	16.66624241	0.06000153	164.90781489	9.89472076	0.00606399	0.10106399	31
32	18.24953544	0.05479592	181.57405731	9.94951668	0.00550739	0.10050739	32
33	19.98324131	0.05004193	199.82359275	9.99955861	0.00500441	0.10000441	33
34	21.88164924	0.04570039	219.80683406	10.04525901	0.00454945	0.09954945	34
35	23.96040591	0.04173552	241.68848330	10.08699453	0.00413756	0.09913756	35
36	26.23664448	0.03811463	265.64888921	10.12510916	0.00376437	0.09876437	36
37	28.72912570	0.03480788	291.88553369	10.15991704	0.00342600	0.09842600	37
38	31.45839264	0.03178802	320.61465939	10.19170506	0.00311901	0.09811901	38
39	34.44693994	0.02903015	352.07305203	10.22073521	0.00284032	0.09784032	39
40	37.71939924	0.02651156	386.51999197	10.24724677	0.00258719	0.09758719	40
41	41.30274216	0.02421147	424.23939121	10.27145824	0.00235716	0.09735716	41
42	45.22650267	0.02211093	465.54213337	10.29356917	0.00214803	0.09714803	42
43	49.52302042	0.02019263	510.76863604	10.31376180	0.00195783	0.09695783	43
44	54.22770736	0.01844076	560.29165647	10.33220255	0.00178478	0.09678478	44
45	59.37933956	0.01684087	614.51936383	10.34904343	0.00162729	0.09662729	45
46	65.02037682	0.01537979	673.89870340	10.36442322	0.00148390	0.09648390	46
47	71.19731262	0.01404547	738.91908022	10.37846870	0.00135333	0.09635333	47
48	77.96105732	0.01282692	810.11639284	10.39129561	0.00123439	0.09623439	48
49	85.36735777	0.01171408	888.07745016	10.40300969	0.00112603	0.09612603	49
50	93.47725675	0.01069779	973.44480793	10.41370748	0.00102728	0.09602728	50

Tables 10 Through 12 (continued). Compound Interest

10% n	Table 10.1. Compound amount	Table 10.2. Present value	Table 11.1. Amount of annuity	Table 11.2. Present value of annuity	Table 12.1. Sinking fund	Table 12.2. Amortization	10% n
1	1.10000000	0.90909091	1.00000000	0.90909091	1.00000000	1.10000000	1
2	1.21000000	0.82644628	2.10000000	1.73553719	0.47619048	0.57619048	2
3	1.33100000	0.75131480	3.31000000	2.48685199	0.30211480	0.40211480	3
4	1.46410000	0.68301346	4.64100000	3.16986545	0.21547080	0.31547080	4
5	1.61051000	0.62092132	6.10510000	3.79078677	0.16379748	0.26379748	5
6	1.77156100	0.56447393	7.71561000	4.35526070	0.12960738	0.22960738	6
7	1.94871710	0.51315812	9.48717100	4.86841882	0.10540550	0.20540550	7
8	2.14358881	0.46650738	11.43588810	5.33492620	0.08744402	0.18744402	8
9	2.35794769	0.42409762	13.57947691	5.75902382	0.07364054	0.17364054	9
10	2.59374246	0.38554329	15.93742460	6.14456711	0.06274539	0.16274539	10
11	2.85311671	0.35049390	18.53116706	6.49506101	0.05396314	0.15396314	11
12	3.13842838	0.31863082	21.38428377	6.81369182	0.04676332	0.14676332	12
13	3.45227121	0.28966438	24.52271214	7.10335620	0.04077852	0.14077852	13
14	3.79749834	0.26333125	27.97498336	7.36668746	0.03574622	0.13574622	14
15	4.17724817	0.23939205	31.77248169	7.60607951	0.03147378	0.13147378	15
16	4.59497299	0.21762914	35.94972986	7.82370864	0.02781662	0.12781662	16
17	5.05447028	0.19784467	40.54470285	8.02155331	0.02466413	0.12466413	17
18	5.55991731	0.17985879	45.59917313	8.20141210	0.02193022	0.12193022	18
19	6.11590904	0.16350799	51.15909045	8.36492009	0.01954687	0.11954687	19
20	6.72749995	0.14864363	57.27499949	8.51356372	0.01745962	0.11745962	20
21	7.40024994	0.13513057	64.00249944	8.64869429	0.01562439	0.11562439	21
22	8.14027494	0.12284597	71.40274939	8.77154026	0.01400506	0.11400506	22
23	8.95430243	0.11167816	79.54302433	8.88321842	0.01257181	0.11257181	23
24	9.84973268	0.10152560	88.49732676	8.98474402	0.01129978	0.11129978	24
25	10.83470594	0.09229600	98.34705943	9.07704002	0.01016807	0.11016807	25
26	11.91817654	0.08390545	109.18176538	9.16094547	0.00915904	0.10915904	26
27	13.10999419	0.07627768	121.09994191	9.23722316	0.00825764	0.10825764	27
28	14.42099361	0.06934335	134.20993611	9.30656651	0.00745101	0.10745101	28
29	15.86309297	0.06303941	148.63092972	9.36960591	0.00672807	0.10672807	29
30	17.44940227	0.05730855	164.49402269	9.42691447	0.00607925	0.10607925	30
31	19.19434250	0.05209868	181.94342496	9.47901315	0.00549621	0.10549621	31
32	21.11377675	0.04736244	201.13776745	9.52637559	0.00497172	0.10497172	32
33	23.22515442	0.04305676	222.25154420	9.56943236	0.00449941	0.10449941	33
34	25.54766986	0.03914251	245.47669862	9.60857487	0.00407371	0.10407371	34
35	28.10243685	0.03558410	271.02436848	9.64415897	0.00368971	0.10368971	35
36	30.91268053	0.03234918	299.12680533	9.67650816	0.00334306	0.10334306	36
37	34.00394859	0.02940835	330.03948586	9.70591651	0.00302994	0.10302994	37
38	37.40434344	0.02673486	364.04343445	9.73265137	0.00274692	0.10274692	38
39	41.14477779	0.02430442	401.44777789	9.75695579	0.00249098	0.10249098	39
40	45.25925557	0.02209493	442.59255568	9.77905072	0.00225941	0.10225941	40
41	49.78518112	0.02008630	487.85181125	9.79913702	0.00204980	0.10204980	41
42	54.76369924	0.01826027	537.63699237	9.81739729	0.00185999	0.10185999	42
43	60.24006916	0.01660025	592.40069161	9.83399753	0.00168805	0.10168805	43
44	66.26407608	0.01509113	652.64076077	9.84908867	0.00153224	0.10153224	44
45	72.89048369	0.01371921	718.90483685	9.86280788	0.00139100	0.10139100	45
46	80.17953205	0.01247201	791.79532054	9.87527989	0.00126295	0.10126295	46
47	88.19748526	0.01133819	871.97485259	9.88661808	0.00114682	0.10114682	47
48	97.01723378	0.01030745	960.17233785	9.89692553	0.00104148	0.10104148	48
49	106.71895716	0.00937041	1057.18957163	9.90629594	0.00094590	0.10094590	49
50	117.39085288	0.00851855	1163.90852880	9.91481449	0.00085917	0.10085917	50

Tables 10 Through 12 (continued). Compound Interest

11% n	Table 10.1. Compound amount	Table 10.2. Present value	Table 11.1. Amount of annuity	Table 11.2. Present value of annuity	Table 12.1. Sinking fund	Table 12.2. Amortization	11% n
1	1.11000000	0.90090090	1.00000000	0.90090090	1.00000000	1.11000000	1
2	1.23210000	0.81162243	2.11000000	1.71252333	0.47393365	0.58393365	2
3	1.36763100	0.73119138	3.34210000	2.44371472	0.29921307	0.40921307	3
4	1.51807041	0.65873097	4.70973100	3.10244569	0.21232635	0.32232635	4
5	1.68505816	0.59345133	6.22780141	3.69589702	0.16057031	0.27057031	5
6	1.87041455	0.53464084	7.91285957	4.23053785	0.12637656	0.23637656	6
7	2.07616015	0.48165841	9.78327412	4.71219626	0.10221527	0.21221527	7
8	2.30453777	0.43392650	11.85943427	5.14612276	0.08432105	0.19432105	8
9	2.55803692	0.39092477	14.16397204	5.53704753	0.07060166	0.18060166	9
10	2.83942099	0.35218448	16.72200896	5.88923201	0.05980143	0.16980143	10
11	3.15175729	0.31728331	19.56142995	6.20651533	0.05112101	0.16112101	11
12	3.49845060	0.28584082	22.71318724	6.49235615	0.04402729	0.15402729	12
13	3.88328016	0.25751426	26.21163784	6.74987040	0.03815099	0.14815099	13
14	4.31044098	0.23199482	30.09491800	6.98186523	0.03322820	0.14322820	14
15	4.78458949	0.20900435	34.40535898	7.19086958	0.02906524	0.13906524	15
16	5.31089433	0.18829220	39.18994847	7.37916178	0.02551675	0.13551675	16
17	5.89509271	0.16963262	44.50084281	7.54879440	0.02247148	0.13247148	17
18	6.54355291	0.15282218	50.39593551	7.70161657	0.01984287	0.12984287	18
19	7.26334373	0.13767764	56.93948842	7.83929421	0.01756250	0.12756250	19
20	8.06231154	0.12403391	64.20283215	7.96332812	0.01557564	0.12557564	20
21	8.94916581	0.11174226	72.26514368	8.07507038	0.01383793	0.12383793	21
22	9.93357404	0.10066870	81.21430949	8.17573908	0.01231310	0.12231310	22
23	11.02626719	0.09069252	91.14788353	8.26643160	0.01097118	0.12097118	23
24	12.23915658	0.08170498	102.17415072	8.34813658	0.00978721	0.11978721	24
25	13.58546380	0.07360809	114.41330730	8.42174466	0.00874024	0.11874024	25
26	15.07986482	0.06631359	127.99877110	8.48805826	0.00781258	0.11781258	26
27	16.73864995	0.05974197	143.07863592	8.54780023	0.00698916	0.11698916	27
28	18.57990145	0.05382160	159.81728587	8.60162183	0.00625715	0.11625715	28
29	20.62369061	0.04848793	178.39718732	8.65010976	0.00560547	0.11560547	29
30	22.89229657	0.04368282	199.02087793	8.69379257	0.00502460	0.11502460	30
31	25.41044919	0.03935389	221.91317450	8.73314646	0.00450627	0.11450627	31
32	28.20559861	0.03545395	247.32362369	8.76860042	0.00404329	0.11404329	32
33	31.30821445	0.03194050	275.52922230	8.80054092	0.00362938	0.11362938	33
34	34.75211804	0.02877522	306.83743675	8.82931614	0.00325905	0.11325905	34
35	38.57485103	0.02592363	341.58955480	8.85523977	0.00292749	0.11292749	35
36	42.81808464	0.02335462	380.16440582	8.87859438	0.00263044	0.11263044	36
37	47.52807395	0.02104020	422.98249046	8.89963458	0.00236416	0.11236416	37
38	52.75616209	0.01895513	470.51056441	8.91858971	0.00212535	0.11212535	38
39	58.55933991	0.01707670	523.26672650	8.93566641	0.00191107	0.11191107	39
40	65.00086731	0.01538441	581.82606641	8.95105082	0.00171873	0.11171873	40
41	72.15096271	0.01385983	646.82693372	8.96491065	0.00154601	0.11154601	41
42	80.08756861	0.01248633	718.97789643	8.97739698	0.00139086	0.11139086	42
43	88.89720115	0.01124895	799.06546504	8.98864593	0.00125146	0.11125146	43
44	98.67589328	0.01013419	887.96266619	8.99878011	0.00112617	0.11112617	44
45	109.53024154	0.00912990	986.63855947	9.00791001	0.00101354	0.11101354	45
46	121.57856811	0.00822513	1096.16880101	9.01613515	0.00091227	0.11091227	46
47	134.95221060	0.00741003	1217.74736912	9.02354518	0.00082119	0.11082119	47
48	149.79695377	0.00667570	1352.69957973	9.03022088	0.00073926	0.11073926	48
49	166.27461868	0.00601415	1502.49653350	9.03623503	0.00066556	0.11066556	49
50	184.56482674	0.00541815	1668.77115218	9.04165318	0.00059924	0.11059924	50

Tables 10 Through 12 (continued). Compound Interest

12% n	Table 10.1. Compound amount	Table 10.2. Present value	Table 11.1. Amount of annuity	Table 11.2. Present value of annuity	Table 12.1. Sinking fund	Table 12.2. Amortization	12% n
1	1.12000000	0.89285714	1.00000000	0.89285714	1.00000000	1.12000000	1
2	1.25440000	0.79719388	2.12000000	1.69005102	0.47169811	0.59169811	2
3	1.40492800	0.71178025	3.37440000	2.40183127	0.29634898	0.41634898	3
4	1.57351936	0.63551808	4.77932800	3.03734935	0.20923444	0.32923444	4
5	1.76234168	0.56742686	6.35284736	3.60477620	0.15740973	0.27740973	5
6	1.97382269	0.50663112	8.11518904	4.11140732	0.12322572	0.24322572	6
7	2.21068141	0.45234922	10.08901173	4.56375654	0.09911774	0.21911774	7
8	2.47596318	0.40388323	12.29969314	4.96763977	0.08130284	0.20130284	8
9	2.77307876	0.36061002	14.77565631	5.32824979	0.06767889	0.18767889	9
10	3.10584821	0.32197324	17.54873507	5.65022303	0.05698416	0.17698416	10
11	3.47854999	0.28747610	20.65458328	5.93769913	0.04841540	0.16841540	11
12	3.89597599	0.25667509	24.13313327	6.19437423	0.04143681	0.16143681	12
13	4.36349311	0.22917419	28.02910926	6.42354842	0.03567720	0.15567720	13
14	4.88711229	0.20461981	32.39260238	6.62816823	0.03087125	0.15087125	14
15	5.47356576	0.18269626	37.27971466	6.81086449	0.02682424	0.14682424	15
16	6.13039365	0.16312166	42.75328042	6.97398615	0.02339002	0.14339002	16
17	6.86604089	0.14564434	48.88367407	7.11963049	0.02045673	0.14045673	17
18	7.68996580	0.13003959	55.74971496	7.24967008	0.01793731	0.13793731	18
19	8.61276169	0.11610678	63.43968075	7.36577686	0.01576300	0.13576300	19
20	9.64629309	0.10366677	72.05244244	7.46944362	0.01387878	0.13387878	20
21	10.80384826	0.09255961	81.69873554	7.56200324	0.01224009	0.13224009	21
22	12.10031006	0.08264251	92.50258380	7.64464575	0.01081051	0.13081051	22
23	13.55234726	0.07378796	104.60289386	7.71843370	0.00955996	0.12955996	23
24	15.17862893	0.06588210	118.15524112	7.78431581	0.00846344	0.12846344	24
25	17.00006441	0.05882331	133.33387006	7.84313911	0.00749997	0.12749997	25
26	19.04007214	0.05252081	150.33393446	7.89565992	0.00665186	0.12665186	26
27	21.32488079	0.04689358	169.37400660	7.94255350	0.00590409	0.12590409	27
28	23.88386649	0.04186927	190.69888739	7.98442277	0.00524387	0.12524387	28
29	26.74993047	0.03738327	214.58275388	8.02180604	0.00466021	0.12466021	29
30	29.95992212	0.03337792	241.33268434	8.05518397	0.00414366	0.12414366	30
31	33.55511278	0.02980172	271.29260646	8.08498569	0.00368606	0.12368606	31
32	37.58172631	0.02660868	304.84771924	8.11159436	0.00328033	0.12328033	32
33	42.09153347	0.02375775	342.42944555	8.13535211	0.00292031	0.12292031	33
34	47.14251748	0.02121227	384.52097901	8.15656438	0.00260064	0.12260064	34
35	52.79961958	0.01893953	431.66349649	8.17550391	0.00231662	0.12231662	35
36	59.13557393	0.01691029	484.46311607	8.19241421	0.00206414	0.12206414	36
37	66.23184280	0.01509848	543.59869000	8.20751269	0.00183959	0.12183959	37
38	74.17966394	0.01348078	609.83053280	8.22099347	0.00163980	0.12163980	38
39	83.08122361	0.01203641	684.01019674	8.23302988	0.00146197	0.12146197	39
40	93.05097044	0.01074680	767.09142034	8.24377668	0.00130363	0.12130363	40
41	104.21708689	0.00959536	860.14239079	8.25337204	0.00116260	0.12116260	41
42	116.72313732	0.00856728	964.35947768	8.26193932	0.00103696	0.12103696	42
43	130.72991380	0.00764936	1081.08261500	8.26958868	0.00092500	0.12092500	43
44	146.41750346	0.00682978	1211.81252880	8.27641846	0.00082521	0.12082521	44
45	163.98760387	0.00609802	1358.23003226	8.28251648	0.00073625	0.12073625	45
46	183.66611634	0.00544466	1522.21763613	8.28796115	0.00065694	0.12065694	46
47	205.70605030	0.00486131	1705.88375247	8.29282245	0.00058621	0.12058621	47
48	230.39077633	0.00434045	1911.58980276	8.29716290	0.00052312	0.12052312	48
49	258.03766949	0.00387540	2141.98057909	8.30103831	0.00046686	0.12046686	49
50	289.00218983	0.00346018	2400.01824858	8.30449849	0.00041666	0.12041666	50

Tables 10 Through 12 (continued). Compound Interest

13%	Table 10.1. Compound amount	Table 10.2. Present value	Table 11.1. Amount of annuity	Table 11.2. Present value of annuity	Table 12.1. Sinking fund	Table 12.2. Amortization	13%
n							n
1	1.13000000	0.88495575	1.00000000	0.88495575	1.00000000	1.13000000	1
2	1.27690000	0.78314668	2.13000000	1.66810244	0.46948357	0.59948357	2
3	1.44289700	0.69305016	3.40690000	2.36115260	0.29352197	0.42352197	3
4	1.63047361	0.61331873	4.84979700	2.97447133	0.20619420	0.33619420	4
5	1.84243518	0.54275994	6.48027061	3.51723126	0.15431454	0.28431454	5
6	2.08195175	0.48031853	8.32270579	3.99754979	0.12015323	0.25015323	6
7	2.35260548	0.42506064	10.40465754	4.42261043	0.09611080	0.22611080	7
8	2.65844419	0.37615986	12.75726302	4.79877029	0.07838672	0.20838672	8
9	3.00404194	0.33288483	15.41570722	5.13165513	0.06486890	0.19486890	9
10	3.39456739	0.29458835	18.41974915	5.42624348	0.05428956	0.18428956	10
11	3.83586115	0.26069765	21.81431654	5.68694113	0.04584145	0.17584145	11
12	4.33452310	0.23070589	25.65017769	5.91764702	0.03898608	0.16898608	12
13	4.89801110	0.20416450	29.98470079	6.12181152	0.03335034	0.16335034	13
14	5.53475255	0.18067655	34.88271190	6.30248807	0.02866750	0.15866750	14
15	6.25427038	0.15989075	40.41746444	6.46237882	0.02474178	0.15474178	15
16	7.06732553	0.14149624	46.67173482	6.60387506	0.02142624	0.15142624	16
17	7.98607785	0.12521791	53.73906035	6.72909298	0.01860844	0.14860844	17
18	9.02426797	0.11081231	61.72513819	6.83990529	0.01620085	0.14620085	18
19	10.19742280	0.09806399	70.74940616	6.93796928	0.01413439	0.14413439	19
20	11.52308776	0.08678229	80.94682896	7.02475158	0.01235379	0.14235379	20
21	13.02108917	0.07679849	92.46991672	7.10155007	0.01081433	0.14081433	21
22	14.71383077	0.06796327	105.49100590	7.16951334	0.00947948	0.13947948	22
23	16.62662877	0.06014448	120.20483667	7.22965782	0.00831913	0.13831913	23
24	18.78809051	0.05322521	136.83146543	7.28288303	0.00730826	0.13730826	24
25	21.23054227	0.04710195	155.61955594	7.32998498	0.00642593	0.13642593	25
26	23.99051277	0.04168314	176.85009821	7.37166812	0.00565451	0.13565451	26
27	27.10927943	0.03688774	200.84061098	7.40855586	0.00497907	0.13497907	27
28	30.63348575	0.03264402	227.94989040	7.44119988	0.00438693	0.13438693	28
29	34.61583890	0.02888851	258.58337616	7.47008839	0.00386722	0.13386722	29
30	39.11589796	0.02556505	293.19921506	7.49565344	0.00341065	0.13341065	30
31	44.20096469	0.02262394	332.31511301	7.51827738	0.00300919	0.13300919	31
32	49.94709010	0.02002119	376.51607771	7.53829857	0.00265593	0.13265593	32
33	56.44021181	0.01771786	426.46316781	7.55601643	0.00234487	0.13234487	33
34	63.77743935	0.01567953	482.90337962	7.57169596	0.00207081	0.13207081	34
35	72.06850647	0.01387569	546.68081897	7.58557164	0.00182922	0.13182922	35
36	81.43741231	0.01227937	618.74932544	7.59785101	0.00161616	0.13161616	36
37	92.02427591	0.01086670	700.18673775	7.60871771	0.00142819	0.13142819	37
38	103.98743178	0.00961655	792.21101365	7.61833426	0.00126229	0.13126229	38
39	117.50579791	0.00851022	896.19844543	7.62684447	0.00111582	0.13111582	39
40	132.78155163	0.00753117	1013.70424333	7.63437564	0.00098648	0.13098648	40
41	150.04315335	0.00666475	1146.48579497	7.64104039	0.00087223	0.13087223	41
42	169.54876328	0.00589801	1296.52894831	7.64693840	0.00077129	0.13077129	42
43	191.59010251	0.00521948	1466.07771159	7.65215787	0.00068209	0.13068209	43
44	216.49681583	0.00461901	1657.66781410	7.65677688	0.00060326	0.13060326	44
45	244.64140189	0.00408762	1874.16462994	7.66086450	0.00053357	0.13053357	45
46	276.44478414	0.00361736	2118.80603183	7.66448185	0.00047196	0.13047196	46
47	312.38260608	0.00320120	2395.25081596	7.66768306	0.00041749	0.13041749	47
48	352.99234487	0.00283292	2707.63342204	7.67051598	0.00036933	0.13036933	48
49	398.88134970	0.00250701	3060.62576691	7.67302299	0.00032673	0.13032673	49
50	450.73592516	0.00221859	3459.50711660	7.67524158	0.00028906	0.13028906	50

Tables 10 Through 12 (continued). Compound Interest

14% n	Table 10.1. Compound amount	Table 10.2. Present value	Table 11.1. Amount of annuity	Table 11.2. Present value of annuity	Table 12.1. Sinking fund	Table 12.2. Amortization	14% n
1	1.14000000	0.87719298	1.00000000	0.87719298	1.00000000	1.14000000	1
2	1.29960000	0.76946753	2.14000000	1.64666051	0.46728972	0.60728972	2
3	1.48154400	0.67497152	3.43960000	2.32163203	0.29073148	0.43073148	3
4	1.68896016	0.59208028	4.92114400	2.91371230	0.20320478	0.34320478	4
5	1.92541458	0.51936866	6.61010416	3.43308097	0.15128355	0.29128355	5
6	2.19497262	0.45558655	8.53551874	3.88866752	0.11715750	0.25715750	6
7	2.50226879	0.39963732	10.73049137	4.28830484	0.09319238	0.23319238	7
8	2.85258642	0.35055905	13.23276016	4.63886389	0.07557002	0.21557002	8
9	3.25194852	0.30750794	16.08534658	4.94637184	0.06216838	0.20216838	9
10	3.70722131	0.26974381	19.33729510	5.21611565	0.05171354	0.19171354	10
11	4.22623230	0.23661738	23.04451641	5.45273302	0.04339427	0.18339427	11
12	4.81790482	0.20755910	27.27074871	5.66029213	0.03666933	0.17666933	12
13	5.49241149	0.18206939	32.08865353	5.84236151	0.03116366	0.17116366	13
14	6.26134910	0.15970999	37.58106503	6.00207150	0.02660914	0.16660914	14
15	7.13793798	0.14009648	43.84241413	6.14216799	0.02280896	0.16280896	15
16	8.13724930	0.12289165	50.98035211	6.26505964	0.01961540	0.15961540	16
17	9.27646420	0.10779969	59.11760141	6.37285933	0.01691544	0.15691544	17
18	10.57516918	0.09456113	68.39406560	6.46742046	0.01462115	0.15462115	18
19	12.05569287	0.08294836	78.96923479	6.55036883	0.01266316	0.15266316	19
20	13.74348987	0.07276172	91.02492766	6.62313055	0.01098600	0.15098600	20
21	15.66757845	0.06382607	104.76841753	6.68695662	0.00954486	0.14954486	21
22	17.86103944	0.05598778	120.43599598	6.74294441	0.00830317	0.14830317	22
23	20.36158496	0.04911209	138.29703542	6.79205650	0.00723081	0.14723081	23
24	23.21220685	0.04308078	158.65862038	6.83513728	0.00630284	0.14630284	24
25	26.46191581	0.03779016	181.87082723	6.87292744	0.00549841	0.14549841	25
26	30.16658403	0.03314926	208.33274304	6.90607670	0.00480001	0.14480001	26
27	34.38990579	0.02907830	238.49932707	6.93515500	0.00419288	0.14419288	27
28	39.20449260	0.02550728	272.88923286	6.96066228	0.00366449	0.14366449	28
29	44.69312156	0.02237481	312.09372546	6.98303709	0.00320417	0.14320417	29
30	50.95015858	0.01962702	356.78684702	7.00266411	0.00280279	0.14280279	30
31	58.08318078	0.01721669	407.73700561	7.01988080	0.00245256	0.14245256	31
32	66.21482609	0.01510236	465.82018639	7.03498316	0.00214675	0.14214675	32
33	75.48490175	0.01324768	532.03501249	7.04823084	0.00187958	0.14187958	33
34	86.05278799	0.01162077	607.51991423	7.05985161	0.00164604	0.14164604	34
35	98.10017831	0.01019366	693.57270223	7.07004528	0.00144181	0.14144181	35
36	111.83420328	0.00894181	791.67288054	7.07898708	0.00126315	0.14126315	36
37	127.49099173	0.00784369	903.50708382	7.08683078	0.00110680	0.14110680	37
38	145.33973058	0.00688043	1030.99807555	7.09371121	0.00096993	0.14096993	38
39	165.68729286	0.00603547	1176.33780613	7.09974667	0.00085010	0.14085010	39
40	188.88351386	0.00529427	1342.02509898	7.10504094	0.00074514	0.14074514	40
41	215.32720580	0.00464410	1530.90861284	7.10968504	0.00065321	0.14065321	41
42	245.47301461	0.00407377	1746.23581864	7.11375880	0.00057266	0.14057266	42
43	279.83923665	0.00357348	1991.70883325	7.11733228	0.00050208	0.14050208	43
44	319.01672979	0.00313463	2271.54806990	7.12046692	0.00044023	0.14044023	44
45	363.67907196	0.00274968	2590.56479969	7.12321659	0.00038602	0.14038602	45
46	414.59414203	0.00241200	2954.24387165	7.12562859	0.00033850	0.14033850	46
47	472.63732191	0.00211579	3368.83801368	7.12774438	0.00029684	0.14029684	47
48	538.80654698	0.00185595	3841.47533559	7.12960033	0.00026032	0.14026032	48
49	614.23946356	0.00162803	4380.28188258	7.13122836	0.00022830	0.14022830	49
50	700.23298846	0.00142810	4994.52134614	7.13265646	0.00020022	0.14020022	50

Tables 10 Through 12 (continued). Compound Interest

15%	Table 10.1. Compound amount	Table 10.2. Present value	Table 11.1. Amount of annuity	Table 11.2. Present value of annuity	Table 12.1. Sinking fund	Table 12.2. Amortization	15%
n							n
1	1.15000000	0.86956522	1.00000000	0.86956522	1.00000000	1.15000000	1
2	1.32250000	0.75614367	2.15000000	1.62570888	0.46511628	0.61511628	2
3	1.52087500	0.65751623	3.47250000	2.28322512	0.28797696	0.43797696	3
4	1.74900625	0.57175325	4.99337500	2.85497836	0.20026535	0.35026535	4
5	2.01135719	0.49717674	6.74238125	3.35215510	0.14831555	0.29831555	5
6	2.31306077	0.43232760	8.75373844	3.78448269	0.11423691	0.26423691	6
7	2.66001988	0.37593704	11.06679920	4.16041973	0.09036036	0.24036036	7
8	3.05902286	0.32690177	13.72681908	4.48732151	0.07285009	0.22285009	8
9	3.51787629	0.28426241	16.78584195	4.77158392	0.05957402	0.20957402	9
10	4.04555774	0.24718471	20.30371824	5.01876863	0.04925206	0.19925206	10
11	4.65239140	0.21494322	24.34927597	5.23371185	0.04106898	0.19106898	11
12	5.35025011	0.18690715	29.00166737	5.42061900	0.03448078	0.18448078	12
13	6.15278762	0.16252796	34.35191748	5.58314696	0.02911046	0.17911046	13
14	7.07570576	0.14132866	40.50470510	5.72447561	0.02468849	0.17468849	14
15	8.13706163	0.12289449	47.58041086	5.84737010	0.02101705	0.17101705	15
16	9.35762087	0.10686477	55.71747249	5.95423487	0.01794769	0.16794769	16
17	10.76126400	0.09292589	65.07509336	6.04716076	0.01536686	0.16536686	17
18	12.37545361	0.08080512	75.83635737	6.12796587	0.01318629	0.16318629	18
19	14.23177165	0.07026532	88.21181097	6.19823119	0.01133635	0.16133635	19
20	16.36653739	0.06110028	102.44358262	6.25933147	0.00976147	0.15976147	20
21	18.82151800	0.05313068	118.81012001	6.31246215	0.00841679	0.15841679	21
22	21.64474570	0.04620059	137.63163801	6.35866274	0.00726577	0.15726577	22
23	24.89145756	0.04017443	159.27638372	6.39883717	0.00627839	0.15627839	23
24	28.62517619	0.03493428	184.16784127	6.43377145	0.00542983	0.15542983	24
25	32.91895262	0.03037764	212.79301747	6.46414909	0.00469940	0.15469940	25
26	37.85679551	0.02641534	245.71197009	6.49056442	0.00406981	0.15406981	26
27	43.53531484	0.02296986	283.56876560	6.51353428	0.00352648	0.15352648	27
28	50.06561207	0.01997379	327.10408044	6.53350807	0.00305713	0.15305713	28
29	57.57545388	0.01736851	377.16969250	6.55087658	0.00265133	0.15265133	29
30	66.21177196	0.01510305	434.74514638	6.56597964	0.00230020	0.15230020	30
31	76.14353775	0.01313309	500.95691834	6.57911273	0.00199618	0.15199618	31
32	87.56506841	0.01142008	577.10045609	6.59053281	0.00173280	0.15173280	32
33	100.69982867	0.00993050	664.66552450	6.60046331	0.00150452	0.15150452	33
34	115.80480298	0.00863522	765.36535317	6.60909853	0.00130657	0.15130657	34
35	133.17552342	0.00750889	881.17015615	6.61660742	0.00113485	0.15113485	35
36	153.15185194	0.00652947	1014.34567957	6.62313689	0.00098586	0.15098586	36
37	176.12462973	0.00567780	1167.49753151	6.62881468	0.00085653	0.15085653	37
38	202.54332419	0.00493722	1343.62216123	6.63375190	0.00074426	0.15074426	38
39	232.92482281	0.00429323	1546.16548542	6.63804513	0.00064676	0.15064676	39
40	267.86354623	0.00373324	1779.09030823	6.64177837	0.00056209	0.15056209	40
41	308.04307817	0.00324630	2046.95385447	6.64502467	0.00048853	0.15048853	41
42	354.24953990	0.00282287	2354.99693264	6.64784754	0.00042463	0.15042463	42
43	407.38697088	0.00245467	2709.24647253	6.65030221	0.00036911	0.15036911	43
44	468.49501651	0.00213449	3116.63344341	6.65243670	0.00032086	0.15032086	44
45	538.76926899	0.00185608	3585.12845992	6.65429279	0.00027893	0.15027893	45
46	619.58465934	0.00161398	4123.89772891	6.65590677	0.00024249	0.15024249	46
47	712.52235824	0.00140346	4743.48238825	6.65731024	0.00021082	0.15021082	47
48	819.40071197	0.00122040	5456.00474648	6.65853064	0.00018328	0.15018328	48
49	942.31081877	0.00106122	6275.40545846	6.65959186	0.00015935	0.15015935	49
50	1083.65744158	0.00092280	7217.71627723	6.66051466	0.00013855	0.15013855	50

Tables 10 Through 12 (continued). Compound Interest

16%	Table 10.1. Compound amount	Table 10.2. Present value	Table 11.1. Amount of annuity	Table 11.2. Present value of annuity	Table 12.1. Sinking fund	Table 12.2. Amortization	16%
n							n
1	1.16000000	0.86206897	1.00000000	0.86206897	1.00000000	1.16000000	1
2	1.34560000	0.74316290	2.16000000	1.60523187	0.46296296	0.62296296	2
3	1.56089600	0.64065767	3.50560000	2.24588954	0.28525787	0.44525787	3
4	1.81063936	0.55229110	5.06649600	2.79818064	0.19737507	0.35737507	4
5	2.10034166	0.47611302	6.87713536	3.27429365	0.14540938	0.30540938	5
6	2.43639632	0.41044225	8.97747702	3.68473591	0.11138987	0.27138987	6
7	2.82621973	0.35382953	11.41387334	4.03856544	0.08761268	0.24761268	7
8	3.27841489	0.30502546	14.24009307	4.34359090	0.07022426	0.23022426	8
9	3.80296127	0.26295298	17.51850797	4.60654388	0.05708249	0.21708249	9
10	4.41143508	0.22668360	21.32146924	4.83322748	0.04690108	0.20690108	10
11	5.11726469	0.19541690	25.73290432	5.02864438	0.03886075	0.19886075	11
12	5.93602704	0.16846284	30.85016901	5.19710722	0.03241473	0.19241473	12
13	6.88579137	0.14522659	36.78619605	5.34233381	0.02718411	0.18718411	13
14	7.98751799	0.12519534	43.67198742	5.46752915	0.02289797	0.18289797	14
15	9.26552087	0.10792701	51.65950541	5.57545616	0.01935752	0.17935752	15
16	10.74800420	0.09304053	60.92502627	5.66849669	0.01641362	0.17641362	16
17	12.46768488	0.08020735	71.67303048	5.74870404	0.01395225	0.17395225	17
18	14.46251446	0.06914427	84.14071536	5.81784831	0.01188485	0.17188485	18
19	16.77651677	0.05960713	98.60322981	5.87745544	0.01014166	0.17014166	19
20	19.46075945	0.05138546	115.37974658	5.92884090	0.00866703	0.16866703	20
21	22.57448097	0.04429781	134.84050604	5.97313871	0.00741617	0.16741617	21
22	26.18639792	0.03818776	157.41498700	6.01132647	0.00635264	0.16635264	22
23	30.37622159	0.03292049	183.60138492	6.04424696	0.00544658	0.16544658	23
24	35.23641704	0.02837973	213.97760651	6.07262669	0.00467339	0.16467339	24
25	40.87424377	0.02446528	249.21402355	6.09709197	0.00401262	0.16401262	25
26	47.41412277	0.02109076	290.08826732	6.11818273	0.00344723	0.16344723	26
27	55.00038241	0.01818169	337.50239009	6.13636443	0.00296294	0.16296294	27
28	63.80044360	0.01567387	392.50277250	6.15203830	0.00254775	0.16254775	28
29	74.00851458	0.01351196	456.30321610	6.16555026	0.00219153	0.16219153	29
30	85.84987691	0.01164824	530.31173068	6.17719850	0.00188568	0.16188568	30
31	99.58585721	0.01004159	616.16160759	6.18724008	0.00162295	0.16162295	31
32	115.51959437	0.00865654	715.74746480	6.19589662	0.00139714	0.16139714	32
33	134.00272947	0.00746253	831.26705917	6.20335916	0.00120298	0.16120298	33
34	155.44316618	0.00643322	965.26978864	6.20979238	0.00103598	0.16103598	34
35	180.31407277	0.00554588	1120.71295482	6.21533826	0.00089229	0.16089229	35
36	209.16432441	0.00478093	1301.02702759	6.22011919	0.00076862	0.16076862	36
37	242.63016632	0.00412149	1510.19135201	6.22424068	0.00066217	0.16066217	37
38	281.45151493	0.00355301	1752.82196833	6.22779369	0.00057051	0.16057051	38
39	326.48375732	0.00306294	2034.27348326	6.23085663	0.00049158	0.16049158	39
40	378.72115849	0.00264047	2360.75724058	6.23349709	0.00042359	0.16042359	40
41	439.31654385	0.00227626	2739.47839907	6.23577336	0.00036503	0.16036503	41
42	509.60719087	0.00196230	3178.79494293	6.23773565	0.00031458	0.16031458	42
43	591.14434141	0.00169163	3688.40213380	6.23942729	0.00027112	0.16027112	43
44	685.72743603	0.00145831	4279.54647520	6.24088559	0.00023367	0.16023367	44
45	795.44382580	0.00125716	4965.27391123	6.24214275	0.00020140	0.16020140	45
46	922.71483793	0.00108376	5760.71773703	6.24322651	0.00017359	0.16017359	46
47	1070.34921199	0.00093427	6683.43257496	6.24416078	0.00014962	0.16014962	47
48	1241.60508591	0.00080541	7753.78178695	6.24496619	0.00012897	0.16012897	48
49	1440.26189966	0.00069432	8995.38687286	6.24566051	0.00011117	0.16011117	49
50	1670.70380360	0.00059855	10435.64877252	6.24625906	0.00009583	0.16009583	50

Tables 10 Through 12 (continued). Compound Interest

17%	Table 10.1. Compound amount	Table 10.2. Present value	Table 11.1. Amount of annuity	Table 11.2. Present value of annuity	Table 12.1. Sinking fund	Table 12.2. Amortization	17%
n							n
1	1.17000000	0.85470085	1.00000000	0.85470085	1.00000000	1.17000000	1
2	1.36890000	0.7305 1355	2.17000000	1.58521441	0 46082949	0.63082949	2
3	1.60161300	0.62437056	3.53890000	2.20958496	0.28257368	0.45257368	3
4	1.87388721	0.53365005	5.14051300	2.74323501	0.19453311	0.36453311	4
5	2.19244804	0.45611115	7.01440021	3.19934616	0.14256386	0.31256386	5
6	2.56516420	0.38983859	9.20684825	3.58918475	0.10861480	0.27861480	6
7	3.00124212	0.33319538	11.77201245	3.92238013	0.08494724	0.25494724	7
8	3.51145328	0.28478237	14.77325456	4.20716251	0.06768989	0.23768989	8
9	4.10840033	0.24340374	18.28470784	4.45056624	0.05469051	0.22469051	9
10	4.80682839	0.20803738	22.39310817	4.65860363	0.04465660	0.21465660	10
11	5.62398922	0.17780973	27.19993656	4.83641336	0.03676479	0.20676479	11
12	6.58006738	0.15197413	32.82392578	4.98838748	0.03046558	0.20046558	12
13	7.69867884	0.12989242	39.40399316	5.11827990	0.02537814	0.19537814	13
14	9.00745424	0.11101916	47.10267200	5.22929906	0.02123022	0.19123022	14
15	10.53872146	0.09488817	56.11012623	5.32418723	0.01782209	0.18782209	15
16	12.33030411	0.08110100	66.64884769	5.40528823	0.01500401	0.18500401	16
17	14.42645581	0.06931709	78.97915180	5.47460533	0.01266157	0.18266157	17
18	16.87895329	0.05924538	93.40560761	5.53385071	0.01070600	0.18070600	18
19	19.74837535	0.05063708	110.28456090	5.58448778	0.00906745	0.17906745	19
20	23.10559916	0.04327955	130.03293626	5.62776734	0.00769036	0.17769036	20
21	27.03355102	0.03699107	153.13853542	5.66475841	0.00653004	0.17653004	21
22	31.62925470	0.03161630	180.17208644	5.69637471	0.00555025	0.17555025	22
23	37.00622799	0.02702248	211.80134114	5.72339719	0.00472141	0.17472141	23
24	43.29728675	0.02309614	248.80756913	5.74649332	0.00401917	0.17401917	24
25	50.65782550	0.01974029	292.10485588	5.76623361	0.00342343	0.17342343	25
26	59.26965584	0.01687204	342.76268138	5.78310565	0.00291747	0.17291747	26
27	69.34549733	0.01442055	402.03233722	5.79752619	0.00248736	0.17248736	27
28	81.13423187	0.01232525	471.37783454	5.80985145	0.00212144	0.17212144	28
29	94.92705129	0.01053440	552.51206642	5.82038585	0.00180992	0.17180992	29
30	111.06465001	0.00900376	647.43911771	5.82938962	0.00154455	0.17154455	30
31	129.94564051	0.00769553	758.50376772	5.83708514	0.00131839	0.17131839	31
32	152.03639940	0.00657737	888.44940823	5.84366252	0.00112556	0.17112556	32
33	177.88258730	0.00562169	1040.48580763	5.84928420	0.00096109	0.17096109	33
34	208.12262714	0.00480486	1218.36839493	5.85408906	0.00082077	0.17082077	34
35	243.50347375	0.00410672	1426.49102206	5.85819578	0.00070102	0.17070102	35
36	284.89906429	0.00351002	1669.99449581	5.86170579	0.00059880	0.17059880	36
37	333.33190522	0.00300001	1954.89356010	5.86470581	0.00051154	0.17051154	37
38	389.99832910	0.00256411	2288.22546532	5.86726992	0.00043702	0.17043702	38
39	456.29804505	0.00219155	2678.22379443	5.86946147	0.00037338	0.17037338	39
40	533.86871271	0.00187312	3134.52183948	5.87133459	0.00031903	0.17031903	40
41	624.62639387	0.00160096	3668.39055219	5.87293555	0.00027260	0.17027260	41
42	730.81288083	0.00136834	4293.01694606	5.87430389	0.00023294	0.17023294	42
43	855.05107057	0.00116952	5023.82982689	5.87547341	0.00019905	0.17019905	43
44	1000.40975257	0.00099959	5878.88089746	5.87647300	0.00017010	0.17017010	44
45	1170.47941051	0.00085435	6879.29065003	5.87732735	0.00014536	0.17014536	45
46	1369.46091029	0.00073021	8049.77006054	5.87805756	0.00012423	0.17012423	46
47	1602.26926504	0.00062411	9419.23097083	5.87868168	0.00010617	0.17010617	47
48	1874.65504010	0.00053343	11021.50023587	5.87921511	0.00009073	0.17009073	48
49	2193.34639691	0.00045592	12896.15527597	5.87967103	0.00007754	0.17007754	49
50	2566.21528439	0.00038968	15089.50167288	5.88006071	0.00006627	0.17006627	50

Tables 10 Through 12 (continued). Compound Interest

18% n	Table 10.1. Compound amount	Table 10.2. Present value	Table 11.1. Amount of annuity	Table 11.2. Present value of annuity	Table 12.1. Sinking fund	Table 12.2. Amortization	18% n
1	1.18000000	0.84745763	1.00000000	0.84745763	1.00000000	1.18000000	1
2	1.39240000	0.71818443	2.18000000	1.56564206	0.45871560	0.63871560	2
3	1.64303200	0.60863087	3.57240000	2.17427293	0.27992386	0.45992386	3
4	1.93877776	0.51578888	5.21543200	2.69006180	0.19173867	0.37173867	4
5	2.28775776	0.43710922	7.15420976	3.12717102	0.13977784	0.31977784	5
6	2.69955415	0.37043154	9.44196752	3.49760256	0.10591013	0.28591013	6
7	3.18547390	0.31392503	12.14152167	3.81152759	0.08236200	0.26236200	7
8	3.75885920	0.26603816	15.32699557	4.07756576	0.06524436	0.24524436	8
9	4.43545386	0.22545607	19.08585477	4.30302183	0.05239482	0.23239482	9
10	5.23383555	0.19106447	23.52130863	4.49408629	0.04251464	0.22251464	10
11	6.17592595	0.16191904	28.75514419	4.65600533	0.03477639	0.21477639	11
12	7.28759263	0.13721953	34.93107014	4.79322486	0.02862781	0.20862781	12
13	8.59935930	0.11628773	42.21866276	4.90951259	0.02368621	0.20368621	13
14	10.14724397	0.09854893	50.81802206	5.00806152	0.01967806	0.19967806	14
15	11.97374789	0.08351604	60.96526603	5.09157756	0.01640278	0.19640278	15
16	14.12902251	0.07077630	72.93901392	5.16235386	0.01371008	0.19371008	16
17	16.67224656	0.05997992	87.06803642	5.22233378	0.01148527	0.19148527	17
18	19.67325094	0.05083044	103.74028298	5.27316422	0.00963946	0.18963946	18
19	23.21443611	0.04307664	123.41353392	5.31624087	0.00810284	0.18810284	19
20	27.39303460	0.03650563	146.62797002	5.35274650	0.00681998	0.18681998	20
21	32.32378083	0.03093698	174.02100463	5.38368347	0.00574643	0.18574643	21
22	38.14206138	0.02621778	206.34478546	5.40990125	0.00484626	0.18484626	22
23	45.00763243	0.02221845	244.48684684	5.43211970	0.00409020	0.18409020	23
24	53.10900627	0.01882920	289.49447928	5.45094890	0.00345430	0.18345430	24
25	62.66862740	0.01595695	342.60348554	5.46690585	0.00291883	0.18291883	25
26	73.94898033	0.01352284	405.27211294	5.48042868	0.00246748	0.18246748	26
27	87.25979679	0.01146003	479.22109327	5.49188872	0.00208672	0.18208672	27
28	102.96656021	0.00971189	566.48089006	5.50160061	0.00176528	0.18176528	28
29	121.50054105	0.00823042	669.44745027	5.50983102	0.00149377	0.18149377	29
30	143.37063844	0.00697493	790.94799132	5.51680595	0.00126431	0.18126431	30
31	169.17735336	0.00591096	934.31862976	5.52271691	0.00107030	0.18107030	31
32	199.62927696	0.00500929	1103.49598312	5.52772619	0.00090621	0.18090621	32
33	235.56254681	0.00424516	1303.12526008	5.53197135	0.00076739	0.18076739	33
34	277.96380524	0.00359759	1538.68780689	5.53556894	0.00064990	0.18064990	34
35	327.99729018	0.00304881	1816.65161213	5.53861775	0.00055046	0.18055046	35
36	387.03680242	0.00258373	2144.64890232	5.54120148	0.00046628	0.18046628	36
37	456.70342685	0.00218960	2531.68570473	5.54339108	0.00039499	0.18039499	37
38	538.91004369	0.00185560	2988.38913158	5.54524668	0.00033463	0.18033463	38
39	635.91385155	0.00157254	3527.29917527	5.54681922	0.00028350	0.18028350	39
40	750.37834483	0.00133266	4163.21302682	5.54815188	0.00024020	0.18024020	40
41	885.44644690	0.00112937	4913.59137165	5.54928126	0.00020352	0.18020352	41
42	1044.82680734	0.00095710	5799.03781854	5.55023835	0.00017244	0.18017244	42
43	1232.89563266	0.00081110	6843.86462588	5.55104945	0.00014612	0.18014612	43
44	1454.81684654	0.00068737	8076.76025854	5.55173682	0.00012381	0.18012381	44
45	1716.68387891	0.00058252	9531.57710507	5.55231934	0.00010491	0.18010491	45
46	2025.68697712	0.00049366	11248.26098399	5.55281300	0.00008890	0.18008890	46
47	2390.31063300	0.00041836	13273.94796110	5.55323136	0.00007534	0.18007534	47
48	2820.56654694	0.00035454	15664.25859410	5.55358590	0.00006384	0.18006384	48
49	3328.26852539	0.00030046	18484.82514104	5.55388635	0.00005410	0.18005410	49
50	3927.35685996	0.00025462	21813.09366643	5.55414098	0.00004584	0.18004584	50

Tables 10 Through 12 (continued). Compound Interest

19%	Table 10.1. Compound amount	Table 10.2. Present value	Table 11.1. Amount of annuity	Table 11.2. Present value of annuity	Table 12.1. Sinking fund	Table 12.2. Amortization	19%
n							n
1	1.19000000	0.84033613	1.00000000	0.84033613	1.00000000	1.19000000	1
2	1.41610000	0.70616482	2.19000000	1.54650095	0.45662100	0.64662100	2
3	1.68515900	0.59341581	3.60610000	2.13991677	0.27730789	0.46730789	3
4	2.00533921	0.49866875	5.29125900	2.63858552	0.18899094	0.37899094	4
5	2.38635366	0.41904937	7.29659821	3.05763489	0.13705017	0.32705017	5
6	2.83976086	0.35214233	9.68295187	3.40977722	0.10327429	0.29327429	6
7	3.37931542	0.29591792	12.52271273	3.70569514	0.07985490	0.26985490	7
8	4.02138535	0.24867052	15.90202814	3.95436567	0.06288506	0.25288506	8
9	4.78544856	0.20896683	19.92341349	4.16333249	0.05019220	0.24019220	9
10	5.69468379	0.17560238	24.70886205	4.33893487	0.04047131	0.23047131	10
11	6.77667371	0.14756502	30.40354584	4.48649989	0.03289090	0.22289090	11
12	8.06424172	0.12400422	37.18021955	4.61050411	0.02689602	0.21689602	12
13	9.59644764	0.10420523	45.24446127	4.71470933	0.02210215	0.21210215	13
14	11.41977269	0.08756742	54.84090891	4.80227675	0.01823456	0.20823456	14
15	13.58952950	0.07358606	66.26068160	4.87586282	0.01509191	0.20509191	15
16	16.17154011	0.06183703	79.85021111	4.93769985	0.01252345	0.20252345	16
17	19.24413273	0.05196389	96.02175122	4.98966374	0.01041431	0.20041431	17
18	22.90051795	0.04366713	115.26588395	5.03333087	0.00867559	0.19867559	18
19	27.25161636	0.03669507	138.16640190	5.07002594	0.00723765	0.19723765	19
20	32.42942347	0.03083619	165.41801826	5.10086214	0.00604529	0.19604529	20
21	38.59101393	0.02591277	197.84744173	5.12677490	0.00505440	0.19505440	21
22	45.92330658	0.02177544	236.43845566	5.14855034	0.00422943	0.19422943	22
23	54.64873482	0.01829869	282.36176223	5.16684902	0.00354156	0.19354156	23
24	65.03199444	0.01537705	337.01049706	5.18222607	0.00296727	0.19296727	24
25	77.38807338	0.01292189	402.04249150	5.19514796	0.00248730	0.19248730	25
26	92.09180733	0.01085873	479.43056488	5.20600669	0.00208581	0.19208581	26
27	109.58925072	0.00912498	571.52237221	5.21513167	0.00174971	0.19174971	27
28	130.41120836	0.00766805	681.11162293	5.22279972	0.00146819	0.19146819	28
29	155.18933794	0.00644374	811.52283129	5.22924347	0.00123225	0.19123225	29
30	184.67531215	0.00541491	966.71216923	5.23465837	0.00103443	0.19103443	30
31	219.76362146	0.00455034	1151.38748139	5.23920872	0.00086852	0.19086852	31
32	261.51870954	0.00382382	1371.15110285	5.24303254	0.00072931	0.19072931	32
33	311.20726435	0.00321329	1632.66981239	5.24624583	0.00061249	0.19061249	33
34	370.33664458	0.00270025	1943.87707675	5.24894607	0.00051444	0.19051444	34
35	440.70060705	0.00226911	2314.21372133	5.25121519	0.00043211	0.19043211	35
36	524.43372239	0.00190682	2754.91432838	5.25312201	0.00036299	0.19036299	36
37	624.07612965	0.00160237	3279.34805077	5.25472438	0.00030494	0.19030494	37
38	742.65059428	0.00134653	3903.42418042	5.25607090	0.00025619	0.19025619	38
39	883.75420719	0.00113154	4646.07477470	5.25720244	0.00021524	0.19021524	39
40	1051.66750656	0.00095087	5529.82898189	5.25815331	0.00018084	0.19018084	40
41	1251.48433281	0.00079905	6581.49648845	5.25895236	0.00015194	0.19015194	41
42	1489.26635604	0.00067147	7832.98082126	5.25962383	0.00012767	0.19012767	42
43	1772.22696369	0.00056426	9322.24717730	5.26018810	0.00010727	0.19010727	43
44	2108.95008679	0.00047417	11094.47414099	5.26066227	0.00009013	0.19009013	44
45	2509.65060328	0.00039846	13203.42422777	5.26106073	0.00007574	0.19007574	45
46	2986.48421790	0.00033484	15713.07483105	5.26139557	0.00006364	0.19006364	46
47	3553.91621930	0.00028138	18699.55904895	5.26167695	0.00005348	0.19005348	47
48	4229.16030097	0.00023645	22253.47526825	5.26191340	0.00004494	0.19004494	48
49	5032.70075815	0.00019870	26482.63556922	5.26211210	0.00003776	0.19003776	49
50	5988.91390220	0.00016698	31515.33632737	5.26227908	0.00003173	0.19003173	50

Tables 10 Through 12 (continued). Compound Interest

20% n	Table 10.1. Compound amount	Table 10.2. Present value	Table 11.1. Amount of annuity	Table 11.2. Present value of annuity	Table 12.1. Sinking fund	Table 12.2. Amortization	20% n
1	1.20000000	0.83333333	1.00000000	0.83333333	1.00000000	1.20000000	1
2	1.44000000	0.69444444	2.20000000	1.52777778	0.45454545	0.65454545	2
3	1.72800000	0.57870370	3.64000000	2.10648148	0.27472527	0.47472527	3
4	2.07360000	0.48225309	5.36800000	2.58873457	0.18628912	0.38628912	4
5	2.48832000	0.40187757	7.44160000	2.99061214	0.13437970	0.33437970	5
6	2.98598400	0.33489798	9.92992000	3.32551012	0.10070575	0.30070575	6
7	3.58318080	0.27908165	12.91590400	3.60459176	0.07742393	0.27742393	7
8	4.29981696	0.23256804	16.49908480	3.83715980	0.06060942	0.26060942	8
9	5.15978035	0.19380670	20.79890176	4.03096650	0.04807946	0.24807946	9
10	6.19173642	0.16150558	25.95868211	4.19247209	0.03852276	0.23852276	10
11	7.43008371	0.13458799	32.15041853	4.32706007	0.03110379	0.23110379	11
12	8.91610045	0.11215665	39.58050224	4.43921673	0.02526496	0.22526496	12
13	10.69932054	0.09346388	48.49660269	4.53268061	0.02062000	0.22062000	13
14	12.83918465	0.07788057	59.19592323	4.61056717	0.01689306	0.21689306	14
15	15.40702157	0.06490547	72.03510787	4.67547264	0.01388212	0.21388212	15
16	18.48842589	0.05408789	87.44212945	4.72956054	0.01143614	0.21143614	16
17	22.18611107	0.04507324	105.93055534	4.77463378	0.00944015	0.20944015	17
18	26.62333328	0.03756104	128.11666640	4.81219482	0.00780539	0.20780539	18
19	31.94799994	0.03130086	154.73999969	4.84349568	0.00646245	0.20646245	19
20	38.33759992	0.02608405	186.68799962	4.86957973	0.00535653	0.20535653	20
21	46.00511991	0.02173671	225.02559955	4.89131644	0.00444394	0.20444394	21
22	55.20614389	0.01811393	271.03071946	4.90943037	0.00368962	0.20368962	22
23	66.24737267	0.01509494	326.23686335	4.92452531	0.00306526	0.20306526	23
24	79.49684720	0.01257912	392.48423602	4.93710442	0.00254787	0.20254787	24
25	95.39621664	0.01048260	471.98108322	4.94758702	0.00211873	0.20211873	25
26	114.47545997	0.00873550	567.37729986	4.95632252	0.00176250	0.20176250	26
27	137.37055197	0.00727958	681.85275984	4.96360210	0.00146659	0.20146659	27
28	164.84466236	0.00606632	819.22331180	4.96966841	0.00122067	0.20122067	28
29	197.81359483	0.00505526	984.06797417	4.97472368	0.00101619	0.20101619	29
30	237.37631380	0.00421272	1181.88156900	4.97893640	0.00084611	0.20084611	30
31	284.85157656	0.00351060	1419.25788280	4.98244700	0.00070459	0.20070459	31
32	341.82189187	0.00292550	1704.10945936	4.98537250	0.00058682	0.20058682	32
33	410.18627025	0.00243792	2045.93135123	4.98781042	0.00048877	0.20048877	33
34	492.22352430	0.00203160	2456.11762148	4.98984201	0.00040715	0.20040715	34
35	590.66822915	0.00169300	2948.34114577	4.99153501	0.00033917	0.20033917	35
36	708.80187499	0.00141083	3539.00937493	4.99294584	0.00028256	0.20028256	36
37	850.56224998	0.00117569	4247.81124991	4.99412154	0.00023542	0.20023542	37
38	1020.67469998	0.00097974	5098.37349989	4.99510128	0.00019614	0.20019614	38
39	1224.80963997	0.00081645	6119.04819987	4.99591773	0.00016342	0.20016342	39
40	1469.77156797	0.00068038	7343.85783985	4.99659811	0.00013617	0.20013617	40
41	1763.72588156	0.00056698	8813.62940781	4.99716509	0.00011346	0.20011346	41
42	2116.47105788	0.00047248	10577.35528938	4.99763758	0.00009454	0.20009454	42
43	2539.76526945	0.00039374	12693.82634725	4.99803131	0.00007878	0.20007878	43
44	3047.71832334	0.00032811	15233.59161670	4.99835943	0.00006564	0.20006564	44
45	3657.26198801	0.00027343	18281.30994004	4.99863286	0.00005470	0.20005470	45
46	4388.71438561	0.00022786	21938.57192805	4.99886071	0.00004558	0.20004558	46
47	5266.45726273	0.00018988	26327.28631366	4.99905060	0.00003798	0.20003798	47
48	6319.74871528	0.00015823	31593.74357640	4.99920883	0.00003165	0.20003165	48
49	7583.69845834	0.00013186	37913.49229168	4.99934069	0.00002638	0.20002638	49
50	9100.43815000	0.00010988	45497.19075001	4.99945058	0.00002198	0.20002198	50

Table 14.1. Payroll Taxes: SINGLE Persons — WEEKLY Payroll Period

And the wages are—		And the number of withholding allowances claimed is—										
At least	But less than	0	1	2	3	4	5	6	7	8	9	10
		The amount of income tax to be withheld shall be—										
$0	$30	$0	$0	$0	$0	$0	$0	$0	$0	$0	$0	$0
30	32	1	0	0	0	0	0	0	0	0	0	0
32	34	1	0	0	0	0	0	0	0	0	0	0
34	36	1	0	0	0	0	0	0	0	0	0	0
36	38	1	0	0	0	0	0	0	0	0	0	0
38	40	1	0	0	0	0	0	0	0	0	0	0
40	42	2	0	0	0	0	0	0	0	0	0	0
42	44	2	0	0	0	0	0	0	0	0	0	0
44	46	2	0	0	0	0	0	0	0	0	0	0
46	48	2	0	0	0	0	0	0	0	0	0	0
48	50	3	0	0	0	0	0	0	0	0	0	0
50	52	3	1	0	0	0	0	0	0	0	0	0
52	54	3	1	0	0	0	0	0	0	0	0	0
54	56	3	1	0	0	0	0	0	0	0	0	0
56	58	4	1	0	0	0	0	0	0	0	0	0
58	60	4	1	0	0	0	0	0	0	0	0	0
60	62	4	2	0	0	0	0	0	0	0	0	0
62	64	4	2	0	0	0	0	0	0	0	0	0
64	66	4	2	0	0	0	0	0	0	0	0	0
66	68	5	2	0	0	0	0	0	0	0	0	0
68	70	5	3	0	0	0	0	0	0	0	0	0
70	72	5	3	1	0	0	0	0	0	0	0	0
72	74	6	3	1	0	0	0	0	0	0	0	0
74	76	6	3	1	0	0	0	0	0	0	0	0
76	78	6	4	1	0	0	0	0	0	0	0	0
78	80	6	4	1	0	0	0	0	0	0	0	0
80	82	7	4	2	0	0	0	0	0	0	0	0
82	84	7	4	2	0	0	0	0	0	0	0	0
84	86	7	4	2	0	0	0	0	0	0	0	0
86	88	7	5	2	0	0	0	0	0	0	0	0
88	90	8	5	3	0	0	0	0	0	0	0	0
90	92	8	5	3	1	0	0	0	0	0	0	0
92	94	8	6	3	1	0	0	0	0	0	0	0
94	96	9	6	3	1	0	0	0	0	0	0	0
96	98	9	6	4	1	0	0	0	0	0	0	0
98	100	9	6	4	1	0	0	0	0	0	0	0
100	105	10	7	4	2	0	0	0	0	0	0	0
105	110	10	8	5	2	0	0	0	0	0	0	0
110	115	11	8	5	3	1	0	0	0	0	0	0
115	120	12	9	6	4	1	0	0	0	0	0	0
120	125	13	10	7	4	2	0	0	0	0	0	0
125	130	13	10	8	5	2	0	0	0	0	0	0
130	135	14	11	8	5	3	1	0	0	0	0	0
135	140	15	12	9	6	4	1	0	0	0	0	0
140	145	16	13	10	7	4	2	0	0	0	0	0
145	150	16	13	10	8	5	2	0	0	0	0	0
150	160	18	14	11	9	6	3	1	0	0	0	0
160	170	19	16	13	10	7	4	2	0	0	0	0
170	180	21	18	14	11	9	6	3	1	0	0	0
180	190	22	19	16	13	10	7	4	2	0	0	0
190	200	24	21	18	14	11	9	6	3	1	0	0
200	210	26	22	19	16	13	10	7	4	2	0	0
210	220	27	24	21	18	14	11	9	6	3	1	0
220	230	29	26	22	19	16	13	10	7	4	2	0
230	240	31	27	24	21	18	14	11	9	6	3	1
240	250	33	29	26	22	19	16	13	10	7	4	2
250	260	35	31	27	24	21	18	14	11	9	6	3
260	270	37	33	29	26	22	19	16	13	10	7	4
270	280	39	35	31	27	24	21	18	14	11	9	6
280	290	41	37	33	29	26	22	19	16	13	10	7
290	300	43	39	35	31	27	24	21	18	14	11	9
300	310	46	41	37	33	29	26	22	19	16	13	10
310	320	48	43	39	35	31	27	24	21	18	14	11
320	330	50	46	41	37	33	29	26	22	19	16	13
330	340	53	48	43	39	35	31	27	24	21	18	14
340	350	55	50	46	41	37	33	29	26	22	19	16
350	360	58	53	48	43	39	35	31	27	24	21	18
360	370	60	55	50	46	41	37	33	29	26	22	19
370	380	63	58	53	48	43	39	35	31	27	24	21

(Continued on next page)

Table 14.1. Payroll Taxes: SINGLE Persons — WEEKLY Payroll Period

And the wages are–		And the number of withholding allowances claimed is–										
At least	But less than	0	1	2	3	4	5	6	7	8	9	10
		The amount of income tax to be withheld shall be–										
$380	$390	$65	$60	$55	$50	$46	$41	$37	$33	$29	$26	$22
390	400	68	63	58	53	48	43	39	35	31	27	24
400	410	71	65	60	55	50	46	41	37	33	29	26
410	420	73	68	63	58	53	48	43	39	35	31	27
420	430	76	71	65	60	55	50	46	41	37	33	29
430	440	78	73	68	63	58	53	48	43	39	35	31
440	450	81	76	71	65	60	55	50	46	41	37	33
450	460	84	78	73	68	63	58	53	48	43	39	35
460	470	87	81	76	71	65	60	55	50	46	41	37
470	480	90	84	78	73	68	63	58	53	48	43	39
480	490	93	87	81	76	71	65	60	55	50	46	41
490	500	96	90	84	78	73	68	63	58	53	48	43
500	510	99	93	87	81	76	71	65	60	55	50	46
510	520	102	96	90	84	78	73	68	63	58	53	48
520	530	105	99	93	87	81	76	71	65	60	55	50
530	540	108	102	96	90	84	78	73	68	63	58	53
540	550	111	105	99	93	87	81	76	71	65	60	55
550	560	114	108	102	96	90	84	78	73	68	63	58
560	570	117	111	105	99	93	87	81	76	71	65	60
570	580	121	114	108	102	96	90	84	78	73	68	63
580	590	124	117	111	105	99	93	87	81	76	71	65
590	600	127	121	114	108	102	96	90	84	78	73	68
600	610	131	124	117	111	105	99	93	87	81	76	71
610	620	134	127	121	114	108	102	96	90	84	78	73
620	630	138	131	124	117	111	105	99	93	87	81	76
630	640	141	134	127	121	114	108	102	96	90	84	78
640	650	144	138	131	124	117	111	105	99	93	87	81
650	660	148	141	134	127	121	114	108	102	96	90	84
660	670	151	144	138	131	124	117	111	105	99	93	87
670	680	155	148	141	134	127	121	114	108	102	96	90
680	690	159	151	144	138	131	124	117	111	105	99	93
690	700	162	155	148	141	134	127	121	114	108	102	96
700	710	166	159	151	144	138	131	124	117	111	105	99
710	720	170	162	155	148	141	134	127	121	114	108	102
720	730	173	166	159	151	144	138	131	124	117	111	105
730	740	177	170	162	155	148	141	134	127	121	114	108
740	750	181	173	166	159	151	144	138	131	124	117	111
750	760	184	177	170	162	155	148	141	134	127	121	114
760	770	188	181	173	166	159	151	144	138	131	124	117
770	780	192	184	177	170	162	155	148	141	134	127	121
780	790	196	188	181	173	166	159	151	144	138	131	124
790	800	199	192	184	177	170	162	155	148	141	134	127
800	810	203	196	188	181	173	166	159	151	144	138	131
810	820	207	199	192	184	177	170	162	155	148	141	134
820	830	210	203	196	188	181	173	166	159	151	144	138
830	840	214	207	199	192	184	177	170	162	155	148	141
840	850	218	210	203	196	188	181	173	166	159	151	144
850	860	221	214	207	199	192	184	177	170	162	155	148
860	870	225	218	210	203	196	188	181	173	166	159	151
870	880	229	221	214	207	199	192	184	177	170	162	155
880	890	233	225	218	210	203	196	188	181	173	166	159
890	900	236	229	221	214	207	199	192	184	177	170	162
900	910	240	233	225	218	210	203	196	188	181	173	166
910	920	244	236	229	221	214	207	199	192	184	177	170
920	930	247	240	233	225	218	210	203	196	188	181	173
930	940	251	244	236	229	221	214	207	199	192	184	177
940	950	255	247	240	233	225	218	210	203	196	188	181
950	960	258	251	244	236	229	221	214	207	199	192	184
960	970	262	255	247	240	233	225	218	210	203	196	188
970	980	266	258	251	244	236	229	221	214	207	199	192
980	990	270	262	255	247	240	233	225	218	210	203	196
990	1,000	273	266	258	251	244	236	229	221	214	207	199
1,000	1,010	277	270	262	255	247	240	233	225	218	210	203
1,010	1,020	281	273	266	258	251	244	236	229	221	214	207
1,020	1,030	284	277	270	262	255	247	240	233	225	218	210
37 percent of the excess over $1,030 plus–												
$1,030 and over		286	279	271	264	257	249	242	234	227	220	212

Table 14.1. Payroll Taxes: MARRIED Persons — WEEKLY Payroll Period

And the wages are—		And the number of withholding allowances claimed is—										
At least	But less than	0	1	2	3	4	5	6	7	8	9	10
		The amount of income tax to be withheld shall be—										
$0	$52	$0	$0	$0	$0	$0	$0	$0	$0	$0	$0	$0
52	54	1	0	0	0	0	0	0	0	0	0	0
54	56	1	0	0	0	0	0	0	0	0	0	0
56	58	1	0	0	0	0	0	0	0	0	0	0
58	60	1	0	0	0	0	0	0	0	0	0	0
60	62	1	0	0	0	0	0	0	0	0	0	0
62	64	2	0	0	0	0	0	0	0	0	0	0
64	66	2	0	0	0	0	0	0	0	0	0	0
66	68	2	0	0	0	0	0	0	0	0	0	0
68	70	2	0	0	0	0	0	0	0	0	0	0
70	72	3	0	0	0	0	0	0	0	0	0	0
72	74	3	1	0	0	0	0	0	0	0	0	0
74	76	3	1	0	0	0	0	0	0	0	0	0
76	78	3	1	0	0	0	0	0	0	0	0	0
78	80	3	1	0	0	0	0	0	0	0	0	0
80	82	4	1	0	0	0	0	0	0	0	0	0
82	84	4	2	0	0	0	0	0	0	0	0	0
84	86	4	2	0	0	0	0	0	0	0	0	0
86	88	4	2	0	0	0	0	0	0	0	0	0
88	90	5	2	0	0	0	0	0	0	0	0	0
90	92	5	3	0	0	0	0	0	0	0	0	0
92	94	5	3	1	0	0	0	0	0	0	0	0
94	96	5	3	1	0	0	0	0	0	0	0	0
96	98	5	3	1	0	0	0	0	0	0	0	0
98	100	6	3	1	0	0	0	0	0	0	0	0
100	105	6	4	2	0	0	0	0	0	0	0	0
105	110	7	4	2	0	0	0	0	0	0	0	0
110	115	7	5	3	0	0	0	0	0	0	0	0
115	120	8	6	3	1	0	0	0	0	0	0	0
120	125	9	6	4	2	0	0	0	0	0	0	0
125	130	9	7	4	2	0	0	0	0	0	0	0
130	135	10	7	5	3	0	0	0	0	0	0	0
135	140	10	8	6	3	1	0	0	0	0	0	0
140	145	11	9	6	4	2	0	0	0	0	0	0
145	150	12	9	7	4	2	0	0	0	0	0	0
150	160	13	10	8	5	3	1	0	0	0	0	0
160	170	14	11	9	6	4	2	0	0	0	0	0
170	180	16	13	10	8	5	3	1	0	0	0	0
180	190	17	14	11	9	6	4	2	0	0	0	0
190	200	18	16	13	10	8	5	3	1	0	0	0
200	210	20	17	14	11	9	6	4	2	0	0	0
210	220	21	18	16	13	10	8	5	3	1	0	0
220	230	23	20	17	14	11	9	6	4	2	0	0
230	240	24	21	18	16	13	10	8	5	3	1	0
240	250	26	23	20	17	14	11	9	6	4	2	0
250	260	28	24	21	18	16	13	10	8	5	3	1
260	270	29	26	23	20	17	14	11	9	6	4	2
270	280	31	28	24	21	18	16	13	10	8	5	3
280	290	32	29	26	23	20	17	14	11	9	6	4
290	300	34	31	28	24	21	18	16	13	10	8	5
300	310	36	32	29	26	23	20	17	14	11	9	6
310	320	38	34	31	28	24	21	18	16	13	10	8
320	330	39	36	32	29	26	23	20	17	14	11	9
330	340	41	38	34	31	28	24	21	18	16	13	10
340	350	43	39	36	32	29	26	23	20	17	14	11
350	360	45	41	38	34	31	28	24	21	18	16	13
360	370	47	43	39	36	32	29	26	23	20	17	14
370	380	48	45	41	38	34	31	28	24	21	18	16
380	390	50	47	43	39	36	32	29	26	23	20	17
390	400	52	48	45	41	38	34	31	28	24	21	18
400	410	55	50	47	43	39	36	32	29	26	23	20
410	420	57	52	48	45	41	38	34	31	28	24	21
420	430	59	55	50	47	43	39	36	32	29	26	23
430	440	61	57	52	48	45	41	38	34	31	28	24
440	450	63	59	55	50	47	43	39	36	32	29	26
450	460	66	61	57	52	48	45	41	38	34	31	28
460	470	68	63	59	55	50	47	43	39	36	32	29
470	480	70	66	61	57	52	48	45	41	38	34	31
480	490	73	68	63	59	55	50	47	43	39	36	32

(Continued on next page)

Table 14.1. Payroll Taxes: MARRIED Persons — WEEKLY Payroll Period

And the wages are—		And the number of withholding allowances claimed is—										
At least	But less than	0	1	2	3	4	5	6	7	8	9	10
		The amount of income tax to be withheld shall be—										
$490	$500	$75	$70	$66	$61	$57	$52	$48	$45	$41	$38	$34
500	510	78	73	68	63	59	55	50	47	43	39	36
510	520	80	75	70	66	61	57	52	48	45	41	38
520	530	83	78	73	68	63	59	55	50	47	43	39
530	540	85	80	75	70	66	61	57	52	48	45	41
540	550	88	83	78	73	68	63	59	55	50	47	43
550	560	90	85	80	75	70	66	61	57	52	48	45
560	570	93	88	83	78	73	68	63	59	55	50	47
570	580	95	90	85	80	75	70	66	61	57	52	48
580	590	98	93	88	83	78	73	68	63	59	55	50
590	600	101	95	90	85	80	75	70	66	61	57	52
600	610	103	98	93	88	83	78	73	68	63	59	55
610	620	106	101	95	90	85	80	75	70	66	61	57
620	630	109	103	98	93	88	83	78	73	68	63	59
630	640	112	106	101	95	90	85	80	75	70	66	61
640	650	115	109	103	98	93	88	83	78	73	68	63
650	660	117	112	106	101	95	90	85	80	75	70	66
660	670	120	115	109	103	98	93	88	83	78	73	68
670	680	123	117	112	106	101	95	90	85	80	75	70
680	690	126	120	115	109	103	98	93	88	83	78	73
690	700	129	123	117	112	106	101	95	90	85	80	75
700	710	132	126	120	115	109	103	98	93	88	83	78
710	720	136	129	123	117	112	106	101	95	90	85	80
720	730	139	132	126	120	115	109	103	98	93	88	83
730	740	142	136	129	123	117	112	106	101	95	90	85
740	750	146	139	132	126	120	115	109	103	98	93	88
750	760	149	142	136	129	123	117	112	106	101	95	90
760	770	152	146	139	132	126	120	115	109	103	98	93
770	780	155	149	142	136	129	123	117	112	106	101	95
780	790	159	152	146	139	132	126	120	115	109	103	98
790	800	162	155	149	142	136	129	123	117	112	106	101
800	810	165	159	152	146	139	132	126	120	115	109	103
810	820	169	162	155	149	142	136	129	123	117	112	106
820	830	172	165	159	152	146	139	132	126	120	115	109
830	840	175	169	162	155	149	142	136	129	123	117	112
840	850	179	172	165	159	152	146	139	132	126	120	115
850	860	182	175	169	162	155	149	142	136	129	123	117
860	870	185	179	172	165	159	152	146	139	132	126	120
870	880	188	182	175	169	162	155	149	142	136	129	123
880	890	192	185	179	172	165	159	152	146	139	132	126
890	900	195	188	182	175	169	162	155	149	142	136	129
900	910	199	192	185	179	172	165	159	152	146	139	132
910	920	202	195	188	182	175	169	162	155	149	142	136
920	930	206	199	192	185	179	172	165	159	152	146	139
930	940	210	202	195	188	182	175	169	162	155	149	142
940	950	213	206	199	192	185	179	172	165	159	152	146
950	960	217	210	202	195	188	182	175	169	162	155	149
960	970	221	213	206	199	192	185	179	172	165	159	152
970	980	225	217	210	202	195	188	182	175	169	162	155
980	990	228	221	213	206	199	192	185	179	172	165	159
990	1,000	232	225	217	210	202	195	188	182	175	169	162
1,000	1,010	236	228	221	213	206	199	192	185	179	172	165
1,010	1,020	239	232	225	217	210	202	195	188	182	175	169
1,020	1,030	243	236	228	221	213	206	199	192	185	179	172
1,030	1,040	247	239	232	225	217	210	202	195	188	182	175
1,040	1,050	250	243	236	228	221	213	206	199	192	185	179
1,050	1,060	254	247	239	232	225	217	210	202	195	188	182
1,060	1,070	258	250	243	236	228	221	213	206	199	192	185
1,070	1,080	262	254	247	239	232	225	217	210	202	195	188
1,080	1,090	265	258	250	243	236	228	221	213	206	199	192
1,090	1,100	269	262	254	247	239	232	225	217	210	202	195
1,100	1,110	273	265	258	250	243	236	228	221	213	206	199
1,110	1,120	276	269	262	254	247	239	232	225	217	210	202
1,120	1,130	280	273	265	258	250	243	236	228	221	213	206
1,130	1,140	284	276	269	262	254	247	239	232	225	217	210
		37 percent of the excess over $1,140 plus—										
$1,140 and over		286	278	271	263	256	249	241	234	226	219	212

Table 14.1. Payroll Taxes: SINGLE Persons — BIWEEKLY Payroll Period

And the wages are–		And the number of withholding allowances claimed is–										
At least	But less than	0	1	2	3	4	5	6	7	8	9	10
		The amount of income tax to be withheld shall be–										
$0	$56	$0	$0	$0	$0	$0	$0	$0	$0	$0	$0	$0
56	58	1	0	0	0	0	0	0	0	0	0	0
58	60	1	0	0	0	0	0	0	0	0	0	0
60	62	1	0	0	0	0	0	0	0	0	0	0
62	64	1	0	0	0	0	0	0	0	0	0	0
64	66	1	0	0	0	0	0	0	0	0	0	0
66	68	2	0	0	0	0	0	0	0	0	0	0
68	70	2	0	0	0	0	0	0	0	0	0	0
70	72	2	0	0	0	0	0	0	0	0	0	0
72	74	2	0	0	0	0	0	0	0	0	0	0
74	76	3	0	0	0	0	0	0	0	0	0	0
76	78	3	0	0	0	0	0	0	0	0	0	0
78	80	3	0	0	0	0	0	0	0	0	0	0
80	82	3	0	0	0	0	0	0	0	0	0	0
82	84	3	0	0	0	0	0	0	0	0	0	0
84	86	4	0	0	0	0	0	0	0	0	0	0
86	88	4	0	0	0	0	0	0	0	0	0	0
88	90	4	0	0	0	0	0	0	0	0	0	0
90	92	4	0	0	0	0	0	0	0	0	0	0
92	94	5	0	0	0	0	0	0	0	0	0	0
94	96	5	0	0	0	0	0	0	0	0	0	0
96	98	5	1	0	0	0	0	0	0	0	0	0
98	100	5	1	0	0	0	0	0	0	0	0	0
100	102	5	1	0	0	0	0	0	0	0	0	0
102	104	6	1	0	0	0	0	0	0	0	0	0
104	106	6	1	0	0	0	0	0	0	0	0	0
106	108	6	2	0	0	0	0	0	0	0	0	0
108	110	6	2	0	0	0	0	0	0	0	0	0
110	112	7	2	0	0	0	0	0	0	0	0	0
112	114	7	2	0	0	0	0	0	0	0	0	0
114	116	7	3	0	0	0	0	0	0	0	0	0
116	118	7	3	0	0	0	0	0	0	0	0	0
118	120	8	3	0	0	0	0	0	0	0	0	0
120	124	8	3	0	0	0	0	0	0	0	0	0
124	128	8	4	0	0	0	0	0	0	0	0	0
128	132	9	4	0	0	0	0	0	0	0	0	0
132	136	9	5	0	0	0	0	0	0	0	0	0
136	140	10	5	1	0	0	0	0	0	0	0	0
140	144	10	6	1	0	0	0	0	0	0	0	0
144	148	11	6	2	0	0	0	0	0	0	0	0
148	152	12	7	2	0	0	0	0	0	0	0	0
152	156	12	7	2	0	0	0	0	0	0	0	0
156	160	13	7	3	0	0	0	0	0	0	0	0
160	164	13	8	3	0	0	0	0	0	0	0	0
164	168	14	8	4	0	0	0	0	0	0	0	0
168	172	14	9	4	0	0	0	0	0	0	0	0
172	176	15	9	5	0	0	0	0	0	0	0	0
176	180	16	10	5	1	0	0	0	0	0	0	0
180	184	16	10	6	1	0	0	0	0	0	0	0
184	188	17	11	6	2	0	0	0	0	0	0	0
188	192	17	12	7	2	0	0	0	0	0	0	0
192	196	18	12	7	2	0	0	0	0	0	0	0
196	200	18	13	7	3	0	0	0	0	0	0	0
200	210	19	14	8	4	0	0	0	0	0	0	0
210	220	21	15	10	5	0	0	0	0	0	0	0
220	230	22	17	11	6	1	0	0	0	0	0	0
230	240	24	18	12	7	3	0	0	0	0	0	0
240	250	25	19	14	8	4	0	0	0	0	0	0
250	260	27	21	15	10	5	0	0	0	0	0	0
260	270	28	22	17	11	6	1	0	0	0	0	0
270	280	30	24	18	12	7	3	0	0	0	0	0
280	290	31	25	19	14	8	4	0	0	0	0	0
290	300	33	27	21	15	10	5	0	0	0	0	0
300	320	35	29	23	17	12	7	2	0	0	0	0
320	340	38	32	26	20	14	9	4	0	0	0	0
340	360	41	35	29	23	17	12	7	2	0	0	0
360	380	45	38	32	26	20	14	9	4	0	0	0
380	400	48	41	35	29	23	17	12	7	2	0	0
400	420	51	45	38	32	26	20	14	9	4	0	0
420	440	55	48	41	35	29	23	17	12	7	2	0

(Continued on next page)

Table 14.1. Payroll Taxes: SINGLE Persons — BIWEEKLY Payroll Period

And the wages are–		And the number of withholding allowances claimed is–										
At least	But less than	0	1	2	3	4	5	6	7	8	9	10
		The amount of income tax to be withheld shall be–										
$440	$460	$59	$51	$45	$38	$32	$26	$20	$14	$9	$4	$0
460	480	62	55	48	41	35	29	23	17	12	7	2
480	500	66	59	51	45	38	32	26	20	14	9	4
500	520	70	62	55	48	41	35	29	23	17	12	7
520	540	74	66	59	51	45	38	32	26	20	14	9
540	560	78	70	62	55	48	41	35	29	23	17	12
560	580	82	74	66	59	51	45	38	32	26	20	14
580	600	87	78	70	62	55	48	41	35	29	23	17
600	620	92	82	74	66	59	51	45	38	32	26	20
620	640	96	87	78	70	62	55	48	41	35	29	23
640	660	101	92	82	74	66	59	51	45	38	32	26
660	680	105	96	87	78	70	62	55	48	41	35	29
680	700	110	101	92	82	74	66	59	51	45	38	32
700	720	115	105	96	87	78	70	62	55	48	41	35
720	740	120	110	101	92	82	74	66	59	51	45	38
740	760	126	115	105	96	87	78	70	62	55	48	41
760	780	131	120	110	101	92	82	74	66	59	51	45
780	800	136	126	115	105	96	87	78	70	62	55	48
800	820	141	131	120	110	101	92	82	74	66	59	51
820	840	146	136	126	115	105	96	87	78	70	62	55
840	860	152	141	131	120	110	101	92	82	74	66	59
860	880	157	146	136	126	115	105	96	87	78	70	62
880	900	162	152	141	131	120	110	101	92	82	74	66
900	920	168	157	146	136	126	115	105	96	87	78	70
920	940	174	162	152	141	131	120	110	101	92	82	74
940	960	180	168	157	146	136	126	115	105	96	87	78
960	980	186	174	162	152	141	131	120	110	101	92	82
980	1,000	192	180	168	157	146	136	126	115	105	96	87
1,000	1,020	198	186	174	162	152	141	131	120	110	101	92
1,020	1,040	204	192	180	168	157	146	136	126	115	105	96
1,040	1,060	210	198	186	174	162	152	141	131	120	110	101
1,060	1,080	216	204	192	180	168	157	146	136	126	115	105
1,080	1,100	222	210	198	186	174	162	152	141	131	120	110
1,100	1,120	228	216	204	192	180	168	157	146	136	126	115
1,120	1,140	234	222	210	198	186	174	162	152	141	131	120
1,140	1,160	241	228	216	204	192	180	168	157	146	136	126
1,160	1,180	248	234	222	210	198	186	174	162	152	141	131
1,180	1,200	255	241	228	216	204	192	180	168	157	146	136
1,200	1,220	261	248	234	222	210	198	186	174	162	152	141
1,220	1,240	268	255	241	228	216	204	192	180	168	157	146
1,240	1,260	275	261	248	234	222	210	198	186	174	162	152
1,260	1,280	282	268	255	241	228	216	204	192	180	168	157
1,280	1,300	289	275	261	248	234	222	210	198	186	174	162
1,300	1,320	295	282	268	255	241	228	216	204	192	180	168
1,320	1,340	302	289	275	261	248	234	222	210	198	186	174
1,340	1,360	310	295	282	268	255	241	228	216	204	192	180
1,360	1,380	317	302	289	275	261	248	234	222	210	198	186
1,380	1,400	325	310	295	282	268	255	241	228	216	204	192
1,400	1,420	332	317	302	289	275	261	248	234	222	210	198
1,420	1,440	339	325	310	295	282	268	255	241	228	216	204
1,440	1,460	347	332	317	302	289	275	261	248	234	222	210
1,460	1,480	354	339	325	310	295	282	268	255	241	228	216
1,480	1,500	362	347	332	317	302	289	275	261	248	234	222
1,500	1,520	369	354	339	325	310	295	282	268	255	241	228
1,520	1,540	376	362	347	332	317	302	289	275	261	248	234
1,540	1,560	384	369	354	339	325	310	295	282	268	255	241
1,560	1,580	391	376	362	347	332	317	302	289	275	261	248
1,580	1,600	399	384	369	354	339	325	310	295	282	268	255
1,600	1,620	406	391	376	362	347	332	317	302	289	275	261
1,620	1,640	413	399	384	369	354	339	325	310	295	282	268
1,640	1,660	421	406	391	376	362	347	332	317	302	289	275
1,660	1,680	428	413	399	384	369	354	339	325	310	295	282
1,680	1,700	436	421	406	391	376	362	347	332	317	302	289
1,700	1,720	443	428	413	399	384	369	354	339	325	310	295
1,720	1,740	450	436	421	406	391	376	362	347	332	317	302
		37 percent of the excess over $1,740 plus–										
$1,740 and over		454	439	424	410	395	380	365	350	336	321	306

Table 14.1. Payroll Taxes: MARRIED Persons — BIWEEKLY Payroll Period

And the wages are—		And the number of withholding allowances claimed is—										
At least	But less than	0	1	2	3	4	5	6	7	8	9	10
		The amount of income tax to be withheld shall be—										
$0	$100	$0	$0	$0	$0	$0	$0	$0	$0	$0	$0	$0
100	102	1	0	0	0	0	0	0	0	0	0	0
102	104	1	0	0	0	0	0	0	0	0	0	0
104	106	1	0	0	0	0	0	0	0	0	0	0
106	108	1	0	0	0	0	0	0	0	0	0	0
108	110	1	0	0	0	0	0	0	0	0	0	0
110	112	2	0	0	0	0	0	0	0	0	0	0
112	114	2	0	0	0	0	0	0	0	0	0	0
114	116	2	0	0	0	0	0	0	0	0	0	0
116	118	2	0	0	0	0	0	0	0	0	0	0
118	120	3	0	0	0	0	0	0	0	0	0	0
120	124	3	0	0	0	0	0	0	0	0	0	0
124	128	3	0	0	0	0	0	0	0	0	0	0
128	132	4	0	0	0	0	0	0	0	0	0	0
132	136	4	0	0	0	0	0	0	0	0	0	0
136	140	5	0	0	0	0	0	0	0	0	0	0
140	144	5	1	0	0	0	0	0	0	0	0	0
144	148	5	1	0	0	0	0	0	0	0	0	0
148	152	6	2	0	0	0	0	0	0	0	0	0
152	156	6	2	0	0	0	0	0	0	0	0	0
156	160	7	2	0	0	0	0	0	0	0	0	0
160	164	7	3	0	0	0	0	0	0	0	0	0
164	168	8	3	0	0	0	0	0	0	0	0	0
168	172	8	4	0	0	0	0	0	0	0	0	0
172	176	9	4	0	0	0	0	0	0	0	0	0
176	180	9	5	0	0	0	0	0	0	0	0	0
180	184	9	5	1	0	0	0	0	0	0	0	0
184	188	10	5	1	0	0	0	0	0	0	0	0
188	192	10	6	2	0	0	0	0	0	0	0	0
192	196	11	6	2	0	0	0	0	0	0	0	0
196	200	11	7	2	0	0	0	0	0	0	0	0
200	210	12	8	3	0	0	0	0	0	0	0	0
210	220	13	9	4	0	0	0	0	0	0	0	0
220	230	15	10	5	1	0	0	0	0	0	0	0
230	240	16	11	6	2	0	0	0	0	0	0	0
240	250	17	12	8	3	0	0	0	0	0	0	0
250	260	18	13	9	4	0	0	0	0	0	0	0
260	270	19	15	10	5	1	0	0	0	0	0	0
270	280	21	16	11	6	2	0	0	0	0	0	0
280	290	22	17	12	8	3	0	0	0	0	0	0
290	300	24	18	13	9	4	0	0	0	0	0	0
300	320	26	20	15	10	6	2	0	0	0	0	0
320	340	29	23	18	13	8	4	0	0	0	0	0
340	360	31	26	20	15	10	6	2	0	0	0	0
360	380	34	29	23	18	13	8	4	0	0	0	0
380	400	37	31	26	20	15	10	6	2	0	0	0
400	420	40	34	29	23	18	13	8	4	0	0	0
420	440	43	37	31	26	20	15	10	6	2	0	0
440	460	46	40	34	29	23	18	13	8	4	0	0
460	480	49	43	37	31	26	20	15	10	6	2	0
480	500	52	46	40	34	29	23	18	13	8	4	0
500	520	55	49	43	37	31	26	20	15	10	6	2
520	540	58	52	46	40	34	29	23	18	13	8	4
540	560	62	55	49	43	37	31	26	20	15	10	6
560	580	65	58	52	46	40	34	29	23	18	13	8
580	600	68	62	55	49	43	37	31	26	20	15	10
600	620	71	65	58	52	46	40	34	29	23	18	13
620	640	75	68	62	55	49	43	37	31	26	20	15
640	660	79	71	65	58	52	46	40	34	29	23	18
660	680	82	75	68	62	55	49	43	37	31	26	20
680	700	86	79	71	65	58	52	46	40	34	29	23
700	720	89	82	75	68	62	55	49	43	37	31	26
720	740	93	86	79	71	65	58	52	46	40	34	29
740	760	97	89	82	75	68	62	55	49	43	37	31
760	780	100	93	86	79	71	65	58	52	46	40	34
780	800	105	97	89	82	75	68	62	55	49	43	37
800	820	109	100	93	86	79	71	65	58	52	46	40
820	840	113	105	97	89	82	75	68	62	55	49	43
840	860	118	109	100	93	36	79	71	65	58	52	46
860	880	122	113	105	97	89	82	75	68	62	55	49
880	900	127	118	109	100	93	86	79	71	65	58	52

(Continued on next page)

Table 14.1. Payroll Taxes: MARRIED Persons — BIWEEKLY Payroll Period

And the wages are—		And the number of withholding allowances claimed is—										
At least	But less than	0	1	2	3	4	5	6	7	8	9	10
		The amount of income tax to be withheld shall be—										
$900	$920	$131	$122	$113	$105	$97	$89	$82	$75	$68	$62	$55
920	940	135	127	118	109	100	93	86	79	71	65	58
940	960	140	131	122	113	105	97	89	82	75	68	62
960	980	145	135	127	118	109	100	93	86	79	71	65
980	1,000	150	140	131	122	113	105	97	89	82	75	68
1,000	1,020	155	145	135	127	118	109	100	93	86	79	71
1,020	1,040	160	150	140	131	122	113	105	97	89	82	75
1,040	1,060	165	155	145	135	127	118	109	100	93	86	79
1,060	1,080	170	160	150	140	131	122	113	105	97	89	82
1,080	1,100	175	165	155	145	135	127	118	109	100	93	86
1,100	1,120	180	170	160	150	140	131	122	113	105	97	89
1,120	1,140	185	175	165	155	145	135	127	118	109	100	93
1,140	1,160	190	180	170	160	150	140	131	122	113	105	97
1,160	1,180	195	185	175	165	155	145	135	127	118	109	100
1,180	1,200	201	190	180	170	160	150	140	131	122	113	105
1,200	1,220	207	195	185	175	165	165	145	135	127	118	109
1,220	1,240	212	201	190	180	170	160	150	140	131	122	113
1,240	1,260	218	207	195	185	175	165.	155	145	135	127	118
1,260	1,280	223	212	201	190	180	170	160	150	140	131	122
1,280	1,300	229	218	207	195	185	175	165	155	145	135	127
1,300	1,320	235	223	212	201	190	180	170	160	150	140	131
1,320	1,340	240	229	218	207	195	185	175	165	155	145	135
1,340	1,360	246	235	223	212	201	190	180	170	160	150	140
1,360	1,380	251	240	229	218	207	195	185	175	165	155	145
1,380	1,400	258	246	235	223	212	201	190	180	170	160	150
1,400	1,420	265	251	240	229	218	207	195	185	175	165	155
1,420	1,440	271	258	246	235	223	212	201	190	180	170	160
1,440	1,460	278	265	251	240	229	218	207	195	185	175	165
1,460	1,480	284	271	258	246	235	223	212	201	190	180	170
1,480	1,500	291	278	265	251	240	229	218	207	195	185	175
1,500	1,520	298	284	271	258	246	235	223	212	201	190	180
1,520	1,540	304	291	278	265	251	240	229	218	207	195	185
1,540	1,560	311	298	284	271	258	246	235	223	212	201	190
1,560	1,580	317	304	291	278	265	251	240	229	218	207	195
1,580	1,600	324	311	298	284	271	258	246	235	223	212	201
1,600	1,620	331	317	304	291	278	265	251	240	229	218	207
1,620	1,640	337	324	311	298	284	271	258	246	235	223	212
1,640	1,660	344	331	317	304	291	278	265	251	240	229	218
1,660	1,680	350	337	324	311	298	284	271	258	246	235	223
1,680	1,700	357	344	331	317	304	291	278	265	251	240	229
1,700	1,720	364	350	337	324	311	298	284	271	258	246	235
1,720	1,740	370	357	344	331	317	304	291	278	265	251	240
1,740	1,760	377	364	350	337	324	311	298	284	271	258	246
1,760	1,780	383	370	357	344	331	317	304	291	278	265	251
1,780	1,800	390	377	364	350	337	324	311	298	284	271	258
1,800	1,820	397	383	370	357	344	331	317	304	291	278	265
1,820	1,840	405	390	377	364	350	337	324	311	298	284	271
1,840	1,860	412	397	383	370	357	344	331	317	304	291	278
1,860	1,880	420	405	390	377	364	350	337	324	311	298	284
1,880	1,900	427	412	397	383	370	357	344	331	317	304	291
1,900	1,920	434	420	405	390	377	364	350	337	324	311	298
1,920	1,940	442	427	412	397	383	370	357	344	331	317	304
1,940	1,960	449	434	420	405	390	377	364	350	337	324	311
1,960	1,980	457	442	427	412	397	383	370	357	344	331	317
1,980	2,000	464	449	434	420	405	390	377	364	350	337	324
2,000	2,020	471	457	442	427	412	397	383	370	357	344	331
2,020	2,040	479	464	449	434	420	405	390	377	364	350	337
2,040	2,060	486	471	457	442	427	412	397	383	370	357	344
2,060	2,080	494	479	464	449	434	420	405	390	377	364	350
2,080	2,100	501	486	471	457	442	427	412	397	383	370	357
2,100	2,120	508	494	479	464	449	434	420	405	390	377	364
2,120	2,140	516	501	486	471	457	442	427	412	397	383	370
2,140	2,160	523	508	494	479	464	449	434	420	405	390	377
2,160	2,180	531	516	501	486	471	457	442	427	412	397	383
2,180	2,200	538	523	508	494	479	464	449	434	420	405	390
2,200	2,220	545	531	516	501	486	471	457	442	427	412	397
		37 percent of the excess over $2,220 plus—										
$2,220 and over		549	534	519	505	490	475	460	445	431	416	401

Table 14.1. Payroll Taxes: SINGLE Persons — SEMIMONTHLY Payroll Period

And the wages are—		And the number of withholding allowances claimed is—										
At least	But less than	0	1	2	3	4	5	6	7	8	9	10
		The amount of income tax to be withheld shall be—										
$0	$60	$0	$0	$0	$0	$0	$0	$0	$0	$0	$0	$0
60	62	1	0	0	0	0	0	0	0	0	0	0
62	64	1	0	0	0	0	0	0	0	0	0	0
64	66	1	0	0	0	0	0	0	0	0	0	0
66	68	1	0	0	0	0	0	0	0	0	0	0
68	70	1	0	0	0	0	0	0	0	0	0	0
70	72	2	0	0	0	0	0	0	0	0	0	0
72	74	2	0	0	0	0	0	0	0	0	0	0
74	76	2	0	0	0	0	0	0	0	0	0	0
76	78	2	0	0	0	0	0	0	0	0	0	0
78	80	3	0	0	0	0	0	0	0	0	0	0
80	82	3	0	0	0	0	0	0	0	0	0	0
82	84	3	0	0	0	0	0	0	0	0	0	0
84	86	3	0	0	0	0	0	0	0	0	0	0
86	88	3	0	0	0	0	0	0	0	0	0	0
88	90	4	0	0	0	0	0	0	0	0	0	0
90	92	4	0	0	0	0	0	0	0	0	0	0
92	94	4	0	0	0	0	0	0	0	0	0	0
94	96	4	0	0	0	0	0	0	0	0	0	0
96	98	4	0	0	0	0	0	0	0	0	0	0
98	100	5	0	0	0	0	0	0	0	0	0	0
100	102	5	0	0	0	0	0	0	0	0	0	0
102	104	5	0	0	0	0	0	0	0	0	0	0
104	106	5	1	0	0	0	0	0	0	0	0	0
106	108	6	1	0	0	0	0	0	0	0	0	0
108	110	6	1	0	0	0	0	0	0	0	0	0
110	112	6	1	0	0	0	0	0	0	0	0	0
112	114	6	1	0	0	0	0	0	0	0	0	0
114	116	7	2	0	0	0	0	0	0	0	0	0
116	118	7	2	0	0	0	0	0	0	0	0	0
118	120	7	2	0	0	0	0	0	0	0	0	0
120	124	7	2	0	0	0	0	0	0	0	0	0
124	128	8	3	0	0	0	0	0	0	0	0	0
128	132	8	3	0	0	0	0	0	0	0	0	0
132	136	9	4	0	0	0	0	0	0	0	0	0
136	140	9	4	0	0	0	0	0	0	0	0	0
140	144	10	5	0	0	0	0	0	0	0	0	0
144	148	10	5	0	0	0	0	0	0	0	0	0
148	152	11	6	1	0	0	0	0	0	0	0	0
152	156	11	6	1	0	0	0	0	0	0	0	0
156	160	12	7	2	0	0	0	0	0	0	0	0
160	164	13	7	2	0	0	0	0	0	0	0	0
164	168	13	7	3	0	0	0	0	0	0	0	0
168	172	14	8	3	0	0	0	0	0	0	0	0
172	176	14	8	3	0	0	0	0	0	0	0	0
176	180	15	9	4	0	0	0	0	0	0	0	0
180	184	15	9	4	0	0	0	0	0	0	0	0
184	188	16	10	5	0	0	0	0	0	0	0	0
188	192	16	10	5	0	0	0	0	0	0	0	0
192	196	17	11	6	1	0	0	0	0	0	0	0
196	200	18	11	6	1	0	0	0	0	0	0	0
200	210	19	12	7	2	0	0	0	0	0	0	0
210	220	20	14	8	3	0	0	0	0	0	0	0
220	230	21	15	9	4	0	0	0	0	0	0	0
230	240	23	17	11	5	1	0	0	0	0	0	0
240	250	24	18	12	7	2	0	0	0	0	0	0
250	260	26	19	13	8	3	0	0	0	0	0	0
260	270	27	21	15	9	4	0	0	0	0	0	0
270	280	29	22	16	10	5	0	0	0	0	0	0
280	290	30	24	18	12	6	1	0	0	0	0	0
290	300	32	25	19	13	7	2	0	0	0	0	0
300	320	34	27	21	15	9	4	0	0	0	0	0
320	340	37	30	24	18	12	6	2	0	0	0	0
340	360	40	33	27	21	15	9	4	0	0	0	0
360	380	43	36	30	23	17	11	6	1	0	0	0
380	400	47	40	33	26	20	14	8	3	0	0	0
400	420	50	43	36	29	23	17	11	6	1	0	0
420	440	53	46	39	32	26	20	14	8	3	0	0
440	460	57	49	42	35	29	22	16	10	5	0	0
460	480	60	52	46	39	32	25	19	13	8	3	0
480	500	64	56	49	42	35	28	22	16	10	5	0
500	520	67	60	52	45	38	31	25	19	13	7	2

(Continued on next page)

Table 14.1. Payroll Taxes: SINGLE Persons — SEMIMONTHLY Payroll Period

And the wages are–		And the number of withholding allowances claimed is–										
At least	But less than	0	1	2	3	4	5	6	7	8	9	10
		The amount of income tax to be withheld shall be–										
$520	$540	$71	$63	$55	$48	$41	$34	$28	$22	$15	$10	$4
540	560	75	67	59	51	44	38	31	24	18	12	7
560	580	79	71	63	55	48	41	34	27	21	15	9
580	600	83	75	66	58	51	44	37	30	24	18	12
600	620	87	79	70	62	54	47	40	33	27	21	15
620	640	92	83	74	66	58	50	43	36	30	23	17
640	660	97	87	78	69	61	54	47	40	33	26	20
660	680	101	91	82	73	65	57	50	43	36	29	23
680	700	106	96	86	77	69	61	53	46	39	32	26
700	720	110	100	91	81	73	64	57	49	42	35	29
720	740	115	105	95	85	77	68	60	52	46	39	32
740	760	120	110	100	90	81	72	64	56	49	42	35
760	780	125	114	104	94	85	76	67	60	52	45	38
780	800	130	119	109	99	89	80	71	63	55	48	41
800	820	135	124	114	104	94	84	75	67	59	51	44
820	840	141	129	118	108	98	88	79	71	63	55	48
840	860	146	135	123	113	103	93	83	75	66	58	51
860	880	151	140	128	117	107	97	87	79	70	62	54
880	900	156	145	134	122	112	102	92	83	74	66	58
900	920	161	150	139	128	117	107	97	87	78	69	61
920	940	167	155	144	133	122	111	101	91	82	73	65
940	960	172	161	149	138	127	116	106	96	86	77	69
960	980	177	166	154	143	132	121	110	100	91	81	73
980	1,000	183	171	160	148	137	126	115	105	95	85	77
1,000	1,020	189	176	165	154	142	131	120	110	100	90	81
1,020	1,040	195	182	170	159	148	136	125	114	104	94	85
1,040	1,060	201	188	175	164	153	141	130	119	109	99	89
1,060	1,080	207	194	181	169	158	147	135	124	114	104	94
1,080	1,100	213	200	187	174	163	152	141	129	118	108	98
1,100	1,120	219	206	193	180	168	157	146	135	123	113	103
1,120	1,140	225	212	199	186	174	162	151	140	128	117	107
1,140	1,160	231	218	205	192	179	167	156	145	134	122	112
1,160	1,180	237	224	211	198	185	173	161	150	139	128	117
1,180	1,200	243	230	217	204	191	178	167	155	144	133	122
1,200	1,220	249	236	223	210	197	184	172	161	149	138	127
1,220	1,240	256	242	229	216	203	190	177	166	154	143	132
1,240	1,260	263	248	235	222	209	196	183	171	160	148	137
1,260	1,280	269	255	241	228	215	202	189	176	165	154	142
1,280	1,300	276	261	247	234	221	208	195	182	170	159	148
1,300	1,320	283	268	253	240	227	214	201	188	175	164	153
1,320	1,340	290	275	260	246	233	220	207	194	181	169	158
1,340	1,360	297	282	267	252	239	226	213	200	187	174	163
1,360	1,380	303	289	274	259	245	232	219	206	193	180	168
1,380	1,400	310	295	281	266	251	238	225	212	199	186	174
1,400	1,420	317	302	287	273	258	244	231	218	205	192	179
1,420	1,440	324	309	294	280	265	250	237	224	211	198	185
1,440	1,460	331	316	301	286	272	257	243	230	217	204	191
1,460	1,480	338	323	308	293	278	264	249	236	223	210	197
1,480	1,500	346	330	315	300	285	270	256	242	229	216	203
1,500	1,520	353	337	321	307	292	277	263	248	235	222	209
1,520	1,540	361	345	328	314	299	284	269	255	241	228	215
1,540	1,560	368	352	336	320	306	291	276	261	247	234	221
1,560	1,580	375	359	343	327	312	298	283	268	253	240	227
1,580	1,600	383	367	351	335	319	304	290	275	260	246	233
1,600	1,620	390	374	358	342	326	311	297	282	267	252	239
1,620	1,640	398	382	365	349	333	318	303	289	274	259	245
1,640	1,660	405	389	373	357	341	325	310	295	281	266	251
1,660	1,680	412	396	380	364	348	332	317	302	287	273	258
1,680	1,700	420	404	388	372	356	340	324	309	294	280	265
1,700	1,720	427	411	395	379	363	347	331	316	301	286	272
1,720	1,740	435	419	402	386	370	354	338	323	308	293	278
1,740	1,760	442	426	410	394	378	362	346	330	315	300	285
1,760	1,780	449	433	417	401	385	369	353	337	321	307	292
1,780	1,800	457	441	425	409	393	377	361	345	328	314	299
1,800	1,820	464	448	432	416	400	384	368	352	336	320	306
1,820	1,840	472	456	439	423	407	391	375	359	343	327	312
1,840	1,860	479	463	447	431	415	399	383	367	351	335	319
1,860	1,880	486	470	454	438	422	406	390	374	358	342	326
		37 percent of the excess over $1,880 plus–										
$1,880 and over		490	474	458	442	426	410	394	378	362	346	330

Table 14.1. Payroll Taxes: MARRIED Persons — SEMIMONTHLY Payroll Period

And the wages are—		And the number of withholding allowances claimed is—										
At least	But less than	0	1	2	3	4	5	6	7	8	9	10
		The amount of income tax to be withheld shall be—										
$0	$108	$0	$0	$0	$0	$0	$0	$0	$0	$0	$0	$0
108	110	1	0	0	0	0	0	0	0	0	0	0
110	112	1	0	0	0	0	0	0	0	0	0	0
112	114	1	0	0	0	0	0	0	0	0	0	0
114	116	1	0	0	0	0	0	0	0	0	0	0
116	118	1	0	0	0	0	0	0	0	0	0	0
118	120	2	0	0	0	0	0	0	0	0	0	0
120	124	2	0	0	0	0	0	0	0	0	0	0
124	128	2	0	0	0	0	0	0	0	0	0	0
128	132	3	0	0	0	0	0	0	0	0	0	0
132	136	3	0	0	0	0	0	0	0	0	0	0
136	140	4	0	0	0	0	0	0	0	0	0	0
140	144	4	0	0	0	0	0	0	0	0	0	0
144	148	5	0	0	0	0	0	0	0	0	0	0
148	152	5	0	0	0	0	0	0	0	0	0	0
152	156	5	1	0	0	0	0	0	0	0	0	0
156	160	6	1	0	0	0	0	0	0	0	0	0
160	164	6	2	0	0	0	0	0	0	0	0	0
164	168	7	2	0	0	0	0	0	0	0	0	0
168	172	7	2	0	0	0	0	0	0	0	0	0
172	176	8	3	0	0	0	0	0	0	0	0	0
176	180	8	3	0	0	0	0	0	0	0	0	0
180	184	9	4	0	0	0	0	0	0	0	0	0
184	188	9	4	0	0	0	0	0	0	0	0	0
188	192	9	5	0	0	0	0	0	0	0	0	0
192	196	10	5	0	0	0	0	0	0	0	0	0
196	200	10	6	1	0	0	0	0	0	0	0	0
200	210	11	6	2	0	0	0	0	0	0	0	0
210	220	12	7	3	0	0	0	0	0	0	0	0
220	230	14	9	4	0	0	0	0	0	0	0	0
230	240	15	10	5	0	0	0	0	0	0	0	0
240	250	16	11	6	1	0	0	0	0	0	0	0
250	260	17	12	7	2	0	0	0	0	0	0	0
260	270	18	13	8	3	0	0	0	0	0	0	0
270	280	20	14	9	4	0	0	0	0	0	0	0
280	290	21	16	10	6	1	0	0	0	0	0	0
290	300	22	17	12	7	2	0	0	0	0	0	0
300	320	24	19	13	8	4	0	0	0	0	0	0
320	340	27	21	16	11	6	1	0	0	0	0	0
340	360	30	24	18	13	8	3	0	0	0	0	0
360	380	33	27	21	15	10	5	1	0	0	0	0
380	400	35	29	23	18	13	8	3	0	0	0	0
400	420	38	32	26	20	15	10	5	0	0	0	0
420	440	41	35	29	23	17	12	7	2	0	0	0
440	460	44	38	32	26	20	15	9	5	0	0	0
460	480	47	41	35	28	22	17	12	7	2	0	0
480	500	50	43	37	31	25	19	14	9	4	0	0
500	520	53	46	40	34	28	22	17	11	7	2	0
520	540	56	49	43	37	31	25	19	14	9	4	0
540	560	59	52	46	40	34	28	21	16	11	6	1
560	580	63	56	49	42	36	30	24	19	13	8	4
580	600	66	59	52	45	39	33	27	21	16	11	6
600	620	69	62	55	48	42	36	30	24	18	13	8
620	640	72	65	58	51	45	39	33	27	21	15	10
640	660	75	68	62	55	48	42	35	29	23	18	13
660	680	79	72	65	58	51	44	38	32	26	20	15
680	700	83	75	68	61	54	47	41	35	29	23	17
700	720	86	78	71	64	57	50	44	38	32	26	20
720	740	90	82	74	67	60	54	47	41	35	28	22
740	760	93	86	78	71	64	57	50	43	37	31	25
760	780	97	89	81	74	67	60	53	46	40	34	28
780	800	101	93	85	77	70	63	56	49	43	37	31
800	820	104	96	89	81	73	66	59	52	46	40	34
820	840	108	100	92	84	77	70	63	56	49	42	36
840	860	112	104	96	88	80	73	66	59	52	45	39
860	880	117	107	99	92	84	76	69	62	55	48	42
880	900	121	111	103	95	87	80	72	65	58	51	45
900	920	125	116	107	99	91	83	75	68	62	55	48
920	940	130	120	111	102	95	87	79	72	65	58	51
940	960	134	125	115	106	98	90	83	75	68	61	54
960	980	139	129	119	110	102	94	86	78	71	64	57
980	1,000	143	133	124	114	105	98	90	82	74	67	60
1,000	1,020	147	138	128	119	109	101	93	86	78	71	64

(Continued on next page)

Table 14.1. Payroll Taxes: MARRIED Persons — SEMIMONTHLY Payroll Period

And the wages are—		And the number of withholding allowances claimed is—										
At least	But less than	0	1	2	3	4	5	6	7	8	9	10
		The amount of income tax to be withheld shall be—										
$1,020	$1,040	$152	$142	$133	$123	$114	$105	$97	$89	$81	$74	$67
1,040	1,060	157	147	137	128	118	108	101	93	85	77	70
1,060	1,080	162	151	141	132	122	113	104	96	89	81	73
1,080	1,100	167	156	146	136	127	117	108	100	92	84	77
1,100	1,120	172	161	150	141	131	122	112	104	96	88	80
1,120	1,140	177	166	155	145	136	126	117	107	99	92	84
1,140	1,160	182	171	160	150	140	130	121	111	103	95	87
1,160	1,180	187	176	165	154	144	135	125	116	107	99	91
1,180	1,200	192	181	170	159	149	139	130	120	111	102	95
1,200	1,220	197	186	175	164	154	144	134	125	115	106	98
1,220	1,240	202	191	180	169	159	148	139	129	119	110	102
1,240	1,260	207	196	185	174	164	153	143	133	124	114	105
1,260	1,280	212	201	190	179	169	158	147	138	128	119	109
1,280	1,300	218	206	195	184	174	163	152	142	133	123	114
1,300	1,320	224	211	200	189	179	168	157	147	137	128	118
1,320	1,340	229	217	205	194	184	173	162	151	141	132	122
1,340	1,360	235	223	211	199	189	178	167	156	146	136	127
1,360	1,380	240	228	216	204	194	183	172	161	150	141	131
1,380	1,400	246	234	222	210	199	188	177	166	155	145	136
1,400	1,420	252	239	227	215	204	193	182	171	160	150	140
1,420	1,440	257	245	233	221	209	198	187	176	165	154	144
1,440	1,460	263	251	239	226	214	203	192	181	170	159	149
1,460	1,480	268	256	244	232	220	208	197	186	175	164	154
1,480	1,500	274	262	250	238	225	213	202	191	180	169	159
1,500	1,520	281	267	255	243	231	219	207	196	185	174	164
1,520	1,540	288	273	261	249	237	225	212	201	190	179	169
1,540	1,560	294	280	267	254	242	230	218	206	195	184	174
1,560	1,580	301	286	272	260	248	236	224	211	200	189	179
1,580	1,600	307	293	279	266	253	241	229	217	205	194	184
1,600	1,620	314	300	285	271	259	247	235	223	211	199	189
1,620	1,640	321	306	292	278	265	253	240	228	216	204	194
1,640	1,660	327	313	299	284	270	258	246	234	222	210	199
1,660	1,680	334	319	305	291	277	264	252	239	227	215	204
1,680	1,700	340	326	312	297	283	269	257	245	233	221	209
1,700	1,720	347	333	318	304	290	275	263	251	239	226	214
1,720	1,740	354	339	325	311	296	282	268	256	244	232	220
1,740	1,760	360	346	332	317	303	289	274	262	250	238	225
1,760	1,780	367	352	338	324	310	295	281	267	255	243	231
1,780	1,800	373	359	345	330	316	302	288	273	261	249	237
1,800	1,820	380	366	351	337	323	308	294	280	267	254	242
1,820	1,840	387	372	358	344	329	315	301	286	272	260	248
1,840	1,860	393	379	365	350	336	322	307	293	279	266	253
1,860	1,880	400	385	371	357	343	328	314	300	285	271	259
1,880	1,900	406	392	378	363	349	335	321	306	292	278	265
1,900	1,920	413	399	384	370	356	341	327	313	299	284	270
1,920	1,940	420	405	391	377	362	348	334	319	305	291	277
1,940	1,960	426	412	398	383	369	355	340	326	312	297	283
1,960	1,980	434	418	404	390	376	361	347	333	318	304	290
1,980	2,000	441	425	411	396	382	368	354	339	325	311	296
2,000	2,020	449	433	417	403	389	374	360	346	332	317	303
2,020	2,040	456	440	424	410	395	381	367	352	338	324	310
2,040	2,060	463	447	431	416	402	388	373	359	345	330	316
2,060	2,080	471	455	439	423	409	394	380	366	351	337	323
2,080	2,100	478	462	446	430	415	401	387	372	358	344	329
2,100	2,120	486	470	454	438	422	407	393	379	365	350	336
2,120	2,140	493	477	461	445	429	414	400	385	371	357	343
2,140	2,160	500	484	468	452	436	421	406	392	378	363	349
2,160	2,180	508	492	476	460	444	428	413	399	384	370	356
2,180	2,200	515	499	483	467	451	435	420	405	391	377	362
2,200	2,220	523	507	491	475	459	442	426	412	398	383	369
2,220	2,240	530	514	498	482	466	450	434	418	404	390	376
2,240	2,260	537	521	505	489	473	457	441	425	411	396	382
2,260	2,280	545	529	513	497	481	465	449	433	417	403	389
2,280	2,300	552	536	520	504	488	472	456	440	424	410	395
2,300	2,320	560	544	528	512	496	479	463	447	431	416	402
2,320	2,340	567	551	535	519	503	487	471	455	439	423	409
2,340	2,360	574	558	542	526	510	494	478	462	446	430	415
2,360	2,380	582	566	550	534	518	502	486	470	454	438	422
2,380	2,400	589	573	557	541	525	509	493	477	461	445	429
		37 percent of the excess over $2,400 plus—										
$2,400 and over		593	577	561	545	529	513	497	481	465	449	433

Table 14.2. Percentage Method of Withholding Federal Income Taxes

Percentage Method Income Tax Withholding Table

Payroll Period	One with- holding allowance
Weekly	$20.00
Biweekly	40.00
Semimonthly	43.33
Monthly	86.67
Quarterly	260.00
Semiannually	520.00
Annually	1,040.00
Daily or miscellaneous (each day of the payroll period) .	4.00

—If the Payroll Period With Respect to an Employee is Weekly

(a) SINGLE person—including head of household:

If the amount of wages is:		The amount of income tax to be withheld shall be:	
Not over $27 0			
Over—	But not over—		of excess over—
$27	—$84 . . .	.12%	—$27
$84	—$185 . . .	.$6.84 plus 15%	—$84
$185	—$292 . . .	.$21.99 plus 19%	—$185
$292	—$440 . . .	.$42.32 plus 25%	—$292
$440	—$556 . . .	.$79.32 plus 30%	—$440
$556	—$663 . . .	.$114.12 plus 34%	—$556
$663	. . . .	.$150.50 plus 37%	—$663

(b) MARRIED person—

If the amount of wages is:		The amount of income tax to be withheld shall be:	
Not over $48 0			
Over—	But not over—		of excess over—
$48	—$192 . . .	.12%	—$48
$192	—$384 . . .	.$17.28 plus 17%	—$192
$384	—$472 . . .	.$49.92 plus 22%	—$384
$472	—$578 . . .	.$69.28 plus 25%	—$472
$578	—$684 . . .	.$95.78 plus 28%	—$578
$684	—$897 . . .	.$125.46 plus 33%	—$684
$897	. . . .	.$195.75 plus 37%	—$897

—If the Payroll Period With Respect to an Employee is Biweekly

(a) SINGLE person—including head of household:

If the amount of wages is:		The amount of income tax to be withheld shall be:	
Not over $55 0			
Over—	But not over—		of excess over—
$55	—$168 . . .	.12%	—$55
$168	—$369 . . .	.$13.56 plus 15%	—$168
$369	—$585 . . .	.$43.71 plus 19%	—$369
$585	—$881 . . .	.$84.75 plus 25%	—$585
$881	—$1,113 . . .	.$158.75 plus 30%	—$881
$1,113	—$1,325 . . .	.$228.35 plus 34%	—$1,113
$1,325	. . . .	.$300.43 plus 37%	—$1,325

(b) MARRIED person—

If the amount of wages is:		The amount of income tax to be withheld shall be:	
Not over $96 0			
Over—	But not over—		of excess over—
$96	—$385 . . .	.12%	—$96
$385	—$767 . . .	.$34.68 plus 17%	—$385
$767	—$945 . . .	.$99.62 plus 22%	—$767
$945	—$1,157 . . .	.$138.78 plus 25%	—$945
$1,157	—$1,369 . . .	.$191.78 plus 28%	—$1,157
$1,369	—$1,793 . . .	.$251.14 plus 33%	—$1,369
$1,793	. . . .	.$391.06 plus 37%	—$1,793

—If the Payroll Period With Respect to an Employee is Semimonthly

(a) SINGLE person—including head of household:

If the amount of wages is:		The amount of income tax to be withheld shall be:	
Not over $59 0			
Over—	But not over—		of excess over—
$59	—$182 . . .	.12%	—$59
$182	—$400 . . .	.$14.76 plus 15%	—$182
$400	—$633 . . .	.$47.46 plus 19%	—$400
$633	—$954 . . .	.$91.73 plus 25%	—$633
$954	—$1,205 . . .	.$171.98 plus 30%	—$954
$1,205	—$1,435 . . .	.$247.28 plus 34%	—$1,205
$1,435	. . . .	.$325.48 plus 37%	—$1,435

(b) MARRIED person—

If the amount of wages is:		The amount of income tax to be withheld shall be:	
Not over $104 0			
Over—	But not over—		of excess over—
$104	—$417 . . .	.12%	—$104
$417	—$831 . . .	.$37.56 plus 17%	—$417
$831	—$1,023. . .	.$107.94 plus 22%	—$831
$1,023	—$1,253 . . .	.$150.18 plus 25%	—$1,023
$1,253	—$1,483 . . .	.$207.68 plus 28%	—$1,253
$1,483	—$1,943 . . .	.$272.08 plus 33%	—$1,483
$1,943	. . . .	.$423.88 plus 37%	—$1,943

Table 14.3. Social Security Employee Tax Table

Wages at least	But less than	Tax to be withheld	Wages at least	But less than	Tax to be withheld	Wages at least	But less than	Tax to be withheld	Wages at least	But less than	Tax to be withheld
$0.00	$0.08	$0.00	12.70	12.84	.90	25.47	25.61	1.80	38.23	38.37	2.70
.08	.22	.01	12.84	12.98	.91	25.61	25.75	1.81	38.37	38.52	2.71
.22	.36	.02	12.98	13.13	.92	25.75	25.89	1.82	38.52	38.66	2.72
.36	.50	.03	13.13	13.27	.93	25.89	26.03	1.83	38.66	38.80	2.73
.50	.64	.04	13.27	13.41	.94	26.03	26.18	1.84	38.80	38.94	2.74
.64	.79	.05	13.41	13.55	.95	26.18	26.32	1.85	38.94	39.08	2.75
.79	.93	.06	13.55	13.69	.96	26.32	26.46	1.86	39.08	39.22	2.76
.93	1.07	.07	13.69	13.83	.97	26.46	26.60	1.87	39.22	39.37	2.77
1.07	1.21	.08	13.83	13.98	.98	26.60	26.74	1.88	39.37	39.51	2.78
1.21	1.35	.09	13.98	14.12	.99	26.74	26.88	1.89	39.51	39.65	2.79
1.35	1.49	.10	14.12	14.26	1.00	26.88	27.03	1.90	39.65	39.79	2.80
1.49	1.64	.11	14.26	14.40	1.01	27.03	27.17	1.91	39.79	39.93	2.81
1.64	1.78	.12	14.40	14.54	1.02	27.17	27.31	1.92	39.93	40.08	2.82
1.78	1.92	.13	14.54	14.69	1.03	27.31	27.45	1.93	40.08	40.22	2.83
1.92	2.06	.14	14.69	14.83	1.04	27.45	27.59	1.94	40.22	40.36	2.84
2.06	2.20	.15	14.83	14.97	1.05	27.59	27.74	1.95	40.36	40.50	2.85
2.20	2.35	.16	14.97	15.11	1.06	27.74	27.88	1.96	40.50	40.64	2.86
2.35	2.49	.17	15.11	15.25	1.07	27.88	28.02	1.97	40.64	40.79	2.87
2.49	2.63	.18	15.25	15.40	1.08	28.02	28.16	1.98	40.79	40.93	2.88
2.63	2.77	.19	15.40	15.54	1.09	28.16	28.30	1.99	40.93	41.07	2.89
2.77	2.91	.20	15.54	15.68	1.10	28.30	28.44	2.00	41.07	41.21	2.90
2.91	3.05	.21	15.68	15.82	1.11	28.44	28.59	2.01	41.21	41.35	2.91
3.05	3.20	.22	15.82	15.96	1.12	28.59	28.73	2.02	41.35	41.49	2.92
3.20	3.34	.23	15.96	16.10	1.13	28.73	28.87	2.03	41.49	41.64	2.93
3.34	3.48	.24	16.10	16.25	1.14	28.87	29.01	2.04	41.64	41.78	2.94
3.48	3.62	.25	16.25	16.39	1.15	29.01	29.15	2.05	41.78	41.92	2.95
3.62	3.76	.26	16.39	16.53	1.16	29.15	29.30	2.06	41.92	42.06	2.96
3.76	3.91	.27	16.53	16.67	1.17	29.30	29.44	2.07	42.06	42.20	2.97
3.91	4.05	.28	16.67	16.81	1.18	29.44	29.58	2.08	42.20	42.35	2.98
4.05	4.19	.29	16.81	16.96	1.19	29.58	29.72	2.09	42.35	42.49	2.99
4.19	4.33	.30	16.96	17.10	1.20	29.72	29.86	2.10	42.49	42.63	3.00
4.33	4.47	.31	17.10	17.24	1.21	29.86	30.00	2.11	42.63	42.77	3.01
4.47	4.61	.32	17.24	17.38	1.22	30.00	30.15	2.12	42.77	42.91	3.02
4.61	4.76	.33	17.38	17.52	1.23	30.15	30.29	2.13	42.91	43.05	3.03
4.76	4.90	.34	17.52	17.66	1.24	30.29	30.43	2.14	43.05	43.20	3.04
4.90	5.04	.35	17.66	17.81	1.25	30.43	30.57	2.15	43.20	43.34	3.05
5.04	5.18	.36	17.81	17.95	1.26	30.57	30.71	2.16	43.34	43.48	3.06
5.18	5.32	.37	17.95	18.09	1.27	30.71	30.86	2.17	43.48	43.62	3.07
5.32	5.47	.38	18.09	18.23	1.28	30.86	31.00	2.18	43.62	43.76	3.08
5.47	5.61	.39	18.23	18.37	1.29	31.00	31.14	2.19	43.76	43.91	3.09
5.61	5.75	.40	18.37	18.52	1.30	31.14	31.28	2.20	43.91	44.05	3.10
5.75	5.89	.41	18.52	18.66	1.31	31.28	31.42	2.21	44.05	44.19	3.11
5.89	6.03	.42	18.66	18.80	1.32	31.42	31.57	2.22	44.19	44.33	3.12
6.03	6.18	.43	18.80	18.94	1.33	31.57	31.71	2.23	44.33	44.47	3.13
6.18	6.32	.44	18.94	19.08	1.34	31.71	31.85	2.24	44.47	44.61	3.14
6.32	6.46	.45	19.08	19.22	1.35	31.85	31.99	2.25	44.61	44.76	3.15
6.46	6.60	.46	19.22	19.37	1.36	31.99	32.13	2.26	44.76	44.90	3.16
6.60	6.74	.47	19.37	19.51	1.37	32.13	32.27	2.27	44.90	45.04	3.17
6.74	6.88	.48	19.51	19.65	1.38	32.27	32.42	2.28	45.04	45.18	3.18
6.88	7.03	.49	19.65	19.79	1.39	32.42	32.56	2.29	45.18	45.32	3.19
7.03	7.17	.50	19.79	19.93	1.40	32.56	32.70	2.30	45.32	45.47	3.20
7.17	7.31	.51	19.93	20.08	1.41	32.70	32.84	2.31	45.47	45.61	3.21
7.31	7.45	.52	20.08	20.22	1.42	32.84	32.98	2.32	45.61	45.75	3.22
7.45	7.59	.53	20.22	20.36	1.43	32.98	33.13	2.33	45.75	45.89	3.23
7.59	7.74	.54	20.36	20.50	1.44	33.13	33.27	2.34	45.89	46.03	3.24
7.74	7.88	.55	20.50	20.64	1.45	33.27	33.41	2.35	46.03	46.18	3.25
7.88	8.02	.56	20.64	20.79	1.46	33.41	33.55	2.36	46.18	46.32	3.26
8.02	8.16	.57	20.79	20.93	1.47	33.55	33.69	2.37	46.32	46.46	3.27
8.16	8.30	.58	20.93	21.07	1.48	33.69	33.83	2.38	46.46	46.60	3.28
8.30	8.44	.59	21.07	21.21	1.49	33.83	33.98	2.39	46.60	46.74	3.29
8.44	8.59	.60	21.21	21.35	1.50	33.98	34.12	2.40	46.74	46.88	3.30
8.59	8.73	.61	21.35	21.49	1.51	34.12	34.26	2.41	46.88	47.03	3.31
8.73	8.87	.62	21.49	21.64	1.52	34.26	34.40	2.42	47.03	47.17	3.32
8.87	9.01	.63	21.64	21.78	1.53	34.40	34.54	2.43	47.17	47.31	3.33
9.01	9.15	.64	21.78	21.92	1.54	34.54	34.69	2.44	47.31	47.45	3.34
9.15	9.30	.65	21.92	22.06	1.55	34.69	34.83	2.45	47.45	47.59	3.35
9.30	9.44	.66	22.06	22.20	1.56	34.83	34.97	2.46	47.59	47.74	3.36
9.44	9.58	.67	22.20	22.35	1.57	34.97	35.11	2.47	47.74	47.88	3.37
9.58	9.72	.68	22.35	22.49	1.58	35.11	35.25	2.48	47.88	48.02	3.38
9.72	9.86	.69	22.49	22.63	1.59	35.25	35.40	2.49	48.02	48.16	3.39
9.86	10.00	.70	22.63	22.77	1.60	35.40	35.54	2.50	48.16	48.30	3.40
10.00	10.15	.71	22.77	22.91	1.61	35.54	35.68	2.51	48.30	48.44	3.41
10.15	10.29	.72	22.91	23.05	1.62	35.68	35.82	2.52	48.44	48.59	3.42
10.29	10.43	.73	23.05	23.20	1.63	35.82	35.96	2.53	48.59	48.73	3.43
10.43	10.57	.74	23.20	23.34	1.64	35.96	36.10	2.54	48.73	48.87	3.44
10.57	10.71	.75	23.34	23.48	1.65	36.10	36.25	2.55	48.87	49.01	3.45
10.71	10.86	.76	23.48	23.62	1.66	36.25	36.39	2.56	49.01	49.15	3.46
10.86	11.00	.77	23.62	23.76	1.67	36.39	36.53	2.57	49.15	49.30	3.47
11.00	11.14	.78	23.76	23.91	1.68	36.53	36.67	2.58	49.30	49.44	3.48
11.14	11.28	.79	23.91	24.05	1.69	36.67	36.81	2.59	49.44	49.58	3.49
11.28	11.42	.80	24.05	24.19	1.70	36.81	36.96	2.60	49.58	49.72	3.50
11.42	11.57	.81	24.19	24.33	1.71	36.96	37.10	2.61	49.72	49.86	3.51
11.57	11.71	.82	24.33	24.47	1.72	37.10	37.24	2.62	49.86	50.00	3.52
11.71	11.85	.83	24.47	24.61	1.73	37.24	37.38	2.63	50.00	50.15	3.53
11.85	11.99	.84	24.61	24.76	1.74	37.38	37.52	2.64	50.15	50.29	3.54
11.99	12.13	.85	24.76	24.90	1.75	37.52	37.66	2.65	50.29	50.43	3.55
12.13	12.27	.86	24.90	25.04	1.76	37.66	37.81	2.66	50.43	50.57	3.56
12.27	12.42	.87	25.04	25.18	1.77	37.81	37.95	2.67	50.57	50.71	3.57
12.42	12.56	.88	25.18	25.32	1.78	37.95	38.09	2.68	50.71	50.86	3.58
12.56	12.70	.89	25.32	25.47	1.79	38.09	38.23	2.69	50.86	51.00	3.59

Table 14.3. Social Security Employee Tax Table — Continued

Wages at least	But less than	Tax to be withheld	Wages at least	But less than	Tax to be withheld	Wages at least	But less than	Tax to be withheld	Wages at least	But less than	Tax to be withheld
51.00	51.14	3.60	63.76	63.91	4.50	76.53	76.67	5.40	89.30	89.44	6.30
51.14	51.28	3.61	63.91	64.05	4.51	76.67	76.81	5.41	89.44	89.58	6.31
51.28	51.42	3.62	64.05	64.19	4.52	76.81	76.96	5.42	89.58	89.72	6.32
51.42	51.57	3.63	64.19	64.33	4.53	76.96	77.10	5.43	89.72	89.86	6.33
51.57	51.71	3.64	64.33	64.47	4.54	77.10	77.24	5.44	89.86	90.00	6.34
51.71	51.85	3.65	64.47	64.61	4.55	77.24	77.38	5.45	90.00	90.15	6.35
51.85	51.99	3.66	64.61	64.76	4.56	77.38	77.52	5.46	90.15	90.29	6.36
51.99	52.13	3.67	64.76	64.90	4.57	77.52	77.66	5.47	90.29	90.43	6.37
52.13	52.27	3.68	64.90	65.04	4.58	77.66	77.81	5.48	90.43	90.57	6.38
52.27	52.42	3.69	65.04	65.18	4.59	77.81	77.95	5.49	90.57	90.71	6.39
52.42	52.56	3.70	65.18	65.32	4.60	77.95	78.09	5.50	90.71	90.86	6.40
52.56	52.70	3.71	65.32	65.47	4.61	78.09	78.23	5.51	90.86	91.00	6.41
52.70	52.84	3.72	65.47	65.61	4.62	78.23	78.37	5.52	91.00	91.14	6.42
52.84	52.98	3.73	65.61	65.75	4.63	78.37	78.52	5.53	91.14	91.28	6.43
52.98	53.13	3.74	65.75	65.89	4.64	78.52	78.66	5.54	91.28	91.42	6.44
53.13	53.27	3.75	65.89	66.03	4.65	78.66	78.80	5.55	91.42	91.57	6.45
53.27	53.41	3.76	66.03	66.18	4.66	78.80	78.94	5.56	91.57	91.71	6.46
53.41	53.55	3.77	66.18	66.32	4.67	78.94	79.08	5.57	91.71	91.85	6.47
53.55	53.69	3.78	66.32	66.46	4.68	79.08	79.22	5.58	91.85	91.99	6.48
53.69	53.83	3.79	66.46	66.60	4.69	79.22	79.37	5.59	91.99	92.13	6.49
53.83	53.98	3.80	66.60	66.74	4.70	79.37	79.51	5.60	92.13	92.27	6.50
53.98	54.12	3.81	66.74	66.88	4.71	79.51	79.65	5.61	92.27	92.42	6.51
54.12	54.26	3.82	66.88	67.03	4.72	79.65	79.79	5.62	92.42	92.56	6.52
54.26	54.40	3.83	67.03	67.17	4.73	79.79	79.93	5.63	92.56	92.70	6.53
54.40	54.54	3.84	67.17	67.31	4.74	79.93	80.08	5.64	92.70	92.84	6.54
54.54	54.69	3.85	67.31	67.45	4.75	80.08	80.22	5.65	92.84	92.98	6.55
54.69	54.83	3.86	67.45	67.59	4.76	80.22	80.36	5.66	92.98	93.13	6.56
54.83	54.97	3.87	67.59	67.74	4.77	80.36	80.50	5.67	93.13	93.27	6.57
54.97	55.11	3.88	67.74	67.88	4.78	80.50	80.64	5.68	93.27	93.41	6.58
55.11	55.25	3.89	67.88	68.02	4.79	80.64	80.79	5.69	93.41	93.55	6.59
55.25	55.40	3.90	68.02	68.16	4.80	80.79	80.93	5.70	93.55	93.69	6.60
55.40	55.54	3.91	68.16	68.30	4.81	80.93	81.07	5.71	93.69	93.83	6.61
55.54	55.68	3.92	68.30	68.44	4.82	81.07	81.21	5.72	93.83	93.98	6.62
55.68	55.82	3.93	68.44	68.59	4.83	81.21	81.35	5.73	93.98	94.12	6.63
55.82	55.96	3.94	68.59	68.73	4.84	81.35	81.49	5.74	94.12	94.26	6.64
55.96	56.10	3.95	68.73	68.87	4.85	81.49	81.64	5.75	94.26	94.40	6.65
56.10	56.25	3.96	68.87	69.01	4.86	81.64	81.78	5.76	94.40	94.54	6.66
56.25	56.39	3.97	69.01	69.15	4.87	81.78	81.92	5.77	94.54	94.69	6.67
56.39	56.53	3.98	69.15	69.30	4.88	81.92	82.06	5.78	94.69	94.83	6.68
56.53	56.67	3.99	69.30	69.44	4.89	82.06	82.20	5.79	94.83	94.97	6.69
56.67	56.81	4.00	69.44	69.58	4.90	82.20	82.35	5.80	94.97	95.11	6.70
56.81	56.96	4.01	69.58	69.72	4.91	82.35	82.49	5.81	95.11	95.25	6.71
56.96	57.10	4.02	69.72	69.86	4.92	82.49	82.63	5.82	95.25	95.40	6.72
57.10	57.24	4.03	69.86	70.00	4.93	82.63	82.77	5.83	95.40	95.54	6.73
57.24	57.38	4.04	70.00	70.15	4.94	82.77	82.91	5.84	95.54	95.68	6.74
57.38	57.52	4.05	70.15	70.29	4.95	82.91	83.05	5.85	95.68	95.82	6.75
57.52	57.66	4.06	70.29	70.43	4.96	83.05	83.20	5.86	95.82	95.96	6.76
57.66	57.81	4.07	70.43	70.57	4.97	83.20	83.34	5.87	95.96	96.10	6.77
57.81	57.95	4.08	70.57	70.71	4.98	83.34	83.48	5.88	96.10	96.25	6.78
57.95	58.09	4.09	70.71	70.86	4.99	83.48	83.62	5.89	96.25	96.39	6.79
58.09	58.23	4.10	70.86	71.00	5.00	83.62	83.76	5.90	96.39	96.53	6.80
58.23	58.37	4.11	71.00	71.14	5.01	83.76	83.91	5.91	96.53	96.67	6.81
58.37	58.52	4.12	71.14	71.28	5.02	83.91	84.05	5.92	96.67	96.81	6.82
58.52	58.66	4.13	71.28	71.42	5.03	84.05	84.19	5.93	96.81	96.96	6.83
58.66	58.80	4.14	71.42	71.57	5.04	84.19	84.33	5.94	96.96	97.10	6.84
58.80	58.94	4.15	71.57	71.71	5.05	84.33	84.47	5.95	97.10	97.24	6.85
58.94	59.08	4.16	71.71	71.85	5.06	84.47	84.61	5.96	97.24	97.38	6.86
59.08	59.22	4.17	71.85	71.99	5.07	84.61	84.76	5.97	97.38	97.52	6.87
59.22	59.37	4.18	71.99	72.13	5.08	84.76	84.90	5.98	97.52	97.66	6.88
59.37	59.51	4.19	72.13	72.27	5.09	84.90	85.04	5.99	97.66	97.81	6.89
59.51	59.65	4.20	72.27	72.42	5.10	85.04	85.18	6.00	97.81	97.95	6.90
59.65	59.79	4.21	72.42	72.56	5.11	85.18	85.32	6.01	97.95	98.09	6.91
59.79	59.93	4.22	72.56	72.70	5.12	85.32	85.47	6.02	98.09	98.23	6.92
59.93	60.08	4.23	72.70	72.84	5.13	85.47	85.61	6.03	98.23	98.37	6.93
60.08	60.22	4.24	72.84	72.98	5.14	85.61	85.75	6.04	98.37	98.52	6.94
60.22	60.36	4.25	72.98	73.13	5.15	85.75	85.89	6.05	98.52	98.66	6.95
60.36	60.50	4.26	73.13	73.27	5.16	85.89	86.03	6.06	98.66	98.80	6.96
60.50	60.64	4.27	73.27	73.41	5.17	86.03	86.18	6.07	98.80	98.94	6.97
60.64	60.79	4.28	73.41	73.55	5.18	86.18	86.32	6.08	98.94	99.08	6.98
60.79	60.93	4.29	73.55	73.69	5.19	86.32	86.46	6.09	99.08	99.22	6.99
60.93	61.07	4.30	73.69	73.83	5.20	86.46	86.60	6.10	99.22	99.37	7.00
61.07	61.21	4.31	73.83	73.98	5.21	86.60	86.74	6.11	99.37	99.51	7.01
61.21	61.35	4.32	73.98	74.12	5.22	86.74	86.88	6.12	99.51	99.65	7.02
61.35	61.49	4.33	74.12	74.26	5.23	86.88	87.03	6.13	99.65	99.79	7.03
61.49	61.64	4.34	74.26	74.40	5.24	87.03	87.17	6.14	99.79	99.93	7.04
61.64	61.78	4.35	74.40	74.54	5.25	87.17	87.31	6.15	99.93	100.08	7.05
61.78	61.92	4.36	74.54	74.69	5.26	87.31	87.45	6.16			
61.92	62.06	4.37	74.69	74.83	5.27	87.45	87.59	6.17			
62.06	62.20	4.38	74.83	74.97	5.28	87.59	87.74	6.18			
62.20	62.35	4.39	74.97	75.11	5.29	87.74	87.88	6.19			
62.35	62.49	4.40	75.11	75.25	5.30	87.88	88.02	6.20			
62.49	62.63	4.41	75.25	75.40	5.31	88.02	88.16	6.21			
62.63	62.77	4.42	75.40	75.54	5.32	88.16	88.30	6.22			
62.77	62.91	4.43	75.54	75.68	5.33	88.30	88.44	6.23			
62.91	63.05	4.44	75.68	75.82	5.34	88.44	88.59	6.24			
63.05	63.20	4.45	75.82	75.96	5.35	88.59	88.73	6.25			
63.20	63.34	4.46	75.96	76.10	5.36	88.73	88.87	6.26			
63.34	63.48	4.47	76.10	76.25	5.37	88.87	89.01	6.27			
63.48	63.62	4.48	76.25	76.39	5.38	89.01	89.15	6.28			
63.62	63.76	4.49	76.39	76.53	5.39	89.15	89.30	6.29			

Wages	Taxes
100	$7.50
200	14.10
300	21.15
400	28.20
500	35.25
600	42.30
700	49.35
800	56.40
900	63.45
1,000	70.50

Table 16.4
Recovery Periods for
Personal Property

Class	Types of assets
3-year	Autos Light-duty trucks Other short-lived personal property Research-and-development equipment
5-year	All personal property not included in the three-year category, such as office equipment and heavy machinery
10-year	Certain public utility personal property Amusement parks Mobile homes Railroad tank cars
15-year	Longer-lived public utility property

Table 16.5
Accelerated Cost
Recovery for Personal
Property (Percents)

Year of ownership	Class of investment			
	3-year	5-year	10-year	15-year
1	25	15	8	5
2	38	22	14	10
3	37	21	12	9
4		21	10	8
5		21	10	7
6			10	7
7			9	6
8			9	6
9			9	6
10			9	6
11				6
12				6
13				6
14				6
15				6
Total	100	100	100	100

Table 16.6
Optional Recovery
Periods — Personal
Property

Property class	Extended periods
3-year	3, 5, or 12 years
5-year	5, 12, or 25 years
10-year	10, 25, or 35 years
15-year	15, 35, or 45 years

Table 16.8
Investment Tax Credit

Class of investment	Percent credit
3-year	6
5- 10-, 15-year	10

Table 16.9. Accelerated Cost Recovery for Real Property (Percents)

Year of ownership	Month asset placed in service											
	Jan	Feb	Mar	Apr	May	Jun	Jul	Aug	Sep	Oct	Nov	Dec
1	12	11	10	9	8	7	6	5	4	3	2	1
2	10	10	11	11	11	11	11	11	11	11	11	12
3	9	9	9	9	10	10	10	10	10	10	10	10
4	8	8	8	8	8	8	9	9	9	9	9	9
5	7	7	7	7	7	7	8	8	8	8	8	8
6	6	6	6	6	7	7	7	7	7	7	7	7
7	6	6	6	6	6	6	6	6	6	6	6	6
8	6	6	6	6	6	6	5	6	6	6	6	6
9	6	6	6	6	5	6	5	5	5	6	6	6
10	5	6	5	6	5	5	5	5	5	5	6	5
11	5	5	5	5	5	5	5	5	5	5	5	5
12	5	5	5	5	5	5	5	5	5	5	5	5
13	5	5	5	5	5	5	5	5	5	5	5	5
14	5	5	5	5	5	5	5	5	5	5	5	5
15	5	5	5	5	5	5	5	5	5	5	5	5
16			1	1	2	2	3	3	4	4	4	5
Total	100	100	100	100	100	100	100	100	100	100	100	100

B   Selected Equations

Chapter 4
Percentage
Applications   65

$$BR = P$$

$$P = BR$$

$$R = \frac{P}{B}$$

$$B = \frac{P}{R}$$

Chapter 7
Retail Transactions
                117

Retail equation: $P = C + M$

$$M = P - C$$

$$C = P - M$$

Markup equations: $M_c = \dfrac{M}{C}$

$$M_p = \frac{M}{P}$$

$$\text{Break-even point} = \frac{\text{Overhead}}{\text{Retail price} - \text{variable cost}}$$

Chapter 8
Simple Interest   139

$$Prt = I$$

$$I = Prt$$

$$P = \frac{I}{rt}$$

$$r = \frac{I}{Pt}$$

$$t = \frac{I}{Pr}$$

$$A = P + Prt$$

| Chapter 9 Bank Discounts 161 | $P - Prt = P'$ (P' = proceeds) |

$$P(1 - rt) = P'$$

$$P - P' = I$$

$$P + Prt = A$$

$$A - (Art) = P'$$

Chapter 10
Compound interest
183

$$P(1 + \%)^n = A$$

Chapter 11
Ordinary Annuities
199

$$D \cdot \frac{(1 + \%)^n - 1}{\%} = A_n$$

$$PV \text{ of } A_n = W \cdot \frac{1 - \dfrac{1}{(1 + \%)^n}}{\%}$$

Chapter 12
Sinking Funds and
Amortization 211

$$D = \frac{\%}{(1 + \%)^n - 1} \cdot An$$

$$Py = P \cdot \frac{\%}{1 - \dfrac{1}{(1 + \%)^n}}$$

Chapter 17
Financial Statements
319

Income-statement equation:

Revenues (sales)
−Cost of goods sold
=Gross profit
−Expenses
=Net income

Net sales = Gross sales − Returns and allowances

Gross profit = Revenues − Cost of goods sold

Cost of goods sold:

> Beginning inventory
> +Goods purchased
> =Goods available
> −Ending inventory
> =Cost of goods sold

Balance-sheet equation:

Assets = Liabilities + Owners' equity

Liabilities = Assets − Owners' equity

Owners equity = Assets − Liabilities

**Chapter 18
Financial Ratios** 341

Current ratio: $\dfrac{\text{Current assets}}{\text{Current liabilities}}$

Quick ratio: $\dfrac{\text{Current assets} - \text{Inventory}}{\text{Current liabilities}}$

Working capital: Current assets − Current liabilities

Debt-to-total assets: $\dfrac{\text{Total liabilities}}{\text{Total assets}}$

Times-interest earned: $\dfrac{\text{Pretax profit} + \text{Interest charges}}{\text{Interest charges}}$

Inventory-turnover: $\dfrac{\text{Cost of goods sold}}{\text{Average inventory}}$

Receivables turnover: $\dfrac{\text{Net sales} \times \% \text{ of sales on credit}}{\text{Average accounts receivable}}$

Average age of receivables: $\dfrac{\text{Number of days in a year}}{\text{Receivables turnover}}$

Sales margin: $\dfrac{\text{Net income after taxes}}{\text{Net sales}}$

Return on investment: $\dfrac{\text{Net income after taxes}}{\text{Owners' equity}}$

Chapter 19
Securities Analysis
and Transactions 359

Yield: $\dfrac{\text{Annual dividend}}{\text{Closing price}}$
(stock)

P-E ratio: $\dfrac{\text{Closing price}}{\text{Earnings per share}}$

Yield: $\dfrac{\text{Annual interest}}{\text{Closing price}}$
(bonds)

Yield to maturity: $\dfrac{\text{Annual interest} + \text{Prorated discount}}{\text{Average investment}}$
(discounted bond)

Yield to maturity: $\dfrac{\text{Annual interest} - \text{Prorated premium}}{\text{Average investment}}$
(premium bond)

Chapter 21
Basic Statistics 417

Midpoint: $\dfrac{\text{Sum of class limits}}{2}$

Arithmetic mean: $X = \dfrac{\Sigma x}{n}$
(ungrouped data)

Arithmetic mean: $X = \dfrac{\Sigma fx}{n}$
(grouped data)

Location of median: $\dfrac{n+1}{2}$

Median (M_d): $L + \dfrac{\left(\dfrac{n+1}{2} - F\right)i}{f}$

Standard deviation (S): $\sqrt{\dfrac{\Sigma d^2}{n}}$
(ungrouped data)

Standard deviation (S): $\sqrt{\dfrac{\Sigma fd^2}{n}}$
(grouped data)

**Chapter 22
English and Metric
Measurements   453**

Perimeter of a rectangle (P): $2(l + w)$

Perimeter of a square (P): $4l$

Perimeter of a triangle (P): $a + b + c$

Circumference of a circle (C): πd

Area of a square (A): l^2

Area of a rectangle (A): lw

Area of a triangle (A): $\dfrac{1}{2} bh$

Area of a circle (A): πr^2

Volume of a cube or any
type of rectangular prism (V): lwh

Volume of pyramids and cones (V): $\dfrac{1}{3} Bh$

Volume of a cylinder (V): Bh

Fahrenheit to Celsius: $\dfrac{5}{9} (°F - 32)$

Celsius to Fahrenheit: $\dfrac{9}{5} °C + 32$

C Glossary

Accelerated Cost Recovery System (ACRS), established by the Internal Revenue Service in 1981, offers businesses greater incentives than before for increased investment through the application of more highly accelerated depreciation schedules.

Accounts payable are amounts owed by a company to other businesses for goods and services purchased on credit.

Accounts receivable represent money due a company for credit sales to consumers and business customers.

Accounts-receivable turnover relates credit sales to average accounts receivable to provide an approximation of the number of times that accounts receivable are collected each year.

Accumulated depreciation is the sum of annual depreciation claimed for the current year and for any preceding years. **See also:** Depreciation

After arrival (AA) means that the *cash discount* period does not begin until the products have reached the buyer's warehouse.

Aliquot part is a part of a number by which the number can be divided evenly, that is, without leaving a remainder.

Amortization is a series of periodic payments that not only repays a principal of a loan, but that also pays the interest as it is earned on the unpaid balance.

Annual percentage rate (APR) is the effective (actual) interest rate on a loan. It is the common denominator with which consumers may assess and compare loan offers.

Annuity is a sum of money that is payable at regular intervals.

Annuity certain is an annuity that has definite beginning and ending dates, such as a limited-payment life insurance policy. **See also:** Annuity

Annuity due is an annuity that requires payment be made at the beginning of the periods, such as rental payments on property that are due on the first day of each month. **See also:** Annuity

Arithmetic mean, the most widely used measure of central tendency, is the summation of the values of a set of data divided by the number of values represented.

Array is a series of numbers arranged in order of magnitude.

Assets include the entire property owned by a business, encompassing all items ranging from product inventories to office supplies, from buildings to robots, from land to patents.

Average age of accounts receivable is computed by dividing the number of days in a year by the accounts-receivable turnover.

Average-cost method of inventory valuation bases the cost of inventories by an average of the cost for producing them or of the prices paid for purchasing them.

Average daily balance is a method of calculating the amount of interest based on the sum of the daily balances due in a charge account divided by the number of days in the accounting period.

Balance sheet is a statement of a company's financial position that reveals the value of assets and provides details of the claims of creditors and owners on those assets.

Bank discount is the interest that banks collect in advance, that is, at the beginning of a loan term.

Bar graphs are visual illustrations of numerical data in which one or more boxed areas represent the change in one or more variables. These boxed areas or bars extend to varying degrees either upward (positive data) or downward (negative data).

Base is the whole of whatever is being considered — the total population, the total amount of a sale, the total number of orders received.

Bearer bonds entitle their possessors (bearers), who are unknown to the issuing company, to remove coupons (called "clipping coupons") on the dates that interest payments are due and to cash them at authorized banks.

Bill of lading, a shipping agreement between a manufacturer and transportation company, releases merchandise for shipment, effectively transferring responsibility from the manufacturer to the transportation company.

Bonds are debt securities issued by corporations and governments that promise to repay specific amounts of borrowed money on certain dates, at specified rates of interest.

Book value is the remaining value of an asset as reflected in company records after the scheduled depreciation has been deducted.

Break-even point indicates the level of sales or production at which a business enterprise neither earns a profit nor loses money.

Brokers are producers' agents who negotiate contracts for the purchase and sale of goods and services.

C.O.D. specifies that the transportation company is to collect for the value of merchandise at the time of delivery.

Cwt. means "per hundred weight" and is used extensively with freight rates.

Call provisions in bond indentures entitle the issuing corporations or governments to recall (redeem) the bonds when practical to reissue (refund) them at lower rates.

Capital assets include such items of value as buildings, machinery, vehicles, securities, and land.

Capital gains include any profits realized from the sale of such capital assets as buildings, machinery, and vehicles.

Cash discounts are reductions in the net amount of invoices that businesses may deduct when paying promptly.

Cashier's check is a negotiable instrument that is drawn on a bank's own funds.

Certificate of deposit (CD) is an investment that, in exchange for a relatively high rate of interest compared to regular savings accounts, requires a minimum deposit for a prescribed time period — the higher the imposed minimum deposit and the longer the time commitment, the higher the rate.

Certified check is a check made out to a specific person or business that is certified (stamped and signed) by a bank officer as a guarantee to the recipient that a sufficient amount of money is in the issuer's (payor's) checking account and will be held there until the check clears the bank.

Chain discounts are successive discounts on the purchase of goods, usually as enticements for business customers to order merchandise in relatively large quantities.

Change slip, derived from the change tally, shows the total number of bills and coins that are required to make cash payments to employees on paydays.

Change tally enables a division of net pay into the highest possible denominations of money when paying employees in cash.

Check is a written order directing a financial institution to pay money as directed. The writers issue orders to third parties (bankers) to withdraw money from their (the writers') accounts and give it to the bearers of checks — either in cash or through a transfer of funds from the accounts of the writers to the accounts of the recipients.

Circle graphs are visual illustrations of numerical data in which relationships are compared for only one time period.

Class interval is the size of each class in a frequency distribution.

Class limits are the lowest and highest values of each class of a frequency distribution.

Classes are groups into which given values (numbers) are placed in a frequency distribution.

Closed-end funds are mutual funds with limited memberships that require investors to buy into the funds by purchasing shares from existing members who wish to sell their shares.

Common stock is a transferable security that represents ownership in a company and entitles the owners to share in any dividends that are distributed and to vote in certain company affairs.

Complex fractions are numbers in which the numerators and/or the denominators are fractions.

Compound amount is the principal (beginning value of a deposit or a loan) plus the related interested earned.

Compound interest is interest that is computed not only on the principal of a loan or a deposit, but also on any interest that has accrued.

Contingent annuity is an annuity with either an uncertain beginning date (such as payment to begin at death) or an uncertain ending date (such as payments that are to continue until death). **See also:** Annuity

Conversion privileges in bond indentures entitle bondholders to convert their bonds to common stock at prescribed prices within prescribed time periods.

Corporation is a company that has applied for and received a charter from any of the 50 states and which, once incorporated, has the same legal rights and responsibilities of any citizen.

Cost is the amount paid for products that are to be resold or the amount incurred to produce goods or services.

Cost of goods sold (COGS) is determined by adding to beginning inventory the value of all goods purchased or manufactured during an accounting period and subtracting the value of ending inventory.

Cumulative preferred stock, the most common type of preferred stock, guarantees that preferred shareholders will be paid any missed and current dividends before the company pays current dividends to the holders of common stock.

Current assets include the cash that a business has on hand (including checking account balances) and such near-cash items as merchandise inventories and accounts receivable — assets that can be converted to cash within a one-year period from the date of the balance sheet.

Current liabilities consist of outstanding debts that are payable within a one-year period, and they include such obligations as accounts payable and accrued wages and taxes.

Current ratio is the proportion of current assets to current liabilities.

Current yield is the rate of return that would be realized by an investor who purchased a stock or bond at the closing price, and it is computed by dividing the annual dividend or interest payment by the current (closing) price.

Debentures are bonds that are sold strictly on the financial and operational reputations of corporations, with no collateral behind them.

Debt-equity ratio is the proportion of current and long-term liabilities to owners' equity.

Debt-to-total-assets ratio states total debt as a percent of total assets, which is computed by dividing total liabilities by total assets.

Declining-balance method provides accelerated depreciation by permitting businesses to claim a relatively high portion of a total depreciation expense during the early years of ownership.

Depreciation is the allocation over a period of time of the costs of a business asset that has a useful life of longer than one year, which results in a reduction in value of the asset that a business may claim as tax-free income.

Discount brokers offer virtually no financial advice while processing customer orders to buy and sell securities, but they charge relatively low commission rates. **See also:** Full-service brokers

Draft (also called "bill of exchange") is a written order by the first party (the drawer, who is usually the seller) for the second party (the drawee, who is usually the buyer) to pay a specified sum of money to a third party (usually the seller's bank).

Fair Labor Standards Act establishes minimum wages and standards for employment with respect to maximum hours, overtime pay, and equal pay.

Federal Insurance Contributions Act (FICA), more commonly known as Social Security, provides retirement benefits to eligible people beginning at age 65 (age 62 for reduced benefits), disability and survivor benefits, and, through the Medicare program, health insurance to people over 65 years of age. To cover the costs of these programs, employers not only must withhold a certain percentage from the pay of employees, but also must match the amounts withheld.

Federal Unemployment Tax (FUT) requires businesses to pay a rate of 6.2 percent of the first $7,000 of an employee's gross pay to fund unemployment benefits. Because the federal government permits employers to reduce this rate by a state unemployment tax rate, the effective FUT is 0.08 percent.

Free on board (F.O.B.) the city of origin designates that the buyer (consignee) will assume liability for the goods in transit and pay the shipping costs. **F.O.B. the destination city** means that the shipper pays all shipping costs and retains liability for the goods until they are delivered. If no location is specified following the abbreviation "F.O.B.," the legal interpretation is the same as if it read "F.O.B. (CITY OF ORIGIN)."

Figure is the word used for labeling data that are represented in pictoral form such as graphs, flowcharts, and maps. **See also:** Table

Finished goods are products that are complete and ready for sale.

First-in, First-out (FIFO) is a method of inventory valuation in which the first items received or produced by a company (first in) are the first ones sold (first out). **See also:** Last-in, first-out

Fixed assets are assets that have useful economic lives of longer than one year, such as office equipment and machinery.

Fixed costs are those costs that remain relatively constant at varying production and sales volumes. **See also:** Overhead

Freight bill is an invoice issued by a transportation company to assess charges for moving materials from one location to another. This document may be either prepaid (paid by the shipper) or collect (paid by the consignee).

Freight rates are the prices that transportation companies charge for the movement of materials, the size of a rate depending on the distance involved, the value and fragility of items, and the weight or size of the shipment, as well as competitive factors.

Frequency distribution is an arrangement of a large set of statistical data in which the values are grouped into classes to show how often certain values occur. This classification process is used to derive central tendencies and dispersion.

Front-end-load funds are mutual funds that charge investors for both buying and selling fees at the time of purchase. **See also:** Mutual funds

Full-service brokers provide investors with financial counseling, in addition to the actual buying and selling of securities, at relatively high commission rates. **See also:** Discount brokers

Goods in process are materials presently being used to manufacture products.

Gross pay is the total amount of employee earnings before any deductions have been made by employers.

Gross profit, frequently referred to as "margin," is the balance of income remaining after subtracting the *cost of goods sold* from total revenues received.

Gross sales consist of a total of all sales income before deductions have been made for any returns or allowances.

Horizontal analysis compares each item from two sets of financial statements to reflect the absolute amount and percent of increase or decrease.

Improper fractions are those fractions in which the numerator is larger than the denominator.

Income statement is a financial report that shows profits and losses during a specified period (day, week, month, year) that is commonly referred to as a "profit-and-loss (P & L) statement."

Indentures are contractual segments of bond contracts which include covenants (promises by borrowing corporations and governments) concerning such provisions as interest rates and repayment schedules.

Individual retirement accounts (IRAs) are personal retirement accounts that are available to all taxpayers, even those who are participating in separate pension plans at work, which entitle them to defer income taxes on current income.

Intangible assets consist of such nonphysical properties as patents, goodwill, and trademarks.

Interest is a charge or cost for borrowing money.

Inventory consists of goods and materials on hand such as raw materials, goods in process, and finished goods.

Inventory-turnover relates cost of goods sold to average inventory to reveal the number of times within a one-year period that inventories are sold and replenished.

Investment tax credits are direct reductions in taxes at specified rates, as opposed to less lucrative reductions in taxable income.

Invoice is a bill from a supplier to a business customer for the total value of goods purchased, which may or may not reflect any discounts or prepaid shipping charges.

Last-in, First-out (LIFO) is a method of inventory valuation in which the most recently received shipments or the most recently produced items (last in) are sold first (first out). **See also:** First-in, First-out

Limit orders authorize broker representatives to purchase or sell stock at specified prices. **See also:** Market order

Line graphs are visual illustrations of numerical data in which one or more lines, representing the changes in one or more variables, are drawn to connect points whose coordinates reflect given relationships.

Liquidity refers to cash and near-cash items such as accounts receivable and merchandise inventories, items that are likely to be converted to cash within a relatively short time period.

List prices are the base prices that producers publish, usually in the form of price lists.

Long-term capital gains are profits realized from the sale of capital assets (such as land, buildings, vehicles, and securities) that have been owned by a taxpayer for longer than six months. Under the capital gains provision of the federal tax law, only 40 percent ($100\% - 60\% = 40\%$) of long-term capital gains are taxable.

Long-term liabilities are company debts that will not be paid in their entirety within one year.

Lowest common denominator (LCD) is a number that is divisible by the denominators of fractions being added or subtracted.

Markdown is a reduction in a retail price.

Market orders authorize broker representatives to purchase or sell stock at whatever amount the issue is selling for at the time of transaction. **See also:** Limit orders

Market price is the current or replacement price of an item.

Market intermediaries See: Middlemen

Markup is the amount that retailers add to costs to establish the prices that they charge consumers.

Median, a measure of central tendency, is the value that divides a set of data into two equal parts so that half the values are greater than the median and half are less than the median.

Middlemen, routinely referred to as "marketing intermediaries," are the dealers or agents (including wholesalers, retailers, and brokers) who channel products from manufacturers to consumers.

Midpoint in a class is the central value of a class that is determined by averaging the class limits.

Mixed numbers are combinations of whole numbers and fractions.

Modified mean is an arithmetic mean that is calculated after extreme values are deleted from the data to be averaged. **See also:** Mean

Money market funds represent a pool of deposits by individual investors in special (money market) accounts which bankers and securities brokers reinvest in short-term government securities.

Municipal bonds are tax-exempt bonds that are issued by state and city governments.

Mutual funds are investment companies that sell shares in their own organizations, using the investors' money to purchase government securities and the stocks and bonds of selected corporations.

Negotiable instruments are notes representing claims on present or future payments, claims that may be transferred from an individual or institution to other individuals or institutions.

Net income is the profit (or loss) that results from transactions during an accounting period as reflected on an income statement.

Net (take-home) pay is the amount of income remaining after deducting from gross pay prescribed amounts of money for federal taxes, state taxes, Social Security contributions, and, in some cases, insurance premiums, charitable contributions, and union dues. **See also** Gross pay

Net sales are the total revenues received from the sale of goods or services after adjustments have been made for any items that were returned by customers for credit.

No-load funds are mutual funds that do not assess buying and selling charges, which makes it necessary that investors contact the investment companies directly.

Normal (bell-shaped) curve is a graph showing the normal distribution of data with a dominating central tendency in which most of the values concentrate near the middle and with progressively fewer values to both the left and the right of center.

Normal distribution is a frequency distribution in which the recorded values of a set of data are distributed symmetrically about the mean, with about 68 percent of the data being one standard deviation from the mean, about 95 percent being two standard deviations away, and almost 100 percent falling within three standard deviations.

Notes encompass a variety of financial instruments such as promissory notes and sight drafts that promise to pay specific amounts of money within prescribed time periods, with or without interest charges.

Odd lots are purchases or sales of stock in amounts other than 100 shares.

Open-end funds are mutual funds in which the number of shares that may be sold is unlimited.

Opportunity costs are the returns that could be realized through alternative investments, a factor that should be considered when evaluating the return on investment.

Ordinary annuity is an annuity that calls for payments to be made at the end of related periods, such as salaries paid following the period during which they were earned. **See also:** Annuity

Ordinary interest, also called "approximate interest" and "banker's interest," simplifies interest computations by treating all months as though they contain 30 days and all years as though they contain 360 days. **See also:** Exact interest

Overhead are those business expenses such as rent, insurance, and utilities — expenses that are not readily assignable to specific departments or products.

Owners' equity refers to the amount of the investments of owners in a business.

Par value is the dollar value printed on a stock certificate at the time of issue — a value on which preferred dividends are commonly computed, but a value that usually has no long-term relationship to the market price of the stock.

Partial payments are part payments of invoices which usually entitle business customers to earn at least part of the cash discounts.

Partnership is a business that is owned by two or more people.

Percent, which means "per hundred," is based on a whole of something that is divided into one hundred parts.

Percentage is part of a whole expressed in hundredths.

Periodic inventory control systems are those in which employees rely on actual counts of products on hand. **See also:** Perpetual inventory records

Perpetual inventory records provide current information at all times regarding product availability. **See also:** Periodic inventory control systems

Piecework applies to arrangements in which employers pay employees on the basis of the number of units (pieces) produced.

Population, as used in statistical analysis, refers to the whole (all elements) of whatever is being analyzed.

Preferred stock is a transferable security that represents ownership in a corporation and entitles owners to prior claim over common stockholders on the earnings (confined to a fixed rate) and on the assets in the event of liquidation.

Present value is the quantity of money that is required at some starting date to equal a compound amount at some future date.

Present value of an annuity is the lump sum of money that must be invested to provide a series of withdrawals over a prescribed time period.

Price-earnings (P-E) ratio is the relationship of the current (closing) price of a stock to company earnings. It is calculated by dividing the closing price of the stock by the most recent earnings per share.

Price protection grants to the buyers the discounts on purchases that have been made prior to the beginning of a discount date.

Prime number is one that is divisible by only itself and one.

Principal is the amount of money (loan or deposit) on which an interest charge is computed.

Proceeds is the actual amount of money that the borrower receives from a bank loan.

Promissory note is a written promise to pay a specified amount of money to the payee (bearer) within a prescribed time period.

Proper fractions are those fractions that include numbers in which the numerator is smaller than the denominator. They always denote a portion of a whole.

Prox, an abbreviation for the Latin word *proximo*, is synonymous with the term *end of month*. It indicates that a discount period of ten days begins the first day of the following month.

Purchase order, a form that is submitted by business buyers to their suppliers that specify the items being ordered, their prices, and such details as credit terms and provision for delivery.

Quick ratio, sometimes referred to as the "acid test," is the relationship of current assets, excluding inventories and other relatively nonliquid assets, to current liabilities.

Range is the difference between the highest and lowest values in a grouping of numbers.

Rate is a number that is related to the percent (%) sign or the word *percent*. It also denotes the designated percent of the principal that a lender collects as rent for a borrower's use of money.

Ratio is a comparison in lowest terms of two related numbers.

Raw materials are products that are to be used in a manufacturing process to create final products.

Real property includes land (which cannot be depreciated for tax purposes), buildings, and fixtures that are attached to buildings.

Receipt of goods (ROG) indicates that the *cash discount* period does not begin until the products have reached the buyer's warehouse.

Registered bonds are registered by a representative of the issuing company in the names of purchasers, following which the issuing companies mail interest checks directly to the owners on prescribed payment dates.

Retail price is the amount of money paid by ultimate consumers for the purchase of products from retailers (stores).

Retailers are marketing intermediaries (middlemen) who make final sales to consumers.

Return on investment is calculated by dividing net income after taxes by the owners' investments and is considered to be one of the most important ratios in determining the profitability of investments.

Revenue includes the total income of a business, which may consist of income realized through the sale of goods and services and from other (nonoperating) sources.

Round lots are purchases and sales of stock in amounts of 100 shares or multiples thereof.

Rule of 78, in those states where it is lawful, permits lenders to assess higher interest charges during the early months of loans than during later periods, effectively enabling them to impose restrictive conditions on loans that are "paid off" before maturity dates.

Salary is fixed monetary compensation that is paid regularly to employees for services rendered. Payment is usually based on monthly or annual amounts.

Sales margin is determined by dividing net income after taxes by net sales, which reveals the percent or number of cents from each dollar of sales revenue that are retained by a company as profit.

Sample, as used in statistical analysis, is a representative few of a population, which enables estimations (with a high degree of confidence) regarding characteristics of the entire population.

Secured bonds are bonds that are backed by collateral (such as buildings and equipment), assets that may be sold in the case of default in order to repay bondholders.

Service-hours method of depreciation bases annual depreciation expenses on the number of hours that assets are operational in the production process.

Shipper's order bill of lading is a document that is used when a shipper wishes to collect from the buyer's bank prior to delivery of large shipments, rather than extend credit for the products sold.

Short-term capital gains are profits realized from the sale of capital assets that have been held by investors for six months or less, which must be reported to the Internal Revenue Service as regular income. **See also:** Long-term capital gains

Sight draft is a draft that is payable upon its receipt, without any extensions of credit or assessment of interest charges. **See also:** Draft

Simple interest specifies that the interest is computed strictly on the original amount of money borrowed or deposited. **See also:** Compound interest

Sinking fund is an account that financial managers of businesses establish for the repayment of borrowed money through a series of periodic deposits that earn compound interest.

Sole proprietorship is a business that is owned by one person.

Specific identify identifies each item in inventory evaluation, as opposed to categorizing inventoried items and averaging their costs or prices.

Standard deviation is a mathematical equation that is used to measure dispersion (variation from the arithmetic mean) of a relatively large set of numbers.

State unemployment tax (SUT) requires businesses to pay a rate of 5.4 percent of the first $7,000 of an employee's yearly gross pay to fund unemployment benefits. **See also:** Federal unemployment tax

Statistics is the collection, analysis, interpretation, and presentation of data.

Stock certificate is written proof of ownership which enables investors to sell stock at any brokerage office and to use as collateral to secure relatively low-cost loans. As negotiable instruments, stock certificates must be protected as though they were money.

Stock exchanges are places where the buying and selling needs of investors are identified and paired in a bidding process that may result in a slightly higher or lower price than initially offered.

Straight-line depreciation is the simplest and most logical approach to the depreciation of assets, whereby the value of assets is reduced the same proportion of their total value each year of their useful economic life. **See also:** Depreciation

Sum-of-the-years' digits method depreciates assets at relatively high rates during the early years of ownership.

Table is the word used for labeling data that are listed in rows and columns. **See also:** Figure

Tariffs are price lists that transportation companies publish for different categories of freight, such as canned goods, steel, and lumber.

Time draft is a draft that is payable at some specified date after its receipt. **See also:** Draft

Times-interest-earned ratio is the relationship of profit (before taxes), plus interest charges, to annual interest charges, which indicates the capacity of a company to generate sufficient profits to pay its current debts and to assume additional debt obligations.

Treasury bills are government securities that have a term of only three months and are sold in minimum denominations of $10,000.

Treasury bonds are government securities that have durations of longer than ten years and which may be either bearer or registered.

Units-of-production method depreciates assets on the basis of the number of units produced by a particular piece of equipment, rather than on the simple passage of time. **See also:** Depreciation

U.S. bonds are government securities with varying denominations and maturities that cannot be traded among investors but which may be redeemed at any time.

U.S. treasury notes are government securities that range from $500 to more than $10,000 denominations and have maturity dates ranging from one to ten years.

Usury laws, which are intended to curb exorbitant rates of interest on borrowed money, place upper limits on the rates of interest that stores and other lenders may charge their individual (noncorporate) customers.

Variable costs are those costs that are directly related to the production or the purchase and handling of a particular product. **See also:** Fixed costs

Vertical analysis shows every entry in a financial statement as a percent of one significant figure — such as a percent of net sales in income statements and a percent of total assets in balance sheets.

Wage is a payment of money for labor or services that is usually on an hourly or piecework basis, with the specific rate depending on the importance and difficulty of the job, the availability of qualified applicants, and the level of wages being paid elsewhere for similar work.

Weight-break point exists between any two weight-rate combinations, which is that weight where it becomes less costly for the shipment to be billed (priced) at the next higher minimum weight in order to benefit from a lower rate.

Weighted mean is an arithmetic mean in which the values are assigned relative weights based on their varying degrees of importance.

Wholesalers are middlemen who buy from producers in large quantities and sell to retailers in relatively small quantities. They take physical possession of the products and assume complete responsibility for their resale.

Working capital is the difference between current assets and current liabilities, assuming that current assets are greater than current liabilities.

Yield is the rate of return realized from an investment, and it is calculated by dividing the annual dividend paid by a corporation by the closing price of its common stock.

Yield to maturity is the rate (percent) that the purchaser of a bond realizes from the purchase date to maturity, when taking into account any discount realized or premium paid.

Zero-coupon bonds pay no interest until maturity, at which time the principal of a bond and all accumulated interest become payable.

D Answers to Selected Exercises

1-10	a. 3-1/3; c. 6-1/2; e. 1-1/2; g. 3-1/2; i. 1-19/24
1-11	a. 3/2; c. 11/3; e. 40/17; g. 17/8; i. 67/4
1-12	a. 1/3; c. 1/14; e. 1/4; g. 3/5; i. 1-1/3; k. 5-1/9; m. 6-1/9; o. 1/12
1-13	a. 240; c. 120; e. 180; g. 60; i. 840
1-14	a. 3/4; c. 1; e. 1-7/16; g. 1-8/9; i. 2-14/45; k. 17-23/24; m. 9-7/20
1-15	a. 5/8; c. 11/35; e. 4/15; g. 2-2/9; i. 4-49/99; k. 4-4/35; m. 3-17/35
1-16	a. 7/18; c. 12/25; e. 15/22; g. 1/10; i. 2/7; k. 1-25/32; m. 55-4/5
1-17	a. 1; c. 2-10/21; e. 1-1/2; g. 4-12/13; i. 3-6/7; k. 2-2/19; m. 12-2/5
1-18	a. 1:5; c. 5:1; e. 7:1
1-19	a. 10 barges; c. 5/8 oz; e. 1/12; g. 21-3/8; i. 1:3
2-1	a. 250.0; c. $47.00
2-2	a. Five tenths; c. three and two hundredths
2-3	a. 0.0555 < 0.110; c. 0.11120 < 0.1213; e. 3.875 > 3.785
2-4	a. 40.31; c. 132.751; e. 566.7; g. 908.603
2-5	a. 164.77; c. 1,008.04; e. 4,787.90; g. 34,106.75; i. 222.02; k. 1,099.33
2-6	a. 1,948.1; c. 34.0662; e. 52; g. 88,660; i. 3,125; k. 5,440
2-7	a. 16.70; c. 136.80; e. 7.14; g. 81.63
2-8	a. 403,025.00; b. 376.9; c. 463.46; d. 16.9 (first in each group)
2-9	a. 12,126; c. 1,945,606; e. 25,415.6; g. 8.1808; i. 256.1
2-10	a. 1/2; c. 1-3/1,000; e. 1/20; g. 3-1/1,250; i. 1/4; k. 5-1/4
2-11	a. 0.111; c. 0.429; e. 0.286; g. 0.412; i. 0.167; k. 0.760
2-12	a. 0.5; c. 0.75; e. 0.667; g. 0.20; i. 0.375; k. 0.6
2-13	a. $375; c. $4,800; e. $168.75; g. $195.56
2-15	47-5/8
2-17	$39,200.43
2-19	$31,000
2-21	$3,200
2-23	7,747.5 sq ft
2-25	$150
2-27	$66,225
3-1	a. −24; c. 10; e. 20; g. 1; i. 10
3-2	a. 8; c. 35; e. −14; g. 0.75; i. −30
3-3	a. 40; c. −150; e. −21; g. 25; i. −3x + 15

3-4	a. 5; c. 0.4; e. 1; g. −9; i. −5; k. −5; m. 7; o. 4
3-5	a. −5; c. 10; e. 225; g. 10; i. 2; k. 20; m. 55; o. 2
3-6	a. $x = 5$, $y = 2$; c. $x = 108$, $y = (-48)$
3-7	79
3-9	1,010
3-11	16
3-13	Line 14 = 8,000, Line 15 = 7,000
3-15	344
3-17	18
3-19	11 tons gravel, 41-1/4 tons sand
3-21	1,212
3-23	37 long sleeves, 81 short sleeves
3-25	84 pounds peanuts, 36 pounds raisins
3-27	$97.50
3-29	129,376.34 gal
3-31	6.5 days (indirectly proportional)
3-33	a. 256; c. 2,744; e. 11,390,625; g. 35,831,808; i. 390,625
4-1	a. 0.03; c. 4.0; e. 0.015; g. 0.25125; i. 1.0; k. 2.5; m. 0.215; o. 0.011; q. 0.09; s. 0.005
4-2	a. 50%; c. 5%; e. 20%; g. 325%; i. 225%; k. 137.5%; m. 10%; o. 3,175%; q. 4%; s. 125%
4-3	a. 9/20; c. 1/20; e. 7/200; g. 33/400; i. 1/200; k. 7/100; m. 1/8; o. 1/20; q. 1/200; s. 1/50
4-4	a. 33.3%; c. 20%; e. 12.5%; g. 50%; i. 10%; k. 66-2/3%; m. 87-1/2%; o. 14.3%; q. 62-1/2%; s. 58-1/3%
4-5	a. 13.25%; c. $48.75; e. 729.52; g. 986; i. $275,324; k. $1,541.25; m. 2%; o. $57.50; q. $204; s. 60%; u. 71,142; w. 160%; y. $29,757.35
4-6	a. 13.8%; c. 7.8%; e. 7.1%; g. 0.5% better off; i. 30%
4-7	$578.50
4-9	shoes, $279.36, appliances $467.92
5-2	a. $8,250; c. $32.78; e. 31.8%; g. 1.9%; i. 23.7%; k. $86.90; m. $3,924.97; o. $42.10; q. 16.5%; s. $849.20 and 29¢
5-3	a. $2,450; c. $64,025; e. $34,729.59; g. $90,160; i. $16,747.50
5-4	a. $3,559.36; c. $18,558.35; e. $6,884.65
6-5	a. 8,942 lb; c. $380.00
6-9	$3,389.37
6-11	$14,546.25
6-13	$266.25
7-1	$3.93
7-3	$32.57
7-5	$55.25
7-7	$787.60
7-9	$597.55
7-11	15-1/4%
7-13	29.9%
7-15	$151.20

7-17	$746.99
7-19	52¢
7-21	61.3%
7-23	$115.42
7-25	5,682
7-27	a. 11.27¢ oz; b. 10.45¢ oz; c. 9.76¢ oz
7-29	6.4¢
7-31	$81.59
7-33	$86.09
7-35	$57.34
8-1	$144
8-3	a. $256; b. $531.88; c. $181.91; d. $144.38
8-5	a. 153 days; b. 151 days; c. 512 days; d. 210 days; e. 614 days
8-7	a. $1,531.74; b. $1,538.32
8-9	$5,107.40
8-11	a. $37.13; b. 2-1/2 years; c. $840; d. 7.5%; e. $110,000; f. $32.80; g. 3 months
8-13	9-1/2%
8-15	24%
8-17	$2,702.48
8-19	$46.88
8-21	15%
9-3	$42,500
9-5	a. $107,962.21; b. April 3, following year; c. $107,962.21; d. 15.9%
9-13	a. $990.67; b. $1,000, May 4; c. none; d. none
9-19	23-1/2% or 23-3/4%
9-21	30-1/2%
9-25	$22.71 difference
10-5	$5,962.60
10-7	$18.71
10-9	a. $90,861.47; b. $21,112.16; c. $14,304.35
10-11	a. $11,579.84; b. $4,384.14; c. $750.00
11-3	a. $23,035.57; b. $10,540.74; c. $82,955.64
11-5	$1,833.39
11-7	a. $6,342.09; b. $40,184.78; c. $27,940.36
12-5	a. $693,939; b. $139.08; c. $2,945.23
12-7	Amounts = $2,663.05, $5,539.14, $8,645.32, $12,000.00
12-9	a. $218.59; b. $703.55; c. $39,816.54
12-11	Balance owed — $42,284.27, $33,565.50, $23,713.29, $12,580.29, zero
13-3	37-1/2¢ each
13-5	$5.80
13-7	$87.90
13-17	Closing balance = $402.40
13-27	Ending balance of $421.60
13-29	Ending balance of $376.00

13-31	$19.78
13-33	$34.03
13-41	By switching, better off by $21.71
14-5	$1,250
14-7	$164.92
14-9	$134.00
14-11	$22.36
14-13	a. $36.27; b. $38.31; c. $38.94; d. $34.00; e. $42.74
14-15	$2,053.33
14-17	$43
14-21	$131
14-23	$62.57
14-25	none
14-27	$9.90
14-29	$17.57
14-31	$20.82
14-33	Total gross pay is $1,567.45, total net pay is $1,264.11
14-35	Total net pay is $1,515.72
15-5	Ending balance is 112,520 cases
15-7	$44,622.90
15-11	a. 1,058 units; b. indeterminable from the information given; c. $36,067.22; d. $36,752.74; e. $35,266.20
15-13	$29,314.83
16-7	a. $10,687.50; b. $10,687.50; c. $10,174.50
16-9	a. $31,905 each year; b. $58,009.09 first year
16-11	First-year depreciation $16,800; book value, $25,200
16-13	$7,500
16-19	Straight-line under 5-year property class for 5, 12, or 25 years
16-21	First-year depreciation, $562.50; book value, $3,187.50
16-23	1987 depreciation, $156.25; book value $3,593.75
16-25	1986 depreciation, $7,400; book value, $85,100
16-27	$12,500
16-31	$26,400
16-33	$700
17-5	$307,281.25
17-7	$1,032,429
17-9	a. $98,963; b. $81,322
17-11	$21,876
17-13	1,342,081
17-19	a. Net income is $527,536 (24.0%) and $650,404 (30.8%) b. Net income is $527,536, $650,404 (122,868) (18.9)
17-23	$768
17-25	82-1/2¢
17-27	$1.87
17-33	$1,658,000
17-35	a. Current assets read $821,517, 48.3% and $757,924, 47.8% b. Current assets read $821, 517, $757,924, $63,593, 8.4%

18-7	a. 4.3:1.00; b. 1.4:1.0; c. $205,005
18-9	a. 7.8 times; c. 7.1 times; d. 51 days
18-11	5.2%
18-13	38.9%
18-15	8.2 times or 44.5 days
18-17	Yes, based on current ratio of 3.0 and quick ratio of 1.8
18-19	$412,380
19-7	$2.75
19-15	a. $2,948; b. $505.50; c. $202.20; d. $70.77
19-17	$80.80
19-29	$10,258.80
19-35	11.4%
19-37	a. $8,794.17; b. $8,724.17
19-39	$172.50
19-41	$336.42
19-43	12%
20-27	5.7, 2.7, 4.8, 2.8
21-1	a. 26.6; b. 27.5; c. 28.0
21-3	a. $80.90; b. $80.75; c. no mode
21-5	$150.83
21-7	a. $103; b. $105; c. $65 and $115 (bimodal)
21-9	Median of 10.5
21-13	$30.06
21-15	$2,174.44
21-17	a. 82.83; b. 76.6; c. 50–99
29-19	a. 50%; b. 34%; c. 68%; d. 84%; e. 4,200 cans; f. 16%; g. 2.5%; h. 5%; i. 4,750 cans
21-21	b. 680; c. 950; d. 50
21-23	a. 48.5; b. 24.61
22-1	3.56 yards
22-3	2,160
22-5	764 m^2
22-7	3,166.67 yards
22-9	13.5 dm
22-11	30.615 cm
22-13	$1,388.52
22-15	67.5 dm^2
22-17	2.338 m^2
22-19	5,000 cm
22-21	1.2276 m^3
22-23	4.06 quarts
22-25	0.338 m^3
22-27	22.5 or 23 bottles
22-29	$80.83
22-31	a. 14.51 gallons; b. 4.03 quarts
22-33	33.3° C

INDEX